COLLEGE MATHEMATICS

Custom Edition for
SULLIVAN UNIVERSITY

Taken from:

Introductory Algebra, Tenth Edition
by Marvin L. Bittinger

Custom Publishing

New York   Boston   San Francisco
London   Toronto   Sydney   Tokyo   Singapore   Madrid
Mexico City   Munich   Paris   Cape Town   Hong Kong   Montreal

Taken from:

Introductory Algebra, Tenth Edition
by Marvin L. Bittinger
Copyright © 2007 by Pearson Education, Inc.
Published by Addison-Wesley
Boston, Massachusetts 02116

This special edition published in cooperation with Pearson Custom Publishing.

Printed in the United States of America

10   9   8   7

2008360995

LR

**Pearson
Custom Publishing**
is a division of

www.pearsonhighered.com

ISBN 10: 0-558-02228-6
ISBN 13: 978-0-558-02228-0

Contents

PREALGEBRA REVIEW

INTRODUCTION TO REAL NUMBERS AND ALGEBRAIC EXPRESSIONS

SOLVING EQUATIONS AND INEQUALITIES

GRAPHS OF LINEAR EQUATIONS

SYSTEMS OF EQUATIONS

APPENDIXES

Index of Applications

Index of Study Tips

Preface

It is with great pride and excitement that we present to you the tenth edition of *Introductory Algebra*. The text has evolved dramatically over the past 36 years through your comments, responses, and opinions. This feedback, combined with our overall objective of presenting the material in a clear and accurate manner, drives each revision. It is our hope that *Introductory Algebra,* Tenth Edition, and the supporting supplements will help provide an improved teaching and learning experience by matching the needs of instructors and successfully preparing students for their future.

This text is the third in a series that includes the following:

Bittinger: *Basic Mathematics,* Tenth Edition

Bittinger: *Fundamental Mathematics,* Fourth Edition

Bittinger: *Introductory Algebra,* Tenth Edition

Bittinger: *Intermediate Algebra,* Tenth Edition

Bittinger/Beecher: *Introductory and Intermediate Algebra,* Third Edition

Building Understanding through an Interactive Approach

The pedagogy of this text is designed to provide an interactive learning experience between the student and the exposition, annotated examples, art, margin exercises, and exercise sets. This unique approach, which has been developed and refined over ten editions and is illustrated at right, provides students with a clear set of learning

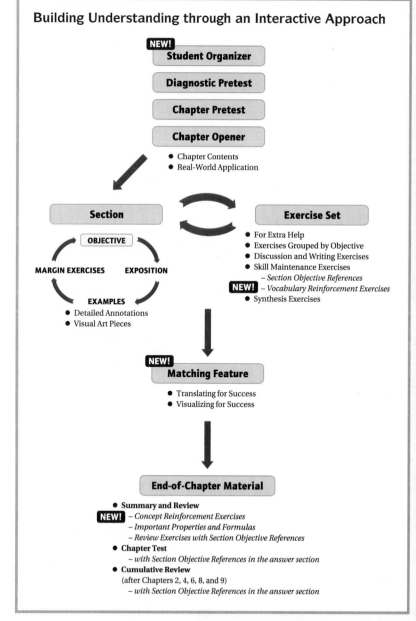

Building Understanding through an Interactive Approach

NEW! Student Organizer

Diagnostic Pretest

Chapter Pretest

Chapter Opener
- Chapter Contents
- Real-World Application

Section
- OBJECTIVE
- MARGIN EXERCISES — EXPOSITION
- EXAMPLES
  - Detailed Annotations
  - Visual Art Pieces

Exercise Set
- For Extra Help
- Exercises Grouped by Objective
- Discussion and Writing Exercises
- Skill Maintenance Exercises
  – Section Objective References
  NEW! – *Vocabulary Reinforcement Exercises*
- Synthesis Exercises

NEW! Matching Feature
- Translating for Success
- Visualizing for Success

End-of-Chapter Material
- **Summary and Review**
  NEW! – *Concept Reinforcement Exercises*
  – *Important Properties and Formulas*
  – *Review Exercises with Section Objective References*
- **Chapter Test**
  – *with Section Objective References in the answer section*
- **Cumulative Review**
  (after Chapters 2, 4, 6, 8, and 9)
  – *with Section Objective References in the answer section*

objectives, involves them with the development of the material, and provides immediate and continual reinforcement and assessment through the margin exercises.

Let's Visit the Tenth Edition

The style, format, and approach of the ninth edition have been strengthened in this new edition in a number of ways. However, the accuracy that the Bittinger books are known for has not changed. This edition, as with all editions, has gone through an exhaustive checking process to ensure accuracy in the problem sets, mathematical art, and accompanying supplements. We know what a critical role the accuracy of a book plays in student learning and we value the reputation for accuracy that we have earned.

 IN THE TENTH EDITION

Each revision gives us the opportunity to incorporate new elements and refine existing elements to provide a better experience for students and teachers alike. Below are four new features designed to help students succeed.

- Student Organizer
- Translating/Visualizing for Success matching exercises
- Vocabulary Reinforcement exercises
- Concept Reinforcement exercises

These features, along with the hallmark features of this book, are discussed in the pages that follow.

In addition, the tenth edition has been designed to be open and flexible, helping students focus their attention on details that are critical at this level through prominent headings, boxed definitions and rules, and clearly labeled objectives.

NEW! CHANGES IN THE TABLE OF CONTENTS

In response to reviewers' suggestions, the two graphing chapters of the ninth edition—Chapter 3, "Graphs of Linear Equations," and Chapter 7, "Graphs, Slope, and Applications"—have been combined into one chapter—Chapter 3, "Graphs of Linear Equations"—in the tenth edition. Sections 3.1 and 3.2 of the ninth edition are now Section 3.1 in the tenth edition. Sections 3.3, 3.4, and 7.1–7.4 of the ninth edition are now Sections 3.2–3.7 of the tenth edition. Section 7.5 of the ninth edition is now Section 6.9 in the tenth edition. These changes were requested primarily so that instructors can cover the topics of graphing and slope in a more efficient manner. In addition, Appendix B ("Finding Equations of Lines: Point–Slope Equation") has been added to extend the coverage of equations of lines in Section 3.4.

Chapter Pretests, now located along with the Diagnostic Pretest in the *Printed Test Bank* and in MyMathLab, diagnose at the section and objective level and can be used to place students in a specific section, or objective, of the chapter, allowing them to concentrate on topics with which they have particular difficulty. Answers to these pretests are available in the *Printed Test Bank* and in MyMathLab.

NEW! STUDENT ORGANIZER

Along with the study tips found throughout the text, we have provided a pull-out card that will help students stay organized and increase their ability to be successful in this course. Students can use this card to keep track of important dates and useful contact information and to access information for technology and to plan class time, study time, work time, travel time, family time, and, sometimes most importantly, relaxation time.

CHAPTER OPENERS

To engage students and prepare them for the upcoming chapter material, gateway chapter openers are designed with exceptional artwork that is tied to a motivating real-world application. (See pages 57, 137, and 223.)

OBJECTIVE BOXES

At the beginning of each section, a boxed list of objectives is keyed by letter not only to section subheadings, but also to the exercises in the Pretest (located in the *Printed Test Bank* and MyMathLab), the section exercise sets, and the Summary and Review exercises, as well as to the answers to the questions in the Chapter Tests and Cumulative Reviews. This correlation enables students to easily find appropriate review material if they need help with a particular exercise or skill at the objective level. (See pages 150, 224, and 426.)

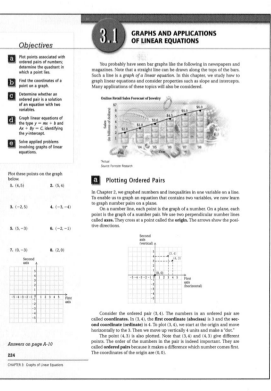

ANNOTATED EXAMPLES

Detailed annotations and color highlights lead the student through the structured steps of the examples. The level of detail in these annotations is a significant reason for students' success with this book. (See pages 152, 378, and 488.)

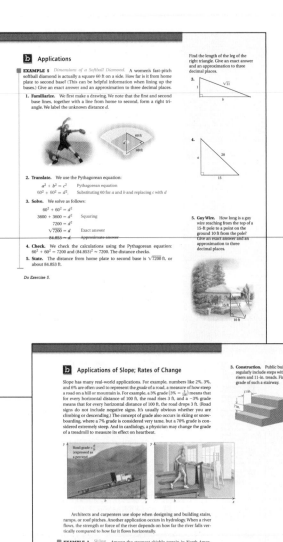

Applications

EXAMPLE 5 *Dimensions of a Softball Diamond.* A women's fast-pitch softball diamond is actually a square 60 ft on a side. How far is it from home plate to second base? (This can be helpful information when lining up the bases.) Give an exact answer and an approximation to three decimal places.

1. Familiarize. We first make a drawing. We note that the first and second base lines, together with a line from home to second, form a right triangle. We label the unknown distance d.

2. Translate. We use the Pythagorean equation:
$a^2 + b^2 = c^2$ Pythagorean equation
$60^2 + 60^2 = d^2$.   Substituting 60 for a and b and replacing c with d

3. Solve. We solve as follows:
$60^2 + 60^2 = d^2$
$3600 + 3600 = d^2$ Squaring
$7200 = d^2$
$\sqrt{7200} = d$ Exact answer
$84.853 \approx d$.   Approximate answer

4. Check. We check the calculations using the Pythagorean equation:
$60^2 + 60^2 = 7200$ and $(84.853)^2 \approx 7200$. The distance checks.
5. State. The distance from home plate to second base is $\sqrt{7200}$ ft, or about 84.853 ft.

Do Exercise 5.

Find the length of the leg of the right triangle. Give an exact answer and an approximation to three decimal places.

3.

4.

5. Guy Wire. How long is a guy wire reaching from the top of a 15-ft pole to a point on the ground 10 ft from the pole? Give an exact answer and an approximation to three decimal places.

Solve.
9. $7y + 5 = 2y + 10$

10. $5 - 2y = 3y - 5$

Solve.
11. $7x - 17 + 2x = 2 - 8x + 15$

12. $3x - 15 = 5x + 2 - 4x$

EXAMPLE 6 Solve: $2x - 2 = -3x + 3$.
$2x - 2 = -3x + 3$
$2x - 2 + 2 = -3x + 3 + 2$ Adding 2
$2x = -3x + 5$ Collecting like terms
$2x + 3x = -3x + 3x + 5$ Adding $3x$
$5x = 5$ Simplifying
$\dfrac{5x}{5} = \dfrac{5}{5}$ Dividing by 5
$x = 1$ Simplifying

Check: $2x - 2 = -3x + 3$
$2 \cdot 1 - 2 \;?\; -3 \cdot 1 + 3$ Substituting in the original equation
$2 - 2 \;|\; -3 + 3$
$0 \;|\; 0$ TRUE

The solution is 1.

Do Exercises 9 and 10.

In Example 6, we used the addition principle to get all terms with a variable on one side and all numbers on the other side. Then we collected like terms and proceeded as before. If there are like terms on one side at the outset, they should be collected before proceeding.

EXAMPLE 7 Solve: $6x + 5 - 7x = 10 - 4x + 3$.
$6x + 5 - 7x = 10 - 4x + 3$
$-x + 5 = 13 - 4x$ Collecting like terms
$4x - x + 5 = 13 - 4x + 4x$ Adding $4x$ to get all terms with a variable on one side
$3x + 5 = 13$ Simplifying; that is, collecting like terms
$3x + 5 - 5 = 13 - 5$ Subtracting 5
$3x = 8$ Simplifying
$\dfrac{3x}{3} = \dfrac{8}{3}$ Dividing by 3
$x = \dfrac{8}{3}$ Simplifying

The number $\frac{8}{3}$ checks, so it is the solution.

Do Exercises 11 and 12.

CLEARING FRACTIONS AND DECIMALS

In general, equations are easier to solve if they do not contain fractions or decimals. Consider, for example,

$$\frac{1}{2}x + 5 = \frac{3}{4} \quad \text{and} \quad 2.3x + 7 = 5.4.$$

Answers on page A-8

MARGIN EXERCISES

Throughout the text, students are directed to numerous margin exercises that provide immediate practice and reinforcement of the concepts covered in each section. Answers are provided at the back of the book so students can immediately self-assess their understanding of the skill or concept at hand. (See pages 207, 369, and 439.)

Applications of Slope; Rates of Change

Slope has many real-world applications. For example, numbers like 2%, 3%, and 6% are often used to represent the *grade* of a road, a measure of how steep a road on a hill or mountain is. For example, a 3% grade ($3\% = \frac{3}{100}$) means that for every horizontal distance of 100 ft, the road rises 3 ft, and a −3% grade means that for every horizontal distance of 100 ft, the road drops 3 ft. (Road signs do not include negative signs. It's usually obvious whether you are climbing or descending.) The concept of grade also occurs in skiing or snowboarding, where a 7% grade is considered very tame, but a 70% grade is considered extremely steep. And in cardiology, a physician may change the grade of a treadmill to measure its effect on heartbeat.

Road grade = $\frac{a}{b}$ (expressed as a percent)

Architects and carpenters use slope when designing and building stairs, ramps, or roof pitches. Another application occurs in hydrology. When a river flows, the strength or force of the river depends on how far it falls vertically compared to how far it flows horizontally.

EXAMPLE 2 *Skiing.* Among the steepest skiable terrain in North America, the Headwall on Mount Washington, in New Hampshire, drops 720 ft over a horizontal distance of 900 ft. Find the grade of the Headwall.

Mt. Washington
The Headwall
720 ft
900 ft

The grade of the Headwall is its slope, expressed as a percent:

$m = \dfrac{720}{900}$ ← Vertical change
       ← Horizontal change
$= \dfrac{8}{10} = 80\%$.

Do Exercise 3.

3. Construction. Public buildings regularly include steps with 7-in. risers and 11-in. treads. Find the grade of such a stairway.

11 in.
7 in.

Answer on page A-18

REAL-DATA APPLICATIONS

This text encourages students to see and interpret the mathematics that appears every day in the world around them. Throughout the writing process, an extensive and energetic search for real-data applications was conducted, and the result is a variety of examples and exercises that connect the mathematical content with the real world. A large number of the applications are new to this edition, and many are drawn from the fields of business and economics, life and physical sciences, social sciences, and areas of general interest such as sports and daily life. To further encourage students to understand the relevance of mathematics, many applications are enhanced by graphs and drawings similar to those found in today's newspapers and magazines, and feature source lines as well. (See pages 88, 162, and 257.)

TRANSLATING/VISUALIZING FOR SUCCESS

Translating for Success The goal of the matching exercises in this new feature is to practice step two, *Translate,* of the five-step problem-solving process. Students translate each of ten problems to an equation or an inequality and select the correct translation from fifteen given equations and inequalities. This feature appears once in each chapter that contains problems that can be solved using the five-step problem-solving process and reviews skills and concepts with problems from all preceding chapters. (See pages 189, 526, and 654.)

Visualizing for Success This new feature provides students with an opportunity to match an equation with its graph by focusing on characteristics of the equation or inequality and the corresponding attributes of the graph. This feature appears at least once in each chapter that contains graphing instruction and reviews graphing skills and concepts with exercises from all preceding chapters. (See pages 248, 362, and 709.)

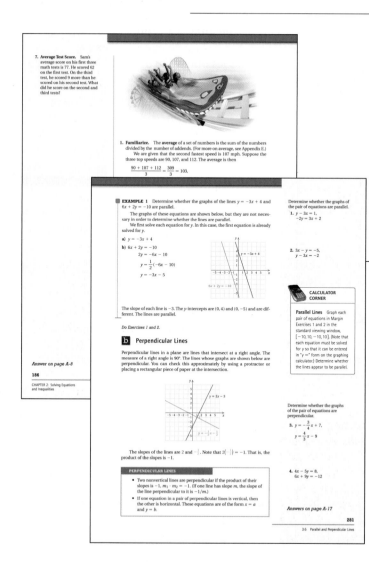

ART PROGRAM

Today's students are often visually oriented and their approach to a printed page is no exception. The art program is designed to improve the visualization of the mathematical concepts and to enhance the real-data applications. (See pages 190, 454, and 520.)

The use of color is carried out in a methodical and precise manner so that it conveys a consistent meaning, which enhances the readability of the text. For example, the use of both red and blue in mathematical art increases understanding of the concepts. When two lines are graphed using the same set of axes, one is usually red and the other blue. Note that equation labels are the same color as the corresponding line to aid in understanding.

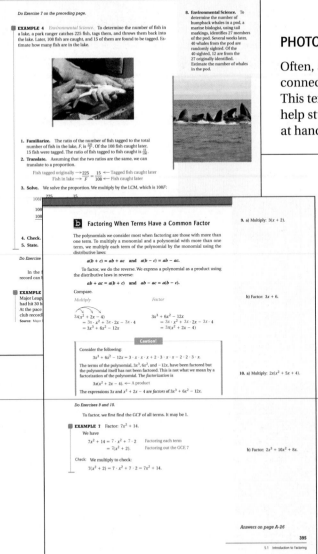

Do Exercise 7 on the preceding page.

◾ **EXAMPLE 4** *Environmental Science.* To determine the number of fish in a lake, a park ranger catches 225 fish, tags them, and throws them back into the lake. Later, 108 fish are caught, and 15 of them are found to be tagged. Estimate how many fish are in the lake.

1. **Familiarize.** The ratio of the number of fish tagged to the total number of fish in the lake, F, is $\frac{225}{F}$. Of the 108 fish caught later, 15 fish were tagged. The ratio of fish tagged to fish caught is $\frac{15}{108}$.
2. **Translate.** Assuming that the two ratios are the same, we can translate to a proportion.

Fish tagged originally $\longrightarrow \dfrac{225}{F} = \dfrac{15}{108} \longleftarrow$ Tagged fish caught later
Fish in lake $\longrightarrow \phantom{\dfrac{225}{F}}$ $\phantom{=\dfrac{15}{108}} \longleftarrow$ Fish caught later

3. **Solve.** We solve the proportion. We multiply by the LCM, which is 108F:

4. **Check.**
5. **State.**

Do Exercise

In the
record can

◾ **EXAMPLE**
Major Leag
had hit 30 h
At the pace
club record
Source: Major

8. **Environmental Science.** To determine the number of humpback whales in a pod, a marine biologist, using tail markings, identifies 27 members of the pod. Several weeks later, 40 whales from the pod are randomly sighted. Of the 40 sighted, 12 are from the 27 originally identified. Estimate the number of whales in the pod.

PHOTOGRAPHS

Often, an application becomes relevant to students when the connection to the real world is illustrated with a photograph. This text has numerous photographs throughout in order to help students see the relevance and visualize the application at hand. (See pages 298, 458, and 523.)

---

b **Factoring When Terms Have a Common Factor**

The polynomials we consider most when factoring are those with more than one term. To multiply a monomial and a polynomial with more than one term, we multiply each term of the polynomial by the monomial using the distributive laws:

$$a(b + c) = ab + ac \quad \text{and} \quad a(b - c) = ab - ac.$$

To factor, we do the reverse. We express a polynomial as a product using the distributive laws in reverse:

$$ab + ac = a(b + c) \quad \text{and} \quad ab - ac = a(b - c).$$

Compare.

Multiply

$3x(x^2 + 2x - 4)$
$= 3x \cdot x^2 + 3x \cdot 2x - 3x \cdot 4$
$= 3x^3 + 6x^2 - 12x$

Factor

$3x^3 + 6x^2 - 12x$
$= 3x \cdot x^2 + 3x \cdot 2x - 3x \cdot 4$
$= 3x(x^2 + 2x - 4)$

Caution!

Consider the following:

$$3x^3 + 6x^2 - 12x = 3 \cdot x \cdot x \cdot x + 2 \cdot 3 \cdot x \cdot x - 2 \cdot 2 \cdot 3 \cdot x.$$

The terms of the polynomial, $3x^3$, $6x^2$, and $-12x$, have been factored but the polynomial itself has not been factored. This is not what we mean by a factorization of the polynomial. The *factorization* is

$$3x(x^2 + 2x - 4). \quad \longleftarrow \text{A product}$$

The expressions $3x$ and $x^2 + 2x - 4$ are *factors* of $3x^3 + 6x^2 - 12x$.

Do Exercises 9 and 10.

To factor, we first find the GCF of all terms. It may be 1.

◾ **EXAMPLE 7** Factor: $7x^2 + 14$.

We have

$7x^2 + 14 = 7 \cdot x^2 + 7 \cdot 2$ Factoring each term
$= 7(x^2 + 2).$ Factoring out the GCF 7

Check: We multiply to check:

$$7(x^2 + 2) = 7 \cdot x^2 + 7 \cdot 2 = 7x^2 + 14.$$

9. a) Multiply: $3(x + 2)$.

b) Factor: $3x + 6$.

10. a) Multiply: $2x(x^2 + 5x + 4)$.

b) Factor: $2x^3 + 10x^2 + 8x$.

Answers on page A-26

395

5.1 Introduction to Factoring

CAUTION BOXES

Found at relevant points throughout the text, boxes with the "Caution!" heading warn students of common misconceptions or errors made in performing a particular mathematics operation or skill. (See pages 229, 395, and 430.)

ALGEBRAIC–GRAPHICAL CONNECTIONS

To provide a visual understanding of algebra, algebraic–graphical connections are included in each chapter beginning with Chapter 3. This feature gives the algebra more meaning by connecting it to a graphical interpretation. (See pages 233, 448, and 510.)

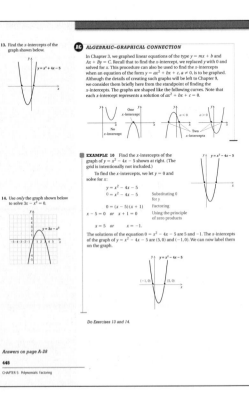

13. Find the x-intercepts of the graph shown below.

AG *ALGEBRAIC–GRAPHICAL CONNECTION*

In Chapter 3, we graphed linear equations of the type $y = mx + b$ and $Ax + By = C$. Recall that to find the x-intercept, we replaced y with 0 and solved for x. This procedure can also be used to find the x-intercepts when an equation of the form $y = ax^2 + bx + c$, $a \neq 0$, is to be graphed. Although the details of creating such graphs will be left to Chapter 9, we consider them briefly here from the standpoint of finding the x-intercepts. The graphs are shaped like the following curves. Note that each x-intercept represents a solution of $ax^2 + bx + c = 0$.

◾ **EXAMPLE 10** Find the x-intercepts of the graph of $y = x^2 - 4x - 5$ shown at right. (The grid is intentionally not included.)

To find the x-intercepts, we let $y = 0$ and solve for x:

$y = x^2 - 4x - 5$
$0 = x^2 - 4x - 5$ Substituting 0 for y
$0 = (x - 5)(x + 1)$ Factoring
$x - 5 = 0 \quad or \quad x + 1 = 0$ Using the principle of zero products
$x = 5 \quad or \quad x = -1.$

The solutions of the equation $0 = x^2 - 4x - 5$ are 5 and -1. The x-intercepts of the graph of $y = x^2 - 4x - 5$ are $(5, 0)$ and $(-1, 0)$. We can now label them on the graph.

14. Use *only* the graph shown below to solve $3x - x^2 = 0$.

Do Exercises 13 and 14.

Answers on page A-28

448

CHAPTER 5: Polynomials: Factoring

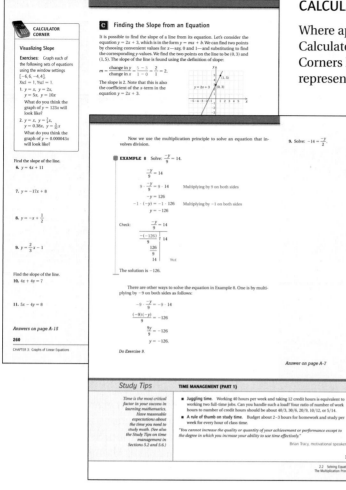

CALCULATOR CORNERS

Where appropriate throughout the text, students will find optional Calculator Corners. Popular in the Ninth Edition, these Calculator Corners have been revised to be more accessible to students and to represent current calculators. (See pages 126, 235, 289, and 512.)

STUDY TIPS

A variety of Study Tips throughout the text give students pointers on how to develop good study habits as they progress through the course. At times short snippets and at other times more lengthy discussions, these Study Tips encourage students to get involved in the learning process. (See pages 147, 275, and 356.)

EXERCISE SETS

The exercise sets are a critical part of any math book. To give students ample opportunity to practice what they have learned, each section is followed by an extensive exercise set designed to reinforce the section concepts. In addition, students also have the opportunity to synthesize the objectives from the current section with those from preceding sections.

For Extra Help Many valuable study aids accompany this text. Located before each exercise set, "For Extra Help" references list appropriate video/CD, tutorial, and Web resources so that students can easily find related support materials.

Exercises Grouped by Objective Exercises in the section exercise sets are keyed by letter to the section objectives for easy review and remediation. This reinforces the objective-based structure of the book. (See pages 203, 310, and 546.)

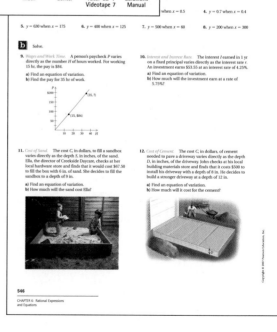

Discussion and Writing Exercises Designed to help students develop a deeper comprehension of critical concepts, Discussion and Writing exercises (indicated by $\mathbf{D_W}$) are suitable for individual or group work. These exercises encourage students to both think and write about key mathematical ideas in the chapter. (See pages 177, 348, and 533.)

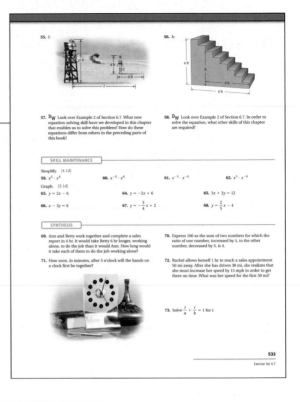

55. l:

56. h:

57. $\mathbf{D_W}$ Look over Example 2 of Section 6.7. What new equation-solving skill have we developed in this chapter that enables us to solve this problem? How do these equations differ from others in the preceding parts of this book?

58. $\mathbf{D_W}$ Look over Example 2 of Section 6.7. In order to solve the equation, what other skills of this chapter are required?

SKILL MAINTENANCE

Simplify. [4.1d]

59. $x^3 \cdot x^6$ **60.** $x^{-5} \cdot x^6$ **61.** $x^{-5} \cdot x^{-6}$ **62.** $x^5 \cdot x^{-6}$

Graph. [3.1d]

63. $y = 2x - 6$ **64.** $y = -2x + 6$ **65.** $3x + 2y = 12$

66. $x - 3y = 6$ **67.** $y = -\frac{3}{4}x + 2$ **68.** $y = \frac{2}{5}x - 4$

SYNTHESIS

69. Ann and Betty work together and complete a sales report in 4 hr. It would take Betty 6 hr longer, working alone, to do the job than it would Ann. How long would it take each of them to do the job working alone?

70. Express 100 as the sum of two numbers for which the ratio of one number, increased by 5, to the other number, decreased by 5, is 4.

71. How soon, in minutes, after 5 o'clock will the hands on a clock first be together?

72. Rachel allows herself 1 hr to reach a sales appointment 50 mi away. After she has driven 30 mi, she realizes that she must increase her speed by 15 mph in order to get there on time. What was her speed for the first 30 mi?

73. Solve $\frac{t}{a} + \frac{t}{b} = 1$ for t.

533

Exercise Set 6.7

SKILL MAINTENANCE

Find the slope of the line containing the given pair of points. [3.3a]

33. $(-2, -6), (8, 7)$ **34.** $(2, -6), (8, -7)$

35. $(4.5, -2.3), (14.5, 4.6)$ **36.** $(-0.8, -2.3), (-4.8, 0.1)$

37. $(-2, -6), (8, -6)$ **38.** $(-2, -6), (-2, 7)$

39. $(11, -1), (11, -4)$ **40.** $(-3, 5), (8, 5)$

41. *Kidney Transplants.* The number of kidney transplants in the United States has increased in recent years, as shown in the following graph. Find the rate of change in the number of kidney transplants with respect to time. Find the slope of the graph. [3.3b]

42. *Liver Transplants.* The number of liver transplants in the United States has increased in recent years, as shown in the following graph. Find the rate of change in the number of liver transplants with respect to time. Find the slope of the graph. [3.3b]

SYNTHESIS

43. *Refrigerator Size.* Kitchen designers recommend that a refrigerator be selected on the basis of the number of people in the household. For 1–2 people, a 16 ft³ model is suggested. For each additional person, an additional 1.5 ft³ is recommended. If x is the number of residents in excess of 2, find the slope–intercept equation for the recommended size of a refrigerator.

44. *Telephone Service.* In a recent promotion, AT&T charged a monthly fee of $3.95 plus 7¢ for each minute of long-distance phone calls. If x is the number of minutes of long-distance calls, find the slope–intercept equation for the monthly bill.

Skill Maintenance Exercises Found in each exercise set, these exercises review concepts from other sections in the text to prepare students for their final examination. Section and objective codes appear next to each Skill Maintenance exercise for easy reference. (See pages 279, 491, and 550.)

45. Graph the point $(-3,$

SKILL MAINTENANCE

VOCABULARY REINFORCEMENT

In each of Exercises 31–38, fill in the blank with the correct term from the given list. Some of the choices may not be used.

31. Equations with the same solutions are called _____. [2.1b]

32. The _____ for equations asserts that when we subtract the same number on both sides of an equation, we get equivalent equations. [2.1b]

33. The _____ for equations asserts that when we multiply or divide by the same nonzero number on both sides of an equation, we get equivalent equations. [2.2a]

34. _____ lines are graphs of equations of the type $y = b$. [3.2b]

35. _____ lines are graphs of equations of the type $x = a$. [3.2b]

36. The _____ of a line is a number that indicates how the line slants. [3.3a]

37. The _____ of a line, if it exists, indicates where the line crosses the x-axis. [3.3a]

38. The _____ of a line, if it exists, indicates where the line crosses the y-axis. [3.2a]

vertical
horizontal
variable
addition principle
multiplication principle
coefficient
equivalent equations
slope
x-intercept
y-intercept
parallel
perpendicular

SYNTHESIS

39. Find an equation of a line that contains the point $(0, 6)$ and is parallel to $y = 3x + 4$.

40. Find an equation of the line that contains the point $(-2, 4)$ and is parallel to $y = 2x - 3$.

41. Find an equation of the line that contains the point $(0, 2)$ and is perpendicular to $3y - x = 0$.

42. Find an equation of the line that contains the point $(1, 0)$ and is perpendicular to $2x + y = -4$.

43. Find an equation of the line that has x-intercept $(-2, 0)$ and is parallel to $4x - 8y = 12$.

44. Find the value of k such that $4y = kx - 6$ and $5x + 20y = 12$ are parallel.

45. Find the value of k such that $4y = kx - 6$ and $5x + 20y = 12$ are perpendicular.

The lines in the graphs in Exercises 46 and 47 are perpendicular and the lines in the graph in Exercise 48 are parallel. Find an equation of each line.

46.   **47.**   **48.**

284

CHAPTER 3: Graphs of Linear Equations

Copyright © 2007 Pearson Education, Inc.

NEW! **Vocabulary Reinforcement Exercises** This new feature checks and reviews students' understanding of the vocabulary introduced throughout the text. It appears once in every chapter, in the Skill Maintenance portion of an exercise set, and is intended to provide a continuing review of the terms that students must know in order to be able to communicate effectively in the language of mathematics. (See pages 284, 382, and 464.)

Synthesis Exercises In most exercise sets, Synthesis exercises help build critical-thinking skills by requiring students to synthesize or combine learning objectives from the current section as well as from preceding text sections. (See pages 279, 375, and 465.)

END-OF-CHAPTER MATERIAL

At the end of each chapter, students can practice all they have learned as well as tie the current chapter content to material covered in earlier chapters.

SUMMARY AND REVIEW

A three-part *Summary and Review* appears at the end of each chapter. The first part includes the Concept Reinforcement Exercises described below. The second part is a list of important properties and formulas, when applicable, and the third part provides an extensive set of review exercises. (See pages 132, 215, and 293.)

NEW! **Concept Reinforcement Exercises**   Found in the Summary and Review of every chapter, these true/false exercises are designed to increase understanding of the concepts rather than merely assess students' skill at memorizing procedures. (See pages 383, 466, and 551.)

Important Properties and Formulas   A list of the important properties and formulas discussed in the chapter is provided for students in an organized manner to help them prioritize topics learned and prepare for chapter tests. This list is only provided in those chapters in which new properties or formulas are presented. (See pages 132, 293, and 466.)

Review Exercises   At the end of each chapter, students are provided with an extensive set of review exercises. Reference codes beside each exercise or direction line allow students to easily refer back to specific, objective-level content for remediation. (See pages 132, 215, and 293.)

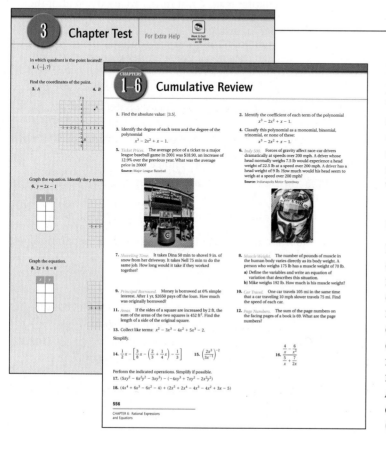

CHAPTER TEST

Following the Review Exercises, a sample Chapter Test allows students to review and test comprehension of chapter skills prior to taking an instructor's exam. Answers to all questions in the Chapter Test are given at the back of the book. Section and objective references for each question are included with the answers. (See pages 135, 218, and 299.)

CUMULATIVE REVIEW

Following Chapters 2, 4, 6, 8, and 9, students encounter a Cumulative Review. This exercise set reviews skills and concepts from all preceding chapters to help students recall previously learned material and prepare for a final exam. At the back of the book are answers to all Cumulative Review exercises, together with section and objective references, so that students know exactly what material to study if they miss a review exercise. Additional Cumulative Review Tests for every chapter are available in the *Printed Test Bank*. (See pages 220, 388, and 556.)

Ancillaries

The following ancillaries are available to help both instructors and students use this text more effectively.

Student Supplements

Student's Solutions Manual   (ISBN 0-321-30599-X)

- By Judith A. Penna, *Indiana University Purdue University Indianapolis*
- Contains completely worked-out solutions with step-by-step annotations for all the odd-numbered exercises in the text, with the exception of the discussion and writing exercises, as well as completely worked-out solutions to all the exercises in the Chapter Reviews, Chapter Tests, and Cumulative Reviews.

Collaborative Learning Activities Manual
(ISBN 0-321-30598-1)

- Features group activities tied to text sections and includes the focus, time estimate, suggested group size and materials, and background notes for each activity.
- Available as a stand-alone supplement sold in the bookstore, as a textbook bundle component for students, or as a classroom activity resource for instructors.

Videotapes   (ISBN 0-321-30608-2)

- To tie student learning to the pedagogy of the text, lectures are organized by objectives, which are indicated on the screen at the start of each new objective.
- Present a series of lectures correlated directly to the content of each section of the text.
- Feature an engaging team of instructors who present material in a format that stresses student interaction, often using examples and exercises from the text.

Digital Video Tutor   (ISBN 0-321-30606-6)

- Complete set of digitized videos (as described above) on CD-ROMs for student use at home or on campus.
- Ideal for distance learning or supplemental instruction.
- Are available with captioning on request. Contact your local Addison-Wesley representative for details.

NEW!   Work It Out! Chapter Test Video on CD
(ISBN 0-321-41638-4)

- Presented by Judith A. Penna and Barbara Johnson
- Provides step-by-step solutions to every exercise in each Chapter Test from the text.
- Helps students prepare for chapter tests and synthesize content.

Math Study Skills for Students Video on CD
(ISBN 0-321-29745-8)

- Presented by author Marvin Bittinger
- Designed to help students make better use of their math study time and improve their retention of concepts and procedures taught in classes from basic mathematics through intermediate algebra.
- Through carefully crafted graphics and comprehensive on-camera explanation, focuses on study skills that are commonly overlooked.

Instructor Supplements

Annotated Instructor's Edition   (ISBN 0-321-30601-5)

- Includes answers to all exercises printed in blue on the same page as those exercises.

Instructor's Solutions Manual   (ISBN 0-321-30603-1)

- By Judith A. Penna, *Indiana University Purdue University Indianapolis*
- Contains brief solutions to the even-numbered exercises in the exercise sets, answers to all discussion and writing exercises, and completely worked-out solutions to all the exercises in the Chapter Reviews, Chapter Tests, and Cumulative Reviews.

Online Answer Book

- By Judith A. Penna, *Indiana University Purdue University Indianapolis*
- Available in electronic form from the instructor resource center. Contact your local Addison-Wesley representative for details.
- Contains answers to all the section exercises in the text.

Printed Test Bank   (ISBN 0-321-30605-8)

- By Laurie Hurley
- Contains one diagnostic test.
- Contains one pretest for each chapter.
- Provides 13 new test forms for every chapter and 8 new test forms for the final exam.
- For the chapter tests, 5 test forms are modeled after the chapter tests in the text, 3 test forms are organized by topic order following the text objectives, 3 test forms are designed for 50-minute class periods and organized so that each objective in the chapter is covered on one of the tests, and 2 test forms are multiple-choice. Chapter tests also include more challenging synthesis questions.
- Contains 2 cumulative tests per chapter beginning with Chapter 2.
- For the final exam, 3 test forms are organized by chapter, 3 test forms are organized by question type, and 2 test forms are multiple-choice.

NEW!   Instructor and Adjunct Support Manual
(ISBN 0-321-30602-3)

- Includes Adjunct Support Manual material.
- Features resources and teaching tips designed to help both new and adjunct faculty with course preparation and classroom management.
- Resources include chapter reviews, extra practice sheets, conversion guide, video index, audio index, and transparency masters.
- Also available electronically so course/adjunct coordinators can customize material specific to their schools.

Student Supplements

Audio Recordings

- By Bill Saler
- Lead students through the material in each section of the text, explaining solution steps to examples, pointing out common errors, and focusing on margin exercises and solutions.
- Audio files are available to download in MP3 format. Contact your local Addison-Wesley representative for details.

Addison-Wesley Math Tutor Center

www.aw-bc.com/tutorcenter

- The Addison-Wesley Math Tutor Center is staffed by qualified mathematics instructors who provide students with tutoring on examples and odd-numbered exercises from the textbook. Tutoring is available via toll-free telephone, toll-free fax, e-mail, or the Internet. White Board technology allows tutors and students to actually see problems worked while they "talk" in real time over the Internet during tutoring sessions.

MathXL® Tutorials on CD   (ISBN 0-321-30611-2)

- Provides algorithmically generated practice exercises that correlate at the objective level to the content of the text.
- Includes an example and a guided solution to accompany every exercise and video clips for selected exercises.
- Recognizes student errors and provides feedback; generates printed summaries of students' progress.

Instructor Supplements

TestGen with Quizmaster   (ISBN 0-321-30607-4)

- Enables instructors to build, edit, print, and administer tests.
- Features a computerized bank of questions developed to cover all text objectives.
- Algorithmically based content allows instructors to create multiple but equivalent versions of the same question or test with a click of a button.
- Instructors can also modify test-bank questions or add new questions by using the built-in question editor, which allows users to create graphs, input graphics, and insert math notation, variable numbers, or text.
- Tests can be printed or administered online via the Internet or another network. Quizmaster allows students to take tests on a local area network.
- Available on a dual-platform Windows/Macintosh CD-ROM.

MathXL®   www.mathxl.com

MathXL is a powerful online homework, tutorial, and assessment system that accompanies Addison-Wesley textbooks in mathematics or statistics. With MathXL, instructors can create, edit, and assign online homework and tests using algorithmically generated exercises correlated at the objective level to the textbook. They can also create and assign their own online exercises and import TestGen tests for added flexibility. All student work is tracked in MathXL's online gradebook. Students can take chapter tests in MathXL and receive personalized study plans based on their test results. The study plan diagnoses weaknesses and links students directly to tutorial exercises for the objectives they need to study and retest. Students can also access supplemental animations and video clips directly from selected exercises. MathXL is available to qualified adopters. For more information, visit our Web site at www.mathxl.com or contact your Addison-Wesley sales representative.

MyMathLab   www.mymathlab.com

MyMathLab is a series of text-specific, easily customizable online courses for Addison-Wesley textbooks in mathematics and statistics. Powered by CourseCompass™ (Pearson Education's online teaching and learning environment) and MathXL® (our online homework, tutorial, and assessment system), MyMathLab gives instructors the tools they need to deliver all or a portion of their course online, whether students are in a lab setting or working from home. MyMathLab provides a rich and flexible set of course materials, featuring free-response exercises that are algorithmically generated for unlimited practice and mastery. Students can also use online tools, such as video lectures, animations, and a multimedia textbook, to independently improve their understanding and performance. Instructors can use MyMathLab's homework and test managers to select and assign online exercises correlated directly to the textbook, and they can also create and assign their own online exercises and import TestGen tests for added flexibility. MyMathLab's online gradebook—designed specifically for mathematics and statistics—automatically tracks students' homework and test results and gives the instructor control over how to calculate final grades. Instructors can also add offline (paper-and-pencil) grades to the gradebook. MyMathLab is available to qualified adopters. For more information, visit our Web site at www.mymathlab.com or contact your Addison-Wesley sales representative.

InterAct Math® Tutorial Web site   www.interactmath.com

Get practice and tutorial help online! This interactive tutorial Web site provides algorithmically generated practice exercises that correlate directly to the exercises in the textbook. Students can retry an exercise as many times as they like with new values each time for unlimited practice and mastery. Every exercise is accompanied by an interactive guided solution that provides helpful feedback for incorrect answers, and students can also view a worked-out sample problem that steps them through an exercise similar to the one they're working on.

ADDISON-WESLEY MATH ADJUNCT SUPPORT CENTER

The Addison-Wesley Math Adjunct Support Center is staffed by qualified mathematics instructors with over 50 years of combined experience at both the community college and university level. Assistance is provided for faculty in the following areas:

- Suggested syllabus consultation
- Tips on using materials packaged with your book
- Book-specific content assistance
- Teaching suggestions including advice on classroom strategies

For more information, visit www.aw-bc.com/tutorcenter/math-adjunct.html

Acknowledgments and Reviewers

Many of you helped to shape the tenth edition by reviewing and spending time with us on your campuses. Our deepest appreciation to all of you and in particular to the following:

Louis Audet, *Augusta Technical College*

Gail Burkett, *Palm Beach Community College*

Jimmy Bullock, *Wilson Technical Community College*

Lucy Dechéne, *Fitchburg State College*

Joe Jordan, *John Tyler Community College*

Susan Meshulam, *Indiana University Purdue University Indianapolis*

Michael Montano, *Riverside Community College City Campus*

Robert Payne, *Stephen F. Austin State University*

Alice Wong, *Miami-Dade College*

Prealgebra Review

Real-World Application

The volume of a truck toolbox is the sum of the volumes of two rectangular solids. The upper portion measures $70\frac{1}{2}$ in. by $20\frac{1}{8}$ in. by $7\frac{1}{2}$ in. The lower portion measures $60\frac{1}{2}$ in. by $20\frac{1}{8}$ in. by $11\frac{1}{4}$ in. Find the total volume of the toolbox.

This problem appears as Example 14 in Section R.6.

Objectives

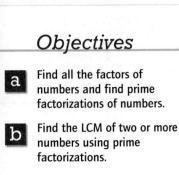

a Find all the factors of numbers and find prime factorizations of numbers.

b Find the LCM of two or more numbers using prime factorizations.

Find all the factors of the number.

1. 9   **2.** 16

3. 24   **4.** 180

To the student:

In the preface, at the front of the text, you will find a Student Organizer card. This pullout card will help you keep track of important dates and useful contact information. You can also use it to plan time for class, study, work, and relaxation. By managing your time wisely, you will provide yourself the best possible opportunity to be successful in this course.

Answers on page A-1

R.1   FACTORING AND LCMS

a   Factors and Prime Factorizations

We begin our review with *factoring*, which is a necessary skill for addition and subtraction with fraction notation. Factoring is also an important skill in algebra. You will eventually learn to factor algebraic expressions.

The numbers we will be factoring are **natural numbers:**

$$1, \quad 2, \quad 3, \quad 4, \quad 5, \quad \text{and so on.}$$

To **factor** a number means to express the number as a product. Consider the product $12 = 3 \cdot 4$. We say that 3 and 4 are **factors** of 12 and that $3 \cdot 4$ is a **factorization** of 12. Since $12 = 12 \cdot 1$, we also know that 12 and 1 are factors of 12 and that $12 \cdot 1$ is a factorization of 12.

EXAMPLE 1   Find all the factors of 12.

We first find some factorizations:

$$12 = 1 \cdot 12, \quad 12 = 2 \cdot 6, \quad 12 = 3 \cdot 4, \quad 12 = 2 \cdot 2 \cdot 3.$$

The factors of 12 are 1, 2, 3, 4, 6, and 12.

EXAMPLE 2   Find all the factors of 150.

We first find some factorizations:

$$150 = 1 \cdot 150, \quad 150 = 2 \cdot 75, \quad 150 = 3 \cdot 50, \quad 150 = 5 \cdot 30,$$
$$150 = 6 \cdot 25, \quad 150 = 10 \cdot 15, \quad 150 = 2 \cdot 5 \cdot 3 \cdot 5.$$

The factors of 150 are 1, 2, 3, 5, 6, 10, 15, 25, 30, 50, 75, and 150.

Note that the word "factor" is used both as a noun and as a verb. You **factor** when you express a number as a product. The numbers you multiply together to get the product are **factors.**

Do Exercises 1–4 (in the margin at left).

PRIME NUMBER

A natural number that has *exactly two different factors*, itself and 1, is called a **prime number.**

EXAMPLE 3   Which of these numbers are prime?   7, 4, 11, 18, 1

7 is prime. It has exactly two different factors, 1 and 7.

4 is *not* prime. It has three different factors, 1, 2, and 4.

11 is prime. It has exactly two different factors, 1 and 11.

18 is *not* prime. It has factors 1, 2, 3, 6, 9, and 18.

1 is *not* prime. It does not have two *different* factors.

Bittinger Student Organizer

WEEKLY PLANNER

Success is planned. On this page, plan a typical week. Consider time allotments for class, study, work, travel, family, and relaxation.

Important Dates

Midterm Exam

_____

Final Exam

_____

Holidays

_____

_____

_____

_____

Other

_____

_____

_____

_____

TIME	Sun.	Mon.	Tues.	Wed.	Thurs.	Fri.	Sat.
6:00 A.M.							
6:30							
7:00							
7:30							
8:00							
8:30							
9:00							
9:30							
10:00							
10:30							
11:00							
11:30							
12:00 P.M.							
12:30							
1:00							
1:30							
2:00							
2:30							
3:00							
3:30							
4:00							
4:30							
5:00							
5:30							
6:00							
6:30							
7:00							
7:30							
8:00							
8:30							
9:00							
9:30							
10:00							
10:30							
11:00							
11:30							
12:00 A.M.							

Study Tips

Throughout this text, you will find a feature called *Study Tips*. We discuss these in the Preface of this text. They are intended to help improve your math study skills. An index of all the *Study Tips* can be found at the front of the book.

For Extra Help

MyMathLab   MathXL

Student's Solutions Manual   Digital Video Tutor CD Videotape

Math Tutor Center   InterAct Math

Additional Resources

Basic Math Review Card
(ISBN 0-321-39476-3)

Algebra Review Card
(ISBN 0-321-39473-9)

Math for Allied Health Reference Card
(ISBN 0-321-39474-7)

Graphing Calculator Reference Card
(ISBN 0-321-39475-5)

Math Study Skills for Students Video on CD
(ISBN 0-321-29745-8)

Go to
www.aw-bc.com/math
for more information.

On the first day of class, complete this chart and the weekly planner that follows on the reverse page.

Instructor Information:

Name _____

Office Hours and Location _____

_____

Phone Number _____

Fax Number _____

E-mail Address _____

Find the names of two students whom you could contact for class information or study questions:

1. Name _____

   Phone Number _____

   Fax Number _____

   E-mail Address _____

2. Name _____

   Phone Number _____

   Fax Number _____

   E-mail Address _____

Math Lab on Campus:

Location _____

Hours _____

Phone Number _____

Tutoring:

Campus Location _____

Hours _____

 To order the Addison-Wesley Math Tutor Center, call 1-888-777-0463.

(*See the Preface for important information concerning this tutoring.*)

Important Supplements: (*See the Preface for a complete list of available supplements.*)

Supplements recommended by the instructor _____

_____

Online Log-in Information (*include access code, password, Web address, etc.*)

_____

_____

We wish to express our heartfelt appreciation to a number of people who have contributed in special ways to the development of this textbook. Our editor, Jennifer Crum, and marketing manager, Jay Jenkins, encouraged our vision and provided marketing insight. Kari Heen, the project manager, deserves special recognition for overseeing every phase of the project and keeping it moving. The unwavering support of the Developmental Math group, including Katie Nopper, project editor, Elizabeth Bernardi and Alison Macdonald, editorial assistants, Ron Hampton, managing editor, Dennis Schaefer, cover designer, and Sharon Smith and Ceci Fleming, media producers, and the endless hours of hard work by Martha Morong and Geri Davis have led to products of which we are immensely proud.

We also want to thank Judy Penna for writing the *Student's* and *Instructor's Solutions Manuals* and for her strong leadership in the preparation of the printed supplements, videotapes, and MyMathLab. Other strong support has come from Laurie Hurley for the *Printed Test Bank,* Bill Saler for the audio recordings, and Barbara Johnson, Vince Koehler, and Juliet Penna for their accuracy checking of the manuscript. We also wish to recognize those who wrote scripts, presented lessons on camera, and checked the accuracy of the videotapes.

To the Student

As your author, I would like to welcome you to this study of *Introductory Algebra.* Whatever your past experiences, I encourage you to look at this mathematics course as a fresh start. Approach this course with a positive attitude about mathematics. Mathematics is a base for life, for many majors, for personal finances, for most careers, or just for pleasure.

You are the most important factor in the success of your learning. In earlier experiences, you may have allowed yourself to sit back and let the instructor "pour in" the learning, with little or no follow-up on your part. But now you must take a more assertive and proactive stance. This may be the first adjustment you make in college. As soon as possible after class, you should thoroughly read the textbook and the supplements and do all you can to learn on your own. In other words, rid yourself of former habits and take responsibility for your own learning. Then, with all the help you have around you, your hard work will lead to success.

One of the most important suggestions I can make is to allow yourself enough *time* to learn. You can have the best book, the best instructor, and the best supplements, but if you do not give yourself time to learn, how can they be of benefit? Many other helpful suggestions are presented in the Study Tips that you will find throughout the book. You may want to read through all the Study Tips before you begin the text. An Index of Study Tips can be found at the front of the book.

M.L.B.

In the margin at right is a table of the prime numbers from 2 to 157. There are more extensive tables, but these prime numbers will be the most helpful to you in this text.

Do Exercise 5.

If a natural number, other than 1, is not prime, we call it **composite.** Every composite number can be factored into a product of prime numbers. Such a factorization is called a **prime factorization.**

EXAMPLE 4 Find the prime factorization of 36.

We begin by factoring 36 any way we can. One way is like this:

$$36 = 4 \cdot 9.$$

The factors 4 and 9 are not prime, so we factor them:

$$36 = \quad 4 \quad \cdot \quad 9$$
$$ = 2 \cdot 2 \cdot 3 \cdot 3$$

The factors in the last factorization are all prime, so we now have the *prime factorization* of 36. Note that 1 is *not* part of this factorization because it is not prime.

Another way to find the prime factorization of 36 is like this:

$$36 = 2 \cdot 18 = 2 \cdot 3 \cdot 6 = 2 \cdot 3 \cdot 2 \cdot 3.$$

In effect, we begin factoring any way we can think of and keep factoring until all factors are prime. Using a **factor tree** might also be helpful.

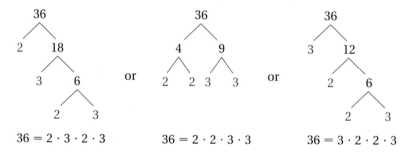

$$36 = 2 \cdot 3 \cdot 2 \cdot 3 \qquad 36 = 2 \cdot 2 \cdot 3 \cdot 3 \qquad 36 = 3 \cdot 2 \cdot 2 \cdot 3$$

No matter which way we begin, the result is the same: The prime factorization of 36 contains two factors of 2 and two factors of 3. Every composite number has a *unique* prime factorization.

EXAMPLE 5 Find the prime factorization of 60.

This time, we use the list of primes from the table. We go through the table until we find a prime that is a factor of 60. The first such prime is 2.

$$60 = 2 \cdot 30$$

We keep dividing by 2 until it is not possible to do so.

$$60 = 2 \cdot 2 \cdot 15$$

Now we go to the next prime in the table that is a factor of 60. It is 3.

$$60 = 2 \cdot 2 \cdot 3 \cdot 5$$

Each factor in $2 \cdot 2 \cdot 3 \cdot 5$ is a prime. Thus this is the prime factorization.

Do Exercises 6–8.

Answers on page A-1

A TABLE OF PRIMES

2, 3, 5, 7, 11, 13, 17, 19, 23, 29, 31, 37, 41, 43, 47, 53, 59, 61, 67, 71, 73, 79, 83, 89, 97, 101, 103, 107, 109, 113, 127, 131, 137, 139, 149, 151, 157

5. Which of these numbers are prime?

    8, 6, 13, 14, 1

Find the prime factorization.

6. 48

7. 50

8. 770

9. Find the common multiples of 3 and 5 by making lists of multiples.

b   Least Common Multiples

Least common multiples are used to add and subtract with fraction notation.

The **multiples** of a number all have that number as a factor. For example, the multiples of 2 are

$$2, \quad 4, \quad 6, \quad 8, \quad 10, \quad 12, \quad 14, \quad 16, \ldots.$$

We could name each of them in such a way as to show 2 as a factor. For example, $14 = 2 \cdot 7$.

The multiples of 3 all have 3 as a factor:

$$3, \quad 6, \quad 9, \quad 12, \quad 15, \quad 18, \ldots.$$

Two or more numbers always have many multiples in common. From lists of multiples, we can find common multiples.

EXAMPLE 6   Find the common multiples of 2 and 3.

We make lists of their multiples and circle the multiples that appear in both lists.

$$2, 4, \textcircled{6}, 8, 10, \textcircled{12}, 14, 16, \textcircled{18}, 20, 22, \textcircled{24}, 26, 28, \textcircled{30}, 32, 34, \textcircled{36}, \ldots;$$
$$3, \textcircled{6}, 9, \textcircled{12}, 15, \textcircled{18}, 21, \textcircled{24}, 27, \textcircled{30}, 33, \textcircled{36}, \ldots.$$

The common multiples of 2 and 3 are

$$6, \quad 12, \quad 18, \quad 24, \quad 30, \quad 36, \ldots.$$

Do Exercises 9 and 10.

10. Find the common multiples of 9 and 15 by making lists of multiples.

In Example 6, we found common multiples of 2 and 3. The *least*, or smallest, of those common multiples is 6. We abbreviate **least common multiple** as **LCM.**

There are several methods that work well for finding the LCM of several numbers. Some of these do not work well in algebra, especially when we consider expressions with variables such as $4ab$ and $12abc$. We now review a method that will work in arithmetic *and in algebra as well*. To see how it works, let's look at the prime factorizations of 9 and 15 in order to find the LCM:

$$9 = 3 \cdot 3, \qquad 15 = 3 \cdot 5.$$

Any multiple of 9 must have *two* 3's as factors. Any multiple of 15 must have *one* 3 and *one* 5 as factors. The smallest multiple of 9 and 15 is

$$\underset{\text{One 3, one 5; 15 is a factor}}{\overset{\text{Two 3's; 9 is a factor}}{3 \cdot 3 \cdot 5 = 45.}}$$

The LCM must have all the factors of 9 and all the factors of 15, *but the factors are not repeated when they are common to both numbers.*

> To find the LCM of several numbers using prime factorizations:
>
> **a)** Write the prime factorization of each number.
> **b)** Form the LCM by writing the product of the different factors from step (a), using each factor the greatest number of times that it occurs in any *one* of the factorizations.

Answers on page A-1

EXAMPLE 7 Find the LCM of 40 and 100.

a) We find the prime factorizations:

$$40 = 2 \cdot 2 \cdot 2 \cdot 5,$$
$$100 = 2 \cdot 2 \cdot 5 \cdot 5.$$

b) The different prime factors are 2 and 5. We write 2 as a factor three times (the greatest number of times that it occurs in any *one* factorization). We write 5 as a factor two times (the greatest number of times that it occurs in any *one* factorization).

The LCM is $2 \cdot 2 \cdot 2 \cdot 5 \cdot 5$, or 200.

Do Exercises 11 and 12.

EXAMPLE 8 Find the LCM of 27, 90, and 84.

a) We factor:

$$27 = 3 \cdot 3 \cdot 3,$$
$$90 = 2 \cdot 3 \cdot 3 \cdot 5,$$
$$84 = 2 \cdot 2 \cdot 3 \cdot 7.$$

b) We write 2 as a factor two times, 3 three times, 5 one time, and 7 one time.

The LCM is $2 \cdot 2 \cdot 3 \cdot 3 \cdot 3 \cdot 5 \cdot 7$, or 3780.

Do Exercise 13.

EXAMPLE 9 Find the LCM of 7 and 21.

Since 7 is prime, it has no prime factorization. It still, however, must be a factor of the LCM:

$$7 = 7,$$
$$21 = 3 \cdot 7.$$

The LCM is $7 \cdot 3$, or 21.

> If one number is a factor of another, then the LCM is the larger of the two numbers.

Do Exercises 14 and 15.

EXAMPLE 10 Find the LCM of 8 and 9.

We have

$$8 = 2 \cdot 2 \cdot 2,$$
$$9 = 3 \cdot 3.$$

The LCM is $2 \cdot 2 \cdot 2 \cdot 3 \cdot 3$, or 72.

> If two or more numbers have no common prime factor, then the LCM is the product of the numbers.

Do Exercises 16 and 17.

Find the LCM by factoring.

11. 8 and 10

12. 18 and 27

13. Find the LCM of 18, 24, and 30.

Find the LCM.

14. 3, 18

15. 12, 24

Find the LCM.

16. 4, 9

17. 5, 6, 7

Answers on page A-1

R.1

EXERCISE SET

For Extra Help

MathXL   MyMathLab   InterAct   Math Tutor   Digital Video   Student's
                       Math   Center   Tutor CD 1   Solutions
                                                 Videotape 1   Manual

Always review the objectives before doing an exercise set. See page 3. Note how the objectives are keyed to the exercises.

a Find all the factors of the number.

1. 20   **2.** 36   **3.** 72   **4.** 81

Find the prime factorization of the number.

5. 15   **6.** 14   **7.** 22   **8.** 33   **9.** 9

10. 25   **11.** 49   **12.** 121   **13.** 18   **14.** 24

15. 40   **16.** 56   **17.** 90   **18.** 120   **19.** 210

20. 330   **21.** 91   **22.** 143   **23.** 119   **24.** 221

b Find the prime factorization of the numbers. Then find the LCM.

25. 4,   5   **26.** 18,   40   **27.** 24,   36   **28.** 24,   27   **29.** 3,   15

30. 20,   40   **31.** 30,   40   **32.** 50,   60   **33.** 13,   23   **34.** 12,   18

35. 18,   30   **36.** 45,   72   **37.** 30,   36   **38.** 30,   50   **39.** 24,   30

40. 60,   70   **41.** 17,   29   **42.** 18,   24   **43.** 12,   28   **44.** 35,   45

45. 2,   3,   5   **46.** 3,   5,   7   **47.** 24,   36,   12   **48.** 8,   16,   22

49. 5,   12,   15   **50.** 12,   18,   40   **51.** 6,   12,   18   **52.** 24,   35,   45

Planet Orbits. The earth, Jupiter, Saturn, and Uranus all revolve around the sun. The earth takes 1 yr, Jupiter 12 yr, Saturn 30 yr, and Uranus 84 yr to make a complete revolution. On a certain night, you look at those three distant planets and wonder how many years it will take before they have the same position again. (*Hint:* To find out, you find the LCM of 12, 30, and 84. It will be that number of years.)

Source: *The Handy Science Answer Book*

53. How often will Jupiter and Saturn have the same position in the night sky as seen from the earth?

54. How often will Jupiter and Uranus have the same position in the night sky as seen from the earth?

55. How often will Saturn and Uranus have the same position in the night sky as seen from the earth?

56. How often will Jupiter, Saturn, and Uranus have the same position in the night sky as seen from the earth?

South African Artistry. In South Africa, the design of every woven handbag, or *gipatsi* (plural, *sipatsi*), is created by repeating two or more geometric patterns. Each pattern encircles the bag, sharing the strands of fabric with any pattern above or below. The length, or period, of each pattern is the number of strands required to construct the pattern. For a gipatsi to be considered beautiful, each individual pattern must fit a whole number of times around the bag.

Source: Gerdes, Paulus. *Women, Art and Geometry in Southern Africa.* Asmara, Eritrea: Africa World Press, Inc., p. 5.

57. A weaver is using two patterns to create a gipatsi. Pattern A is 10 strands long, and pattern B is 3 strands long. What is the smallest number of strands that can be used to complete the gipatsi?

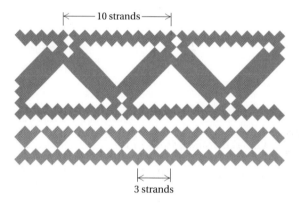

58. A weaver is using a four-strand pattern, a six-strand pattern, and an eight-strand pattern. What is the smallest number of strands that can be used to complete the gipatsi?

To the student and the instructor: The Synthesis exercises found at the end of every exercise set challenge students to combine concepts or skills studied in that section or in preceding parts of the text. Exercises marked with a ▦ symbol are meant to be solved using a calculator.

59. Consider the numbers 8 and 12. Determine whether each of the following is the LCM of 8 and 12. Tell why or why not.

    a) $2 \cdot 2 \cdot 3 \cdot 3$ **b)** $2 \cdot 2 \cdot 2 \cdot 3 \cdot 5$ **c)** $2 \cdot 3 \cdot 3$ **d)** $2 \cdot 2 \cdot 2 \cdot 3$

▦   Use a calculator to find the LCM of the numbers.

60. 288, 324

61. 2700, 7800

Objectives

 Find equivalent fraction expressions by multiplying by 1.

b Simplify fraction notation.

c Add, subtract, multiply, and divide using fraction notation.

We now review fraction notation and its use with addition, subtraction, multiplication, and division of *arithmetic numbers*.

a Equivalent Expressions and Fraction Notation

An example of **fraction notation** for a number is

$$\frac{2}{3} \begin{array}{l} \leftarrow \text{Numerator} \\ \leftarrow \text{Denominator} \end{array}$$

The top number is called the **numerator,** and the bottom number is called the **denominator.**

The **whole numbers** consist of the natural numbers and 0:

0, 1, 2, 3, 4, 5,....

The **arithmetic numbers,** also called the **nonnegative rational numbers,** consist of the whole numbers and the fractions, such as $\frac{2}{3}$ and $\frac{9}{5}$. The arithmetic numbers can also be described as follows.

ARITHMETIC NUMBERS

The **arithmetic numbers** are the whole numbers and the fractions, such as $8, \frac{3}{4},$ and $\frac{6}{5}$. All these numbers can be named with fraction notation $\frac{a}{b}$, where a and b are whole numbers and $b \neq 0$.

Note that all whole numbers can be named with fraction notation. For example, we can name the whole number 8 as $\frac{8}{1}$. We call 8 and $\frac{8}{1}$ **equivalent expressions.**

Being able to find an equivalent expression is critical to a study of algebra. Some simple but powerful properties of numbers that allow us to find equivalent expressions are the identity properties of 0 and 1.

THE IDENTITY PROPERTY OF 0 (ADDITIVE IDENTITY)

For any number a,

$$a + 0 = a.$$

(Adding 0 to any number gives that same number—for example, $12 + 0 = 12$.)

THE IDENTITY PROPERTY OF 1 (MULTIPLICATIVE IDENTITY)

For any number a,

$$a \cdot 1 = a.$$

(Multiplying any number by 1 gives that same number—for example, $\frac{3}{5} \cdot 1 = \frac{3}{5}$.)

Here are some ways to name the number 1:

$$\frac{5}{5}, \quad \frac{3}{3}, \quad \text{and} \quad \frac{26}{26}.$$

The following property allows us to find equivalent fraction expressions, that is, find other names for arithmetic numbers.

EQUIVALENT EXPRESSIONS FOR 1

For any number a, $a \neq 0$,

$$\frac{a}{a} = 1.$$

We can use the identity property of 1 and the preceding result to find equivalent fraction expressions.

EXAMPLE 1 Write a fraction expression equivalent to $\frac{2}{3}$ with a denominator of 15.

Note that $15 = 3 \cdot 5$. We want fraction notation for $\frac{2}{3}$ that has a denominator of 15, but the denominator 3 is missing a factor of 5. We multiply by 1, using $\frac{5}{5}$ as an equivalent expression for 1. Recall from arithmetic that to multiply with fraction notation, we multiply numerators and denominators:

$$\frac{2}{3} = \frac{2}{3} \cdot 1 \qquad \text{Using the identity property of 1}$$

$$= \frac{2}{3} \cdot \frac{5}{5} \qquad \text{Using } \frac{5}{5} \text{ for 1}$$

$$= \frac{10}{15}. \qquad \text{Multiplying numerators and denominators}$$

Do Exercises 1–3.

b Simplifying Expressions

We know that $\frac{1}{2}, \frac{2}{4}, \frac{4}{8}$, and so on, all name the same number. Any arithmetic number can be named in many ways. The **simplest fraction notation** is the notation that has the smallest numerator and denominator. We call the process of finding the simplest fraction notation **simplifying.** We reverse the process of Example 1 by first factoring the numerator and the denominator. Then we factor the fraction expression and remove a factor of 1 using the identity property of 1.

EXAMPLE 2 Simplify: $\dfrac{10}{15}$.

$$\frac{10}{15} = \frac{2 \cdot 5}{3 \cdot 5} \qquad \begin{array}{l}\text{Factoring the numerator and the denominator. In this}\\ \text{case, each is the prime factorization.}\end{array}$$

$$= \frac{2}{3} \cdot \frac{5}{5} \qquad \text{Factoring the fraction expression}$$

$$= \frac{2}{3} \cdot 1$$

$$= \frac{2}{3} \qquad \text{Using the identity property of 1 (removing a factor of 1)}$$

1. Write a fraction expression equivalent to $\frac{2}{3}$ with a denominator of 12.

2. Write a fraction expression equivalent to $\frac{3}{4}$ with a denominator of 28.

3. Multiply by 1 to find three different fraction expressions for $\frac{7}{8}$.

Answers on page A-1

Simplify.

4. $\dfrac{18}{45}$

5. $\dfrac{38}{18}$

6. $\dfrac{72}{27}$

EXAMPLE 3 Simplify: $\dfrac{36}{24}$.

$$\dfrac{36}{24} = \dfrac{2 \cdot 3 \cdot 2 \cdot 3}{2 \cdot 2 \cdot 3 \cdot 2} \quad \text{Factoring the numerator and the denominator}$$

$$= \dfrac{2 \cdot 3 \cdot 2}{2 \cdot 3 \cdot 2} \cdot \dfrac{3}{2} \quad \text{Factoring the fraction expression}$$

$$= 1 \cdot \dfrac{3}{2}$$

$$= \dfrac{3}{2} \quad \text{Removing a factor of 1}$$

It is always a good idea to check at the end to see if you have indeed factored out all the common factors of the numerator and the denominator.

CANCELING

Canceling is a shortcut that you may have used to remove a factor of 1 when working with fraction notation. With *great* concern, we mention it as a possible way to speed up your work. You should use canceling only when removing common factors in numerators and denominators. Each common factor allows us to remove a factor of 1 in a product. **Canceling *cannot* be done when adding.** Our concern is that "canceling" be performed with care and understanding. Example 3 might have been done faster as follows:

$$\dfrac{36}{24} = \dfrac{\cancel{2} \cdot \cancel{3} \cdot \cancel{2} \cdot 3}{\cancel{2} \cdot \cancel{2} \cdot \cancel{3} \cdot 2} = \dfrac{3}{2}, \quad \text{or} \quad \dfrac{36}{24} = \dfrac{3 \cdot \cancel{12}}{2 \cdot \cancel{12}} = \dfrac{3}{2}, \quad \text{or} \quad \dfrac{\overset{3}{\cancel{\underset{\cancel{18}}{36}}}}{\underset{\underset{2}{\cancel{12}}}{\cancel{24}}} = \dfrac{3}{2}.$$

Caution!

The difficulty with canceling is that it is often applied incorrectly in situations like the following:

$$\dfrac{\cancel{2} + 3}{\cancel{2}} = 3; \qquad \dfrac{\cancel{4} + 1}{\cancel{4} + 2} = \dfrac{1}{2}; \qquad \dfrac{1\cancel{5}}{\cancel{5}4} = \dfrac{1}{4}.$$

Wrong!   Wrong!   Wrong!

The correct answers are

$$\dfrac{2 + 3}{2} = \dfrac{5}{2}; \qquad \dfrac{4 + 1}{4 + 2} = \dfrac{5}{6}; \qquad \dfrac{15}{54} = \dfrac{5}{18}.$$

In each situation, the number canceled was not a factor of 1. Factors are parts of products. For example, in $2 \cdot 3$, 2 and 3 are factors, but in $2 + 3$, 2 and 3 are *not* factors. ***Canceling may not be done when sums or differences are in numerators or denominators, as shown here.***

Do Exercises 4–6.

Answers on page A-1

We can always insert the number 1 as a factor. The identity property of 1 allows us to do that.

EXAMPLE 4 Simplify: $\dfrac{18}{72}$.

$$\frac{18}{72} = \frac{2 \cdot 9}{8 \cdot 9} = \frac{2}{8} = \frac{2 \cdot 1}{2 \cdot 4} = \frac{1}{4}, \quad \text{or} \quad \frac{18}{72} = \frac{1 \cdot 18}{4 \cdot 18} = \frac{1}{4}$$

EXAMPLE 5 Simplify: $\dfrac{72}{9}$.

$$\frac{72}{9} = \frac{8 \cdot 9}{1 \cdot 9} \qquad \text{Factoring and inserting a factor of 1 in the denominator}$$

$$= \frac{8 \cdot 9}{1 \cdot 9} \qquad \text{Removing a factor of 1: } \frac{9}{9} = 1$$

$$= \frac{8}{1} = 8 \qquad \text{Simplifying}$$

Do Exercises 7 and 8.

C Multiplication, Addition, Subtraction, and Division

After we have performed an operation of multiplication, addition, subtraction, or division, the answer may or may not be in simplified form. We simplify, if at all possible.

MULTIPLICATION

To multiply using fraction notation, we multiply the numerators to get the new numerator, and we multiply the denominators to get the new denominator.

> **MULTIPLYING FRACTIONS**
>
> To multiply fractions, multiply the numerators and multiply the denominators:
>
> $$\frac{a}{b} \cdot \frac{c}{d} = \frac{a \cdot c}{b \cdot d}.$$

EXAMPLE 6 Multiply and simplify: $\dfrac{5}{6} \cdot \dfrac{9}{25}$.

$$\frac{5}{6} \cdot \frac{9}{25} = \frac{5 \cdot 9}{6 \cdot 25} \qquad \text{Multiplying numerators and denominators}$$

$$= \frac{5 \cdot 3 \cdot 3}{2 \cdot 3 \cdot 5 \cdot 5} \qquad \text{Factoring the numerator and the denominator}$$

$$= \frac{3 \cdot 3 \cdot 3}{3 \cdot 3 \cdot 2 \cdot 5} \qquad \text{Removing a factor of 1: } \frac{3 \cdot 5}{3 \cdot 5} = 1$$

$$= \frac{3}{10} \qquad \text{Simplifying}$$

Do Exercises 9 and 10.

Simplify.

7. $\dfrac{27}{54}$

8. $\dfrac{48}{12}$

Multiply and simplify.

9. $\dfrac{6}{5} \cdot \dfrac{25}{12}$

10. $\dfrac{3}{8} \cdot \dfrac{5}{3} \cdot \dfrac{7}{2}$

Answers on page A-1

ADDITION

When denominators are the same, we can add by adding the numerators and keeping the same denominator.

> **ADDING FRACTIONS WITH LIKE DENOMINATORS**
>
> To add fractions when denominators are the same, add the numerators and keep the same denominator:
>
> $$\frac{a}{c} + \frac{b}{c} = \frac{a+b}{c}.$$

EXAMPLE 7 Add: $\frac{4}{8} + \frac{5}{8}$.

The common denominator is 8. We add the numerators and keep the common denominator:

$$\frac{4}{8} + \frac{5}{8} = \frac{4+5}{8} = \frac{9}{8}.$$

In arithmetic, we generally write $\frac{9}{8}$ as $1\frac{1}{8}$. (See a review of converting from a mixed numeral to fraction notation at left.) In algebra, you will find that *improper fraction* symbols such as $\frac{9}{8}$ are more useful and are quite *proper* for our purposes.

What do we do when denominators are different? We find a common denominator. We can do this by multiplying by 1. Consider adding $\frac{1}{6}$ and $\frac{3}{4}$. There are several common denominators that can be obtained. Let's look at two possibilities.

A.
$$\frac{1}{6} + \frac{3}{4} = \frac{1}{6} \cdot 1 + \frac{3}{4} \cdot 1$$
$$= \frac{1}{6} \cdot \frac{4}{4} + \frac{3}{4} \cdot \frac{6}{6}$$
$$= \frac{4}{24} + \frac{18}{24}$$
$$= \frac{22}{24}$$
$$= \frac{11}{12} \qquad \text{Simplifying}$$

B.
$$\frac{1}{6} + \frac{3}{4} = \frac{1}{6} \cdot 1 + \frac{3}{4} \cdot 1$$
$$= \frac{1}{6} \cdot \frac{2}{2} + \frac{3}{4} \cdot \frac{3}{3}$$
$$= \frac{2}{12} + \frac{9}{12}$$
$$= \frac{11}{12}$$

We had to simplify in (A). We didn't have to simplify in (B). In (B), we used the least common multiple of the denominators, 12. That number is called the **least common denominator,** or **LCD.**

> **ADDING FRACTIONS WITH DIFFERENT DENOMINATORS**
>
> To add fractions when denominators are different:
>
> **a)** Find the least common multiple of the denominators. That number is the least common denominator, LCD.
> **b)** Multiply by 1, using an appropriate notation, n/n, to express each fraction in terms of the LCD.
> **c)** Add the numerators, keeping the same denominator.
> **d)** Simplify, if possible.

To convert from a mixed numeral to fraction notation:

$$3\frac{5}{8} = \frac{29}{8}$$

ⓐ Multiply the whole number by the denominator:

$$3 \cdot 8 = 24.$$

ⓑ Add the result to the numerator:

$$24 + 5 = 29.$$

ⓒ Keep the denominator.

EXAMPLE 8 Add and simplify: $\dfrac{3}{8} + \dfrac{5}{12}$.

The LCM of the denominators, 8 and 12, is 24. Thus the LCD is 24. We multiply each fraction by 1 to obtain the LCD:

$$\frac{3}{8} + \frac{5}{12} = \frac{3}{8} \cdot \frac{3}{3} + \frac{5}{12} \cdot \frac{2}{2}$$

Multiplying by 1. Since $3 \cdot 8 = 24$, we multiply the first number by $\frac{3}{3}$. Since $2 \cdot 12 = 24$, we multiply the second number by $\frac{2}{2}$.

$$= \frac{9}{24} + \frac{10}{24}$$

$$= \frac{9 + 10}{24}$$

Adding the numerators and keeping the same denominator

$$= \frac{19}{24}.$$

EXAMPLE 9 Add and simplify: $\dfrac{11}{30} + \dfrac{5}{18}$.

We first look for the LCM of 30 and 18. That number is then the LCD. We find the prime factorization of each denominator:

$$\frac{11}{30} + \frac{5}{18} = \frac{11}{5 \cdot 2 \cdot 3} + \frac{5}{2 \cdot 3 \cdot 3}.$$

The LCD is $5 \cdot 2 \cdot 3 \cdot 3$, or 90. To get the LCD in the first denominator, we need a factor of 3. To get the LCD in the second denominator, we need a factor of 5. We get these numbers by multiplying by 1:

$$\frac{11}{30} + \frac{5}{18} = \frac{11}{5 \cdot 2 \cdot 3} \cdot \frac{3}{3} + \frac{5}{2 \cdot 3 \cdot 3} \cdot \frac{5}{5}$$

Multiplying by 1

$$= \frac{33}{5 \cdot 2 \cdot 3 \cdot 3} + \frac{25}{2 \cdot 3 \cdot 3 \cdot 5}$$

The denominators are now the LCD.

$$= \frac{58}{5 \cdot 2 \cdot 3 \cdot 3}$$

Adding the numerators and keeping the LCD

$$= \frac{2 \cdot 29}{5 \cdot 2 \cdot 3 \cdot 3}$$

Factoring the numerator and removing a factor of 1

$$= \frac{29}{45}.$$

Simplifying

Do Exercises 11–14.

SUBTRACTION

When subtracting, we also multiply by 1 to obtain the LCD. After we have made the denominators the same, we can subtract by subtracting the numerators and keeping the same denominator.

EXAMPLE 10 Subtract and simplify: $\dfrac{9}{8} - \dfrac{4}{5}$.

$$\frac{9}{8} - \frac{4}{5} = \frac{9}{8} \cdot \frac{5}{5} - \frac{4}{5} \cdot \frac{8}{8}$$

The LCD is 40.

$$= \frac{45}{40} - \frac{32}{40}$$

$$= \frac{45 - 32}{40} = \frac{13}{40}$$

Subtracting the numerators and keeping the same denominator

Add and simplify.

11. $\dfrac{4}{5} + \dfrac{3}{5}$

12. $\dfrac{5}{6} + \dfrac{7}{6}$

13. $\dfrac{5}{6} + \dfrac{7}{10}$

14. $\dfrac{13}{24} + \dfrac{7}{40}$

Answers on page A-1

Subtract and simplify.

15. $\dfrac{7}{8} - \dfrac{2}{5}$

16. $\dfrac{5}{12} - \dfrac{2}{9}$

Find the reciprocal.

17. $\dfrac{4}{11}$

18. $\dfrac{15}{7}$

19. 5

20. $\dfrac{1}{3}$

21. Divide by multiplying by 1:

$$\dfrac{\frac{3}{5}}{\frac{4}{7}}.$$

■ **EXAMPLE 11**   Subtract and simplify: $\dfrac{7}{10} - \dfrac{1}{5}$.

$$\dfrac{7}{10} - \dfrac{1}{5} = \dfrac{7}{10} - \dfrac{1}{5} \cdot \dfrac{2}{2} \qquad \text{The LCD is 10.}$$

$$= \dfrac{7}{10} - \dfrac{2}{10} = \dfrac{7 - 2}{10}$$

$$= \dfrac{5}{10}$$

$$= \dfrac{1 \cdot \cancel{5}}{2 \cdot \cancel{5}} = \dfrac{1}{2} \qquad \text{Removing a factor of 1: } \dfrac{5}{5} = 1$$

Do Exercises 15 and 16.

RECIPROCALS

Two numbers whose product is 1 are called **reciprocals,** or **multiplicative inverses,** of each other. All the arithmetic numbers, except zero, have reciprocals.

■ **EXAMPLES**

12. The reciprocal of $\frac{2}{3}$ is $\frac{3}{2}$ because $\frac{2}{3} \cdot \frac{3}{2} = \frac{6}{6} = 1$.

13. The reciprocal of 9 is $\frac{1}{9}$ because $9 \cdot \frac{1}{9} = \frac{9}{9} = 1$.

14. The reciprocal of $\frac{1}{4}$ is 4 because $\frac{1}{4} \cdot 4 = \frac{4}{4} = 1$.

Do Exercises 17–20.

RECIPROCALS AND DIVISION

Reciprocals and the number 1 can be used to justify a fast way to divide arithmetic numbers. We multiply by 1, carefully choosing the expression for 1.

■ **EXAMPLE 15**   Divide $\dfrac{2}{3}$ by $\dfrac{7}{5}$.

This is a symbol for 1.

$$\dfrac{2}{3} \div \dfrac{7}{5} = \dfrac{\frac{2}{3}}{\frac{7}{5}} = \dfrac{\frac{2}{3}}{\frac{7}{5}} \cdot \dfrac{\frac{5}{7}}{\frac{5}{7}} \qquad \text{Multiplying by } \tfrac{5}{7}. \text{ We use } \tfrac{5}{7} \text{ because it is the reciprocal of } \tfrac{7}{5}.$$

$$= \dfrac{\frac{2}{3} \cdot \frac{5}{7}}{\frac{7}{5} \cdot \frac{5}{7}} \qquad \text{Multiplying numerators and denominators}$$

$$= \dfrac{\frac{10}{21}}{\frac{35}{35}} = \dfrac{\frac{10}{21}}{1} \qquad \tfrac{35}{35} = 1$$

$$= \dfrac{10}{21} \qquad \text{Simplifying}$$

After multiplying, we had a denominator of $\frac{35}{35}$, or 1. That was because we used $\frac{5}{7}$, the reciprocal of the divisor, for both the numerator and the denominator of the symbol for 1.

Do Exercise 21.

When multiplying by 1 to divide, we get a denominator of 1. What do we get in the numerator? In Example 15, we got $\frac{2}{3} \cdot \frac{5}{7}$. This is the product of $\frac{2}{3}$, the dividend, and $\frac{5}{7}$, the reciprocal of the divisor.

DIVIDING FRACTIONS

To divide fractions, multiply by the reciprocal of the divisor:

$$\frac{a}{b} \div \frac{c}{d} = \frac{a}{b} \cdot \frac{d}{c}.$$

EXAMPLE 16 Divide by multiplying by the reciprocal of the divisor: $\frac{1}{2} \div \frac{3}{5}$.

$$\frac{1}{2} \div \frac{3}{5} = \frac{1}{2} \cdot \frac{5}{3} \qquad \text{$\frac{5}{3}$ is the reciprocal of $\frac{3}{5}$}$$

$$= \frac{5}{6} \qquad \text{Multiplying}$$

After dividing, always simplify if possible.

EXAMPLE 17 Divide and simplify: $\dfrac{2}{3} \div \dfrac{4}{9}$.

$$\frac{2}{3} \div \frac{4}{9} = \frac{2}{3} \cdot \frac{9}{4} \qquad \text{$\frac{9}{4}$ is the reciprocal of $\frac{4}{9}$}$$

$$= \frac{2 \cdot 9}{3 \cdot 4} \qquad \text{Multiplying numerators and denominators}$$

$$= \frac{2 \cdot 3 \cdot 3}{3 \cdot 2 \cdot 2} \qquad \text{Removing a factor of 1: $\frac{2 \cdot 3}{2 \cdot 3} = 1$}$$

$$= \frac{3}{2}$$

Do Exercises 22–24.

EXAMPLE 18 Divide and simplify: $\dfrac{5}{6} \div 30$.

$$\frac{5}{6} \div 30 = \frac{5}{6} \div \frac{30}{1} = \frac{5}{6} \cdot \frac{1}{30} = \frac{5 \cdot 1}{6 \cdot 30} = \frac{5 \cdot 1}{6 \cdot 5 \cdot 6} = \frac{1}{6 \cdot 6} = \frac{1}{36}$$

$$\text{Removing a factor of 1: } \frac{5}{5} = 1$$

EXAMPLE 19 Divide and simplify: $24 \div \dfrac{3}{8}$.

$$24 \div \frac{3}{8} = \frac{24}{1} \div \frac{3}{8} = \frac{24}{1} \cdot \frac{8}{3} = \frac{24 \cdot 8}{1 \cdot 3} = \frac{3 \cdot 8 \cdot 8}{1 \cdot 3} = \frac{8 \cdot 8}{1} = 64$$

$$\text{Removing a factor of 1: } \frac{3}{3} = 1$$

Do Exercises 25 and 26.

Divide by multiplying by the reciprocal of the divisor. Then simplify.

22. $\dfrac{4}{3} \div \dfrac{7}{2}$

23. $\dfrac{5}{4} \div \dfrac{3}{2}$

24. $\dfrac{\frac{2}{9}}{\frac{5}{12}}$

Divide and simplify.

25. $\dfrac{7}{8} \div 56$

26. $36 \div \dfrac{4}{9}$

Answers on page A-1

CALCULATOR CORNER

Graphing Calculators and Operations on Fractions   Although a calculator is *not* required for this textbook, the book contains a series of *optional* discussions on using a graphing calculator. The keystrokes for a TI-84 Plus graphing calculator will be shown throughout. For keystrokes for other models of calculators, consult the user's manual for your particular calculator.

Note that there are options above the keys as well as on them. To access the option written on a key, simply press the key. The options written in blue above the keys are accessed by first pressing the blue **2ND** key and then pressing the key corresponding to the desired option. The green options are accessed by first pressing the green **ALPHA** key.

To turn the calculator on, press the **ON** key at the bottom left-hand corner of the keypad. You should see a blinking rectangle, or cursor, on the screen. If you do not see the cursor, try adjusting the display contrast. To do this, first press **2ND** and then press and hold ⌃ to increase the contrast or ⌄ to decrease the contrast.

To turn the calculator off, press **2ND** **OFF**. (OFF is the second operation associated with the **ON** key.) The calculator will turn itself off automatically after about five minutes of no activity.

Press **MODE** to display the MODE settings. Initially, you should select the settings on the left side of the display.

```
NORMAL  SCI  ENG
FLOAT  0123456789
RADIAN  DEGREE
FUNC  PAR  POL  SEQ
CONNECTED  DOT
SEQUENTIAL  SIMUL
REAL  a+bi  re^θi
FULL  HORIZ  G-T
```

To change a setting on the MODE screen, use ⌄ or ⌃ to move the cursor to the line of that setting. Then use ▷ or ◁ to move the blinking cursor to the desired setting and press **ENTER** . Press **CLEAR** or **2ND** **QUIT** to leave the MODE screen. QUIT is the second operation associated with the **MODE** key.) Pressing **CLEAR** or **2ND** **QUIT** will take you to the **home screen** where computations are performed.

We can perform operations on fractions on a graphing calculator. To find $\frac{3}{4} + \frac{1}{2}$ and express the result as a fraction, we press ③ ÷ ④ + ① ÷ ② **MATH** ① **ENTER** . The keystrokes **MATH** ① select the ▷FRAC option from the MATH menu, causing the result to be expressed in fraction form. The calculator display is shown below.

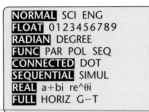

```
3/4+1/2▶Frac
                    5/4
```

Exercises: Perform each calculation. Give the answer in fraction notation.

1. $\frac{1}{3} + \frac{1}{4}$

2. $\frac{5}{6} + \frac{7}{8}$

3. $\frac{7}{5} - \frac{3}{10}$

4. $\frac{31}{16} - \frac{4}{7}$

5. $\frac{15}{4} \cdot \frac{7}{12}$

6. $\frac{3}{2} \cdot \frac{8}{9}$

7. $\frac{4}{5} \div \frac{8}{3}$

8. $\frac{5}{4} \div \frac{3}{7}$

a   Write an equivalent expression for each of the following. Use the indicated name for 1.

1. $\dfrac{3}{4}$ $\left(\text{Use } \dfrac{3}{3} \text{ for } 1.\right)$

2. $\dfrac{5}{6}$ $\left(\text{Use } \dfrac{10}{10} \text{ for } 1.\right)$

3. $\dfrac{3}{5}$ $\left(\text{Use } \dfrac{20}{20} \text{ for } 1.\right)$

4. $\dfrac{8}{9}$ $\left(\text{Use } \dfrac{4}{4} \text{ for } 1.\right)$

5. $\dfrac{13}{20}$ $\left(\text{Use } \dfrac{8}{8} \text{ for } 1.\right)$

6. $\dfrac{13}{32}$ $\left(\text{Use } \dfrac{40}{40} \text{ for } 1.\right)$

Write an equivalent expression with the given denominator.

7. $\dfrac{7}{8}$ (Denominator: 24)

8. $\dfrac{5}{6}$ (Denominator: 48)

9. $\dfrac{5}{4}$ (Denominator: 16)

10. $\dfrac{2}{9}$ (Denominator: 54)

11. $\dfrac{17}{19}$ (Denominator: 437)

12. $\dfrac{15}{23}$ (Denominator: 437)

b   Simplify.

13. $\dfrac{18}{27}$

14. $\dfrac{49}{56}$

15. $\dfrac{56}{14}$

16. $\dfrac{48}{27}$

17. $\dfrac{6}{42}$

18. $\dfrac{13}{104}$

19. $\dfrac{56}{7}$

20. $\dfrac{132}{11}$

21. $\dfrac{19}{76}$

22. $\dfrac{17}{51}$

23. $\dfrac{100}{20}$

24. $\dfrac{150}{25}$

25. $\dfrac{425}{525}$

26. $\dfrac{625}{325}$

27. $\dfrac{2600}{1400}$

28. $\dfrac{4800}{1600}$

29. $\dfrac{8 \cdot x}{6 \cdot x}$

30. $\dfrac{13 \cdot v}{39 \cdot v}$

c   Compute and simplify.

31. $\dfrac{1}{3} \cdot \dfrac{1}{4}$

32. $\dfrac{15}{16} \cdot \dfrac{8}{5}$

33. $\dfrac{15}{4} \cdot \dfrac{3}{4}$

34. $\dfrac{10}{11} \cdot \dfrac{11}{10}$

35. $\dfrac{1}{3} + \dfrac{1}{3}$

36. $\dfrac{1}{4} + \dfrac{1}{3}$

37. $\dfrac{4}{9} + \dfrac{13}{18}$

38. $\dfrac{4}{5} + \dfrac{8}{15}$

39. $\dfrac{3}{10} + \dfrac{8}{15}$

40. $\dfrac{9}{8} + \dfrac{7}{12}$

41. $\dfrac{7}{30} + \dfrac{5}{12}$ **42.** $\dfrac{3}{16} - \dfrac{1}{18}$ **43.** $\dfrac{5}{4} - \dfrac{3}{4}$ **44.** $\dfrac{12}{5} - \dfrac{2}{5}$ **45.** $\dfrac{11}{12} - \dfrac{3}{8}$

46. $\dfrac{15}{16} - \dfrac{5}{12}$ **47.** $\dfrac{11}{12} - \dfrac{2}{5}$ **48.** $\dfrac{15}{16} - \dfrac{2}{3}$ **49.** $\dfrac{7}{6} \div \dfrac{3}{5}$ **50.** $\dfrac{7}{5} \div \dfrac{3}{4}$

51. $\dfrac{8}{9} \div \dfrac{4}{15}$ **52.** $\dfrac{3}{4} \div \dfrac{3}{7}$ **53.** $\dfrac{1}{8} \div \dfrac{1}{4}$ **54.** $\dfrac{1}{20} \div \dfrac{1}{5}$ **55.** $\dfrac{\frac{13}{12}}{\frac{39}{5}}$

56. $\dfrac{\frac{17}{6}}{\frac{3}{8}}$ **57.** $100 \div \dfrac{1}{5}$ **58.** $78 \div \dfrac{1}{6}$ **59.** $\dfrac{3}{4} \div 10$ **60.** $\dfrac{5}{6} \div 15$

To the student and the instructor: The Discussion and Writing exercises denoted by the symbol D_W are meant to be answered with one or more sentences. They can be discussed and answered collaboratively by the entire class or by small groups. Because of their open-ended nature, the answers to these exercises do not appear at the back of the book.

61. D_W Explain in your own words when it *is* possible to cancel and when it is *not* possible to cancel.

62. D_W A student incorrectly insists that $\frac{12}{35} \div \frac{4}{5}$ is $\frac{7}{3}$. What mistake is the student likely making?

This heading indicates that the exercises that follow are *Skill Maintenance exercises,* which review any skill previously studied in the text. You can expect such exercises in every exercise set. Answers to *all* skill maintenance exercises are found at the back of the book. If you miss an exercise, restudy the objective shown in red.

Find the prime factorization.   [R.1a]

63. 28   **64.** 56   **65.** 1000   **66.** 192   **67.** 2001

Find the LCM.   [R.1b]

68. 18,   63   **69.** 16,   24   **70.** 28,   49,   56   **71.** 48,   64,   96   **72.** 25,   75,   150

SYNTHESIS

Simplify.

73. $\dfrac{192}{256}$ **74.** $\dfrac{p \cdot q}{r \cdot q}$ **75.** $\dfrac{64 \cdot a \cdot b}{16 \cdot a \cdot b}$

76. $\dfrac{4 \cdot 9 \cdot 24}{2 \cdot 8 \cdot 15}$ **77.** $\dfrac{36 \cdot (2 \cdot h)}{8 \cdot (9 \cdot h)}$ **78.** $\dfrac{256 \cdot a \cdot b \cdot c \cdot d}{192 \cdot b \cdot c \cdot d}$

18

CHAPTER R: Prealgebra Review

Copyright © 2007 Pearson Education, Inc.

DECIMAL NOTATION

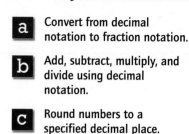

Objectives

a Convert from decimal notation to fraction notation.

b Add, subtract, multiply, and divide using decimal notation.

c Round numbers to a specified decimal place.

Let's say that the cost of a sound system is

$1768.95.

This amount is given in **decimal notation.** The following place-value chart shows the place value of each digit in 1768.95.

PLACE-VALUE CHART								
Ten Thousands	Thousands	Hundreds	Tens	Ones	Tenths	Hundredths	Thousandths	Ten-Thousandths
10,000	1000	100	10	1	$\frac{1}{10}$	$\frac{1}{100}$	$\frac{1}{1000}$	$\frac{1}{10,000}$
	1	7	6	8 . 9	5			

a ## Converting from Decimal Notation to Fraction Notation

When we multiply by 1, a number is not changed. If we choose the notation $\frac{10}{10}, \frac{100}{100}, \frac{1000}{1000}$, and so on for 1, we can move a decimal point in a numerator to the right to convert from decimal notation to fraction notation.

Look for a pattern in the following products:

$$0.1 = 0.1 \times 1 = 0.1 \times \frac{10}{10} = \frac{0.1 \times 10}{10} = \frac{1}{10};$$

$$0.6875 = 0.6875 \times 1 = 0.6875 \times \frac{10,000}{10,000} = \frac{0.6875 \times 10,000}{10,000} = \frac{6875}{10,000};$$

$$53.47 = 53.47 \times 1 = 53.47 \times \frac{100}{100} = \frac{53.47 \times 100}{100} = \frac{5347}{100}.$$

To convert from decimal notation to fraction notation:

a) Count the number of decimal places.

4.98

2 places

b) Move the decimal point that many places to the right.

$4.98.$

Move 2 places.

c) Write the result over a denominator with that number of zeros.

$\frac{498}{100}$

2 zeros

EXAMPLE 1 Convert 0.876 to fraction notation. Do not simplify.

0.876 $0.876.$ $0.876 = \frac{876}{1000}$

3 places   3 places   3 zeros

Convert to fraction notation. Do not simplify.

1. 0.568

2. 2.3

3. 89.04

Answers on page A-1

Convert to decimal notation.

4. $\dfrac{4131}{1000}$

EXAMPLE 2 Convert 1.5018 to fraction notation. Do not simplify.

$$1.5018 \qquad \underset{\text{4 places}}{1.5018.} \qquad 1.5018 = \underset{\text{4 zeros}}{\dfrac{15,018}{10,000}}$$

Do Exercises 1–3 on the preceding page.

To convert from fraction notation to decimal notation when the denominator is a number like 10, 100, or 1000:

a) Count the number of zeros.

$$\underset{\text{3 zeros}}{\dfrac{8679}{1000}}$$

5. $\dfrac{4131}{10,000}$

b) Move the decimal point that number of places to the left. Leave off the denominator.

$$\underset{\text{Move 3 places.}}{8.679.}$$

EXAMPLE 3 Convert to decimal notation: $\dfrac{123,067}{10,000}$.

6. $\dfrac{573}{100}$

$$\underset{\text{4 zeros}}{\dfrac{123,067}{10,000}} \qquad \underset{\text{4 places}}{12.3067.} \qquad \dfrac{123,067}{10,000} = 12.3067$$

Do Exercises 4–6.

Addition, Subtraction, Multiplication, and Division

Add.

7. $69 + 1.785 + 213.67$

ADDITION WITH DECIMAL NOTATION

Adding with decimal notation is similar to adding whole numbers. First, line up the decimal points. Then add the thousandths, then the hundredths, and so on, carrying if necessary.

EXAMPLE 4 Add: $74 + 26.46 + 0.998$.

$$\begin{array}{r} \overset{1\ 1\ 1}{7\ 4.} \\ 2\ 6.4\ 6 \\ +\quad 0.9\ 9\ 8 \\ \hline 1\ 0\ 1.4\ 5\ 8 \end{array}$$

8. $17.95 + 14.68 + 236$

You can place extra zeros to the right of any decimal point so that there are the same number of decimal places in all the addends, but this is not necessary. If you did, the preceding problem would look like this:

$$\begin{array}{r} \overset{1\ 1\ 1}{7\ 4.0\ 0\ 0} \quad \text{Adding zeros to 74} \\ 2\ 6.4\ 6\ 0 \quad \text{Adding zeros to 26.46} \\ +\quad 0.9\ 9\ 8 \\ \hline 1\ 0\ 1.4\ 5\ 8 \end{array}$$

Answers on page A-1

Do Exercises 7 and 8.

SUBTRACTION WITH DECIMAL NOTATION

Subtracting with decimal notation is similar to subtracting whole numbers. First, line up the decimal points. Then subtract the thousandths, then the hundredths, the tenths, and so on, borrowing if necessary. Extra zeros can be added if needed.

EXAMPLES

5. Subtract: $76.14 - 18.953$.

$$
\begin{array}{r}
\overset{15\ 10\ 13}{\overset{6\ \cancel{5}\ \cancel{0}\ \cancel{3}\ 10}{7\cancel{6}.\cancel{1}\cancel{4}\cancel{0}}} \\
-\ 1\ 8.9\ 5\ 3 \\
\hline
5\ 7.1\ 8\ 7
\end{array}
$$

6. Subtract: $200 - 0.68$.

$$
\begin{array}{r}
\overset{1\ 9\ 9\ 9\ 10}{2\cancel{0}\cancel{0}.\cancel{0}\cancel{0}} \\
-\ \ \ \ 0.6\ 8 \\
\hline
1\ 9\ 9.3\ 2
\end{array}
$$

Do Exercises 9–12.

Look at this product.

$$
\underset{\substack{\uparrow\\2\ \text{places}}}{5.14} \times \underset{\substack{\uparrow\\1\ \text{place}}}{0.8} = \frac{514}{100} \times \frac{8}{10} = \frac{514 \times 8}{100 \times 10} = \frac{4112}{1000} = \underset{\substack{\uparrow\\3\ \text{places}}}{4.\underset{\smile}{112}}
$$

We can also do this calculation more quickly by multiplying the whole numbers 8 and 514 and then determining the position of the decimal point.

MULTIPLICATION WITH DECIMAL NOTATION

a) Ignore the decimal points and multiply as whole numbers.
b) Place the decimal point in the result of step (a) by adding the number of decimal places in the original factors.

EXAMPLE 7 Multiply: 5.14×0.8.

a) Ignore the decimal points and multiply as whole numbers.

$$
\begin{array}{r}
\overset{1\ \ 3}{5.1\ 4} \\
\times\ \ \ \ 0.8 \\
\hline
4\ 1\ 1\ 2
\end{array}
$$

b) Place the decimal point in the result of step (a) by adding the number of decimal places in the original factors.

$$
\begin{array}{r}
5.1\ 4 \longleftarrow 2\ \text{decimal places} \\
\times\ \ \ \ 0.8 \longleftarrow 1\ \text{decimal place} \\
\hline
4.1\ 1\ 2
\end{array}
$$

$\quad\quad\quad\quad\quad\quad\uparrow$
$\quad\quad\quad\quad\quad\quad$ 3 decimal places

Do Exercises 13–15.

Subtract.

9. $29.35 - 1.674$

10. $92.375 - 27.692$

11. $100 - 0.41$

12. $240 - 0.117$

Multiply.

13.
$$
\begin{array}{r}
6.5\ 2 \\
\times\ \ \ 0.9 \\
\hline
\end{array}
$$

14.
$$
\begin{array}{r}
6.5\ 2 \\
\times\ 0.0\ 9 \\
\hline
\end{array}
$$

15.
$$
\begin{array}{r}
5\ 6.7\ 6 \\
\times\ 0.9\ 0\ 8 \\
\hline
\end{array}
$$

Answers on page A-1

Divide.

16. $7 \overline{)\ 3\ 4\ 2.3}$

17. $1\ 6 \overline{)\ 2\ 5\ 3.1\ 2}$

Divide.

18. $2\ 5 \overline{)\ 3\ 2}$

19. $3\ 8 \overline{)\ 6\ 8\ 2.1}$

Divide.

20. $0.0\ 2\ 4 \overline{)\ 2\ 0.5\ 4\ 4}$

21. $4.6 \overline{)\ 3.9\ 1}$

Convert to decimal notation.

22. $\dfrac{5}{8}$

23. $\dfrac{2}{3}$

24. $\dfrac{84}{11}$

Note that $37.6 \div 8 = 4.7$ because $8 \times 4.7 = 37.6$. If we write this as shown at right, we see how the following method can be used to divide by a whole number.

$$
\begin{array}{r}
4.7 \\
8 \overline{)\ 3\ 7.6} \\
3\ 2 \\
\hline
5\ 6 \\
5\ 6 \\
\hline
0
\end{array}
$$

> **DIVIDING WHEN THE DIVISOR IS A WHOLE NUMBER**
>
> a) Place the decimal point in the quotient directly above the decimal point in the dividend.
> b) Divide as whole numbers.

EXAMPLE 8 Divide: $216.75 \div 25$.

a)
$$
25 \overline{)\ 2\ 1\ 6.7\ 5}
$$
Place the decimal point.

b)
$$
\begin{array}{r}
8.6\ 7 \\
25 \overline{)\ 2\ 1\ 6.7\ 5} \\
2\ 0\ 0 \\
\hline
1\ 6\ 7 \\
1\ 5\ 0 \\
\hline
1\ 7\ 5 \\
1\ 7\ 5 \\
\hline
0
\end{array}
$$
Divide as though dividing whole numbers.

Do Exercises 16 and 17.

Sometimes it is helpful to write extra zeros to the right of the decimal point. Doing so does not change the answer. Remember that the decimal point for a whole number, though not normally written, is to the right of the number.

EXAMPLE 9 Divide: $54 \div 8$.

a)
$$
8 \overline{)\ 5\ 4.}
$$

b)
$$
\begin{array}{r}
6.7\ 5 \\
8 \overline{)\ 5\ 4.0\ 0} \\
4\ 8 \\
\hline
6\ 0 \\
5\ 6 \\
\hline
4\ 0 \\
4\ 0 \\
\hline
0
\end{array}
$$
Extra zeros are written to the right of the decimal point as needed.

Do Exercises 18 and 19.

> **DIVIDING WHEN THE DIVISOR IS NOT A WHOLE NUMBER**
>
> a) Move the decimal point in the divisor as many places to the right as it takes to make it a whole number. Move the decimal point in the dividend the same number of places to the right and place the decimal point in the quotient.
> b) Divide as whole numbers, inserting zeros if necessary.

EXAMPLE 10 Divide: $83.79 \div 0.098$.

a)

$$0.098.\overline{)\,83.790.}$$

b)

$$\begin{array}{r} 8\ 5\ 5. \\ 0.098_\wedge\overline{)\,83.790_\wedge} \\ 7\ 8\ 4 \\ \hline 5\ 3\ 9 \\ 4\ 9\ 0 \\ \hline 4\ 9\ 0 \\ 4\ 9\ 0 \\ \hline 0 \end{array}$$

Do Exercises 20 and 21 on the preceding page.

CONVERTING FROM FRACTION NOTATION TO DECIMAL NOTATION

To convert from fraction notation to decimal notation when the denominator is not a number like 10, 100, or 1000, we divide the numerator by the denominator.

EXAMPLE 11 Convert to decimal notation: $\dfrac{5}{16}$.

$$\begin{array}{r} 0.3\ 1\ 2\ 5 \\ 16\overline{)\,5.0\ 0\ 0\ 0} \\ 4\ 8 \\ \hline 2\ 0 \\ 1\ 6 \\ \hline 4\ 0 \\ 3\ 2 \\ \hline 8\ 0 \\ 8\ 0 \\ \hline 0 \end{array}$$

If we get a remainder of 0, the decimal *terminates*. Thus, $\frac{5}{16} = 0.3125$.

EXAMPLE 12 Convert to decimal notation: $\dfrac{7}{12}$.

$$\begin{array}{r} 0.5\ 8\ 3\ 3 \\ 12\overline{)\,7.0\ 0\ 0\ 0} \\ 6\ 0 \\ \hline 1\ 0\ 0 \\ 9\ 6 \\ \hline 4\ 0 \\ 3\ 6 \\ \hline 4\ 0 \\ 3\ 6 \\ \hline 4 \end{array}$$

The number 4 repeats as a remainder, so the digit 3 will repeat in the quotient. Therefore,

$$\frac{7}{12} = 0.583333\ldots.$$

Instead of dots, we often put a bar over the repeating part—in this case, only the 3. Thus,

$$\frac{7}{12} = 0.58\overline{3}.$$

Do Exercises 22–24 on the preceding page.

Round to the nearest tenth.

25. 2.76

26. 13.85

27. 7.009

Round to the nearest hundredth.

28. 7.834

29. 34.675

30. 0.025

Round to the nearest thousandth.

31. 0.9434

32. 8.0038

33. 43.1119

34. 37.4005

Round 7459.3549 to the nearest:

35. thousandth.

36. hundredth.

37. tenth.

38. one.

39. ten.

Answers on page A-1

When working with decimal notation in real-life situations, we often shorten notation by **rounding.** Although there are many rules for rounding, we will use the following.

ROUNDING DECIMAL NOTATION

To round to a certain place:

a) Locate the digit in that place.
b) Consider the digit to its right.
c) If the digit to the right is 5 or higher, round up; if the digit to the right is less than 5, round down.

EXAMPLE 13   Round 3872.2459 to the nearest tenth.

a) We locate the digit in the tenths place, 2.

3 8 7 2.2 4 5 9
     ↑

b) Then we consider the next digit to the right, 4.

3 8 7 2.2 4 5 9
         ↑

c) Since that digit, 4, is less than 5, we round down.

3 8 7 2.2 ← This is the answer.

EXAMPLE 14   Round 3872.2459 to the nearest thousandth, hundredth, tenth, one, ten, hundred, and thousand.

thousandth:	3872.246
hundredth:	3872.25
tenth:	3872.2
one:	3872
ten:	3870
hundred:	3900
thousand:	4000

Do Exercises 25–39.

In rounding, we sometimes use the symbol ≈, which means "is approximately equal to." Thus,

$$46.124 \approx 46.1.$$

a Convert to fraction notation. Do not simplify.

1. 5.3

2. 2.7

3. 0.67

4. 0.93

5. 2.0007

6. 4.0008

7. 7889.8

8. 1122.3

Convert to decimal notation.

9. $\dfrac{1}{10}$

10. $\dfrac{1}{100}$

11. $\dfrac{1}{10,000}$

12. $\dfrac{1}{1000}$

13. $\dfrac{9999}{1000}$

14. $\dfrac{39}{10,000}$

15. $\dfrac{4578}{10,000}$

16. $\dfrac{94}{100,000}$

b Add.

17.
$$
\begin{array}{r}
4\ 1\ 5.7\ 8 \\
+\ \ \ 2\ 9.1\ 6 \\
\hline
\end{array}
$$

18.
$$
\begin{array}{r}
7\ 0\ 8.9\ 9 \\
+\ \ \ \ 7\ 5.4\ 8 \\
\hline
\end{array}
$$

19.
$$
\begin{array}{r}
2\ 3\ 4.0\ 0\ 0 \\
+\ 1\ 5\ 6.6\ 1\ 7 \\
\hline
\end{array}
$$

20.
$$
\begin{array}{r}
1\ 3\ 4\ 5.1\ 2 \\
+\ \ \ \ 5\ 6\ 6.9\ 8 \\
\hline
\end{array}
$$

21. 85 + 67.95 + 2.774

22. 119 + 43.74 + 18.876

23. 17.95 + 16.99 + 28.85

24. 14.59 + 16.79 + 19.95

Subtract.

25.
$$
\begin{array}{r}
7\ 8.1\ 1\ 0 \\
-\ 4\ 5.8\ 7\ 6 \\
\hline
\end{array}
$$

26.
$$
\begin{array}{r}
1\ 4.0\ 8\ 0 \\
-\ \ \ 9.1\ 9\ 9 \\
\hline
\end{array}
$$

27.
$$
\begin{array}{r}
3\ 8.7 \\
-\ 1\ 1.8\ 6\ 5 \\
\hline
\end{array}
$$

28.
$$
\begin{array}{r}
3\ 0\ 0. \\
-\ \ \ 2\ 4.6\ 7\ 7 \\
\hline
\end{array}
$$

29. 57.86 − 9.95

30. 2.6 − 1.08

31. 3 − 1.0807

32. 5 − 3.4051

Multiply.

33.
$$
\begin{array}{r}
7.3\ 4 \\
\times\ \ \ \ 1.8 \\
\hline
\end{array}
$$

34.
$$
\begin{array}{r}
6.5\ 5 \\
\times\ \ \ \ 3.2 \\
\hline
\end{array}
$$

35.
$$
\begin{array}{r}
0.8\ 6 \\
\times\ 0.9\ 3 \\
\hline
\end{array}
$$

36.
$$
\begin{array}{r}
0.0\ 2\ 8 \\
\times\ 7.4\ 0\ 9 \\
\hline
\end{array}
$$

37.
$$
\begin{array}{r}
1\ 7.9\ 5 \\
\times\ \ \ \ \ \ 1\ 0 \\
\hline
\end{array}
$$

38.
$$
\begin{array}{r}
1\ 8.9\ 4 \\
\times\ \ \ \ \ 0.1 \\
\hline
\end{array}
$$

39.
$$
\begin{array}{r}
0.4\ 5\ 7 \\
\times\ \ \ \ 3.0\ 8 \\
\hline
\end{array}
$$

40.
$$
\begin{array}{r}
0.0\ 0\ 2\ 4 \\
\times\ \ \ 0.0\ 1\ 5 \\
\hline
\end{array}
$$

41.
$$
\begin{array}{r}
3.6\ 4\ 2 \\
\times\ \ \ 0.9\ 9 \\
\hline
\end{array}
$$

42.
$$
\begin{array}{r}
2\ 8\ 7.4 \\
\times\ \ \ \ 1.0\ 8 \\
\hline
\end{array}
$$

Divide.

43. $7\,2\,\overline{)\,1\,6\,5.6}$ **44.** $5.2\,\overline{)\,4\,4.2}$ **45.** $8.5\,\overline{)\,4\,4.2}$ **46.** $7.8\,\overline{)\,7\,2.5\,4}$

47. $9.9\,\overline{)\,0.2\,2\,7\,7}$ **48.** $1\,0\,0\,\overline{)\,9\,5}$ **49.** $0.6\,4\,\overline{)\,1\,2}$ **50.** $1.6\,\overline{)\,7\,5}$

51. $1.0\,5\,\overline{)\,6\,9\,3}$ **52.** $2\,5\,\overline{)\,4}$ **53.** $8.6\,\overline{)\,5.8\,4\,8}$ **54.** $0.4\,7\,\overline{)\,0.1\,2\,2\,2}$

Convert to decimal notation.

55. $\dfrac{11}{32}$ **56.** $\dfrac{17}{32}$ **57.** $\dfrac{13}{11}$ **58.** $\dfrac{17}{12}$

59. $\dfrac{5}{9}$ **60.** $\dfrac{5}{6}$ **61.** $\dfrac{19}{9}$ **62.** $\dfrac{9}{11}$

C Round to the nearest hundredth, tenth, one, ten, and hundred.

63. 745.06534 **64.** 317.18565 **65.** 6780.50568 **66.** 840.15493

Round to the nearest cent and to the nearest dollar (nearest one).

67. $17.988 **68.** $20.492 **69.** $346.075 **70.** $4.718

Round to the nearest dollar.

71. $16.95 **72.** $17.50 **73.** $189.50 **74.** $567.24

Divide and round to the nearest ten-thousandth, thousandth, hundredth, tenth, and one.

75. $\dfrac{1000}{81}$ **76.** $\dfrac{23}{17}$ **77.** $\dfrac{23}{39}$ **78.** $\dfrac{8467}{5603}$

79. $\mathbf{D_W}$ A student insists that $5.367 \div 0.1$ is 0.5367. How could you convince this student that a mistake has been made?

80. $\mathbf{D_W}$ A student rounds 536.448 to the nearest one and gets 537. Explain the possible error.

SKILL MAINTENANCE

Calculate. [R.2c]

81. $\dfrac{7}{8} + \dfrac{5}{32}$ **82.** $\dfrac{15}{16} - \dfrac{11}{12}$ **83.** $\dfrac{15}{16} \cdot \dfrac{11}{12}$ **84.** $\dfrac{15}{32} \div \dfrac{3}{8}$

85. $\dfrac{9}{70} + \dfrac{8}{15}$ **86.** $\dfrac{11}{21} + \dfrac{13}{16}$ **87.** $\dfrac{9}{10} + \dfrac{1}{100} + \dfrac{113}{1000}$ **88.** $\dfrac{1}{7} + \dfrac{4}{21} + \dfrac{9}{10}$

Find the prime factorization. [R.1a]

89. 208 **90.** 128 **91.** 1250 **92.** 2560

R.4 PERCENT NOTATION

Objectives

a   Convert from percent notation to decimal notation.

b   Convert from percent notation to fraction notation.

c   Convert from decimal notation to percent notation.

d   Convert from fraction notation to percent notation.

a   Converting to Decimal Notation

Of all the major causes of mortality of people age 15 to 24, homicide accounts for 15.5%. What does this mean? It means that of every 100 deaths, 15.5 are from homicide. Thus, 15.5% is a ratio of 15.5 to 100.

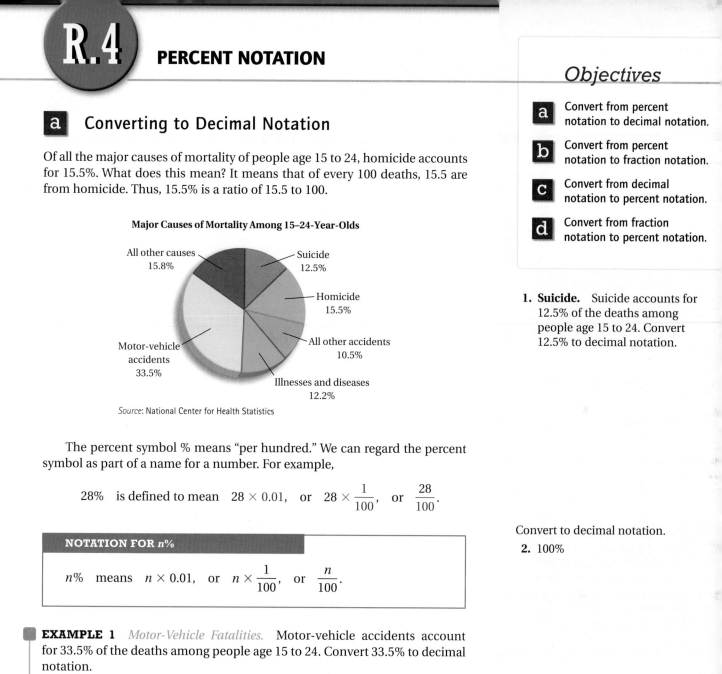

Major Causes of Mortality Among 15–24-Year-Olds

All other causes 15.8%
Suicide 12.5%
Homicide 15.5%
All other accidents 10.5%
Illnesses and diseases 12.2%
Motor-vehicle accidents 33.5%

Source: National Center for Health Statistics

The percent symbol % means "per hundred." We can regard the percent symbol as part of a name for a number. For example,

$$28\% \quad \text{is defined to mean} \quad 28 \times 0.01, \quad \text{or} \quad 28 \times \frac{1}{100}, \quad \text{or} \quad \frac{28}{100}.$$

> **NOTATION FOR $n\%$**
>
> $n\%$ means $n \times 0.01$,   or $n \times \dfrac{1}{100}$,   or $\dfrac{n}{100}$.

EXAMPLE 1   *Motor-Vehicle Fatalities.*   Motor-vehicle accidents account for 33.5% of the deaths among people age 15 to 24. Convert 33.5% to decimal notation.

$$33.5\% = 33.5 \times 0.01 \qquad \text{Replacing \% with} \times 0.01$$
$$= 0.335$$

> **FROM PERCENT NOTATION TO DECIMAL NOTATION**
>
> To convert from percent notation to decimal notation, move the decimal point *two* places to the *left* and drop the percent symbol.

EXAMPLE 2   Convert 43.67% to decimal notation.

43.67%   0.43.67   43.67% = 0.4367

Move the decimal point two places to the left.

Do Exercises 1–3.

1. **Suicide.** Suicide accounts for 12.5% of the deaths among people age 15 to 24. Convert 12.5% to decimal notation.

Convert to decimal notation.

2. 100%

3. 66.67%

Answers on page A-2

4. Water in Watermelon.
Watermelon is 90% water. Convert 90% to fraction notation.

Convert to fraction notation.
5. 53%   **6.** 45.9%

7. 0.23%

Answers on page A-2

b Converting to Fraction Notation

EXAMPLE 3 Convert 88% to fraction notation.

$$88\% = 88 \times \frac{1}{100} \qquad \text{Replacing \% with } \times \frac{1}{100}$$

$$= \frac{88}{100} \qquad \text{Multiplying. You need not simplify.}$$

EXAMPLE 4 Convert 34.8% to fraction notation.

$$34.8\% = 34.8 \times \frac{1}{100} \qquad \text{Replacing \% with } \times \frac{1}{100}$$

$$= \frac{34.8}{100}$$

$$= \frac{34.8}{100} \cdot \frac{10}{10} \qquad \begin{array}{l}\text{Multiplying by 1 to get a whole number} \\ \text{in the numerator}\end{array}$$

$$= \frac{348}{1000} \qquad \text{You need not simplify.}$$

Do Exercises 4–7.

c Converting from Decimal Notation

By applying the definition of percent in reverse, we can convert from decimal notation to percent notation. We multiply by 1, expressing it as 100×0.01 and replacing $\times 0.01$ with %.

EXAMPLE 5 *Digital Photography.* From 2000 to 2004, the use of film for photographs decreased by 0.191. Convert 0.191 to percent notation.

$$\begin{aligned} 0.191 &= 0.191 \times 1 & \text{Identity property of 1} \\ &= 0.191 \times (100 \times 0.01) & \text{Expressing 1 as } 100 \times 0.01 \\ &= (0.191 \times 100) \times 0.01 \\ &= 19.1 \times 0.01 \\ &= 19.1\% & \text{Replacing } \times 0.01 \text{ with \%} \end{aligned}$$

**FROM DECIMAL NOTATION
TO PERCENT NOTATION**

To convert from decimal notation to percent notation, move the decimal point *two* places to the *right* and write the percent symbol.

EXAMPLE 6 Convert 0.082 to percent notation.

$$0.082 \qquad 0.08.2 \qquad 0.082 = 8.2\%$$

Move the decimal point two places to the right.

Do Exercises 8–10.

8. Coal and Electrical Energy.
Of all the means of producing electrical energy, 0.51 of the electrical energy comes from coal. Convert 0.51 to percent notation.
Source: U.S. Department of Energy

Convert to percent notation.
9. 6.77   **10.** 0.9944

d Converting from Fraction Notation

We can convert from fraction notation to percent notation by converting first to decimal notation. Then we move the decimal point two places to the *right* and write a percent symbol.

EXAMPLE 7 Convert $\dfrac{5}{8}$ to percent notation.

$$\frac{5}{8} = 0.625 = 62.5\%$$

EXAMPLE 8 *Water Content.* The human body is about $\frac{2}{3}$ water. Water is the single most abundant chemical in the body. Convert $\frac{2}{3}$ to percent notation.

a) Find decimal notation for $\frac{2}{3}$ using long division.

$$
\begin{array}{r}
0.6\ 6\ 6 \\
3\ \overline{)\ 2.0\ 0\ 0} \\
\underline{1\ 8} \\
2\ 0 \\
\underline{1\ 8} \\
2\ 0 \\
\underline{1\ 8} \\
2
\end{array}
$$

We get a repeating decimal: $0.66\overline{6}$.

b) Convert the answer to percent notation.

$$0.66.\overline{6}$$

$$\frac{2}{3} = 66.\overline{6}\%, \text{ or } 66\tfrac{2}{3}\%$$

Do Exercises 11–13.

11. **Deaths from Heart Attack.** Of all those who have heart attacks, approximately $\frac{1}{3}$ of them die within one year of an initial heart attack. Convert $\frac{1}{3}$ to percent notation.
Source: American Heart Association

Convert to percent notation.

12. $\dfrac{1}{4}$

13. $\dfrac{7}{8}$

Answers on page A-2

R.4

EXERCISE SET | For Extra Help

MathXL | MyMathLab | InterAct Math | Math Tutor Center | Digital Video Tutor CD 1 Videotape 1 | Student's Solutions Manual

a   Convert the percent notation in the sentence to decimal notation.

1. *Nuclear Energy.*   Nuclear energy accounts for 21% of electrical power.
Source: U.S. Department of Energy

2. *Oil.*   Oil accounts for 3% of electrical power.
Source: U.S. Department of Energy

3. *CD Rates.*   A recent interest rate on a five-year certificate of deposit was 3.45%.
Source: Bank Rate Monitor

4. *CD Rates.*   A recent interest rate on a two-year certificate of deposit was 2.15%.
Source: Bank Rate Monitor

Convert to decimal notation.

5. 63%

6. 64%

7. 94.1%

8. 34.6%

9. 1%

10. 100%

11. 0.61%

12. 125%

13. 240%

14. 0.73%

15. 3.25%

16. 2.3%

b   Convert the percent notation in the sentence to fraction notation.

17. *Dehydration.*   A 2% drop in water content of the body can affect one's ability to study mathematics.
Source: High Performance Nutrition

18. *Hispanic Graduates.*   It is estimated that by 2008, 21% of the public high school graduates in the United States will be Hispanic.
Source: Western Interstate Commission for Higher Education

19. *Live Births.*   From 1950 to 2001, the number of live births per year in the United States increased 10.9%.
Source: U.S. Bureau of the Census

20. *Female Basketball Players.*   In a recent year, 9.6% of all female college athletes participated in basketball.
Source: National Collegiate Athletic Association

21. *Wealth in the Aged.*   Those 60 and older own 77% of the nation's financial assets.

22. *Wealth in the Aged.*   Those 60 and older make up 66% of the nation's stockholders.

Convert to fraction notation.

23. 60%

24. 40%

25. 28.9%

26. 37.5%

27. 110%

28. 120%

29. 0.042%

30. 0.68%

31. 250%

32. 3.2%

33. 3.47%

34. 12.557%

c   Convert the decimal notation in the sentence to percent notation.

35. *NASCAR Fans.*   In a poll of NASCAR fans, 0.73 of those questioned said that a sponsor's participation in the sport influences their purchasing decisions.
Source: Performance Research, Inc.

36. *NASCAR Fans.*   Of those who are fans of NASCAR racing, 0.42 of them earn more than $50,000 per year.
Source: Scott Racing, Inc.

37. *NASCAR Fans.*   Of those who are fans of NASCAR racing, 0.41 of them have attended college or beyond.
Source: TKO Motorsports

38. *NASCAR Fans.*   Of all NASCAR fans, 0.40 are women.

Convert to percent notation.

39. 1

40. 8.56

41. 0.996

42. 0.83

43. 0.0047

44. 2

45. 0.072

46. 1.34

47. 9.2

48. 0.013

49. 0.0068

50. 0.675

d   Convert to percent notation.

51. $\frac{1}{6}$

52. $\frac{1}{5}$

53. $\frac{13}{20}$

54. $\frac{14}{25}$

55. $\frac{29}{100}$

56. $\frac{123}{100}$

57. $\frac{8}{10}$

58. $\frac{7}{10}$

59. $\frac{3}{5}$

60. $\frac{17}{50}$

61. $\frac{2}{3}$

62. $\frac{7}{8}$

63. $\frac{7}{4}$

64. $\frac{3}{8}$

65. $\frac{3}{4}$

66. $\frac{99.4}{100}$

Convert the fraction notation in the sentence to percent notation.

67. *Heart-Disease Death Rate.* Of those people living in Florida, 118.6 of every 100,000 will die of heart disease.
Source: "Reforming the Health Care System; State Profiles 1999," AARP

68. *Cancer Death Rate.* Of those people living in Florida, 125.7 of every 100,000 will die of cancer.
Source: "Reforming the Health Care System; State Profiles 1999," AARP

Women at Work. The following table lists the percentages of people in various professions who are women. Fill in the blanks in the table.

WOMEN IN THE WORKPLACE

	PROFESSION	DECIMAL NOTATION	FRACTION NOTATION	PERCENT NOTATION
69.	Editor/reporter			49%
70.	Physician			31%
71.	Lawyer	0.29		
72.	Engineer	0.11		
73.	Chemist		$\frac{3}{10}$	
74.	College/university teacher		$\frac{43}{100}$	
75.	Musician/composer			36%
76.	Real-estate salesperson			55%

Source: Statistical Abstract of the United States, 2003

77. **D_W** 🖩 What would you do to an entry on a calculator in order to get percent notation?

78. **D_W** Is it always best to convert from fraction notation to percent notation by first finding decimal notation? Why or why not?

SKILL MAINTENANCE

Convert to decimal notation. [R.3b]

79. $\frac{9}{4}$ **80.** $\frac{11}{8}$ **81.** $\frac{17}{12}$ **82.** $\frac{8}{9}$ **83.** $\frac{10}{11}$ **84.** $\frac{17}{11}$

Calculate. [R.3b]
85. 23.458×7.03 **86.** $7.8\overline{)440.154}$ **87.** $809.569 + 86.99$ **88.** $809.569 - 86.99$

SYNTHESIS

Simplify. Express the answer in percent notation.

89. $18\% + 14\%$ **90.** $84\% - 12\%$ **91.** $1 - 30\%$ **92.** $92\% - 10\%$ **93.** $27 \times 100\%$

94. $42\% - (1 - 58\%)$ **95.** $3(1 + 15\%)$ **96.** $7(1\% + 13\%)$ **97.** $\frac{100\%}{40}$ **98.** $\frac{3}{4} + 20\%$

CHAPTER R: Prealgebra Review

Objectives

a	Write exponential notation for a product.
b	Evaluate exponential expressions.
c	Simplify expressions using the rules for order of operations.

a Exponential Notation

Exponents provide a shorter way of writing products. An abbreviation for a product in which the factors are the same is called a **power.** For

$$10 \cdot 10 \cdot 10, \quad \text{we write} \quad 10^3.$$

3 factors

This is read "ten to the third power." We call the number 3 an **exponent** and we say that 10 is the **base.** An exponent of 2 or greater tells how many times the base is used as a factor. For example,

$$a \cdot a \cdot a \cdot a = a^4.$$

In this case, the exponent is 4 and the base is a. An expression for a power is called **exponential notation.**

This is the exponent.

$$a^n$$

This is the base.

EXAMPLE 1 Write exponential notation for $10 \cdot 10 \cdot 10 \cdot 10 \cdot 10$.

$$10 \cdot 10 \cdot 10 \cdot 10 \cdot 10 = 10^5$$

Do Exercises 1–3.

b Evaluating Exponential Expressions

EXAMPLE 2 Evaluate: 5^2.

$$5^2 = 5 \cdot 5 = 25$$

EXAMPLE 3 Evaluate: 3^4.

We have

$$3^4 = 3 \cdot 3 \cdot 3 \cdot 3 = 9 \cdot 9 = 81.$$

We could also carry out the calculation as follows:

$$3^4 = 3 \cdot 3 \cdot 3 \cdot 3 = 9 \cdot 3 \cdot 3 = 27 \cdot 3 = 81.$$

EXPONENTIAL NOTATION

For any natural number n greater than or equal to 2,

n factors

$$b^n = b \cdot b \cdot b \cdot b \cdots b.$$

Do Exercises 4–6.

Write exponential notation.

1. $4 \cdot 4 \cdot 4$

2. $6 \cdot 6 \cdot 6 \cdot 6 \cdot 6$

3. 1.08×1.08

Evaluate.

4. 10^4

5. 8^3

6. $(1.1)^3$

Answers on page A-2

Exponents and Powers   We use the $\wedge$ key to evaluate exponential notation on a graphing calculator.

To find 3^5, for example, we press ③ $\wedge$ ⑤ **ENTER**. To find $\left(\dfrac{5}{8}\right)^3$ and express the result in fraction notation, we press

(⑤ **÷** ⑧ **)** $\wedge$ ③ **MATH** ① **ENTER**. Note that the parentheses are necessary in this calculation. If they were not used, we would be calculating $5 \div 8^3$, or $5 \div 512$. The results of these computations are shown on the left below.

```
3^5
                    243
(5/8)^3►Frac
                125/512
```

```
2.4²
                   5.76
2.4^2
                   5.76
```

The calculator has a special **x²** key that can be used to raise a number to the second power. To find 2.4^2, for example, we press ② **·** ④ **x²** **ENTER**, as shown on the right above. We could also use the $\wedge$ key to do this calculation, pressing ② **·** ④ $\wedge$ ② **ENTER**.

Exercises: Evaluate.

1. 4^5

2. 7^9

3. 19^2

4. 5.718^2

5. 1.8^4

6. 23.4^3

7. $\left(\dfrac{3}{4}\right)^5$

8. $\left(\dfrac{2}{3}\right)^6$

Calculate.

7. $16 - 3 \times 5 + 4$

8. $4 + 5 \times 2$

C Order of Operations

What does $4 + 5 \times 2$ mean? If we add 4 and 5 and multiply the result by 2, we get 18. If we multiply 5 and 2 and add 4 to the result, we get 14. Since the results are different, we see that the order in which we carry out operations is important. To indicate which operation is to be done first, we use grouping symbols such as parentheses ( ), or brackets [ ], or braces { }. For example, $(3 \times 5) + 6 = 15 + 6 = 21$, but $3 \times (5 + 6) = 3 \times 11 = 33$.

Grouping symbols tell us what to do first. If there are no grouping symbols, we have agreements about the order in which operations should be done.

RULES FOR ORDER OF OPERATIONS

1. Do all calculations within grouping symbols before operations outside.
2. Evaluate all exponential expressions.
3. Do all multiplications and divisions in order from left to right.
4. Do all additions and subtractions in order from left to right.

EXAMPLE 4   Calculate: $15 - 2 \times 5 + 3$.

$$\begin{aligned}
15 - 2 \times 5 + 3 &= 15 - 10 + 3 \qquad &\text{Multiplying} \\
&= 5 + 3 \qquad &\text{Subtracting} \\
&= 8 \qquad &\text{Adding}
\end{aligned}$$

Do Exercises 7 and 8.

Answers on page A-2

Always calculate within parentheses first. When there are exponents and no parentheses, simplify powers before multiplying or dividing.

EXAMPLE 5 Calculate: $(3 \times 4)^2$.

$$(3 \times 4)^2 = (12)^2 \qquad \text{Working within parentheses first}$$
$$= 144 \qquad \text{Evaluating the exponential expression}$$

EXAMPLE 6 Calculate: 3×4^2.

$$3 \times 4^2 = 3 \times 16 \qquad \text{Evaluating the exponential expression}$$
$$= 48 \qquad \text{Multiplying}$$

Note that $(3 \times 4)^2 \neq 3 \times 4^2$.

EXAMPLE 7 Calculate: $7 + 3 \times 29 - 4^2$.

$$7 + 3 \times 29 - 4^2 = 7 + 3 \times 29 - 16 \qquad \begin{array}{l}\text{There are no parentheses,}\\ \text{so we find } 4^2 \text{ first.}\end{array}$$
$$= 7 + 87 - 16 \qquad \text{Multiplying}$$
$$= 94 - 16 \qquad \text{Adding}$$
$$= 78 \qquad \text{Subtracting}$$

Do Exercises 9–12.

EXAMPLE 8 Calculate: $2.56 \div 1.6 \div 0.4$.

$$2.56 \div 1.6 \div 0.4 = 1.6 \div 0.4 \qquad \begin{array}{l}\text{Doing the divisions in order from}\\ \text{left to right}\end{array}$$
$$= 4 \qquad \text{Doing the second division}$$

EXAMPLE 9 Calculate: $1000 \div \frac{1}{10} \cdot \frac{4}{5}$.

$$1000 \div \frac{1}{10} \cdot \frac{4}{5} = (1000 \cdot 10) \cdot \frac{4}{5} \qquad \text{Doing the division first}$$
$$= 10{,}000 \cdot \frac{4}{5} \qquad \text{Multiplying}$$
$$= 8000 \qquad \text{Multiplying}$$

Do Exercises 13 and 14.

Sometimes combinations of grouping symbols are used, as in

$$5[4 + (8 - 2)].$$

The rules still apply. We begin with the innermost grouping symbols—in this case, the parentheses—and work to the outside.

EXAMPLE 10 Calculate: $5[4 + (8 - 2)]$.

$$5[4 + (8 - 2)] = 5[4 + 6] \qquad \text{Subtracting within the parentheses first}$$
$$= 5[10] \qquad \text{Adding inside the brackets}$$
$$= 50 \qquad \text{Multiplying}$$

Calculate.

9. $18 - 4 \times 3 + 7$

10. $(2 \times 5)^3$

11. 2×5^3

12. $8 + 2 \times 5^3 - 4 \cdot 20$

Calculate.

13. $51.2 \div 0.64 \div 40$

14. $1000 \cdot \frac{1}{10} \div \frac{4}{5}$

Answers on page A-2

Calculate.

15. $4[(8 - 3) + 7]$

16. $\dfrac{13(10 - 6) + 4 \cdot 9}{5^2 - 3^2}$

Answers on page A-2

A fraction bar can play the role of a grouping symbol.

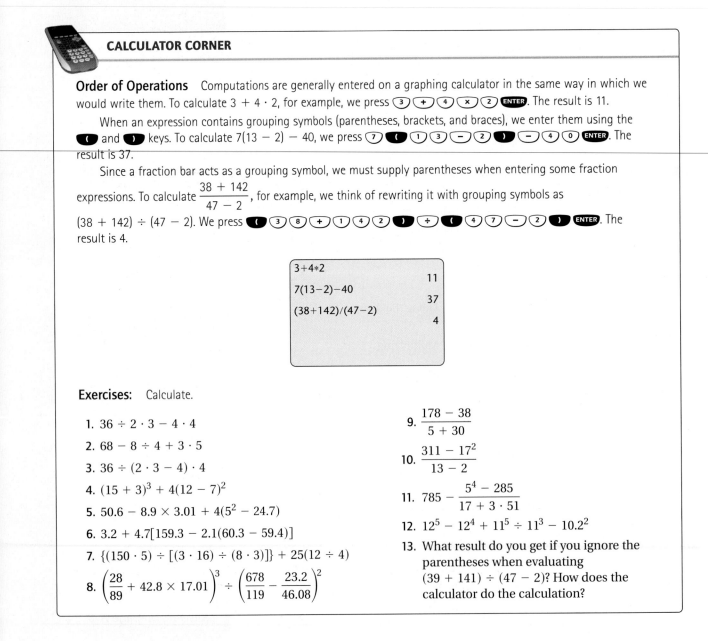

EXAMPLE 11 Calculate: $\dfrac{12(9 - 7) + 4 \cdot 5}{3^3 - 2^4}$.

An equivalent expression with brackets as grouping symbols is

$$[12(9 - 7) + 4 \cdot 5] \div [3^3 - 2^4].$$

What this shows, in effect, is that we do the calculations first in the numerator and then in the denominator, and then divide the results:

$$\frac{12(9 - 7) + 4 \cdot 5}{3^3 - 2^4} = \frac{12(2) + 4 \cdot 5}{27 - 16} = \frac{24 + 20}{11} = \frac{44}{11} = 4.$$

Do Exercises 15 and 16.

CALCULATOR CORNER

Order of Operations Computations are generally entered on a graphing calculator in the same way in which we would write them. To calculate $3 + 4 \cdot 2$, for example, we press ③ ➕ ④ ✖ ② **ENTER**. The result is 11.

When an expression contains grouping symbols (parentheses, brackets, and braces), we enter them using the **(** and **)** keys. To calculate $7(13 - 2) - 40$, we press ⑦ **(** ① ③ ➖ ② **)** ➖ ④ ⓪ **ENTER**. The result is 37.

Since a fraction bar acts as a grouping symbol, we must supply parentheses when entering some fraction expressions. To calculate $\dfrac{38 + 142}{47 - 2}$, for example, we think of rewriting it with grouping symbols as $(38 + 142) \div (47 - 2)$. We press **(** ③ ⑧ ➕ ① ④ ② **)** ➗ **(** ④ ⑦ ➖ ② **)** **ENTER**. The result is 4.

```
3+4*2
               11
7(13−2)−40
               37
(38+142)/(47−2)
               4
```

Exercises: Calculate.

1. $36 \div 2 \cdot 3 - 4 \cdot 4$

2. $68 - 8 \div 4 + 3 \cdot 5$

3. $36 \div (2 \cdot 3 - 4) \cdot 4$

4. $(15 + 3)^3 + 4(12 - 7)^2$

5. $50.6 - 8.9 \times 3.01 + 4(5^2 - 24.7)$

6. $3.2 + 4.7[159.3 - 2.1(60.3 - 59.4)]$

7. $\{(150 \cdot 5) \div [(3 \cdot 16) \div (8 \cdot 3)]\} + 25(12 \div 4)$

8. $\left(\dfrac{28}{89} + 42.8 \times 17.01\right)^3 \div \left(\dfrac{678}{119} - \dfrac{23.2}{46.08}\right)^2$

9. $\dfrac{178 - 38}{5 + 30}$

10. $\dfrac{311 - 17^2}{13 - 2}$

11. $785 - \dfrac{5^4 - 285}{17 + 3 \cdot 51}$

12. $12^5 - 12^4 + 11^5 \div 11^3 - 10.2^2$

13. What result do you get if you ignore the parentheses when evaluating $(39 + 141) \div (47 - 2)$? How does the calculator do the calculation?

a   Write exponential notation.

1. $5 \times 5 \times 5 \times 5$

2. $3 \times 3 \times 3 \times 3 \times 3$

3. $10 \cdot 10 \cdot 10$

4. $1 \cdot 1 \cdot 1$

5. $10 \times 10 \times 10 \times 10 \times 10 \times 10$

6. $18 \cdot 18$

b   Evaluate.

7. 7^2

8. 4^3

9. 9^5

10. 12^4

11. 10^2

12. 1^5

13. 1^4

14. $(1.8)^2$

15. $(2.3)^2$

16. $(0.1)^3$

17. $(0.2)^3$

18. $(14.8)^2$

19. $(20.4)^2$

20. $\left(\dfrac{4}{5}\right)^2$

21. $\left(\dfrac{3}{8}\right)^2$

22. 2^4

23. 5^3

24. $(1.4)^3$

25. $1000 \times (1.02)^3$

26. $2000 \times (1.06)^2$

c   Calculate.

27. $9 + 2 \times 8$

28. $14 + 6 \times 6$

29. $9(8) + 7(6)$

30. $30(5) + 2(2)$

31. $39 - 4 \times 2 + 2$

32. $14 - 2 \times 6 + 7$

33. $9 \div 3 + 16 \div 8$

34. $32 - 8 \div 4 - 2$

35. $7 + 10 - 10 \div 2$

36. $(5 \cdot 4)^2$

37. $(6 \cdot 3)^2$

38. $3 \cdot 2^3$

39. $4 \cdot 5^2$

40. $(7 + 3)^2$

41. $(8 + 2)^3$

42. $7 + 2^2$

43. $6 + 4^2$

44. $(5 - 2)^2$

45. $(3 - 2)^2$

46. $10 - 3^2$

47. $4^3 \div 8 - 4$

48. $20 + 4^3 \div 8 - 4$

49. $120 - 3^3 \cdot 4 \div 6$

50. $7 \times 3^4 + 18$

51. $6[9 + (3 + 4)]$

52. $8[(13 + 6) - 11]$

53. $8 + (7 + 9)$

54. $(8 + 7) + 9$

55. $15(4 + 2)$

56. $15 \cdot 4 + 15 \cdot 2$

57. $12 - (8 - 4)$

58. $(12 - 8) - 4$

59. $1000 \div 100 \div 10$

60. $256 \div 32 \div 4$

61. $2000 \div \dfrac{3}{50} \cdot \dfrac{3}{2}$

62. $400 \times 0.64 \div 3.2$

63. $75 \div 15 \cdot 4 \cdot 8 \div 32$

64. $84 \div 12 \cdot 10 \div 35 \cdot 8 \cdot 2 \div 16$

65. $16 \cdot 5 \div 80 \div 12 \cdot 36 \cdot 9$

66. $20 \cdot 45 \div 15 \div 15 \cdot 60 \div 12$

67. $\dfrac{80 - 6^2}{9^2 + 3^2}$

68. $\dfrac{5^2 + 4^3 - 3}{9^2 - 2^2 + 1^5}$

69. $\dfrac{3(6 + 7) - 5 \cdot 4}{6 \cdot 7 + 8(4 - 1)}$

70. $\dfrac{20(8 - 3) - 4(10 - 3)}{10(6 + 2) + 2(5 + 2)}$

71. $8 \cdot 2 - (12 - 0) \div 3 - (5 - 2)$

72. $95 - 2^3 \cdot 5 \div (24 - 4)$

73. **D$_W$** The expression $(3 \cdot 4)^2$ contains parentheses. Are they necessary? Why or why not?

74. **D$_W$** The expression $9 - (4 \cdot 2)$ contains parentheses. Are they necessary? Why or why not?

SKILL MAINTENANCE

Find percent notation.   [R.4d]

75. $\dfrac{5}{16}$

76. $\dfrac{11}{6}$

Simplify.   [R.2b]

77. $\dfrac{9}{2001}$

78. $\dfrac{2005}{3640}$

79. Find the prime factorization of 48.   [R.1a]

80. Find the LCM of 12, 24, and 56.   [R.1b]

SYNTHESIS

Write each of the following with a single exponent.

81. $\dfrac{10^5}{10^3}$

82. $\dfrac{10^7}{10^2}$

83. $5^4 \cdot 5^2$

84. $\dfrac{2^8}{8^2}$

85. *Five 5's.*   We can use five 5's and grouping symbols to represent the numbers 0 through 10. For example,

$$0 = 5 \cdot 5 \cdot 5(5 - 5), \qquad 1 = \frac{5 + 5}{5} - \frac{5}{5}, \qquad 2 = \frac{5 \cdot 5 - 5}{5 + 5}.$$

Often more than one way to make a representation is possible. Use five 5's to represent the numbers 3 through 10.

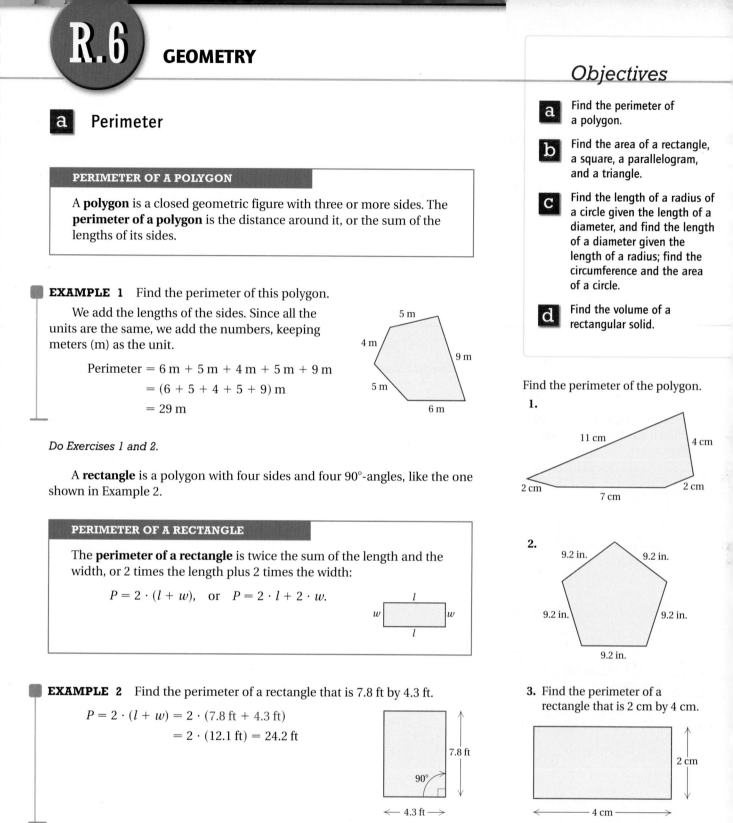

R.6 GEOMETRY

Objectives

a Find the perimeter of a polygon.

b Find the area of a rectangle, a square, a parallelogram, and a triangle.

c Find the length of a radius of a circle given the length of a diameter, and find the length of a diameter given the length of a radius; find the circumference and the area of a circle.

d Find the volume of a rectangular solid.

a Perimeter

PERIMETER OF A POLYGON

A **polygon** is a closed geometric figure with three or more sides. The **perimeter of a polygon** is the distance around it, or the sum of the lengths of its sides.

EXAMPLE 1 Find the perimeter of this polygon.

We add the lengths of the sides. Since all the units are the same, we add the numbers, keeping meters (m) as the unit.

$$\text{Perimeter} = 6\,\text{m} + 5\,\text{m} + 4\,\text{m} + 5\,\text{m} + 9\,\text{m}$$
$$= (6 + 5 + 4 + 5 + 9)\,\text{m}$$
$$= 29\,\text{m}$$

Do Exercises 1 and 2.

A **rectangle** is a polygon with four sides and four 90°-angles, like the one shown in Example 2.

PERIMETER OF A RECTANGLE

The **perimeter of a rectangle** is twice the sum of the length and the width, or 2 times the length plus 2 times the width:

$$P = 2 \cdot (l + w), \quad \text{or} \quad P = 2 \cdot l + 2 \cdot w.$$

EXAMPLE 2 Find the perimeter of a rectangle that is 7.8 ft by 4.3 ft.

$$P = 2 \cdot (l + w) = 2 \cdot (7.8\,\text{ft} + 4.3\,\text{ft})$$
$$= 2 \cdot (12.1\,\text{ft}) = 24.2\,\text{ft}$$

Do Exercises 3 and 4.

Find the perimeter of the polygon.

1.

2.

3. Find the perimeter of a rectangle that is 2 cm by 4 cm.

4. Find the perimeter of a rectangle that is 5.25 yd by 3.5 yd.

Answers on page A-2

5. Find the perimeter of a square with sides of length 10 km.

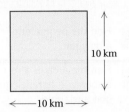

10 km

←——10 km——→

A **square** is a rectangle with all sides the same length.

PERIMETER OF A SQUARE

The **perimeter of a square** is four times the length of a side:

$$P = 4 \cdot s.$$

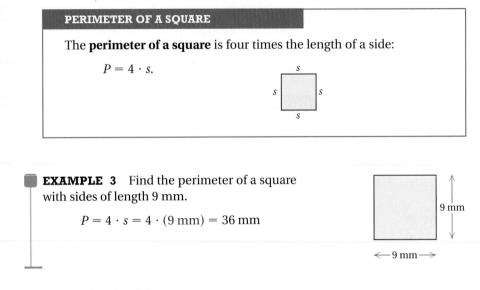

EXAMPLE 3 Find the perimeter of a square with sides of length 9 mm.

$$P = 4 \cdot s = 4 \cdot (9 \text{ mm}) = 36 \text{ mm}$$

9 mm

←—9 mm—→

6. Find the perimeter of a square with sides of length $5\frac{1}{4}$ yd.

Do Exercises 5 and 6.

7. What is the area of this region? Count the number of square centimeters.

2 cm

4 cm

b Area

RECTANGLES

We can find the area of a rectangle by filling it with square units. Two such units, a *square inch* and a *square centimeter*, are shown below.

Square inch

←———1 in.———→

Square centimeter

1 cm

8. Find the area of a rectangle that is 7 km by 8 km.

AREA OF A RECTANGLE

The **area of a rectangle** is the product of the length *l* and the width *w*:

$$A = l \cdot w.$$

w

l

---

9. Find the area of a rectangle that is 5.3 yd by 3.2 yd.

EXAMPLE 4 Find the area of a rectangle that is 7 yd by 4 yd.

$$A = l \cdot w = 7 \text{ yd} \cdot 4 \text{ yd} = 7 \cdot 4 \cdot \text{yd} \cdot \text{yd} = 28 \text{ yd}^2$$

We think of yd · yd as $(\text{yd})^2$ and denote it yd^2. Thus we read "28 yd^2" as "28 square yards."

Answers on page A-2

Do Exercises 7–9.

SQUARES

10. Find the area of a square with sides of length 10.9 m.

AREA OF A SQUARE

The **area of a square** is the square of the length of a side:

$$A = s \cdot s, \quad \text{or} \quad A = s^2.$$

EXAMPLE 5 Find the area of a square with sides of length 20.3 m.

$$A = s \cdot s = 20.3 \text{ m} \times 20.3 \text{ m}$$
$$= 20.3 \times 20.3 \times \text{m} \times \text{m} = 412.09 \text{ m}^2$$

Do Exercises 10 and 11.

PARALLELOGRAMS

A **parallelogram** is a four-sided polygon with two pairs of parallel sides, as shown below.

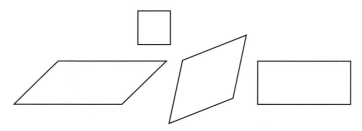

11. Find the area of a square with sides of length $\frac{5}{8}$ yd.

To find the area of a parallelogram, consider the one below.

If we cut off a piece and move it to the other end, we get a rectangle.

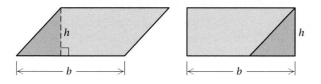

We can find the area by multiplying the length b, called a **base,** by h, called the **height.** The height forms a 90° angle with the base.

AREA OF A PARALLELOGRAM

The **area of a parallelogram** is the product of a base b and the height h:

$$A = b \cdot h.$$

Answers on page A-2

Find the area.

12.

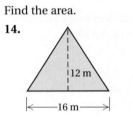
6 cm
7.3 cm

EXAMPLE 6 Find the area of this parallelogram.

$A = b \cdot h$
$= 7 \text{ km} \cdot 5 \text{ km}$
$= 35 \text{ km}^2$

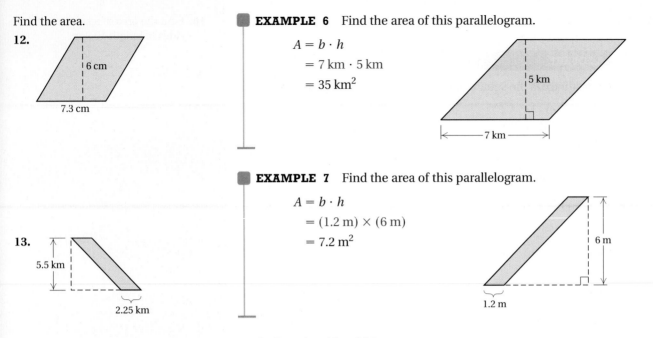
5 km
7 km

EXAMPLE 7 Find the area of this parallelogram.

$A = b \cdot h$
$= (1.2 \text{ m}) \times (6 \text{ m})$
$= 7.2 \text{ m}^2$

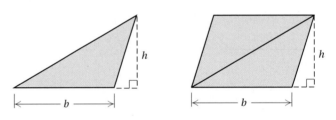
6 m
1.2 m

13.

5.5 km
2.25 km

Do Exercises 12 and 13.

TRIANGLES

To find the area of a triangle, think of cutting out another just like it. Then place the second one as shown in the figure on the right.

Find the area.

14.

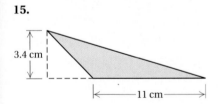
12 m
16 m

h
b
h
b

The resulting figure is a parallelogram whose area is $b \cdot h$. The triangle we started with has half the area of the parallelogram, or $\frac{1}{2} \cdot b \cdot h$.

AREA OF A TRIANGLE

The **area of a triangle** is half the length of the base times the height:

$$A = \frac{1}{2} \cdot b \cdot h.$$

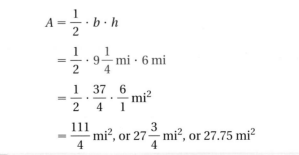
h
b

15.

3.4 cm
11 cm

EXAMPLE 8 Find the area of this triangle.

$A = \frac{1}{2} \cdot b \cdot h$

$= \frac{1}{2} \cdot 9\frac{1}{4} \text{ mi} \cdot 6 \text{ mi}$

$= \frac{1}{2} \cdot \frac{37}{4} \cdot \frac{6}{1} \text{ mi}^2$

$= \frac{111}{4} \text{ mi}^2, \text{ or } 27\frac{3}{4} \text{ mi}^2, \text{ or } 27.75 \text{ mi}^2$

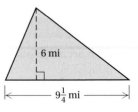
6 mi
$9\frac{1}{4}$ mi

Answers on page A-2

EXAMPLE 9 Find the area of this triangle.

$$A = \frac{1}{2} \cdot b \cdot h$$

$$= \frac{1}{2} \times 6.25 \text{ ft} \times 5.5 \text{ ft}$$

$$= 0.5 \times 6.25 \times 5.5 \text{ ft}^2$$

$$= 17.1875 \text{ ft}^2$$

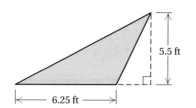

Do Exercises 14 and 15 on the preceding page.

C Circles

DIAMETER AND RADIUS OF A CIRCLE

Shown at right is a circle with center O. Segment $\overline{AC}$ is a *diameter*. A **diameter** is a segment that passes through the center of the circle and has endpoints on the circle. Segment $\overline{OB}$ is called a *radius*. A **radius** is a segment with one endpoint on the center and the other endpoint on the circle.

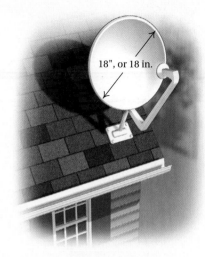

DIAMETER AND RADIUS

Suppose that d is the diameter of a circle and r is the radius. Then

$$d = 2 \cdot r \quad \text{and} \quad r = \frac{d}{2}.$$

Do Exercises 16 and 17.

CIRCUMFERENCE OF A CIRCLE

The **circumference** of a circle is the distance around it. Calculating circumference is similar to finding the perimeter of a polygon. For any circle, if we divide the circumference C by the diameter d, we get the same number. We call this number π (pi):

$$\pi = \frac{C}{d}.$$

CIRCUMFERENCE OF A CIRCLE

The **circumference** C of a circle is given by

$$C = \pi \cdot d, \quad \text{or} \quad C = 2 \cdot \pi \cdot r,$$

where d is the diameter and r is the radius. The number π is about 3.14, or about $\frac{22}{7}$.

EXAMPLE 10 Find the circumference of this circle. Use 3.14 for π.

$$C = \pi \cdot d$$

$$\approx 3.14 \times 6 \text{ cm}$$

$$= 18.84 \text{ cm}$$

The circumference is about 18.84 cm.

16. Find the length of a radius.

17. Find the length of a diameter.

18. Find the circumference of this circle. Use 3.14 for π.

19. Find the circumference of this circle. Use $\frac{22}{7}$ for π.

Answers on page A-2

20. Find the area of this circle. Use $\frac{22}{7}$ for π.

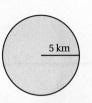

5 km

21. Find the area of this circle. Use 3.14 for π. Round to the nearest hundredth.

10.4 cm

Answers on page A-2

EXAMPLE 11   Find the circumference of this circle. Use $\frac{22}{7}$ for π.

$$C = 2 \cdot \pi \cdot r$$

$$\approx 2 \cdot \frac{22}{7} \cdot 70 \text{ in.}$$

$$= 2 \cdot 22 \cdot \frac{70}{7} \text{ in.}$$

$$= 44 \cdot 10 \text{ in.}$$

$$= 440 \text{ in.}$$

The circumference is about 440 in.

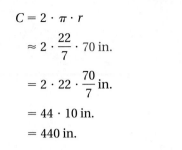

70 in.

Do Exercises 18 and 19 on the preceding page.

AREA OF A CIRCLE

Now we consider a formula for the area of a circle.

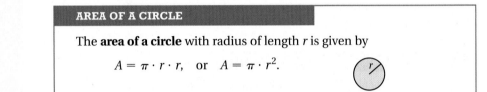

AREA OF A CIRCLE

The **area of a circle** with radius of length r is given by

$$A = \pi \cdot r \cdot r, \quad \text{or} \quad A = \pi \cdot r^2.$$

r

CALCULATOR CORNER

Using the Pi Key   On certain calculators, there is a pi key, $\boxed{\pi}$. You can use a $\boxed{\pi}$ key for most computations instead of stopping to round the value of π. Rounding, if necessary, is done at the end.

Exercises:

1. If you have a $\boxed{\pi}$ key on your calculator, to how many places does this key give the value of π?

2. Find the circumference and the area of a circle with a radius of 225.68 in.

3. Find the area of a circle with a diameter of 46.6 in.

4. Find the area of a large irrigated farming circle with a diameter of 400 ft.

EXAMPLE 12   Find the area of this circle. Use $\frac{22}{7}$ for π.

$$A = \pi \cdot r \cdot r$$

$$\approx \frac{22}{7} \cdot 14 \text{ cm} \cdot 14 \text{ cm}$$

$$= \frac{22}{7} \cdot 196 \text{ cm}^2$$

$$= 616 \text{ cm}^2$$

The area is about 616 cm^2.

14 cm

Do Exercise 20.

EXAMPLE 13   Find the area of this circle. Use 3.14 for π. Round to the nearest hundredth.

$$A = \pi \cdot r \cdot r$$

$$\approx 3.14 \times 2.1 \text{ m} \times 2.1 \text{ m}$$

$$= 3.14 \times 4.41 \text{ m}^2$$

$$= 13.8474 \text{ m}^2$$

$$\approx 13.85 \text{ m}^2$$

The area is about 13.85 m^2.

2.1 m

Do Exercise 21.

d Volume

The **volume of a rectangular solid** is the number of unit cubes needed to fill it.

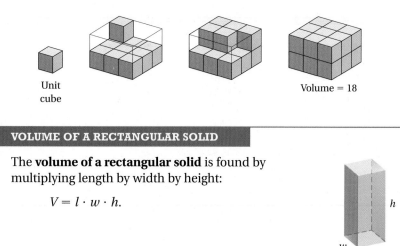

Unit
cube

Volume = 18

VOLUME OF A RECTANGULAR SOLID

The **volume of a rectangular solid** is found by multiplying length by width by height:

$$V = l \cdot w \cdot h.$$

22. Cord of Wood. A cord of wood is 4 ft by 4 ft by 8 ft. What is the volume of a cord of wood?

Source: *The American Heritage Dictionary of the English Language*

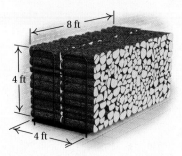

8 ft

4 ft

4 ft

EXAMPLE 14 *Truck Toolbox.* The volume of a truck toolbox is the sum of the volumes of two rectangular solids. The upper portion measures $70\frac{1}{2}$ in. by $20\frac{1}{8}$ in. by $7\frac{1}{2}$ in. The lower portion measures $60\frac{1}{2}$ in. by $20\frac{1}{8}$ in. by $11\frac{1}{4}$ in. Find the total volume of the toolbox.

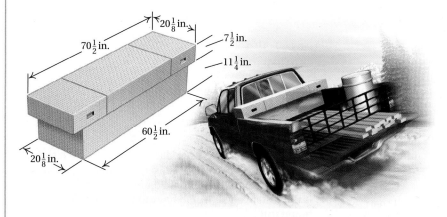

We use the formula

$$V = l \cdot w \cdot h.$$

The volume of the upper portion is

$$V = 70\frac{1}{2} \text{ in.} \times 20\frac{1}{8} \text{ in.} \times 7\frac{1}{2} \text{ in.}$$
$$= \frac{141}{2} \times \frac{161}{8} \times \frac{15}{2} \text{ in}^3 = \frac{340,515}{32} \text{ in}^3 = 10{,}641\frac{3}{32} \text{ in}^3.$$

The volume of the lower portion is

$$V = 60\frac{1}{2} \text{ in.} \times 20\frac{1}{8} \text{ in.} \times 11\frac{1}{4} \text{ in.}$$
$$= \frac{121}{2} \times \frac{161}{8} \times \frac{45}{4} \text{ in}^3 = \frac{876,645}{64} \text{ in}^3 = 13{,}697\frac{37}{64} \text{ in}^3.$$

The total volume of the toolbox is

$$10{,}641\tfrac{3}{32} \text{ in}^3 + 13{,}697\tfrac{37}{64} \text{ in}^3 = 10{,}641\tfrac{6}{64} \text{ in}^3 + 13{,}697\tfrac{37}{64} \text{ in}^3 = 24{,}338\tfrac{43}{64} \text{ in}^3.$$

Answer on page A-2

Do Exercise 22.

45

R.6   Geometry

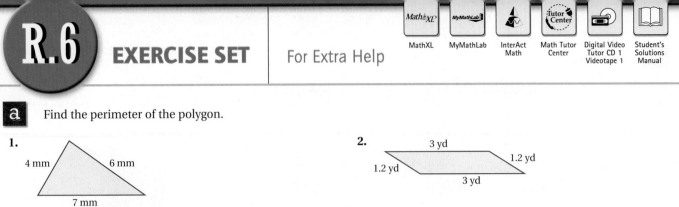

R.6 EXERCISE SET For Extra Help

a Find the perimeter of the polygon.

1.

4 mm 6 mm

7 mm

2.

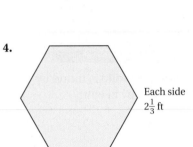

3 yd

1.2 yd

1.2 yd

3 yd

3.

3.5 in. 3.5 in.

3.5 in. 4.25 in.

3.5 in.

0.5 in.

4.

Each side
$2\frac{1}{3}$ ft

Find the perimeter of the rectangle.

5. 5 ft by 10 ft

6. 2.5 m by 100 m

7. 34.67 cm by 4.9 cm

8. 3.5 yd by 4.5 yd

Find the perimeter of the square.

9. $20\frac{3}{8}$ ft on a side

10. 56.9 km on a side

11. 45.5 mm on a side

12. $\frac{1}{8}$ yd on a side

13. *Rain Gutters.* A rain gutter is to be installed around the house shown in the figure.

  a) Find the perimeter of the house.
  b) If the gutter costs $4.59 per foot, what is the total cost of the gutter?

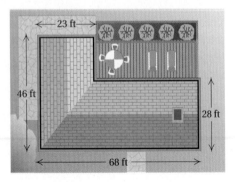

23 ft

46 ft

28 ft

68 ft

14. *Softball Diamond.* A standard-sized slow-pitch softball diamond is a square with sides of length 65 ft. What is the perimeter of this softball diamond? (This is the distance you would have to run if you hit a home run.)

65 ft

65 ft

b Find the area.

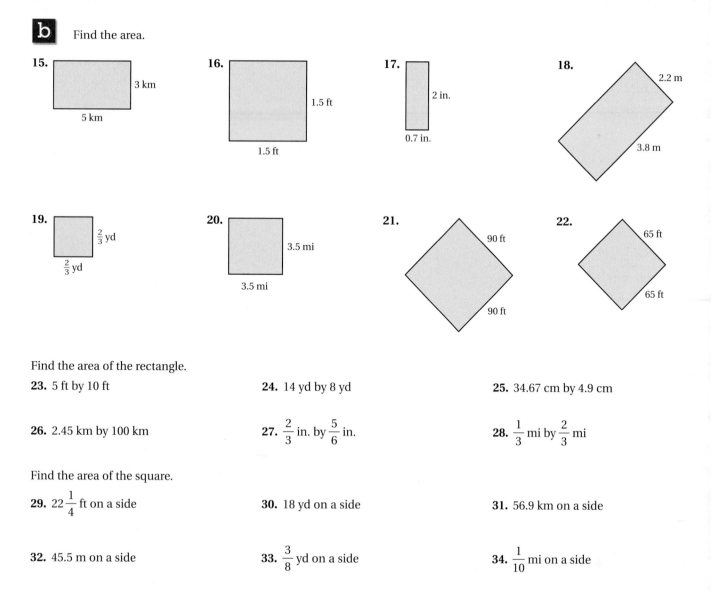

15.
3 km
5 km

16.
1.5 ft
1.5 ft

17.
2 in.
0.7 in.

18.
2.2 m
3.8 m

19.
$\frac{2}{3}$ yd
$\frac{2}{3}$ yd

20.
3.5 mi
3.5 mi

21.
90 ft
90 ft

22.
65 ft
65 ft

Find the area of the rectangle.

23. 5 ft by 10 ft

24. 14 yd by 8 yd

25. 34.67 cm by 4.9 cm

26. 2.45 km by 100 km

27. $\frac{2}{3}$ in. by $\frac{5}{6}$ in.

28. $\frac{1}{3}$ mi by $\frac{2}{3}$ mi

Find the area of the square.

29. $22\frac{1}{4}$ ft on a side

30. 18 yd on a side

31. 56.9 km on a side

32. 45.5 m on a side

33. $\frac{3}{8}$ yd on a side

34. $\frac{1}{10}$ mi on a side

35. *Sidewalk Area.* Franklin Construction Company builds a sidewalk around two sides of the Municipal Trust Bank building, as shown in the figure. What is the area of the sidewalk?

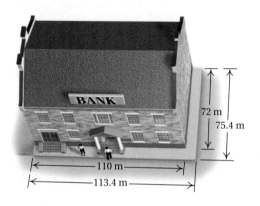

72 m
75.4 m
110 m
113.4 m

36. *Yard Maintenance.* A square sandbox 4.5 ft on a side is placed on a 60-ft by $93\frac{2}{3}$-ft yard.

a) Find the area of the yard excluding the sandbox.
b) It costs $0.03 per square foot for yard maintenance. What is the total cost of the yard maintenance?

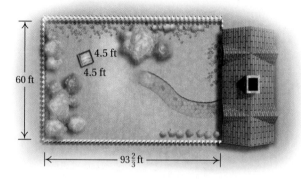

4.5 ft
4.5 ft
60 ft
$93\frac{2}{3}$ ft

Find the area.

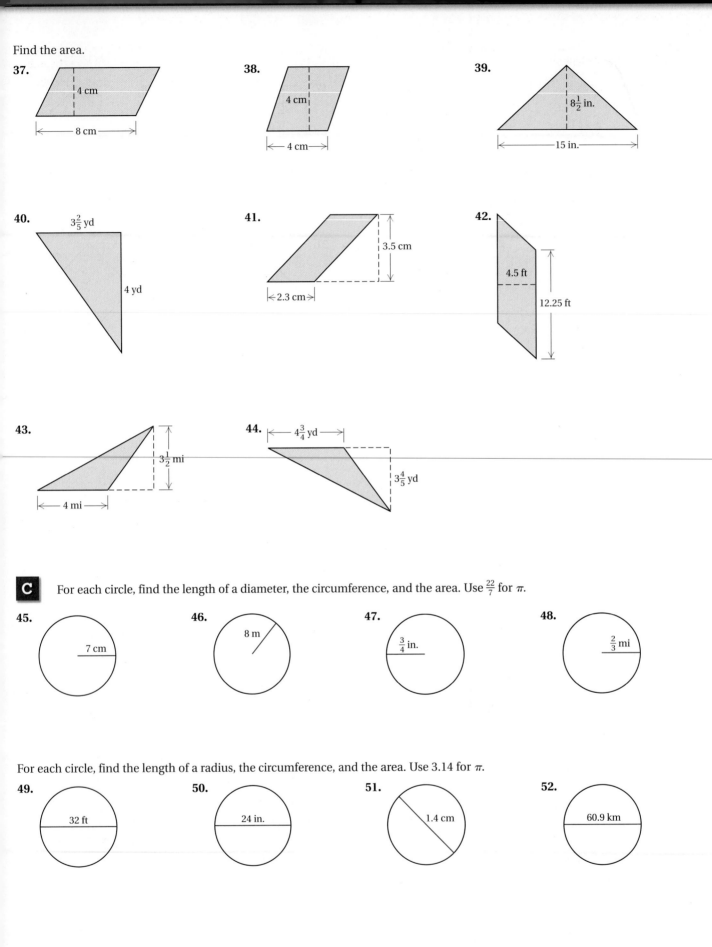

37.

4 cm

8 cm

38.

4 cm

4 cm

39.

$8\frac{1}{2}$ in.

15 in.

40.

$3\frac{2}{5}$ yd

4 yd

41.

3.5 cm

2.3 cm

42.

4.5 ft

12.25 ft

43.

$3\frac{1}{2}$ mi

4 mi

44.

$4\frac{3}{4}$ yd

$3\frac{4}{5}$ yd

C For each circle, find the length of a diameter, the circumference, and the area. Use $\frac{22}{7}$ for π.

45.

7 cm

46.

8 m

47.

$\frac{3}{4}$ in.

48.

$\frac{2}{3}$ mi

For each circle, find the length of a radius, the circumference, and the area. Use 3.14 for π.

49.

32 ft

50.

24 in.

51.

1.4 cm

52.

60.9 km

53. *Trampoline.* The standard backyard trampoline is circular with a diameter of 14 ft. What is its area? Use $\frac{22}{7}$ for π.

Source: International Trampoline Industry Association, Inc.

54. *Roller-Rink Floor.* A roller-rink floor is shown below. Each end is a semicircle. What is its area? If hardwood flooring costs $32.50 per square meter, how much will the flooring cost? Use 3.14 for π.

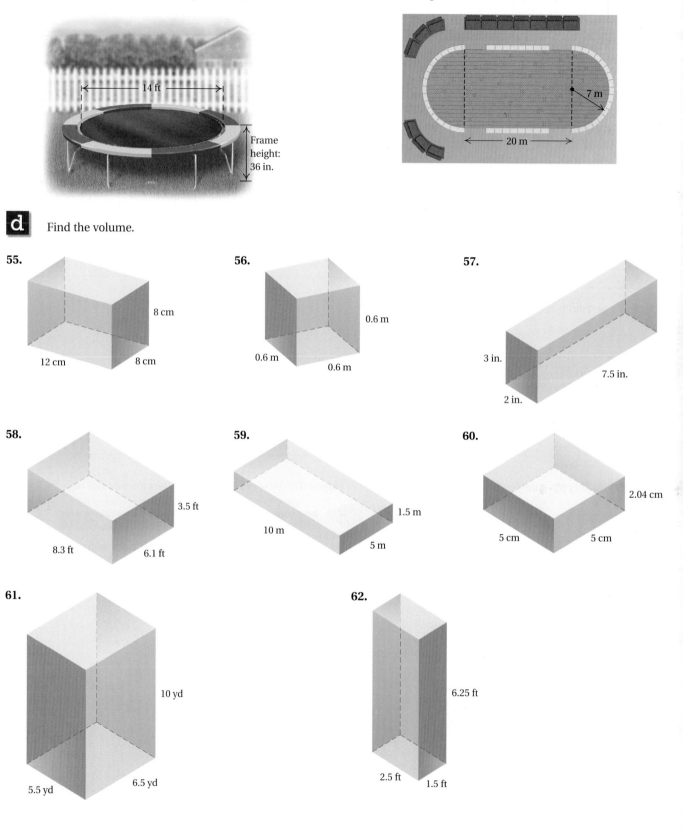

d   Find the volume.

55.

8 cm

12 cm   8 cm

56.

0.6 m

0.6 m

0.6 m

57.

3 in.

7.5 in.

2 in.

58.

3.5 ft

8.3 ft   6.1 ft

59.

10 m

1.5 m

5 m

60.

2.04 cm

5 cm   5 cm

61.

10 yd

5.5 yd   6.5 yd

62.

6.25 ft

2.5 ft   1.5 ft

63. *Carry-On Luggage.* The largest piece of luggage that you can carry on an airplane measures 22 in. by 9 in. by 14 in. Find the volume of this solid.

Source: Northwest Airlines

64. *Toolbox.* A three-drawer toolbox measures $23\frac{1}{4}$ in. by $11\frac{1}{2}$ in. by $13\frac{3}{8}$ in. Find the volume of the toolbox.

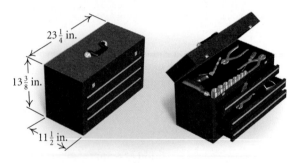

65. $\mathbf{D_W}$ Explain how the area of a parallelogram can be found by considering the area of a rectangle.

66. $\mathbf{D_W}$ Explain why a 16-in. diameter pizza that costs $16.25 is a better buy than a 10-in. diameter pizza that costs $7.85.

SKILL MAINTENANCE

Convert to percent notation.   [R.4c]

67. 0.875

68. $0.\overline{6}$

Convert to percent notation.   [R.4d]

69. $\dfrac{3}{8}$

70. $\dfrac{1}{3}$

Compute and simplify.   [R.2c]

71. $\dfrac{17}{72} + \dfrac{13}{60}$

72. $\dfrac{53}{54} + \dfrac{19}{36}$

73. $\dfrac{49}{54} - \dfrac{19}{36}$

74. $\dfrac{53}{72} - \dfrac{23}{60}$

SYNTHESIS

Circular cylinders have bases of equal area that lie in parallel planes. The bases of circular cylinders are circular regions.

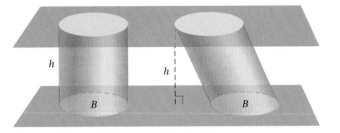

> **VOLUME OF A CIRCULAR CYLINDER**
>
> The **volume of a circular cylinder** is the product of the area of the base B and the height h:
> $$V = B \cdot h, \quad \text{or} \quad V = \pi \cdot r^2 \cdot h.$$

Find the volume of the circular cylinder. Use 3.14 for π in Exercises 75–77. Use $\frac{22}{7}$ for π in Exercise 78.

75.   **76.**   **77.**   **78.**

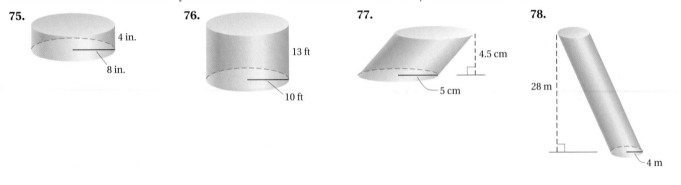

The review that follows is meant to prepare you for a chapter exam. It consists of three parts. The first part, Concept Reinforcement, is designed to increase understanding of the concepts through true/false exercises. The second part is a list of important properties and formulas. The third part is the Review Exercises. These provide practice exercises for the exam, together with references to section objectives so you can go back and review. Before beginning, stop and look back over the skills you have obtained. What skills in mathematics do you have now that you did not have before studying this chapter?

CONCEPT REINFORCEMENT

Determine whether the statement is true or false. Answers are given at the back of the book.

_____ **1.** The least common multiple of two numbers is always larger than or equal to the larger number.

_____ **2.** To add fractions when denominators are the same, keep the numerator and add the denominators.

_____ **3.** To convert from decimal notation to percent notation, move the decimal point two places to the left and write the percent symbol.

_____ **4.** The number 1 is not prime.

_____ **5.** The area of a circle is given by the formula $A = \pi r^2$, or $\frac{1}{4}\pi d^2$.

IMPORTANT PROPERTIES AND FORMULAS

Identity Property of 0:	$a + 0 = a$	*Area of a Rectangle:*	$A = l \cdot w$
Identity Property of 1:	$a \cdot 1 = a$	*Area of a Square:*	$A = s \cdot s$, or $A = s^2$
Equivalent Expressions for 1:	$\frac{a}{a} = 1, \quad a \neq 0$	*Area of a Parallelogram:*	$A = b \cdot h$
$n\% = n \times 0.01 = n \times \frac{1}{100} = \frac{n}{100}$		*Area of a Triangle:*	$A = \frac{1}{2} \cdot b \cdot h$
Exponential Notation:	$a^n = \underbrace{a \cdot a \cdot a \cdots a}_{n \text{ factors}}$	*Radius and Diameter of a Circle:*	$d = 2 \cdot r$, or $r = \frac{d}{2}$
		Circumference of a Circle:	$C = \pi \cdot d$, or $C = 2 \cdot \pi \cdot r$
Perimeter of a Rectangle:	$P = 2 \cdot (l + w)$, or $P = 2 \cdot l + 2 \cdot w$	*Area of a Circle:*	$A = \pi \cdot r \cdot r$, or $A = \pi \cdot r^2$
Perimeter of a Square:	$P = 4 \cdot s$	*Volume of a Rectangular Solid:*	$V = l \cdot w \cdot h$

Review Exercises

The review exercises that follow are for practice. Answers are at the back of the book. If you miss an exercise, restudy the objective indicated in red next to the exercise or direction line that precedes it.

Find the prime factorization. [R.1a]

1. 92   **2.** 1400

Find the LCM. [R.1b]

3. 13, 32   **4.** 5, 18, 45

Write an equivalent expression using the indicated number for 1. [R.2a]

5. $\frac{2}{5}$ $\left(\text{Use } \frac{6}{6} \text{ for 1.}\right)$ **6.** $\frac{12}{23}$ $\left(\text{Use } \frac{8}{8} \text{ for 1.}\right)$

Write an equivalent expression with the given denominator. [R.2a]

7. $\dfrac{5}{8}$ (Denominator: 64)   **8.** $\dfrac{13}{12}$ (Denominator: 84)

Simplify. [R.2b]

9. $\dfrac{20}{48}$ **10.** $\dfrac{1020}{1820}$

Compute and simplify. [R.2c]

11. $\dfrac{4}{9} + \dfrac{5}{12}$ **12.** $\dfrac{3}{4} \div 3$

13. $\dfrac{2}{3} - \dfrac{1}{15}$ **14.** $\dfrac{9}{10} \cdot \dfrac{16}{5}$

15. $\dfrac{11}{18} + \dfrac{13}{16}$ **16.** $\dfrac{35}{36} + \dfrac{23}{24}$

17. $\dfrac{25}{27} + \dfrac{17}{18}$ **18.** $\dfrac{29}{42} + \dfrac{17}{28}$

19. $\dfrac{35}{36} - \dfrac{19}{24}$ **20.** $\dfrac{13}{16} - \dfrac{11}{18}$

21. $\dfrac{29}{42} - \dfrac{17}{28}$ **22.** $\dfrac{11}{36} - \dfrac{1}{20}$

23. Convert to fraction notation: 17.97. [R.3a]

24. Convert to decimal notation: $\dfrac{2337}{10,000}$. [R.3a]

Add. [R.3b]

25.
```
   2 3 4 4.5 6
 +     9 8.3 4 5
```

26. $6.04 + 78 + 1.9898$

Subtract. [R.3b]

27. $20.4 - 11.058$

28.
```
   7 8 9.0 3 2
 - 6 5 5.7 6 8
```

Multiply. [R.3b]

29.
```
   1 7.9 5
 ×     2 4
```

30.
```
   5 6.9 5
 ×   1.9 4
```

Divide. [R3.b]

31. $2.8 \overline{)\,1\,5\,5.6\,8}$

32. $5\,2 \overline{)\,2\,3.4}$

33. Convert to decimal notation: $\dfrac{19}{12}$. [R.3b]

34. Round to the nearest tenth: 34.067. [R.3c]

35. *Homicides.* Homicides account for 15.5% of the deaths among people age 15 to 24. Convert 15.5% to decimal notation. [R.4a]
Source: National Center for Health Statistics

36. *Foreign Student Enrollment.* Of all the foreign students studying in the United States in the academic year 2002–2003, 0.127 are from India. Convert 0.127 to percent notation. [R.4c]
Source: Institute of International Education

37. *Twin Birth Rate.* The twin birth rate has continued its steady climb. In 2002, twins accounted for 3.11% of all births. Convert 3.11% to fraction notation.   [R.4b]

38. *Heart-Disease Death Rate.* Of those people living in California, 114.1 of every 100,000 will die of heart disease. Convert $\frac{114.1}{100,000}$ to percent notation.   [R.4d]

Source: "Reforming the Health Care System; State Profiles 1999," AARP

Convert to percent notation.   [R.4d]

39. $\frac{5}{8}$ **40.** $\frac{29}{25}$

41. Write exponential notation: $6 \cdot 6 \cdot 6$.   [R.5a]

42. Evaluate: $(1.06)^2$.   [R.5b]

Calculate.   [R.5c]

43. $120 - 6^2 \div 4 + 8$

44. $64 \div 16 \cdot 32 \div 48 \div 12 \cdot 18$

45. $(120 - 6^2) \div 4 + 8$

46. $64 \cdot 16 \div 32 \div 48 \div 12 \cdot 18$

47. $(120 - 6^2) \div (4 + 8)$

48. $8^2 \cdot 2^4 \div 2^2 \cdot 8 \div 48 \div 12 \cdot 18$

49. Calculate: $\dfrac{4(18 - 8) + 7 \cdot 9}{9^2 - 8^2}$.   [R.5c]

Find the perimeter.   [R.6a]

50.

51.

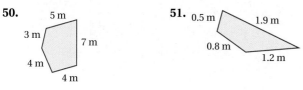

52. *Tennis Court.* The dimensions of a standard-sized tennis court are 78 ft by 36 ft. Find the perimeter and the area of the tennis court.   [R.6a, b]

Find the perimeter and the area.   [R.6a, b]

53.

9 ft

9 ft

54.

1.8 cm

7 cm

Find the area.   [R.6b]

55.

5 cm

12 cm

56.

3 m

15 m

57.

5 cm

11 cm

58.

6 in.

21 in.

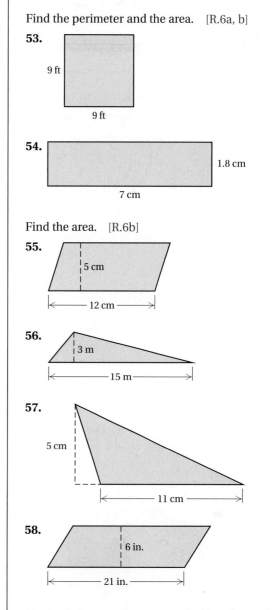

59. *Seeded Area.* A grassy section is to be seeded around three sides of a building and has equal width on the three sides, as shown below. What is the area of this grassy section?   [R.6b]

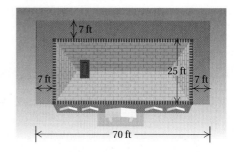

7 ft

25 ft

7 ft

7 ft

70 ft

Find the length of a radius of the circle. [R.6c]

60.

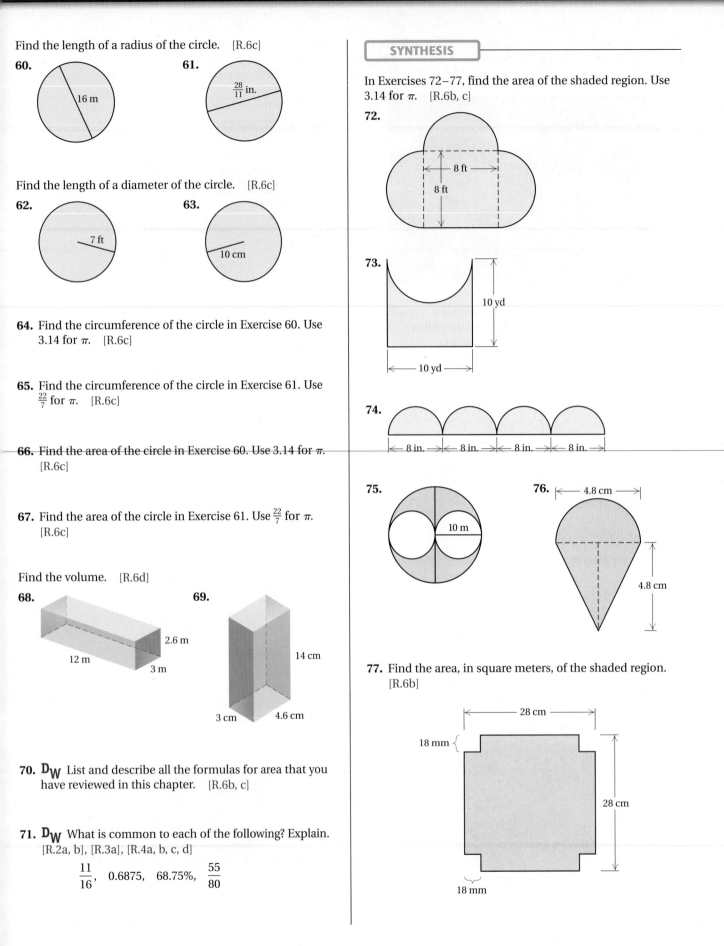

61.

Find the length of a diameter of the circle. [R.6c]

62.

63.

64. Find the circumference of the circle in Exercise 60. Use 3.14 for π. [R.6c]

65. Find the circumference of the circle in Exercise 61. Use $\frac{22}{7}$ for π. [R.6c]

66. Find the area of the circle in Exercise 60. Use 3.14 for π. [R.6c]

67. Find the area of the circle in Exercise 61. Use $\frac{22}{7}$ for π. [R.6c]

Find the volume. [R.6d]

68.

69.

70. $\mathbf{D_W}$ List and describe all the formulas for area that you have reviewed in this chapter. [R.6b, c]

71. $\mathbf{D_W}$ What is common to each of the following? Explain. [R.2a, b], [R.3a], [R.4a, b, c, d]

$$\frac{11}{16}, \quad 0.6875, \quad 68.75\%, \quad \frac{55}{80}$$

In Exercises 72–77, find the area of the shaded region. Use 3.14 for π. [R.6b, c]

72.

73.

74.

75.

76.

77. Find the area, in square meters, of the shaded region. [R.6b]

1. Find the prime factorization of 300.

2. Find the LCM of 15, 24, and 60.

3. Write an expression equivalent to $\frac{3}{7}$ using $\frac{7}{7}$ as a name for 1.

4. Write an equivalent expression with the given denominator:

$$\frac{11}{16}. \text{ (Denominator: 48)}$$

Simplify.

5. $\frac{16}{24}$

6. $\frac{925}{1525}$

Compute and simplify.

7. $\frac{10}{27} \div \frac{8}{3}$

8. $\frac{9}{10} - \frac{5}{8}$

9. $\frac{11}{12} + \frac{17}{18}$

10. $\frac{10}{27} \cdot \frac{3}{8}$

11. Convert to fraction notation (do not simplify): 6.78.

12. Convert to decimal notation: $\frac{1895}{1000}$.

13. Add: 7.14 + 89 + 2.8787.

14. Subtract: 1800 − 3.42.

15. Multiply:
$$\begin{array}{r} 1\ 2\ 3.6 \\ \times \quad 3.5\ 2 \\ \hline \end{array}$$

16. Divide: $7.2 \overline{)\ 1\ 1.5\ 2}$

17. Convert to decimal notation: $\frac{23}{11}$.

18. Round 234.7284 to the nearest tenth.

19. Round 234.7284 to the nearest thousandth.

20. Convert to decimal notation: 0.7%.

21. Convert to fraction notation: 91%.

22. Convert to percent notation: $\frac{11}{25}$.

23. Evaluate: 5^4.

24. Evaluate: $(1.2)^2$.

25. Calculate: $200 - 2^3 + 5 \times 10$.

26. Calculate: $8000 \div 0.16 \div 2.5$.

27. *Heart-Disease Death Rate.* Of those people living in Colorado, 101.4 of every 100,000 will die of cancer. Convert $\frac{101.4}{100,000}$ to percent notation.

Source: "Reforming the Health Care System; State Profiles 1999," AARP

28. *CD Rates.* A recent interest rate on a 6-month certificate of deposit was 2.14%. Convert 2.14% to decimal notation.

Source: Bank Rate Monitor

Find the perimeter and the area.

29.

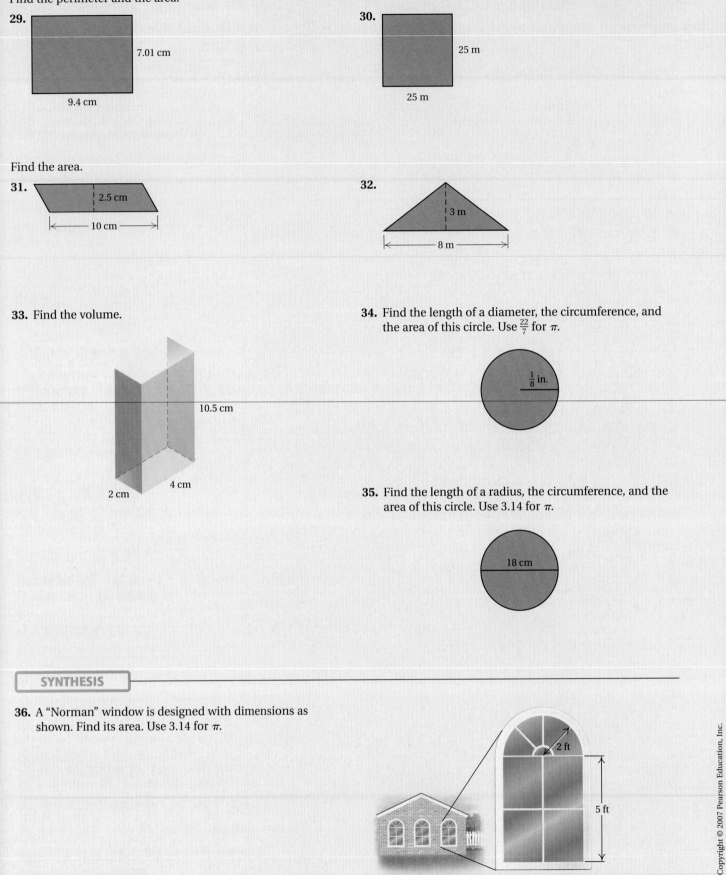

7.01 cm

9.4 cm

30.

25 m

25 m

Find the area.

31.

2.5 cm

10 cm

32.

3 m

8 m

33. Find the volume.

10.5 cm

4 cm

2 cm

34. Find the length of a diameter, the circumference, and the area of this circle. Use $\frac{22}{7}$ for π.

$\frac{1}{8}$ in.

35. Find the length of a radius, the circumference, and the area of this circle. Use 3.14 for π.

18 cm

SYNTHESIS

36. A "Norman" window is designed with dimensions as shown. Find its area. Use 3.14 for π.

2 ft

5 ft

Introduction to Real Numbers and Algebraic Expressions

1

Real-World Application

Surface temperatures on Mars vary from $-128°C$ during polar night to $27°C$ at the equator during midday at the closest point in orbit to the sun. Find the difference between the highest value and the lowest value in this temperature range.

Source: Mars Institute

This problem appears as Example 13 in Section 1.4.

Objectives

a Evaluate algebraic expressions by substitution.

b Translate phrases to algebraic expressions.

The study of algebra involves the use of equations to solve problems. Equations are constructed from algebraic expressions. The purpose of this section is to introduce you to the types of expressions encountered in algebra.

a Evaluating Algebraic Expressions

In arithmetic, you have worked with expressions such as

$$49 + 75, \quad 8 \times 6.07, \quad 29 - 14, \quad \text{and} \quad \frac{5}{6}.$$

In algebra, we use certain letters for numbers and work with *algebraic expressions* such as

$$x + 75, \quad 8 \times y, \quad 29 - t, \quad \text{and} \quad \frac{a}{b}.$$

Sometimes a letter can represent various numbers. In that case, we call the letter a **variable.** Let $a =$ your age. Then a is a variable since a changes from year to year. Sometimes a letter can stand for just one number. In that case, we call the letter a **constant.** Let $b =$ your date of birth. Then b is a constant.

Where do algebraic expressions occur? Most often we encounter them when we are solving applied problems. For example, consider the bar graph shown at left, one that we might find in a book or magazine. Suppose we want to know how much higher Mt. McKinley is than Mt. Evans. Using arithmetic, we might simply subtract. But let's see how we can find this out using algebra. We translate the problem into a statement of equality, an equation. It could be done as follows:

$$\underbrace{\text{Height of Mt. Evans}}_{14{,}264} \;\; \underbrace{\text{plus}}_{+} \;\; \underbrace{\text{How much more}}_{x} \;\; \underbrace{\text{is}}_{=} \;\; \underbrace{\text{Height of Mt. McKinley}}_{20{,}320.}$$

Note that we have an algebraic expression, $14{,}264 + x$, on the left of the equals sign. To find the number x, we can subtract $14{,}264$ on both sides of the equation:

$$14{,}264 + x = 20{,}320$$
$$14{,}264 + x - 14{,}264 = 20{,}320 - 14{,}264$$
$$x = 6056.$$

This value of x gives the answer, 6056 ft.

We call $14{,}264 + x$ an *algebraic expression* and $14{,}264 + x = 20{,}320$ an *algebraic equation.* Note that there is no equals sign, $=$, in an algebraic expression.

In arithmetic, you probably would do this subtraction without ever considering an equation. *In algebra, more complex problems are difficult to solve without first writing an equation.*

1. Translate this problem to an equation. Use the graph below.

Mountain Peaks.   There are 92 mountain peaks in the United States higher than 14,000 ft. The bar graph below shows data for six of these. How much higher is Mt. Fairweather than Mt. Rainer?

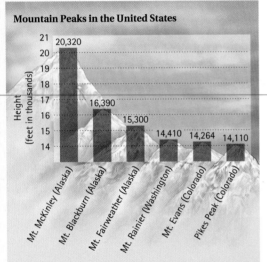

Mountain Peaks in the United States

Source: U.S. Department of the Interior, Geological Survey

Answer on page A-3

Do Exercise 1.

An **algebraic expression** consists of variables, constants, numerals, and operation signs. When we replace a variable with a number, we say that we are **substituting** for the variable. This process is called **evaluating the expression.**

EXAMPLE 1 Evaluate $x + y$ when $x = 37$ and $y = 29$.

We substitute 37 for x and 29 for y and carry out the addition:

$$x + y = 37 + 29 = 66.$$

The number 66 is called the **value** of the expression.

Algebraic expressions involving multiplication can be written in several ways. For example, "8 times a" can be written as

$$8 \times a, \quad 8 \cdot a, \quad (8a), \quad \text{or simply} \quad 8a.$$

Two letters written together without an operation symbol, such as ab, also indicate a multiplication.

EXAMPLE 2 Evaluate $3y$ when $y = 14$.

$$3y = 3(14) = 42$$

Do Exercises 2–4.

EXAMPLE 3 *Area of a Rectangle.* The area A of a rectangle of length l and width w is given by the formula $A = lw$. Find the area when l is 24.5 in. and w is 16 in.

We substitute 24.5 in. for l and 16 in. for w and carry out the multiplication:

$$
\begin{aligned}
A = lw &= (24.5 \text{ in.})(16 \text{ in.})\\
&= (24.5)(16)(\text{in.})(\text{in.})\\
&= 392 \text{ in}^2, \text{ or } 392 \text{ square inches.}
\end{aligned}
$$

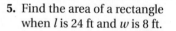

Do Exercise 5.

Algebraic expressions involving division can also be written in several ways. For example, "8 divided by t" can be written as

$$8 \div t, \quad \frac{8}{t}, \quad 8/t, \quad \text{or} \quad 8 \cdot \frac{1}{t},$$

where the fraction bar is a division symbol.

EXAMPLE 4 Evaluate $\dfrac{a}{b}$ when $a = 63$ and $b = 9$.

We substitute 63 for a and 9 for b and carry out the division:

$$\frac{a}{b} = \frac{63}{9} = 7.$$

---

2. Evaluate $a + b$ when $a = 38$ and $b = 26$.

3. Evaluate $x - y$ when $x = 57$ and $y = 29$.

4. Evaluate $4t$ when $t = 15$.

5. Find the area of a rectangle when l is 24 ft and w is 8 ft.

6. Evaluate a/b when $a = 200$ and $b = 8$.

7. Evaluate $10p/q$ when $p = 40$ and $q = 25$.

Answers on page A-3

8. Motorcycle Travel. Find the time it takes to travel 660 mi if the speed is 55 mph.

EXAMPLE 5 Evaluate $\frac{12m}{n}$ when $m = 8$ and $n = 16$.

$$\frac{12m}{n} = \frac{12 \cdot 8}{16} = \frac{96}{16} = 6$$

Do Exercises 6 and 7 on the preceding page.

EXAMPLE 6 *Motorcycle Travel.* Ed takes a trip on his motorcycle. He wants to travel 660 mi on a particular day. The time t, in hours, that it takes to travel 660 mi is given by

$$t = \frac{660}{r},$$

where r is the speed of Ed's motorcycle. Find the time of travel if the speed r is 60 mph.

We substitute 60 for r and carry out the division:

$$t = \frac{660}{r} = \frac{660}{60} = 11 \text{ hr.}$$

Do Exercise 8.

CALCULATOR CORNER

Evaluating Algebraic Expressions   *To the student and the instructor:* This book contains a series of *optional* discussions on using a calculator. A calculator is *not* a requirement for this textbook. There are many kinds of calculators and different instructions for their usage. We have included instructions here for the scientific keys on a graphing calculator such as a TI-84 Plus. Be sure to consult your user's manual as well. Also, check with your instructor about whether you are allowed to use a calculator in the course.

We can evaluate algebraic expressions on a calculator by making the appropriate substitutions, keeping in mind the rules for order of operations, and then carrying out the resulting calculations. To evaluate $12m/n$ when $m = 8$ and $n = 16$, as in Example 5, we enter $12 \cdot 8/16$ by pressing ① ② ✕ ⑧ ÷ ① ⑥ **ENTER** . The result is 6.

Exercises: Evaluate.

1. $\frac{12m}{n}$, when $m = 42$ and $n = 9$

2. $a + b$, when $a = 8.2$ and $b = 3.7$

3. $b - a$, when $a = 7.6$ and $b = 9.4$

4. $27xy$, when $x = 12.7$ and $y = 100.4$

5. $3a + 2b$, when $a = 2.9$ and $b = 5.7$

6. $2a + 3b$, when $a = 7.3$ and $b = 5.1$

Answer on page A-3

b Translating to Algebraic Expressions

In algebra, we translate problems to equations. The different parts of an equation are translations of word phrases to algebraic expressions. It is easier to translate if we know that certain words often translate to certain operation symbols.

KEY WORDS, PHRASES, AND CONCEPTS

ADDITION (+)	SUBTRACTION (−)	MULTIPLICATION (·)	DIVISION (÷)
add	subtract	multiply	divide
added to	subtracted from	multiplied by	divided by
sum	difference	product	quotient
total	minus	times	
plus	less than	of	
more than	decreased by		
increased by	take away		

EXAMPLE 7 Translate to an algebraic expression:

Twice (or two times) some number.

Think of some number, say, 8. We can write 2 times 8 as 2×8, or $2 \cdot 8$. We multiplied by 2. Do the same thing using a variable. We can use any variable we wish, such as x, y, m, or n. Let's use y to stand for some number. If we multiply by 2, we get an expression

$$y \times 2, \quad 2 \times y, \quad 2 \cdot y, \quad \text{or} \quad 2y.$$

In algebra, $2y$ is the expression generally used.

EXAMPLE 8 Translate to an algebraic expression:

Thirty-eight percent of some number.

Let $n = $ the number. The word "of" translates to a multiplication symbol, so we get the following expressions as a translation:

$$38\% \cdot n, \quad 0.38 \times n, \quad \text{or} \quad 0.38n.$$

EXAMPLE 9 Translate to an algebraic expression:

Seven less than some number.

We let

x represent the number.

Now if the number were 23, then 7 less than 23 is 16, that is, $(23 - 7)$, not $(7 - 23)$. If we knew the number to be 345, then the translation would be $345 - 7$. If the number is x, then the translation is

$$x - 7.$$

> **Caution!**
>
> Note that $7 - x$ is *not* a correct translation of the expression in Example 9. The expression $7 - x$ is a translation of "seven minus some number" or "some number less than seven."

61

Translate to an algebraic expression.

9. Eight less than some number

10. Eight more than some number

11. Four less than some number

12. Half of a number

13. Six more than eight times some number

14. The difference of two numbers

15. Fifty-nine percent of some number

16. Two hundred less than the product of two numbers

17. The sum of two numbers

EXAMPLE 10 Translate to an algebraic expression:

Eighteen more than a number.

We let

t = the number.

Now if the number were 26, then the translation would be $26 + 18$, or $18 + 26$. If we knew the number to be 174, then the translation would be $174 + 18$, or $18 + 174$. If the number is t, then the translation is

$$t + 18, \quad \text{or} \quad 18 + t.$$

EXAMPLE 11 Translate to an algebraic expression:

A number divided by 5.

We let

m = the number.

Now if the number were 76, then the translation would be $76 \div 5$, or $76/5$, or $\frac{76}{5}$. If the number were 213, then the translation would be $213 \div 5$, or $213/5$, or $\frac{213}{5}$. If the number is m, then the translation is

$$m \div 5, \quad m/5, \quad \text{or} \quad \frac{m}{5}.$$

EXAMPLE 12 Translate each phrase to an algebraic expression.

PHRASE	ALGEBRAIC EXPRESSION
Five more than some number	$n + 5$, or $5 + n$
Half of a number	$\frac{1}{2}t$, $\frac{t}{2}$, or $t/2$
Five more than three times some number	$3p + 5$, or $5 + 3p$
The difference of two numbers	$x - y$
Six less than the product of two numbers	$mn - 6$
Seventy-six percent of some number	$76\%z$, or $0.76z$
Four less than twice some number	$2x - 4$

Do Exercises 9–17.

Answers on page A-3

a   Substitute to find values of the expressions in each of the following applied problems.

1. *Commuting Time.* It takes Erin 24 min less time to commute to work than it does George. Suppose that the variable x stands for the time it takes George to get to work. Then $x - 24$ stands for the time it takes Erin to get to work. How long does it take Erin to get to work if it takes George 56 min? 93 min? 105 min?

2. *Enrollment Costs.* At Emmett Community College, it costs $600 to enroll in the 8 A.M. section of Elementary Algebra. Suppose that the variable n stands for the number of students who enroll. Then $600n$ stands for the total amount of money collected for this course. How much is collected if 34 students enroll? 78 students? 250 students?

3. *Area of a Triangle.* The area A of a triangle with base b and height h is given by $A = \frac{1}{2}bh$. Find the area when $b = 45$ m (meters) and $h = 86$ m.

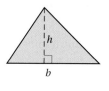

4. *Area of a Parallelogram.* The area A of a parallelogram with base b and height h is given by $A = bh$. Find the area of the parallelogram when the height is 15.4 cm (centimeters) and the base is 6.5 cm.

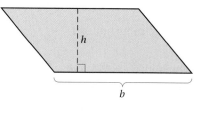

5. *Distance Traveled.* A driver who drives at a constant speed of r mph for t hr will travel a distance d mi given by $d = rt$ mi. How far will a driver travel at a speed of 65 mph for 4 hr?

6. *Simple Interest.* The simple interest I on a principal of P dollars at interest rate r for time t, in years, is given by $I = Prt$. Find the simple interest on a principal of $4800 at 9% for 2 yr. (*Hint*: 9% = 0.09.)

7. *Hockey Goal.* The front of a regulation hockey goal is a rectangle that is 6 ft wide and 4 ft high. Find its area.
Source: National Hockey League

8. *Zoology.* A great white shark has triangular teeth. Each tooth measures about 5 cm across the base and has a height of 6 cm. Find the surface area of one side of one tooth. (See Exercise 3.)

Evaluate.

9. $8x$, when $x = 7$

10. $6y$, when $y = 7$

11. $\dfrac{c}{d}$, when $c = 24$ and $d = 3$

12. $\dfrac{p}{q}$, when $p = 16$ and $q = 2$

13. $\dfrac{3p}{q}$, when $p = 2$ and $q = 6$

14. $\dfrac{5y}{z}$, when $y = 15$ and $z = 25$

15. $\dfrac{x + y}{5}$, when $x = 10$ and $y = 20$

16. $\dfrac{p + q}{2}$, when $p = 2$ and $q = 16$

17. $\dfrac{x - y}{8}$, when $x = 20$ and $y = 4$

18. $\dfrac{m - n}{5}$, when $m = 16$ and $n = 6$

b   Translate each phrase to an algebraic expression. Use any letter for the variable unless directed otherwise.

19. Seven more than some number

20. Nine more than some number

21. Twelve less than some number

22. Fourteen less than some number

23. Some number increased by four

24. Some number increased by thirteen

25. b more than a

26. c more than d

27. x divided by y

28. c divided by h

29. x plus w

30. s added to t

31. m subtracted from n

32. p subtracted from q

33. The sum of two numbers

34. The sum of nine and some number

35. Twice some number

36. Three times some number

37. Three multiplied by some number

38. The product of eight and some number

39. Six more than four times some number

40. Two more than six times some number

41. Eight less than the product of two numbers

42. The product of two numbers minus seven

43. Five less than twice some number

44. Six less than seven times some number

45. Three times some number plus eleven

46. Some number times 8 plus 5

47. The sum of four times a number plus three times another number

48. Five times a number minus eight times another number

CHAPTER 1: Introduction to Real Numbers
and Algebraic Expressions

49. The product of 89% and your salary

50. 67% of the women attending

51. Your salary after a 5% salary increase if your salary before the increase was s

52. The price of a blouse after a 30% reduction if the price before the reduction was P

53. Danielle drove at a speed of 65 mph for t hours. How far did Danielle travel?

54. Juan has d dollars before spending $29.95 on a DVD of the movie *Chicago*. How much did Juan have after the purchase?

55. Lisa had $50 before spending x dollars on pizza. How much money remains?

56. Dino drove his pickup truck at 55 mph for t hours. How far did he travel?

To the student and the instructor: The Discussion and Writing exercises are meant to be answered with one or more sentences. They can be discussed and answered collaboratively by the entire class or by small groups. Because of their open-ended nature, the answers to these exercises do not appear at the back of the book. They are denoted by the symbol **D**$_\mathbf{W}$.

57. **D**$_\mathbf{W}$ If the length of a rectangle is doubled, does the area double? Why or why not?

58. **D**$_\mathbf{W}$ If the height and the base of a triangle are doubled, what happens to the area? Explain.

Find the prime factorization.   [R.1a]

59. 54   **60.** 32   **61.** 108   **62.** 192   **63.** 1023

Find the LCM.   [R.1b]

64. 6, 18   **65.** 6, 24, 32   **66.** 10, 20, 30   **67.** 16, 24, 32   **68.** 18, 36, 44

Evaluate.

69. $\dfrac{a - 2b + c}{4b - a}$, when $a = 20$, $b = 10$, and $c = 5$

70. $\dfrac{x}{y} - \dfrac{5}{x} + \dfrac{2}{y}$, when $x = 30$ and $y = 6$

71. $\dfrac{12 - c}{c + 12b}$, when $b = 1$ and $c = 12$

72. $\dfrac{2w - 3z}{7y}$, when $w = 5$, $y = 6$, and $z = 1$

1.2 THE REAL NUMBERS

Objectives

a State the integer that corresponds to a real-world situation.

b Graph rational numbers on a number line.

c Convert from fraction notation to decimal notation for a rational number.

d Determine which of two real numbers is greater and indicate which, using < or >; given an inequality like $a > b$, write another inequality with the same meaning. Determine whether an inequality like $-3 \le 5$ is true or false.

e Find the absolute value of a real number.

Study Tips

THE AW MATH TUTOR CENTER

www.aw-bc.com/tutorcenter

The AW Math Tutor Center is staffed by highly qualified mathematics instructors who provide students with tutoring on text examples and odd-numbered exercises. Tutoring is provided free to students who have bought a new text-book with a special access card bound with the book. Tutoring is available by toll-free telephone, toll-free fax, e-mail, and the Internet. White-board technology allows tutors and students to actually see problems worked while they "talk" live in real time during the tutoring sessions. If you purchased a book without this card, you can purchase an access code through your bookstore using ISBN 0-201-72170-8. (This is also discussed in the Preface.)

A **set** is a collection of objects. (See Appendix D for more on sets.) For our purposes, we will most often be considering sets of numbers. One way to name a set uses what is called **roster notation.** For example, roster notation for the set containing the numbers 0, 2, and 5 is {0, 2, 5}.

Sets that are part of other sets are called **subsets.** In this section, we become acquainted with the set of *real numbers* and its various subsets.

Two important subsets of the real numbers are listed below using roster notation.

NATURAL NUMBERS

The set of **natural numbers** = $\{1, 2, 3, \ldots\}$. These are the numbers used for counting.

WHOLE NUMBERS

The set of **whole numbers** = $\{0, 1, 2, 3, \ldots\}$. This is the set of natural numbers with 0 included.

We can represent these sets on a number line. The natural numbers are those to the right of zero. The whole numbers are the natural numbers and zero.

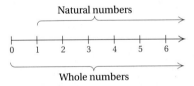

We create a new set, called the *integers*, by starting with the whole numbers, 0, 1, 2, 3, and so on. For each natural number 1, 2, 3, and so on, we obtain a new number to the left of zero on the number line:

For the number 1, there will be an *opposite* number -1 (negative 1).

For the number 2, there will be an *opposite* number -2 (negative 2).

For the number 3, there will be an *opposite* number -3 (negative 3), and so on.

The **integers** consist of the whole numbers and these new numbers.

INTEGERS

The set of **integers** = $\{\ldots, -5, -4, -3, -2, -1, 0, 1, 2, 3, 4, 5, \ldots\}$.

CHAPTER 1: Introduction to Real Numbers and Algebraic Expressions

We picture the integers on a number line as follows.

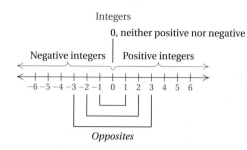

Integers
0, neither positive nor negative

Negative integers | Positive integers

−6 −5 −4 −3 −2 −1 0 1 2 3 4 5 6

Opposites

We call these new numbers to the left of 0 **negative integers.** The natural numbers are also called **positive integers.** Zero is neither positive nor negative. We call −1 and 1 **opposites** of each other. Similarly, −2 and 2 are opposites, −3 and 3 are opposites, −100 and 100 are opposites, and 0 is its own opposite. Pairs of opposite numbers like −3 and 3 are the same distance from 0. The integers extend infinitely on the number line to the left and right of zero.

a Integers and the Real World

Integers correspond to many real-world problems and situations. The following examples will help you get ready to translate problem situations that involve integers to mathematical language.

EXAMPLE 1 Tell which integer corresponds to this situation: The temperature is 4 degrees below zero.

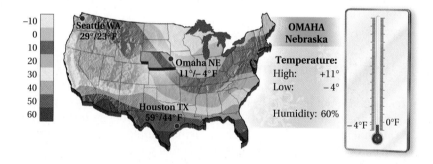

The integer −4 corresponds to the situation. The temperature is −4°.

EXAMPLE 2 *"Jeopardy."* Tell which integer corresponds to this situation: A contestant missed a $600 question on the television game show "Jeopardy."

Missing a $600 question means −600.

Missing a $600 question causes a $600 loss on the score—that is, the contestant earns −600 dollars.

State the integers that correspond to the given situation.

1. The halfback gained 8 yd on the first down. The quarterback was sacked for a 5-yd loss on the second down.

2. **Temperature High and Low.** The highest recorded temperature in Nevada is 125°F on June 29, 1994, in Laughlin. The lowest recorded temperature in Nevada is 50°F below zero on June 8, 1937, in San Jacinto.

   Sources: National Climatic Data Center, Asheville, NC, and Storm Phillips, STORMFAX, INC.

3. **Stock Decrease.** The price of Wendy's stock decreased from $41 per share to $38 per share over a recent time period.

   Source: The New York Stock Exchange

4. At 10 sec before liftoff, ignition occurs. At 156 sec after liftoff, the first stage is detached from the rocket.

5. A submarine dove 120 ft, rose 50 ft, and then dove 80 ft.

Answers on page A-4

EXAMPLE 3 *Elevation.* Tell which integer corresponds to this situation: The shores of California's largest lake, the Salton Sea, are 227 ft below sea level.

Source: *National Geographic*, February 2005, p. 88. Salton Sea, by Joel K. Bourne, Jr., Senior Writer.

The integer −227 corresponds to the situation. The elevation is −227 ft.

EXAMPLE 4 *Stock Price Change.* Tell which integers correspond to this situation: The price of Pearson Education stock decreased from $27 per share to $11 per share over a recent time period. The price of Safeway stock increased from $20 per share to $22 per share over a recent time period.

Source: The New York Stock Exchange

The integer −16 corresponds to the decrease in the stock value. The integer 2 represents the increase in stock value.

Do Exercises 1–5.

b   The Rational Numbers

We created the set of integers by obtaining a negative number for each natural number and also including 0. To create a larger number system, called the set of **rational numbers,** we consider quotients of integers with nonzero divisors. The following are some examples of rational numbers:

$$\frac{2}{3}, \quad -\frac{2}{3}, \quad \frac{7}{1}, \quad 4, \quad -3, \quad 0, \quad \frac{23}{-8}, \quad 2.4, \quad -0.17, \quad 10\frac{1}{2}.$$

The number $-\frac{2}{3}$ (read "negative two-thirds") can also be named $\frac{-2}{3}$ or $\frac{2}{-3}$; that is,

$$-\frac{a}{b} = \frac{-a}{b} = \frac{a}{-b}.$$

The number 2.4 can be named $\frac{24}{10}$ or $\frac{12}{5}$, and −0.17 can be named $-\frac{17}{100}$. We can describe the set of rational numbers as follows.

RATIONAL NUMBERS

The set of **rational numbers** = the set of numbers $\dfrac{a}{b}$, where a and b are integers and b is not equal to 0 ($b \neq 0$).

Note that this new set of numbers, the rational numbers, contains the whole numbers, the integers, the arithmetic numbers (also called the non-negative rational numbers), and the negative rational numbers.

We picture the rational numbers on a number line as follows.

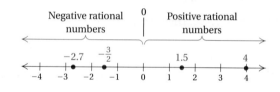

To **graph** a number means to find and mark its point on the number line. Some rational numbers are graphed in the preceding figure.

EXAMPLE 5 Graph: $\frac{5}{2}$.

The number $\frac{5}{2}$ can be named $2\frac{1}{2}$, or 2.5. Its graph is halfway between 2 and 3.

EXAMPLE 6 Graph: -3.2.

The graph of -3.2 is $\frac{2}{10}$ of the way from -3 to -4.

EXAMPLE 7 Graph: $\frac{13}{8}$.

The number $\frac{13}{8}$ can be named $1\frac{5}{8}$, or 1.625. The graph is $\frac{5}{8}$ of the way from 1 to 2.

Do Exercises 6–8.

C Notation for Rational Numbers

Each rational number can be named using fraction or decimal notation.

EXAMPLE 8 Convert to decimal notation: $-\frac{5}{8}$.

We first find decimal notation for $\frac{5}{8}$. Since $\frac{5}{8}$ means $5 \div 8$, we divide.

$$
\begin{array}{r}
0.6\,2\,5 \\
8 \overline{)5.0\,0\,0} \\
\underline{4\,8} \\
2\,0 \\
\underline{1\,6} \\
4\,0 \\
\underline{4\,0} \\
0
\end{array}
$$

Thus, $\frac{5}{8} = 0.625$, so $-\frac{5}{8} = -0.625$.

Graph on a number line.

6. $-\frac{7}{2}$

<-6 -5 -4 -3 -2 -1 0 1 2 3 4 5 6>

7. -1.4

<-6 -5 -4 -3 -2 -1 0 1 2 3 4 5 6>

8. $\frac{11}{4}$

<-6 -5 -4 -3 -2 -1 0 1 2 3 4 5 6>

Answers on page A-4

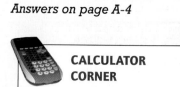

CALCULATOR CORNER

Negative Numbers on a Calculator; Converting to Decimal Notation We use the opposite key (−) to enter negative numbers on a graphing calculator. Note that this is different from the (−) key, which is used for the operation of subtraction. To convert $-\frac{5}{8}$ to decimal notation, as in Example 8, we press (−) 5 ÷ 8 ENTER. The result is -0.625.

```
-5/8
              -.625
```

Exercises: Convert each of the following negative numbers to decimal notation.

1. $-\frac{3}{4}$ 2. $-\frac{9}{20}$

3. $-\frac{1}{8}$ 4. $-\frac{9}{5}$

5. $-\frac{27}{40}$ 6. $-\frac{11}{16}$

7. $-\frac{7}{2}$ 8. $-\frac{19}{25}$

69

Convert to decimal notation.

9. $-\dfrac{3}{8}$

10. $-\dfrac{6}{11}$

11. $\dfrac{4}{3}$

Answers on page A-4

CALCULATOR
CORNER

Approximating Square Roots and π Square roots are found by pressing **2ND** **√**. ($\sqrt{}$ is the second operation associated with the **x²** key.)

To find an approximation for $\sqrt{48}$, we press **2ND** **√** **4** **8** **ENTER**. The approximation 6.92820323 is displayed.

To find $8 \cdot \sqrt{13}$, we press **8** **2ND** **√** **1** **3** **ENTER**. The approximation 28.8444102 is displayed. The number π is used widely enough to have its own key. (π is the second operation associated with the **⌒** key.)

To approximate π, we press **2ND** **π** **ENTER**. The approximation 3.141592654 is displayed.

Exercises: Approximate.

1. $\sqrt{76}$ 2. $\sqrt{317}$

3. $15 \cdot \sqrt{20}$

4. $29 + \sqrt{42}$

5. π 6. $29 \cdot \pi$

7. $\pi \cdot 13^2$

8. $5 \cdot \pi + 8 \cdot \sqrt{237}$

Decimal notation for $-\dfrac{5}{8}$ is -0.625. We consider -0.625 to be a **terminating decimal.** Decimal notation for some numbers repeats.

EXAMPLE 9 Convert to decimal notation: $\dfrac{7}{11}$.

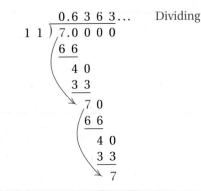

We can abbreviate repeating decimal notation by writing a bar over the repeating part—in this case, $0.\overline{63}$. Thus, $\dfrac{7}{11} = 0.\overline{63}$.

> Each rational number can be expressed in either terminating or repeating decimal notation.

The following are other examples to show how each rational number can be named using fraction or decimal notation:

$$0 = \frac{0}{8}, \qquad \frac{27}{100} = 0.27, \qquad -8\frac{3}{4} = -8.75, \qquad -\frac{13}{6} = -2.1\overline{6}.$$

Do Exercises 9–11.

d The Real Numbers and Order

Every rational number has a point on the number line. However, there are some points on the line for which there is no rational number. These points correspond to what are called **irrational numbers.**

What kinds of numbers are irrational? One example is the number π, which is used in finding the area and the circumference of a circle: $A = \pi r^2$ and $C = 2\pi r$.

Another example of an irrational number is the square root of 2, named $\sqrt{2}$. It is the length of the diagonal of a square with sides of length 1. It is also the number that when multiplied by itself gives 2—that is, $\sqrt{2} \cdot \sqrt{2} = 2$. There is no rational number that can be multiplied by itself to get 2. But the following are rational *approximations*:

1.4 is an approximation of $\sqrt{2}$ because $(1.4)^2 = 1.96$;

1.41 is a better approximation because $(1.41)^2 = 1.9881$;

1.4142 is an even better approximation because $(1.4142)^2 = 1.99996164$.

We can find rational approximations for square roots using a calculator.

Decimal notation for rational numbers *either* terminates *or* repeats. Decimal notation for irrational numbers *neither* terminates *nor* repeats.

Some other examples of irrational numbers are $\sqrt{3}$, $-\sqrt{8}$, $\sqrt{11}$, and $0.121221222122221\ldots$. Whenever we take the square root of a number that is not a perfect square, we will get an irrational number.

The rational numbers and the irrational numbers together correspond to all the points on a number line and make up what is called the **real-number system.**

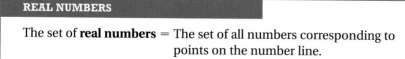

REAL NUMBERS

The set of **real numbers** = The set of all numbers corresponding to points on the number line.

The real numbers consist of the rational numbers and the irrational numbers. The following figure shows the relationships among various kinds of numbers.

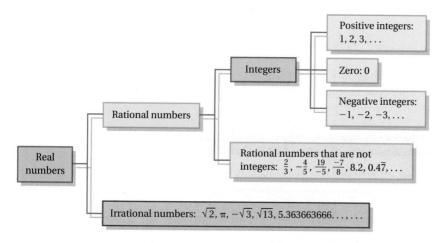

ORDER

Real numbers are named in order on the number line, with larger numbers named farther to the right. For any two numbers on the line, the one to the left is less than the one to the right.

We use the symbol **<** to mean "**is less than.**" The sentence $-8 < 6$ means "-8 is less than 6." The symbol **>** means "**is greater than.**" The sentence $-3 > -7$ means "-3 is greater than -7." The sentences $-8 < 6$ and $-3 > -7$ are **inequalities.**

Use either $<$ or $>$ for $\square$ to write a true sentence.

12. $-3 \;\square\; 7$

13. $-8 \;\square\; -5$

14. $7 \;\square\; -10$

15. $3.1 \;\square\; -9.5$

16. $-\dfrac{2}{3} \;\square\; -1$

17. $-\dfrac{11}{8} \;\square\; \dfrac{23}{15}$

18. $-\dfrac{2}{3} \;\square\; -\dfrac{5}{9}$

19. $-4.78 \;\square\; -5.01$

Answers on page A-4

Write another inequality with the same meaning.

20. $-5 < 7$

21. $x > 4$

Write true or false.

22. $-4 \leq -6$

23. $7.8 \geq 7.8$

24. $-2 \leq \dfrac{3}{8}$

EXAMPLES Use either $<$ or $>$ for ☐ to write a true sentence.

10. $2 \:\square\: 9$ Since 2 is to the left of 9, 2 is less than 9, so $2 < 9$.

11. $-7 \:\square\: 3$ Since -7 is to the left of 3, we have $-7 < 3$.

12. $6 \:\square\: -12$ Since 6 is to the right of -12, then $6 > -12$.

13. $-18 \:\square\: -5$ Since -18 is to the left of -5, we have $-18 < -5$.

14. $-2.7 \:\square\: -\frac{3}{2}$ The answer is $-2.7 < -\frac{3}{2}$.

15. $1.5 \:\square\: -2.7$ The answer is $1.5 > -2.7$.

16. $1.38 \:\square\: 1.83$ The answer is $1.38 < 1.83$.

17. $-3.45 \:\square\: 1.32$ The answer is $-3.45 < 1.32$.

18. $-4 \:\square\: 0$ The answer is $-4 < 0$.

19. $5.8 \:\square\: 0$ The answer is $5.8 > 0$.

20. $\frac{5}{8} \:\square\: \frac{7}{11}$ We convert to decimal notation: $\frac{5}{8} = 0.625$ and $\frac{7}{11} = 0.6363\ldots$. Thus, $\frac{5}{8} < \frac{7}{11}$.

21. $-\frac{1}{2} \:\square\: -\frac{1}{3}$ The answer is $-\frac{1}{2} < -\frac{1}{3}$.

22. $-2\frac{3}{5} \:\square\: -\frac{11}{4}$ The answer is $-2\frac{3}{5} > -\frac{11}{4}$.

Do Exercises 12–19 on the preceding page.

Note that both $-8 < 6$ and $6 > -8$ are true. Every true inequality yields another true inequality when we interchange the numbers or variables and reverse the direction of the inequality sign.

ORDER; $>$, $<$

$a < b$ also has the meaning $b > a$.

EXAMPLES Write another inequality with the same meaning.

23. $-3 > -8$ The inequality $-8 < -3$ has the same meaning.

24. $a < -5$ The inequality $-5 > a$ has the same meaning.

A helpful mental device is to think of an inequality sign as an "arrow" with the arrow pointing to the smaller number.

Do Exercises 20 and 21.

Answers on page A-4

CHAPTER 1: Introduction to Real Numbers and Algebraic Expressions

Note that all positive real numbers are greater than zero and all negative real numbers are less than zero.

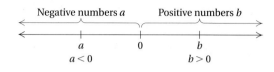

If b is a positive real number, then $b > 0$.
If a is a negative real number, then $a < 0$.

Expressions like $a \leq b$ and $b \geq a$ are also inequalities. We read **$a \leq b$** as "**a is less than or equal to b.**" We read **$a \geq b$** as "**a is greater than or equal to b.**"

EXAMPLES Write true or false for the statement.

25. $-3 \leq 5.4$ True since $-3 < 5.4$ is true
26. $-3 \leq -3$ True since $-3 = -3$ is true
27. $-5 \geq 1\frac{2}{3}$ False since neither $-5 > 1\frac{2}{3}$ nor $-5 = 1\frac{2}{3}$ is true

Do Exercises 22–24 on the preceding page.

e   Absolute Value

From the number line, we see that numbers like 4 and -4 are the same distance from zero. Distance is always a nonnegative number. We call the distance of a number from zero on a number line the **absolute value** of the number.

The distance of -4 from 0 is 4. The absolute value of -4 is 4.

The distance of 4 from 0 is 4. The absolute value of 4 is 4.

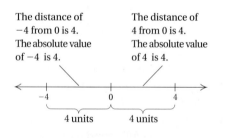

4 units   4 units

ABSOLUTE VALUE

The **absolute value** of a number is its distance from zero on a number line. We use the symbol $|x|$ to represent the absolute value of a number x.

Find the absolute value.

25. $|8|$ **26.** $|-9|$

27. $\left|-\dfrac{2}{3}\right|$ **28.** $|5.6|$

FINDING ABSOLUTE VALUE

a) If a number is negative, its absolute value is positive.
b) If a number is positive or zero, its absolute value is the same as the number.

EXAMPLES   Find the absolute value.

28. $|-7|$ The distance of -7 from 0 is 7, so $|-7| = 7$.
29. $|12|$ The distance of 12 from 0 is 12, so $|12| = 12$.
30. $|0|$ The distance of 0 from 0 is 0, so $|0| = 0$.
31. $\left|\dfrac{3}{2}\right| = \dfrac{3}{2}$
32. $|-2.73| = 2.73$

Do Exercises 25–28.

Study Tips

USING THIS TEXTBOOK

You will find many Study Tips throughout the book. An index of all Study Tips can be found at the front of the book. One of the most important ways to improve your math study skills is to learn the proper use of the textbook. Here we highlight a few points that we consider most helpful.

- **Be sure to note the special symbols** a , b , c **, and so on, that correspond to the objectives you are to be able to perform.**   The first time you see them is in the margin at the beginning of each section; the second time is in the subheadings of each section; and the third time is in the exercise set for the section. You will also find them next to the skill maintenance exercises in each exercise set and in the review exercises at the end of the chapter, as well as in the answers to the chapter tests and the cumulative reviews. These objective symbols allow you to refer to the appropriate place in the text whenever you need to review a topic.

- **Read and study each step of each example.**   The examples include important side comments that explain each step. These carefully chosen examples and notes prepare you for success in the exercise set.

- **Stop and do the margin exercises as you study a section.**   Doing the margin exercises is one of the most effective ways to enhance your ability to learn mathematics from this text. Don't deprive yourself of its benefits!

- **Note the icons listed at the top of each exercise set.**   These refer to the many distinctive multimedia study aids that accompany the book.

- **Odd-numbered exercises.**   Usually an instructor assigns some odd-numbered exercises. When you complete these, you can check your answers at the back of the book. If you miss any, check your work in the *Student's Solutions Manual* or ask your instructor for guidance.

- **Even-numbered exercises.**   Whether or not your instructor assigns the even-numbered exercises, always do some on your own. Remember, there are no answers given for the class tests, so you need to practice doing exercises without answers. Check your answers later with a friend or your instructor.

CHAPTER 1: Introduction to Real Numbers
and Algebraic Expressions

1.2 EXERCISE SET   For Extra Help

a State the integers that correspond to the situation.

1. *Pollution Fine.* In 2003, The Colonial Pipeline Company was fined a record $34 million for pollution.
Source: greenconsumerguide.com

2. *Lake Powell.* The water level of Lake Powell, a desert reservoir behind Glen Canyon Dam in northern Arizona and southeastern Utah, has dropped 130 ft since 2000.

3. On Wednesday, the temperature was 24° above zero. On Thursday, it was 2° below zero.

4. A student deposited her tax refund of $750 in a savings account. Two weeks later, she withdrew $125 to pay sorority fees.

5. *Temperature Extremes.* The highest temperature ever created on Earth was 950,000,000°F. The lowest temperature ever created was approximately 460°F below zero.
Source: *Guinness Book of World Records*

6. *Extreme Climate.* Verkhoyansk, a river port in northeast Siberia, has the most extreme climate on the planet. Its average monthly winter temperature is 58.5°F below zero, and its average monthly summer temperature is 56.5°F.
Source: *Guinness Book of World Records*

7. In bowling, the Alley Cats are 34 pins behind the Strikers going into the last frame. Describe the situation of each team.

8. During a video game, Maggie intercepted a missile worth 20 points, lost a starship worth 150 points, and captured a landing base worth 300 points.

b Graph the number on the number line.

9. $\dfrac{10}{3}$

10. $-\dfrac{17}{4}$

11. -5.2

12. 4.78

13. $-4\dfrac{2}{5}$

14. $2\dfrac{6}{11}$

C Convert to decimal notation.

15. $-\dfrac{7}{8}$

16. $-\dfrac{3}{16}$

17. $\dfrac{5}{6}$

18. $\dfrac{5}{3}$

19. $-\dfrac{7}{6}$

20. $-\dfrac{5}{12}$

21. $\dfrac{2}{3}$

22. $-\dfrac{11}{9}$

23. $\dfrac{1}{10}$

24. $\dfrac{1}{4}$

25. $-\dfrac{1}{2}$

26. $\dfrac{9}{8}$

27. $\dfrac{4}{25}$

28. $-\dfrac{7}{20}$

d Use either $<$ or $>$ for $\square$ to write a true sentence.

29. $8 \ \square \ 0$

30. $3 \ \square \ 0$

31. $-8 \ \square \ 3$

32. $6 \ \square \ -6$

33. $-8 \ \square \ 8$

34. $0 \ \square \ -9$

35. $-8 \ \square \ -5$

36. $-4 \ \square \ -3$

37. $-5 \ \square \ -11$

38. $-3 \ \square \ -4$

39. $-6 \ \square \ -5$

40. $-10 \ \square \ -14$

41. $2.14 \ \square \ 1.24$

42. $-3.3 \ \square \ -2.2$

43. $-14.5 \ \square \ 0.011$

44. $17.2 \ \square \ -1.67$

45. $-12.88 \ \square \ -6.45$

46. $-14.34 \ \square \ -17.88$

47. $-\dfrac{1}{2} \ \square \ -\dfrac{2}{3}$

48. $-\dfrac{5}{4} \ \square \ -\dfrac{3}{4}$

49. $-\dfrac{2}{3} \ \square \ \dfrac{1}{3}$

50. $\dfrac{3}{4} \ \square \ -\dfrac{5}{4}$

51. $\dfrac{5}{12} \ \square \ \dfrac{11}{25}$

52. $-\dfrac{13}{16} \ \square \ -\dfrac{5}{9}$

CHAPTER 1: Introduction to Real Numbers
and Algebraic Expressions

Write true or false.

53. $-3 \geq -11$ **54.** $5 \leq -5$ **55.** $0 \geq 8$ **56.** $-5 \leq 7$

Write an inequality with the same meaning.

57. $-6 > x$ **58.** $x < 8$ **59.** $-10 \leq y$ **60.** $12 \geq t$

e   Find the absolute value.

61. $|-3|$ **62.** $|-7|$ **63.** $|10|$ **64.** $|11|$ **65.** $|0|$

66. $|-2.7|$ **67.** $|-30.4|$ **68.** $|325|$ **69.** $\left|-\dfrac{2}{3}\right|$ **70.** $\left|-\dfrac{10}{7}\right|$

71. $\left|\dfrac{0}{4}\right|$ **72.** $|14.8|$ **73.** $\left|-3\dfrac{5}{8}\right|$ **74.** $\left|-7\dfrac{4}{5}\right|$

75. $\mathbf{D_W}$ ▦ When Jennifer's calculator gives a decimal approximation for $\sqrt{2}$ and that approximation is promptly squared, the result is 2. Yet, when that same approximation is entered by hand and then squared, the result is not exactly 2. Why do you suppose this happens?

76. $\mathbf{D_W}$ How many rational numbers are there between 0 and 1? Why?

SKILL MAINTENANCE

Convert to decimal notation.   [R.4a]

77. 63%   **78.** $23\dfrac{4}{5}\%$ **79.** 110%   **80.** 22.76%

Convert to percent notation.   [R.4d]

81. $\dfrac{13}{25}$ **82.** $\dfrac{5}{4}$ **83.** $\dfrac{5}{6}$ **84.** $\dfrac{19}{32}$

SYNTHESIS

List in order from the least to the greatest.

85. $-\dfrac{2}{3}, \dfrac{1}{2}, -\dfrac{3}{4}, -\dfrac{5}{6}, \dfrac{3}{8}, \dfrac{1}{6}$

86. $\dfrac{2}{3}, -\dfrac{1}{7}, \dfrac{1}{3}, -\dfrac{2}{7}, -\dfrac{2}{3}, \dfrac{2}{5}, -\dfrac{1}{3}, -\dfrac{2}{5}, \dfrac{9}{8}$

87. $-5.16, -4.24, -8.76, 5.23, 1.85, -2.13$

88. $-8\dfrac{7}{8}, 7^1, -5, |-6|, 4, |3|, -8\dfrac{5}{8}, -100, 0, 1^7, \dfrac{14}{4}, -\dfrac{67}{8}$

Given that $0.\overline{3} = \frac{1}{3}$ and $0.\overline{6} = \frac{2}{3}$, express each of the following as a quotient or ratio of two integers.

89. $0.\overline{1}$ **90.** $0.\overline{9}$ **91.** $5.\overline{5}$

Objectives

a Add real numbers without using a number line.

b Find the opposite, or additive inverse, of a real number.

c Solve applied problems involving addition of real numbers.

In this section, we consider addition of real numbers. First, to gain an understanding, we add using a number line. Then we consider rules for addition.

ADDITION ON A NUMBER LINE

To do the addition $a + b$ on a number line, we start at 0. Then we move to a and then move according to b.

a) If b is positive, we move from a to the right.

b) If b is negative, we move from a to the left.

c) If b is 0, we stay at a.

Add using a number line.

1. $0 + (-3)$

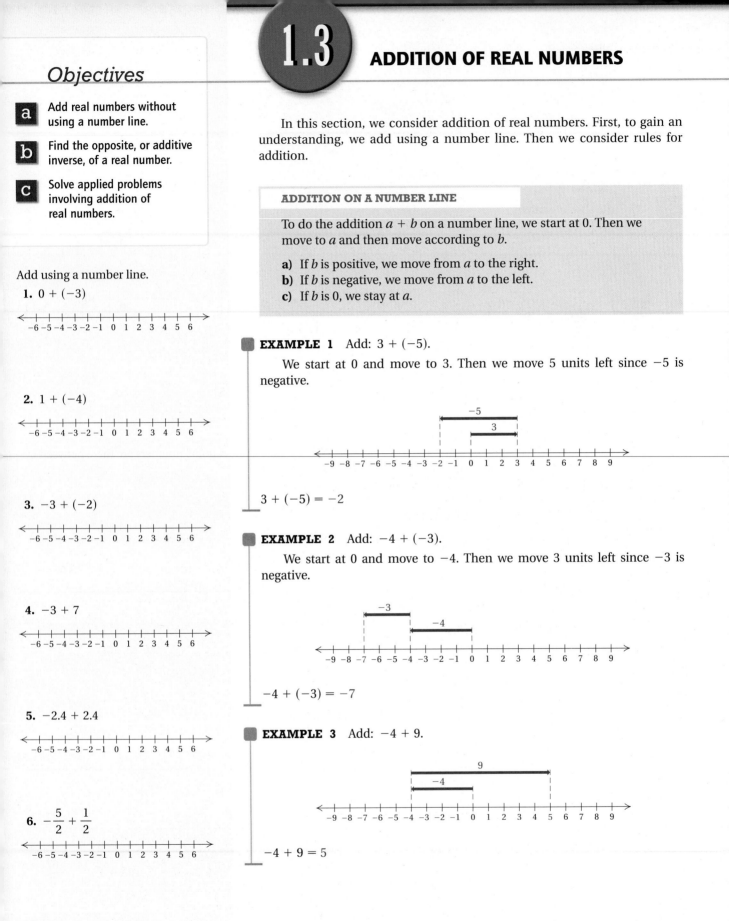

2. $1 + (-4)$

3. $-3 + (-2)$

4. $-3 + 7$

5. $-2.4 + 2.4$

6. $-\dfrac{5}{2} + \dfrac{1}{2}$

EXAMPLE 1 Add: $3 + (-5)$.

We start at 0 and move to 3. Then we move 5 units left since -5 is negative.

$$3 + (-5) = -2$$

EXAMPLE 2 Add: $-4 + (-3)$.

We start at 0 and move to -4. Then we move 3 units left since -3 is negative.

$$-4 + (-3) = -7$$

EXAMPLE 3 Add: $-4 + 9$.

$$-4 + 9 = 5$$

Answers on page A-4

EXAMPLE 4 Add: $-5.2 + 0$.

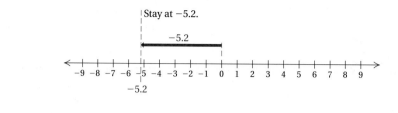

Stay at -5.2.

-5.2

-5.2

$-5.2 + 0 = -5.2$

Do Exercises 1–6 on the preceding page.

a Adding Without a Number Line

You may have noticed some patterns in the preceding examples. These lead us to rules for adding without using a number line that are more efficient for adding larger numbers.

> **RULES FOR ADDITION OF REAL NUMBERS**
>
> 1. *Positive numbers*: Add the same as arithmetic numbers. The answer is positive.
> 2. *Negative numbers*: Add absolute values. The answer is negative.
> 3. *A positive and a negative number*: Subtract the smaller absolute value from the larger. Then:
>   a) If the positive number has the greater absolute value, the answer is positive.
>   b) If the negative number has the greater absolute value, the answer is negative.
>   c) If the numbers have the same absolute value, the answer is 0.
> 4. *One number is zero*: The sum is the other number.

Rule 4 is known as the **identity property of 0.** It says that for any real number a, $a + 0 = a$.

EXAMPLES Add without using a number line.

5. $-12 + (-7) = -19$ Two negatives. Add the absolute values: $|-12| + |-7| = 12 + 7 = 19$. Make the answer *negative*: -19.

6. $-1.4 + 8.5 = 7.1$ One negative, one positive. Find the absolute values: $|-1.4| = 1.4$; $|8.5| = 8.5$. Subtract the smaller absolute value from the larger: $8.5 - 1.4 = 7.1$. The *positive* number, 8.5, has the larger absolute value, so the answer is *positive*: 7.1.

7. $-36 + 21 = -15$ One negative, one positive. Find the absolute values: $|-36| = 36$, $|21| = 21$. Subtract the smaller absolute value from the larger: $36 - 21 = 15$. The *negative* number, -36, has the larger absolute value, so the answer is *negative*: -15.

Add without using a number line.

7. $-5 + (-6)$

8. $-9 + (-3)$

9. $-4 + 6$

10. $-7 + 3$

11. $5 + (-7)$

12. $-20 + 20$

13. $-11 + (-11)$

14. $10 + (-7)$

15. $-0.17 + 0.7$

16. $-6.4 + 8.7$

17. $-4.5 + (-3.2)$

18. $-8.6 + 2.4$

19. $\dfrac{5}{9} + \left(-\dfrac{7}{9}\right)$

20. $-\dfrac{1}{5} + \left(-\dfrac{3}{4}\right)$

Answers on page A-4

Add.

21. $(-15) + (-37) + 25 + 42 + (-59) + (-14)$

22. $42 + (-81) + (-28) + 24 + 18 + (-31)$

23. $-2.5 + (-10) + 6 + (-7.5)$

24. $-35 + 17 + 14 + (-27) + 31 + (-12)$

Find the opposite, or additive inverse, of each of the following.

25. -4

26. 8.7

27. -7.74

28. $-\dfrac{8}{9}$

29. 0

30. 12

Answers on page A-4

8. $1.5 + (-1.5) = 0$ The numbers have the same absolute value. The sum is 0.

9. $-\dfrac{7}{8} + 0 = -\dfrac{7}{8}$ One number is zero. The sum is $-\dfrac{7}{8}$.

10. $-9.2 + 3.1 = -6.1$

11. $-\dfrac{3}{2} + \dfrac{9}{2} = \dfrac{6}{2} = 3$

12. $-\dfrac{2}{3} + \dfrac{5}{8} = -\dfrac{16}{24} + \dfrac{15}{24} = -\dfrac{1}{24}$

Do Exercises 7–20 on the preceding page.

Suppose we want to add several numbers, some positive and some negative, as follows. How can we proceed?

$$15 + (-2) + 7 + 14 + (-5) + (-12)$$

We can change grouping and order as we please when adding. For instance, we can group the positive numbers together and the negative numbers together and add them separately. Then we add the two results.

EXAMPLE 13   Add: $15 + (-2) + 7 + 14 + (-5) + (-12)$.

a) $15 + 7 + 14 = 36$ Adding the positive numbers

b) $-2 + (-5) + (-12) = -19$ Adding the negative numbers

    $36 + (-19) = 17$ Adding (a) and (b)

We can also add the numbers in any other order we wish, say, from left to right as follows:

$$
\begin{aligned}
15 + (-2) + 7 + 14 + (-5) + (-12) &= 13 + 7 + 14 + (-5) + (-12) \\
&= 20 + 14 + (-5) + (-12) \\
&= 34 + (-5) + (-12) \\
&= 29 + (-12) \\
&= 17
\end{aligned}
$$

Do Exercises 21–24.

b   Opposites, or Additive Inverses

Suppose we add two numbers that are **opposites,** such as 6 and -6. The result is 0. When opposites are added, the result is always 0. Such numbers are also called **additive inverses.** Every real number has an opposite, or additive inverse.

> **OPPOSITES, OR ADDITIVE INVERSES**
>
> Two numbers whose sum is 0 are called **opposites,** or **additive inverses,** of each other.

EXAMPLES Find the opposite, or additive inverse, of each number.

14. 34   The opposite of 34 is -34 because $34 + (-34) = 0$.

15. -8 The opposite of -8 is 8 because $-8 + 8 = 0$.

16. 0   The opposite of 0 is 0 because $0 + 0 = 0$.

17. $-\dfrac{7}{8}$ The opposite of $-\dfrac{7}{8}$ is $\dfrac{7}{8}$ because $-\dfrac{7}{8} + \dfrac{7}{8} = 0$.

Do Exercises 25–30 on the preceding page.

To name the opposite, we use the symbol $-$, as follows.

> **SYMBOLIZING OPPOSITES**
>
> The opposite, or additive inverse, of a number a can be named $-a$ (read "the opposite of a," or "the additive inverse of a").

Note that if we take a number, say, 8, and find its opposite, -8, and then find the opposite of the result, we will have the original number, 8, again.

> **THE OPPOSITE OF AN OPPOSITE**
>
> The **opposite of the opposite** of a number is the number itself. (The additive inverse of the additive inverse of a number is the number itself.) That is, for any number a,
>
> $$-(-a) = a.$$

EXAMPLE 18 Evaluate $-x$ and $-(-x)$ when $x = 16$.

If $x = 16$, then $-x = -16$.   The opposite of 16 is -16.

If $x = 16$, then $-(-x) = -(-16) = 16$.   The opposite of the opposite of 16 is 16.

EXAMPLE 19 Evaluate $-x$ and $-(-x)$ when $x = -3$.

If $x = -3$, then $-x = -(-3) = 3$.

If $x = -3$, then $-(-x) = -(-(-3)) = -(3) = -3$.

Note that in Example 19 we used a second set of parentheses to show that we are substituting the negative number -3 for x. Symbolism like $--x$ is not considered meaningful.

Do Exercises 31–36.

A symbol such as -8 is usually read "negative 8." It could be read "the additive inverse of 8," because the additive inverse of 8 is negative 8. It could also be read "the opposite of 8," because the opposite of 8 is -8. Thus a symbol like -8 can be read in more than one way. It is never correct to read -8 as "minus 8."

> **Caution!**
>
> A symbol like $-x$, which has a variable, should be read "the opposite of x" or "the additive inverse of x" and *not* "negative x," because we do not know whether x represents a positive number, a negative number, or 0. You can check this in Examples 18 and 19.

Evaluate $-x$ and $-(-x)$ when:

31. $x = 14$.

32. $x = 1$.

33. $x = -19$.

34. $x = -1.6$.

35. $x = \dfrac{2}{3}$.

36. $x = -\dfrac{9}{8}$.

Answers on page A-4

Find the opposite. (Change the sign.)

37. −4

38. −13.4

39. 0

40. $\dfrac{1}{4}$

41. Change in Class Size. During the first two weeks of the semester in Jim's algebra class, 4 students withdrew, 8 students enrolled in the class, and 6 students were dropped as "no shows." By how many students had the class size changed at the end of the first two weeks?

Answers on page A-4

We can use the symbolism $-a$ to restate the definition of opposite, or additive inverse.

THE SUM OF OPPOSITES

For any real number a, the **opposite,** or **additive inverse,** of a, expressed as $-a$, is such that

$$a + (-a) = (-a) + a = 0.$$

SIGNS OF NUMBERS

A negative number is sometimes said to have a "negative sign." A positive number is said to have a "positive sign." When we replace a number with its opposite, we can say that we have "changed its sign."

EXAMPLES Find the opposite. (Change the sign.)

20. −3 $-(-3) = 3$

21. $-\dfrac{2}{13}$ $-\left(-\dfrac{2}{13}\right) = \dfrac{2}{13}$

22. 0 $-(0) = 0$

23. 14 $-(14) = -14$

Do Exercises 37–40.

C   Applications and Problem Solving

Addition of real numbers occurs in many real-world situations.

EXAMPLE 24 *Lake Level.* In the course of one four-month period, the water level of Lake Champlain went down 2 ft, up 1 ft, down 5 ft, and up 3 ft. How much had the lake level changed at the end of the four months?

We let $T =$ the total change in the level of the lake. Then the problem translates to a sum:

Total change	is	1st change	plus	2nd change	plus	3rd change	plus	4th change.
T	$=$	-2	$+$	1	$+$	(-5)	$+$	3

Adding from left to right, we have

$$T = -2 + 1 + (-5) + 3 = -1 + (-5) + 3$$
$$= -6 + 3$$
$$= -3.$$

The lake level has dropped 3 ft at the end of the four-month period.

Do Exercise 41.

EXERCISE SET | For Extra Help

a   Add. Do not use a number line except as a check.

1. $2 + (-9)$ **2.** $-5 + 2$ **3.** $-11 + 5$ **4.** $4 + (-3)$ **5.** $-6 + 6$

6. $8 + (-8)$ **7.** $-3 + (-5)$ **8.** $-4 + (-6)$ **9.** $-7 + 0$ **10.** $-13 + 0$

11. $0 + (-27)$ **12.** $0 + (-35)$ **13.** $17 + (-17)$ **14.** $-15 + 15$ **15.** $-17 + (-25)$

16. $-24 + (-17)$ **17.** $18 + (-18)$ **18.** $-13 + 13$ **19.** $-28 + 28$ **20.** $11 + (-11)$

21. $8 + (-5)$ **22.** $-7 + 8$ **23.** $-4 + (-5)$ **24.** $10 + (-12)$ **25.** $13 + (-6)$

26. $-3 + 14$ **27.** $-25 + 25$ **28.** $50 + (-50)$ **29.** $53 + (-18)$ **30.** $75 + (-45)$

31. $-8.5 + 4.7$ **32.** $-4.6 + 1.9$ **33.** $-2.8 + (-5.3)$ **34.** $-7.9 + (-6.5)$ **35.** $-\dfrac{3}{5} + \dfrac{2}{5}$

36. $-\dfrac{4}{3} + \dfrac{2}{3}$ **37.** $-\dfrac{2}{9} + \left(-\dfrac{5}{9}\right)$ **38.** $-\dfrac{4}{7} + \left(-\dfrac{6}{7}\right)$ **39.** $-\dfrac{5}{8} + \dfrac{1}{4}$ **40.** $-\dfrac{5}{6} + \dfrac{2}{3}$

41. $-\dfrac{5}{8} + \left(-\dfrac{1}{6}\right)$ **42.** $-\dfrac{5}{6} + \left(-\dfrac{2}{9}\right)$ **43.** $-\dfrac{3}{8} + \dfrac{5}{12}$ **44.** $-\dfrac{7}{16} + \dfrac{7}{8}$

45. $-\dfrac{1}{6} + \dfrac{7}{10}$ **46.** $-\dfrac{11}{18} + \left(-\dfrac{3}{4}\right)$ **47.** $\dfrac{7}{15} + \left(-\dfrac{1}{9}\right)$ **48.** $-\dfrac{4}{21} + \dfrac{3}{14}$

49. $76 + (-15) + (-18) + (-6)$

50. $29 + (-45) + 18 + 32 + (-96)$

51. $-44 + \left(-\dfrac{3}{8}\right) + 95 + \left(-\dfrac{5}{8}\right)$

52. $24 + 3.1 + (-44) + (-8.2) + 63$

53. $98 + (-54) + 113 + (-998) + 44 + (-612)$

54. $-458 + (-124) + 1025 + (-917) + 218$

b   Find the opposite, or additive inverse.

55. 24

56. -64

57. -26.9

58. 48.2

Evaluate $-x$ when:

59. $x = 8.$

60. $x = -27.$

61. $x = -\dfrac{13}{8}.$

62. $x = \dfrac{1}{236}.$

Evaluate $-(-x)$ when:

63. $x = -43.$

64. $x = 39.$

65. $x = \dfrac{4}{3}.$

66. $x = -7.1.$

Find the opposite. (Change the sign.)

67. -24

68. -12.3

69. $-\dfrac{3}{8}$

70. 10

c   Solve.

71. *Tallest Mountain.*   The tallest mountain in the world, when measured from base to peak, is Mauna Kea (White Mountain) in Hawaii. From its base 19,684 ft below sea level in the Hawaiian Trough, it rises 33,480 ft. What is the elevation of the peak above sea level?

Source: *The Guinness Book of Records*

72. *Telephone Bills.*   Erika's cell-phone bill for July was $82. She sent a check for $50 and then made $37 worth of calls in August. How much did she then owe on her cell-phone bill?

73. *Temperature Changes.*   One day the temperature in Lawrence, Kansas, is 32°F at 6:00 A.M. It rises 15° by noon, but falls 50° by midnight when a cold front moves in. What is the final temperature?

74. *Stock Changes.*   On a recent day, the price of a stock opened at a value of $61.38. During the day, it rose $4.75, dropped $7.38, and rose $5.13. Find the value of the stock at the end of the day.

75. *Profits and Losses.* A business expresses a profit as a positive number and refers to it as operating "in the black." A loss is expressed as a negative number and is referred to as operating "in the red." The profits and losses of Xponent Corporation over various years are shown in the bar graph below. Find the sum of the profits and losses.

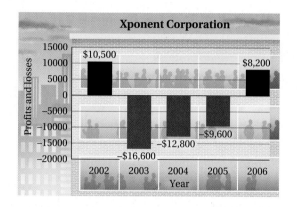

76. *Football Yardage.* In a college football game, the quarterback attempted passes with the following results. Find the total gain or loss.

TRY	GAIN OR LOSS
1st	13-yd gain
2nd	12-yd loss
3rd	21-yd gain

77. *Credit Card Bills.* On August 1, Lyle's credit card bill shows that he owes $470. During the month of August, Lyle sends a check for $45 to the credit card company, charges another $160 in merchandise, and then pays off another $500 of his bill. What is the new balance of Lyle's account at the end of August?

78. *Account Balance.* Leah has $460 in a checking account. She writes a check for $530, makes a deposit of $75, and then writes a check for $90. What is the balance in her account?

79. D_W Without actually performing the addition, explain why the sum of all integers from -50 to 50 is 0.

80. D_W Explain in your own words why the sum of two negative numbers is always negative.

SKILL MAINTENANCE

Convert to decimal notation.   [R.4a]

81. 71.3%

82. $92\frac{7}{8}\%$

Convert to percent notation.   [R.4d]

83. $\frac{1}{8}$

84. $\frac{13}{32}$

85. Divide and simplify: $\frac{2}{3} \div \frac{5}{12}$.   [R.2c]

86. Subtract and simplify: $\frac{2}{3} - \frac{5}{12}$.   [R.2c]

SYNTHESIS

87. For what numbers x is $-x$ negative?

88. For what numbers x is $-x$ positive?

For each of Exercises 89 and 90, choose the correct answer from the selections given.

89. If a is positive and b is negative, then $-a + b$ is:
   a) Positive.   **b)** Negative.
   c) 0.   **d)** Cannot be determined without more information

90. If $a = b$ and a and b are negative, then $-a + (-b)$ is:
   a) Positive.   **b)** Negative.
   c) 0.   **d)** Cannot be determined without more information

1.4 SUBTRACTION OF REAL NUMBERS

Objectives

a Subtract real numbers and simplify combinations of additions and subtractions.

b Solve applied problems involving subtraction of real numbers.

a Subtraction

We now consider subtraction of real numbers.

> **SUBTRACTION**
>
> The difference $a - b$ is the number c for which $a = b + c$.

Consider, for example, $45 - 17$. *Think*: What number can we add to 17 to get 45? Since $45 = 17 + 28$, we know that $45 - 17 = 28$. Let's consider an example whose answer is a negative number.

EXAMPLE 1 Subtract: $3 - 7$.

Think: What number can we add to 7 to get 3? The number must be negative. Since $7 + (-4) = 3$, we know the number is -4: $3 - 7 = -4$. That is, $3 - 7 = -4$ because $7 + (-4) = 3$.

Subtract.

1. $-6 - 4$

Think: What number can be added to 4 to get -6:

$$\square + 4 = -6?$$

2. $-7 - (-10)$

Think: What number can be added to -10 to get -7:

$$\square + (-10) = -7?$$

Do Exercises 1–3.

The definition above does not provide the most efficient way to do subtraction. We can develop a faster way to subtract. As a rationale for the faster way, let's compare $3 + 7$ and $3 - 7$ on a number line.

To find $3 + 7$ on a number line, we move 3 units to the right from 0 since 3 is positive. Then we move 7 units farther to the right since 7 is positive.

3. $-7 - (-2)$

Think: What number can be added to -2 to get -7:

$$\square + (-2) = -7?$$

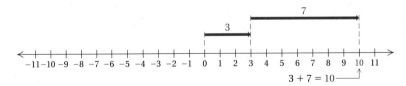

To find $3 - 7$, we do the "opposite" of adding 7: We move 7 units to the *left* to do the subtracting. This is the same as *adding* the opposite of 7, -7, to 3.

Subtract. Use a number line, doing the "opposite" of addition.

4. $-4 - (-3)$

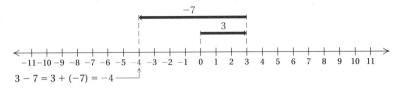

Do Exercises 4–6.

5. $-4 - (-6)$

6. $5 - 9$

Look for a pattern in the examples shown at right.

SUBTRACTING	ADDING AN OPPOSITE
$5 - 8 = -3$	$5 + (-8) = -3$
$-6 - 4 = -10$	$-6 + (-4) = -10$
$-7 - (-2) = -5$	$-7 + 2 = -5$

Answers on page A-4

Do Exercises 7–10 on the following page.

Perhaps you have noticed that we can subtract by adding the opposite of the number being subtracted. This can always be done.

SUBTRACTING BY ADDING THE OPPOSITE

For any real numbers a and b,

$$a - b = a + (-b).$$

(To subtract, add the opposite, or additive inverse, of the number being subtracted.)

This is the method generally used for quick subtraction of real numbers.

EXAMPLES Subtract.

2. $2 - 6 = 2 + (-6) = -4$ 　　The opposite of 6 is -6. We change the subtraction to addition and add the opposite. *Check*: $-4 + 6 = 2$.

3. $4 - (-9) = 4 + 9 = 13$ 　　The opposite of -9 is 9. We change the subtraction to addition and add the opposite. *Check*: $13 + (-9) = 4$.

4. $-4.2 - (-3.6) = -4.2 + 3.6 = -0.6$ 　　Adding the opposite. *Check*: $-0.6 + (-3.6) = -4.2$.

5. $-\dfrac{1}{2} - \left(-\dfrac{3}{4}\right) = -\dfrac{1}{2} + \dfrac{3}{4}$ 　　Adding the opposite.
$$= -\dfrac{2}{4} + \dfrac{3}{4} = \dfrac{1}{4}$$
Check: $\dfrac{1}{4} + \left(-\dfrac{3}{4}\right) = -\dfrac{1}{2}$.

Do Exercises 11–16.

EXAMPLES Read each of the following. Then subtract by adding the opposite of the number being subtracted.

6. $3 - 5$ 　　Read "three minus five is three plus the opposite of five"
$3 - 5 = 3 + (-5) = -2$

7. $\dfrac{1}{8} - \dfrac{7}{8}$ 　　Read "one-eighth minus seven-eighths is one-eighth plus the opposite of seven-eighths"
$\dfrac{1}{8} - \dfrac{7}{8} = \dfrac{1}{8} + \left(-\dfrac{7}{8}\right) = -\dfrac{6}{8}$, or $-\dfrac{3}{4}$

8. $-4.6 - (-9.8)$ 　　Read "negative four point six minus negative nine point eight is negative four point six plus the opposite of negative nine point eight"
$-4.6 - (-9.8) = -4.6 + 9.8 = 5.2$

9. $-\dfrac{3}{4} - \dfrac{7}{5}$ 　　Read "negative three-fourths minus seven-fifths is negative three-fourths plus the opposite of seven-fifths"
$-\dfrac{3}{4} - \dfrac{7}{5} = -\dfrac{3}{4} + \left(-\dfrac{7}{5}\right) = -\dfrac{15}{20} + \left(-\dfrac{28}{20}\right) = -\dfrac{43}{20}$

Do Exercises 17–21 on the following page.

Complete the addition and compare with the subtraction.

7. $4 - 6 = -2$;
$4 + (-6) = \underline{\hspace{2cm}}$

8. $-3 - 8 = -11$;
$-3 + (-8) = \underline{\hspace{2cm}}$

9. $-5 - (-9) = 4$;
$-5 + 9 = \underline{\hspace{2cm}}$

10. $-5 - (-3) = -2$;
$-5 + 3 = \underline{\hspace{2cm}}$

Subtract.

11. $2 - 8$

12. $-6 - 10$

13. $12.4 - 5.3$

14. $-8 - (-11)$

15. $-8 - (-8)$

16. $\dfrac{2}{3} - \left(-\dfrac{5}{6}\right)$

Answers on page A-4

Read each of the following. Then subtract by adding the opposite of the number being subtracted.

17. $3 - 11$

18. $12 - 5$

19. $-12 - (-9)$

20. $-12.4 - 10.9$

21. $-\dfrac{4}{5} - \left(-\dfrac{4}{5}\right)$

Simplify.

22. $-6 - (-2) - (-4) - 12 + 3$

23. $\dfrac{2}{3} - \dfrac{4}{5} - \left(-\dfrac{11}{15}\right) + \dfrac{7}{10} - \dfrac{5}{2}$

24. $-9.6 + 7.4 - (-3.9) - (-11)$

25. Temperature Extremes. The highest temperature ever recorded in the United States is 134°F in Greenland Ranch, California, on July 10, 1913. The lowest temperature ever recorded is −80°F in Prospect Creek, Alaska, on January 23, 1971. How much higher was the temperature in Greenland Ranch than that in Prospect Creek?

Source: National Oceanographic and Atmospheric Administration

When several additions and subtractions occur together, we can make them all additions.

■ **EXAMPLES** Simplify.

10. $8 - (-4) - 2 - (-4) + 2 = 8 + 4 + (-2) + 4 + 2$ Adding the
$$= 16$$ opposite

11. $8.2 - (-6.1) + 2.3 - (-4) = 8.2 + 6.1 + 2.3 + 4 = 20.6$

12. $\dfrac{3}{4} - \left(-\dfrac{1}{12}\right) - \dfrac{5}{6} - \dfrac{2}{3} = \dfrac{9}{12} + \dfrac{1}{12} + \left(-\dfrac{10}{12}\right) + \left(-\dfrac{8}{12}\right)$

$$= \dfrac{9 + 1 + (-10) + (-8)}{12}$$

$$= \dfrac{-8}{12} = -\dfrac{8}{12} = -\dfrac{2}{3}$$

Do Exercises 22–24.

b   Applications and Problem Solving

Let's now see how we can use subtraction of real numbers to solve applied problems.

■ **EXAMPLE 13** *Surface Temperatures on Mars.* Surface temperatures on Mars vary from −128°C during polar night to 27°C at the equator during midday at the closest point in orbit to the sun. Find the difference between the highest value and the lowest value in this temperature range.

Source: Mars Institute

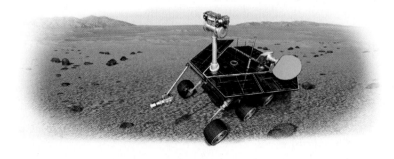

We let $D =$ the difference in the temperatures. Then the problem translates to the following subtraction:

Difference in temperature	is	Highest temperature	minus	Lowest temperature
↓	↓	↓	↓	↓
D	$=$	27	$-$	(-128)

$$D = 27 + 128 = 155$$

The difference in the temperatures is 155°C.

Do Exercise 25.

Answers on page A-4

a Subtract.

1. $2 - 9$

2. $3 - 8$

3. $-8 - (-2)$

4. $-6 - (-8)$

5. $-11 - (-11)$

6. $-6 - (-6)$

7. $12 - 16$

8. $14 - 19$

9. $20 - 27$

10. $30 - 4$

11. $-9 - (-3)$

12. $-7 - (-9)$

13. $-40 - (-40)$

14. $-9 - (-9)$

15. $7 - (-7)$

16. $4 - (-4)$

17. $8 - (-3)$

18. $-7 - 4$

19. $-6 - 8$

20. $6 - (-10)$

21. $-4 - (-9)$

22. $-14 - 2$

23. $-6 - (-5)$

24. $-4 - (-3)$

25. $8 - (-10)$

26. $5 - (-6)$

27. $-5 - (-2)$

28. $-3 - (-1)$

29. $-7 - 14$

30. $-9 - 16$

31. $0 - (-5)$

32. $0 - (-1)$

33. $-8 - 0$

34. $-9 - 0$

35. $7 - (-5)$

36. $7 - (-4)$

37. $2 - 25$

38. $18 - 63$

39. $-42 - 26$

40. $-18 - 63$

41. $-71 - 2$

42. $-49 - 3$

43. $24 - (-92)$

44. $48 - (-73)$

45. $-50 - (-50)$

46. $-70 - (-70)$

47. $-\dfrac{3}{8} - \dfrac{5}{8}$

48. $\dfrac{3}{9} - \dfrac{9}{9}$

49. $\dfrac{3}{4} - \dfrac{2}{3}$

50. $\dfrac{5}{8} - \dfrac{3}{4}$

51. $-\dfrac{3}{4} - \dfrac{2}{3}$

52. $-\dfrac{5}{8} - \dfrac{3}{4}$

53. $-\dfrac{5}{8} - \left(-\dfrac{3}{4}\right)$

54. $-\dfrac{3}{4} - \left(-\dfrac{2}{3}\right)$

55. $6.1 - (-13.8)$

56. $1.5 - (-3.5)$

57. $-2.7 - 5.9$

58. $-3.2 - 5.8$

59. $0.99 - 1$

60. $0.87 - 1$

61. $-79 - 114$

62. $-197 - 216$

63. $0 - (-500)$

64. $500 - (-1000)$

65. $-2.8 - 0$

66. $6.04 - 1.1$

67. $7 - 10.53$

68. $8 - (-9.3)$

69. $\dfrac{1}{6} - \dfrac{2}{3}$

70. $-\dfrac{3}{8} - \left(-\dfrac{1}{2}\right)$

71. $-\dfrac{4}{7} - \left(-\dfrac{10}{7}\right)$

72. $\dfrac{12}{5} - \dfrac{12}{5}$

73. $-\dfrac{7}{10} - \dfrac{10}{15}$

74. $-\dfrac{4}{18} - \left(-\dfrac{2}{9}\right)$

75. $\dfrac{1}{5} - \dfrac{1}{3}$

76. $-\dfrac{1}{7} - \left(-\dfrac{1}{6}\right)$

77. $\dfrac{5}{12} - \dfrac{7}{16}$

78. $-\dfrac{1}{35} - \left(-\dfrac{9}{40}\right)$

79. $-\dfrac{2}{15} - \dfrac{7}{12}$

80. $\dfrac{2}{21} - \dfrac{9}{14}$

CHAPTER 1: Introduction to Real Numbers
and Algebraic Expressions

Simplify.

81. $18 - (-15) - 3 - (-5) + 2$

82. $22 - (-18) + 7 + (-42) - 27$

83. $-31 + (-28) - (-14) - 17$

84. $-43 - (-19) - (-21) + 25$

85. $-34 - 28 + (-33) - 44$

86. $39 + (-88) - 29 - (-83)$

87. $-93 - (-84) - 41 - (-56)$

88. $84 + (-99) + 44 - (-18) - 43$

89. $-5.4 - (-30.9) + 30.8 + 40.2 - (-12)$

90. $14.9 - (-50.7) + 20 - (-32.8)$

91. $-\dfrac{7}{12} + \dfrac{3}{4} - \left(-\dfrac{5}{8}\right) - \dfrac{13}{24}$

92. $-\dfrac{11}{16} + \dfrac{5}{32} - \left(-\dfrac{1}{4}\right) + \dfrac{7}{8}$

b Solve.

93. *Ocean Depth.* The deepest point in the Pacific Ocean is the Marianas Trench, with a depth of 10,924 m. The deepest point in the Atlantic Ocean is the Puerto Rico Trench, with a depth of 8605 m. What is the difference in the elevation of the two trenches?

Source: *The World Almanac and Book of Facts*

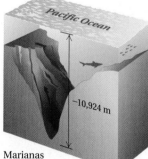
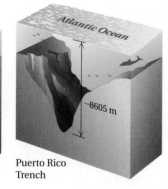

Pacific Ocean

Atlantic Ocean

−10,924 m

−8605 m

Marianas
Trench

Puerto Rico
Trench

94. *Elevations in Africa.* The elevation of the highest point in Africa, Mt. Kilimanjaro, Tanzania, is 19,340 ft. The lowest elevation, at Lake Assal, Djibouti, is −512 ft. What is the difference in the elevations of the two locations?

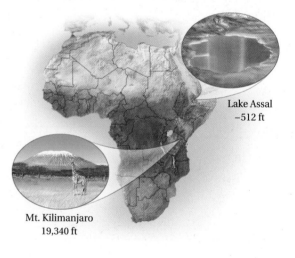

Lake Assal
−512 ft

Mt. Kilimanjaro
19,340 ft

95. Claire has a charge of $476.89 on her credit card, but she then returns a sweater that cost $128.95. How much does she now owe on her credit card?

96. Chris has $720 in a checking account. He writes a check for $970 to pay for a sound system. What is the balance in his checking account?

97. *Home-Run Differential.* In baseball, the difference between the number of home runs hit by a team's players and the number allowed by its pitchers is called the *home-run differential,* that is,

Home run differential = $\dfrac{\text{Number of}}{\text{home runs hit}} - \dfrac{\text{Number of home}}{\text{runs allowed}}$.

Teams strive for a positive home-run differential.

a) In a recent year, Atlanta hit 197 home runs and allowed 120. Find its home-run differential.

b) In a recent year, San Francisco hit 153 home runs and allowed 194. Find its home-run differential.

Source: Major League Baseball

98. *Temperature Records.* The greatest recorded temperature change in one 24-hour period occurred between January 23 and January 24, 1916, in Browning, Montana, where the temperature fell from 44°F to −56°F. By how much did the temperature drop?

Source: *The Guinness Book of Records,* 2004

99. *Low Points on Continents.* The lowest point in Africa is Lake Assal, which is 512 ft below sea level. The lowest point in South America is the Valdes Peninsula, which is 131 ft below sea level. How much lower is Lake Assal than the Valdes Peninsula?

Source: National Geographic Society

100. *Elevation Changes.* The lowest elevation in North America, Death Valley, California, is 282 ft below sea level. The highest elevation in North America, Mount McKinley, Alaska, is 20,320 ft. Find the difference in elevation between the highest point and the lowest.

Source: National Geographic Society

101. **D**$_\mathbf{W}$ If a negative number is subtracted from a positive number, will the result always be positive? Why or why not?

102. **D**$_\mathbf{W}$ Write a problem for a classmate to solve. Design the problem so that the solution is "The temperature dropped to −9°."

SKILL MAINTENANCE

Simplify. [R.5c]

103. $256 \div 64 \div 2^3 + 100$

104. $5 \cdot 6 + (7 \cdot 2)^2$

105. $2^5 \div 4 + 20 \div 2^2$

106. $65 - 5^2 \div 5 - 5 \cdot 2$

107. Add and simplify: $\dfrac{1}{8} + \dfrac{7}{12} + \dfrac{5}{24}$. [R.2c]

108. Simplify: $\dfrac{164}{256}$. [R.2b]

SYNTHESIS

Tell whether the statement is true or false for all integers a and b. If false, give an example to show why.

109. $a - 0 = 0 - a$

110. $0 - a = a$

111. If $a \neq b$, then $a - b \neq 0$.

112. If $a = -b$, then $a + b = 0$.

113. If $a + b = 0$, then a and b are opposites.

114. If $a - b = 0$, then $a = -b$.

1.5 MULTIPLICATION OF REAL NUMBERS

Objectives

a Multiply real numbers.

b Solve applied problems involving multiplication of real numbers.

a Multiplication

Multiplication of real numbers is very much like multiplication of arithmetic numbers. The only difference is that we must determine whether the answer is positive or negative.

MULTIPLICATION OF A POSITIVE NUMBER AND A NEGATIVE NUMBER

To see how to multiply a positive number and a negative number, consider the pattern of the following.

This number decreases by 1 each time.

$$4 \cdot 5 = 20$$
$$3 \cdot 5 = 15$$
$$2 \cdot 5 = 10$$
$$1 \cdot 5 = 5$$
$$0 \cdot 5 = 0$$
$$-1 \cdot 5 = -5$$
$$-2 \cdot 5 = -10$$
$$-3 \cdot 5 = -15$$

This number decreases by 5 each time.

Do Exercise 1.

According to this pattern, it looks as though the product of a negative number and a positive number is negative. That is the case, and we have the first part of the rule for multiplying numbers.

> **THE PRODUCT OF A POSITIVE AND A NEGATIVE NUMBER**
>
> To multiply a positive number and a negative number, multiply their absolute values. The answer is negative.

EXAMPLES Multiply.

1. $8(-5) = -40$ **2.** $-\dfrac{1}{3} \cdot \dfrac{5}{7} = -\dfrac{5}{21}$ **3.** $(-7.2)5 = -36$

Do Exercises 2–7.

MULTIPLICATION OF TWO NEGATIVE NUMBERS

How do we multiply two negative numbers? Again, we look for a pattern.

This number decreases by 1 each time.

$$4 \cdot (-5) = -20$$
$$3 \cdot (-5) = -15$$
$$2 \cdot (-5) = -10$$
$$1 \cdot (-5) = -5$$
$$0 \cdot (-5) = 0$$
$$-1 \cdot (-5) = 5$$
$$-2 \cdot (-5) = 10$$
$$-3 \cdot (-5) = 15$$

This number increases by 5 each time.

1. Complete, as in the example.

$$4 \cdot 10 = 40$$
$$3 \cdot 10 = 30$$
$$2 \cdot 10 =$$
$$1 \cdot 10 =$$
$$0 \cdot 10 =$$
$$-1 \cdot 10 =$$
$$-2 \cdot 10 =$$
$$-3 \cdot 10 =$$

Multiply.

2. $-3 \cdot 6$

3. $20 \cdot (-5)$

4. $4 \cdot (-20)$

5. $-\dfrac{2}{3} \cdot \dfrac{5}{6}$

6. $-4.23(7.1)$

7. $\dfrac{7}{8}\left(-\dfrac{4}{5}\right)$

8. Complete, as in the example.

$$3 \cdot (-10) = -30$$
$$2 \cdot (-10) = -20$$
$$1 \cdot (-10) =$$
$$0 \cdot (-10) =$$
$$-1 \cdot (-10) =$$
$$-2 \cdot (-10) =$$
$$-3 \cdot (-10) =$$

Answers on page A-5

Multiply.

9. $-9 \cdot (-3)$

10. $-16 \cdot (-2)$

11. $-7 \cdot (-5)$

12. $-\dfrac{4}{7}\left(-\dfrac{5}{9}\right)$

13. $-\dfrac{3}{2}\left(-\dfrac{4}{9}\right)$

14. $-3.25(-4.14)$

Multiply.

15. $5(-6)$

16. $(-5)(-6)$

17. $(-3.2) \cdot 0$

18. $\left(-\dfrac{4}{5}\right)\left(\dfrac{10}{3}\right)$

19. $0 \cdot (-34.2)$

20. $23 \cdot 0 \cdot \left(-4\frac{2}{3}\right)$

Do Exercise 8 on the preceding page.

According to the pattern, it appears that the product of two negative numbers is positive. That is actually so, and we have the second part of the rule for multiplying real numbers.

> **THE PRODUCT OF TWO NEGATIVE NUMBERS**
>
> To multiply two negative numbers, multiply their absolute values. The answer is positive.

Do Exercises 9–14.

The following is another way to consider the rules we have for multiplication.

> To multiply two nonzero real numbers:
>
> **a)** Multiply the absolute values.
> **b)** If the signs are the same, the answer is positive.
> **c)** If the signs are different, the answer is negative.

MULTIPLICATION BY ZERO

The only case that we have not considered is multiplying by zero. As with other numbers, the product of any real number and 0 is 0.

> **THE MULTIPLICATION PROPERTY OF ZERO**
>
> For any real number a,
>
> $$a \cdot 0 = 0 \cdot a = 0.$$
>
> (The product of 0 and any real number is 0.)

EXAMPLES Multiply.

4. $(-3)(-4) = 12$

5. $-1.6(2) = -3.2$

6. $-19 \cdot 0 = 0$

7. $\left(-\dfrac{5}{6}\right)\left(-\dfrac{1}{9}\right) = \dfrac{5}{54}$

8. $0 \cdot (-452) = 0$

9. $23 \cdot 0 \cdot \left(-8\frac{2}{3}\right) = 0$

Do Exercises 15–20.

Answers on page A-5

MULTIPLYING MORE THAN TWO NUMBERS

When multiplying more than two real numbers, we can choose order and grouping as we please.

■ **EXAMPLES** Multiply.

10. $-8 \cdot 2(-3) = -16(-3)$ Multiplying the first two numbers

$$= 48$$

11. $-8 \cdot 2(-3) = 24 \cdot 2$ Multiplying the negatives. Every pair of negative numbers gives a positive product.

$$= 48$$

12. $-3(-2)(-5)(4) = 6(-5)(4)$ Multiplying the first two numbers

$$= (-30)4$$

$$= -120$$

13. $\left(-\dfrac{1}{2}\right)(8)\left(-\dfrac{2}{3}\right)(-6) = (-4)4$ Multiplying the first two numbers and the last two numbers

$$= -16$$

14. $-5 \cdot (-2) \cdot (-3) \cdot (-6) = 10 \cdot 18 = 180$

15. $(-3)(-5)(-2)(-3)(-6) = (-30)(18) = -540$

Considering that the product of a pair of negative numbers is positive, we see the following pattern.

> The product of an even number of negative numbers is positive.
> The product of an odd number of negative numbers is negative.

Do Exercises 21–26.

■ **EXAMPLE 16** Evaluate $2x^2$ when $x = 3$ and when $x = -3$.

$$2x^2 = 2(3)^2 = 2(9) = 18;$$

$$2x^2 = 2(-3)^2 = 2(9) = 18$$

Let's compare the expressions $(-x)^2$ and $-x^2$.

■ **EXAMPLE 17** Evaluate $(-x)^2$ and $-x^2$ when $x = 5$.

$(-x)^2 = (-5)^2 = (-5)(-5) = 25;$ Substitute 5 for x. Then evaluate the power.

$-x^2 = -(5)^2 = -25$ Substitute 5 for x. Evaluate the power. Then find the opposite.

■ **EXAMPLE 18** Evaluate $(-a)^2$ and $-a^2$ when $a = -4$.

To make sense of the substitutions and computations, we introduce extra brackets into the expressions.

$$(-a)^2 = [-(-4)]^2 = [4]^2 = 16;$$

$$-a^2 = -(-4)^2 = -(16) = -16$$

Multiply.

21. $5 \cdot (-3) \cdot 2$

22. $-3 \times (-4.1) \times (-2.5)$

23. $-\dfrac{1}{2} \cdot \left(-\dfrac{4}{3}\right) \cdot \left(-\dfrac{5}{2}\right)$

24. $-2 \cdot (-5) \cdot (-4) \cdot (-3)$

25. $(-4)(-5)(-2)(-3)(-1)$

26. $(-1)(-1)(-2)(-3)(-1)(-1)$

27. Evaluate $(-x)^2$ and $-x^2$ when $x = 2$.

28. Evaluate $(-x)^2$ and $-x^2$ when $x = -3$.

29. Evaluate $3x^2$ when $x = 4$ and when $x = -4$.

Answers on page A-5

30. Chemical Reaction. During a chemical reaction, the temperature in the beaker increased by 3°C every minute until 1:34 P.M. If the temperature was −17°C at 1:10 P.M., when the reaction began, what was the temperature at 1:34 P.M.?

The expressions $(-x)^2$ and $-x^2$ are *not* equivalent. That is, they do not have the same value for every allowable replacement of the variable by a real number. To find $(-x)^2$, we take the opposite and then square. To find $-x^2$, we find the square and then take the opposite.

Do Exercises 27–29 on the preceding page.

b Applications and Problem Solving

We now consider multiplication of real numbers in real-world applications.

EXAMPLE 19 *Chemical Reaction.* During a chemical reaction, the temperature in the beaker decreased by 2°C every minute until 10:23 A.M. If the temperature was 17°C at 10:00 A.M., when the reaction began, what was the temperature at 10:23 A.M.?

This is a multistep problem. We first find the total number of degrees that the temperature dropped, using −2° for each minute. Since it dropped 2° for each of the 23 minutes, we know that the total drop d is given by

$$d = 23 \cdot (-2) = -46.$$

To determine the temperature after this time period, we find the sum of 17 and −46, or

$$T = 17 + (-46) = -29.$$

Thus the temperature at 10:23 A.M. was −29°C.

Answer on page A-5

Do Exercise 30.

a   Multiply.

1. $-4 \cdot 2$

2. $-3 \cdot 5$

3. $-8 \cdot 6$

4. $-5 \cdot 2$

5. $8 \cdot (-3)$

6. $9 \cdot (-5)$

7. $-9 \cdot 8$

8. $-10 \cdot 3$

9. $-8 \cdot (-2)$

10. $-2 \cdot (-5)$

11. $-7 \cdot (-6)$

12. $-9 \cdot (-2)$

13. $15 \cdot (-8)$

14. $-12 \cdot (-10)$

15. $-14 \cdot 17$

16. $-13 \cdot (-15)$

17. $-25 \cdot (-48)$

18. $39 \cdot (-43)$

19. $-3.5 \cdot (-28)$

20. $97 \cdot (-2.1)$

21. $9 \cdot (-8)$

22. $7 \cdot (-9)$

23. $4 \cdot (-3.1)$

24. $3 \cdot (-2.2)$

25. $-5 \cdot (-6)$

26. $-6 \cdot (-4)$

27. $-7 \cdot (-3.1)$

28. $-4 \cdot (-3.2)$

29. $\frac{2}{3} \cdot \left(-\frac{3}{5}\right)$

30. $\frac{5}{7} \cdot \left(-\frac{2}{3}\right)$

31. $-\frac{3}{8} \cdot \left(-\frac{2}{9}\right)$

32. $-\frac{5}{8} \cdot \left(-\frac{2}{5}\right)$

33. -6.3×2.7

34. -4.1×9.5

35. $-\frac{5}{9} \cdot \frac{3}{4}$

36. $-\frac{8}{3} \cdot \frac{9}{4}$

37. $7 \cdot (-4) \cdot (-3) \cdot 5$

38. $9 \cdot (-2) \cdot (-6) \cdot 7$

39. $-\frac{2}{3} \cdot \frac{1}{2} \cdot \left(-\frac{6}{7}\right)$

40. $-\frac{1}{8} \cdot \left(-\frac{1}{4}\right) \cdot \left(-\frac{3}{5}\right)$

41. $-3 \cdot (-4) \cdot (-5)$

42. $-2 \cdot (-5) \cdot (-7)$

43. $-2 \cdot (-5) \cdot (-3) \cdot (-5)$

44. $-3 \cdot (-5) \cdot (-2) \cdot (-1)$

45. $\frac{1}{5}\left(-\frac{2}{9}\right)$

46. $-\frac{3}{5}\left(-\frac{2}{7}\right)$

47. $-7 \cdot (-21) \cdot 13$

48. $-14 \cdot (34) \cdot 12$

49. $-4 \cdot (-1.8) \cdot 7$

50. $-8 \cdot (-1.3) \cdot (-5)$

51. $-\dfrac{1}{9}\left(-\dfrac{2}{3}\right)\left(\dfrac{5}{7}\right)$

52. $-\dfrac{7}{2}\left(-\dfrac{5}{7}\right)\left(-\dfrac{2}{5}\right)$

53. $4 \cdot (-4) \cdot (-5) \cdot (-12)$

54. $-2 \cdot (-3) \cdot (-4) \cdot (-5)$

55. $0.07 \cdot (-7) \cdot 6 \cdot (-6)$

56. $80 \cdot (-0.8) \cdot (-90) \cdot (-0.09)$

57. $\left(-\dfrac{5}{6}\right)\left(\dfrac{1}{8}\right)\left(-\dfrac{3}{7}\right)\left(-\dfrac{1}{7}\right)$

58. $\left(\dfrac{4}{5}\right)\left(-\dfrac{2}{3}\right)\left(-\dfrac{15}{7}\right)\left(\dfrac{1}{2}\right)$

59. $(-14) \cdot (-27) \cdot 0$

60. $7 \cdot (-6) \cdot 5 \cdot (-4) \cdot 3 \cdot (-2) \cdot 1 \cdot 0$

61. $(-8)(-9)(-10)$

62. $(-7)(-8)(-9)(-10)$

63. $(-6)(-7)(-8)(-9)(-10)$

64. $(-5)(-6)(-7)(-8)(-9)(-10)$

65. $(-1)^{12}$

66. $(-1)^9$

67. Evaluate $(-x)^2$ and $-x^2$ when $x = 4$ and when $x = -4$.

68. Evaluate $(-x)^2$ and $-x^2$ when $x = 10$ and when $x = -10$.

69. Evaluate $(-3x)^2$ and $-3x^2$ when $x = 7$.

70. Evaluate $(-2x)^2$ and $-2x^2$ when $x = 3$.

71. Evaluate $5x^2$ when $x = 2$ and when $x = -2$.

72. Evaluate $2x^2$ when $x = 5$ and when $x = -5$.

73. Evaluate $-2x^3$ when $x = 1$ and when $x = -1$.

74. Evaluate $-3x^3$ when $x = 2$ and when $x = -2$.

b Solve.

75. *Lost Weight.*   Dave lost 2 lb each week for a period of 10 weeks. Express his total weight change as an integer.

76. *Stock Loss.*   Emma lost $3 each day for a period of 5 days in the value of a stock she owned. Express her total loss as an integer.

77. *Chemical Reaction.*   The temperature of a chemical compound was 0°C at 11:00 A.M. During a reaction, it dropped 3°C per minute until 11:18 A.M. What was the temperature at 11:18 A.M.?

78. *Chemical Reaction.*   The temperature in a chemical compound was −5°C at 3:20 P.M. During a reaction, it increased 2°C per minute until 3:52 P.M. What was the temperature at 3:52 P.M.?

79. *Stock Price.* The price of ePDQ.com began the day at $23.75 per share and dropped $1.38 per hour for 8 hr. What was the price of the stock after 8 hr?

80. *Population Decrease.* The population of a rural town was 12,500. It decreased 380 each year for 4 yr. What was the population of the town after 4 yr?

81. *Diver's Position.* After diving 95 m below the sea level, a diver rises at a rate of 7 meters per minute for 9 min. Where is the diver in relation to the surface?

82. *Checking Account Balance.* Karen had $68 in her checking account. After she had written checks to make seven purchases at $13 each, what was the balance in her checking account?

83. D_W Multiplication can be thought of as repeated addition. Using this concept and a number line, explain why $3 \cdot (-5) = -15$.

84. D_W What rule have we developed that would tell you the sign of $(-7)^8$ and $(-7)^{11}$ without doing the computations? Explain.

SKILL MAINTENANCE

85. Find the LCM of 36 and 60. [R.1b]

86. Find the prime factorization of 4608. [R.1a]

Simplify. [R.2b]

87. $\dfrac{26}{39}$

88. $\dfrac{48}{54}$

89. $\dfrac{264}{484}$

90. $\dfrac{1025}{6625}$

91. $\dfrac{275}{800}$

92. $\dfrac{111}{201}$

93. $\dfrac{11}{264}$

94. $\dfrac{78}{13}$

SYNTHESIS

For each of Exercises 95 and 96, choose the correct answer from the selections given.

95. If a is positive and b is negative, then $-ab$ is:

  a) Positive.
  b) Negative.
  c) 0.
  d) Cannot be determined without more information

96. If a is positive and b is negative, then $(-a)(-b)$ is:

  a) Positive.
  b) Negative.
  c) 0.
  d) Cannot be determined without more information

97. Below is a number line showing 0 and two positive numbers x and y. Use a compass or ruler to locate as best you can the following:

$$2x, \quad 3x, \quad 2y, \quad -x, \quad -y, \quad x + y, \quad x - y, \quad x - 2y.$$

98. Of all possible quotients of the numbers 10, $-\frac{1}{2}$, -5, and $\frac{1}{5}$, which two produce the largest quotient? Which two produce the smallest quotient?

Objectives

a Divide integers.

b Find the reciprocal of a real number.

c Divide real numbers.

d Solve applied problems involving division of real numbers.

We now consider division of real numbers. The definition of division results in rules for division that are the same as those for multiplication.

a Division of Integers

> **DIVISION**
>
> The quotient $a \div b$, or $\dfrac{a}{b}$, where $b \neq 0$, is that unique real number c for which $a = b \cdot c$.

Let's use the definition to divide integers.

EXAMPLES Divide, if possible. Check your answer.

1. $14 \div (-7) = -2$ *Think*: What number multiplied by -7 gives 14? That number is -2. *Check*: $(-2)(-7) = 14$.

2. $\dfrac{-32}{-4} = 8$ *Think*: What number multiplied by -4 gives -32? That number is 8. *Check*: $8(-4) = -32$.

3. $\dfrac{-10}{7} = -\dfrac{10}{7}$ *Think*: What number multiplied by 7 gives -10? That number is $-\frac{10}{7}$. *Check*: $-\frac{10}{7} \cdot 7 = 10$.

4. $\dfrac{-17}{0}$ is **not defined.**   *Think*: What number multiplied by 0 gives -17? There is no such number because the product of 0 and *any* number is 0.

The rules for division are the same as those for multiplication.

> To multiply or divide two real numbers (where the divisor is nonzero):
>
> **a)** Multiply or divide the absolute values.
> **b)** If the signs are the same, the answer is positive.
> **c)** If the signs are different, the answer is negative.

Do Exercises 1–6.

EXCLUDING DIVISION BY 0

Example 4 shows why we cannot divide -17 by 0. We can use the same argument to show why we cannot divide any nonzero number b by 0. Consider $b \div 0$. We look for a number that when multiplied by 0 gives b. There is no such number because the product of 0 and any number is 0. Thus we cannot divide a nonzero number b by 0.

On the other hand, if we divide 0 by 0, we look for a number c such that $0 \cdot c = 0$. But $0 \cdot c = 0$ for any number c. Thus it appears that $0 \div 0$ could be any number we choose. Getting any answer we want when we divide 0 by 0 would be very confusing. Thus we agree that division by zero is not defined.

Divide.

1. $6 \div (-3)$

Think: What number multiplied by -3 gives 6?

2. $\dfrac{-15}{-3}$

Think: What number multiplied by -3 gives -15?

3. $-24 \div 8$

Think: What number multiplied by 8 gives -24?

4. $\dfrac{-48}{-6}$

5. $\dfrac{30}{-5}$

6. $\dfrac{30}{-7}$

Answers on page A-5

EXCLUDING DIVISION BY 0

Division by 0 is not defined.

$a \div 0$, or $\dfrac{a}{0}$, is not defined for all real numbers a.

DIVIDING 0 BY OTHER NUMBERS

Note that

$0 \div 8 = 0$ because $0 = 0 \cdot 8;$ $\qquad \dfrac{0}{-5} = 0$ because $0 = 0 \cdot (-5).$

DIVIDENDS OF 0

Zero divided by any nonzero real number is 0:

$\dfrac{0}{a} = 0;$ $\qquad a \neq 0.$

EXAMPLES Divide.

5. $0 \div (-6) = 0$ $\qquad$ **6.** $\dfrac{0}{12} = 0$ $\qquad$ **7.** $\dfrac{-3}{0}$ is not defined.

Do Exercises 7 and 8.

b Reciprocals

When two numbers like $\frac{1}{2}$ and 2 are multiplied, the result is 1. Such numbers are called **reciprocals** of each other. Every nonzero real number has a reciprocal, also called a **multiplicative inverse.**

RECIPROCALS

Two numbers whose product is 1 are called **reciprocals,** or **multiplicative inverses,** of each other.

EXAMPLES Find the reciprocal.

8. $\dfrac{7}{8}$ $\qquad$ The reciprocal of $\dfrac{7}{8}$ is $\dfrac{8}{7}$ because $\dfrac{7}{8} \cdot \dfrac{8}{7} = 1.$

9. -5 $\qquad$ The reciprocal of -5 is $-\dfrac{1}{5}$ because $-5\left(-\dfrac{1}{5}\right) = 1.$

10. 3.9 $\qquad$ The reciprocal of 3.9 is $\dfrac{1}{3.9}$ because $3.9\left(\dfrac{1}{3.9}\right) = 1.$

11. $-\dfrac{1}{2}$ $\qquad$ The reciprocal of $-\dfrac{1}{2}$ is -2 because $\left(-\dfrac{1}{2}\right)(-2) = 1.$

12. $-\dfrac{2}{3}$ $\qquad$ The reciprocal of $-\dfrac{2}{3}$ is $-\dfrac{3}{2}$ because $\left(-\dfrac{2}{3}\right)\left(-\dfrac{3}{2}\right) = 1.$

13. $\dfrac{1}{3/4}$ $\qquad$ The reciprocal of $\dfrac{1}{3/4}$ is $\dfrac{3}{4}$ because $\left(\dfrac{1}{3/4}\right)\left(\dfrac{3}{4}\right) = 1.$

Divide, if possible.

7. $\dfrac{-5}{0}$

8. $\dfrac{0}{-3}$

Find the reciprocal.

9. $\dfrac{2}{3}$

10. $-\dfrac{5}{4}$

11. -3

12. $-\dfrac{1}{5}$

13. 1.6

14. $\dfrac{1}{2/3}$

Answers on page A-5

101

15. Complete the following table.

NUMBER	OPPOSITE	RECIPROCAL
$\dfrac{2}{3}$		
$-\dfrac{5}{4}$		
0		
1		
−8		
−4.5		

Do Exercises 9–14 on the preceding page.

RECIPROCAL PROPERTIES

For $a \neq 0$, the reciprocal of a can be named $\dfrac{1}{a}$ and the reciprocal of $\dfrac{1}{a}$ is a.

The reciprocal of a nonzero number $\dfrac{a}{b}$ can be named $\dfrac{b}{a}$.

The number 0 has no reciprocal.

The reciprocal of a positive number is also a positive number, because their product must be the positive number 1. The reciprocal of a negative number is also a negative number, because their product must be the positive number 1.

THE SIGN OF A RECIPROCAL

The reciprocal of a number has the same sign as the number itself.

Caution!

It is important *not* to confuse *opposite* with *reciprocal*. Keep in mind that the opposite, or additive inverse, of a number is what we add to the number to get 0. The reciprocal, or multiplicative inverse, is what we multiply the number by to get 1.

Compare the following.

NUMBER	OPPOSITE (Change the sign.)	RECIPROCAL (Invert but do not change the sign.)
$-\dfrac{3}{8}$	$\dfrac{3}{8}$	$-\dfrac{8}{3}$
19	−19	$\dfrac{1}{19}$
$\dfrac{18}{7}$	$-\dfrac{18}{7}$	$\dfrac{7}{18}$
−7.9	7.9	$-\dfrac{1}{7.9}$, or $-\dfrac{10}{79}$
0	0	Not defined

$$\left(-\dfrac{3}{8}\right)\left(-\dfrac{8}{3}\right) = 1$$

$$-\dfrac{3}{8} + \dfrac{3}{8} = 0$$

Do Exercise 15.

Study Tips

TAKE THE TIME!

The foundation of all your study skills is *time*! If you invest your time, we will help you achieve success.

"Nine-tenths of wisdom is being wise in time."

Theodore Roosevelt

CHAPTER 1: Introduction to Real Numbers and Algebraic Expressions

C Division of Real Numbers

We know that we can subtract by adding an opposite. Similarly, we can divide by multiplying by a reciprocal.

> ### RECIPROCALS AND DIVISION
>
> For any real numbers a and b, $b \neq 0$,
>
> $$a \div b = \frac{a}{b} = a \cdot \frac{1}{b}.$$
>
> (To divide, multiply by the reciprocal of the divisor.)

EXAMPLES Rewrite the division as a multiplication.

14. $-4 \div 3$ $-4 \div 3$ is the same as $-4 \cdot \frac{1}{3}$

15. $\frac{6}{-7}$ $\frac{6}{-7} = 6\left(-\frac{1}{7}\right)$

16. $\frac{x+2}{5}$ $\frac{x+2}{5} = (x+2)\frac{1}{5}$ Parentheses are necessary here.

17. $\frac{-17}{1/b}$ $\frac{-17}{1/b} = -17 \cdot b$

18. $\frac{3}{5} \div \left(-\frac{9}{7}\right)$ $\frac{3}{5} \div \left(-\frac{9}{7}\right) = \frac{3}{5}\left(-\frac{7}{9}\right)$

Do Exercises 16–20.

When actually doing division calculations, we sometimes multiply by a reciprocal and we sometimes divide directly. With fraction notation, it is usually better to multiply by a reciprocal. With decimal notation, it is usually better to divide directly.

EXAMPLES Divide by multiplying by the reciprocal of the divisor.

19. $\frac{2}{3} \div \left(-\frac{5}{4}\right) = \frac{2}{3} \cdot \left(-\frac{4}{5}\right) = -\frac{8}{15}$

20. $-\frac{5}{6} \div \left(-\frac{3}{4}\right) = -\frac{5}{6} \cdot \left(-\frac{4}{3}\right) = \frac{20}{18} = \frac{10 \cdot 2}{9 \cdot 2} = \frac{10}{9} \cdot \frac{2}{2} = \frac{10}{9}$

> ### Caution!
>
> Be careful not to change the sign when taking a reciprocal!

21. $-\frac{3}{4} \div \frac{3}{10} = -\frac{3}{4} \cdot \left(\frac{10}{3}\right) = -\frac{30}{12} = -\frac{5}{2} \cdot \frac{6}{6} = -\frac{5}{2}$

Rewrite the division as a multiplication.

16. $\frac{4}{7} \div \left(-\frac{3}{5}\right)$

17. $\frac{5}{-8}$

18. $\frac{a-b}{7}$

19. $\frac{-23}{1/a}$

20. $-5 \div 7$

Divide by multiplying by the reciprocal of the divisor.

21. $\frac{4}{7} \div \left(-\frac{3}{5}\right)$

22. $-\frac{8}{5} \div \frac{2}{3}$

23. $-\frac{12}{7} \div \left(-\frac{3}{4}\right)$

24. Divide: $21.7 \div (-3.1)$.

Answers on page A-5

Find two equal expressions for the number with negative signs in different places.

25. $\dfrac{-5}{6}$

26. $-\dfrac{8}{7}$

27. $\dfrac{10}{-3}$

Answers on page A-5

With decimal notation, it is easier to carry out long division than to multiply by the reciprocal.

EXAMPLES Divide.

22. $-27.9 \div (-3) = \dfrac{-27.9}{-3} = 9.3$ Do the long division $3\overline{)27.9}$ giving 9.3. The answer is positive.

23. $-6.3 \div 2.1 = -3$ Do the long division $2.1\overline{)6.3}$ giving $3.$ The answer is negative.

Do Exercises 21–24 on the preceding page.

Consider the following:

1. $\dfrac{2}{3} = \dfrac{2}{3} \cdot 1 = \dfrac{2}{3} \cdot \dfrac{-1}{-1} = \dfrac{2(-1)}{3(-1)} = \dfrac{-2}{-3}.$ Thus, $\dfrac{2}{3} = \dfrac{-2}{-3}.$

(A negative number divided by a negative number is positive.)

2. $-\dfrac{2}{3} = -1 \cdot \dfrac{2}{3} = \dfrac{-1}{1} \cdot \dfrac{2}{3} = \dfrac{-1 \cdot 2}{1 \cdot 3} = \dfrac{-2}{3}.$ Thus, $-\dfrac{2}{3} = \dfrac{-2}{3}.$

(A negative number divided by a positive number is negative.)

3. $\dfrac{-2}{3} = \dfrac{-2}{3} \cdot 1 = \dfrac{-2}{3} \cdot \dfrac{-1}{-1} = \dfrac{-2(-1)}{3(-1)} = \dfrac{2}{-3}.$ Thus, $-\dfrac{2}{3} = \dfrac{2}{-3}.$

(A positive number divided by a negative number is negative.)

We can use the following properties to make sign changes in fraction notation.

SIGN CHANGES IN FRACTION NOTATION

For any numbers a and b, $b \neq 0$:

1. $\dfrac{-a}{-b} = \dfrac{a}{b}$

(The opposite of a number a divided by the opposite of another number b is the same as the quotient of the two numbers a and b.)

2. $\dfrac{-a}{b} = \dfrac{a}{-b} = -\dfrac{a}{b}$

(The opposite of a number a divided by another number b is the same as the number a divided by the opposite of the number b, and both are the same as the opposite of a divided by b.)

Do Exercises 25–27.

d | Applications and Problem Solving

EXAMPLE 24 *Chemical Reaction.* During a chemical reaction, the temperature in the beaker decreased every minute by the same number of degrees. The temperature was 56°F at 10:10 A.M. By 10:42 A.M., the temperature had dropped to −12°F. By how many degrees did it change each minute?

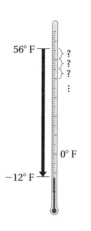

We first determine by how many degrees d the temperature changed altogether. We subtract −12 from 56:

$$d = 56 - (-12) = 56 + 12 = 68.$$

The temperature changed a total of 68°. We can express this as −68° since the temperature dropped.

The amount of time t that passed was 42 − 10, or 32 min. Thus the number of degrees T that the temperature dropped each minute is given by

$$T = \frac{d}{t} = \frac{-68}{32} = -2.125.$$

The change was −2.125°F per minute.

Do Exercise 28.

28. Chemical Reaction. During a chemical reaction, the temperature in the beaker decreased every minute by the same number of degrees. The temperature was 71°F at 2:12 P.M. By 2:37 P.M., the temperature had changed to −14°F. By how many degrees did it change each minute?

Answer on page A-5

CALCULATOR CORNER

Operations on the Real Numbers We can perform operations on the real numbers on a graphing calculator. Recall that negative numbers are entered using the opposite key, (−), rather than the subtraction operation key, (−). Consider the sum −5 + (−3.8). We use parentheses when we write this sum in order to separate the addition symbol and the "opposite of" symbol and thus make the expression more easily read. When we enter this calculation on a graphing calculator, however, the parentheses are not necessary. We can press (−) (5) (+) (−) (3) (·) (8) **ENTER**. The result is −8.8. Note that it is not incorrect to enter the parentheses. The result will be the same if this is done.

To find the difference 10 − (−17), we press (1)(0) (−) (−)(1)(7) **ENTER**. The result is 27. We can also multiply and divide real numbers. To find −5 · (−7), we press (−)(5) (×) (−)(7) **ENTER**, and to find 45 ÷ (−9), we press (4)(5) (÷) (−)(9) **ENTER**. Note that it is not necessary to use parentheses in any of these calculations.

```
-5+-3.8
              -8.8
-5+(-3.8)
              -8.8
```

```
10--17
               27
-5*-7
               35
45/-9
               -5
```

Exercises: Use a calculator to perform the operation.

1. −8 + 4	5. −8 − 4	9. −8 · 4	13. −8 ÷ 4
2. 1.2 + (−1.5)	6. 1.2 − (−1.5)	10. 1.2 · (−1.5)	14. 1.2 ÷ (−1.5)
3. −7 + (−5)	7. −7 − (−5)	11. −7 · (−5)	15. −7 ÷ (−5)
4. −7.6 + (−1.9)	8. −7.6 − (−1.9)	12. −7.6 · (−1.9)	16. −7.6 ÷ (−1.9)

a   Divide, if possible. Check each answer.

1. $48 \div (-6)$

2. $\dfrac{42}{-7}$

3. $\dfrac{28}{-2}$

4. $24 \div (-12)$

5. $\dfrac{-24}{8}$

6. $-18 \div (-2)$

7. $\dfrac{-36}{-12}$

8. $-72 \div (-9)$

9. $\dfrac{-72}{9}$

10. $\dfrac{-50}{25}$

11. $-100 \div (-50)$

12. $\dfrac{-200}{8}$

13. $-108 \div 9$

14. $\dfrac{-63}{-7}$

15. $\dfrac{200}{-25}$

16. $-300 \div (-16)$

17. $\dfrac{75}{0}$

18. $\dfrac{0}{-5}$

19. $\dfrac{0}{-2.6}$

20. $\dfrac{-23}{0}$

b   Find the reciprocal.

21. $\dfrac{15}{7}$

22. $\dfrac{3}{8}$

23. $-\dfrac{47}{13}$

24. $-\dfrac{31}{12}$

25. 13

26. -10

27. 4.3

28. -8.5

29. $\dfrac{1}{-7.1}$

30. $\dfrac{1}{-4.9}$

31. $\dfrac{p}{q}$

32. $\dfrac{s}{t}$

33. $\dfrac{1}{4y}$

34. $\dfrac{-1}{8a}$

35. $\dfrac{2a}{3b}$

36. $\dfrac{-4y}{3x}$

37. $4 \div 17$

38. $5 \div (-8)$

39. $\dfrac{8}{-13}$

40. $-\dfrac{13}{47}$

41. $\dfrac{13.9}{-1.5}$

42. $-\dfrac{47.3}{21.4}$

43. $\dfrac{x}{\dfrac{1}{y}}$

44. $\dfrac{13}{x}$

45. $\dfrac{3x + 4}{5}$

46. $\dfrac{4y - 8}{-7}$

47. $\dfrac{5a - b}{5a + b}$

48. $\dfrac{2x + x^2}{x - 5}$

Divide.

49. $\dfrac{3}{4} \div \left(-\dfrac{2}{3} \right)$

50. $\dfrac{7}{8} \div \left(-\dfrac{1}{2} \right)$

51. $-\dfrac{5}{4} \div \left(-\dfrac{3}{4} \right)$

52. $-\dfrac{5}{9} \div \left(-\dfrac{5}{6} \right)$

53. $-\dfrac{2}{7} \div \left(-\dfrac{4}{9} \right)$

54. $-\dfrac{3}{5} \div \left(-\dfrac{5}{8} \right)$

55. $-\dfrac{3}{8} \div \left(-\dfrac{8}{3} \right)$

56. $-\dfrac{5}{8} \div \left(-\dfrac{6}{5} \right)$

57. $-6.6 \div 3.3$

58. $-44.1 \div (-6.3)$

59. $\dfrac{-11}{-13}$

60. $\dfrac{-1.9}{20}$

61. $\dfrac{48.6}{-3}$

62. $\dfrac{-17.8}{3.2}$

63. $\dfrac{-9}{17 - 17}$

64. $\dfrac{-8}{-5 + 5}$

d *Percent of Increase or Decrease in Employment.* A percent of increase is generally positive and a percent of decrease is generally negative. The following table lists estimates of the number of job opportunities for various occupations in 2002 and 2012. In Exercises 65–68, find the missing numbers.

	OCCUPATION	NUMBER OF JOBS IN 2002 (in thousands)	NUMBER OF JOBS IN 2012 (in thousands)	CHANGE	PERCENT OF INCREASE OR DECREASE
	Electrician	659	814	155	23.5%
	Travel agent	118	102	−16	−13.6%
65.	Fitness trainer/ aerobic instructor	183	264	81	
66.	Child-care worker	1211	1353	142	
67.	Telemarketer	428	406	−22	
68.	Aerospace engineer	78	74	−4	

Source: U.S. Bureau of Labor Statistics

69. D$_W$ Explain how multiplication can be used to justify why a negative number divided by a positive number is negative.

70. D$_W$ Explain how multiplication can be used to justify why a negative number divided by a negative number is positive.

Simplify. [R.5c]

71. $2^3 − 5 \cdot 3 + 8 \cdot 10 \div 2$

72. $16 \cdot 2^3 − 5 \cdot 3 + 80 \div 10 \cdot 2$

73. $1000 \div 100 \div 10$

74. $216 \cdot 6^3 \div 6^2$

75. Simplify: $\dfrac{264}{468}$. [R.2b]

76. Convert to decimal notation: 47.7%. [R.4a]

77. Convert to percent notation: $\dfrac{7}{8}$. [R.4d]

78. Simplify: $\dfrac{40}{60}$. [R.2b]

79. Divide and simplify: $\dfrac{12}{25} \div \dfrac{32}{75}$. [R.2c]

80. Multiply and simplify: $\dfrac{12}{25} \cdot \dfrac{32}{75}$. [R.2c]

81. Find the reciprocal of $−10.5$. What happens if you take the reciprocal of the result?

82. Determine those real numbers a for which the opposite of a is the same as the reciprocal of a.

Tell whether the expression represents a positive number or a negative number when a and b are negative.

83. $\dfrac{-a}{b}$

84. $\dfrac{-a}{-b}$

85. $-\left(\dfrac{a}{-b}\right)$

86. $-\left(\dfrac{-a}{b}\right)$

87. $-\left(\dfrac{-a}{-b}\right)$

PROPERTIES OF REAL NUMBERS

Objectives

a	Find equivalent fraction expressions and simplify fraction expressions.
b	Use the commutative and associative laws to find equivalent expressions.
c	Use the distributive laws to multiply expressions like 8 and $x - y$.
d	Use the distributive laws to factor expressions like $4x - 12 + 24y$.
e	Collect like terms.

a Equivalent Expressions

In solving equations and doing other kinds of work in algebra, we manipulate expressions in various ways. For example, instead of $x + x$, we might write $2x$, knowing that the two expressions represent the same number for any allowable replacement of x. In that sense, the expressions $x + x$ and $2x$ are **equivalent,** as are $\dfrac{3}{x}$ and $\dfrac{3x}{x^2}$, even though 0 is not an allowable replacement because division by 0 is not defined.

EQUIVALENT EXPRESSIONS

Two expressions that have the same value for all allowable replacements are called **equivalent.**

The expressions $x + 3x$ and $5x$ are *not* equivalent.

Do Exercises 1 and 2.

In this section, we will consider several laws of real numbers that will allow us to find equivalent expressions. The first two laws are the *identity properties of 0 and 1.*

THE IDENTITY PROPERTY OF 0

For any real number a,

$$a + 0 = 0 + a = a.$$

(The number 0 is the *additive identity.*)

THE IDENTITY PROPERTY OF 1

For any real number a,

$$a \cdot 1 = 1 \cdot a = a.$$

(The number 1 is the *multiplicative identity.*)

We often refer to the use of the identity property of 1 as "multiplying by 1." We can use this method to find equivalent fraction expressions. Recall from arithmetic that to multiply with fraction notation, we multiply numerators and denominators. (See also Section R.2.)

EXAMPLE 1 Write a fraction expression equivalent to $\frac{2}{3}$ with a denominator of $3x$:

$$\frac{2}{3} = \frac{\square}{3x}.$$

Complete the table by evaluating each expression for the given values.

1.

Value	$x + x$	$2x$
$x = 3$		
$x = -6$		
$x = 4.8$		

2.

Value	$x + 3x$	$5x$
$x = 2$		
$x = -6$		
$x = 4.8$		

Answers on page A-6

3. Write a fraction expression equivalent to $\frac{3}{4}$ with a denominator of 8:

$$\frac{3}{4} = \frac{\square}{8}.$$

Note that $3x = 3 \cdot x$. We want fraction notation for $\frac{2}{3}$ that has a denominator of $3x$, but the denominator 3 is missing a factor of x. Thus we multiply by 1, using x/x as an equivalent expression for 1:

$$\frac{2}{3} = \frac{2}{3} \cdot 1 = \frac{2}{3} \cdot \frac{x}{x} = \frac{2x}{3x}.$$

The expressions $2/3$ and $2x/3x$ are equivalent. They have the same value for any allowable replacement. Note that $2x/3x$ is not defined for a replacement of 0, but for all nonzero real numbers, the expressions $2/3$ and $2x/3x$ have the same value.

4. Write a fraction expression equivalent to $\frac{3}{4}$ with a denominator of $4t$:

$$\frac{3}{4} = \frac{\square}{4t}.$$

Do Exercises 3 and 4.

In algebra, we consider an expression like $2/3$ to be "simplified" from $2x/3x$. To find such simplified expressions, we use the identity property of 1 to remove a factor of 1. (See also Section R.2.)

EXAMPLE 2 Simplify: $-\dfrac{20x}{12x}$.

Simplify.

5. $\dfrac{3y}{4y}$

6. $-\dfrac{16m}{12m}$

$$-\frac{20x}{12x} = -\frac{5 \cdot 4x}{3 \cdot 4x} \qquad \text{We look for the largest factor common to both the numerator and the denominator and factor each.}$$

$$= -\frac{5}{3} \cdot \frac{4x}{4x} \qquad \text{Factoring the fraction expression}$$

$$= -\frac{5}{3} \cdot 1 \qquad \frac{4x}{4x} = 1$$

$$= -\frac{5}{3} \qquad \text{Removing a factor of 1 using the identity property of 1}$$

7. $\dfrac{5xy}{40y}$

8. $\dfrac{18p}{24pq}$

EXAMPLE 3 Simplify: $\dfrac{14ab}{56a}$.

$$\frac{14ab}{56a} = \frac{14a \cdot b}{14a \cdot 4} = \frac{14a}{14a} \cdot \frac{b}{4} = 1 \cdot \frac{b}{4} = \frac{b}{4}$$

Do Exercises 5–8.

9. Evaluate $x + y$ and $y + x$ when $x = -2$ and $y = 3$.

b The Commutative and Associative Laws

THE COMMUTATIVE LAWS

Let's examine the expressions $x + y$ and $y + x$, as well as xy and yx.

EXAMPLE 4 Evaluate $x + y$ and $y + x$ when $x = 4$ and $y = 3$.

We substitute 4 for x and 3 for y in both expressions:

$$x + y = 4 + 3 = 7; \qquad y + x = 3 + 4 = 7.$$

10. Evaluate xy and yx when $x = -2$ and $y = 5$.

EXAMPLE 5 Evaluate xy and yx when $x = 23$ and $y = -12$.

We substitute 23 for x and -12 for y in both expressions:

$$xy = 23 \cdot (-12) = -276; \qquad yx = (-12) \cdot 23 = -276.$$

Answers on page A-6

CHAPTER 1: Introduction to Real Numbers
and Algebraic Expressions

Do Exercises 9 and 10 on the preceding page.

Note that the expressions $x + y$ and $y + x$ have the same values no matter what the variables stand for. Thus they are equivalent. Therefore, when we add two numbers, the order in which we add does not matter. Similarly, the expressions xy and yx are equivalent. They also have the same values, no matter what the variables stand for. Therefore, when we multiply two numbers, the order in which we multiply does not matter.

The following are examples of general patterns or laws.

THE COMMUTATIVE LAWS

Addition.   For any numbers a and b,

$$a + b = b + a.$$

(We can change the order when adding without affecting the answer.)

Multiplication.   For any numbers a and b,

$$ab = ba.$$

(We can change the order when multiplying without affecting the answer.)

Using a commutative law, we know that $x + 2$ and $2 + x$ are equivalent. Similarly, $3x$ and $x(3)$ are equivalent. Thus, in an algebraic expression, we can replace one with the other and the result will be equivalent to the original expression.

EXAMPLE 6   Use the commutative laws to write an expression equivalent to $y + 5$, ab, and $7 + xy$.

An expression equivalent to $y + 5$ is $5 + y$ by the commutative law of addition.

An expression equivalent to ab is ba by the commutative law of multiplication.

An expression equivalent to $7 + xy$ is $xy + 7$ by the commutative law of addition. Another expression equivalent to $7 + xy$ is $7 + yx$ by the commutative law of multiplication. Another equivalent expression is $yx + 7$.

Do Exercises 11–13.

THE ASSOCIATIVE LAWS

Now let's examine the expressions $a + (b + c)$ and $(a + b) + c$. Note that these expressions involve the use of parentheses as *grouping* symbols, and they also involve three numbers. Calculations within parentheses are to be done first.

EXAMPLE 7   Calculate and compare: $3 + (8 + 5)$ and $(3 + 8) + 5$.

$$3 + (8 + 5) = 3 + 13 \qquad \text{Calculating within parentheses first;}$$
$$\text{adding the 8 and 5}$$
$$= 16;$$
$$(3 + 8) + 5 = 11 + 5 \qquad \text{Calculating within parentheses first;}$$
$$\text{adding the 3 and 8}$$
$$= 16$$

Use a commutative law to write an equivalent expression.

11. $x + 9$

12. pq

13. $xy + t$

Answers on page A-6

14. Calculate and compare:

$8 + (9 + 2)$ and $(8 + 9) + 2$.

The two expressions in Example 7 name the same number. Moving the parentheses to group the additions differently does not affect the value of the expression.

> **EXAMPLE 8** Calculate and compare: $3 \cdot (4 \cdot 2)$ and $(3 \cdot 4) \cdot 2$.
>
> $$3 \cdot (4 \cdot 2) = 3 \cdot 8 = 24; \qquad (3 \cdot 4) \cdot 2 = 12 \cdot 2 = 24$$

Do Exercises 14 and 15.

You may have noted that when only addition is involved, parentheses can be placed any way we please without affecting the answer. When only multiplication is involved, parentheses also can be placed any way we please without affecting the answer.

15. Calculate and compare:

$10 \cdot (5 \cdot 3)$ and $(10 \cdot 5) \cdot 3$.

THE ASSOCIATIVE LAWS

Addition. For any numbers a, b, and c,

$$a + (b + c) = (a + b) + c.$$

(Numbers can be grouped in any manner for addition.)

Multiplication. For any numbers a, b, and c,

$$a \cdot (b \cdot c) = (a \cdot b) \cdot c.$$

(Numbers can be grouped in any manner for multiplication.)

Use an associative law to write an equivalent expression.

16. $r + (s + 7)$

> **EXAMPLE 9** Use an associative law to write an expression equivalent to $(y + z) + 3$ and $8(xy)$.
>
> An expression equivalent to $(y + z) + 3$ is $y + (z + 3)$ by the associative law of addition.
>
> An expression equivalent to $8(xy)$ is $(8x)y$ by the associative law of multiplication.

Do Exercises 16 and 17.

The associative laws say parentheses can be placed any way we please when only additions or only multiplications are involved. Thus we often omit them. For example,

$$x + (y + 2) \quad \text{means} \quad x + y + 2, \quad \text{and} \quad (lw)h \quad \text{means} \quad lwh.$$

17. $9(ab)$

USING THE COMMUTATIVE AND ASSOCIATIVE LAWS TOGETHER

> **EXAMPLE 10** Use the commutative and associative laws to write at least three expressions equivalent to $(x + 5) + y$.
>
> **a)** $(x + 5) + y = x + (5 + y)$ Using the associative law first and then using
> $= x + (y + 5)$ the commutative law
>
> **b)** $(x + 5) + y = y + (x + 5)$ Using the commutative law first and then the
> $= y + (5 + x)$ commutative law again
>
> **c)** $(x + 5) + y = (5 + x) + y$ Using the commutative law first and then the
> $= 5 + (x + y)$ associative law

Answers on page A-6

Use the commutative and associative laws to write at least three equivalent expressions.

EXAMPLE 11 Use the commutative and associative laws to write at least three expressions equivalent to $(3x)y$.

a) $(3x)y = 3(xy)$ Using the associative law first and then using the commutative law

$= 3(yx)$

18. $4(tu)$

b) $(3x)y = y(3x)$ Using the commutative law twice

$= y(x \cdot 3)$

c) $(3x)y = (x \cdot 3)y$ Using the commutative law, and then the associative law, and then the commutative law again

$= x(3y)$

$= x(y \cdot 3)$

19. $r + (2 + s)$

Do Exercises 18 and 19.

c The Distributive Laws

The *distributive laws* are the basis of many procedures in both arithmetic and algebra. They are probably the most important laws that we use to manipulate algebraic expressions. The distributive law of multiplication over addition involves two operations: addition and multiplication.

Let's begin by considering a multiplication problem from arithmetic:

$$\begin{array}{r} 4\ 5 \\ \times\ \ \ 7 \\ \hline 3\ 5 \\ 2\ 8\ 0 \\ \hline 3\ 1\ 5 \end{array}$$

$\leftarrow$ This is $7 \cdot 5$.
$\leftarrow$ This is $7 \cdot 40$.
$\leftarrow$ This is the sum $7 \cdot 40 + 7 \cdot 5$.

To carry out the multiplication, we actually added two products. That is,

$$7 \cdot 45 = 7(40 + 5) = 7 \cdot 40 + 7 \cdot 5.$$

Let's examine this further. If we wish to multiply a sum of several numbers by a factor, we can either add and then multiply, or multiply and then add.

EXAMPLE 12 Compute in two ways: $5 \cdot (4 + 8)$.

a) $5 \cdot (4 + 8)$ Adding within parentheses first, and then multiplying

$= 5 \cdot \quad 12$

$= 60$

b) $(5 \cdot 4) + (5 \cdot 8)$ Distributing the multiplication to terms within parentheses first and then adding

$= \quad 20 \quad + \quad 40$

$= \quad 60$

Do Exercises 20–22.

> **THE DISTRIBUTIVE LAW OF MULTIPLICATION OVER ADDITION**
>
> For any numbers a, b, and c,
>
> $$a(b + c) = ab + ac.$$

Use the commutative and associative laws to write at least three equivalent expressions.

18. $4(tu)$

19. $r + (2 + s)$

Compute.

20. a) $7 \cdot (3 + 6)$

b) $(7 \cdot 3) + (7 \cdot 6)$

21. a) $2 \cdot (10 + 30)$

b) $(2 \cdot 10) + (2 \cdot 30)$

22. a) $(2 + 5) \cdot 4$

b) $(2 \cdot 4) + (5 \cdot 4)$

Answers on page A-6

Calculate.

23. a) $4(5 - $

b) $4 \cdot 5 - $

24. a) $-2 \cdot ($

b) $-2 \cdot 5$

25. a) $5 \cdot (2 $

b) $5 \cdot 2 - $

What are the expression?

26. $5x - 8y +$

27. $-4y - 2x$

Multiply.

28. $3(x - 5)$

29. $5(x + 1)$

30. $\dfrac{3}{5}(p + q$

Answers on
114
CHAPTER 1: Intro and Algebraic Exp

Factor.

41. $6x - 12$

42. $3x - 6y + 9$

43. $bx + by - bz$

44. $16a - 36b + 42$

45. $\dfrac{3}{8}x - \dfrac{5}{8}y + \dfrac{7}{8}$

46. $-12x + 32y - 16z$

Answers on page A-6

116
CHAPTER 1: Introduction to Real Numbers and Algebraic Expressions

We generally remove the largest common factor. In this case, that factor is 9. Thus,

$$9x - 45 = 9 \cdot x - 9 \cdot 5$$
$$= 9(x - 5).$$

Remember that an expression has been factored when we have found an equivalent expression that is a product. Above, we note that $9x - 45$ and $9(x - 5)$ are equivalent expressions. The expression $9x - 45$ is the difference of $9x$ and 45; the expression $9(x - 5)$ is the product of 9 and $(x - 5)$.

EXAMPLES Factor.

25. $5x - 10 = 5 \cdot x - 5 \cdot 2$ Try to do this step mentally.
           $= 5(x - 2)$ You can check by multiplying.

26. $ax - ay + az = a(x - y + z)$

27. $9x + 27y - 9 = 9 \cdot x + 9 \cdot 3y - 9 \cdot 1 = 9(x + 3y - 1)$

Note in Example 27 that you might, at first, just factor out a 3, as follows:

$$9x + 27y - 9 = 3 \cdot 3x + 3 \cdot 9y - 3 \cdot 3$$
$$= 3(3x + 9y - 3).$$

At this point, the mathematics is correct, but the answer is not because there is another factor of 3 that can be factored out, as follows:

$$3 \cdot 3x + 3 \cdot 9y - 3 \cdot 3 = 3(3x + 9y - 3)$$
$$= 3(3 \cdot x + 3 \cdot 3y - 3 \cdot 1)$$
$$= 3 \cdot 3(x + 3y - 1)$$
$$= 9(x + 3y - 1).$$

We now have a correct answer, but it took more work than we did in Example 27. Thus it is better to look for the greatest common factor at the outset.

EXAMPLES Factor. Try to write just the answer, if you can.

28. $5x - 5y = 5(x - y)$

29. $-3x + 6y - 9z = -3(x - 2y + 3z)$

We usually factor out a negative factor when the first term is negative. The way we factor can depend on the situation in which we are working. We might also factor the expression in Example 29 as follows:

$$-3x + 6y - 9z = 3(-x + 2y - 3z).$$

30. $18z - 12x - 24 = 6(3z - 2x - 4)$

31. $\frac{1}{2}x + \frac{3}{2}y - \frac{1}{2} = \frac{1}{2}(x + 3y - 1)$

Remember that you can always check factoring by multiplying. Keep in mind that an expression is factored when it is written as a product.

Do Exercises 41–46.

e Collecting Like Terms

Terms such as $5x$ and $-4x$, whose variable factors are exactly the same, are called **like terms.** Similarly, numbers, such as -7 and 13, are like terms. Also, $3y^2$ and $9y^2$ are like terms because the variables are raised to the same power. Terms such as $4y$ and $5y^2$ are not like terms, and $7x$ and $2y$ are not like terms.

The process of **collecting like terms** is also based on the distributive laws. We can apply the distributive law when a factor is on the right because of the commutative law of multiplication.

Later in this text, terminology like "collecting like terms" and "combining like terms" will also be referred to as "simplifying."

EXAMPLES Collect like terms. Try to write just the answer, if you can.

32. $4x + 2x = (4 + 2)x = 6x$ 　　Factoring out the x using a distributive law

33. $2x + 3y - 5x - 2y = 2x - 5x + 3y - 2y$
$$= (2 - 5)x + (3 - 2)y = -3x + y$$

34. $3x - x = 3x - 1x = (3 - 1)x = 2x$

35. $x - 0.24x = 1 \cdot x - 0.24x = (1 - 0.24)x = 0.76x$

36. $x - 6x = 1 \cdot x - 6 \cdot x = (1 - 6)x = -5x$

37. $4x - 7y + 9x - 5 + 3y - 8 = 13x - 4y - 13$

38. $\frac{2}{3}a - b + \frac{4}{5}a + \frac{1}{4}b - 10 = \frac{2}{3}a - 1 \cdot b + \frac{4}{5}a + \frac{1}{4}b - 10$
$$= \left(\frac{2}{3} + \frac{4}{5}\right)a + \left(-1 + \frac{1}{4}\right)b - 10$$
$$= \left(\frac{10}{15} + \frac{12}{15}\right)a + \left(-\frac{4}{4} + \frac{1}{4}\right)b - 10$$
$$= \frac{22}{15}a - \frac{3}{4}b - 10$$

Do Exercises 47–53.

Collect like terms.

47. $6x - 3x$

48. $7x - x$

49. $x - 9x$

50. $x - 0.41x$

51. $5x + 4y - 2x - y$

52. $3x - 7x - 11 + 8y + 4 - 13y$

53. $-\dfrac{2}{3} - \dfrac{3}{5}x + y + \dfrac{7}{10}x - \dfrac{2}{9}y$

Answers on page A-6

Study Tips

LEARNING RESOURCES

Are you aware of all the learning resources that exist for this textbook? Many details are given in the Preface.

■ The *Student's Solutions Manual* contains fully worked-out solutions to the odd-numbered exercises in the exercise sets, with the exception of the discussion and writing exercises, as well as solutions to all exercises in Chapter Reviews, Chapter Tests, and Cumulative Reviews. You can order this through the bookstore or by calling 1-800-282-0693.

■ An extensive set of *videotapes* supplements this text. These are available on CD-ROM by calling 1-800-282-0693.

■ *Tutorial software* called InterAct Math also accompanies this text. If it is not available in the campus learning center, you can order it by calling 1-800-282-0693.

■ The Addison-Wesley *Math Tutor Center* is available for help with the odd-numbered exercises. You can order this service by calling 1-800-824-7799.

■ Extensive help is available online via MyMathLab and/or MathXL. Ask your instructor for information about these or visit MyMathLab.com and MathXL.com.

a Find an equivalent expression with the given denominator.

1. $\dfrac{3}{5} = \dfrac{\square}{5y}$

2. $\dfrac{5}{8} = \dfrac{\square}{8t}$

3. $\dfrac{2}{3} = \dfrac{\square}{15x}$

4. $\dfrac{6}{7} = \dfrac{\square}{14y}$

5. $\dfrac{2}{x} = \dfrac{\square}{x^2}$

6. $\dfrac{4}{9x} = \dfrac{\square}{9xy}$

Simplify.

7. $-\dfrac{24a}{16a}$

8. $-\dfrac{42t}{18t}$

9. $-\dfrac{42ab}{36ab}$

10. $-\dfrac{64pq}{48pq}$

11. $\dfrac{20st}{15t}$

12. $\dfrac{21w}{7wz}$

b Write an equivalent expression. Use a commutative law.

13. $y + 8$

14. $x + 3$

15. mn

16. ab

17. $9 + xy$

18. $11 + ab$

19. $ab + c$

20. $rs + t$

Write an equivalent expression. Use an associative law.

21. $a + (b + 2)$

22. $3(vw)$

23. $(8x)y$

24. $(y + z) + 7$

25. $(a + b) + 3$

26. $(5 + x) + y$

27. $3(ab)$

28. $(6x)y$

Use the commutative and associative laws to write three equivalent expressions.

29. $(a + b) + 2$

30. $(3 + x) + y$

31. $5 + (v + w)$

32. $6 + (x + y)$

33. $(xy)3$

34. $(ab)5$

35. $7(ab)$

36. $5(xy)$

c Multiply.

37. $2(b + 5)$

38. $4(x + 3)$

39. $7(1 + t)$

40. $4(1 + y)$

41. $6(5x + 2)$

42. $9(6m + 7)$

43. $7(x + 4 + 6y)$

44. $4(5x + 8 + 3p)$

45. $7(x - 3)$

46. $15(y - 6)$

47. $-3(x - 7)$

48. $1.2(x - 2.1)$

49. $\dfrac{2}{3}(b - 6)$

50. $\dfrac{5}{8}(y + 16)$

51. $7.3(x - 2)$

52. $5.6(x - 8)$

53. $-\dfrac{3}{5}(x - y + 10)$

54. $-\dfrac{2}{3}(a + b - 12)$

55. $-9(-5x - 6y + 8)$

56. $-7(-2x - 5y + 9)$

57. $-4(x - 3y - 2z)$

58. $8(2x - 5y - 8z)$

59. $3.1(-1.2x + 3.2y - 1.1)$

60. $-2.1(-4.2x - 4.3y - 2.2)$

List the terms of the expression.

61. $4x + 3z$

62. $8x - 1.4y$

63. $7x + 8y - 9z$

64. $8a + 10b - 18c$

d Factor. Check by multiplying.

65. $2x + 4$

66. $5y + 20$

67. $30 + 5y$

68. $7x + 28$

69. $14x + 21y$

70. $18a + 24b$

71. $5x + 10 + 15y$

72. $9a + 27b + 81$

73. $8x - 24$

74. $10x - 50$

75. $-4y + 32$

76. $-6m + 24$

77. $8x + 10y - 22$

78. $9a + 6b - 15$

79. $ax - a$

80. $by - 9b$

81. $ax - ay - az$

82. $cx + cy - cz$

83. $-18x + 12y + 6$

84. $-14x + 21y + 7$

85. $\frac{2}{3}x - \frac{5}{3}y + \frac{1}{3}$

86. $\frac{3}{5}a + \frac{4}{5}b - \frac{1}{5}$

ⓔ Collect like terms.

87. $9a + 10a$

88. $12x + 2x$

89. $10a - a$

90. $-16x + x$

91. $2x + 9z + 6x$

92. $3a - 5b + 7a$

93. $7x + 6y^2 + 9y^2$

94. $12m^2 + 6q + 9m^2$

95. $41a + 90 - 60a - 2$

96. $42x - 6 - 4x + 2$

97. $23 + 5t + 7y - t - y - 27$

98. $45 - 90d - 87 - 9d + 3 + 7d$

99. $\frac{1}{2}b + \frac{1}{2}b$

100. $\frac{2}{3}x + \frac{1}{3}x$

101. $2y + \frac{1}{4}y + y$

102. $\frac{1}{2}a + a + 5a$

103. $11x - 3x$

104. $9t - 17t$

105. $6n - n$

106. $100t - t$

107. $y - 17y$

108. $3m - 9m + 4$

109. $-8 + 11a - 5b + 6a - 7b + 7$

110. $8x - 5x + 6 + 3y - 2y - 4$

111. $9x + 2y - 5x$

112. $8y - 3z + 4y$

113. $11x + 2y - 4x - y$

114. $13a + 9b - 2a - 4b$

115. $2.7x + 2.3y - 1.9x - 1.8y$

116. $6.7a + 4.3b - 4.1a - 2.9b$

117. $\dfrac{13}{2}a + \dfrac{9}{5}b - \dfrac{2}{3}a - \dfrac{3}{10}b - 42$

118. $\dfrac{11}{4}x + \dfrac{2}{3}y - \dfrac{4}{5}x - \dfrac{1}{6}y + 12$

119. **D**_{**W**} The distributive law was introduced before the discussion on collecting like terms. Why do you think this was done?

120. **D**_{**W**} Find two algebraic expressions for the total area of this figure. Explain the equivalence of the expressions in terms of the distributive law.

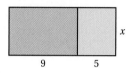

Find the LCM.   [R.1b]

121. 16, 18

122. 18, 24

123. 16, 18, 24

124. 12, 15, 20

125. 16, 32

126. 24, 72

127. 15, 45, 90

128. 18, 54, 108

129. Add and simplify: $\dfrac{11}{12} + \dfrac{15}{16}$.   [R.2c]

130. Subtract and simplify: $\dfrac{7}{8} - \dfrac{2}{3}$.   [R.2c]

131. Subtract and simplify: $\dfrac{1}{8} - \dfrac{1}{3}$.   [R.2c], [1.4a]

132. Convert to percent notation: $\dfrac{3}{10}$.   [R.4d]

Tell whether the expressions are equivalent. Give an example if they are not.

133. $3t + 5$ and $3 \cdot 5 + t$

134. $4x$ and $x + 4$

135. $5m + 6$ and $6 + 5m$

136. $(x + y) + z$ and $z + (x + y)$

137. Factor: $q + qr + qrs + qrst$.

138. Collect like terms:
$$21x + 44xy + 15y - 16x - 8y - 38xy + 2y + xy.$$

a Find an equivalent expression for an opposite without parentheses, where an expression has several terms.

b Simplify expressions by removing parentheses and collecting like terms.

c Simplify expressions with parentheses inside parentheses.

d Simplify expressions using rules for order of operations.

Find an equivalent expression without parentheses.

1. $-(x + 2)$

2. $-(5x + 2y + 8)$

Answers on page A-6

1.8 SIMPLIFYING EXPRESSIONS; ORDER OF OPERATIONS

We now expand our ability to manipulate expressions by first considering opposites of sums and differences. Then we simplify expressions involving parentheses.

a Opposites of Sums

What happens when we multiply a real number by -1? Consider the following products:

$$-1(7) = -7, \qquad -1(-5) = 5, \qquad -1(0) = 0.$$

From these examples, it appears that when we multiply a number by -1, we get the opposite, or additive inverse, of that number.

THE PROPERTY OF -1

For any real number a,

$$-1 \cdot a = -a.$$

(Negative one times a is the opposite, or additive inverse, of a.)

The property of -1 enables us to find certain expressions equivalent to opposites of sums.

EXAMPLES Find an equivalent expression without parentheses.

1.
$$
\begin{aligned}
-(3 + x) &= -1(3 + x) &&\text{Using the property of } -1 \\
&= -1 \cdot 3 + (-1)x &&\text{Using a distributive law, multiplying each} \\
& &&\text{term by } -1 \\
&= -3 + (-x) &&\text{Using the property of } -1 \\
&= -3 - x
\end{aligned}
$$

2.
$$
\begin{aligned}
-(3x + 2y + 4) &= -1(3x + 2y + 4) &&\text{Using the property} \\
& &&\text{of } -1 \\
&= -1(3x) + (-1)(2y) + (-1)4 &&\text{Using a distributive law} \\
&= -3x - 2y - 4 &&\text{Using the property} \\
& &&\text{of } -1
\end{aligned}
$$

Do Exercises 1 and 2.

Suppose we want to remove parentheses in an expression like

$$-(x - 2y + 5).$$

We can first rewrite any subtractions inside the parentheses as additions. Then we take the opposite of each term:

$$
\begin{aligned}
-(x - 2y + 5) &= -[x + (-2y) + 5] \\
&= -x + 2y - 5.
\end{aligned}
$$

The most efficient method for removing parentheses is to replace each term in the parentheses with its opposite ("change the sign of every term"). Doing so for $-(x - 2y + 5)$, we obtain $-x + 2y - 5$ as an equivalent expression.

EXAMPLES   Find an equivalent expression without parentheses.

3. $-(5 - y) = -5 + y = y + (-5) = y - 5$ Changing the sign of each term

4. $-(2a - 7b - 6) = -2a + 7b + 6$

5. $-(-3x + 4y + z - 7w - 23) = 3x - 4y - z + 7w + 23$

Do Exercises 3–6.

b   Removing Parentheses and Simplifying

When a sum is added, as in $5x + (2x + 3)$, we can simply remove, or drop, the parentheses and collect like terms because of the associative law of addition:

$$5x + (2x + 3) = 5x + 2x + 3 = 7x + 3.$$

On the other hand, when a sum is subtracted, as in $3x - (4x + 2)$, no "associative" law applies. However, we can subtract by adding an opposite. We then remove parentheses by changing the sign of each term inside the parentheses and collecting like terms.

EXAMPLE 6   Remove parentheses and simplify.

$$3x - (4x + 2) = 3x + [-(4x + 2)] \quad \text{Adding the opposite of } (4x + 2)$$
$$= 3x + (-4x - 2) \quad \text{Changing the sign of each term inside the parentheses}$$
$$= 3x - 4x - 2$$
$$= -x - 2 \quad \text{Collecting like terms}$$

> **Caution!**
>
> Note that $3x - (4x + 2) \neq 3x - 4x + 2$. That is, $3x - (4x + 2)$ is *not* equivalent to $3x - 4x + 2$. You cannot simply drop the parentheses.

Do Exercises 7 and 8.

In practice, the first three steps of Example 6 are usually combined by changing the sign of each term in parentheses and then collecting like terms.

EXAMPLES   Remove parentheses and simplify.

7. $5y - (3y + 4) = 5y - 3y - 4$ Removing parentheses by changing the sign of every term inside the parentheses

$$= 2y - 4 \quad \text{Collecting like terms}$$

8. $3x - 2 - (5x - 8) = 3x - 2 - 5x + 8$
$$= -2x + 6, \text{ or } 6 - 2x$$

9. $(3a + 4b - 5) - (2a - 7b + 4c - 8)$
$$= 3a + 4b - 5 - 2a + 7b - 4c + 8$$
$$= a + 11b - 4c + 3$$

Do Exercises 9–11.

Find an equivalent expression without parentheses. Try to do this in one step.

3. $-(6 - t)$

4. $-(x - y)$

5. $-(-4a + 3t - 10)$

6. $-(18 - m - 2n + 4z)$

Remove parentheses and simplify.

7. $5x - (3x + 9)$

8. $5y - 2 - (2y - 4)$

Remove parentheses and simplify.

9. $6x - (4x + 7)$

10. $8y - 3 - (5y - 6)$

11. $(2a + 3b - c) - (4a - 5b + 2c)$

Answers on page A-6

Remove parentheses and simplify.

12. $y - 9(x + y)$

13. $5a - 3(7a - 6)$

14. $4a - b - 6(5a - 7b + 8c)$

15. $5x - \dfrac{1}{4}(8x + 28)$

16. $4.6(5x - 3y) - 5.2(8x + y)$

Simplify.

17. $12 - (8 + 2)$

18. $\{9 - [10 - (13 + 6)]\}$

19. $[24 \div (-2)] \div (-2)$

20. $5(3 + 4) - \{8 - [5 - (9 + 6)]\}$

Answers on page A-6

Next, consider subtracting an expression consisting of several terms multiplied by a number other than 1 or -1.

EXAMPLE 10   Remove parentheses and simplify.

$$\begin{aligned}
x - 3(x + y) &= x + [-3(x + y)] &&\text{Adding the opposite of } 3(x + y) \\
&= x + [-3x - 3y] &&\text{Multiplying } x + y \text{ by } -3 \\
&= x - 3x - 3y \\
&= -2x - 3y &&\text{Collecting like terms}
\end{aligned}$$

EXAMPLES   Remove parentheses and simplify.

11. $3y - 2(4y - 5) = 3y - 8y + 10$ Multiplying each term in parentheses by -2

$$= -5y + 10$$

12. $(2a + 3b - 7) - 4(-5a - 6b + 12)$

$$= 2a + 3b - 7 + 20a + 24b - 48 = 22a + 27b - 55$$

13. $2y - \frac{1}{3}(9y - 12) = 2y - 3y + 4 = -y + 4$

14. $6.4(5x - 3y) - 2.5(8x + y) = 32x - 19.2y - 20x - 2.5y = 12x - 21.7y$

Do Exercises 12–16.

C   **Parentheses Within Parentheses**

In addition to parentheses, some expressions contain other grouping symbols such as brackets [ ] and braces { }.

> When more than one kind of grouping symbol occurs, do the computations in the innermost ones first. Then work from the inside out.

EXAMPLES   Simplify.

15. $[3 - (7 + 3)] = [3 - 10] = -7$

16. $\{8 - [9 - (12 + 5)]\} = \{8 - [9 - 17]\}$ Computing $12 + 5$

$$= \{8 - [-8]\} \qquad \text{Computing } 9 - 17$$
$$= 8 + 8 = 16$$

17. $\left[(-4) \div \left(-\frac{1}{4}\right)\right] \div \frac{1}{4} = [(-4) \cdot (-4)] \div \frac{1}{4}$ Working within the brackets; computing $(-4) \div \left(-\frac{1}{4}\right)$

$$= 16 \div \frac{1}{4}$$
$$= 16 \cdot 4 = 64$$

18. $4(2 + 3) - \{7 - [4 - (8 + 5)]\}$

$$= 4 \cdot 5 - \{7 - [4 - 13]\} \qquad \text{Working with the innermost parentheses first}$$

$$= 20 - \{7 - [-9]\} \qquad \text{Computing } 4 \cdot 5 \text{ and } 4 - 13$$

$$= 20 - 16 \qquad \text{Computing } 7 - [-9]$$

$$= 4$$

Do Exercises 17–20.

EXAMPLE 19 Simplify.

$$[5(x + 2) - 3x] - [3(y + 2) - 7(y - 3)]$$
$$= [5x + 10 - 3x] - [3y + 6 - 7y + 21] \quad \text{Working with the innermost parentheses first}$$
$$= [2x + 10] - [-4y + 27] \quad \text{Collecting like terms within brackets}$$
$$= 2x + 10 + 4y - 27 \quad \text{Removing brackets}$$
$$= 2x + 4y - 17 \quad \text{Collecting like terms}$$

Do Exercise 21.

21. Simplify:

$$[3(x + 2) + 2x] - [4(y + 2) - 3(y - 2)].$$

d   Order of Operations

When several operations are to be done in a calculation or a problem, we apply the same rules that we did in Section R.5. We repeat them here for review. (If you did not study that section earlier, you should do so now.)

RULES FOR ORDER OF OPERATIONS

1. Do all calculations within grouping symbols before operations outside.
2. Evaluate all exponential expressions.
3. Do all multiplications and divisions in order from left to right.
4. Do all additions and subtractions in order from left to right.

Simplify.
22. $23 - 42 \cdot 30$

These rules are consistent with the way in which most computers and scientific calculators perform calculations.

23. $32 \div 8 \cdot 2$

EXAMPLE 20 Simplify: $-34 \cdot 56 - 17$.

There are no parentheses or powers, so we start with the third step.

$$-34 \cdot 56 - 17 = -1904 - 17 \quad \text{Doing all multiplications and divisions in order from left to right}$$
$$= -1921 \quad \text{Doing all additions and subtractions in order from left to right}$$

24. $-24 \div 3 - 48 \div (-4)$

EXAMPLE 21 Simplify: $25 \div (-5) + 50 \div (-2)$.

There are no calculations inside parentheses or powers. The parentheses with (-5) and (-2) are used only to represent the negative numbers. We begin by doing all multiplications and divisions.

$$\underbrace{25 \div (-5)}_{\downarrow} + \underbrace{50 \div (-2)}_{\downarrow}$$
$$= -5 + (-25) \quad \text{Doing all multiplications and divisions in order from left to right}$$
$$= -30 \quad \text{Doing all additions and subtractions in order from left to right.}$$

Do Exercises 22–24.

Answers on page A-6

EXAMPLE 22 Simplify: $-2^4 + 51 \cdot 4 - (37 + 23 \cdot 2)$.

$$-2^4 + 51 \cdot 4 - (37 + 23 \cdot 2)$$

$= -2^4 + 51 \cdot 4 - (37 + 46)$	Following the rules for order of operations within the parentheses first
$= -2^4 + 51 \cdot 4 - 83$	Completing the addition inside parentheses
$= -16 + 51 \cdot 4 - 83$	Evaluating exponential expressions. Note that $-2^4 \neq (-2)^4$.
$= -16 + 204 - 83$	Doing all multiplications
$= 188 - 83$	Doing all additions and subtractions in order from left to right
$= 105$	

CALCULATOR CORNER

Order of Operations and Grouping Symbols   Parentheses are necessary in some calculations in order to ensure that operations are performed in the desired order. To simplify $-5(3 - 6) - 12$, we press (-) 5 (3 (-) 6) (-) 1 2 ENTER. The result is 3. Without parentheses, the computation is $-5 \cdot 3 - 6 - 12$, and the result is -33.

```
-5(3-6)-12
                    3
-5*3-6-12
                  -33
```

When a negative number is raised to an even power, parentheses must also be used. To find $(-3)^4$, we press ((-) 3) ^ 4 ENTER. The result is 81. Without parentheses, the computation is $-3^4 = -1 \cdot 3^4 = -1 \cdot 81 = -81$.

```
(-3)^4
                   81
-3^4
                  -81
```

To simplify an expression like $\dfrac{49 - 104}{7 + 4}$, we must enter it as

$(49 - 104) \div (7 + 4)$. We press (4 9 (-) 1 0 4) ÷ (7 + 4) ENTER. The result is -5.

```
(49-104)/(7+4)
                   -5
```

Exercises: Calculate.

1. $-8 + 4(7 - 9) + 5$

2. $-3[2 + (-5)]$

3. $7[4 - (-3)] + 5[3^2 - (-4)]$

4. $(-7)^6$

5. $(-17)^5$

6. $(-104)^3$

7. -7^6

8. -17^5

9. -104^3

10. $\dfrac{38 - 178}{5 + 30}$

11. $\dfrac{311 - 17^2}{2 - 13}$

12. $785 - \dfrac{285 - 5^4}{17 + 3 \cdot 51}$

A fraction bar can play the role of a grouping symbol, although such a symbol is not as evident as the others.

EXAMPLE 23 Simplify: $\dfrac{-64 \div (-16) \div (-2)}{2^3 - 3^2}$.

An equivalent expression with brackets as grouping symbols is

$$[-64 \div (-16) \div (-2)] \div [2^3 - 3^2].$$

This shows, in effect, that we do the calculations in the numerator and then in the denominator, and divide the results:

$$\frac{-64 \div (-16) \div (-2)}{2^3 - 3^2} = \frac{4 \div (-2)}{8 - 9} = \frac{-2}{-1} = 2.$$

Do Exercises 25 and 26.

Simplify.

25. $-4^3 + 52 \cdot 5 + 5^3 - (4^2 - 48 \div 4)$

26. $\dfrac{5 - 10 - 5 \cdot 23}{2^3 + 3^2 - 7}$

Answers on page A-6

Study Tips

TEST PREPARATION

You are probably ready to begin preparing for your first test. Here are some test-taking study tips.

■ **Make up your own test questions as you study.**   After you have done your homework over a particular objective, write one or two questions on your own that you think might be on a test. You will be amazed at the insight this will provide.

■ **Do an overall review of the chapter, focusing on the objectives and the examples.**   This should be accompanied by a study of any class notes you may have taken.

■ **Do the review exercises at the end of the chapter.**   Check your answers at the back of the book. If you have trouble with an exercise, use the objective symbol as a guide to go back and do further study of that objective.

■ **Call the AW Math Tutor Center if you need extra help at 1-888-777-0463.**

■ **Do the chapter test at the end of the chapter.**   Check the answers and use the objective symbols at the back of the book as a reference for where to review.

■ **Ask former students for old exams.**   Working such exams can be very helpful and allows you to see what various professors think is important.

■ **When taking a test, read each question carefully and try to do all the questions the first time through, but pace yourself.**   Answer all the questions, and mark those to recheck if you have time at the end. Very often, your first hunch will be correct.

■ **Try to write your test in a neat and orderly manner.**   Very often, your instructor tries to give you partial credit when grading an exam. If your test paper is sloppy and disorderly, it is difficult to verify the partial credit. Doing your work neatly can ease such a task for the instructor.

1.8 EXERCISE SET

For Extra Help

a Find an equivalent expression without parentheses.

1. $-(2x + 7)$

2. $-(8x + 4)$

3. $-(8 - x)$

4. $-(a - b)$

5. $-(4a - 3b + 7c)$

6. $-(x - 4y - 3z)$

7. $-(6x - 8y + 5)$

8. $-(4x + 9y + 7)$

9. $-(3x - 5y - 6)$

10. $-(6a - 4b - 7)$

11. $-(-8x - 6y - 43)$

12. $-(-2a + 9b - 5c)$

b Remove parentheses and simplify.

13. $9x - (4x + 3)$

14. $4y - (2y + 5)$

15. $2a - (5a - 9)$

16. $12m - (4m - 6)$

17. $2x + 7x - (4x + 6)$

18. $3a + 2a - (4a + 7)$

19. $2x - 4y - 3(7x - 2y)$

20. $3a - 9b - 1(4a - 8b)$

21. $15x - y - 5(3x - 2y + 5z)$

22. $4a - b - 4(5a - 7b + 8c)$

23. $(3x + 2y) - 2(5x - 4y)$

24. $(-6a - b) - 5(2b + a)$

25. $(12a - 3b + 5c) - 5(-5a + 4b - 6c)$

26. $(-8x + 5y - 12) - 6(2x - 4y - 10)$

CHAPTER 1: Introduction to Real Numbers
and Algebraic Expressions

Simplify.

27. $[9 - 2(5 - 4)]$ **28.** $[6 - 5(8 - 4)]$ **29.** $8[7 - 6(4 - 2)]$ **30.** $10[7 - 4(7 - 5)]$

31. $[4(9 - 6) + 11] - [14 - (6 + 4)]$ **32.** $[7(8 - 4) + 16] - [15 - (7 + 8)]$

33. $[10(x + 3) - 4] + [2(x - 1) + 6]$ **34.** $[9(x + 5) - 7] + [4(x - 12) + 9]$

35. $[7(x + 5) - 19] - [4(x - 6) + 10]$ **36.** $[6(x + 4) - 12] - [5(x - 8) + 14]$

37. $3\{[7(x - 2) + 4] - [2(2x - 5) + 6]\}$ **38.** $4\{[8(x - 3) + 9] - [4(3x - 2) + 6]\}$

39. $4\{[5(x - 3) + 2] - 3[2(x + 5) - 9]\}$ **40.** $3\{[6(x - 4) + 5] - 2[5(x + 8) - 3]\}$

d Simplify.

41. $8 - 2 \cdot 3 - 9$ **42.** $8 - (2 \cdot 3 - 9)$ **43.** $(8 - 2 \cdot 3) - 9$ **44.** $(8 - 2)(3 - 9)$

45. $[(-24) \div (-3)] \div \left(-\frac{1}{2}\right)$ **46.** $[32 \div (-2)] \div \left(-\frac{1}{4}\right)$

47. $16 \cdot (-24) + 50$ **48.** $10 \cdot 20 - 15 \cdot 24$

49. $2^4 + 2^3 - 10$

50. $40 - 3^2 - 2^3$

51. $5^3 + 26 \cdot 71 - (16 + 25 \cdot 3)$

52. $4^3 + 10 \cdot 20 + 8^2 - 23$

53. $4 \cdot 5 - 2 \cdot 6 + 4$

54. $4 \cdot (6 + 8)/(4 + 3)$

55. $4^3/8$

56. $5^3 - 7^2$

57. $8(-7) + 6(-5)$

58. $10(-5) + 1(-1)$

59. $19 - 5(-3) + 3$

60. $14 - 2(-6) + 7$

61. $9 \div (-3) + 16 \div 8$

62. $-32 - 8 \div 4 - (-2)$

63. $-4^2 + 6$

64. $-5^2 + 7$

65. $-8^2 - 3$

66. $-9^2 - 11$

67. $12 - 20^3$

68. $20 + 4^3 \div (-8)$

69. $2 \cdot 10^3 - 5000$

70. $-7(3^4) + 18$

71. $6[9 - (3 - 4)]$

72. $8[(6 - 13) - 11]$

73. $-1000 \div (-100) \div 10$

74. $256 \div (-32) \div (-4)$

75. $8 - (7 - 9)$

76. $(8 - 7) - 9$

77. $\dfrac{10 - 6^2}{9^2 + 3^2}$

78. $\dfrac{5^2 - 4^3 - 3}{9^2 - 2^2 - 1^5}$

79. $\dfrac{3(6 - 7) - 5 \cdot 4}{6 \cdot 7 - 8(4 - 1)}$

80. $\dfrac{20(8 - 3) - 4(10 - 3)}{10(2 - 6) - 2(5 + 2)}$

CHAPTER 1: Introduction to Real Numbers
and Algebraic Expressions

81. $\dfrac{|2^3 - 3^2| + |12 \cdot 5|}{-32 \div (-16) \div (-4)}$

82. $\dfrac{|3 - 5|^2 - |7 - 13|}{|12 - 9| + |11 - 14|}$

83. $\mathbf{D_W}$ ▦ Jake keys in $18/2 \cdot 3$ on his calculator and expects the result to be 3. What mistake is he making?

84. $\mathbf{D_W}$ Determine whether $|-x|$ and $|x|$ are equivalent. Explain.

SKILL MAINTENANCE

↪ VOCABULARY REINFORCEMENT

In each of Exercises 85–92, fill in the blank with the correct term from the given list. Some of the choices may not be used and some may be used more than once.

85. The set of _____ is
$\{\ldots, -5, -4, -3, -2, -1, 0, 1, 2, 3, \ldots\}$.   [1.2a]

86. Two numbers whose sum is 0 are called _____ of each other.   [1.3b]

87. The _____ of addition says that $a + b = b + a$ for any real numbers a and b.   [1.7b]

88. The _____ states that for any real number a, $a \cdot 1 = 1 \cdot a = a$.   [1.7a]

89. The _____ of addition says that $a + (b + c) = (a + b) + c$ for any real numbers a, b, and c.   [1.7b]

90. The _____ of multiplication says that $a(bc) = (ab)c$ for any real numbers a, b, and c.   [1.7b]

91. Two numbers whose product is 1 are called _____ of each other.   [1.6b]

92. The equation $y + 0 = y$ illustrates the _____.   [1.7a]

natural numbers

multiplicative inverses

distributive law

associative law

whole numbers

additive inverses

identity property of 0

property of -1

integers

commutative law

identity property of 1

real numbers

SYNTHESIS

Find an equivalent expression by enclosing the last three terms in parentheses preceded by a minus sign.

93. $6y + 2x - 3a + c$

94. $x - y - a - b$

95. $6m + 3n - 5m + 4b$

Simplify.

96. $z - \{2z - [3z - (4z - 5z) - 6z] - 7z\} - 8z$

97. $\{x - [f - (f - x)] + [x - f]\} - 3x$

98. $x - \{x - 1 - [x - 2 - (x - 3 - \{x - 4 - [x - 5 - (x - 6)]\})]\}$

99. ▦ Use your calculator to do the following.
 a) Evaluate $x^2 + 3$ when $x = 7$, when $x = -7$, and when $x = -5.013$.
 b) Evaluate $1 - x^2$ when $x = 5$, when $x = -5$, and when $x = -10.455$.

100. Express $3^3 + 3^3 + 3^3$ as a power of 3.

Find the average.

101. $-15, \ 20, \ 50, \ -82, \ -7, \ -2$

102. $-1, \ 1, \ 2, \ -2, \ 3, \ -8, \ -10$

The review that follows is meant to prepare you for a chapter exam. It consists of three parts. The first part, Concept Reinforcement, is designed to increase understanding of the concepts through true/false exercises. The second part is a list of important properties and formulas. The third part is the Review Exercises. These provide practice exercises for the exam, together with references to section objectives so you can go back and review. Before beginning, stop and look back over the skills you have obtained. What skills in mathematics do you have now that you did not have before studying this chapter?

☞ CONCEPT REINFORCEMENT

Determine whether the statement is true or false. Answers are given at the back of the book.

_____ **1.** The set of whole numbers is a subset of the set of integers.

_____ **2.** All rational numbers can be named using fraction or decimal notation.

_____ **3.** The product of an even number of negative numbers is negative.

_____ **4.** The operation of subtraction is not commutative.

_____ **5.** The product of a number and its multiplicative inverse is -1.

_____ **6.** Decimal notation for irrational numbers neither repeats nor terminates.

_____ **7.** $a < b$ also has the meaning $b \geq a$.

IMPORTANT PROPERTIES AND FORMULAS

Properties of the Real-Number System

The Commutative Laws: $a + b = b + a, \quad ab = ba$

The Associative Laws: $a + (b + c) = (a + b) + c, \quad a(bc) = (ab)c$

The Identity Properties: $a + 0 = 0 + a = a, \quad a \cdot 1 = 1 \cdot a = a$

The Inverse Properties: For any real number a, there is an opposite $-a$ such that $a + (-a) = (-a) + a = 0$.

For any nonzero real number a, there is a reciprocal $\dfrac{1}{a}$ such that $a \cdot \dfrac{1}{a} = \dfrac{1}{a} \cdot a = 1$.

The Distributive Laws: $a(b + c) = ab + ac, \quad a(b - c) = ab - ac$

Review Exercises

The review exercises that follow are for practice. Answers are at the back of the book. If you miss an exercise, restudy the objective indicated in red after the exercise or the direction line that precedes it.

1. Evaluate $\dfrac{x - y}{3}$ when $x = 17$ and $y = 5$. [1.1a]

2. Translate to an algebraic expression: [1.1b]

Nineteen percent of some number.

3. Tell which integers correspond to this situation: [1.2a]

David has a debt of $45 and Joe has $72 in his savings account.

4. Find: $|-38|$. [1.2e]

Graph the number on a number line.   [1.2b]

5. −2.5

6. $\dfrac{8}{9}$

Use either < or > for ☐ to write a true sentence.   [1.2d]

7. −3 ☐ 10

8. −1 ☐ −6

9. 0.126 ☐ −12.6

10. $-\dfrac{2}{3}$ ☐ $-\dfrac{1}{10}$

Find the opposite.   [1.3b]

11. 3.8

12. $-\dfrac{3}{4}$

Find the reciprocal.   [1.6b]

13. $\dfrac{3}{8}$

14. −7

15. Evaluate −x when $x = -34$.   [1.3b]

16. Evaluate −(−x) when $x = 5$.   [1.3b]

Compute and simplify.

17. 4 + (−7)   [1.3a]

18. 6 + (−9) + (−8) + 7   [1.3a]

19. −3.8 + 5.1 + (−12) + (−4.3) + 10   [1.3a]

20. −3 − (−7) + 7 − 10   [1.4a]

21. $-\dfrac{9}{10} - \dfrac{1}{2}$ [1.4a]

22. −3.8 − 4.1   [1.4a]

23. −9 · (−6)   [1.5a]

24. −2.7(3.4)   [1.5a]

25. $\dfrac{2}{3} \cdot \left(-\dfrac{3}{7}\right)$ [1.5a]

26. 3 · (−7) · (−2) · (−5)   [1.5a]

27. 35 ÷ (−5)   [1.6a]

28. −5.1 ÷ 1.7   [1.6c]

29. $-\dfrac{3}{11} \div \left(-\dfrac{4}{11}\right)$ [1.6c]

Simplify.   [1.8d]

30. (−3.4 − 12.2) − 8(−7)

31. $\dfrac{-12(-3) - 2^3 - (-9)(-10)}{3 \cdot 10 + 1}$

32. −16 ÷ 4 − 30 ÷ (−5)

33. $\dfrac{9[(7 - 14) - 13]}{|-2(8) - 4|}$

Solve.

34. On the first, second, and third downs, a football team had these gains and losses: 5-yd gain, 12-yd loss, and 15-yd gain, respectively. Find the total gain (or loss). [1.3c]

35. Kaleb's total assets are $170. He borrows $300. What are his total assets now?   [1.4b]

36. *Stock Price.* The value of EFX Corp. stock began the day at $17.68 per share and dropped $1.63 per hour for 8 hr. What was the price of the stock after 8 hr? [1.5b]

37. *Checking Account Balance.* Yuri had $68 in his checking account. After writing checks to make seven purchases of DVDs at the same price for each, the balance in his account was −$64.65. What was the price of each DVD? [1.6d]

Multiply. [1.7c]

38. $5(3x - 7)$

39. $-2(4x - 5)$

40. $10(0.4x + 1.5)$

41. $-8(3 - 6x)$

Factor. [1.7d]

42. $2x - 14$

43. $-6x + 6$

44. $5x + 10$

45. $-3x + 12y - 12$

Collect like terms. [1.7e]

46. $11a + 2b - 4a - 5b$

47. $7x - 3y - 9x + 8y$

48. $6x + 3y - x - 4y$

49. $-3a + 9b + 2a - b$

Remove parentheses and simplify.

50. $2a - (5a - 9)$ [1.8b]

51. $3(b + 7) - 5b$ [1.8b]

52. $3[11 - 3(4 - 1)]$ [1.8c]

53. $2[6(y - 4) + 7]$ [1.8c]

54. $[8(x + 4) - 10] - [3(x - 2) + 4]$ [1.8c]

55. $5\{[6(x - 1) + 7] - [3(3x - 4) + 8]\}$ [1.8c]

Answer True or False. [1.2d]

56. $-9 \leq 11$

57. $-11 \geq -3$

58. Write another inequality with the same meaning as $-3 < x$. [1.2d]

59. **D$_W$** Explain the notion of the opposite of a number in as many ways as possible. [1.3b]

60. **D$_W$** Is the absolute value of a number always positive? Why or why not? [1.2e]

SYNTHESIS

Simplify. [1.2e], [1.4a], [1.6a], [1.8d]

61. $-\left| \dfrac{7}{8} - \left(-\dfrac{1}{2} \right) - \dfrac{3}{4} \right|$

62. $(|2.7 - 3| + 3^2 - |-3|) \div (-3)$

63. $2000 - 1990 + 1980 - 1970 + \cdots + 20 - 10$

64. Find a formula for the perimeter of the following figure. [R.6a], [1.7e]

1. Evaluate $\dfrac{3x}{y}$ when $x = 10$ and $y = 5$.

2. Write an algebraic expression: Nine less than some number.

3. Find the area of a triangle when the height h is 30 ft and the base b is 16 ft.

Use either $<$ or $>$ for ☐ to write a true sentence.

4. -4 ☐ 0

5. -3 ☐ -8

6. -0.78 ☐ -0.87

7. $-\dfrac{1}{8}$ ☐ $\dfrac{1}{2}$

Find the absolute value.

8. $|-7|$

9. $\left|\dfrac{9}{4}\right|$

10. $|-2.7|$

Find the opposite.

11. $\dfrac{2}{3}$

12. -1.4

13. Evaluate $-x$ when $x = -8$.

Find the reciprocal.

14. -2

15. $\dfrac{4}{7}$

Compute and simplify.

16. $3.1 - (-4.7)$

17. $-8 + 4 + (-7) + 3$

18. $-\dfrac{1}{5} + \dfrac{3}{8}$

19. $2 - (-8)$

20. $3.2 - 5.7$

21. $\dfrac{1}{8} - \left(-\dfrac{3}{4}\right)$

22. $4 \cdot (-12)$

23. $-\dfrac{1}{2} \cdot \left(-\dfrac{3}{8}\right)$

24. $-45 \div 5$

25. $-\dfrac{3}{5} \div \left(-\dfrac{4}{5}\right)$

26. $4.864 \div (-0.5)$

27. $-2(16) - |2(-8) - 5^3|$

28. $-20 \div (-5) + 36 \div (-4)$

29. *Antarctica Highs and Lows.* The continent of Antarctica, which lies in the southern hemisphere, experiences winter in July. The average high temperature is −67°F and the average low temperature is −81°F. How much higher is the average high than the average low?

Source: National Climatic Data Center

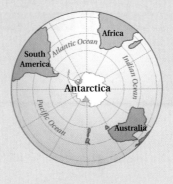

30. Maureen is a stockbroker. She kept track of the changes in the stock market over a period of 5 weeks. By how many points had the market risen or fallen over this time?

WEEK 1	WEEK 2	WEEK 3	WEEK 4	WEEK 5
Down 13 pts	Down 16 pts	Up 36 pts	Down 11 pts	Up 19 pts

31. *Population Decrease.* The population of a city was 18,600. It dropped 420 each year for 6 yr. What was the population of the city after 6 yr?

32. *Chemical Experiment.* During a chemical reaction, the temperature in the beaker decreased every minute by the same number of degrees. The temperature was 16°C at 11:08 A.M. By 11:43 A.M., the temperature had dropped to −17°C. By how many degrees did it drop each minute?

Multiply.

33. $3(6 - x)$

34. $-5(y - 1)$

Factor.

35. $12 - 22x$

36. $7x + 21 + 14y$

Simplify.

37. $6 + 7 - 4 - (-3)$

38. $5x - (3x - 7)$

39. $4(2a - 3b) + a - 7$

40. $4\{3[5(y - 3) + 9] + 2(y + 8)\}$

41. $256 \div (-16) \div 4$

42. $2^3 - 10[4 - (-2 + 18)3]$

43. Write an inequality with the same meaning as $x \le -2$.

SYNTHESIS

Simplify.

44. $|-27 - 3(4)| - |-36| + |-12|$

45. $a - \{3a - [4a - (2a - 4a)]\}$

46. Find a formula for the perimeter of the figure shown here.

Solving Equations and Inequalities

Real-World Application

The average top speed of the three fastest roller coasters in the world is 109 mph. The third fastest roller coaster, Superman the Escape (at Six Flags Magic Mountain, Los Angeles, CA) reaches a top speed of 20 mph less than the fastest roller coaster, Top Thrill Dragster (in Cedar Point, Sandusky, OH). The second fastest roller coaster, Dodonpa (in Fujikyu Highlands, Japan), has a top speed of 107 mph. What is the top speed of the fastest roller coaster?

Source: Fortune Small Business, June 2004, p. 48

This problem appears as Example 7 in Section 2.6.

Objectives

a Determine whether a given number is a solution of a given equation.

b Solve equations using the addition principle.

Determine whether the equation is true, false, or neither.

1. $5 - 8 = -4$

2. $12 + 6 = 18$

3. $x + 6 = 7 - x$

Answers on page A-7

a Equations and Solutions

In order to solve problems, we must learn to solve equations.

> **EQUATION**
>
> An **equation** is a number sentence that says that the expressions on either side of the equals sign, =, represent the same number.

Here are some examples:

$$3 + 2 = 5, \quad 14 - 10 = 1 + 3, \quad x + 6 = 13, \quad 3x - 2 = 7 - x.$$

Equations have expressions on each side of the equals sign. The sentence "$14 - 10 = 1 + 3$" asserts that the expressions $14 - 10$ and $1 + 3$ name the same number.

Some equations are true. Some are false. Some are neither true nor false.

EXAMPLES Determine whether the equation is true, false, or neither.

1. $3 + 2 = 5$ The equation is *true*.

2. $7 - 2 = 4$ The equation is *false*.

3. $x + 6 = 13$ The equation is *neither* true nor false, because we do not know what number x represents.

Do Exercises 1–3.

> **SOLUTION OF AN EQUATION**
>
> Any replacement for the variable that makes an equation true is called a **solution** of the equation. To solve an equation means to find *all* of its solutions.

One way to determine whether a number is a solution of an equation is to evaluate the expression on each side of the equals sign by substitution. If the values are the same, then the number is a solution.

EXAMPLE 4 Determine whether 7 is a solution of $x + 6 = 13$.

We have

$$\begin{array}{c|l} x + 6 = 13 & \text{Writing the equation} \\ \hline 7 + 6 \ ? \ 13 & \text{Substituting 7 for } x \\ 13 \ | & \text{TRUE} \end{array}$$

Since the left-hand and the right-hand sides are the same, we have a solution. No other number makes the equation true, so the only solution is the number 7.

EXAMPLE 5 Determine whether 19 is a solution of $7x = 141$.

$$
\begin{array}{ll}
7x = 141 & \text{Writing the equation} \\
\overline{7(19)\ ?\ 141} & \text{Substituting 19 for } x \\
133\ | & \text{FALSE}
\end{array}
$$

Since the left-hand and the right-hand sides are not the same, we do not have a solution.

Do Exercises 4–7.

b   Using the Addition Principle

Consider the equation

$$x = 7.$$

We can easily see that the solution of this equation is 7. If we replace x with 7, we get

$$7 = 7, \quad \text{which is true.}$$

Now consider the equation of Example 4:

$$x + 6 = 13.$$

In Example 4, we discovered that the solution of this equation is also 7, but the fact that 7 is the solution is not as obvious. We now begin to consider principles that allow us to start with an equation like $x + 6 = 13$ and end up with an *equivalent equation,* like $x = 7$, in which the variable is alone on one side and for which the solution is easier to find.

EQUIVALENT EQUATIONS

Equations with the same solutions are called **equivalent equations.**

One of the principles that we use in solving equations involves adding. An equation $a = b$ says that a and b stand for the same number. Suppose this is true, and we add a number c to the number a. We get the same answer if we add c to b, because a and b are the same number.

**THE ADDITION PRINCIPLE
FOR EQUATIONS**

For any real numbers a, b, and c,

$$a = b \quad \text{is equivalent to} \quad a + c = b + c.$$

Let's again solve the equation $x + 6 = 13$ using the addition principle. We want to get x alone on one side. To do so, we use the addition principle, choosing to add -6 because $6 + (-6) = 0$:

$$
\begin{array}{ll}
x + 6 = 13 & \\
x + 6 + (-6) = 13 + (-6) & \text{Using the addition principle: adding } -6 \\
& \text{on both sides} \\
x + 0 = 7 & \text{Simplifying} \\
x = 7. & \text{Identity property of 0: } x + 0 = x
\end{array}
$$

The solution of $x + 6 = 13$ is 7.

Determine whether the given number is a solution of the given equation.

4. 8; $x + 4 = 12$

5. 0; $x + 4 = 12$

6. -3; $7 + x = -4$

7. $-\dfrac{3}{5}$; $-5x = 3$

Answers on page A-7

8. Solve using the addition principle:

$$x + 2 = 11.$$

Do Exercise 8.

When we use the addition principle, we sometimes say that we "add the same number on both sides of the equation." This is also true for subtraction, since we can express every subtraction as an addition. That is, since

$$a - c = b - c \quad \text{is equivalent to} \quad a + (-c) = b + (-c),$$

the addition principle tells us that we can "subtract the same number on both sides of the equation."

EXAMPLE 6 Solve: $x + 5 = -7$.

We have

$$\begin{aligned} x + 5 &= -7 \\ x + 5 - 5 &= -7 - 5 \qquad &\text{Using the addition principle: adding } -5 \text{ on} \\ & &\text{both sides or subtracting 5 on both sides} \\ x + 0 &= -12 \qquad &\text{Simplifying} \\ x &= -12. \qquad &\text{Identity property of 0} \end{aligned}$$

9. Solve using the addition principle, subtracting 5 on both sides:

$$x + 5 = -8.$$

To check the answer, we substitute -12 in the original equation.

Check:
$$\begin{array}{c} x + 5 = -7 \\ \hline -12 + 5 \; ? \; -7 \\ -7 \; \Big| \qquad \text{TRUE} \end{array}$$

The solution of the original equation is -12.

In Example 6, to get x alone, we used the addition principle and subtracted 5 on both sides. This eliminated the 5 on the left. We started with $x + 5 = -7$, and, using the addition principle, we found a simpler equation $x = -12$ for which it was easy to *"see"* the solution. The equations $x + 5 = -7$ and $x = -12$ are *equivalent*.

Do Exercise 9.

Now we use the addition principle to solve an equation that involves a subtraction.

10. Solve: $t - 3 = 19$.

EXAMPLE 7 Solve: $a - 4 = 10$.

We have

$$\begin{aligned} a - 4 &= 10 \\ a - 4 + 4 &= 10 + 4 \qquad &\text{Using the addition principle: adding 4 on} \\ & &\text{both sides} \\ a + 0 &= 14 \qquad &\text{Simplifying} \\ a &= 14. \qquad &\text{Identity property of 0} \end{aligned}$$

Check:
$$\begin{array}{c} a - 4 = 10 \\ \hline 14 - 4 \; ? \; 10 \\ 10 \; \Big| \qquad \text{TRUE} \end{array}$$

The solution is 14.

Do Exercise 10.

EXAMPLE 8 Solve: $-6.5 = y - 8.4$.

We have

$$-6.5 = y - 8.4$$

$$-6.5 + 8.4 = y - 8.4 + 8.4$$ Using the addition principle: adding 8.4 on both sides to eliminate -8.4 on the right

$$1.9 = y.$$

Check:
$$-6.5 = y - 8.4$$
$$\overline{-6.5 \; ? \; 1.9 - 8.4}$$
$$\quad | \; -6.5 \qquad \text{TRUE}$$

The solution is 1.9.

Note that equations are reversible. That is, if $a = b$ is true, then $b = a$ is true. Thus when we solve $-6.5 = y - 8.4$, we can reverse it and solve $y - 8.4 = -6.5$ if we wish.

Do Exercises 11 and 12.

EXAMPLE 9 Solve: $-\dfrac{2}{3} + x = \dfrac{5}{2}$.

We have

$$-\frac{2}{3} + x = \frac{5}{2}$$

$$\frac{2}{3} - \frac{2}{3} + x = \frac{2}{3} + \frac{5}{2}$$ Adding $\frac{2}{3}$ on both sides

$$x = \frac{2}{3} + \frac{5}{2}$$

$$x = \frac{2}{3} \cdot \frac{2}{2} + \frac{5}{2} \cdot \frac{3}{3}$$ Multiplying by 1 to obtain equivalent fraction expressions with the least common denominator 6

$$x = \frac{4}{6} + \frac{15}{6}$$

$$x = \frac{19}{6}.$$

Check:
$$-\frac{2}{3} + x = \frac{5}{2}$$
$$\overline{-\frac{2}{3} + \frac{19}{6} \; ? \; \frac{5}{2}}$$
$$-\frac{4}{6} + \frac{19}{6}$$
$$\frac{15}{6}$$
$$\frac{5}{2} \qquad \text{TRUE}$$

The solution is $\dfrac{19}{6}$.

Do Exercises 13 and 14.

Solve.

11. $8.7 = n - 4.5$

12. $y + 17.4 = 10.9$

Solve.

13. $x + \dfrac{1}{2} = -\dfrac{3}{2}$

14. $t - \dfrac{13}{4} = \dfrac{5}{8}$

Answers on page A-7

2.1 Solving Equations: The Addition Principle

a Determine whether the given number is a solution of the given equation.

1. 15; $x + 17 = 32$

2. 35; $t + 17 = 53$

3. 21; $x - 7 = 12$

4. 36; $a - 19 = 17$

5. -7; $6x = 54$

6. -9; $8y = -72$

7. 30; $\dfrac{x}{6} = 5$

8. 49; $\dfrac{y}{8} = 6$

9. 19; $5x + 7 = 107$

10. 9; $9x + 5 = 86$

11. -11; $7(y - 1) = 63$

12. -18; $x + 3 = 3 + x$

b Solve using the addition principle. Don't forget to check!

13. $x + 2 = 6$

Check: $x + 2 = 6$
$$\overline{}$$
?

14. $y + 4 = 11$

Check: $y + 4 = 11$
$$\overline{}$$
?

15. $x + 15 = -5$

Check: $x + 15 = -5$
$$\overline{}$$
?

16. $t + 10 = 44$

Check: $t + 10 = 44$
$$\overline{}$$
?

17. $x + 6 = -8$

Check: $x + 6 = -8$
$$\overline{}$$
?

18. $z + 9 = -14$

19. $x + 16 = -2$

20. $m + 18 = -13$

21. $x - 9 = 6$

22. $x - 11 = 12$

23. $x - 7 = -21$

24. $x - 3 = -14$

25. $5 + t = 7$

26. $8 + y = 12$

27. $-7 + y = 13$

28. $-8 + y = 17$

29. $-3 + t = -9$

30. $-8 + t = -24$

31. $x + \dfrac{1}{2} = 7$

32. $24 = -\dfrac{7}{10} + r$

33. $12 = a - 7.9$

34. $2.8 + y = 11$

35. $r + \dfrac{1}{3} = \dfrac{8}{3}$

36. $t + \dfrac{3}{8} = \dfrac{5}{8}$

37. $m + \dfrac{5}{6} = -\dfrac{11}{12}$

38. $x + \dfrac{2}{3} = -\dfrac{5}{6}$

39. $x - \dfrac{5}{6} = \dfrac{7}{8}$

40. $y - \dfrac{3}{4} = \dfrac{5}{6}$

41. $-\dfrac{1}{5} + z = -\dfrac{1}{4}$

42. $-\dfrac{1}{8} + y = -\dfrac{3}{4}$

43. $7.4 = x + 2.3$

44. $8.4 = 5.7 + y$

45. $7.6 = x - 4.8$

46. $8.6 = x - 7.4$

47. $-9.7 = -4.7 + y$

48. $-7.8 = 2.8 + x$

49. $5\dfrac{1}{6} + x = 7$

50. $5\dfrac{1}{4} = 4\dfrac{2}{3} + x$

51. $q + \dfrac{1}{3} = -\dfrac{1}{7}$

52. $52\dfrac{3}{8} = -84 + x$

53. D_W Explain the difference between equivalent expressions and equivalent equations.

54. D_W When solving an equation using the addition principle, how do you determine which number to add or subtract on both sides of the equation?

SKILL MAINTENANCE

55. Add: $-3 + (-8)$. [1.3a]

56. Subtract: $-3 - (-8)$. [1.4a]

57. Multiply: $-\dfrac{2}{3} \cdot \dfrac{5}{8}$. [1.5a]

58. Divide: $-\dfrac{3}{7} \div \left(-\dfrac{9}{7}\right)$. [1.6c]

59. Divide: $\dfrac{2}{3} \div \left(-\dfrac{4}{9}\right)$. [1.6c]

60. Add: $-8.6 + 3.4$. [1.3a]

61. Subtract: $-\dfrac{2}{3} - \left(-\dfrac{5}{8}\right)$. [1.4a]

62. Multiply: $(-25.4)(-6.8)$. [1.5a]

Translate to an algebraic expression. [1.1b]

63. Jane had $83 before paying x dollars for a pair of tennis shoes. How much does she have left?

64. Justin drove his S-10 pickup truck 65 mph for t hours. How far did he drive?

SYNTHESIS

Solve.

65. $-356.788 = -699.034 + t$

66. $-\dfrac{4}{5} + \dfrac{7}{10} = x - \dfrac{3}{4}$

67. $x + \dfrac{4}{5} = -\dfrac{2}{3} - \dfrac{4}{15}$

68. $8 - 25 = 8 + x - 21$

69. $16 + x - 22 = -16$

70. $x + x = x$

71. $x + 3 = 3 + x$

72. $x + 4 = 5 + x$

73. $-\dfrac{3}{2} + x = -\dfrac{5}{17} - \dfrac{3}{2}$

74. $|x| = 5$

75. $|x| + 6 = 19$

2.2 SOLVING EQUATIONS: THE MULTIPLICATION PRINCIPLE

Objective

a Solve equations using the multiplication principle.

1. Solve. Multiply on both sides.

$$6x = 90$$

a Using the Multiplication Principle

Suppose that $a = b$ is true, and we multiply a by some number c. We get the same number if we multiply b by c, because a and b are the same number.

> **THE MULTIPLICATION PRINCIPLE FOR EQUATIONS**
>
> For any real numbers a, b, and c, $c \neq 0$,
>
> $$a = b \quad \text{is equivalent to} \quad a \cdot c = b \cdot c.$$

When using the multiplication principle, we sometimes say that we "multiply on both sides of the equation by the same number."

EXAMPLE 1 Solve: $5x = 70$.

To get x alone, we multiply by the *multiplicative inverse*, or *reciprocal*, of 5. Then we get the *multiplicative identity* 1 times x, or $1 \cdot x$, which simplifies to x. This allows us to eliminate 5 on the left.

$$5x = 70 \qquad \text{The reciprocal of 5 is } \tfrac{1}{5}.$$

$$\frac{1}{5} \cdot 5x = \frac{1}{5} \cdot 70 \qquad \text{Multiplying by } \tfrac{1}{5} \text{ to get } 1 \cdot x \text{ and eliminate 5 on the left}$$

$$1 \cdot x = 14 \qquad \text{Simplifying}$$

$$x = 14 \qquad \text{Identity property of 1: } 1 \cdot x = x$$

2. Solve. Divide on both sides.

$$4x = -7$$

Check:
$$\frac{5x = 70}{5 \cdot 14 \;?\; 70}$$
$$70 \;|\quad \text{TRUE}$$

The solution is 14.

The multiplication principle also tells us that we can "divide on both sides of the equation by a nonzero number." This is because division is the same as multiplying by a reciprocal. That is,

$$\frac{a}{c} = \frac{b}{c} \quad \text{is equivalent to} \quad a \cdot \frac{1}{c} = b \cdot \frac{1}{c}, \quad \text{when } c \neq 0.$$

In an expression like $5x$ in Example 1, the number 5 is called the **coefficient.** Example 1 could be done as follows, dividing on both sides by 5, the coefficient of x.

EXAMPLE 2 Solve: $5x = 70$.

$$5x = 70$$

$$\frac{5x}{5} = \frac{70}{5} \qquad \text{Dividing by 5 on both sides}$$

$$1 \cdot x = 14 \qquad \text{Simplifying}$$

$$x = 14 \qquad \text{Identity property of 1}$$

Answers on page A-7

CHAPTER 2: Solving Equations and Inequalities

Do Exercises 1 and 2 on the preceding page.

3. Solve: $-6x = 108$.

EXAMPLE 3 Solve: $-4x = 92$.

We have

$$-4x = 92$$

$$\frac{-4x}{-4} = \frac{92}{-4}$$ Using the multiplication principle. Dividing by -4 on both sides is the same as multiplying by $-\frac{1}{4}$.

$$1 \cdot x = -23$$ Simplifying

$$x = -23.$$ Identity property of 1

Check: $$\frac{-4x = 92}{-4(-23) \; ? \; 92}$$
$$92 \; | \qquad \text{TRUE}$$

The solution is -23.

Do Exercise 3.

4. Solve: $-x = -10$.

EXAMPLE 4 Solve: $-x = 9$.

We have

$$-x = 9$$

$$-1 \cdot x = 9$$ Using the property of -1: $-x = -1 \cdot x$

$$\frac{-1 \cdot x}{-1} = \frac{9}{-1}$$ Dividing by -1 on both sides

$$1 \cdot x = -9$$

$$x = -9.$$

Check: $$\frac{-x = 9}{-(-9) \; ? \; 9}$$
$$9 \; | \qquad \text{TRUE}$$

The solution is -9.

Do Exercise 4.

5. Solve: $-x = -10$.

We can also solve the equation $-x = 9$ by multiplying as follows.

EXAMPLE 5 Solve: $-x = 9$.

We have

$$-x = 9$$

$$-1(-x) = -1 \cdot 9$$ Multiplying by -1 on both sides

$$-1 \cdot (-1) \cdot x = -9$$

$$1 \cdot x = -9$$

$$x = -9.$$

The solution is -9.

Do Exercise 5.

Answers on page A-7

6. Solve: $\dfrac{2}{3} = -\dfrac{5}{6}\,y.$

In practice, it is generally more convenient to divide on both sides of the equation if the coefficient of the variable is in decimal notation or is an integer. If the coefficient is in fraction notation, it is more convenient to multiply by a reciprocal.

EXAMPLE 6 Solve: $\dfrac{3}{8} = -\dfrac{5}{4}x.$

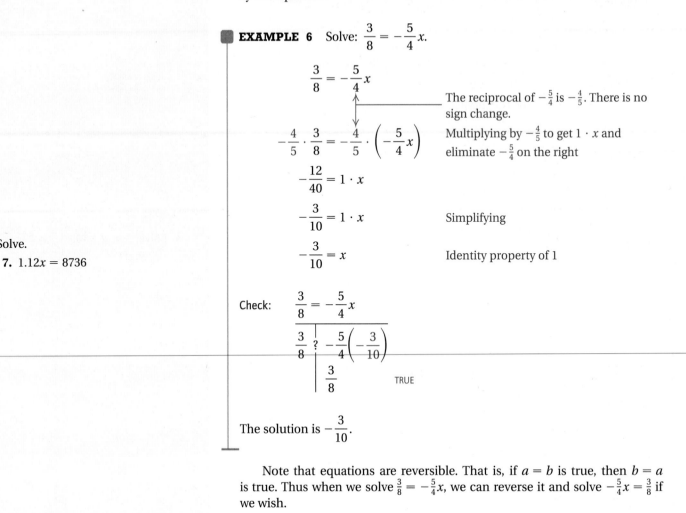

$$\frac{3}{8} = -\frac{5}{4}x$$

The reciprocal of $-\frac{5}{4}$ is $-\frac{4}{5}$. There is no sign change.

$$-\frac{4}{5} \cdot \frac{3}{8} = -\frac{4}{5} \cdot \left(-\frac{5}{4}x\right)$$

Multiplying by $-\frac{4}{5}$ to get $1 \cdot x$ and eliminate $-\frac{5}{4}$ on the right

$$-\frac{12}{40} = 1 \cdot x$$

$$-\frac{3}{10} = 1 \cdot x$$ Simplifying

$$-\frac{3}{10} = x$$ Identity property of 1

Check:
$$\frac{3}{8} = -\frac{5}{4}x$$

$$\frac{3}{8} \;\overset{?}{\mid}\; -\frac{5}{4}\left(-\frac{3}{10}\right)$$

$$\frac{3}{8} \qquad \text{TRUE}$$

The solution is $-\dfrac{3}{10}$.

Note that equations are reversible. That is, if $a = b$ is true, then $b = a$ is true. Thus when we solve $\frac{3}{8} = -\frac{5}{4}x$, we can reverse it and solve $-\frac{5}{4}x = \frac{3}{8}$ if we wish.

Do Exercise 6.

EXAMPLE 7 Solve: $1.16y = 9744.$

$$1.16y = 9744$$

$$\frac{1.16y}{1.16} = \frac{9744}{1.16}$$ Dividing by 1.16 on both sides

$$y = \frac{9744}{1.16}$$

$$y = 8400$$ Using a calculator to divide

Check:
$$1.16y = 9744$$

$$1.16(8400) \;\overset{?}{\mid}\; 9744$$

$$9744 \;\mid\; \qquad \text{TRUE}$$

The solution is 8400.

Solve.

7. $1.12x = 8736$

8. $6.3 = -2.1y$

Answers on page A-7

Do Exercises 7 and 8.

Now we use the multiplication principle to solve an equation that involves division.

EXAMPLE 8 Solve: $\dfrac{-y}{9} = 14$.

$$\frac{-y}{9} = 14$$

$$9 \cdot \frac{-y}{9} = 9 \cdot 14 \qquad \text{Multiplying by 9 on both sides}$$

$$-y = 126$$

$$-1 \cdot (-y) = -1 \cdot 126 \qquad \text{Multiplying by } -1 \text{ on both sides}$$

$$y = -126$$

Check:
$$\frac{-y}{9} = 14$$

$$\frac{-(-126)}{9} \; ? \; 14$$

$$\frac{126}{9}$$

$$14 \qquad \text{TRUE}$$

The solution is -126.

9. Solve: $-14 = \dfrac{-y}{2}$.

There are other ways to solve the equation in Example 8. One is by multiplying by -9 on both sides as follows:

$$-9 \cdot \frac{-y}{9} = -9 \cdot 14$$

$$\frac{(-9)(-y)}{9} = -126$$

$$\frac{9y}{9} = -126$$

$$y = -126.$$

Do Exercise 9.

Answer on page A-7

Study Tips **TIME MANAGEMENT (PART 1)**

Time is the most critical factor in your success in learning mathematics. Have reasonable expectations about the time you need to study math. (See also the Study Tips on time management in Sections 5.2 and 5.6.)

- **Juggling time.** Working 40 hours per week and taking 12 credit hours is equivalent to working two full-time jobs. Can you handle such a load? Your ratio of number of work hours to number of credit hours should be about 40/3, 30/6, 20/9, 10/12, or 5/14.

- **A rule of thumb on study time.** Budget about 2–3 hours for homework and study per week for every hour of class time.

"You cannot increase the quality or quantity of your achievement or performance except to the degree in which you increase your ability to use time effectively."

Brian Tracy, motivational speaker

147

2.2 Solving Equations:
The Multiplication Principle

2.2

EXERCISE SET

For Extra Help

Math XL   MyMathLab   InterAct   Math Tutor   Digital Video   Student's
                        Math   Center   Tutor CD 2   Solutions
MathXL   MyMathLab   Videotape 3   Manual

a   Solve using the multiplication principle. Don't forget to check!

1. $6x = 36$

Check: $6x = 36$
$$\overline{}$$
$?$

2. $3x = 51$

Check: $3x = 51$
$$\overline{}$$
$?$

3. $5x = 45$

Check: $5x = 45$
$$\overline{}$$
$?$

4. $8x = 72$

Check: $8x = 72$
$$\overline{}$$
$?$

5. $84 = 7x$

6. $63 = 9x$

7. $-x = 40$

8. $53 = -x$

9. $-x = -1$

10. $-47 = -t$

11. $7x = -49$

12. $8x = -56$

13. $-12x = 72$

14. $-15x = 105$

15. $-21x = -126$

16. $-13x = -104$

17. $\dfrac{t}{7} = -9$

18. $\dfrac{y}{-8} = 11$

19. $\dfrac{3}{4}x = 27$

20. $\dfrac{4}{5}x = 16$

21. $\dfrac{-t}{3} = 7$

22. $\dfrac{-x}{6} = 9$

23. $-\dfrac{m}{3} = \dfrac{1}{5}$

24. $\dfrac{1}{8} = -\dfrac{y}{5}$

25. $-\dfrac{3}{5}r = \dfrac{9}{10}$

26. $\dfrac{2}{5}y = -\dfrac{4}{15}$

27. $-\dfrac{3}{2}r = -\dfrac{27}{4}$

28. $-\dfrac{3}{8}x = -\dfrac{15}{16}$

CHAPTER 2: Solving Equations
and Inequalities

29. $6.3x = 44.1$

30. $2.7y = 54$

31. $-3.1y = 21.7$

32. $-3.3y = 6.6$

33. $38.7m = 309.6$

34. $29.4m = 235.2$

35. $-\dfrac{2}{3}y = -10.6$

36. $-\dfrac{9}{7}y = 12.06$

37. $\dfrac{-x}{5} = 10$

38. $\dfrac{-x}{8} = -16$

39. $-\dfrac{t}{2} = 7$

40. $\dfrac{m}{-3} = 10$

41. $\mathbf{D_W}$ When solving an equation using the multiplication principle, how do you determine by what number to multiply or divide on both sides of the equation?

42. $\mathbf{D_W}$ Are the equations $x = 5$ and $x^2 = 25$ equivalent? Why or why not?

SKILL MAINTENANCE

Collect like terms.   [1.7e]

43. $3x + 4x$

44. $6x + 5 - 7x$

45. $-4x + 11 - 6x + 18x$

46. $8y - 16y - 24y$

Remove parentheses and simplify.   [1.8b]

47. $3x - (4 + 2x)$

48. $2 - 5(x + 5)$

49. $8y - 6(3y + 7)$

50. $-2a - 4(5a - 1)$

Translate to an algebraic expression.   [1.1b]

51. Patty drives her van for 8 hr at a speed of r mph. How far does she drive?

52. A triangle has a height of 10 meters and a base of b meters. What is the area of the triangle?

SYNTHESIS

Solve.

53. $-0.2344m = 2028.732$

54. $0 \cdot x = 0$

55. $0 \cdot x = 9$

56. $4|x| = 48$

57. $2|x| = -12$

Solve for x.

58. $ax = 5a$

59. $3x = \dfrac{b}{a}$

60. $cx = a^2 + 1$

61. $\dfrac{a}{b}x = 4$

62. A student makes a calculation and gets an answer of 22.5. On the last step, she multiplies by 0.3 when she should have divided by 0.3. What is the correct answer?

149

Objectives

a Solve equations using both the addition and the multiplication principles.

b Solve equations in which like terms may need to be collected.

c Solve equations by first removing parentheses and collecting like terms; solve equations with no solutions and equations with an infinite number of solutions.

1. Solve: $9x + 6 = 51$.

Solve.

2. $8x - 4 = 28$

3. $-\frac{1}{2}x + 3 = 1$

2.3 USING THE PRINCIPLES TOGETHER

a Applying Both Principles

Consider the equation $3x + 4 = 13$. It is more complicated than those we discussed in the preceding two sections. In order to solve such an equation, we first isolate the x-term, $3x$, using the addition principle. Then we apply the multiplication principle to get x by itself.

EXAMPLE 1 Solve: $3x + 4 = 13$.

$$3x + 4 = 13$$
$$3x + 4 - 4 = 13 - 4 \qquad \text{Using the addition principle: subtracting 4 on both sides}$$

First isolate the x-term. $\longrightarrow 3x = 9$ Simplifying

$$\frac{3x}{3} = \frac{9}{3} \qquad \text{Using the multiplication principle: dividing by 3 on both sides}$$

Then isolate x. $\longrightarrow x = 3$ Simplifying

Check: $\dfrac{3x + 4 = 13}{\begin{array}{c|c} 3 \cdot 3 + 4 \ ? \ 13 \\ 9 + 4 \\ 13 \end{array}}$ TRUE We use the rules for order of operations to carry out the check. We find the product $3 \cdot 3$. Then we add 4.

The solution is 3.

Do Exercise 1.

EXAMPLE 2 Solve: $-5x - 6 = 16$.

$$-5x - 6 = 16$$
$$-5x - 6 + 6 = 16 + 6 \qquad \text{Adding 6 on both sides}$$
$$-5x = 22$$
$$\frac{-5x}{-5} = \frac{22}{-5} \qquad \text{Dividing by } -5 \text{ on both sides}$$
$$x = -\frac{22}{5}, \text{ or } -4\frac{2}{5} \qquad \text{Simplifying}$$

Check: $\dfrac{-5x - 6 = 16}{\begin{array}{c|c} -5\left(-\dfrac{22}{5}\right) - 6 \ ? \ 16 \\ 22 - 6 \\ 16 \end{array}}$ TRUE

The solution is $-\dfrac{22}{5}$.

Do Exercises 2 and 3.

Answers on page A-8

EXAMPLE 3 Solve: $45 - t = 13$.

$$45 - t = 13$$
$$-45 + 45 - t = -45 + 13 \qquad \text{Adding } -45 \text{ on both sides}$$
$$-t = -32$$
$$-1(-t) = -1(-32) \qquad \text{Multiplying by } -1 \text{ on both sides}$$
$$t = 32$$

The number 32 checks and is the solution.

Do Exercise 4.

EXAMPLE 4 Solve: $16.3 - 7.2y = -8.18$.

$$16.3 - 7.2y = -8.18$$
$$-16.3 + 16.3 - 7.2y = -16.3 + (-8.18) \qquad \begin{array}{l}\text{Adding } -16.3 \text{ on} \\ \text{both sides}\end{array}$$
$$-7.2y = -24.48$$
$$\frac{-7.2y}{-7.2} = \frac{-24.48}{-7.2} \qquad \begin{array}{l}\text{Dividing by } -7.2 \text{ on} \\ \text{both sides}\end{array}$$
$$y = 3.4$$

Check: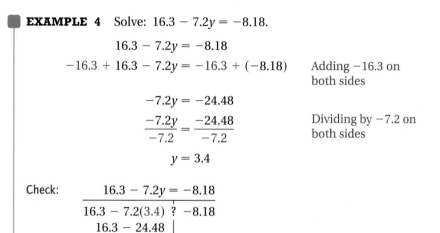

$$\begin{array}{c} 16.3 - 7.2y = -8.18 \\ \hline 16.3 - 7.2(3.4) \ ? \ -8.18 \\ 16.3 - 24.48 \ \Big| \\ -8.18 \ \Big| \qquad \text{TRUE} \end{array}$$

The solution is 3.4.

Do Exercises 5 and 6.

---

b Collecting Like Terms

If there are like terms on one side of the equation, we collect them before using the addition or the multiplication principle.

EXAMPLE 5 Solve: $3x + 4x = -14$.

$$3x + 4x = -14$$
$$7x = -14 \qquad \text{Collecting like terms}$$
$$\frac{7x}{7} = \frac{-14}{7} \qquad \text{Dividing by 7 on both sides}$$
$$x = -2$$

The number -2 checks, so the solution is -2.

Do Exercises 7 and 8.

If there are like terms on opposite sides of the equation, we get them on the same side by using the addition principle. Then we collect them. In other words, we get all terms with a variable on one side and all numbers on the other.

4. Solve: $-18 - m = -57$.

Solve.

5. $-4 - 8x = 8$

6. $41.68 = 4.7 - 8.6y$

Solve.

7. $4x + 3x = -21$

8. $x - 0.09x = 728$

Answers on page A-8

Solve.

9. $7y + 5 = 2y + 10$

10. $5 - 2y = 3y - 5$

EXAMPLE 6 Solve: $2x - 2 = -3x + 3$.

$$2x - 2 = -3x + 3$$
$$2x - 2 + 2 = -3x + 3 + 2 \qquad \text{Adding 2}$$
$$2x = -3x + 5 \qquad \text{Collecting like terms}$$
$$2x + 3x = -3x + 3x + 5 \qquad \text{Adding } 3x$$
$$5x = 5 \qquad \text{Simplifying}$$
$$\frac{5x}{5} = \frac{5}{5} \qquad \text{Dividing by 5}$$
$$x = 1 \qquad \text{Simplifying}$$

Check:

$$\begin{array}{c|c} \multicolumn{2}{c}{2x - 2 = -3x + 3} \\ \hline 2 \cdot 1 - 2 \;?\; -3 \cdot 1 + 3 & \text{Substituting in the original equation} \\ 2 - 2 \;|\; -3 + 3 \\ 0 \;|\; 0 & \text{TRUE} \end{array}$$

The solution is 1.

Do Exercises 9 and 10.

In Example 6, we used the addition principle to get all terms with a variable on one side and all numbers on the other side. Then we collected like terms and proceeded as before. If there are like terms on one side at the outset, they should be collected before proceeding.

Solve.

11. $7x - 17 + 2x = 2 - 8x + 15$

12. $3x - 15 = 5x + 2 - 4x$

EXAMPLE 7 Solve: $6x + 5 - 7x = 10 - 4x + 3$.

$$6x + 5 - 7x = 10 - 4x + 3$$
$$-x + 5 = 13 - 4x \qquad \text{Collecting like terms}$$
$$4x - x + 5 = 13 - 4x + 4x \qquad \begin{array}{l} \text{Adding } 4x \text{ to get all terms with a} \\ \text{variable on one side} \end{array}$$
$$3x + 5 = 13 \qquad \begin{array}{l} \text{Simplifying; that is, collecting} \\ \text{like terms} \end{array}$$
$$3x + 5 - 5 = 13 - 5 \qquad \text{Subtracting 5}$$
$$3x = 8 \qquad \text{Simplifying}$$
$$\frac{3x}{3} = \frac{8}{3} \qquad \text{Dividing by 3}$$
$$x = \frac{8}{3} \qquad \text{Simplifying}$$

The number $\frac{8}{3}$ checks, so it is the solution.

Do Exercises 11 and 12.

CLEARING FRACTIONS AND DECIMALS

In general, equations are easier to solve if they do not contain fractions or decimals. Consider, for example,

$$\frac{1}{2}x + 5 = \frac{3}{4} \quad \text{and} \quad 2.3x + 7 = 5.4.$$

Answers on page A-8

If we multiply by 4 on both sides of the first equation and by 10 on both sides of the second equation, we have

$$4\left(\frac{1}{2}x + 5\right) = 4 \cdot \frac{3}{4} \quad \text{and} \qquad 10(2.3x + 7) = 10 \cdot 5.4$$

$$4 \cdot \frac{1}{2}x + 4 \cdot 5 = 4 \cdot \frac{3}{4} \quad \text{and} \quad 10 \cdot 2.3x + 10 \cdot 7 = 10 \cdot 5.4$$

$$2x + 20 = 3 \qquad \text{and} \qquad 23x + 70 = 54.$$

The first equation has been "cleared of fractions" and the second equation has been "cleared of decimals." Both resulting equations are equivalent to the original equations and are easier to solve. *It is your choice* whether to clear fractions or decimals, but doing so often eases computations.

The easiest way to clear an equation of fractions is to multiply *every term on both sides* by the **least common multiple of all the denominators.**

EXAMPLE 8 Solve: $\frac{2}{3}x - \frac{1}{6} + \frac{1}{2}x = \frac{7}{6} + 2x$.

The number 6 is the least common multiple of all the denominators. We multiply by 6 on both sides.

$$6\left(\frac{2}{3}x - \frac{1}{6} + \frac{1}{2}x\right) = 6\left(\frac{7}{6} + 2x\right) \qquad \text{Multiplying by 6 on both sides}$$

$$6 \cdot \frac{2}{3}x - 6 \cdot \frac{1}{6} + 6 \cdot \frac{1}{2}x = 6 \cdot \frac{7}{6} + 6 \cdot 2x \qquad \begin{array}{l}\text{Using the distributive law}\\ (\textit{Caution!} \text{ Be sure to multiply}\\ \textit{all} \text{ the terms by 6.)}\end{array}$$

$4x - 1 + 3x = 7 + 12x$	Simplifying. Note that the fractions are cleared.
$7x - 1 = 7 + 12x$	Collecting like terms
$7x - 1 - 12x = 7 + 12x - 12x$	Subtracting $12x$
$-5x - 1 = 7$	Collecting like terms
$-5x - 1 + 1 = 7 + 1$	Adding 1
$-5x = 8$	Collecting like terms
$\dfrac{-5x}{-5} = \dfrac{8}{-5}$	Dividing by -5
$x = -\dfrac{8}{5}$	

Check:

$$\frac{2}{3}x - \frac{1}{6} + \frac{1}{2}x = \frac{7}{6} + 2x$$

$$\frac{2}{3}\left(-\frac{8}{5}\right) - \frac{1}{6} + \frac{1}{2}\left(-\frac{8}{5}\right) \; ? \; \frac{7}{6} + 2\left(-\frac{8}{5}\right)$$

$$-\frac{16}{15} - \frac{1}{6} - \frac{8}{10} \; \Big| \; \frac{7}{6} - \frac{16}{5}$$

$$-\frac{32}{30} - \frac{5}{30} - \frac{24}{30} \; \Big| \; \frac{35}{30} - \frac{96}{30}$$

$$\frac{-32 - 5 - 24}{30} \; \Big| \; -\frac{61}{30}$$

$$-\frac{61}{30} \; \Big| \qquad\qquad \text{TRUE}$$

13. Solve: $\frac{7}{8}x - \frac{1}{4} + \frac{1}{2}x = \frac{3}{4} + x.$

The solution is $-\frac{8}{5}$.

Do Exercise 13.

To illustrate clearing decimals, we repeat Example 4, but this time we clear the equation of decimals first. Compare both methods.

To clear an equation of decimals, we count the greatest number of decimal places in any one number. If the greatest number of decimal places is 1, we multiply every term on both sides by 10; if it is 2, we multiply by 100; and so on.

14. Solve: $41.68 = 4.7 - 8.6y.$

EXAMPLE 9 Solve: $16.3 - 7.2y = -8.18.$

The greatest number of decimal places in any one number is *two*. Multiplying by 100, which has *two* 0's, will clear all decimals.

$$100(16.3 - 7.2y) = 100(-8.18) \qquad \text{Multiplying by 100 on both sides}$$

$$100(16.3) - 100(7.2y) = 100(-8.18) \qquad \text{Using the distributive law}$$

$$1630 - 720y = -818 \qquad \text{Simplifying}$$

$$1630 - 720y - 1630 = -818 - 1630 \qquad \text{Subtracting 1630}$$

$$-720y = -2448 \qquad \text{Collecting like terms}$$

$$\frac{-720y}{-720} = \frac{-2448}{-720} \qquad \text{Dividing by } -720$$

Solve.

15. $2(2y + 3) = 14$

$$y = \frac{17}{5}, \text{ or } 3.4$$

The number $\frac{17}{5}$, or 3.4, checks, as shown in Example 4, so it is the solution.

Do Exercise 14.

C Equations Containing Parentheses

To solve certain kinds of equations that contain parentheses, we first use the distributive laws to remove the parentheses. Then we proceed as before.

EXAMPLE 10 Solve: $8x = 2(12 - 2x).$

16. $5(3x - 2) = 35$

$$8x = 2(12 - 2x)$$

$$8x = 24 - 4x \qquad \text{Using the distributive laws to multiply and remove parentheses}$$

$$8x + 4x = 24 - 4x + 4x \qquad \text{Adding } 4x \text{ to get all the } x\text{-terms on one side}$$

$$12x = 24 \qquad \text{Collecting like terms}$$

$$\frac{12x}{12} = \frac{24}{12} \qquad \text{Dividing by 12}$$

$$x = 2$$

The number 2 checks, so the solution is 2.

Answers on page A-8

Do Exercises 15 and 16.

Here is a procedure for solving the types of equation discussed in this section.

AN EQUATION-SOLVING PROCEDURE

1. Multiply on both sides to clear the equation of fractions or decimals. (This is optional, but it can ease computations.)
2. If parentheses occur, multiply to remove them using the *distributive laws*.
3. Collect like terms on each side, if necessary.
4. Get all terms with variables on one side and all numbers (constant terms) on the other side, using the *addition principle*.
5. Collect like terms again, if necessary.
6. Multiply or divide to solve for the variable, using the *multiplication principle*.
7. Check all possible solutions in the original equation.

EXAMPLE 11 Solve: $2 - 5(x + 5) = 3(x - 2) - 1$.

$$2 - 5(x + 5) = 3(x - 2) - 1$$
$$2 - 5x - 25 = 3x - 6 - 1 \qquad \text{Using the distributive laws to multiply and remove parentheses}$$
$$-5x - 23 = 3x - 7 \qquad \text{Collecting like terms}$$
$$-5x - 23 + 5x = 3x - 7 + 5x \qquad \text{Adding } 5x$$
$$-23 = 8x - 7 \qquad \text{Collecting like terms}$$
$$-23 + 7 = 8x - 7 + 7 \qquad \text{Adding } 7$$
$$-16 = 8x \qquad \text{Collecting like terms}$$
$$\frac{-16}{8} = \frac{8x}{8} \qquad \text{Dividing by 8}$$
$$-2 = x$$

Check:
$$\begin{array}{c|c} \multicolumn{2}{c}{2 - 5(x + 5) = 3(x - 2) - 1} \\ \hline 2 - 5(-2 + 5) \ ? \ 3(-2 - 2) - 1 \\ 2 - 5(3) & 3(-4) - 1 \\ 2 - 15 & -12 - 1 \\ -13 & -13 \qquad \text{TRUE} \end{array}$$

The solution is -2.

Do Exercises 17 and 18.

EQUATIONS WITH INFINITELY MANY SOLUTIONS

The types of equations we have considered thus far in Sections 2.1–2.3 have all had exactly one solution. We now look at two other possibilities.
    Consider

$$3 + x = x + 3.$$

Let's explore the solutions in Margin Exercises 19–22.

Do Exercises 19–22.

Solve.

17. $3(7 + 2x) = 30 + 7(x - 1)$

18. $4(3 + 5x) - 4 = 3 + 2(x - 2)$

Determine whether the given number is a solution of the given equation.

19. $10; \quad 3 + x = x + 3$

20. $-7; \quad 3 + x = x + 3$

21. $\dfrac{1}{2}; \quad 3 + x = x + 3$

22. $0; \quad 3 + x = x + 3$

Answers on page A-8

Determine whether the given number is a solution of the given equation.

23. 10; $3 + x = x + 8$

24. -7; $3 + x = x + 8$

25. $\dfrac{1}{2}$; $3 + x = x + 8$

26. 0; $3 + x = x + 8$

Solve.

27. $30 + 5(x + 3) = -3 + 5x + 48$

28. $2x + 7(x - 4) = 13 + 9x$

Answers on page A-8

We know by the commutative law of addition that this equation holds for any replacement of x with a real number. (See Section 1.7.) We have confirmed some of these solutions in Margin Exercises 19–22. Suppose we try to solve this equation using the addition principle:

$$3 + x = x + 3$$
$$-x + 3 + x = -x + x + 3 \qquad \text{Adding } -x$$
$$3 = 3. \qquad \text{TRUE}$$

We end with a true equation. The original equation holds for all real-number replacements. Every real number is a solution. Thus the number of solutions is **infinite.**

EXAMPLE 12 Solve: $7x - 17 = 4 + 7(x - 3)$.

$$7x - 17 = 4 + 7(x - 3)$$
$$7x - 17 = 4 + 7x - 21 \qquad \text{Using the distributive law to multiply and remove parentheses}$$
$$7x - 17 = 7x - 17 \qquad \text{Collecting like terms}$$
$$-7x + 7x - 17 = -7x + 7x - 17 \qquad \text{Adding } -7x$$
$$-17 = -17 \qquad \text{TRUE}$$

Every real number is a solution. There are infinitely many solutions.

EQUATIONS WITH NO SOLUTION

Now consider

$$3 + x = x + 8.$$

Let's explore the solutions in Margin Exercises 23–26.

Do Exercises 23–26.

None of the replacements in Margin Exercises 23–26 is a solution of the given equation. In fact, there are no solutions. Let's try to solve this equation using the addition principle:

$$3 + x = x + 8$$
$$-x + 3 + x = -x + x + 8 \qquad \text{Adding } -x$$
$$3 = 8. \qquad \text{FALSE}$$

We end with a false equation. The original equation is false for all real-number replacements. Thus it has **no** solutions.

EXAMPLE 13 Solve: $3x + 4(x + 2) = 11 + 7x$.

$$3x + 4(x + 2) = 11 + 7x$$
$$3x + 4x + 8 = 11 + 7x \qquad \text{Using the distributive law to multiply and remove parentheses}$$
$$7x + 8 = 11 + 7x \qquad \text{Collecting like terms}$$
$$7x + 8 - 7x = 11 + 7x - 7x \qquad \text{Subtracting } 7x$$
$$8 = 11 \qquad \text{FALSE}$$

There are no solutions.

Do Exercises 27 and 28.

The following is a guideline for solving linear equations of the types that we have considered in Sections 2.1–2.3.

RESULTING EQUATION	NUMBER OF SOLUTIONS	SOLUTION(S)
$x = a$, where a is a real number	One	The number a
A true equation such as $3 = 3$, $-11 = -11$, or $0 = 0$	Infinitely many	Every real number is a solution.
A false equation such as $3 = 8$, $-4 = 5$, or $0 = -5$	Zero	There are no solutions.

CALCULATOR CORNER

Checking Possible Solutions To check the possible solutions of an equation on a calculator, we can substitute and carry out the calculations on each side of the equation just as we do when we check by hand. To check the possible solution -2 in Example 11, for instance, we first substitute -2 for x in the expression on the left side of the equation. We press ② ⊖ ⑤ ❨ ⊝ ②
⊕ ⑤ ❩ **ENTER**. We get -13. Next, we substitute -2 for x in the expression on the right side of the equation. We then press ③ ❨ ⊝ ② ⊖ ② ❩
⊖ ① **ENTER**. Again we get -13. Since the two sides of the equation have the same value when x is -2, we know that -2 is the solution of the equation.

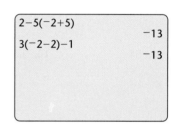

A table can also be used to check the possible solutions of an equation. First, we enter the left side and the right side of the equation on the Y = or equation editor screen. To do this, we first press ⟨Y=⟩. If an expression for Y1 is currently entered, we place the cursor on it and press **CLEAR** to delete it. We do the same for any other entries that are present.

Next, we position the cursor to the right of Y1 = and enter the left side of the equation by pressing ② ⊖
⑤ ❨ X,T,θ,n ⊕ ⑤ ❩. Then we position the cursor beside Y2 = and enter the right side of the equation by pressing ③ ❨ X,T,θ,n ⊖ ② ❩ ⊖ ①. Now we press **2ND** ⟨TBLSET⟩ to display the Table Setup screen. (TBLSET is the second operation associated with the ⟨WINDOW⟩ key.) On the Indpnt line, we position the cursor on "Ask" and press **ENTER** to set up a table in ASK mode. (The settings for TblStart and ΔTbl are irrelevant in ASK mode.)

Now we press **2ND** ⟨TABLE⟩ to display the table. (TABLE is the second operation associated with the ⟨GRAPH⟩ key.) We then enter the possible solution, -2, by pressing ⊝ ② **ENTER**. We see that Y1 $= -13 =$ Y2 for this value of x. This confirms that the left and right sides of the equation have the same value for $x = -2$, so -2 is the solution of the equation.

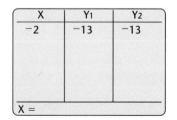

```
Plot1   Plot2   Plot3
\Y1 ▇ 2−5(X+5)
\Y2 ▇ 3(X−2)−1
\Y3 =
\Y4 =
\Y5 =
\Y6 =
\Y7 =
```

```
TABLE SETUP
 TblStart=1
 ΔTbl=1
Indpnt: Auto  [Ask]
Depend: [Auto]  Ask
```

X	Y1	Y2
−2	−13	−13
X =		

Exercises:

1. Use substitution to check the solutions found in Examples 6, 7, and 10.

2. Use a table set in ASK mode to check the solutions found in Examples 6, 7, and 10.

a Solve. Don't forget to check!

1. $5x + 6 = 31$

Check: $5x + 6 = 31$

2. $7x + 6 = 13$

Check: $7x + 6 = 13$

3. $8x + 4 = 68$

Check: $8x + 4 = 68$

4. $4y + 10 = 46$

Check: $4y + 10 = 46$

5. $4x - 6 = 34$

6. $5y - 2 = 53$

7. $3x - 9 = 33$

8. $4x - 19 = 5$

9. $7x + 2 = -54$

10. $5x + 4 = -41$

11. $-45 = 3 + 6y$

12. $-91 = 9t + 8$

13. $-4x + 7 = 35$

14. $-5x - 7 = 108$

15. $-8x - 24 = -29\dfrac{1}{3}$

16. $\dfrac{3}{2}x - 24 = -36$

b Solve.

17. $5x + 7x = 72$

Check: $5x + 7x = 72$

18. $8x + 3x = 55$

Check: $8x + 3x = 55$

19. $8x + 7x = 60$

Check: $8x + 7x = 60$

20. $8x + 5x = 104$

Check: $8x + 5x = 104$

21. $4x + 3x = 42$

22. $7x + 18x = 125$

23. $-6y - 3y = 27$

24. $-5y - 7y = 144$

25. $-7y - 8y = -15$

26. $-10y - 3y = -39$

27. $x + \dfrac{1}{3}x = 8$

28. $x + \dfrac{1}{4}x = 10$

29. $10.2y - 7.3y = -58$

30. $6.8y - 2.4y = -88$

31. $8y - 35 = 3y$

32. $4x - 6 = 6x$

33. $8x - 1 = 23 - 4x$

34. $5y - 2 = 28 - y$

35. $2x - 1 = 4 + x$

36. $4 - 3x = 6 - 7x$

37. $6x + 3 = 2x + 11$

38. $14 - 6a = -2a + 3$

39. $5 - 2x = 3x - 7x + 25$

40. $-7z + 2z - 3z - 7 = 17$

41. $4 + 3x - 6 = 3x + 2 - x$

42. $5 + 4x - 7 = 4x - 2 - x$

43. $4y - 4 + y + 24 = 6y + 20 - 4y$

44. $5y - 7 + y = 7y + 21 - 5y$

Solve. Clear fractions or decimals first.

45. $\dfrac{7}{2}x + \dfrac{1}{2}x = 3x + \dfrac{3}{2} + \dfrac{5}{2}x$

46. $\dfrac{7}{8}x - \dfrac{1}{4} + \dfrac{3}{4}x = \dfrac{1}{16} + x$

47. $\dfrac{2}{3} + \dfrac{1}{4}t = \dfrac{1}{3}$

48. $-\dfrac{3}{2} + x = -\dfrac{5}{6} - \dfrac{4}{3}$

49. $\dfrac{2}{3} + 3y = 5y - \dfrac{2}{15}$

50. $\dfrac{1}{2} + 4m = 3m - \dfrac{5}{2}$

51. $\dfrac{5}{3} + \dfrac{2}{3}x = \dfrac{25}{12} + \dfrac{5}{4}x + \dfrac{3}{4}$

52. $1 - \dfrac{2}{3}y = \dfrac{9}{5} - \dfrac{y}{5} + \dfrac{3}{5}$

53. $2.1x + 45.2 = 3.2 - 8.4x$

54. $0.96y - 0.79 = 0.21y + 0.46$

55. $1.03 - 0.62x = 0.71 - 0.22x$

56. $1.7t + 8 - 1.62t = 0.4t - 0.32 + 8$

57. $\dfrac{2}{7}x - \dfrac{1}{2}x = \dfrac{3}{4}x + 1$

58. $\dfrac{5}{16}y + \dfrac{3}{8}y = 2 + \dfrac{1}{4}y$

C   Solve.

59. $3(2y - 3) = 27$

60. $8(3x + 2) = 30$

61. $40 = 5(3x + 2)$

62. $9 = 3(5x - 2)$

63. $-23 + y = y + 25$

64. $17 - t = -t + 68$

65. $-23 + x = x - 23$

66. $y - \dfrac{2}{3} = -\dfrac{2}{3} + y$

67. $2(3 + 4m) - 9 = 45$

68. $5x + 5(4x - 1) = 20$

69. $5r - (2r + 8) = 16$

70. $6b - (3b + 8) = 16$

71. $6 - 2(3x - 1) = 2$

72. $10 - 3(2x - 1) = 1$

73. $5x + 5 - 7x = 15 - 12x + 10x - 10$

74. $3 - 7x + 10x - 14 = 9 - 6x + 9x - 20$

75. $22x - 5 - 15x + 3 = 10x - 4 - 3x + 11$

76. $11x - 6 - 4x + 1 = 9x - 8 - 2x + 12$

77. $5(d + 4) = 7(d - 2)$

78. $3(t - 2) = 9(t + 2)$

79. $8(2t + 1) = 4(7t + 7)$

80. $7(5x - 2) = 6(6x - 1)$

81. $3(r - 6) + 2 = 4(r + 2) - 21$

82. $5(t + 3) + 9 = 3(t - 2) + 6$

83. $19 - (2x + 3) = 2(x + 3) + x$

84. $13 - (2c + 2) = 2(c + 2) + 3c$

85. $2[4 - 2(3 - x)] - 1 = 4[2(4x - 3) + 7] - 25$

86. $5[3(7 - t) - 4(8 + 2t)] - 20 = -6[2(6 + 3t) - 4]$

87. $11 - 4(x + 1) - 3 = 11 + 2(4 - 2x) - 16$

88. $6(2x - 1) - 12 = 7 + 12(x - 1)$

89. $22x - 1 - 12x = 5(2x - 1) + 4$

90. $2 + 14x - 9 = 7(2x + 1) - 14$

91. $0.7(3x + 6) = 1.1 - (x + 2)$

92. $0.9(2x + 8) = 20 - (x + 5)$

93. $\mathbf{D_W}$ What procedure would you follow to solve an equation like $0.23x + \frac{17}{3} = -0.8 + \frac{3}{4}x$? Could your procedure be streamlined? If so, how?

94. $\mathbf{D_W}$ You are trying to explain to a classmate how equations can arise with infinitely many solutions and with no solutions. Give such an explanation. Does having no solution mean that 0 is a solution? Explain.

SKILL MAINTENANCE

95. Divide: $-22.1 \div 3.4$.　[1.6c]

96. Multiply: $-22.1(3.4)$.　[1.5a]

97. Factor: $7x - 21 - 14y$.　[1.7d]

98. Factor: $8y - 88x + 8$.　[1.7d]

Simplify.

99. $-3 + 2(-5)^2(-3) - 7$　[1.8d]

100. $3x + 2[4 - 5(2x - 1)]$　[1.8c]

101. $23(2x - 4) - 15(10 - 3x)$　[1.8b]

102. $256 \div 64 \div 4^2$　[1.8d]

SYNTHESIS

Solve.

103. $\frac{2}{3}\left(\frac{7}{8} - 4x\right) - \frac{5}{8} = \frac{3}{8}$

104. $\frac{1}{4}(8y + 4) - 17 = -\frac{1}{2}(4y - 8)$

105. $\frac{4 - 3x}{7} = \frac{2 + 5x}{49} - \frac{x}{14}$

106. The width of a rectangle is 5 ft, its length is $(3x + 2)$ ft, and its area is 75 ft². Find x.

Objectives

a Evaluate a formula.

b Solve a formula for a specified letter.

---

1. Storm Distance. Suppose that it takes the sound of thunder 14 sec to reach you. How far away is the storm?

---

2. Socks from Cotton. Referring to Example 2, find the number of socks that can be made from 65 bales of cotton.

---

a Evaluating Formulas

A **formula** is a "recipe" for doing a certain type of calculation. Formulas are often given as equations. When we replace the variables in an equation with numbers and calculate the result, we are **evaluating** the formula. We did some evaluating in Section 1.1.

Let's consider another example. A formula that has to do with weather is $M = \frac{1}{5}t$. You see a flash of lightning. After a few seconds you hear the thunder associated with that flash. How far away was the lightning?

Your distance from the storm is M miles. You can find that distance by counting the number of seconds t that it takes the sound of the thunder to reach you and then multiplying by $\frac{1}{5}$.

EXAMPLE 1 *Storm Distance.* Consider the formula $M = \frac{1}{5}t$. It takes 10 sec for the sound of thunder to reach you after you have seen a flash of lightning. How far away is the storm?

We substitute 10 for t and calculate M:

$$M = \frac{1}{5}t = \frac{1}{5}(10) = 2.$$

The storm is 2 mi away.

EXAMPLE 2 *Socks from Cotton.* Consider the formula $S = 4321x$, where S is the number of socks of normal size that can be produced from x bales of cotton. You see a shipment of 300 bales of cotton taken off a ship. How many socks can be made from the cotton?

Source: *Country Woman Magazine*

We substitute 300 for x and calculate S:

$$S = 4321x = 4321(300) = 1{,}296{,}300.$$

Thus, 1,296,300 socks can be made from 300 bales of cotton.

Do Exercises 1 and 2.

Answers on page A-8

EXAMPLE 3 *Distance, Rate, and Time.* The distance d that a car will travel at a rate, or speed, r in time t is given by

$$d = rt.$$

A car travels at 75 miles per hour (mph) for 4.5 hr. How far will it travel?

We substitute 75 for r and 4.5 for t and calculate d:

$$d = rt = (75)(4.5) = 337.5 \text{ mi.}$$

The car will travel 337.5 mi.

Do Exercise 3.

b | Solving Formulas

Refer to Example 2. Suppose a clothing company wants to produce S socks and needs to know how many bales of cotton to order. If this calculation is to be repeated many times, it might be helpful to first solve the formula for x:

$$S = 4321x$$

$$\frac{S}{4321} = x. \qquad \text{Dividing by 4321}$$

Then we can substitute a number for S and calculate x. For example, if the number of socks S to be produced is 432,100, then

$$x = \frac{S}{4321} = \frac{432,100}{4321} = 100.$$

The company would need to order 100 bales of cotton.

EXAMPLE 4 Solve for t: $M = \frac{1}{5}t$.

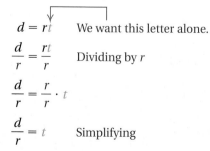

$$M = \frac{1}{5}t \qquad \text{We want this letter alone.}$$
$$5 \cdot M = 5 \cdot \frac{1}{5}t \qquad \text{Multiplying by 5 on both sides}$$
$$5M = t$$

For $M = 2$ in Example 4, $t = 5M = 5(2)$, or 10.

EXAMPLE 5 *Distance, Rate, and Time.* Solve for t: $d = rt$.

$$d = rt \qquad \text{We want this letter alone.}$$
$$\frac{d}{r} = \frac{rt}{r} \qquad \text{Dividing by } r$$
$$\frac{d}{r} = \frac{r}{r} \cdot t$$
$$\frac{d}{r} = t \qquad \text{Simplifying}$$

Do Exercises 4–6.

3. **Distance, Rate, and Time.** A car travels at 55 mph for 6.2 hr. How far will it travel?

4. Solve for q: $B = \frac{1}{3}q$.

5. **Distance, Rate, and Time.** Solve for r: $d = rt$.

6. **Electricity.** Solve for I: $E = IR$. (This formula relates voltage E, current I, and resistance R.)

Answers on page A-8

Solve for x.

7. $y = x + 5$

8. $y = x - 7$

9. $y = x - b$

10. Solve for y: $9y = 5x$.

11. Solve for p: $ap = bq$.

12. Solve for x: $y = mx + b$.

13. Solve for Q: $tQ - p = a$.

Answers on page A-8

EXAMPLE 6 Solve for x: $y = x + 3$.

$$y = x + 3 \qquad \text{We want this letter alone.}$$
$$y - 3 = x + 3 - 3 \qquad \text{Subtracting 3}$$
$$y - 3 = x \qquad \text{Simplifying}$$

EXAMPLE 7 Solve for x: $y = x - a$.

$$y = x - a \qquad \text{We want this letter alone.}$$
$$y + a = x - a + a \qquad \text{Adding } a$$
$$y + a = x \qquad \text{Simplifying}$$

Do Exercises 7–9.

EXAMPLE 8 Solve for y: $6y = 3x$.

$$6y = 3x \qquad \text{We want this letter alone.}$$
$$\frac{6y}{6} = \frac{3x}{6} \qquad \text{Dividing by 6}$$
$$y = \frac{1}{2}x \qquad \text{Simplifying}$$

EXAMPLE 9 Solve for y: $by = ax$.

$$by = ax \qquad \text{We want this letter alone.}$$
$$\frac{by}{b} = \frac{ax}{b} \qquad \text{Dividing by } b$$
$$y = \frac{ax}{b} \qquad \text{Simplifying}$$

Do Exercises 10 and 11.

EXAMPLE 10 Solve for x: $ax + b = c$.

$$ax + b = c \qquad \text{We want this letter alone.}$$
$$ax + b - b = c - b \qquad \text{Subtracting } b$$
$$ax = c - b \qquad \text{Simplifying}$$
$$\frac{ax}{a} = \frac{c - b}{a} \qquad \text{Dividing by } a$$
$$x = \frac{c - b}{a} \qquad \text{Simplifying}$$

Do Exercises 12 and 13.

To solve a formula for a given letter, identify the letter and:

1. Multiply on both sides to clear fractions or decimals, if that is needed.
2. Collect like terms on each side, if necessary.
3. Get all terms with the letter to be solved for on one side of the equation and all other terms on the other side.
4. Collect like terms again, if necessary.
5. Solve for the letter in question.

EXAMPLE 11 *Circumference.* Solve for r: $C = 2\pi r$. This is a formula for the circumference C of a circle of radius r.

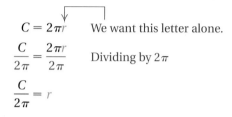

$C = 2\pi r$ We want this letter alone.

$\dfrac{C}{2\pi} = \dfrac{2\pi r}{2\pi}$ Dividing by 2π

$\dfrac{C}{2\pi} = r$

EXAMPLE 12 *Averages.* Solve for a: $A = \dfrac{a + b + c}{3}$. This is a formula for the average A of three numbers a, b, and c.

$A = \dfrac{a + b + c}{3}$ We want the letter a alone.

$3 \cdot A = 3 \cdot \dfrac{a + b + c}{3}$ Multiplying by 3 on both sides

$3A = a + b + c$ Simplifying

$3A - b - c = a$ Subtracting b and c

Do Exercises 14 and 15.

14. Circumference. Solve for D:

$$C = \pi D.$$

(This is a formula for the circumference C of a circle of diameter D.)

15. Averages. Solve for c:

$$A = \frac{a + b + c + d}{4}.$$

Answers on page A-8

Study Tips   HIGHLIGHTING

Reading and highlighting a section before your instructor lectures on it allows you to maximize your learning and understanding during the lecture.

- **Try to keep one section ahead of your syllabus.** If you study ahead of your lectures, you can concentrate on what is being explained in them, rather than trying to write everything down. You can then take notes only of special points or of questions related to what is happening in class.

- **Highlight important points.** You are probably used to highlighting key points as you study. If that works for you, continue to do so. But you will notice many design features throughout this book that already highlight important points. Thus you may not need to highlight as much as you generally do.

- **Highlight points that you do not understand.** Use a unique mark to indicate trouble spots that can lead to questions to be asked during class, in a tutoring session, or when calling or contacting the AW Math Tutor Center.

2.4

EXERCISE SET

For Extra Help

Math XL   MyMathLab   InterAct   Math Tutor   Digital Video   Student's
                        Math   Center   Tutor CD 2   Solutions
MathXL   MyMathLab   InterAct   Videotape 3   Manual
                      Math

a , b   Solve.

1. *Furnace Output.* The formula

$$B = 30a$$

is used in New England to estimate the minimum furnace output B, in Btu's, for a modern house with a square feet of flooring.

Source: U.S. Department of Energy

a) Determine the minimum furnace output for a 1900-ft^2 modern house.

b) Solve for a. That is, solve $B = 30a$ for a.

2. *Furnace Output.* The formula

$$B = 50a$$

is used in New England to estimate the minimum furnace output B, in Btu's, for an old, poorly insulated house with a square feet of flooring.

Source: U.S. Department of Energy

a) Determine the minimum furnace output for a 3200-ft^2 old, poorly insulated house.

b) Solve for a. That is, solve $B = 50a$ for a.

3. *Distance from a Storm.* The formula

$$M = \tfrac{1}{5}t$$

can be used to determine how far M, in miles, you are from lightning when its thunder takes t seconds to reach your ears.

a) It takes 8 sec for the sound of thunder to reach you after you have seen the lightning. How far away is the storm?

b) Solve for t.

4. *Electrical Power.* The power rating P, in watts, of an electrical appliance is determined by

$$P = I \cdot V,$$

where I is the current, in amperes, and V is measured in volts.

a) A kitchen requires 30 amps of current and the voltage in the house is 115 volts. What is the wattage of the kitchen?

b) Solve for I; for V.

5. *College Enrollment.* At many colleges, the number of "full-time-equivalent" students f is given by

$$f = \frac{n}{15},$$

where n is the total number of credits for which students have enrolled in a given semester.

a) Determine the number of full-time-equivalent students on a campus in which students registered for a total of 21,345 credits.

b) Solve for n.

6. *Surface Area of a Cube.* The surface area A of a cube with side s is given by

$$A = 6s^2.$$

a) Find the surface area of a cube with sides of 3 in.

b) Solve for s^2.

7. *Calorie Density.* The calorie density D, in calories per ounce, of a food that contains c calories and weighs w ounces is given by

$$D = \frac{c}{w}.$$

Eight ounces of fat-free milk contains 84 calories. Find the calorie density of fat-free milk.

Source: *Nutrition Action Healthletter*, March 2000, p. 9. Center for Science in the Public Interest, Suite 300; 1875 Connecticut Ave NW, Washington, D.C. 20008.

8. *Wavelength of a Musical Note.* The wavelength w, in meters per cycle, of a musical note is given by

$$w = \frac{r}{f},$$

where r is the speed of the sound, in meters per second, and f is the frequency, in cycles per second. The speed of sound in air is 344 m/sec. What is the wavelength of a note whose frequency in air is 24 cycles per second?

9. *Size of a League Schedule.* When all n teams in a league play every other team twice, a total of N games are played, where

$$N = n^2 - n.$$

A soccer league has 7 teams and all teams play each other twice. How many games are played?

10. *Size of a League Schedule.* When all n teams in a league play every other team twice, a total of N games are played, where

$$N = n^2 - n.$$

A basketball league has 11 teams and all teams play each other twice. How many games are played?

b   Solve for the indicated letter.

11. $y = 5x$, for x

12. $d = 55t$, for t

13. $a = bc$, for c

14. $y = mx$, for x

15. $y = 13 + x$, for x

16. $y = x - \frac{2}{3}$, for x

17. $y = x + b$, for x

18. $y = x - A$, for x

19. $y = 5 - x$, for x

20. $y = 10 - x$, for x

21. $y = a - x$, for x

22. $y = q - x$, for x

23. $8y = 5x$, for y

24. $10y = -5x$, for y

25. $By = Ax$, for x

26. $By = Ax$, for y

27. $W = mt + b$, for t

28. $W = mt - b$, for t

29. $y = bx + c$, for x

30. $y = bx - c$, for x

31. $A = \dfrac{a + b + c}{3}$, for b

32. $A = \dfrac{a + b + c}{3}$, for c

33. $A = at + b$, for t

34. $S = rx + s$, for x

35. *Area of a Parallelogram:*
$$A = bh, \quad \text{for } h$$
(Area A, base b, height h)

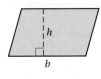

36. *Distance, Rate, Time:*
$$d = rt, \quad \text{for } r$$
(Distance d, speed r, time t)

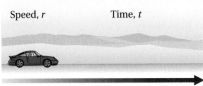
Speed, r Time, t

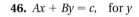
Distance, d

37. *Perimeter of a Rectangle:*
$$P = 2l + 2w, \quad \text{for } w$$
(Perimeter P, length l, width w)

38. *Area of a Circle:*
$$A = \pi r^2, \quad \text{for } r^2$$
(Area A, radius r)

39. *Average of Two Numbers:*
$$A = \dfrac{a + b}{2}, \quad \text{for } a$$

a $A = \dfrac{a+b}{2}$ b

40. *Area of a Triangle:*
$$A = \dfrac{1}{2}bh, \quad \text{for } b$$

41. *Force:*
$$F = ma, \quad \text{for } a$$
(Force F, mass m, acceleration a)

42. *Simple Interest:*
$$I = Prt, \quad \text{for } P$$
(Interest I, principal P, interest rate r, time t)

43. *Relativity:*
$$E = mc^2, \quad \text{for } c^2$$
(Energy E, mass m, speed of light c)

44. $Q = \dfrac{p - q}{2}$, for p

45. $Ax + By = c$, for x

46. $Ax + By = c$, for y

47. $v = \dfrac{3k}{t}$, for t

48. $P = \dfrac{ab}{c}$, for c

49. D_W Devise an application in which it would be useful to solve the equation $d = rt$ for r. (See Exercise 36.)

50. D_W The equations

$$P = 2l + 2w \quad \text{and} \quad w = \frac{P}{2} - l$$

are equivalent formulas involving the perimeter P, the length l, and the width w of a rectangle. (See Exercise 37.) Devise a problem for which the second of the two formulas would be more useful.

51. Convert to decimal notation: $\frac{23}{25}$. [R.3a]

52. Add: $-23 + (-67)$. [1.3a]

53. Add: $0.082 + (-9.407)$. [1.3a]

54. Subtract: $-23 - (-67)$. [1.4a]

55. Subtract: $-45.8 - (-32.6)$. [1.4a]

56. Remove parentheses and simplify: [1.8b]

$$4a - 8b - 5(5a - 4b).$$

Convert to decimal notation. [R.4a]

57. 3.1%

58. 67.1%

59. Add: $-\frac{2}{3} + \frac{5}{6}$. [1.3a]

60. Subtract: $-\frac{2}{3} - \frac{5}{6}$. [1.4a]

61. *Female Caloric Needs.*   The number of calories K needed each day by a moderately active woman who weighs w pounds, is h inches tall, and is a years old can be estimated by the formula

$$K = 917 + 6(w + h - a).$$

Source: Parker, M., *She Does Math.* Mathematical Association of America, p. 96

a) Elaine is moderately active, weighs 120 lb, is 67 in. tall, and is 23 yr old. What are her caloric needs?
b) Solve the formula for a; for h; for w.

62. *Male Caloric Needs.*   The number of calories K needed each day by a moderately active man who weighs w kilograms, is h centimeters tall, and is a years old can be estimated by the formula

$$K = 19.18w + 7h - 9.52a + 92.4.$$

Source: Parker, M., *She Does Math.* Mathematical Association of America, p. 96

a) Marv is moderately active, weighs 97 kg, is 185 cm tall, and is 55 yr old. What are his caloric needs?
b) Solve the formula for a; for h; for w.

Solve.

63. $H = \dfrac{2}{a - b}$,   for b; for a

64. $P = 4m + 7mn$,   for m

65. In $A = lw$, l and w both double. What is the effect on A?

66. In $P = 2a + 2b$, P doubles. Do a and b necessarily both double?

67. In $A = \frac{1}{2}bh$, b increases by 4 units and h does not change. What happens to A?

68. Solve for F: $D = \dfrac{1}{E + F}$.

Objective

a Solve applied problems involving percent.

a Translating and Solving

Many applied problems involve percent. Here we begin to see how equation solving can enhance our problem-solving skills. For background on the manipulative skills of percent notation, see Section R.4.

In solving percent problems, we first *translate* the problem to an equation. Then we *solve* the equation using the techniques discussed in Sections 2.1–2.3. The key words in the translation are as follows.

> **KEY WORDS IN PERCENT TRANSLATIONS**
>
> "**Of**" translates to "·" or "×".
>
> "**Is**" translates to "=".
>
> "**What number**" translates to any letter.
>
> **%** translates to "$\times \frac{1}{100}$" or "$\times 0.01$".

Translate to an equation. Do not solve.

1. 13% of 80 is what number?

2. What number is 60% of 70?

3. 43 is 20% of what number?

4. 110% of what number is 30?

5. 16 is what percent of 80?

6. What percent of 94 is 10.5?

EXAMPLE 1 Translate:

28%   of   5   is   what number?
↓   ↓   ↓   ↓   ↓
28%   ·   5   = a This is a percent equation.

EXAMPLE 2 Translate:

45%   of   what number   is   28?
↓   ↓   ↓   ↓   ↓
45%   × b =   28

EXAMPLE 3 Translate:

What percent   of   90   is   7?
    ↓   ↓   ↓   ↓   ↓
    n ·   90   =   7

Do Exercises 1–6.

Percent problems are actually of three different types. Although the method we present does *not* require that you be able to identify which type we are studying, it is helpful to know them.

We know that

15 is 25% of 60,   or

15 = 25% × 60.

We can think of this as:

> Amount = Percent number × Base.

Answers on page A-8

Each of the three types of percent problems depends on which of the three pieces of information is missing.

1. Finding the **amount** (the result of taking the percent)

   Example: What number is 25% of 60?

   Translation: y $=$ 25% $\cdot$ 60

2. Finding the **base** (the number you are taking the percent of)

   Example: 15 is 25% of what number?

   Translation: 15 $=$ 25% $\cdot$ y

3. Finding the **percent number** (the percent itself)

   Example: 15 is what percent of 60?

   Translation: 15 $=$ y $\cdot$ 60

FINDING THE AMOUNT

EXAMPLE 4 What number is 11% of 49?

What number is 11% of 49?

Translate: a $=$ 11% $\times$ 49

Solve: The letter is by itself. To solve the equation, we need only convert 11% to decimal notation and multiply:

$$a = 11\% \times 49 = 0.11 \times 49 = 5.39.$$

Thus, 5.39 is 11% of 49. The answer is 5.39.

Do Exercise 7.

FINDING THE BASE

EXAMPLE 5 3 is 16% of what number?

3 is 16% of what number?

Translate: 3 $=$ 16% $\times$ b

$3 = 0.16 \times b$ Converting 16% to decimal notation

Solve: In this case, the letter is not by itself. To solve the equation, we divide by 0.16 on both sides:

$$3 = 0.16 \times b$$

$$\frac{3}{0.16} = \frac{0.16 \times b}{0.16}$$ Dividing by 0.16

$$18.75 = b.$$ Simplifying

The answer is 18.75.

Do Exercise 8.

7. What number is 2.4% of 80?

8. 25.3 is 22% of what number?

Answers on page A-8

Answers on page A-8

Study Tips

USING THE SUPPLEMENTS

The new mathematical skills and concepts presented in the lectures will be of increased value to you if you begin the homework assignment as soon as possible after the lecture. Then if you still have difficulty with any of the exercises, you have time to access supplementary resources such as:

- *Student's Solutions Manual*
- Videotapes
- Digital Video Tutor
- MathXL Tutorials on CD
- AW Math Tutor Center
- MyMathLab
- MathXL
- Work It Out! Chapter Test Video on CD

9. What percent of $50 is $18?

10. Areas of Alaska and Arizona.
The area of Arizona is 19% of the area of Alaska. The area of Alaska is 586,400 mi². What is the area of Arizona?

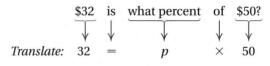

FINDING THE PERCENT NUMBER

In solving these problems, you *must* remember to convert to percent notation after you have solved the equation.

EXAMPLE 6 $32 is what percent of $50?

$$\text{Translate:} \quad \underbrace{\$32}_{32} \quad \underbrace{\text{is}}_{=} \quad \underbrace{\text{what percent}}_{p} \quad \underbrace{\text{of}}_{\times} \quad \underbrace{\$50?}_{50}$$

Solve: To solve the equation, we divide by 50 on both sides and convert the answer to percent notation:

$$32 = p \times 50$$
$$\frac{32}{50} = \frac{p \times 50}{50} \qquad \text{Dividing by 50}$$
$$0.64 = p$$
$$64\% = p. \qquad \text{Converting to percent notation}$$

Thus, $32 is 64% of $50. The answer is 64%.

Do Exercise 9.

EXAMPLE 7 *Coronary Heart Disease.* In 2001, there were about 206 million people age 20 or older in the United States. About 6.4% of them had coronary heart disease. How many had coronary heart disease?

Source: American Heart Association

To solve the problem, we first reword and then translate. We let $a =$ the number of people age 20 or older in the United States with coronary heart disease.

$$\text{Rewording:} \quad \underbrace{\text{What number}}_{a} \quad \underbrace{\text{is}}_{=} \quad \underbrace{6.4\%}_{6.4\%} \quad \underbrace{\text{of}}_{\times} \quad \underbrace{206?}_{206}$$

Solve: The letter is by itself. To solve the equation, we need only convert 6.4% to decimal notation and multiply:

$$a = 6.4\% \times 206 = 0.064 \times 206 = 13.184.$$

Thus, 13.184 million is 6.4% of 206 million, so in 2001 about 13.184 million people age 20 or older in the United States had coronary heart disease.

Do Exercise 10.

EXAMPLE 8 *Digital Camera.* At one time, Best Buy had a Canon Power-Shot digital camera on sale for $349.99. This was 87.5% of the list price. What was the list price?

To solve the problem, we first reword and then translate. We let $L =$ the list price.

$$\text{Rewording:} \quad \underbrace{\$349.99}_{349.99} \quad \underbrace{\text{is}}_{=} \quad \underbrace{87.5\%}_{87.5\%} \quad \underbrace{\text{of}}_{\times} \quad \underbrace{\text{what number?}}_{L}$$

Answers on page A-8

Solve: To solve the equation, we convert 87.5% to decimal notation and divide by 0.875 on both sides:

$$349.99 = 87.5\% \times L$$

$$349.99 = 0.875 \times L \qquad \text{Converting to decimal notation}$$

$$\frac{349.99}{0.875} = \frac{0.875 \times L}{0.875} \qquad \text{Dividing by 0.875}$$

$$399.99 \approx L. \qquad \text{Simplifying using a calculator and rounding to the nearest cent}$$

The list price was about $399.99.

Do Exercise 11.

EXAMPLE 9 *Apple iPod.* An Apple iPod 20.0 GB digital audio player was on sale at Best Buy for $249.99, decreased from a normal list price of $299.99. What was the percent of decrease?

To solve the problem, we must first determine the amount of decrease from the original price:

Original price	minus	Sale price	=	Decrease
↓	↓	↓	↓	↓
$299.99	−	$249.99	=	$50.00.

Using the $50 decrease, we reword and translate. We let p = the percent of decrease. We want to know, "What percent of the *original* price is $50?"

Rewording:	$50	is	what percent	of	$299.99?
	↓	↓	↓	↓	↓
Translate:	50	=	p	×	299.99

Solve: To solve the equation, we divide by 299.99 on both sides and convert the answer to percent notation:

$$50 = p \times 299.99$$

$$\frac{50}{299.99} = \frac{p \times 299.99}{299.99} \qquad \text{Dividing by 299.99}$$

$$0.167 \approx p \qquad \text{Simplifying and converting to percent notation}$$

$$16.7\% = p.$$

Thus the percent of decrease was about 16.7%.

Do Exercise 12.

11. Population of Nevada. The population of Nevada was 2.2 million in 2002. This was 183.3% of its population in 1990. What was the population in 1990?

Source: U.S. Bureau of the Census

12. Job Opportunities. There were 252 thousand medical assistants in 1998. Job opportunities are expected to grow to 398 thousand by 2008. What is the percent of increase?

Source: *Handbook of U.S. Labor Statistics*

Answers on page A-8

a   Solve.

1. What percent of 180 is 36?

2. What percent of 76 is 19?

3. 45 is 30% of what number?

4. 20.4 is 24% of what number?

5. What number is 65% of 840?

6. What number is 50% of 50? (This was a $500.00 question on the "Who Wants To Be a Millionaire?" television quiz show.)

7. 30 is what percent of 125?

8. 57 is what percent of 300?

9. 12% of what number is 0.3?

10. 7 is 175% of what number?

11. 2 is what percent of 40?

12. 40 is 2% of what number?

13. What percent of 68 is 17?

14. What percent of 150 is 39?

15. What number is 35% of 240?

16. What number is 1% of one million?

17. What percent of 125 is 30?

18. What percent of 60 is 75?

19. What percent of 300 is 48?

20. What percent of 70 is 70?

21. 14 is 30% of what number?

22. 54 is 24% of what number?

23. What number is 2% of 40?

24. What number is 40% of 2?

25. 0.8 is 16% of what number?

26. 25 is what percent of 50?

27. 54 is 135% of what number?

28. 8 is 2% of what number?

Costs of Owning a Dog. The American Pet Products Manufacturers Association estimates that the total cost of owning a dog for its lifetime is $6600. The following circle graph shows the relative costs of raising a dog from birth to death.

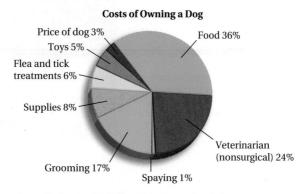

Costs of Owning a Dog

Price of dog 3%
Toys 5%
Flea and tick treatments 6%
Supplies 8%
Grooming 17%
Spaying 1%
Veterinarian (nonsurgical) 24%
Food 36%

Source: The American Pet Products Manufacturers Association

Complete the following table of costs of owning a dog for its lifetime.

	EXPENSE ITEM	COST		EXPENSE ITEM	COST
29.	Price of dog		**30.**	Food	
31.	Veterinarian		**32.**	Grooming	
33.	Supplies		**34.**	Flea and tick treatments	

35. *Car Sales.* In 2002, there were 8,317,954 retail sales of cars in the United States. Of that total, 2,268,093 were imported. Japan manufactured 1,003,745 of those imports, and Germany manufactured 564,910 of them. What percent of the imported cars were manufactured in Japan? in Germany?

Source: Ward's Communications, *World Almanac and Book of Facts* 2004

36. *Truck Sales.* In 2002, 17,118,000 new motor vehicles were sold in the United States. Of these, 9,036,000 were trucks. Imported trucks made up 1,061,000 of those sales. What percent of the motor vehicles sold were trucks? What percent of the truck sales were imported trucks?

Source: U.S. Bureau of Economic Analysis

37. *Batting Average.* At one point in a recent season, Sammy Sosa of the Chicago Cubs had 193 hits. His batting average was 0.320, or 32%. That is, of the total number of at-bats, 32% were hits. How many at-bats did he have?

Source: Major League Baseball

38. *Pass Completions.* At one point in a recent season, Peyton Manning of the Indianapolis Colts had completed 357 passes. This was 62.5% of his attempts. How many attempts did he make?

Source: National Football League

39. *Student Loans.* To finance her community college education, Sarah takes out a Stafford loan for $6500. After a year, Sarah decides to pay off the interest, which is 3% of $6500. How much will she pay?

40. *Student Loans.* Paul takes out a federal Stafford loan for $5400. After a year, Paul decides to pay off the interest, which is 4.5% of $5400. How much will he pay?

41. *Tipping.* Leon left a $4 tip for a meal that cost $25.

a) What percent of the cost of the meal was the tip?
b) What was the total cost of the meal including the tip?

42. *Tipping.* Selena left a $12.76 tip for a meal that cost $58.

a) What percent of the cost of the meal was the tip?
b) What was the total cost of the meal including the tip?

43. *Tipping.* Leon left a 15% tip for a meal that cost $25.

    a) How much was the tip?
    b) What was the total cost of the meal including the tip?

44. *Tipping.* Sam, Selena, Rachel, and Clement left a 15% tip for a meal that cost $58.

    a) How much was the tip?
    b) What was the total cost of the meal including the tip?

45. *Tipping.* Leon left a 15% tip of $4.32 for a meal.

    a) What was the cost of the meal before the tip?
    b) What was the total cost of the meal including the tip?

46. *Tipping.* Selena left a 15% tip of $8.40 for a meal.

    a) What was the cost of the meal before the tip?
    b) What was the total cost of the meal including the tip?

47. In a medical study of a group of pregnant women with "poor" diets, 16 of the women, or 8%, had babies who were in good or excellent health. How many women were in the original study?

48. In a medical study of a group of pregnant women with "good-to-excellent" diets, 285 of the women, or 95%, had babies who were in good or excellent health. How many women were in the original study?

49. *Body Fat.* The author of this text exercises regularly at a local YMCA that recently offered a body-fat percentage test to its members. The device used measures the passage of a very low voltage of electricity through the body. The author's body-fat percentage was found to be 16.5% and he weighs 191 lb. What part, in pounds, of his body weight is fat?

50. *Junk Mail.* The U.S. Postal Service reports that we open and read 78% of the junk mail that we receive. A sports instructional videotape company sends out 10,500 advertising brochures.

    Source: U.S. Postal Service

    a) How many of the brochures can it expect to be opened and read?
    b) The company sells videos to 189 of the people who receive the brochure. What percent of the 10,500 people who receive the brochure buy the video?

Life Insurance Rates for Smokers and Nonsmokers. The data in the following table illustrate how yearly rates (premiums) for a $500,000 term life insurance policy are increased for smokers. Complete the table by finding the missing numbers. Round to the nearest percent and dollar.

TYPICAL INSURANCE PREMIUMS (IN DOLLARS)

	AGE	RATE FOR NONSMOKER	RATE FOR SMOKER	RATE INCREASE	PERCENT OF INCREASE FOR SMOKER
	35	$255	$680	$425	167%
51.	40	$335	$990		
52.	45	$485			208%
53.	50	$735			198%
54.	55	$945	$3330		
55.	60	$1510	$5445		
56.	65	$2545			242%

Source: Faith Financial Planners, Inc.

57. D_W The 80/20 rule is commonly quoted in the field of business. It asserts that 80% of your results will come from 20% of your activities. Discuss how this might affect you as a student and as an employee.

58. D_W Comment on the following quote by Yogi Berra, a famous Major League Hall of Fame baseball player: "Ninety percent of hitting is mental. The other half is physical."

SKILL MAINTENANCE

Compute. [R.3b]

59. $9.076 \div 0.05$

60. 9.076×0.05

61. $1.089 + 10.89 + 0.1089$

62. $1000.23 - 156.0893$

Remove parentheses and simplify. [1.8b]

63. $-5a + 3c - 2(c - 3a)$

64. $4(x - 2y) - (y - 3x)$

Add. [1.3a]

65. $-6.5 + 2.6$

66. $-\dfrac{3}{8} + (-5) + \dfrac{1}{4} + (-1)$

Fill in the blank with a word that makes the statement true.

67. To simplify the calculation $18 - 24 \div 3 - 48 \div (-4)$, do all the _____ calculations first, and then the _____ calculations.

68. To simplify the calculation $18 - 24^3 \div 48 \div (-4)^2$, do all the _____ calculations first, and then the _____ calculations, and finally the _____ calculation.

SYNTHESIS

69. It has been determined that at the age of 15, a boy has reached 96.1% of his final adult height. Jaraan is 6 ft 4 in. at the age of 15. What will his final adult height be?

70. It has been determined that at the age of 10, a girl has reached 84.4% of her final adult height. Dana is 4 ft 8 in. at the age of 10. What will her final adult height be?

APPLICATIONS AND PROBLEM SOLVING

Objective

a Solve applied problems by translating to equations.

a Five Steps for Solving Problems

We have discussed many new equation-solving tools in this chapter and used them for applications and problem solving. Here we consider a five-step strategy that can be very helpful in solving problems.

> **FIVE STEPS FOR PROBLEM SOLVING IN ALGEBRA**
>
> 1. *Familiarize* yourself with the problem situation.
> 2. *Translate* the problem to an equation.
> 3. *Solve* the equation.
> 4. *Check* the answer in the original problem.
> 5. *State* the answer to the problem clearly.

Of the five steps, the most important is probably the first one: becoming familiar with the problem situation. The table below lists some hints for familiarization.

> **TO FAMILIARIZE YOURSELF WITH A PROBLEM**
>
> - If a problem is given in words, read it carefully. Reread the problem, perhaps aloud. Try to verbalize the problem as if you were explaining it to someone else.
> - Choose a variable (or variables) to represent the unknown and clearly state what the variable represents. Be descriptive! For example, let L = the length, d = the distance, and so on.
> - Make a drawing and label it with known information, using specific units if given. Also, indicate unknown information.
> - Find further information. Look up formulas or definitions with which you are not familiar. (Geometric formulas appear on the inside back cover of this text.) Consult a reference librarian or the Internet.
> - Create a table that lists all the information you have available. Look for patterns that may help in the translation to an equation.
> - Think of a possible answer and check the guess. Note the manner in which the guess is checked.

EXAMPLE 1 *Hiking.* In 1998, at age 79, Earl Shaffer became the oldest person to through-hike all 2100 miles of the Appalachian Trail—from Springer Mountain, Georgia, to Mount Katahdin, Maine. Shaffer through-hiked the trail three times, in 1948 (Georgia to Maine), in 1965 (Maine to Georgia), and in 1998 (Georgia to Maine) near the 50th anniversary of his first hike. At one point in 1998, Shaffer stood atop Big Walker Mountain, Virginia, which is three times as far from the northern end as from the southern end. How far was Shaffer from each end of the trail?

Source: Appalachian Trail Conference; Earl Shaffer Foundation

1. Familiarize. Let's consider a drawing.

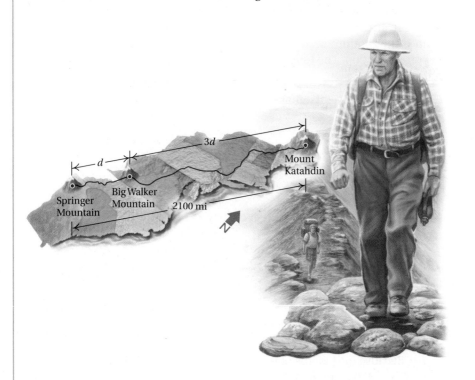

1. Running. In 1997, Yiannis Kouros of Australia set the record for the greatest distance run in 24 hr by running 188 mi. After 8 hr, he was approximately twice as far from the finish line as he was from the start. How far had he run?

Source: *Guinness World Records,* 2004

To become familiar with the problem, let's guess a possible distance that Shaffer stood from Springer Mountain—say, 600 mi. Three times 600 mi is 1800 mi. Since 600 mi + 1800 mi = 2400 mi and 2400 mi is greater than 2100 mi, we see that our guess is too large. Rather than guess again, let's use the skills we have obtained in the ability to solve equations. We let

$d =$ the distance, in miles, to the southern end, and

$3d =$ the distance, in miles, to the northern end.

(We could also let $x =$ the distance to the northern end and $\frac{1}{3}x =$ the distance to the southern end.)

2. Translate. From the drawing, we see that the lengths of the two parts of the trail must add up to 2100 mi. This leads to our translation.

$$
\underbrace{\text{Distance to southern end}}_{d} \quad \underbrace{\text{plus}}_{+} \quad \underbrace{\text{Distance to northern end}}_{3d} \quad \underbrace{\text{is}}_{=} \quad \underbrace{\text{2100 mi}}_{2100}
$$

3. Solve. We solve the equation:

$$d + 3d = 2100$$

$$4d = 2100 \qquad \text{Collecting like terms}$$

$$\frac{4d}{4} = \frac{2100}{4} \qquad \text{Dividing by 4}$$

$$d = 525.$$

4. Check. As expected, d is less than 600 mi. If $d = 525$ mi, then $3d = 1575$ mi. Since 525 mi + 1575 mi = 2100 mi, we have a check.

5. State. Atop Big Walker Mountain, Shaffer stood 525 mi from Springer Mountain and 1575 mi from Mount Katahdin.

Do Exercise 1.

Answer on page A-8

EXAMPLE 2 *Rocket Sections.* A rocket is divided into three sections: the payload and navigation section in the top, the fuel section in the middle, and the rocket engine section in the bottom. The top section is one-sixth the length of the bottom section. The middle section is one-half the length of the bottom section. The total length of the rocket is 240 ft. Find the length of each section.

1. **Familiarize.** We first make a drawing.

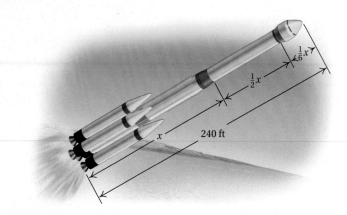

Because the lengths of the top and the middle sections are expressed in terms of the length of the bottom section, we let

$x = $ the length of the bottom section.

Then $\dfrac{1}{6}x = $ the length of the top section

and $\dfrac{1}{2}x = $ the length of the middle section.

2. **Translate.** From the statement of the problem and the drawing, we see that the lengths add up to 240 ft. That gives us our translation:

Length of bottom section	plus	Length of middle section	plus	Length of top section	is	Total length
x	$+$	$\dfrac{1}{2}x$	$+$	$\dfrac{1}{6}x$	$=$	$240.$

3. **Solve.** We begin by clearing fractions and then solving as follows:

$$x + \frac{1}{2}x + \frac{1}{6}x = 240 \qquad \text{The LCM of all the denominators is 6.}$$

$$6\left(x + \frac{1}{2}x + \frac{1}{6}x\right) = 6 \cdot 240 \qquad \text{Multiplying by the LCM, 6}$$

$$6 \cdot x + 6 \cdot \frac{1}{2}x + 6 \cdot \frac{1}{6}x = 6 \cdot 240 \qquad \text{Using the distributive law}$$

$$6x + 3x + x = 1440 \qquad \text{Simplifying}$$

$$10x = 1440 \qquad \text{Collecting like terms}$$

$$\frac{10x}{10} = \frac{1440}{10} \qquad \text{Dividing by 10}$$

$$x = 144.$$

4. Check. Do we have an answer to the *problem*? If the length of the bottom section is 144 ft, then the length of the middle section is $\frac{1}{2} \cdot 144$ ft, or 72 ft, and the length of the top section is $\frac{1}{6} \cdot 144$ ft, or 24 ft. These lengths add up to 240 ft. Our answer checks.

5. State. The length of the bottom section is 144 ft, the length of the middle section is 72 ft, and the length of the top section is 24 ft. (Note the importance of including the unit, feet, in the answer.)

Do Exercise 2.

Recall that the set of integers $= \{\ldots, -5, -4, -3, -2, -1, 0, 1, 2, 3, 4, 5, \ldots\}$. Before we solve the next problem, we need to learn some additional terminology regarding integers.

The following are examples of **consecutive integers:** 16, 17, 18, 19, 20; and $-31, -30, -29, -28$. Note that consecutive integers can be represented in the form $x, x + 1, x + 2$, and so on.

The following are examples of **consecutive even integers:** 16, 18, 20, 22, 24; and $-52, -50, -48, -46$. Note that consecutive even integers can be represented in the form $x, x + 2, x + 4$, and so on.

The following are examples of **consecutive odd integers:** 21, 23, 25, 27, 29; and $-71, -69, -67, -65$. Note that consecutive odd integers can be represented in the form $x, x + 2, x + 4$, and so on.

EXAMPLE 3 *Interstate Mile Markers.* U.S. interstate highways post numbered markers every mile to indicate location in case of an accident or breakdown. In many states, the numbers on the markers increase from west to east. The sum of two consecutive mile markers on I-70 in Kansas is 559. Find the numbers on the markers.

Source: Federal Highway Administration, Ed Rotalewski

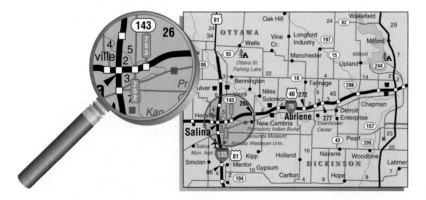

1. Familiarize. The numbers on the mile markers are consecutive positive integers. Thus if we let $x =$ the smaller number, then $x + 1 =$ the larger number.

To become familiar with the problem, we can make a table. First, we guess a value for x; then we find $x + 1$. Finally, we add the two numbers and check the sum.

x	$x + 1$	Sum of x and $x + 1$
114	115	229
252	253	505
302	303	605

2. Gourmet Sandwiches. A gourmet sandwich shop located near a college campus specializes in sandwiches prepared in buns of length 18 in. Suppose Jenny, Emma, and Sarah buy one of these sandwiches and take it back to their apartment. Since they have different appetites, Jenny cuts the sandwich in such a way that Emma gets half of what Jenny gets and Sarah gets three-fourths of what Jenny gets. Find the length of each person's sandwich.

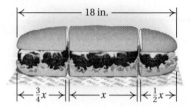

Answer on page A-8

3. Interstate Mile Markers. The sum of two consecutive mile markers on I-90 in upstate New York is 627. (On I-90 in New York, the marker numbers increase from east to west.) Find the numbers on the markers.

Source: New York State Department of Transportation

From the table, we see that the first marker will be between 252 and 302. We could continue guessing and solve the problem this way, but let's work on developing our algebra skills.

2. Translate. We reword the problem and translate as follows.

$$\underbrace{\text{First integer}}_{x} \quad \underbrace{\text{plus}}_{+} \quad \underbrace{\text{Second integer}}_{(x + 1)} \quad \underbrace{\text{is}}_{=} \quad \underbrace{559}_{559} \qquad \begin{array}{l}\text{Rewording} \\ \\ \text{Translating}\end{array}$$

3. Solve. We solve the equation:

$$x + (x + 1) = 559$$
$$2x + 1 = 559 \qquad \text{Collecting like terms}$$
$$2x + 1 - 1 = 559 - 1 \qquad \text{Subtracting 1}$$
$$2x = 558$$
$$\frac{2x}{2} = \frac{558}{2} \qquad \text{Dividing by 2}$$
$$x = 279.$$

If x is 279, then $x + 1$ is 280.

4. Check. Our possible answers are 279 and 280. These are consecutive positive integers and $279 + 280 = 559$, so the answers check.

5. State. The mile markers are 279 and 280.

Do Exercise 3.

EXAMPLE 4 *Copy Machine Rental.* It costs $225 per month plus 1.2¢ per copy to rent a copy machine. A law firm needs to lease a copy machine for use during a special case that they anticipate will take 3 months. If they allot a budget of $1100, how many copies can they make?

Copy Machine Rental
$225 per month
Plus 1.2¢ per copy

1. Familiarize. Suppose that the law firm makes 20,000 copies. Then the cost is monthly charges plus copy charges, or

$$\underbrace{3(\$225)}_{\$675} \quad \underbrace{\text{plus}}_{+} \quad \underbrace{\text{Cost per copy}}_{\$0.012} \quad \underbrace{\text{times}}_{\cdot} \quad \underbrace{\text{Number of copies}}_{20{,}000,}$$

Answer on page A-8

which is $915. This process familiarizes us with the way in which a calculation is made. Note that we convert 1.2¢ to $0.012 so that all information is in the same unit, dollars. Otherwise, we will not get the correct answer.

We let c = the number of copies that can be made for the budget of $1100.

2. **Translate.** We reword the problem and translate as follows.

Monthly cost plus Cost per copy times Number of copies is Budget
$$3(\$225) \quad + \quad \$0.012 \quad \cdot \quad c \quad = \quad \$1100$$

3. **Solve.** We solve the equation:

$$3(225) + 0.012c = 1100$$
$$675 + 0.012c = 1100$$
$$0.012c = 425 \qquad \text{Subtracting 675}$$
$$\frac{0.012c}{0.012} = \frac{425}{0.012} \qquad \text{Dividing by 0.012}$$
$$c \approx 35,417. \qquad \text{Rounding to the nearest one}$$

4. **Check.** We check in the original problem. The cost for 35,417 pages is 35,417($0.012) = $425.004. The rental for 3 months is 3($225) = $675. The total cost is then $425.004 + $675 ≈ $1100, which is the $1100 that was allotted.

5. **State.** The law firm can make 35,417 copies on the copy rental allotment of $1100.

Do Exercise 4.

EXAMPLE 5 *Perimeter of NBA Court.* The perimeter of an NBA basketball court is 288 ft. The length is 44 ft longer than the width. Find the dimensions of the court.

Source: National Basketball Association

1. **Familiarize.** We first make a drawing.

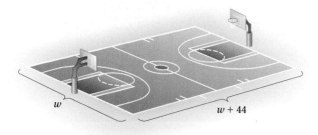

We let w = the width of the rectangle. Then $w + 44$ = the length. The perimeter P of a rectangle is the distance around the rectangle and is given by the formula $2l + 2w = P$, where

l = the length and w = the width.

4. **Copy Machine Rental.** The law firm in Example 4 decides to increase its budget to $1400 for the 3-month period. How many copies can they make for $1400?

Answer on page A-8

5. Perimeter of High School Basketball Court. The perimeter of a standard high school basketball court is 268 ft. The length is 34 ft longer than the width. Find the dimensions of the court.

Source: Indiana High School Athletic Association

2. Translate. To translate the problem, we substitute $w + 44$ for l and 288 for P:

$$2l + 2w = P$$
$$2(w + 44) + 2w = 288.$$

Caution!
Parentheses are important here.

3. Solve. We solve the equation:

$$2(w + 44) + 2w = 288$$

$$2 \cdot w + 2 \cdot 44 + 2w = 288 \qquad \text{Using the distributive law}$$

$$4w + 88 = 288 \qquad \text{Collecting like terms}$$

$$4w + 88 - 88 = 288 - 88 \qquad \text{Subtracting 88}$$

$$4w = 200$$

$$\frac{4w}{4} = \frac{200}{4} \qquad \text{Dividing by 4}$$

$$w = 50.$$

Thus possible dimensions are

$$w = 50 \text{ ft} \quad \text{and} \quad l = w + 44 = 50 + 44, \text{ or } 94 \text{ ft}.$$

4. Check. If the width is 50 ft and the length is 94 ft, then the perimeter is $2(50 \text{ ft}) + 2(94 \text{ ft})$, or 288 ft. This checks.

5. State. The width is 50 ft and the length is 94 ft.

Do Exercise 5.

EXAMPLE 6 *Roof Gable.* In a triangular gable end of a roof, the angle of the peak is twice as large as the angle of the back side of the house. The measure of the angle on the front side is 20° greater than the angle on the back side. How large are the angles?

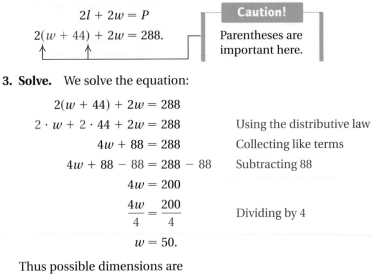

Peak angle
$2x$
Front angle
$x + 20$
x
Back angle

1. Familiarize. We first make a drawing as shown above. We let

measure of back angle = x.

Then   measure of peak angle = $2x$

and   measure of front angle = $x + 20$.

Answer on page A-8

2. Translate. To translate, we need to recall a geometric fact. (You might, as part of step 1, look it up in a geometry book or in the list of formulas on the inside back cover.) Remember, the measures of the angles of a triangle total 180°.

$$\underbrace{\text{Measure of}}_{x}\ \underset{+}{\text{plus}}\ \underbrace{\text{Measure of}}_{2x}\ \underset{+}{\text{plus}}\ \underbrace{\text{Measure of}}_{(x+20)}\ \underset{=}{\text{is}}\ \underset{180°}{180°}$$

Measure of back angle plus Measure of peak angle plus Measure of front angle is 180°

x + $2x$ + $(x + 20)$ = 180°

3. Solve. We solve the equation:

$$x + 2x + (x + 20) = 180$$
$$4x + 20 = 180$$
$$4x + 20 - 20 = 180 - 20$$
$$4x = 160$$
$$\frac{4x}{4} = \frac{160}{4}$$
$$x = 40.$$

Possible measures for the angles are as follows:

Back angle: $x = 40°$;

Peak angle: $2x = 2(40) = 80°$;

Front angle: $x + 20 = 40 + 20 = 60°$.

4. Check. Consider our answers: 40°, 80°, and 60°. The peak is twice the back and the front is 20° greater than the back. The sum is 180°. The angles check.

5. State. The measures of the angles are 40°, 80°, and 60°.

Caution!

Units are important in answers. Remember to include them, where appropriate.

Do Exercise 6.

Caution!

Always be sure to answer the original problem completely. For instance, in Example 1, we need to find *two* numbers: the distances from *each* end of the trail to the hiker. Similarly, in Example 3, we need to find two mile markers, and in Example 5, we need to find two dimensions, not just the width.

EXAMPLE 7 *Top Speeds of Roller Coasters.* The average top speed of the three fastest roller coasters in the world is 109 mph. The third fastest roller coaster, Superman the Escape (at Six Flags Magic Mountain, Los Angeles, CA) reaches a top speed of 20 mph less than the fastest roller coaster, Top Thrill Dragster (in Cedar Point, Sandusky, OH). The second fastest roller coaster, Dodonpa (in Fujikyu Highlands, Japan) has a top speed of 107 mph. What is the top speed of the fastest roller coaster?

Source: *Fortune Small Business*, June 2004, p. 48

6. The second angle of a triangle is three times as large as the first. The third angle measures 30° more than the first angle. Find the measures of the angles.

Answer on page A-8

7. Average Test Score. Sam's average score on his first three math tests is 77. He scored 62 on the first test. On the third test, he scored 9 more than he scored on his second test. What did he score on the second and third tests?

1. **Familiarize.** The **average** of a set of numbers is the sum of the numbers divided by the number of addends. (For more on average, see Appendix E.)

    We are given that the second fastest speed is 107 mph. Suppose the three top speeds are 90, 107, and 112. The average is then

    $$\frac{90 + 107 + 112}{3} = \frac{309}{3} = 103,$$

    which is too low. Instead of continuing to guess, let's use the equation-solving skills we have learned in this chapter. We let x represent the top speed of the fastest roller coaster. Then $x - 20$ is the top speed of the third fastest roller coaster.

2. **Translate.** We reword the problem and translate as follows:

    $$\frac{\begin{array}{ccc}\text{Speed of} & \text{Speed of} & \text{Speed of} \\ \text{fastest} & + \text{second} & + \text{third} \\ \text{coaster} & \text{fastest} & \text{fastest} \\ & \text{coaster} & \text{coaster}\end{array}}{\text{Number of roller coasters}} = \begin{array}{c}\text{Average speed of three} \\ \text{fastest roller coasters}\end{array}$$

    $$\frac{x + 107 + (x - 20)}{3} = 109.$$

3. **Solve.** We solve as follows:

    $$\frac{x + 107 + (x - 20)}{3} = 109$$

    $$3 \cdot \frac{x + 107 + (x - 20)}{3} = 3 \cdot 109 \qquad \begin{array}{l}\text{Multiplying by 3 on both} \\ \text{sides to clear the fraction}\end{array}$$

    $$x + 107 + (x - 20) = 327$$

    $$2x + 87 = 327 \qquad \text{Collecting like terms}$$

    $$2x = 240 \qquad \text{Subtracting 87}$$

    $$x = 120. \qquad \text{Dividing by 2}$$

4. **Check.** If the top speed of the fastest roller coaster is 120 mph, then the top speed of the third fastest is $120 - 20$, or 100 mph. The average of the top speeds of the three fastest is $(120 + 107 + 100) \div 3 = 327 \div 3$, or 109 mph. The answer checks.

5. **State.** The speed of the fastest roller coaster in the world is 120 mph.

Do Exercise 7.

Answer on page A-8

EXAMPLE 8 *Simple Interest.* An investment is made at 6% simple interest for 1 year. It grows to $768.50. How much was originally invested (the principal)?

1. **Familiarize.** Suppose that $100 was invested. Recalling the formula for simple interest, $I = Prt$, we know that the interest for 1 year on $100 at 6% simple interest is given by $I = \$100 \cdot 0.06 \cdot 1 = \$6$. Then, at the end of the year, the amount in the account is found by adding the principal and the interest:

$$\begin{array}{ccccc} \text{Principal} & + & \text{Interest} & = & \text{Amount} \\ \downarrow & & \downarrow & & \downarrow \\ \$100 & + & \$6 & = & \$106. \end{array}$$

In this problem, we are working backward. We are trying to find the principal, which is the original investment. We let $x =$ the principal. Then the interest earned is 6%x.

2. **Translate.** We reword the problem and then translate.

$$\begin{array}{ccccc} \text{Principal} & + & \text{Interest} & = & \text{Amount} \\ \downarrow & & \downarrow & & \downarrow \\ x & + & 6\%x & = & 768.50 \end{array}$$

Interest is 6% of the principal.

3. **Solve.** We solve the equation:

$$\begin{aligned} x + 6\%x &= 768.50 \\ x + 0.06x &= 768.50 \quad &\text{Converting to decimal notation} \\ 1x + 0.06x &= 768.50 \quad &\text{Identity property of 1} \\ 1.06x &= 768.50 \quad &\text{Collecting like terms} \\ \frac{1.06x}{1.06} &= \frac{768.50}{1.06} \quad &\text{Dividing by 1.06} \\ x &= 725. \end{aligned}$$

4. **Check.** We check by taking 6% of $725 and adding it to $725:

$$6\% \times \$725 = 0.06 \times 725 = \$43.50.$$

Then $725 + $43.50 = $768.50, so $725 checks.

5. **State.** The original investment was $725.

Do Exercise 8.

EXAMPLE 9 *Selling a Home.* The Landers are planning to sell their home. If they want to be left with $117,500 after paying 6% of the selling price to a realtor as a commission, for how much must they sell the house?

1. **Familiarize.** Suppose the Landers sell the house for $120,000. A 6% commission can be determined by finding 6% of $120,000:

$$6\% \text{ of } \$120,000 = 0.06(\$120,000) = \$7200.$$

Subtracting this commission from $120,000 would leave the Landers with

$$\$120,000 - \$7200 = \$112,800.$$

This shows that in order for the Landers to clear $117,500, the house must sell for more than $120,000. To determine what the sale price must be, we could check more guesses. Instead, we let $x =$ the selling price, in dollars. With a 6% commission, the realtor would receive 0.06x.

8. Simple Interest. An investment is made at 7% simple interest for 1 year. It grows to $8988. How much was originally invested (the principal)?

Answer on page A-8

9. Price Before Sale. The price of a suit was decreased to a sale price of $526.40. This was a 20% reduction. What was the former price?

2. Translate. We reword the problem and translate as follows.

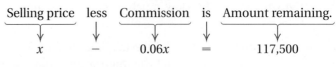

Selling price less Commission is Amount remaining.

$$x \quad - \quad 0.06x \quad = \quad 117{,}500$$

3. Solve. We solve the equation:

$$x - 0.06x = 117{,}500$$
$$1x - 0.06x = 117{,}500$$
$$0.94x = 117{,}500 \qquad \text{Collecting like terms. Had we noted that after the commission has been paid, 94\% remains, we could have begun with this equation.}$$

$$\frac{094x}{0.94} = \frac{117{,}500}{0.94} \qquad \text{Dividing by 0.94}$$

$$x = 125{,}000.$$

4. Check. To check, we first find 6% of $125,000:

$$6\% \text{ of } \$125{,}000 = 0.06(\$125{,}000) = \$7500. \qquad \text{This is the commission.}$$

Next, we subtract the commission to find the remaining amount:

$$\$125{,}000 - \$7500 = \$117{,}500.$$

Since, after the commission, the Landers are left with $117,500, our answer checks. Note that the $125,000 selling price is greater than $120,000, as predicted in the *Familiarize* step.

5. State. To be left with $117,500, the Landers must sell the house for $125,000.

Do Exercise 9.

Caution!

The problem in Example 9 is easy to solve with algebra. Without algebra, it is not. A common error in such a problem is to take 6% of the price after commission and then subtract or add. Note that 6% of the selling price ($6\% \cdot \$125{,}000 = \$7500$) is not equal to 6% of the amount that the Landers want to be left with ($6\% \cdot \$117{,}500 = \$7050$).

Answer on page A-8

Study Tips

PROBLEM-SOLVING TIPS

The more problems you solve, the more your skills will improve.

1. Look for patterns when solving problems. Each time you study an example in a text, you may observe a pattern for problems that you will encounter later in the exercise sets or in other practical situations.

2. When translating in mathematics, consider the dimensions of the variables and constants in the equation. The variables that represent length should all be in the same unit, those that represent money should all be in dollars or all in cents, and so on.

3. Make sure that units appear in the answer whenever appropriate and that you have completely answered the original problem.

Translating for Success

1. *Angle Measures.* The measure of the second angle of a triangle is 51° more than that of the first angle. The measure of the third angle is 3° less than twice the first angle. Find the measures of the angles.

2. *Sales Tax.* Tina paid $3976 for a used car. This amount included 5% for sales tax. How much did the car cost before tax?

3. *Perimeter.* The perimeter of a rectangle is 2347 ft. The length is 28 ft greater than the width. Find the length and the width.

4. *Fraternity or Sorority Membership.* At Arches Tech University, 3976 students belong to a fraternity or a sorority. This is 35% of the total enrollment. What is the total enrollment at Arches Tech?

5. *Fraternity or Sorority Membership.* At Moab Tech University, thirty-five percent of the students belong to a fraternity or a sorority. The total enrollment of the university is 11,360 students. How many students belong to either a fraternity or a sorority?

The goal of these matching questions is to practice step (2), *Translate*, of the five-step problem-solving process. Translate each word problem to an equation and select a correct translation from equations A–O.

A. $x + (x - 3) + \frac{4}{5}x - 384$

B. $x + (x + 51) + (2x - 3) = 180$

C. $x + (x + 96) = 180$

D. $2 \cdot 96 + 2x = 3976$

E. $x + (x + 1) + (x + 2) = 384$

F. $3976 = x \cdot 11{,}360$

G. $2x + 2(x + 28) = 2347$

H. $3976 = x + 5\%x$

I. $x + (x + 28) = 2347$

J. $x = 35\% \cdot 11{,}360$

K. $x + 96 = 3976$

L. $x + (x + 3) + \frac{4}{5}x = 384$

M. $x + (x + 2) + (x + 4) = 384$

N. $35\% \cdot x = 3976$

O. $x + (x + 28) = 2347$

Answers on page A-8

6. *Island Population.* There are 180 thousand people living on a small Caribbean island. The women outnumber the men by 96 thousand. How many men live on the island?

7. *Wire Cutting.* A 384-m wire is cut into three pieces. The second piece is 3 m longer than the first. The third is four-fifths as long as the first. How long is each piece?

8. *Locker Numbers.* The numbers on three adjoining lockers are consecutive integers whose sum is 384. Find the integers.

9. *Fraternity or Sorority Membership.* The total enrollment at Canyonlands Tech University is 11,360 students. Of these, 3976 students belong to a fraternity or a sorority. What percent of the students belong to a fraternity or sorority?

10. *Width of a Rectangle.* The length of a rectangle is 96 ft. The perimeter of the rectangle is 3976 ft. Find the width.

2.6

EXERCISE SET

For Extra Help

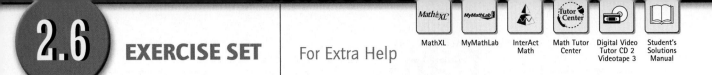

MathXL   MyMathLab   InterAct   Math Tutor   Digital Video   Student's
                       Math   Center   Tutor CD 2   Solutions
                                             Videotape 3   Manual

a Solve. *Even though you might find the answer quickly in some other way, practice using the five-step problem-solving strategy.*

1. *Pipe Cutting.* A 240-in. pipe is cut into two pieces. One piece is three times the length of the other. Find the lengths of the pieces.

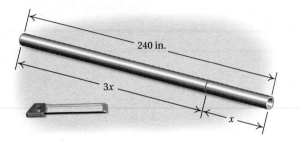

240 in.

$3x$

x

2. *Board Cutting.* A 72-in. board is cut into two pieces. One piece is 2 in. longer than the other. Find the lengths of the pieces.

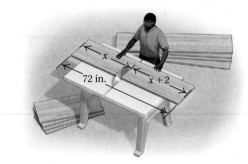

x

72 in.

$x + 2$

3. *Cinnamon Life.* Recently, the cost of four 21-oz boxes of Cinnamon Life cereal was $17.16. What was the cost of one box?

4. *Area of Lake Ontario.* The area of Lake Superior is about four times the area of Lake Ontario. The area of Lake Superior is 30,172 mi². What is the area of Lake Ontario?

Lake Ontario x mi²

CANADA

Lake Superior

Lake Huron

Lake Ontario

Lake Superior 30,172 mi²

Lake Michigan

Lake Erie

UNITED STATES

5. *Women's Dresses.* In a recent year, the total amount spent on women's blouses was $6.5 billion. This was $0.2 billion more than what was spent on women's dresses. How much was spent on women's dresses?

6. *Statue of Liberty.* The height of the Eiffel Tower is 974 ft, which is about 669 ft higher than the Statue of Liberty. What is the height of the Statue of Liberty?

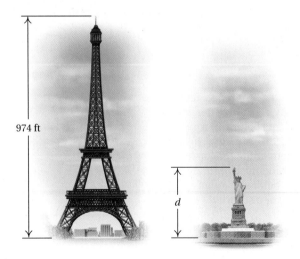

974 ft

d

7. *Iditarod Race.* The Iditarod sled dog race extends for 1049 mi from Anchorage to Nome. If a musher is twice as far from Anchorage as from Nome, how many miles of the race has the musher completed?

Source: Iditarod Trail Commission

8. *Home Remodeling.* In a recent year, Americans spent a total of $35 billion to remodel bathrooms and kitchens. Twice as much was spent on kitchens as bathrooms. How much was spent on each?

9. *Consecutive Apartment Numbers.* The apartments in Vincent's apartment house are numbered consecutively on each floor. The sum of his number and his next-door neighbor's number is 2409. What are the two numbers?

10. *Consecutive Post Office Box Numbers.* The sum of the numbers on two consecutive post office boxes is 547. What are the numbers?

11. *Consecutive Ticket Numbers.* The numbers on Sam's three raffle tickets are consecutive integers. The sum of the numbers is 126. What are the numbers?

12. *Consecutive Ages.* The ages of Whitney, Wesley, and Wanda are consecutive integers. The sum of their ages is 108. What are their ages?

13. *Consecutive Odd Integers.* The sum of three consecutive odd integers is 189. What are the integers?

14. *Consecutive Integers.* Three consecutive integers are such that the first plus one-half the second plus seven less than twice the third is 2101. What are the integers?

15. *Standard Billboard Sign.* A standard rectangular highway billboard sign has a perimeter of 124 ft. The length is 6 ft more than three times the width. Find the dimensions of the sign.

16. *Two-by-Four.* The perimeter of a cross section or end of a "two-by-four" piece of lumber is 10 in. The length is 2 in. more than the width. Find the actual dimensions of the cross section of a two-by-four.

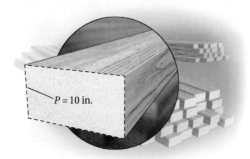

17. *Price of Sneakers.* Amy paid $63.75 for a pair of New Balance 903 running shoes during a 15%-off sale. What was the regular price?

18. *Price of a CD Player.* Doug paid $72 for a shockproof portable CD player during a 20%-off sale. What was the regular price?

19. *Price of a Textbook.* Evelyn paid $89.25, including 5% tax, for her biology textbook. How much did the book itself cost?

20. *Price of a Printer.* Jake paid $100.70, including 6% tax, for a color printer. How much did the printer itself cost?

21. *Parking Costs.* A hospital parking lot charges $1.50 for the first hour or part thereof, and $1.00 for each additional hour or part thereof. A weekly pass costs $27.00 and allows unlimited parking for 7 days. Suppose that each visit Ed makes to the hospital lasts $1\frac{1}{2}$ hr. What is the minimum number of times that Ed would have to visit per week to make it worthwhile for him to buy the pass?

22. *Van Rental.* Value Rent-A-Car rents vans at a daily rate of $84.95 plus 60 cents per mile. Molly rents a van to deliver electrical parts to her customers. She is allotted a daily budget of $320. How many miles can she drive for $320? (*Hint*: 60¢ = $0.60.)

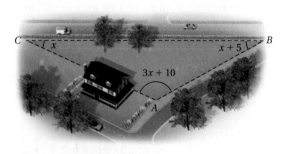

23. *Triangular Field.* The second angle of a triangular field is three times as large as the first angle. The third angle is 40° greater than the first angle. How large are the angles?

24. *Triangular Parking Lot.* The second angle of a triangular parking lot is four times as large as the first angle. The third angle is 45° less than the sum of the other two angles. How large are the angles?

25. *Triangular Backyard.* A home has a triangular backyard. The second angle of the triangle is 5° more than the first angle. The third angle is 10° more than three times the first angle. Find the angles of the triangular yard.

26. *Boarding Stable.* A rancher needs to form a triangular horse pen using ropes next to a stable. The second angle is three times the first angle. The third angle is 15° less than the first angle. Find the angles of the triangular pen.

27. *Stock Prices.* Sarah's investment in AOL/Time Warner stock grew 28% to $448. How much did she invest?

28. *Savings Interest.* Sharon invested money in a savings account at a rate of 6% simple interest. After 1 yr, she has $6996 in the account. How much did Sharon originally invest?

29. *Credit Cards.* The balance in Will's Mastercard® account grew 2%, to $870, in one month. What was his balance at the beginning of the month?

30. *Loan Interest.* Alvin borrowed money from a cousin at a rate of 10% simple interest. After 1 yr, $7194 paid off the loan. How much did Alvin borrow?

31. *Taxi Fares.* In Beniford, taxis charge $3 plus 75¢ per mile for an airport pickup. How far from the airport can Courtney travel for $12?

32. *Taxi Fares.* In Cranston, taxis charge $4 plus 90¢ per mile for an airport pickup. How far from the airport can Ralph travel for $17.50?

33. *Tipping.* Leon left a 15% tip for a meal. The total cost of the meal, including the tip, was $41.40. What was the cost of the meal before the tip was added?

34. *Tipping.* Selena left an 18% tip for a meal. The total cost of the meal, including the tip, was $40.71. What was the cost of the meal before the tip was added?

35. *Average Price.* Tom paid an average of $34 per tie for a recent purchase of three ties. The price of one tie was twice as much as another, and the remaining tie cost $27. What were the prices of the other two ties?

36. *Average Test Score.* Jaci averaged 84 on her first three history exams. The first score was 67. The second score was 7 less than the third score. What did she score on the second and third exams?

37. **D$_W$** Write a problem for a classmate to solve so that it can be translated to the equation
$$\tfrac{2}{3}x + (x + 5) + x = 375.$$

38. **D$_W$** Erin returns a tent that she bought during a storewide 35%-off sale that has ended. She is offered store credit for 125% of what she paid (not to be used on sale items). Is this fair to Erin? Why or why not?

SKILL MAINTENANCE

Calculate.

39. $-\dfrac{4}{5} - \dfrac{3}{8}$ [1.4a]

40. $-\dfrac{4}{5} + \dfrac{3}{8}$ [1.3a]

41. $-\dfrac{4}{5} \cdot \dfrac{3}{8}$ [1.5a]

42. $-\dfrac{4}{5} \div \dfrac{3}{8}$ [1.6c]

43. $\dfrac{1}{10} \div \left(-\dfrac{1}{100}\right)$ [1.6c]

44. $-25.6 \div (-16)$ [1.6c]

45. $-25.6(-16)$ [1.5a]

46. $-25.6 - (-16)$ [1.4a]

47. $-25.6 + (-16)$ [1.3a]

48. $(-0.02) \div (-0.2)$ [1.6c]

SYNTHESIS

49. Apples are collected in a basket for six people. One-third, one-fourth, one-eighth, and one-fifth are given to four people, respectively. The fifth person gets ten apples with one apple remaining for the sixth person. Find the original number of apples in the basket.

50. *Test Questions.* A student scored 78 on a test that had 4 seven-point fill-ins and 24 three-point multiple-choice questions. The student had one fill-in wrong. How many multiple-choice questions did the student answer correctly?

51. The area of this triangle is 2.9047 in². Find x.

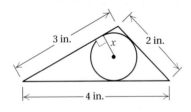

52. A storekeeper goes to the bank to get $10 worth of change. She requests twice as many quarters as half dollars, twice as many dimes as quarters, three times as many nickels as dimes, and no pennies or dollars. How many of each coin did the storekeeper get?

53. In one city, a sales tax of 9% was added to the price of gasoline as registered on the pump. Suppose a driver asked for $10 worth of gas. The attendant filled the tank until the pump read $9.10 and charged the driver $10. Something was wrong. Use algebra to correct the error.

2.7 SOLVING INEQUALITIES

Objectives

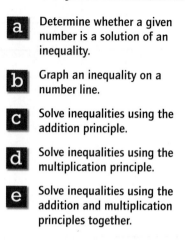

a Determine whether a given number is a solution of an inequality.

b Graph an inequality on a number line.

c Solve inequalities using the addition principle.

d Solve inequalities using the multiplication principle.

e Solve inequalities using the addition and multiplication principles together.

We now extend our equation-solving principles to the solving of inequalities.

a Solutions of Inequalities

In Section 1.2, we defined the symbols $>$ (is greater than), $<$ (is less than), $\geq$ (is greater than or equal to), and $\leq$ (is less than or equal to). For example, $3 \leq 4$ and $3 \leq 3$ are both true, but $-3 \leq -4$ and $0 \geq 2$ are both false.

An **inequality** is a number sentence with $>, <, \geq,$ or $\leq$ as its verb—for example,

$$-4 > t, \quad x < 3, \quad 2x + 5 \geq 0, \quad \text{and} \quad -3y + 7 \leq -8.$$

Some replacements for a variable in an inequality make it true and some make it false.

> **SOLUTION**
>
> A replacement that makes an inequality true is called a **solution.** The set of all solutions is called the **solution set.** When we have found the set of all solutions of an inequality, we say that we have **solved** the inequality.

EXAMPLES Determine whether the number is a solution of $x < 2$.

1. -2.7 Since $-2.7 < 2$ is true, -2.7 is a solution.
2. 2 Since $2 < 2$ is false, 2 is not a solution.

EXAMPLES Determine whether the number is a solution of $y \geq 6$.

3. 6 Since $6 \geq 6$ is true, 6 is a solution.
4. $-\frac{4}{3}$ Since $-\frac{4}{3} \geq 6$ is false, $-\frac{4}{3}$ is not a solution.

Do Exercises 1 and 2.

b Graphs of Inequalities

Some solutions of $x < 2$ are $-3, 0, 1, 0.45, -8.9, -\pi, \frac{5}{8}$, and so on. In fact, there are infinitely many real numbers that are solutions. Because we cannot list them all individually, it is helpful to make a drawing that represents all the solutions.

A **graph** of an inequality is a drawing that represents its solutions. An inequality in one variable can be graphed on a number line. An inequality in two variables can be graphed on a coordinate plane; we will study such graphs in Chapter 3.

Determine whether each number is a solution of the inequality.

1. $x > 3$

   a) 2   b) 0

   c) -5 d) 15.4

   e) 3   f) $-\frac{2}{5}$

2. $x \leq 6$

   a) 6   b) 0

   c) -4.3 d) 25

   e) -6 f) $\frac{5}{8}$

Answers on page A-9

Graph.

3. $x \le 4$

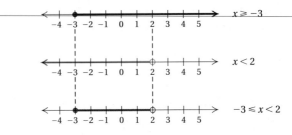

4. $x > -2$

5. $-2 < x \le 4$

Answers on page A-9

EXAMPLE 5   Graph: $x < 2$.

The solutions of $x < 2$ are all those numbers less than 2. They are shown on the graph by shading all points to the left of 2. The open circle at 2 indicates that 2 is *not* part of the graph.

EXAMPLE 6   Graph: $x \ge -3$.

The solutions of $x \ge -3$ are shown on the number line by shading the point for -3 and all points to the right of -3. The closed circle at -3 indicates that -3 *is* part of the graph.

EXAMPLE 7   Graph: $-3 \le x < 2$.

The inequality $-3 \le x < 2$ is read "-3 is less than or equal to x *and* x is less than 2," or "x is greater than or equal to -3 *and* x is less than 2." In order to be a solution of this inequality, a number must be a solution of both $-3 \le x$ and $x < 2$. The number 1 is a solution, as are -1.7, 0, 1.5, and $\frac{3}{8}$. We can see from the graphs below that the solution set consists of the numbers that overlap in the two solution sets in Examples 5 and 6:

The open circle at 2 means that 2 is *not* part of the graph. The closed circle at -3 means that -3 *is* part of the graph. The other solutions are shaded.

Do Exercises 3–5.

C   Solving Inequalities Using the Addition Principle

Consider the true inequality $3 < 7$. If we add 2 on both sides, we get another true inequality:

$$3 + 2 < 7 + 2, \quad \text{or} \quad 5 < 9.$$

Similarly, if we add -4 on both sides of $x + 4 < 10$, we get an *equivalent* inequality:

$$x + 4 + (-4) < 10 + (-4),$$

or
$$x < 6.$$

To say that $x + 4 < 10$ and $x < 6$ are **equivalent** is to say that they have the same solution set. For example, the number 3 is a solution of $x + 4 < 10$. It is also a solution of $x < 6$. The number -2 is a solution of $x < 6$. It is also a solution of $x + 4 < 10$. Any solution of one is a solution of the other—they are equivalent.

For any real numbers a, b, and c:

$a < b$ is equivalent to $a + c < b + c$;

$a > b$ is equivalent to $a + c > b + c$;

$a \leq b$ is equivalent to $a + c \leq b + c$;

$a \geq b$ is equivalent to $a + c \geq b + c$.

In other words, when we add or subtract the same number on both sides of an inequality, the direction of the inequality symbol is not changed.

As with equation solving, when solving inequalities, our goal is to isolate the variable on one side. Then it is easier to determine the solution set.

EXAMPLE 8   Solve: $x + 2 > 8$. Then graph.

We use the addition principle, subtracting 2 on both sides:

$$x + 2 - 2 > 8 - 2$$
$$x > 6.$$

From the inequality $x > 6$, we can determine the solutions directly. Any number greater than 6 makes the last sentence true and is a solution of that sentence. Any such number is also a solution of the original sentence. Thus the inequality is solved. The graph is as follows:

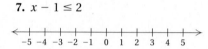

We cannot check all the solutions of an inequality by substitution, as we can check solutions of equations, because there are too many of them. A partial check can be done by substituting a number greater than 6 — say, 7 — into the original inequality:

$$\frac{x + 2 > 8}{7 + 2 \mid 8}$$
$$9 \quad \text{TRUE}$$

Since $9 > 8$ is true, 7 is a solution. Any number greater than 6 is a solution.

EXAMPLE 9   Solve: $3x + 1 \leq 2x - 3$. Then graph.

We have

$$3x + 1 \leq 2x - 3$$
$$3x + 1 - 1 \leq 2x - 3 - 1 \qquad \text{Subtracting 1}$$
$$3x \leq 2x - 4 \qquad \text{Simplifying}$$
$$3x - 2x \leq 2x - 4 - 2x \qquad \text{Subtracting } 2x$$
$$x \leq -4. \qquad \text{Simplifying}$$

The graph is as follows:

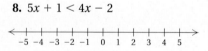

Remember that the graph is a drawing that represents the solutions of the original inequality.

Solve. Then graph.

6. $x + 3 > 5$

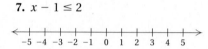

7. $x - 1 \leq 2$

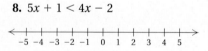

8. $5x + 1 < 4x - 2$

Answers on page A-9

Solve.

9. $x + \dfrac{2}{3} \geq \dfrac{4}{5}$

10. $5y + 2 \leq -1 + 4y$

In Example 9, any number less than or equal to -4 is a solution. The following are some solutions:

$$-4, \quad -5, \quad -6, \quad -\dfrac{13}{3}, \quad -204.5, \quad \text{and} \quad -18\pi.$$

Besides drawing a graph, we can also describe all the solutions of an inequality using **set notation.** We could just begin to list them in a set using roster notation (see p. 66), as follows:

$$\left\{ -4, -5, -6, -\dfrac{13}{3}, -204.5, -18\pi, \ldots \right\}.$$

We can never list them all this way, however. Seeing this set without knowing the inequality makes it difficult for us to know what real numbers we are considering. There is, however, another kind of notation that we can use. It is

$$\{x \,|\, x \leq -4\},$$

which is read

"The set of all x such that x is less than or equal to -4."

This shorter notation for sets is called **set-builder notation.**
From now on, we will use this notation when solving inequalities.

Do Exercises 6–8 on the preceding page.

EXAMPLE 10 Solve: $x + \frac{1}{3} > \frac{5}{4}$.

We have

$$x + \tfrac{1}{3} > \tfrac{5}{4}$$
$$x + \tfrac{1}{3} - \tfrac{1}{3} > \tfrac{5}{4} - \tfrac{1}{3} \qquad \text{Subtracting } \tfrac{1}{3}$$
$$x > \tfrac{5}{4} \cdot \tfrac{3}{3} - \tfrac{1}{3} \cdot \tfrac{4}{4} \qquad \begin{array}{l}\text{Multiplying by 1 to obtain}\\ \text{a common denominator}\end{array}$$
$$x > \tfrac{15}{12} - \tfrac{4}{12}$$
$$x > \tfrac{11}{12}.$$

Any number greater than $\frac{11}{12}$ is a solution. The solution set is

$$\left\{ x \,\middle|\, x > \tfrac{11}{12} \right\},$$

which is read

"The set of all x such that x is greater than $\frac{11}{12}$."

When solving inequalities, you may obtain an answer like $\frac{11}{12} < x$. Recall from Chapter 1 that this has the same meaning as $x > \frac{11}{12}$. Thus the solution set in Example 10 can be described as $\left\{ x \,\middle|\, \frac{11}{12} < x \right\}$ or as $\left\{ x \,\middle|\, x > \frac{11}{12} \right\}$. The latter is used most often.

Do Exercises 9 and 10.

d Solving Inequalities Using the Multiplication Principle

There is a multiplication principle for inequalities that is similar to that for equations, but it must be modified. When we are multiplying on both sides by a negative number, the direction of the inequality symbol must be changed.

Answers on page A-9

Let's see what happens. Consider the true inequality $3 < 7$. If we multiply on both sides by a *positive* number, like 2, we get another true inequality:

$$3 \cdot 2 < 7 \cdot 2, \quad \text{or} \quad 6 < 14. \qquad \text{True}$$

If we multiply on both sides by a *negative* number, like -2, and we do not change the direction of the inequality symbol, we get a *false* inequality:

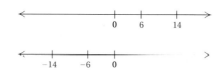

$$3 \cdot (-2) < 7 \cdot (-2), \quad \text{or} \quad -6 < -14. \qquad \text{False}$$

The fact that $6 < 14$ is true but $-6 < -14$ is false stems from the fact that the negative numbers, in a sense, mirror the positive numbers. That is, whereas 14 is to the *right* of 6 on a number line, the number -14 is to the *left* of -6. Thus, if we reverse (change the direction of) the inequality symbol, we get a *true* inequality: $-6 > -14$.

(Two number line illustrations)

THE MULTIPLICATION PRINCIPLE FOR INEQUALITIES

For any real numbers a and b, and any *positive* number c:

$a < b$ is equivalent to $ac < bc$;
$a > b$ is equivalent to $ac > bc$.

For any real numbers a and b, and any *negative* number c:

$a < b$ is equivalent to $ac > bc$;
$a > b$ is equivalent to $ac < bc$.

Similar statements hold for $\leq$ and $\geq$.

In other words, when we multiply or divide by a positive number on both sides of an inequality, the direction of the inequality symbol stays the same. When we multiply or divide by a negative number on both sides of an inequality, the direction of the inequality symbol is reversed.

EXAMPLE 11 Solve: $4x < 28$. Then graph.

We have

$$4x < 28$$

$$\frac{4x}{4} < \frac{28}{4} \qquad \text{Dividing by 4}$$

The symbol stays the same.

$$x < 7. \qquad \text{Simplifying}$$

The solution set is $\{x \mid x < 7\}$. The graph is as follows:

(Number line graph from -4 to 8 with open circle at 7)

Do Exercises 11 and 12.

Solve. Then graph.

11. $8x < 64$

(Number line from -12 to 12)

12. $5y \geq 160$

(Number line from -80 to 80)

Answers on page A-9

Solve.

13. $-4x \leq 24$

14. $-5y > 13$

15. Solve: $7 - 4x < 8$.

EXAMPLE 12 Solve: $-2y < 18$. Then graph.

$$-2y < 18$$

$$\frac{-2y}{-2} > \frac{18}{-2} \qquad \text{Dividing by } -2$$

The symbol must be reversed!

$$y > -9. \qquad \text{Simplifying}$$

The solution set is $\{y \mid y > -9\}$. The graph is as follows:

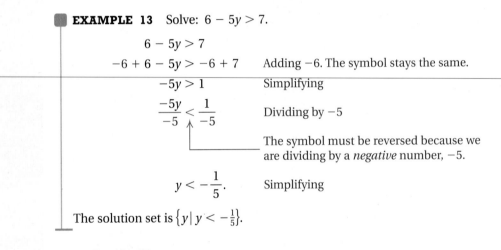

Do Exercises 13 and 14.

e Using the Principles Together

All of the equation-solving techniques used in Sections 2.1–2.3 can be used with inequalities, provided we remember to reverse the inequality symbol when multiplying or dividing on both sides by a negative number.

EXAMPLE 13 Solve: $6 - 5y > 7$.

$$6 - 5y > 7$$

$$-6 + 6 - 5y > -6 + 7 \qquad \text{Adding } -6. \text{ The symbol stays the same.}$$

$$-5y > 1 \qquad \text{Simplifying}$$

$$\frac{-5y}{-5} < \frac{1}{-5} \qquad \text{Dividing by } -5$$

The symbol must be reversed because we are dividing by a *negative* number, -5.

$$y < -\frac{1}{5}. \qquad \text{Simplifying}$$

The solution set is $\left\{y \mid y < -\frac{1}{5}\right\}$.

Do Exercise 15.

EXAMPLE 14 Solve: $8y - 5 > 17 - 5y$.

$$-17 + 8y - 5 > -17 + 17 - 5y \qquad \text{Adding } -17. \text{ The symbol stays the same.}$$

$$8y - 22 > -5y \qquad \text{Simplifying}$$

$$-8y + 8y - 22 > -8y - 5y \qquad \text{Adding } -8y$$

$$-22 > -13y \qquad \text{Simplifying}$$

$$\frac{-22}{-13} < \frac{-13y}{-13} \qquad \text{Dividing by } -13$$

The symbol must be reversed because we are dividing by a *negative* number, -13.

$$\frac{22}{13} < y.$$

The solution set is $\left\{y \mid \frac{22}{13} < y\right\}$, or $\left\{y \mid y > \frac{22}{13}\right\}$.

Do Exercise 16.

It is typical to try to solve an inequality by isolating the variable on the left side of the inequality. Although this is not necessary, it does prevent having to reverse the inequality symbol at the end. Let's solve the inequality in Example 14 again, but this time we will isolate the variable on the left.

EXAMPLE 15   Solve: $8y - 5 > 17 - 5y$.

Note that if we add $5y$ on both sides, the coefficient of the y-term will be positive after like terms have been collected.

$$8y - 5 + 5y > 17 - 5y + 5y \qquad \text{Adding } 5y$$
$$13y - 5 > 17 \qquad\qquad \text{Simplifying}$$
$$13y - 5 + 5 > 17 + 5 \qquad \text{Adding } 5$$
$$13y > 22 \qquad\qquad \text{Simplifying}$$
$$\frac{13y}{13} > \frac{22}{13} \qquad\qquad \begin{array}{l}\text{Dividing by 13. We leave the}\\ \text{inequality symbol the same because}\\ \text{we are dividing by a positive number.}\end{array}$$

$$y > \frac{22}{13}$$

The solution set is $\left\{ y \,\middle|\, y > \frac{22}{13} \right\}$.

Do Exercise 17.

EXAMPLE 16   Solve: $3(x - 2) - 1 < 2 - 5(x + 6)$.

We have

$$3(x - 2) - 1 < 2 - 5(x + 6)$$
$$3x - 6 - 1 < 2 - 5x - 30 \qquad \begin{array}{l}\text{Using the distributive law to multiply}\\ \text{and remove parentheses}\end{array}$$
$$3x - 7 < -5x - 28 \qquad \text{Simplifying}$$
$$3x + 5x < -28 + 7 \qquad \begin{array}{l}\text{Adding } 5x \text{ and 7 to get all } x\text{-terms on}\\ \text{one side and all other terms on the}\\ \text{other side}\end{array}$$
$$8x < -21 \qquad\qquad \text{Simplifying}$$
$$x < \frac{-21}{8}, \text{ or } -\frac{21}{8}. \qquad \text{Dividing by 8}$$

The solution set is $\left\{ x \,\middle|\, x < -\frac{21}{8} \right\}$.

Do Exercise 18.

16. Solve. Use a method like the one used in Example 14.

$$24 - 7y \le 11y - 14$$

17. Solve. Use a method like the one used in Example 15.

$$24 - 7y \le 11y - 14$$

18. Solve:

$$3(7 + 2x) \le 30 + 7(x - 1).$$

Answers on page A-9

19. Solve:

$$2.1x + 43.2 \geq 1.2 - 8.4x.$$

EXAMPLE 17   Solve: $16.3 - 7.2p \leq -8.18$.

The greatest number of decimal places in any one number is *two*. Multiplying by 100, which has two 0's, will clear decimals. Then we proceed as before.

$$16.3 - 7.2p \leq -8.18$$

$100(16.3 - 7.2p) \leq 100(-8.18)$	Multiplying by 100
$100(16.3) - 100(7.2p) \leq 100(-8.18)$	Using the distributive law
$1630 - 720p \leq -818$	Simplifying
$1630 - 720p - 1630 \leq -818 - 1630$	Subtracting 1630
$-720p \leq -2448$	Simplifying
$\dfrac{-720p}{-720} \geq \dfrac{-2448}{-720}$	Dividing by -720

The symbol must be reversed.

$$p \geq 3.4$$

The solution set is $\{p \mid p \geq 3.4\}$.

Do Exercise 19.

20. Solve:

$$\frac{3}{4} + x < \frac{7}{8}x - \frac{1}{4} + \frac{1}{2}x.$$

EXAMPLE 18   Solve: $\dfrac{2}{3}x - \dfrac{1}{6} + \dfrac{1}{2}x > \dfrac{7}{6} + 2x$.

The number 6 is the least common multiple of all the denominators. Thus we multiply by 6 on both sides.

$$\frac{2}{3}x - \frac{1}{6} + \frac{1}{2}x > \frac{7}{6} + 2x$$

$6\left(\dfrac{2}{3}x - \dfrac{1}{6} + \dfrac{1}{2}x\right) > 6\left(\dfrac{7}{6} + 2x\right)$	Multiplying by 6 on both sides
$6 \cdot \dfrac{2}{3}x - 6 \cdot \dfrac{1}{6} + 6 \cdot \dfrac{1}{2}x > 6 \cdot \dfrac{7}{6} + 6 \cdot 2x$	Using the distributive law
$4x - 1 + 3x > 7 + 12x$	Simplifying
$7x - 1 > 7 + 12x$	Collecting like terms
$7x - 1 - 12x > 7 + 12x - 12x$	Subtracting $12x$
$-5x - 1 > 7$	Collecting like terms
$-5x - 1 + 1 > 7 + 1$	Adding 1
$-5x > 8$	Simplifying
$\dfrac{-5x}{-5} < \dfrac{8}{-5}$	Dividing by -5

The symbol must be reversed.

$$x < -\frac{8}{5}$$

The solution set is $\left\{x \mid x < -\frac{8}{5}\right\}$.

Do Exercise 20.

Answers on page A-9

CHAPTER 2: Solving Equations
and Inequalities

2.7

EXERCISE SET

For Extra Help

MathXL MyMathLab InterAct Math Tutor Digital Video Student's
                     Math   Center   Tutor CD 2   Solutions
                                          Videotape 3   Manual

a   Determine whether each number is a solution of the given inequality.

1. $x > -4$
  a) 4
  b) 0
  c) -4
  d) 6
  e) 5.6

2. $x \le 5$
  a) 0
  b) 5
  c) -1
  d) -5
  e) $7\frac{1}{4}$

3. $x \ge 6.8$
  a) -6
  b) 0
  c) 6
  d) 8
  e) $-3\frac{1}{2}$

4. $x < 8$
  a) 8
  b) -10
  c) 0
  d) 11
  e) -4.7

b   Graph on a number line.

5. $x > 4$

6. $x < 0$

7. $t < -3$

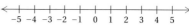

8. $y > 5$

9. $m \ge -1$

10. $x \le -2$

11. $-3 < x \le 4$

12. $-5 \le x < 2$

13. $0 < x < 3$

14. $-5 \le x \le 0$

c   Solve using the addition principle. Then graph.

15. $x + 7 > 2$

16. $x + 5 > 2$

17. $x + 8 \le -10$

18. $x + 8 \le -11$

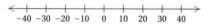

Solve using the addition principle.

19. $y - 7 > -12$

20. $y - 9 > -15$

21. $2x + 3 > x + 5$

22. $2x + 4 > x + 7$

23. $3x + 9 \leq 2x + 6$

24. $3x + 18 \leq 2x + 16$

25. $5x - 6 < 4x - 2$

26. $9x - 8 < 8x - 9$

27. $-9 + t > 5$

28. $-8 + p > 10$

29. $y + \dfrac{1}{4} \leq \dfrac{1}{2}$

30. $x - \dfrac{1}{3} \leq \dfrac{5}{6}$

31. $x - \dfrac{1}{3} > \dfrac{1}{4}$

32. $x + \dfrac{1}{8} > \dfrac{1}{2}$

d Solve using the multiplication principle. Then graph.

33. $5x < 35$

34. $8x \geq 32$

35. $-12x > -36$

36. $-16x > -64$

Solve using the multiplication principle.

37. $5y \geq -2$

38. $3x < -4$

39. $-2x \leq 12$

40. $-3x \leq 15$

41. $-4y \geq -16$

42. $-7x < -21$

43. $-3x < -17$

44. $-5y > -23$

45. $-2y > \dfrac{1}{7}$

46. $-4x \leq \dfrac{1}{9}$

47. $-\dfrac{6}{5} \leq -4x$

48. $-\dfrac{7}{9} > 63x$

CHAPTER 2: Solving Equations
and Inequalities

Solve using the addition and multiplication principles.

49. $4 + 3x < 28$

50. $3 + 4y < 35$

51. $3x - 5 \leq 13$

52. $5y - 9 \leq 21$

53. $13x - 7 < -46$

54. $8y - 6 < -54$

55. $30 > 3 - 9x$

56. $48 > 13 - 7y$

57. $4x + 2 - 3x \leq 9$

58. $15x + 5 - 14x \leq 9$

59. $-3 < 8x + 7 - 7x$

60. $-8 < 9x + 8 - 8x - 3$

61. $6 - 4y > 4 - 3y$

62. $9 - 8y > 5 - 7y + 2$

63. $5 - 9y \leq 2 - 8y$

64. $6 - 18x \leq 4 - 12x - 5x$

65. $19 - 7y - 3y < 39$

66. $18 - 6y - 4y < 63 + 5y$

67. $2.1x + 45.2 > 3.2 - 8.4x$

68. $0.96y - 0.79 \leq 0.21y + 0.46$

69. $\dfrac{x}{3} - 2 \leq 1$

70. $\dfrac{2}{3} + \dfrac{x}{5} < \dfrac{4}{15}$

71. $\dfrac{y}{5} + 1 \leq \dfrac{2}{5}$

72. $\dfrac{3x}{4} - \dfrac{7}{8} \geq -15$

73. $3(2y - 3) < 27$

74. $4(2y - 3) > 28$

75. $2(3 + 4m) - 9 \geq 45$

76. $3(5 + 3m) - 8 \leq 88$

77. $8(2t + 1) > 4(7t + 7)$

78. $7(5y - 2) > 6(6y - 1)$

79. $3(r - 6) + 2 < 4(r + 2) - 21$

80. $5(x + 3) + 9 \leq 3(x - 2) + 6$

81. $0.8(3x + 6) \geq 1.1 - (x + 2)$

82. $0.4(2x + 8) \geq 20 - (x + 5)$

83. $\dfrac{5}{3} + \dfrac{2}{3}x < \dfrac{25}{12} + \dfrac{5}{4}x + \dfrac{3}{4}$

84. $1 - \dfrac{2}{3}y \geq \dfrac{9}{5} - \dfrac{y}{5} + \dfrac{3}{5}$

85. $\mathbf{D_W}$ Are the inequalities $3x - 4 < 10 - 4x$ and $2(x - 5) > 3(2x - 6)$ equivalent? Why or why not?

86. $\mathbf{D_W}$ Explain in your own words why it is necessary to reverse the inequality symbol when multiplying on both sides of an inequality by a negative number.

Add or subtract.　[1.3a], [1.4a]

87. $-56 + (-18)$

88. $-2.3 + 7.1$

89. $-\dfrac{3}{4} + \dfrac{1}{8}$

90. $8.12 - 9.23$

91. $-56 - (-18)$

92. $-\dfrac{3}{4} - \dfrac{1}{8}$

93. $-2.3 - 7.1$

94. $-8.12 + 9.23$

Simplify.

95. $5 - 3^2 + (8 - 2)^2 \cdot 4$　[1.8d]

96. $10 \div 2 \cdot 5 - 3^2 + (-5)^2$　[1.8d]

97. $5(2x - 4) - 3(4x + 1)$　[1.8b]

98. $9(3 + 5x) - 4(7 + 2x)$　[1.8b]

---

99. Determine whether each number is a solution of the inequality $|x| < 3$.

　a) 0　　　　　　　b) -2
　c) -3　　　　　 d) 4
　e) 3　　　　　　　f) 1.7
　g) -2.8

100. Graph $|x| < 3$ on a number line.

Solve.

101. $x + 3 < 3 + x$

102. $x + 4 > 3 + x$

CHAPTER 2: Solving Equations
and Inequalities

2.8 APPLICATIONS AND PROBLEM SOLVING WITH INEQUALITIES

Objectives

a Translate number sentences to inequalities.

b Solve applied problems using inequalities.

The five steps for problem solving can be used for problems involving inequalities.

a Translating to Inequalities

Before solving problems that involve inequalities, we list some important phrases to look for. Sample translations are listed as well.

IMPORTANT WORDS	SAMPLE SENTENCE	TRANSLATION
is at least	Bill is at least 21 years old.	$b \geq 21$
is at most	At most 5 students dropped the course.	$n \leq 5$
cannot exceed	To qualify, earnings cannot exceed $12,000.	$r \leq 12,000$
must exceed	The speed must exceed 15 mph.	$s > 15$
is less than	Tucker's weight is less than 50 lb.	$w < 50$
is more than	Boston is more than 200 miles away.	$d > 200$
is between	The film was between 90 and 100 minutes long.	$90 < t < 100$
no more than	Bing weighs no more than 90 lb.	$w \leq 90$
no less than	Valerie scored no less than 8.3.	$s \geq 8.3$

The following phrases deserve special attention.

> **TRANSLATING "AT LEAST" AND "AT MOST"**
>
> A quantity x is at least some amount q: $x \geq q$.
>   (If x is at least q, it cannot be less than q.)
>
> A quantity x is at most some amount q: $x \leq q$.
>   (If x is at most q, it cannot be more than q.)

Do Exercises 1–10.

b Solving Problems

EXAMPLE 1 *Catering Costs.* To cater a party, Curtis' Barbeque charges a $50 setup fee plus $15 per person. The cost of Hotel Pharmacy's end-of-season softball party cannot exceed $450. How many people can attend the party?

Source: Curtis' All American Barbeque, Putney, Vermont

1. **Familiarize.** Suppose that 20 people were to attend the party. The cost would then be $50 + $15 · 20, or $350. This shows that more than 20 people could attend without exceeding $450. Instead of making another guess, we let n = the number of people in attendance.

Translate.
1. Maggie scored no less than 92 on her English exam.

2. The average credit card holder is at least $4000 in debt.

3. The price of that PT Cruiser is at most $21,900.

4. The time of the test was between 45 and 55 min.

5. Normandale Community College is more than 15 mi away.

6. Tania's weight is less than 110 lb.

7. That number is greater than −2.

8. The costs of production of that CD-ROM cannot exceed $12,500.

9. At most, 11.4% of all deaths in Arizona are from cancer.

10. Yesterday, at least 23 people got tickets for speeding.

Answers on page A-9

11. Butter Temperatures. Butter stays solid at Fahrenheit temperatures below 88°. The formula

$$F = \tfrac{9}{5}C + 32$$

can be used to convert Celsius temperatures C to Fahrenheit temperatures F. Determine (in terms of an inequality) those Celsius temperatures for which butter stays solid.

Answer on page A-9

2. Translate. The cost of the party will be $50 for the setup fee plus $15 times the number of people attending. We can reword and translate to an inequality as follows:

Rewording:	The setup fee	plus	the cost of the meals	cannot exceed	$450.
	↓	↓	↓	↓	↓
Translating:	50	+	15 · n	≤	450

3. Solve. We solve the inequality for n:

$$50 + 15n \le 450$$

$50 + 15n - 50 \le 450 - 50$	Subtracting 50
$15n \le 400$	Simplifying
$\dfrac{15n}{15} \le \dfrac{400}{15}$	Dividing by 15
$n \le \dfrac{400}{15}$	
$n \le 26\tfrac{2}{3}.$	Simplifying

4. Check. Although the solution set of the inequality is all numbers less than or equal to $26\tfrac{2}{3}$, since $n =$ the number of people in attendance, we round *down* to 26. If 26 people attend, the cost will be $50 + $15 · 26$, or $440, and if 27 attend, the cost will exceed $450.

5. State. At most 26 people can attend the party.

Do Exercise 11.

> **Caution!**
>
> Solutions of problems should always be checked using the original wording of the problem. In some cases, answers might need to be whole numbers or integers or rounded off in a particular direction.

EXAMPLE 2 *Nutrition.* The U.S. Department of Agriculture recommends that for a typical 2000-calorie daily diet, no more than 20 g of saturated fat be consumed. In the first three days of a four-day vacation, Anthony consumed 26 g, 17 g, and 22 g of saturated fat. Determine (in terms of an inequality) how many grams of saturated fat Anthony can consume on the fourth day if he is to average no more than 20 g of saturated fat per day.

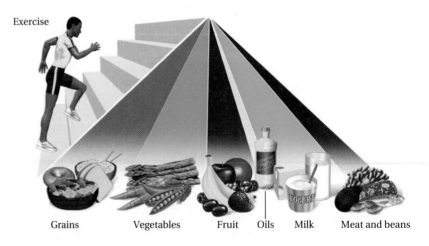

Exercise

Grains · Vegetables · Fruit · Oils · Milk · Meat and beans

Sources: U.S. Department of Health and Human Services and Department of Agriculture

1. **Familiarize.** Suppose Anthony consumed 19 g of saturated fat on the fourth day. His daily average for the vacation would then be

$$\frac{26\text{ g} + 17\text{ g} + 22\text{ g} + 19\text{ g}}{4} = 21\text{ g}.$$

This shows that Anthony cannot consume 19 g of saturated fat on the fourth day, if he is to average no more than 20 g of fat per day. We let x = the number of grams of fat that Anthony consumes on the fourth day.

2. **Translate.** We reword the problem and translate to an inequality as follows:

Rewording: The average consumption of saturated fat   should be no more than   20 g.

Translating: $\dfrac{26 + 17 + 22 + x}{4}$ $\leq$ 20

3. **Solve.** Because of the fraction expression, it is convenient to use the multiplication principle first to solve the inequality:

$$\frac{26 + 17 + 22 + x}{4} \leq 20$$

$$4\left(\frac{26 + 17 + 22 + x}{4}\right) \leq 4 \cdot 20 \qquad \text{Multiplying by 4}$$

$$26 + 17 + 22 + x \leq 80$$

$$65 + x \leq 80 \qquad \text{Simplifying}$$

$$x \leq 15. \qquad \text{Subtracting 65}$$

4. **Check.** As a partial check, we show that Anthony can consume 15 g of saturated fat on the fourth day and not exceed a 20-g average for the four days:

$$\frac{26 + 17 + 22 + 15}{4} = \frac{80}{4} = 20.$$

5. **State.** Anthony's average intake of saturated fat for the vacation will not exceed 20 g per day if he consumes no more than 15 g of saturated fat on the fourth day.

Do Exercise 12.

Translate to an inequality and solve.

12. **Test Scores.** A pre-med student is taking a chemistry course in which four tests are given. To get an A, she must average at least 90 on the four tests. The student got scores of 91, 86, and 89 on the first three tests. Determine (in terms of an inequality) what scores on the last test will allow her to get an A.

Answer on page A-9

Study Tips

The foundation of all your study skills is TIME!

CHECKLIST

☐ Are you approaching your study of mathematics with an assertive, positive attitude?

☐ Are you making use of the textbook supplements, such as the AW Math Tutor Center, the *Student's Solutions Manual*, and the videotapes?

☐ Have you determined the location of the learning resource centers on your campus, such as a math lab, tutor center, and your instructor's office?

☐ Are you stopping to work the margin exercises when directed to do so?

☐ Are you keeping one section ahead in your syllabus?

a Translate to an inequality.

1. A number is at least 7.

2. A number is greater than or equal to 5.

3. The baby weighs more than 2 kilograms (kg).

4. Between 75 and 100 people attended the concert.

5. The speed of the train was between 90 and 110 mph.

6. At least 400,000 people attended the Million Man March.

7. At most 1,200,000 people attended the Million Man March.

8. The amount of acid is not to exceed 40 liters (L).

9. The cost of gasoline is no less than $1.50 per gallon.

10. The temperature is at most −2°.

11. A number is greater than 8.

12. A number is less than 5.

13. A number is less than or equal to −4.

14. A number is greater than or equal to 18.

15. The number of people is at least 1300.

16. The cost is at most $4857.95.

17. The amount of acid is not to exceed 500 liters.

18. The cost of gasoline is no less than 94 cents per gallon.

19. Two more than three times a number is less than 13.

20. Five less than one-half a number is greater than 17.

b Solve.

21. *Test Scores.* A student is taking a literature course in which four tests are given. To get a B, he must average at least 80 on the four tests. The student got scores of 82, 76, and 78 on the first three tests. Determine (in terms of an inequality) what scores on the last test will allow him to get at least a B.

22. *Test Scores.* Your quiz grades are 73, 75, 89, and 91. Determine (in terms of an inequality) what scores on the last quiz will allow you to get an average quiz grade of at least 85.

23. *Gold Temperatures.* Gold stays solid at Fahrenheit temperatures below 1945.4°. Determine (in terms of an inequality) those Celsius temperatures for which gold stays solid. Use the formula given in Margin Exercise 11.

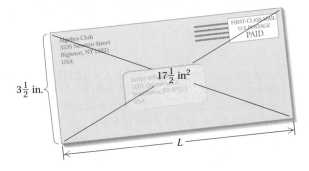

24. *Body Temperatures.* The human body is considered to be fevered when its temperature is higher than 98.6°F. Using the formula given in Margin Exercise 11, determine (in terms of an inequality) those Celsius temperatures for which the body is fevered.

25. *World Records in the 1500-m Run.* The formula

$$R = -0.075t + 3.85$$

can be used to predict the world record in the 1500-m run t years after 1930. Determine (in terms of an inequality) those years for which the world record will be less than 3.5 min.

26. *World Records in the 200-m Dash.* The formula

$$R = -0.028t + 20.8$$

can be used to predict the world record in the 200-m dash t years after 1920. Determine (in terms of an inequality) those years for which the world record will be less than 19.0 sec.

27. *Sizes of Envelopes.* Rhetoric Advertising is a direct-mail company. It determines that for a particular campaign, it can use any envelope with a fixed width of $3\frac{1}{2}$ in. and an area of at least $17\frac{1}{2}$ in². Determine (in terms of an inequality) those lengths that will satisfy the company constraints.

28. *Sizes of Packages.* An overnight delivery service accepts packages of up to 165 in. in length and girth combined. (Girth is the distance around the package.) A package has a fixed girth of 53 in. Determine (in terms of an inequality) those lengths for which a package is acceptable.

29. *Blueprints.* To make copies of blueprints, Vantage Reprographics charges a $5 setup fee plus $4 per copy. Myra can spend no more than $65 for the copying. What numbers of copies will allow her to stay within budget?

30. *Banquet Costs.* The women's volleyball team can spend at most $450 for its awards banquet at a local restaurant. If the restaurant charges a $40 setup fee plus $16 per person, at most how many can attend?

31. *Phone Costs.*   Simon claims that it costs him at least $3.00 every time he calls an overseas customer. If his typical call costs 75¢ plus 45¢ for each minute, how long do his calls typically last? (*Hint*: 75¢ = $0.75.)

32. *Parking Costs.*   Laura is certain that every time she parks in the municipal garage it costs her at least $2.20. If the garage charges 45¢ plus 25¢ for each half hour, for how long is Laura's car generally parked?

33. *College Tuition.*   Angelica's financial aid stipulates that her tuition not exceed $1000. If her local community college charges a $35 registration fee plus $375 per course, what is the greatest number of courses for which Angelica can register?

34. *Furnace Repairs.*   RJ's Plumbing and Heating charges $25 plus $30 per hour for emergency service. Gary remembers being billed over $100 for an emergency call. How long was RJ's there?

35. *Nutrition.*   Following the guidelines of the Food and Drug Administration, Dale tries to eat at least 5 servings of fruits or vegetables each day. For the first six days of one week, he had 4, 6, 7, 4, 6, and 4 servings. How many servings of fruits or vegetables should Dale eat on Saturday, in order to average at least 5 servings per day for the week?

36. *College Course Load.*   To remain on financial aid, Millie needs to complete an average of at least 7 credits per quarter each year. In the first three quarters of 2005, Millie completed 5, 7, and 8 credits. How many credits of course work must Millie complete in the fourth quarter if she is to remain on financial aid?

37. *Perimeter of a Rectangle.*   The width of a rectangle is fixed at 8 ft. What lengths will make the perimeter at least 200 ft? at most 200 ft?

38. *Perimeter of a Triangle.*   One side of a triangle is 2 cm shorter than the base. The other side is 3 cm longer than the base. What lengths of the base will allow the perimeter to be greater than 19 cm?

39. *Area of a Rectangle.*   The width of a rectangle is fixed at 4 cm. For what lengths will the area be less than 86 cm^2?

40. *Area of a Rectangle.*   The width of a rectangle is fixed at 16 yd. For what lengths will the area be at least 264 yd^2?

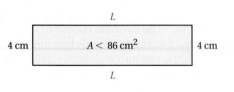

41. *Insurance-covered Repairs.* Most insurance companies will replace a vehicle if an estimated repair exceeds 80% of the "blue-book" value of the vehicle. Michelle's insurance company paid $8500 for repairs to her Subaru after an accident. What can be concluded about the blue-book value of the car?

42. *Insurance-covered Repairs.* Following an accident, Jeff's Ford pickup was replaced by his insurance company because the damage was so extensive. Before the damage, the blue-book value of the truck was $21,000. How much would it have cost to repair the truck? (See Exercise 41.)

43. *Fat Content in Foods.* Reduced Fat Skippy® peanut butter contains 12 g of fat per serving. In order for a food to be labeled "reduced fat," it must have at least 25% less fat than the regular item. What can you conclude about the number of grams of fat in a serving of the regular Skippy peanut butter?
Source: Best Foods

44. *Fat Content in Foods.* Reduced Fat Chips Ahoy!® cookies contain 5 g of fat per serving. What can you conclude about the number of grams of fat in regular Chips Ahoy! cookies (see Exercise 43)?
Source: Nabisco Brands, Inc.

45. *Pond Depth.* On July 1, Garrett's Pond was 25 ft deep. Since that date, the water level has dropped $\frac{2}{3}$ ft per week. For what dates will the water level not exceed 21 ft?

46. *Weight Gain.* A 3-lb puppy is gaining weight at a rate of $\frac{3}{4}$ lb per week. When will the puppy's weight exceed $22\frac{1}{2}$ lb?

47. *Area of a Triangular Flag.* As part of an outdoor education course, Wanda needs to make a bright-colored triangular flag with an area of at least 3 ft². What heights can the triangle be if the base is $1\frac{1}{2}$ ft?

48. *Area of a Triangular Sign.* Zoning laws in Harrington prohibit displaying signs with areas exceeding 12 ft². If Flo's Marina is ordering a triangular sign with an 8-ft base, how tall can the sign be?

49. *Electrician Visits.* Dot's Electric made 17 customer calls last week and 22 calls this week. How many calls must be made next week in order to maintain an average of at least 20 for the three-week period?

50. *Volunteer Work.* George and Joan do volunteer work at a hospital. Joan worked 3 more hr than George, and together they worked more than 27 hr. What possible numbers of hours did each work?

51. D_W If f represents Fran's age and t represents Todd's age, write a sentence that would translate to $t + 3 < f$.

52. D_W Explain how the meanings of "Five more than a number" and "Five is more than a number" differ.

SKILL MAINTENANCE

VOCABULARY REINFORCEMENT

In each of Exercises 53–60, fill in the blank with the correct term from the given list. Some of the choices may not be used.

53. The product of a(n) _____ number of negative numbers is always positive. [1.5a]

54. The product of a(n) _____ number of negative numbers is always negative. [1.5a]

55. The _____ inverse of a negative number is always positive. [1.3b]

56. The _____ inverse of a negative number is always negative. [1.6b]

57. Equations with the same solutions are called _____ equations. [2.1b]

58. The _____ for equations asserts that when we add the same number to the expressions on each side of the equation, we get equivalent equations. [2.1b]

59. The _____ for inequalities asserts that when we multiply or divide by a negative number on both sides of an inequality, the direction of the inequality symbol _____. [2.7d]

60. Any replacement for the variable that makes an equation true is called a(n) _____ of the equation. [2.1a]

addition principle

multiplication principle

solution

replacement

variable

is reversed

stays the same

even

odd

multiplicative

additive

equivalent

SYNTHESIS

61. *Ski Wax.*   Green ski wax works best between 5° and 15° Fahrenheit. Determine those Celsius temperatures for which green ski wax works best.

62. *Parking Fees.*   Mack's Parking Garage charges $4.00 for the first hour and $2.50 for each additional hour. For how long has a car been parked when the charge exceeds $16.50?

63. *Nutritional Standards.*   In order for a food to be labeled "lowfat," it must have fewer than 3 g of fat per serving. Reduced fat Tortilla Pops® contain 60% less fat than regular nacho cheese tortilla chips, but still cannot be labeled lowfat. What can you conclude about the fat content of a serving of nacho cheese tortilla chips?

64. *Parking Fees.*   When asked how much the parking charge is for a certain car (see Exercise 62), Mack replies "between 14 and 24 dollars." For how long has the car been parked?

The review that follows is meant to prepare you for a chapter exam. It consists of three parts. The first part, Concept Reinforcement, is designed to increase understanding of the concepts through true/false exercises. The second part is a list of important properties and formulas. The third part is the Review Exercises. These provide practice exercises for the exam, together with references to section objectives so you can go back and review. Before beginning, stop and look back over the skills you have obtained. What skills in mathematics do you have now that you did not have before studying this chapter?

✋ CONCEPT REINFORCEMENT

Determine whether the statement is true or false. Answers are given at the back of the book.

———— **1.** If $x > y$, then $-x < -y$.

———— **2.** Consecutive odd integers are 2 units apart.

———— **3.** For any number n, $n \geq n$.

———— **4.** $3 - x = 4x$ and $5x = -3$ are equivalent equations.

———— **5.** Some equations have no solution.

———— **6.** $2x - 7 < 11$ and $x < -9$ are equivalent inequalities.

IMPORTANT PROPERTIES AND FORMULAS

The Addition Principle for Equations: For any real numbers a, b, and c: $a = b$ is equivalent to $a + c = b + c$.

The Multiplication Principle for Equations: For any real numbers a, b, and c, $c \neq 0$: $a = b$ is equivalent to $a \cdot c = b \cdot c$.

The Addition Principle for Inequalities: For any real numbers a, b, and c:
$a < b$ is equivalent to $a + c < b + c$;
$a > b$ is equivalent to $a + c > b + c$;
$a \leq b$ is equivalent to $a + c \leq b + c$;
$a \geq b$ is equivalent to $a + c \geq b + c$.

The Multiplication Principle for Inequalities: For any real numbers a and b, and any *positive* number c:
$a < b$ is equivalent to $ac < bc$; $a > b$ is equivalent to $ac > bc$.

For any real numbers a and b, and any *negative* number c:
$a < b$ is equivalent to $ac > bc$; $a > b$ is equivalent to $ac < bc$.

Review Exercises

Solve. [2.1b]

1. $x + 5 = -17$

2. $n - 7 = -6$

3. $x - 11 = 14$

4. $y - 0.9 = 9.09$

Solve. [2.2a]

5. $-\dfrac{2}{3}x = -\dfrac{1}{6}$

6. $-8x = -56$

7. $-\dfrac{x}{4} = 48$

8. $15x = -35$

9. $\dfrac{4}{5}y = -\dfrac{3}{16}$

Solve.   [2.3a]

10. $5 - x = 13$

11. $\dfrac{1}{4}x - \dfrac{5}{8} = \dfrac{3}{8}$

Solve.   [2.3b, c]

12. $5t + 9 = 3t - 1$

13. $7x - 6 = 25x$

14. $14y = 23y - 17 - 10$

15. $0.22y - 0.6 = 0.12y + 3 - 0.8y$

16. $\dfrac{1}{4}x - \dfrac{1}{8}x = 3 - \dfrac{1}{16}x$

17. $14y + 17 + 7y = 9 + 21y + 8$

Solve.   [2.3c]

18. $4(x + 3) = 36$

19. $3(5x - 7) = -66$

20. $8(x - 2) - 5(x + 4) = 20 + x$

21. $-5x + 3(x + 8) = 16$

22. $6(x - 2) - 16 = 3(2x - 5) + 11$

Determine whether the given number is a solution of the inequality $x \le 4$.   [2.7a]

23. -3

24. 7

25. 4

Solve. Write set notation for the answers.   [2.7c, d, e]

26. $y + \dfrac{2}{3} \ge \dfrac{1}{6}$

27. $9x \ge 63$

28. $2 + 6y > 14$

29. $7 - 3y \ge 27 + 2y$

30. $3x + 5 < 2x - 6$

31. $-4y < 28$

32. $4 - 8x < 13 + 3x$

33. $-4x \le \dfrac{1}{3}$

Graph on a number line.   [2.7b, e]

34. $4x - 6 < x + 3$

<+++++++++++>
−5 −4 −3 −2 −1 0 1 2 3 4 5

35. $-2 < x \le 5$

<+++++++++++>
−5 −4 −3 −2 −1 0 1 2 3 4 5

36. $y > 0$

<+++++++++++>
−5 −4 −3 −2 −1 0 1 2 3 4 5

Solve.   [2.4b]

37. $C = \pi d$, for d

38. $V = \dfrac{1}{3}Bh$, for B

39. $A = \dfrac{a + b}{2}$, for a

40. $y = mx + b$, for x

Solve.   [2.6a]

41. *Dimensions of Wyoming.*   The state of Wyoming is roughly in the shape of a rectangle whose perimeter is 1280 mi. The length is 90 mi more than the width. Find the dimensions.

42. *Interstate Mile Markers.*   The sum of two consecutive mile markers on I-5 in California is 691. Find the numbers on the markers.

43. An entertainment center sold for $2449 in June. This was $332 more than the cost in February. Find the cost in February.

44. Ty is paid a commission of $4 for each appliance he sells. One week, he received $108 in commissions. How many appliances did he sell?

45. The measure of the second angle of a triangle is 50° more than that of the first angle. The measure of the third angle is 10° less than twice the first angle. Find the measures of the angles.

Solve. [2.5a]

46. What number is 20% of 75?

47. Fifteen is what percent of 80?

48. 18 is 3% of what number?

49. *Job Opportunities.* There were 905 thousand child-care workers in 1998. Job opportunities are expected to grow to 1141 thousand by 2008. What is the percent of increase?

Source: *Handbook of U.S. Labor Statistics*

Solve. [2.6a]

50. After a 30% reduction, a bread maker is on sale for $154. What was the marked price (the price before the reduction)?

51. A hotel manager's salary is $61,410, which is a 15% increase over the previous year's salary. What was the previous salary?

52. A tax-exempt charity received a bill of $145.90 for a sump pump. The bill incorrectly included sales tax of 5%. How much does the charity actually owe?

Solve. [2.8b]

53. *Test Scores.* Your test grades are 71, 75, 82, and 86. What is the lowest grade that you can get on the next test and still have an average test score of at least 80?

54. The length of a rectangle is 43 cm. What widths will make the perimeter greater than 120 cm?

55. **D**w Would it be better to receive a 5% raise and then an 8% raise or the other way around? Why?   [2.5a]

56. **D**w Are the inequalities $x > -5$ and $-x < 5$ equivalent? Why or why not?   [2.7d]

SYNTHESIS

Solve.

57. $2|x| + 4 = 50$ [1.2e], [2.3a]

58. $|3x| = 60$ [1.2e], [2.2a]

59. $y = 2a - ab + 3$, for a [2.4b]

Solve.

1. $x + 7 = 15$

2. $t - 9 = 17$

3. $3x = -18$

4. $-\dfrac{4}{7}x = -28$

5. $3t + 7 = 2t - 5$

6. $\dfrac{1}{2}x - \dfrac{3}{5} = \dfrac{2}{5}$

7. $8 - y = 16$

8. $-\dfrac{2}{5} + x = -\dfrac{3}{4}$

9. $3(x + 2) = 27$

10. $-3x - 6(x - 4) = 9$

11. $0.4p + 0.2 = 4.2p - 7.8 - 0.6p$

12. $4(3x - 1) + 11 = 2(6x + 5) - 8$

13. $-2 + 7x + 6 = 5x + 4 + 2x$

Solve. Write set notation for the answers.

14. $x + 6 \le 2$

15. $14x + 9 > 13x - 4$

16. $12x \le 60$

17. $-2y \ge 26$

18. $-4y \le -32$

19. $-5x \ge \dfrac{1}{4}$

20. $4 - 6x > 40$

21. $5 - 9x \ge 19 + 5x$

Graph on a number line.

22. $y \le 9$

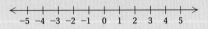

23. $6x - 3 < x + 2$

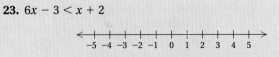

24. $-2 \le x \le 2$

Solve.

25. What number is 24% of 75?

26. 15.84 is what percent of 96?

27. 800 is 2% of what number?

28. *Job Opportunities.* Job opportunities for physician's assistants are expected to increase from 58,000 in 2000 to 89,000 in 2010. What is the percent of increase?

Source: *Monthly Labor Review*, November 2001

29. *Perimeter of a Photograph.* The perimeter of a rectangular photograph is 36 cm. The length is 4 cm greater than the width. Find the width and the length.

30. *Charitable Contributions.* About 35.9% of all charitable contributions are made to religious organizations. In 2003, about $86.4 billion was given to religious organizations. How much was given to charities in general?

Source: AAFRC Trust for Philanthropy/Giving USA 2004

31. *Raffle Tickets.* The numbers on three raffle tickets are consecutive integers whose sum is 7530. Find the integers.

32. *Savings Account.* Money is invested in a savings account at 5% simple interest. After 1 year, there is $924 in the account. How much was originally invested?

33. *Board Cutting.* An 8-m board is cut into two pieces. One piece is 2 m longer than the other. How long are the pieces?

34. *Lengths of a Rectangle.* The width of a rectangle is 96 yd. Find all possible lengths such that the perimeter of the rectangle will be at least 540 yd.

$x + 2$

8 m

x

35. *Budgeting.* Jason has budgeted an average of $95 a month for entertainment. For the first five months of the year, he has spent $98, $89, $110, $85, and $83. How much can Jason spend in the sixth month without exceeding his average budget?

36. *Copy Machine Rental.* It costs $225 per month plus 1.2¢ per copy to rent a copy machine. A catalog publisher needs to lease a copy machine for use during a special project that they anticipate will take 3 months. They decide to rent the copier, but must stay within a budget of $2400 for copies. Determine (in terms of an inequality) the number of copies they can make and still remain within budget.

37. Solve $A = 2\pi rh$ for r.

38. Solve $y = 8x + b$ for x.

SYNTHESIS

39. Solve $c = \dfrac{1}{a - d}$ for d.

40. Solve: $3|w| - 8 = 37$.

41. A movie theater had a certain number of tickets to give away. Five people got the tickets. The first got one-third of the tickets, the second got one-fourth of the tickets, and the third got one-fifth of the tickets. The fourth person got eight tickets, and there were five tickets left for the fifth person. Find the total number of tickets given away.

Cumulative Review

Evaluate.

1. $\dfrac{y-x}{4}$, when $y = 12$ and $x = 6$

2. $\dfrac{3x}{y}$, when $x = 5$ and $y = 4$

3. $x - 3$, when $x = 3$

4. Translate to an algebraic expression: Four less than twice w.

Use $<$ or $>$ for $\square$ to write a true sentence.

5. $-4 \; \square \; -6$

6. $0 \; \square \; -5$

7. $-8 \; \square \; 7$

8. Find the opposite and the reciprocal of $\dfrac{2}{5}$.

Find the absolute value.

9. $|3|$

10. $\left| -\dfrac{3}{4} \right|$

11. $|0|$

Compute and simplify.

12. $-6.7 + 2.3$

13. $-\dfrac{1}{6} - \dfrac{7}{3}$

14. $-\dfrac{5}{8}\left(-\dfrac{4}{3}\right)$

15. $(-7)(5)(-6)(-0.5)$

16. $81 \div (-9)$

17. $-10.8 \div 3.6$

18. $-\dfrac{4}{5} \div -\dfrac{25}{8}$

Multiply.

19. $5(3x + 5y + 2z)$

20. $4(-3x - 2)$

21. $-6(2y - 4x)$

Factor.

22. $64 + 18x + 24y$

23. $16y - 56$

24. $5a - 15b + 25$

Collect like terms.

25. $9b + 18y + 6b + 4y$

26. $3y + 4 + 6z + 6y$

27. $-4d - 6a + 3a - 5d + 1$

28. $3.2x + 2.9y - 5.8x - 8.1y$

Simplify.

29. $7 - 2x - (-5x) - 8$

30. $-3x - (-x + y)$

31. $-3(x - 2) - 4x$

32. $10 - 2(5 - 4x)$

33. $[3(x + 6) - 10] - [5 - 2(x - 8)]$

Solve.

34. $x + 1.75 = 6.25$

35. $\dfrac{5}{2} y = \dfrac{2}{5}$

36. $-2.6 + x = 8.3$

37. $4\dfrac{1}{2} + y = 8\dfrac{1}{3}$

38. $-\dfrac{3}{4} x = 36$

39. $-2.2y = -26.4$

40. $5.8x = -35.96$

41. $-4x + 3 = 15$

42. $-3x + 5 = -8x - 7$

43. $4y - 4 + y = 6y + 20 - 4y$

44. $-3(x - 2) = -15$

45. $\dfrac{1}{3} x - \dfrac{5}{6} = \dfrac{1}{2} + 2x$

46. $-3.7x + 6.2 = -7.3x - 5.8$

47. $4(x + 2) = 4(x - 2) + 16$

48. $0(x + 3) + 4 = 0$

49. $5(7 + x) = (x + 7)5$

50. $3x - 1 < 2x + 1$

51. $5 - y \le 2y - 7$

52. $3y + 7 > 5y + 13$

53. $H = 65 - m$, for m
(To determine the number of heating degree days H for a day with m degrees Fahrenheit as the average temperature)

54. $I = Prt$, for P
(Simple-interest formula, where I is interest, P is principal, r is interest rate, and t is time)

Solve.

55. What number is 24% of 105?

56. 39.6 is what percent of 88?

57. $163.60 is 45% of what number?

58. *Overweight Americans.* In 2004, there were 291 million people in the United States. About 60% of them were considered overweight. How many people were overweight?
Source: U.S. Centers for Disease Control

59. *Grade Average.* Nadia is taking a literature course in which four tests are given. To get a B, a student must average at least 80 on the four tests. Nadia scored 82, 76, and 78 on the first three tests. What scores on the last test will earn her at least a B?

60. *Rollerblade Costs.* Susan and Melinda purchased rollerblades for a total of $107. Susan paid $17 more for her rollerblades than Melinda did. What did Melinda pay?

61. *Savings Investment.* Money is invested in a savings account at 8% simple interest. After 1 year, there is $1134 in the account. How much was originally invested?

62. *Wire Cutting.* A 143-m wire is cut into three pieces. The second piece is 3 m longer than the first. The third is four-fifths as long as the first. How long is each piece?

63. *Truck Rentals.* Truck-Rite Rentals rents trucks at a daily rate of $49.95 plus 39¢ per mile. Concert Productions has budgeted $100 for renting a truck to haul equipment to an upcoming concert. How far can they travel in one day and stay within their budget?

64. *Price Reduction.* After a 25% reduction, a tie is on sale for $18.45. What was the price before reduction?

For each of Exercises 65–67, choose the correct answer from the selections given.

65. Simplify: $-125 \div 25 \cdot 625 \div 5$.

   a) $-390,625$ **b)** -125

   c) -625 **d)** 25

   e) None of these

66. Remove parentheses and simplify:

$$[5(2x + 6) - 7] - [2(x + 4) + 5].$$

   a) $8x + 36$ **b)** $8x - 10$

   c) $8x + 8$ **d)** $8x + 10$

   e) None of these

67. Solve $V = IR$ for I.

   a) $I = V - R$ **b)** $I = \dfrac{V}{R}$

   c) $I = \dfrac{R}{V}$ **d)** $I = VR$

   e) None of these

SYNTHESIS

68. An engineer's salary at the end of a year is $48,418.24. This reflects a 4% salary increase and a later 3% cost-of-living adjustment during the year. What was the salary at the beginning of the year?

69. Nadia needs to use a copier to reduce a drawing to fit on a page. The original drawing is 9 in. long and it must fit into a space that is 6.3 in. long. By what percent should she reduce the drawing on the copier?

Solve.

70. $4|x| - 13 = 3$

71. $\dfrac{2 + 5x}{4} = \dfrac{11}{28} + \dfrac{8x + 3}{7}$

72. $p = \dfrac{2}{m + Q}$, for Q

Graphs of Linear Equations

Real-World Application

The online retail sales of jewelry y, in billions of dollars, is predicted by

$$y = 0.81x + 2,$$

where x is the number of years since 2003. Determine the online retail sales of jewelry in 2003, in 2008, and in 2015.

   Graph the equation and use the graph to estimate online sales in 2010. Then determine the year in which sales will be $9.29 billion.

Source: Forrester Research

This problem appears as Example 11 in Section 3.1.

Objectives

Plot these points on the graph below.

1. $(4, 5)$ **2.** $(5, 4)$

3. $(-2, 5)$ **4.** $(-3, -4)$

5. $(5, -3)$ **6.** $(-2, -1)$

7. $(0, -3)$ **8.** $(2, 0)$

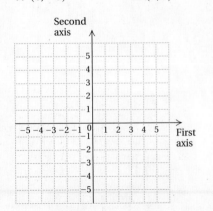

Answers on page A-10

3.1 GRAPHS AND APPLICATIONS OF LINEAR EQUATIONS

You probably have seen bar graphs like the following in newspapers and magazines. Note that a straight line can be drawn along the tops of the bars. Such a line is a *graph of a linear equation*. In this chapter, we study how to graph linear equations and consider properties such as slope and intercepts. Many applications of these topics will also be considered.

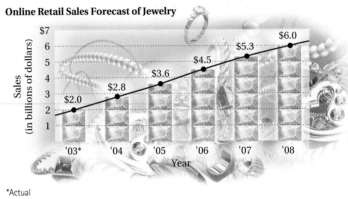

Online Retail Sales Forecast of Jewelry

*Actual

Source: Forrester Research

a Plotting Ordered Pairs

In Chapter 2, we graphed numbers and inequalities in one variable on a line. To enable us to graph an equation that contains two variables, we now learn to graph number pairs on a plane.

On a number line, each point is the graph of a number. On a plane, each point is the graph of a number pair. We use two perpendicular number lines called **axes.** They cross at a point called the **origin.** The arrows show the positive directions.

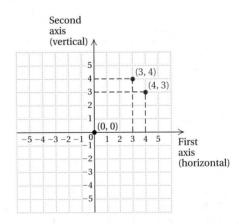

Consider the ordered pair $(3, 4)$. The numbers in an ordered pair are called **coordinates.** In $(3, 4)$, the **first coordinate (abscissa)** is 3 and the **second coordinate (ordinate)** is 4. To plot $(3, 4)$, we start at the origin and move horizontally to the 3. Then we move up vertically 4 units and make a "dot."

The point $(4, 3)$ is also plotted. Note that $(3, 4)$ and $(4, 3)$ give different points. The order of the numbers in the pair is indeed important. They are called **ordered pairs** because it makes a difference which number comes first. The coordinates of the origin are $(0, 0)$.

EXAMPLE 1 Plot the point $(-5, 2)$.

The first number, -5, is negative. Starting at the origin, we move -5 units in the horizontal direction (5 units to the left). The second number, 2, is positive. We move 2 units in the vertical direction (up).

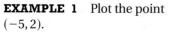

Caution!

The *first* coordinate of an ordered pair is always graphed in a *horizontal* direction and the *second* coordinate is always graphed in a *vertical* direction.

Do Exercises 1–8 on the preceding page.

The figure below shows some points and their coordinates. In region I (the *first quadrant*), both coordinates of any point are positive. In region II (the *second quadrant*), the first coordinate is negative and the second positive. In region III (the *third quadrant*), both coordinates are negative. In region IV (the *fourth quadrant*), the first coordinate is positive and the second is negative.

EXAMPLE 2 In which quadrant, if any, are the points $(-4, 5)$, $(5, -5)$, $(2, 4)$, $(-2, -5)$, and $(-5, 0)$ located?

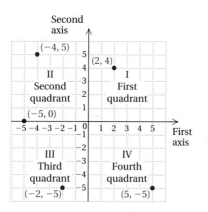

The point $(-4, 5)$ is in the second quadrant. The point $(5, -5)$ is in the fourth quadrant. The point $(2, 4)$ is in the first quadrant. The point $(-2, -5)$ is in the third quadrant. The point $(-5, 0)$ is on an axis and is *not* in any quadrant.

Do Exercises 9–15.

b Finding Coordinates

To find the coordinates of a point, we see how far to the right or left of zero it is located and how far up or down from zero.

---

9. What can you say about the coordinates of a point in the third quadrant?

10. What can you say about the coordinates of a point in the fourth quadrant?

In which quadrant, if any, is the point located?

11. $(5, 3)$

12. $(-6, -4)$

13. $(10, -14)$

14. $(-13, 9)$

15. $(0, -3)$

16. Find the coordinates of points A, B, C, D, E, F, and G on the graph below.

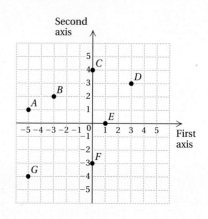

Answers on page A-10

17. Determine whether $(2, -4)$ is a solution of $4q - 3p = 22$.

EXAMPLE 3 Find the coordinates of points A, B, C, D, E, F, and G.

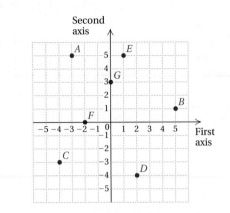

Point A is 3 units to the left (horizontal direction) and 5 units up (vertical direction). Its coordinates are $(-3, 5)$. Point D is 2 units to the right and 4 units down. Its coordinates are $(2, -4)$. The coordinates of the other points are as follows:

B: $(5, 1)$; C: $(-4, -3)$;

E: $(1, 5)$; F: $(-2, 0)$; G: $(0, 3)$.

Do Exercise 16 on the preceding page.

C   Solutions of Equations

18. Determine whether $(2, -4)$ is a solution of $7a + 5b = -6$.

Now we begin to learn how graphs can be used to represent solutions of equations. When an equation contains two variables, the solutions of the equation are *ordered pairs* in which each number in the pair corresponds to a letter in the equation. Unless stated otherwise, to determine whether a pair is a solution, we use the first number in each pair to replace the variable that occurs first *alphabetically*.

EXAMPLE 4 Determine whether each of the following pairs is a solution of $4q - 3p = 22$: $(2, 7)$ and $(-1, 6)$.

For $(2, 7)$, we substitute 2 for p and 7 for q (using alphabetical order of variables):

$$\frac{4q - 3p = 22}{4 \cdot 7 - 3 \cdot 2 \;?\; 22}$$
$$\begin{array}{c|c} 28 - 6 & \\ 22 & \text{TRUE} \end{array}$$

Thus, $(2, 7)$ is a solution of the equation.
For $(-1, 6)$, we substitute -1 for p and 6 for q:

$$\frac{4q - 3p = 22}{4 \cdot 6 - 3 \cdot (-1) \;?\; 22}$$
$$\begin{array}{c|c} 24 + 3 & \\ 27 & \text{FALSE} \end{array}$$

Thus, $(-1, 6)$ is *not* a solution of the equation.

Answers on page A-10

Do Exercises 17 and 18.

EXAMPLE 5 Show that the pairs (3, 7), (0, 1), and (−3, −5) are solutions of $y = 2x + 1$. Then graph the three points and use the graph to determine another pair that is a solution.

19. Use the graph in Example 5 to find at least two more points that are solutions of $y = 2x + 1$.

To show that a pair is a solution, we substitute, replacing x with the first coordinate and y with the second coordinate of each pair:

$$\frac{y = 2x + 1}{7 \; ? \; 2 \cdot 3 + 1}$$
$$\begin{array}{c|c} & 6 + 1 \\ & 7 \qquad \text{TRUE} \end{array}$$

$$\frac{y = 2x + 1}{1 \; ? \; 2 \cdot 0 + 1}$$
$$\begin{array}{c|c} & 0 + 1 \\ & 1 \qquad \text{TRUE} \end{array}$$

$$\frac{y = 2x + 1}{-5 \; ? \; 2(-3) + 1}$$
$$\begin{array}{c|c} & -6 + 1 \\ & -5 \qquad \text{TRUE} \end{array}$$

In each of the three cases, the substitution results in a true equation. Thus the pairs are all solutions.

We plot the points as shown at right. The order of the points follows the alphabetical order of the variables. That is, x comes before y, so x-values are first coordinates and y-values are second coordinates. Similarly, we also label the horizontal axis as the x-axis and the vertical axis as the y-axis.

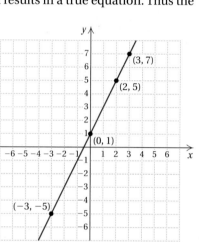

Note that the three points appear to "line up." That is, they appear to be on a straight line. Will other points that line up with these points also represent solutions of $y = 2x + 1$? To find out, we use a straightedge and lightly sketch a line passing through (3, 7), (0, 1), and (−3, −5).

The line appears to pass through (2, 5) as well. Let's see if this pair is a solution of $y = 2x + 1$:

$$\frac{y = 2x + 1}{5 \; ? \; 2 \cdot 2 + 1}$$
$$\begin{array}{c|c} & 4 + 1 \\ & 5 \qquad \text{TRUE} \end{array}$$

Thus, (2, 5) is a solution.

Do Exercise 19.

Example 5 leads us to suspect that any point on the line that passes through (3, 7), (0, 1), and (−3, −5) represents a solution of $y = 2x + 1$. In fact, every solution of $y = 2x + 1$ is represented by a point on that line and every point on that line represents a solution. The line is the *graph* of the equation.

Answer on page A-10

Complete the table and graph.

20. $y = -2x$

x	y	(x, y)
-3		
-1		
0		
1		
3		

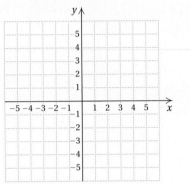

GRAPH OF AN EQUATION

The **graph** of an equation is a drawing that represents all its solutions.

d Graphs of Linear Equations

Equations like $y = 2x + 1$ and $4q - 3p = 22$ are said to be **linear** because the graph of each equation is a straight line. In general, any equation equivalent to one of the form $y = mx + b$ or $Ax + By = C$, where m, b, A, B, and C are constants (not variables) and A and B are not both 0, is linear.

To graph a linear equation:

1. Select a value for one variable and calculate the corresponding value of the other variable. Form an ordered pair using alphabetical order as indicated by the variables.
2. Repeat step (1) to obtain at least two other ordered pairs. Two points are essential to determine a straight line. A third point serves as a check.
3. Plot the ordered pairs and draw a straight line passing through the points.

In general, calculating three (or more) ordered pairs is not difficult for equations of the form $y = mx + b$. We simply substitute values for x and calculate the corresponding values for y.

EXAMPLE 6 Graph: $y = 2x$.

First, we find some ordered pairs that are solutions. We choose *any* number for x and then determine y by substitution. Since $y = 2x$, we find y by doubling x. Suppose that we choose 3 for x. Then

$$y = 2x = 2 \cdot 3 = 6.$$

We get a solution: the ordered pair $(3, 6)$.

Suppose that we choose 0 for x. Then

$$y = 2x = 2 \cdot 0 = 0.$$

We get another solution: the ordered pair $(0, 0)$.

For a third point, we make a negative choice for x. If x is -3, we have

$$y = 2x = 2 \cdot (-3) = -6.$$

We now have enough points to plot the line, but if we wish, we can compute more. If a number takes us off the graph paper, we either do not use it or we use larger paper or rescale the axes. Continuing in this manner, we create a table like the one shown below.

21. $y = \frac{1}{2}x$

x	y	(x, y)
4		
2		
0		
-2		
-4		
-1		

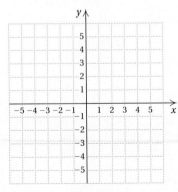

Answers on page A-10

Now we plot these points. We draw the line, or graph, with a straightedge and label it $y = 2x$.

	y	
x	$y = 2x$	(x, y)
3	6	$(3, 6)$
1	2	$(1, 2)$
0	0	$(0, 0)$
-2	-4	$(-2, -4)$
-3	-6	$(-3, -6)$

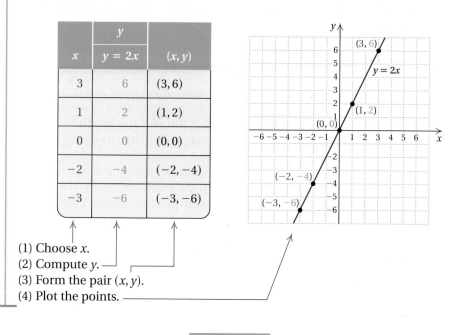

(1) Choose x.
(2) Compute y.
(3) Form the pair (x, y).
(4) Plot the points.

Caution!

Keep in mind that you can choose *any* number for x and then compute y. Our choice of certain numbers in the examples does not dictate the ones you can choose.

Do Exercises 20 and 21 on the preceding page.

EXAMPLE 7 Graph: $y = -3x + 1$.

We select a value for x, compute y, and form an ordered pair. Then we repeat the process for other choices of x.

If $x = 2$,   then $y = -3 \cdot 2 + 1 = -5$,   and $(2, -5)$ is a solution.
If $x = 0$,   then $y = -3 \cdot 0 + 1 = 1$,   and $(0, 1)$ is a solution.
If $x = -1$, then $y = -3 \cdot (-1) + 1 = 4$, and $(-1, 4)$ is a solution.

Results are often listed in a table, as shown below. The points corresponding to each pair are then plotted.

	y	
x	$y = -3x + 1$	(x, y)
2	-5	$(2, -5)$
0	1	$(0, 1)$
-1	4	$(-1, 4)$

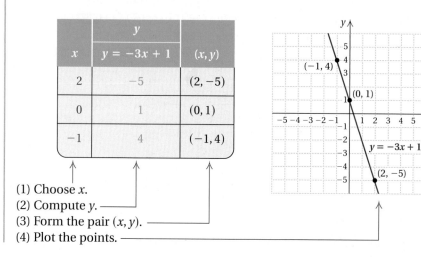

(1) Choose x.
(2) Compute y.
(3) Form the pair (x, y).
(4) Plot the points.

Graph.

22. $y = 2x + 3$

x	y	(x, y)

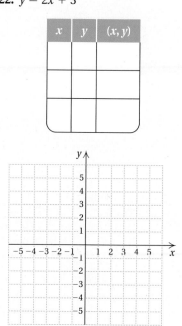

23. $y = -\dfrac{1}{2}x - 3$

x	y	(x, y)

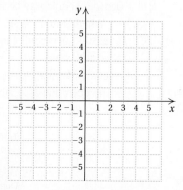

Answers on page A-11

Note that all three points line up. If they did not, we would know that we had made a mistake. When only two points are plotted, a mistake is harder to detect. We use a ruler or other straightedge to draw a line through the points. Every point on the line represents a solution of $y = -3x + 1$.

Do Exercises 22 and 23 on the preceding page.

In Example 6, we saw that $(0, 0)$ is a solution of $y = 2x$. It is also the point at which the graph crosses the y-axis. Similarly, in Example 7, we saw that $(0, 1)$ is a solution of $y = -3x + 1$. It is also the point at which the graph crosses the y-axis. A generalization can be made: If x is replaced with 0 in the equation $y = mx + b$, then the corresponding y-value is $m \cdot 0 + b$, or b. Thus any equation of the form $y = mx + b$ has a graph that passes through the point $(0, b)$. Since $(0, b)$ is the point at which the graph crosses the y-axis, it is called the **y-intercept.** Sometimes, for convenience, we simply refer to b as the y-intercept.

---

y-INTERCEPT

The graph of the equation $y = mx + b$ passes through the **y-intercept** $(0, b)$.

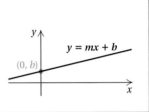

CALCULATOR CORNER

Finding Solutions of Equations   A table of values representing ordered pairs that are solutions of an equation can be displayed on a graphing calculator. To do this for the equation in Example 7, $y = -3x + 1$, we first press ⟨Y=⟩ to access the equation-editor screen. Then we clear any equations that are present. (See the Calculator Corner in Section 2.3 for the procedure for doing this.) Next, we enter the equation by positioning the cursor beside "Y1 =" and pressing ⟨(−)⟩ ⟨3⟩ ⟨X,T,θ,n⟩ ⟨+⟩ ⟨1⟩. Now we press ⟨2ND⟩ ⟨TBLSET⟩ to display the table set-up screen. (TBLSET is the second function associated with the ⟨WINDOW⟩ key.) You can choose to supply the x-values yourself or you can set the calculator to supply them. To supply them yourself, follow the procedure for selecting ASK mode on p. 157. To have the calculator supply the x-values, set "Indpnt" to "Auto" by positioning the cursor over "Auto" and pressing ⟨ENTER⟩. "Depend" should also be set to "Auto."

When "Indpnt" is set to "Auto," the graphing calculator will supply values of x, beginning with the value specified as TBLSTART and continuing by adding the value of △TBL to the preceding value for x. Below, we show a table of values that starts with $x = -2$ and adds 1 to the preceding x-value. We press ⟨(−)⟩ ⟨2⟩ ⟨▽⟩ ⟨1⟩ or ⟨(−)⟩ ⟨2⟩ ⟨ENTER⟩ ⟨1⟩ to select a minimum x-value of -2 and an increment of 1. To display the table, we press ⟨2ND⟩ ⟨TABLE⟩. (TABLE is the second operation associated with the ⟨GRAPH⟩ key.) We can use the ⟨△⟩ and ⟨▽⟩ keys to scroll up and down through the table to see other solutions of the equation.

TABLE SETUP
TblStart=−2
△Tbl=1
Indpnt: **Auto** Ask
Depend: **Auto** Ask

X	Y₁
−2	7
−1	4
0	1
1	−2
2	−5
3	−8
4	−11

X = −2

Exercise:

1. Create a table of ordered pairs that are solutions of the equations in Examples 6 and 8.

EXAMPLE 8 Graph $y = \frac{2}{5}x + 4$ and identify the y-intercept.

We select a value for x, compute y, and form an ordered pair. Then we repeat the process for other choices of x. In this case, using multiples of 5 avoids fractions. We try to avoid graphing ordered pairs with fractions because they are difficult to graph accurately.

If $x = 0$, then $y = \dfrac{2}{5} \cdot 0 + 4 = 4$, and $(0, 4)$ is a solution.

If $x = 5$, then $y = \dfrac{2}{5} \cdot 5 + 4 = 6$, and $(5, 6)$ is a solution.

If $x = -5$, then $y = \dfrac{2}{5} \cdot (-5) + 4 = 2$, and $(-5, 2)$ is a solution.

The following table lists these solutions. Next, we plot the points and see that they form a line. Finally, we draw and label the line.

x	y $y = \frac{2}{5}x + 4$	(x, y)
0	4	$(0, 4)$
5	6	$(5, 6)$
-5	2	$(-5, 2)$

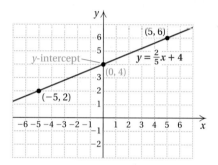

We see that $(0, 4)$ is a solution of $y = \frac{2}{5}x + 4$. It is the y-intercept. Because the equation is in the form $y = mx + b$, we can read the y-intercept directly from the equation as follows:

$$y = \frac{2}{5}x + 4 \qquad (0, 4) \text{ is the } y\text{-intercept.}$$

Do Exercises 24 and 25.

Calculating ordered pairs is generally easiest when y is isolated on one side of the equation, as in $y = mx + b$. To graph an equation in which y is not isolated, we can use the addition and multiplication principles to solve for y (see Section 2.3).

EXAMPLE 9 Graph $3y + 5x = 0$ and identify the y-intercept.

To find an equivalent equation in the form $y = mx + b$, we solve for y:

$$3y + 5x = 0$$
$$3y + 5x - 5x = 0 - 5x \qquad \text{Subtracting } 5x$$
$$3y = -5x \qquad \text{Collecting like terms}$$
$$\frac{3y}{3} = \frac{-5x}{3} \qquad \text{Dividing by 3}$$
$$y = -\frac{5}{3}x.$$

Graph the equation and identify the y-intercept.

24. $y = \dfrac{3}{5}x + 2$

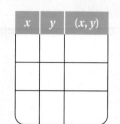

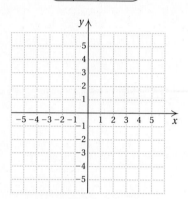

25. $y = -\dfrac{3}{5}x - 1$

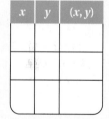

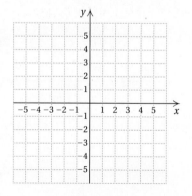

Answers on page A-11

Graph the equation and identify the y-intercept.

26. $5y + 4x = 0$

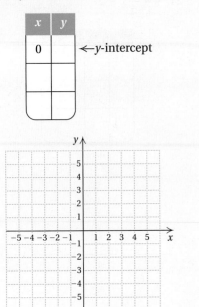

←y-intercept

Because all the equations above are equivalent, we can use $y = -\frac{5}{3}x$ to draw the graph of $3y + 5x = 0$. To graph $y = -\frac{5}{3}x$, we select x-values and compute y-values. In this case, if we select multiples of 3, we can avoid fractions.

$$\text{If } x = 0, \quad \text{then } y = -\frac{5}{3} \cdot 0 = 0.$$

$$\text{If } x = 3, \quad \text{then } y = -\frac{5}{3} \cdot 3 = -5.$$

$$\text{If } x = -3, \quad \text{then } y = -\frac{5}{3} \cdot (-3) = 5.$$

We list these solutions in a table. Next, we plot the points and see that they form a line. Finally, we draw and label the line. The y-intercept is $(0, 0)$.

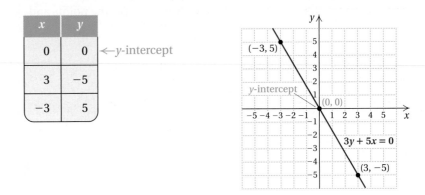

Do Exercises 26 and 27.

27. $4y = 3x$

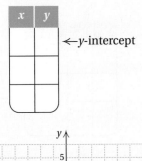

←y-intercept

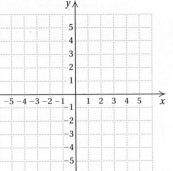

EXAMPLE 10 Graph $4y + 3x = -8$ and identify the y-intercept.

To find an equivalent equation in the form $y = mx + b$, we solve for y:

$$4y + 3x = -8$$

$$4y + 3x - 3x = -8 - 3x \qquad \text{Subtracting } 3x$$

$$4y = -3x - 8 \qquad \text{Simplifying}$$

$$\frac{1}{4} \cdot 4y = \frac{1}{4} \cdot (-3x - 8) \qquad \text{Multiplying by } \tfrac{1}{4} \text{ or dividing by 4}$$

$$y = \frac{1}{4} \cdot (-3x) - \frac{1}{4} \cdot 8 \qquad \text{Using the distributive law}$$

$$y = -\frac{3}{4}x - 2. \qquad \text{Simplifying}$$

Thus, $4y + 3x = -8$ is equivalent to $y = -\frac{3}{4}x - 2$. The y-intercept is $(0, -2)$. We find two other pairs using multiples of 4 for x to avoid fractions. We then complete and label the graph as shown.

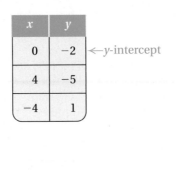

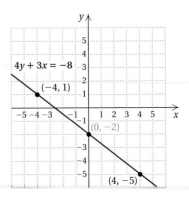

Answers on page A-11

Do Exercises 28 and 29.

e Applications of Linear Equations

Mathematical concepts become more understandable through visualization. Throughout this text, you will occasionally see the heading **AG** Algebraic–Graphical Connection, as in Example 11, which follows. In this feature, the algebraic approach is enhanced and expanded with a graphical connection. Relating a solution of an equation to a graph can often give added meaning to the algebraic solution.

EXAMPLE 11 *Online Retail Sales of Jewelry.* The online retail sales of jewelry y, in billions of dollars, is predicted by

$$y = 0.81x + 2,$$

where x is the number of years since 2003—that is, $x = 0$ corresponds to 2003, $x = 5$ corresponds to 2008, and so on.

Source: Forrester Research

a) Determine the online retail sales of jewelry in 2003, 2008, and 2015.

b) Graph the equation and then use the graph to estimate online retail sales in 2010.

c) In what year would online sales be $9.29 billion?

a) The years 2003, 2008, and 2015 correspond to $x = 0$, $x = 5$, and $x = 12$, respectively. We substitute 0, 5, and 12 for x and then calculate y:

$$y = 0.81(0) + 2 = 0 + 2 = 2;$$
$$y = 0.81(5) + 2 = 4.05 + 2 = 6.05;$$
$$y = 0.81(12) + 2 = 9.72 + 2 = 11.72.$$

Online jewelry sales in 2003, 2008, and 2015 are estimated to be $2.0 billion, $6.05 billion, and $11.72 billion, respectively.

AG ALGEBRAIC–GRAPHICAL CONNECTION

b) We have three ordered pairs from part (a). We plot these points and see that they line up. Thus our calculations are probably correct. Since we are considering only the year 2003 and the number of years since 2003 ($x \geq 0$) and since the sales, in billions of dollars, for those years will be positive ($y > 0$), we need only the first quadrant for the graph. Then we use these points to draw a straight line through them. See Figure 1 on the following page.

Graph the equation and identify the y-intercept.

28. $5y - 3x = -10$

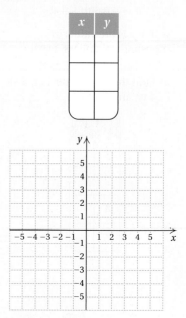

29. $5y + 3x = 20$

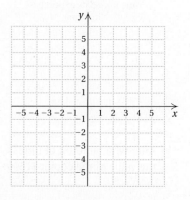

Answers on page A-11

233

30. Value of a Color Copier. The value of Dupliographic's color copier is given by

$$v = -0.68t + 3.4,$$

where v is the value, in thousands of dollars, t years from the date of purchase.

a) Find the value after 1 yr, 2 yr, 4 yr, and 5 yr.

t	v
1	
2	
4	
5	

b) Graph the equation and use the graph to estimate the value of the copier after $2\frac{1}{2}$ yr.

c) After what amount of time is the value of the copier $1500?

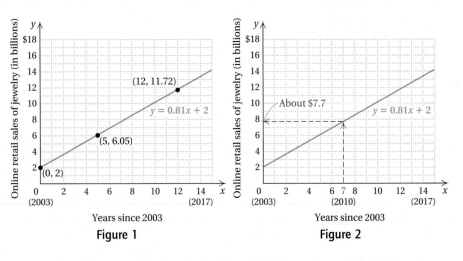

Figure 1

Figure 2

To use the graph to estimate sales in 2010, we first note in Figure 2 that this year corresponds to $x = 7$. We need to determine which y-value is paired with $x = 7$. We locate the point on the graph by moving up vertically from $x = 7$, and then find the value on the y-axis that corresponds to that point. It appears that online jewelry sales in 2010 will be about $7.7 billion.

To find a more accurate value, we can simply substitute into the equation:

$$y = 0.81(7) + 2 = 5.67 + 2 = \$7.67.$$

c) We substitute 9.29 for y and solve for x:

$$y = 0.81x + 2$$

$9.29 = 0.81x + 2$	Substituting
$7.29 = 0.81x$	Subtracting 2
$x = 9.$	Dividing by 0.81

In 9 years, or in 2012, online jewelry sales will be approximately $9.29 billion.

Do Exercise 30.

Many equations in two variables have graphs that are not straight lines. Three such nonlinear graphs are shown below. We will cover some such graphs in the optional Calculator Corners throughout the text and in Chapter 9.

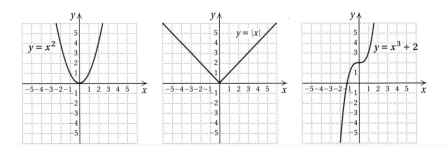

Answers on page A-11

Graphing Equations   Graphs of equations are displayed in the **viewing window** of a graphing calculator. The viewing window is the portion of the coordinate plane that appears on the calculator's screen. It is defined by the minimum and maximum values of x and y: Xmin, Xmax, Ymin, and Ymax. The notation [Xmin, Xmax, Ymin, Ymax] is used to represent these window settings or dimensions. For example, $[-12, 12, -8, 8]$ denotes a window that displays the portion of the x-axis from -12 to 12 and the portion of the y-axis from -8 to 8. In addition, the distance between tick marks on the axes is defined by the settings Xscl and Yscl. The Xres setting indicates the pixel resolution. We usually select Xres = 1. The window corresponding to the settings $[-20, 30, -12, 20]$, Xscl = 5, Yscl = 2, Xres = 1, is shown on the left below. Press (WINDOW) on the top row of the keypad of your calculator to display the current window settings. The settings for the **standard viewing window** are shown on the right below.

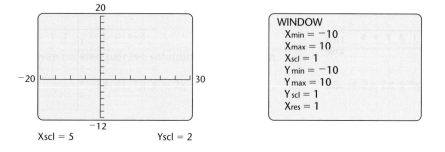

Xscl = 5   Yscl = 2

To change a setting, we position the cursor beside the setting we wish to change and enter the new value. For example, to change from the standard settings to $[-20, 30, -12, 20]$, Xscl = 5, Yscl = 2, on the WINDOW screen, we press (-) (2) (0) (ENTER) (3) (0) (ENTER) (5) (ENTER) (-) (1) (2) (ENTER) (2) (0) (ENTER) (2) (ENTER). The (▽) key can be used instead of (ENTER) after typing each window setting. To see the window, we press (GRAPH) on the top row of the keypad. To return quickly to the standard window setting $[-10, 10, -10, 10]$, Xscl = 1, Yscl = 1, we press (ZOOM) (6).

Equations must be solved for y before they can be graphed on the TI-84 Plus. Consider the equation $3x + 2y = 6$. Solving for y, we get $y = \dfrac{6 - 3x}{2}$. We enter this equation as $y_1 = (6 - 3x)/2$ on the equation-editor screen as described in the Calculator Corner in Section 2.3 (see p. 157). Then we press (ZOOM) (6) to select the standard viewing window and display the graph.

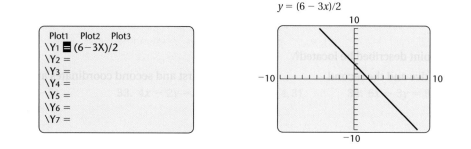

Exercises: Graph each equation in the standard viewing window $[-10, 10, -10, 10]$, Xscl = 1, Yscl = 1.

1. $y = 2x + 1$ 5. $4x - 5y = -10$

2. $y = -3x + 1$ 6. $5y + 5 = -3x$

3. $y = -5x + 3$ 7. $y = 2.085x + 5.08$

4. $y = 4x - 5$ 8. $y = -3.45x - 1.68$

d Graph the equation and identify the *y*-intercept.

35. $y = x + 1$

x	y
-2	
-1	
0	
1	
2	
3	

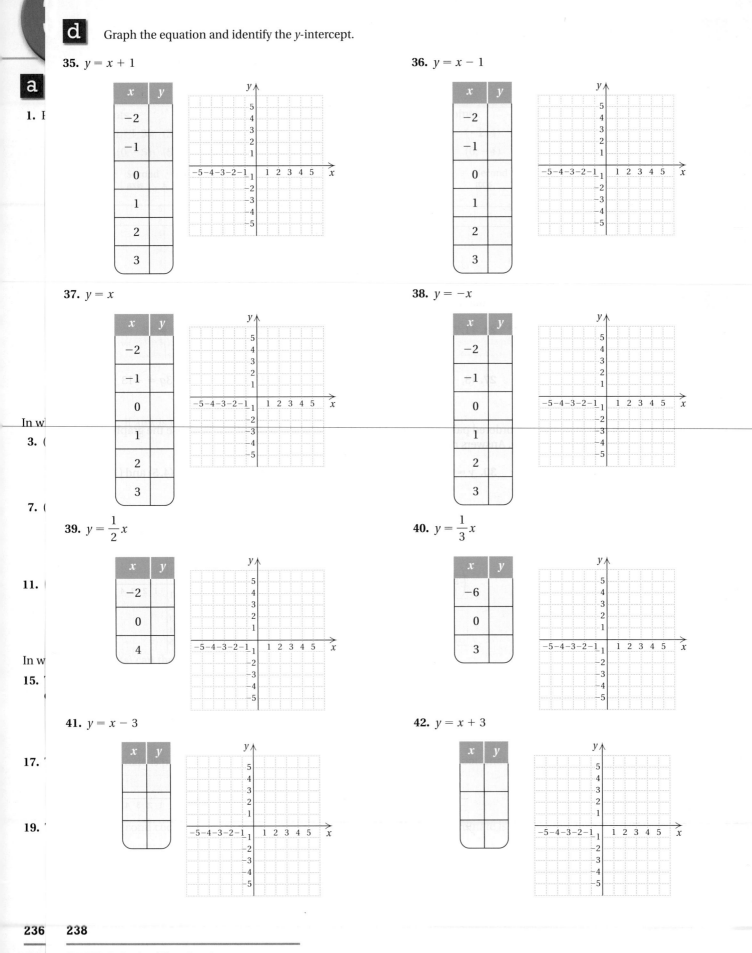

36. $y = x - 1$

x	y
-2	
-1	
0	
1	
2	
3	

37. $y = x$

x	y
-2	
-1	
0	
1	
2	
3	

38. $y = -x$

x	y
-2	
-1	
0	
1	
2	
3	

39. $y = \dfrac{1}{2}x$

x	y
-2	
0	
4	

40. $y = \dfrac{1}{3}x$

x	y
-6	
0	
3	

41. $y = x - 3$

x	y

42. $y = x + 3$

x	y

a

1.

In w

3.

7.

11.

In w

15.

17.

19.

43. $y = 3x - 2$

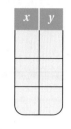

44. $y = 2x + 2$

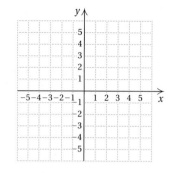

45. $y = \dfrac{1}{2}x + 1$

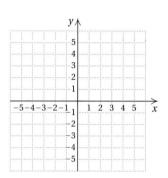

46. $y = \dfrac{1}{3}x - 4$

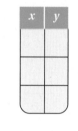

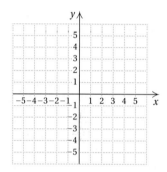

47. $x + y = -5$

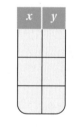

48. $x + y = 4$

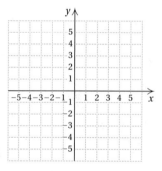

49. $y = \dfrac{5}{3}x - 2$

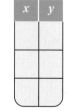

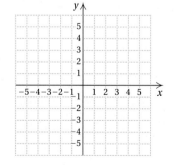

50. $y = \dfrac{5}{2}x + 3$

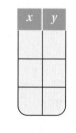

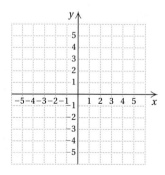

51. $x + 2y = 8$

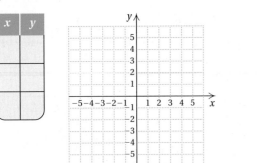

52. $x + 2y = -6$

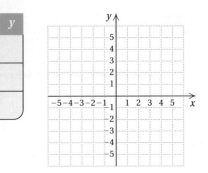

53. $y = \dfrac{3}{2}x + 1$

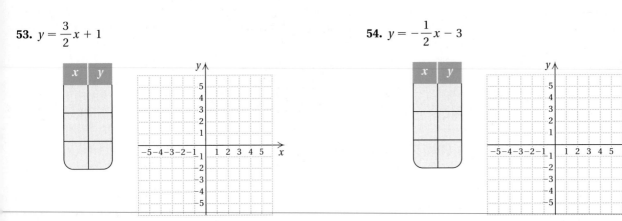

54. $y = -\dfrac{1}{2}x - 3$

55. $8x - 2y = -10$

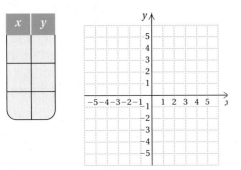

56. $6x - 3y = 9$

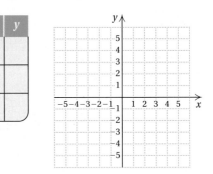

57. $8y + 2x = -4$

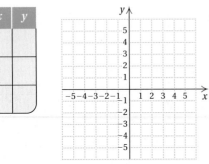

58. $6y + 2x = 8$

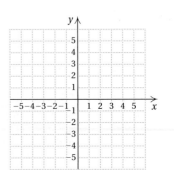

Solve.

59. *Value of Computer Software.* The value V, in dollars, of a shopkeeper's inventory software program is given by $V = -50t + 300$, where t is the number of years since the shopkeeper first bought the program.

a) Find the value of the software after 0 yr, 4 yr, and 6 yr.

b) Graph the equation and then use the graph to estimate the value of the software after 5 yr.

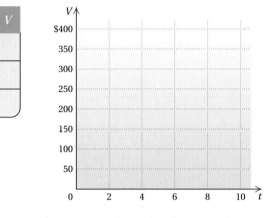

c) After how many years is the value of the software $150?

60. *SAT Math Scores.* The average SAT math scores M of potential college students can be approximated by $M = 1.4t + 518$, where t is the number of years since 2004.

Source: The College Board

a) Find the average SAT math score in 2004 ($t = 0$), 2005 ($t = 1$), and 2010.

b) Graph the equation and then use the graph to estimate the average SAT math score in 2008.

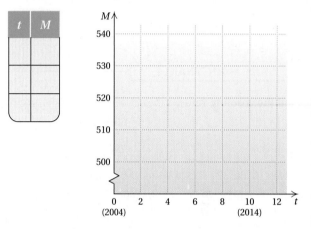

c) In what year will the average SAT math score be 539?

61. *Coffee Consumption.* The number of gallons N of coffee consumed each year by the average U.S. consumer can be approximated by $N = 0.8d + 21.2$, where d is the number of years since 1995.

Source: *Statistical Abstract of the United States,* 2003

a) Find the number of gallons of coffee consumed in 1996 ($d = 1$), 2000, 2006, and 2010.

b) Graph the equation and use the graph to estimate what the coffee consumption was in 2002.

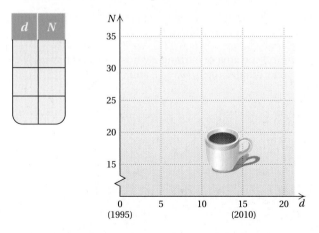

c) In what year will coffee consumption be about 31.6 gal?

62. *Record Temperature Drop.* On 22 January 1943, the temperature T, in degrees Fahrenheit, in Spearfish, South Dakota, could be approximated by $T = -2.15m + 54$, where m is the number of minutes since 9:00 that morning.

Source: *Information Please Almanac*

a) Find the temperature at 9:01 A.M., 9:08 A.M., and 9:20 A.M.

b) Graph the equation and use the graph to estimate the temperature at 9:15 A.M.

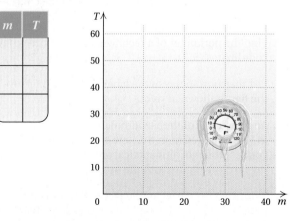

c) The temperature stopped dropping when it reached $-4°F$. At what time did this occur?

63. $\mathbf{D_W}$ The equations $3x + 4y = 8$ and $y = -\frac{3}{4}x + 2$ are equivalent. Which equation is easier to graph and why?

64. $\mathbf{D_W}$ Referring to Exercise 62, discuss why the linear equation no longer described the temperature after the temperature reached $-4°$.

Find the absolute value. [1.2e]

65. $|-12|$

66. $|4.89|$

67. $|0|$

68. $\left|-\frac{4}{5}\right|$

69. $|-3.4|$

70. $\left|\sqrt{2}\right|$

71. $\left|\frac{2}{3}\right|$

72. $\left|-\frac{7}{8}\right|$

Solve. [2.5a]

73. *Baseball Ticket Prices.* In 2004, the average price of a ticket to a major-league baseball game was $19.82. This price was an increase of 17.9% over the price in 2000. What was the average price in 2000?

Source: Major League Baseball

74. *Tipping.* Erin left a 15% tip for a meal. The total cost of the meal, including the tip, was $21.16. What was the cost of the meal before the tip was added?

75. The points $(-1, 1)$, $(4, 1)$, and $(4, -5)$ are three vertices of a rectangle. Find the coordinates of the fourth vertex.

76. Three parallelograms share the vertices $(-2, -3)$, $(-1, 2)$, and $(4, -3)$. Find the fourth vertex of each parallelogram.

77. Graph eight points such that the sum of the coordinates in each pair is 6.

78. Graph eight points such that the first coordinate minus the second coordinate is 1.

79. Find the perimeter of a rectangle whose vertices have coordinates $(5, 3)$, $(5, -2)$, $(-3, -2)$, and $(-3, 3)$.

80. Find the area of a triangle whose vertices have coordinates $(0, 9)$, $(0, -4)$, and $(5, -4)$.

81. List the coordinates of the labeled ordered pairs A–K in the figure shown at right.

82. Add 2 to each of the x-coordinates of the ordered pairs in Exercise 81. Graph the new ordered pairs and connect them in alphabetical order with lines. Compare the resulting figure with the original.

83. Subtract 3 from each of the y-coordinates of the ordered pairs in Exercise 81. Graph the new ordered pairs and connect them in alphabetical order with lines. Compare the resulting figure with the original.

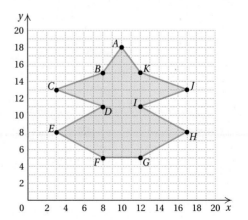

MORE WITH GRAPHING AND INTERCEPTS

Objectives

a Find the intercepts of a linear equation, and graph using intercepts.

b Graph equations equivalent to those of the type $x = a$ and $y = b$.

a   Graphing Using Intercepts

In Section 3.1, we graphed linear equations of the form $Ax + By = C$ by first solving for y to find an equivalent equation in the form $y = mx + b$. We did so because it is then easier to calculate the y-value that corresponds to a given x-value. Another convenient way to graph $Ax + By = C$ is to use **intercepts.** Look at the graph of $-2x + y = 4$ shown below.

The y-intercept is $(0, 4)$. It occurs where the line crosses the y-axis and thus will always have 0 as the first coordinate. The x-intercept is $(-2, 0)$. It occurs where the line crosses the x-axis and thus will always have 0 as the second coordinate.

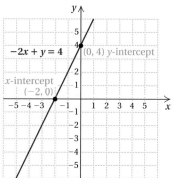

Do Exercise 1.

We find intercepts as follows.

INTERCEPTS

The **y-intercept** is $(0, b)$. To find b, let $x = 0$ and solve the original equation for y.

The **x-intercept** is $(a, 0)$. To find a, let $y = 0$ and solve the original equation for x.

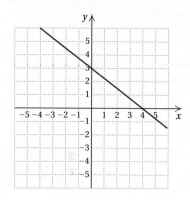

Now let's draw a graph using intercepts.

EXAMPLE 1   Consider $4x + 3y = 12$. Find the intercepts. Then graph the equation using the intercepts.

To find the y-intercept, we let $x = 0$. Then we solve for y:

$$4 \cdot 0 + 3y = 12$$
$$3y = 12$$
$$y = 4.$$

Thus, $(0, 4)$ is the y-intercept. Note that finding this intercept amounts to covering up the x-term and solving the rest of the equation.

To find the x-intercept, we let $y = 0$. Then we solve for x:

$$4x + 3 \cdot 0 = 12$$
$$4x = 12$$
$$x = 3.$$

1. Look at the graph shown below.

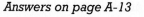

a) Find the coordinates of the y-intercept.

b) Find the coordinates of the x-intercept.

Answers on page A-13

For each equation, find the intercepts. Then graph the equation using the intercepts.

2. $2x + 3y = 6$

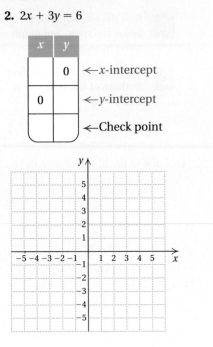

3. $3y - 4x = 12$

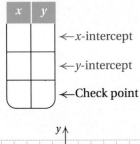

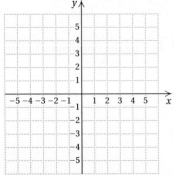

Thus, $(3, 0)$ is the x-intercept. Note that finding this intercept amounts to covering up the y-term and solving the rest of the equation.

We plot these points and draw the line, or graph.

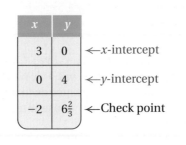

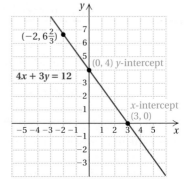

A third point should be used as a check. We substitute any convenient value for x and solve for y. In this case, we choose $x = -2$. Then

$$4(-2) + 3y = 12 \qquad \text{Substituting } -2 \text{ for } x$$
$$-8 + 3y = 12$$
$$3y = 12 + 8 = 20$$
$$y = \frac{20}{3}, \text{ or } 6\frac{2}{3}. \qquad \text{Solving for } y$$

It appears that the point $\left(-2, 6\frac{2}{3}\right)$ is on the graph, though graphing fraction values can be inexact. The graph is probably correct.

Do Exercises 2 and 3.

Graphs of equations of the type $y = mx$ pass through the origin. Thus the x-intercept and the y-intercept are the same, $(0, 0)$. In such cases, we must calculate another point in order to complete the graph. Another point would also have to be calculated if a check is desired.

EXAMPLE 2 Graph: $y = 3x$.

We know that $(0, 0)$ is both the x-intercept and the y-intercept. We calculate values at two other points and complete the graph, knowing that it passes through the origin $(0, 0)$.

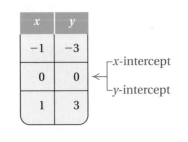

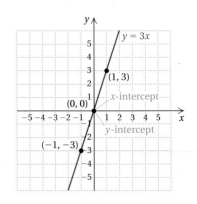

Do Exercises 4 and 5 on the following page.

CALCULATOR CORNER

Viewing the Intercepts Knowing the intercepts of a linear equation helps us to determine a good viewing window for the graph of the equation. For example, when we graph the equation $y = -x + 15$ in the standard window, we see only a small portion of the graph in the upper righthand corner of the screen, as shown on the left below.

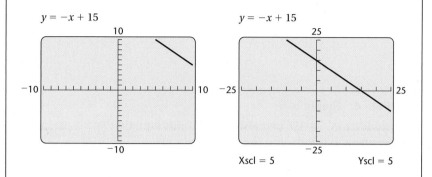

Using algebra, as we did in Example 1, we find that the intercepts of the graph of this equation are $(0, 15)$ and $(15, 0)$. This tells us that, if we are to see more of the graph than is shown on the left above, both Xmax and Ymax should be greater than 15. We can try different window settings until we find one that suits us. One good choice is $[-25, 25, -25, 25]$, Xscl $= 5$, Yscl $= 5$, shown on the right above.

Exercises: Find the intercepts of each equation algebraically. Then graph the equation on a graphing calculator, choosing window settings that allow the intercepts to be seen clearly. (Settings may vary.)

1. $y = -7.5x - 15$
2. $y - 2.15x = 43$
3. $6x - 5y = 150$
4. $y = 0.2x - 4$
5. $y = 1.5x - 15$
6. $5x - 4y = 2$

b Equations Whose Graphs Are Horizontal or Vertical Lines

EXAMPLE 3 Graph: $y = 3$.

Consider $y = 3$. We can also think of this equation as $0 \cdot x + y = 3$. No matter what number we choose for x, we find that y is 3. We make up a table with all 3's in the y-column.

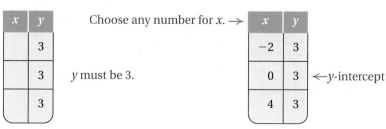

Choose any number for x. →

y must be 3.

←y-intercept

4. $y = 2x$

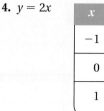

x	y
-1	
0	
1	

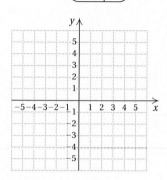

5. $y = -\dfrac{2}{3}x$

x	y

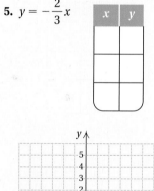

Answers on page A-13

Graph.

6. $x = 5$

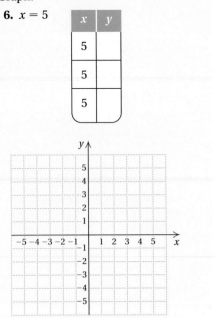

When we plot the ordered pairs $(-2, 3)$, $(0, 3)$, and $(4, 3)$ and connect the points, we obtain a horizontal line. Any ordered pair $(x, 3)$ is a solution. So the line is parallel to the x-axis with y-intercept $(0, 3)$.

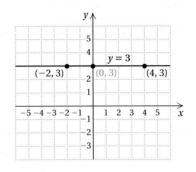

EXAMPLE 4 Graph: $x = -4$.

Consider $x = -4$. We can also think of this equation as $x + 0 \cdot y = -4$. We make up a table with all -4's in the x-column.

x	y
-4	
-4	
-4	
-4	

x must be -4.

Choose any number for y. →

x	y
-4	-5
-4	1
-4	3
-4	0

x-intercept →

When we plot the ordered pairs $(-4, -5)$, $(-4, 1)$, $(-4, 3)$, and $(-4, 0)$ and connect the points, we obtain a vertical line. Any ordered pair $(-4, y)$ is a solution. So the line is parallel to the y-axis with x-intercept $(-4, 0)$.

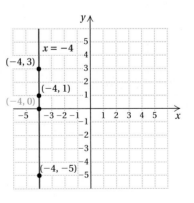

7. $y = -2$

x	y
	-2
	-2
	-2

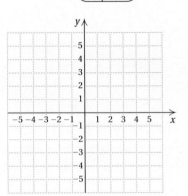

HORIZONTAL AND VERTICAL LINES

The graph of $y = b$ is a **horizontal line.** The y-intercept is $(0, b)$.

The graph of $x = a$ is a **vertical line.** The x-intercept is $(a, 0)$.

Answers on page A-13

Do Exercises 6–9. (Exercises 8 and 9 are on the following page.)

CHAPTER 3: Graphs of Linear Equations

The following is a general procedure for graphing linear equations.

GRAPHING LINEAR EQUATIONS

1. If the equation is of the type $x = a$ or $y = b$, the graph will be a line parallel to an axis; $x = a$ is vertical and $y = b$ is horizontal.

   Examples.

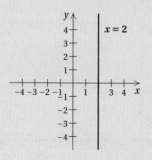

2. If the equation is of the type $y = mx$, both intercepts are the origin, $(0, 0)$. Plot $(0, 0)$ and two other points.

   Example.

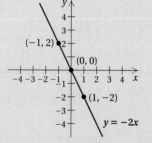

3. If the equation is of the type $y = mx + b$, plot the y-intercept $(0, b)$ and two other points.

   Example.

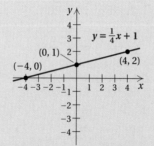

4. If the equation is of the type $Ax + By = C$, but not of the type $x = a$, $y = b$, $y = mx$, or $y = mx + b$, then either solve for y and proceed as with the equation $y = mx + b$, or graph using intercepts. If the intercepts are too close together, choose another point or points farther from the origin.

   Examples.

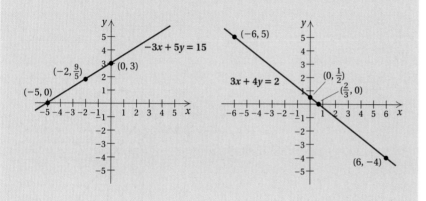

8. $x = 0$

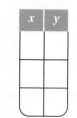

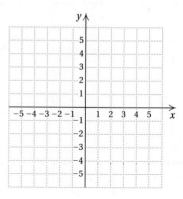

9. $x = -3$

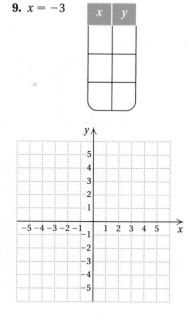

Answers on page A-13

Visualizing for Success

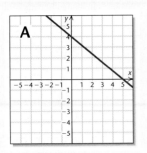

A

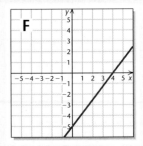

F

Match the equation with its graph.

1. $5y + 20 = 4x$

2. $y = 3$

3. $3x + 5y = 15$

4. $5y + 4x = 20$

5. $5y = 10 - 2x$

6. $4x + 5y + 20 = 0$

7. $5x - 4y = 20$

8. $4y + 5x + 20 = 0$

9. $5y - 4x = 20$

10. $x = -3$

Answers on page A-14

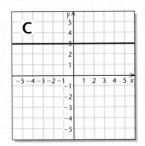

B

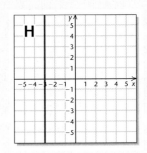

G

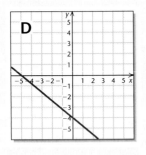

C

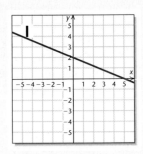

H

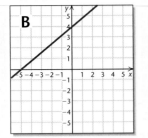

D

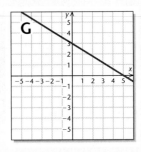

I

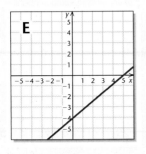

E

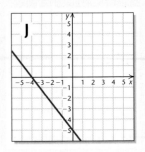

J

3.2 EXERCISE SET

For Extra Help

MathXL · MyMathLab · InterAct Math · Math Tutor Center · Digital Video Tutor CD 2 Videotape 4 · Student's Solutions Manual

a For Exercises 1–4, find **(a)** the coordinates of the *y*-intercept and **(b)** the coordinates of the *x*-intercept.

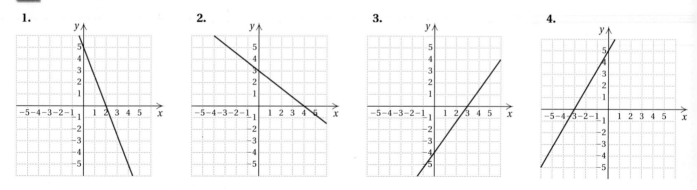

1.

2.

3.

4.

For Exercises 5–12, find **(a)** the coordinates of the *y*-intercept and **(b)** the coordinates of the *x*-intercept. Do not graph.

5. $3x + 5y = 15$

6. $5x + 2y = 20$

7. $7x - 2y = 28$

8. $3x - 4y = 24$

9. $-4x + 3y = 10$

10. $-2x + 3y = 7$

11. $6x - 3 = 9y$

12. $4y - 2 = 6x$

For each equation, find the intercepts. Then use the intercepts to graph the equation.

13. $x + 3y = 6$

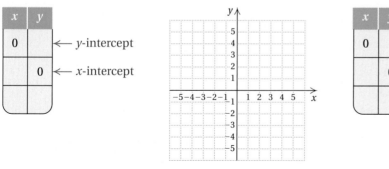

x	y
0	← *y*-intercept
	0 ← *x*-intercept

14. $x + 2y = 2$

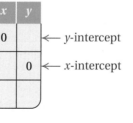

x	y
0	← *y*-intercept
	0 ← *x*-intercept

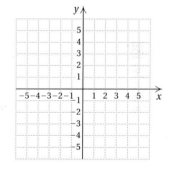

15. $-x + 2y = 4$

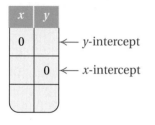

x	y
0	← *y*-intercept
	0 ← *x*-intercept

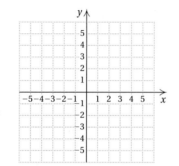

16. $-x + y = 5$

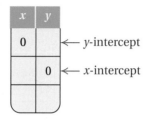

x	y
0	← *y*-intercept
	0 ← *x*-intercept

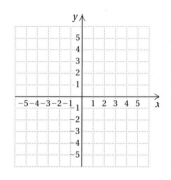

249

17. $3x + y = 6$

x	y
	0	← x-intercept
0		← y-intercept

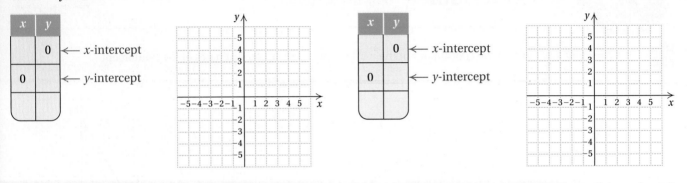

18. $2x + y = 6$

x	y
	0	← x-intercept
0		← y-intercept

19. $2y - 2 = 6x$

x	y
		← x-intercept
		← y-intercept

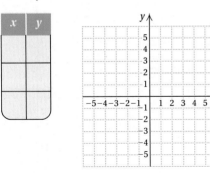

20. $3y - 6 = 9x$

x	y
		← x-intercept
		← y-intercept

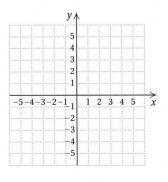

21. $3x - 9 = 3y$

x	y

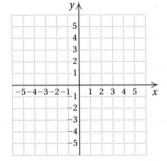

22. $5x - 10 = 5y$

x	y

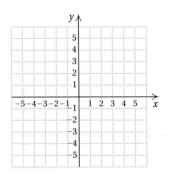

23. $2x - 3y = 6$

x	y

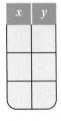

24. $2x - 5y = 10$

x	y

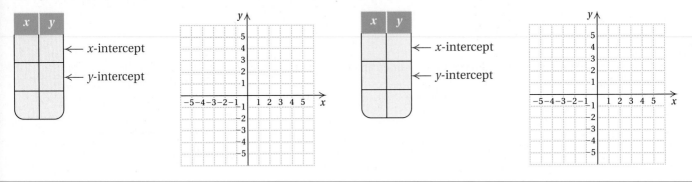

25. $4x + 5y = 20$

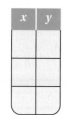

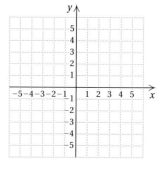

26. $2x + 6y = 12$

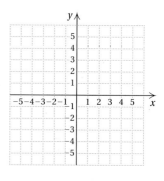

27. $2x + 3y = 8$

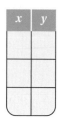

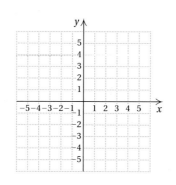

28. $x - 1 = y$

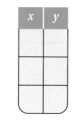

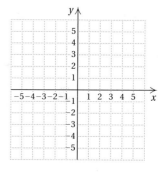

29. $x - 3 = y$

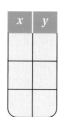

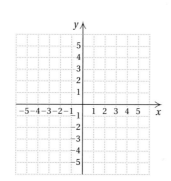

30. $2x - 1 = y$

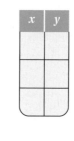

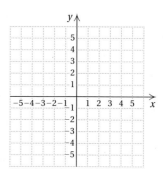

31. $3x - 2 = y$

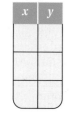

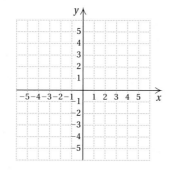

32. $4x - 3y = 12$

33. $6x - 2y = 12$

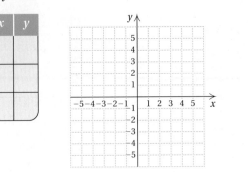

34. $7x + 2y = 6$

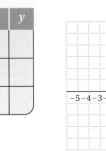

35. $3x + 4y = 5$

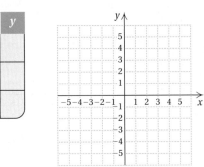

36. $y = -4 - 4x$

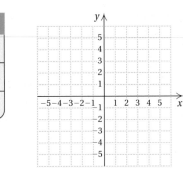

37. $y = -3 - 3x$

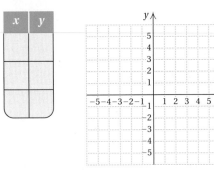

38. $-3x = 6y - 2$

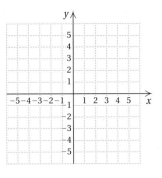

39. $y - 3x = 0$

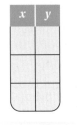

40. $x + 2y = 0$

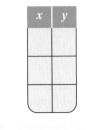

41. $x = -2$

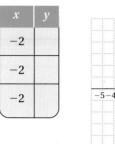

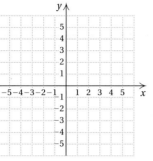

42. $x = 1$

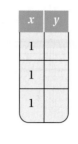

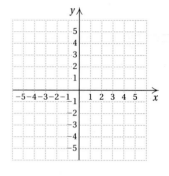

43. $y = 2$

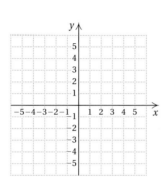

44. $y = -4$

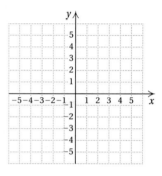

45. $x = 2$

46. $x = 3$

47. $y = 0$

48. $y = -1$

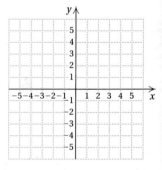

49. $x = \dfrac{3}{2}$

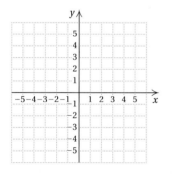

50. $x = -\dfrac{5}{2}$

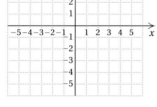

51. $3y = -5$

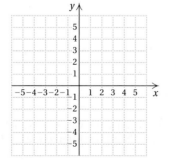

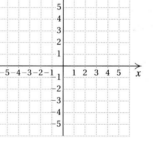

52. $12y = 45$

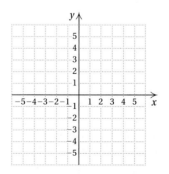

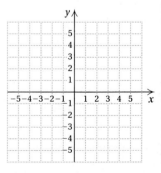

53. $4x + 3 = 0$ **54.** $-3x + 12 = 0$ **55.** $48 - 3y = 0$ **56.** $63 + 7y = 0$

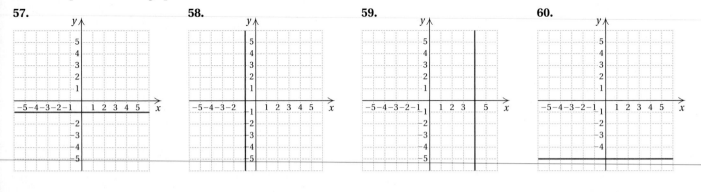

Write an equation for the graph shown.

57.   **58.**   **59.**   **60.**

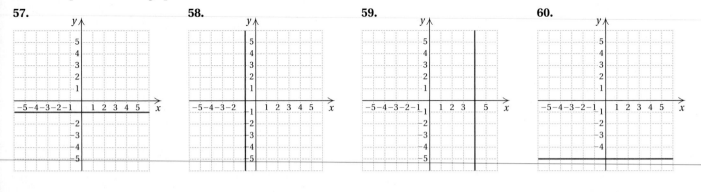

61. $\mathbf{D_W}$ If the graph of the equation $Ax + By = C$ is a horizontal line, what can you conclude about A? Why?

62. $\mathbf{D_W}$ Explain in your own words why the graph of $x = 7$ is a vertical line.

SKILL MAINTENANCE

Solve.   [2.5a]

63. *Desserts.*   If a restaurant sells 250 desserts in an evening, it is typical that 40 of them will be pie. What percent of the desserts sold will be pie?

64. *Tipping.*   Harry left a 20% tip of $6.50 for a meal. What was the cost of the meal before the tip?

Solve.   [2.7e]

65. $-1.6x < 64$

66. $-12x - 71 \geq 13$

67. $x + (x - 1) < (x + 2) - (x + 1)$

68. $6 - 18x \leq 4 - 12x - 5x$

SYNTHESIS

69. Write an equation of a line parallel to the x-axis and passing through $(-3, -4)$.

70. Find the value of m such that the graph of $y = mx + 6$ has an x-intercept of $(2, 0)$.

71. Find the value of k such that the graph of $3x + k = 5y$ has an x-intercept of $(-4, 0)$.

72. Find the value of k such that the graph of $4x = k - 3y$ has a y-intercept of $(0, -8)$.

CHAPTER 3: Graphs of Linear Equations

3.3 SLOPE AND APPLICATIONS

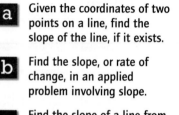

Objectives

a Given the coordinates of two points on a line, find the slope of the line, if it exists.

b Find the slope, or rate of change, in an applied problem involving slope.

c Find the slope of a line from an equation.

a Slope

We have considered two forms of a linear equation,

$$Ax + By = C \quad \text{and} \quad y = mx + b.$$

We found that from the form of the equation $y = mx + b$, we know certain information—namely, that the y-intercept of the line is $(0, b)$.

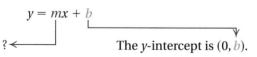

What about the constant m? Does it give us certain information about the line? Look at the following graphs and see if you can make any connection between the constant m and the "slant" of the line.

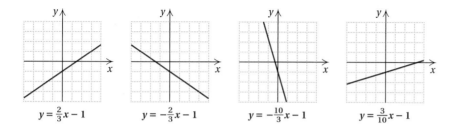

$y = \frac{2}{3}x - 1$ $y = -\frac{2}{3}x - 1$ $y = -\frac{10}{3}x - 1$ $y = \frac{3}{10}x - 1$

The graphs of some linear equations slant upward from left to right. Others slant downward. Some are vertical and some are horizontal. Some slant more steeply than others. We now look for a way to describe such possibilities with numbers.

Consider a line with two points marked P and Q. As we move from P to Q, the y-coordinate changes from 1 to 3 and the x-coordinate changes from 2 to 6. The change in y is $3 - 1$, or 2. The change in x is $6 - 2$, or 4.

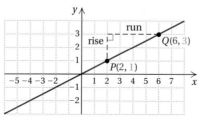

We call the change in y the **rise** and the change in x the **run.** The ratio rise/run is the same for any two points on a line. We call this ratio the **slope.** Slope describes the slant of a line. The slope of the line in the graph above is given by

$$\frac{\text{rise}}{\text{run}} = \frac{\text{the change in } y}{\text{the change in } x}, \text{ or } \frac{2}{4}, \text{ or } \frac{1}{2}.$$

SLOPE

The **slope** of a line containing points (x_1, y_1) and (x_2, y_2) is given by

$$m = \frac{\text{rise}}{\text{run}} = \frac{\text{the change in } y}{\text{the change in } x} = \frac{y_2 - y_1}{x_2 - x_1}.$$

Graph the line containing the points and find the slope in two different ways.

1. $(-2, 3)$ and $(3, 5)$

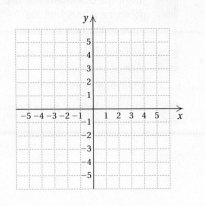

In the preceding definition, (x_1, y_1) and (x_2, y_2)—read "x sub-one, y sub-one and x sub-two, y sub-two"—represent two different points on a line. It does not matter which point is considered (x_1, y_1) and which is considered (x_2, y_2) so long as coordinates are subtracted in the same order in both the numerator and the denominator—for example,

$$\frac{y_2 - y_1}{x_2 - x_1} = \frac{y_1 - y_2}{x_1 - x_2}.$$

EXAMPLE 1 Graph the line containing the points $(-4, 3)$ and $(2, -6)$ and find the slope.

The graph is shown below. We consider (x_1, y_1) to be $(-4, 3)$ and (x_2, y_2) to be $(2, -6)$. From $(-4, 3)$ and $(2, -6)$, we see that the change in y, or the rise, is $-6 - 3$, or -9. The change in x, or the run, is $2 - (-4)$, or 6.

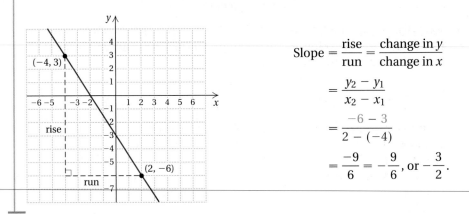

$$\text{Slope} = \frac{\text{rise}}{\text{run}} = \frac{\text{change in } y}{\text{change in } x}$$

$$= \frac{y_2 - y_1}{x_2 - x_1}$$

$$= \frac{-6 - 3}{2 - (-4)}$$

$$= \frac{-9}{6} = -\frac{9}{6}, \text{ or } -\frac{3}{2}.$$

2. $(0, -3)$ and $(-3, 2)$

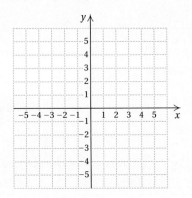

When we use the formula

$$m = \frac{y_2 - y_1}{x_2 - x_1},$$

we must remember to subtract the y-coordinates in the same order that we subtract the x-coordinates. Let's redo Example 1, where we consider (x_1, y_1) to be $(2, -6)$ and (x_2, y_2) to be $(-4, 3)$:

$$\text{Slope} = \frac{\text{change in } y}{\text{change in } x} = \frac{3 - (-6)}{-4 - 2} = \frac{9}{-6} = -\frac{3}{2}.$$

Do Exercises 1 and 2.

The slope of a line tells how it slants. A line with positive slope slants up from left to right. The larger the slope, the steeper the slant. A line with negative slope slants downward from left to right.

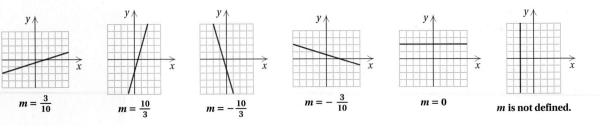

Later in this section, in Examples 10 and 11, we will discuss the slope of a horizontal line and of a vertical line. The slope of a horizontal line is 0. The slope of a vertical line is not defined.

Answers on page A-15

b Applications of Slope; Rates of Change

Slope has many real-world applications. For example, numbers like 2%, 3%, and 6% are often used to represent the *grade* of a road, a measure of how steep a road on a hill or mountain is. For example, a 3% grade $\left(3\% = \frac{3}{100}\right)$ means that for every horizontal distance of 100 ft, the road rises 3 ft, and a −3% grade means that for every horizontal distance of 100 ft, the road drops 3 ft. (Road signs do not include negative signs. It's usually obvious whether you are climbing or descending.) The concept of grade also occurs in skiing or snowboarding, where a 7% grade is considered very tame, but a 70% grade is considered extremely steep. And in cardiology, a physician may change the grade of a treadmill to measure its effect on heartbeat.

Architects and carpenters use slope when designing and building stairs, ramps, or roof pitches. Another application occurs in hydrology. When a river flows, the strength or force of the river depends on how far the river falls vertically compared to how far it flows horizontally.

EXAMPLE 2 *Skiing.* Among the steepest skiable terrain in North America, the Headwall on Mount Washington, in New Hampshire, drops 720 ft over a horizontal distance of 900 ft. Find the grade of the Headwall.

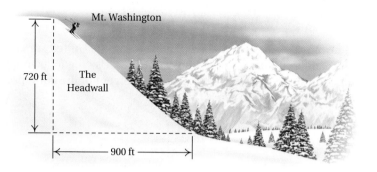

The grade of the Headwall is its slope, expressed as a percent:

$$m = \frac{720 \; \leftarrow \; \text{Vertical change}}{900 \; \leftarrow \; \text{Horizontal change}}$$

$$= \frac{8}{10} = 80\%.$$

Do Exercise 3.

---

3. **Construction.** Public buildings regularly include steps with 7-in. risers and 11-in. treads. Find the grade of such a stairway.

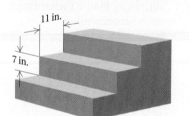

Answer on page A-15

4. Cost of a Telephone Call. The following graph shows data of interstate long-distance calling offered by AmeriCom in the Simplicity Plan. At what rate is the customer billed?

Source: AmeriCom

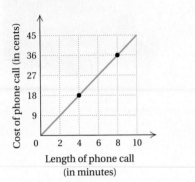

Slope can also be considered as a **rate of change.**

EXAMPLE 3 *Haircutting.* Kiddie Kutters has a graph displaying data from a recent day's work. Use the graph to determine the slope, or the rate of change, of the number of haircuts with respect to time.

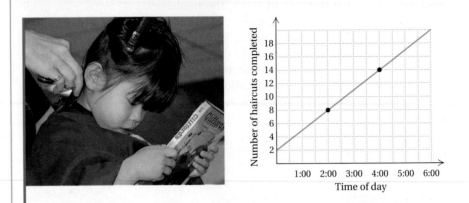

The vertical axis of the graph shows the number of haircuts and the horizontal axis the time, in units of one hour. We can describe the rate of change in the number of haircuts with respect to time as

$$\frac{\text{Haircuts}}{\text{Hour}}, \quad \text{or} \quad \textit{number of haircuts per hour.}$$

This value is the slope of the line. We determine two ordered pairs on the graph—in this case,

(2:00, 8 haircuts)   and   (4:00, 14 haircuts).

This tells us that in the 2 hr between 2:00 and 4:00, 6 haircuts were completed. Thus,

$$\text{Rate of change} = \frac{14 \text{ haircuts} - 8 \text{ haircuts}}{4:00 - 2:00} = \frac{6 \text{ haircuts}}{2 \text{ hours}} = 3 \text{ haircuts per hour.}$$

Do Exercise 4.

EXAMPLE 4 *Decreased Smoking.* Each year in the United States, the percent of the adult population who smoke declines. Use the following graph to determine the slope, or rate of change of the percent of the adult population who smoke with respect to time.

Source: U.S. Centers for Disease Control and Prevention

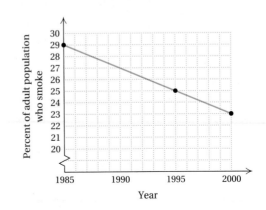

Answer on page A-15

The vertical axis of the graph shows the percent of the adult population who smoke and the horizontal axis shows the years. We can describe the rate of change in the percent who smoke with respect to time as

$$\frac{\text{Percent who smoke}}{\text{Years}}, \quad \text{or} \quad \text{percent who smoke per year.}$$

This value is the slope of the line. We determine two ordered pairs on the graph—in this case,

(1995, 25)   and   (2000, 23).

This tells us that in the 5 yr from 1995 to 2000, the percent dropped from 25% to 23%. Thus

$$\text{Rate of change} = \frac{23\% - 25\%}{2000 - 1995} = \frac{-2\%}{5 \text{ yr}} = -\frac{2}{5}\% \text{ per year.}$$

Do Exercise 5.

Answer on page A-15

5. Death by Firearms. Find the rate of change in the number of deaths by firearms.

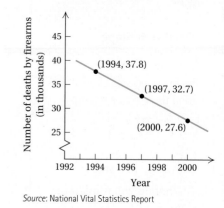

Source: National Vital Statistics Report

Study Tips

SMALL STEPS LEAD TO GREAT SUCCESS (PART 2)

Chris Widener is a popular motivational speaker and writer. In his article "A Little Equation That Creates Big Results," he proposes the following equation: "Your Short-Term Actions Multiplied By Time = Your Long-Term Accomplishments."

Think of the major or career toward which you are working as a long-term accomplishment. We (your authors and instructors) are at a point in life where we realize the long-term benefits of learning mathematics. For you as students, it may be more difficult to see those long-term results. But make an effort to do so.

Widener goes on to say, "We need to take action on our dreams and beliefs every day." Think of the long-term goal as you do the short-term tasks of homework in math, studying for tests, and completing this course so you can move on to what it prepares you for.

Who writes best-selling novels? The person who only dreams of becoming a best-selling author or the one who also spends 4 hours a day doing research and working at a computer?

Who loses weight? The person who thinks about being thin or the one who also plans a healthy diet and runs 3 miles a day?

Who is successful at math? The person who only knows all the benefits of math or the one who also spends at least 2 hours studying outside of class for every hour spent inside class?

"The purpose of man is in action, not thought."

Thomas Carlyle, British historian/essayist

"Prepare for your success in little ways and you will eventually see results in big ways. It's almost magical."

Tom Morris, public philosopher/speaker

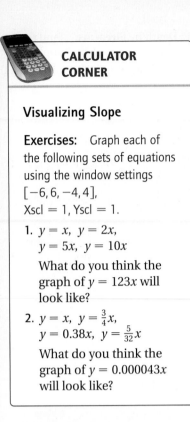
Find the slope of the line.

6. $y = 4x + 11$

7. $y = -17x + 8$

8. $y = -x + \frac{1}{2}$

9. $y = \frac{2}{3}x - 1$

Find the slope of the line.

10. $4x + 4y = 7$

11. $5x - 4y = 8$

Answers on page A-15

C Finding the Slope from an Equation

It is possible to find the slope of a line from its equation. Let's consider the equation $y = 2x + 3$, which is in the form $y = mx + b$. We can find two points by choosing convenient values for x—say, 0 and 1—and substituting to find the corresponding y-values. We find the two points on the line to be $(0, 3)$ and $(1, 5)$. The slope of the line is found using the definition of slope:

$$m = \frac{\text{change in } y}{\text{change in } x} = \frac{5 - 3}{1 - 0} = \frac{2}{1} = 2.$$

The slope is 2. Note that this is also the coefficient of the x-term in the equation $y = 2x + 3$.

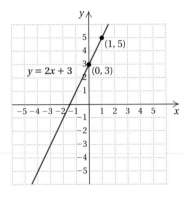

DETERMINING SLOPE FROM THE EQUATION $y = mx + b$

The slope of the line $y = mx + b$ is m. To find the slope of a nonvertical line, solve the linear equation in x and y for y and get the resulting equation in the form $y = mx + b$. The coefficient of the x-term, m, is the slope of the line.

EXAMPLES Find the slope of the line.

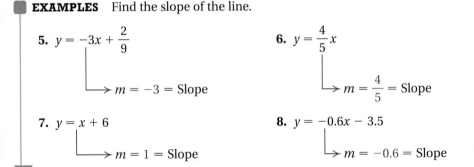

5. $y = -3x + \dfrac{2}{9}$ $\quad\longrightarrow m = -3 = \text{Slope}$

6. $y = \dfrac{4}{5}x$ $\quad\longrightarrow m = \dfrac{4}{5} = \text{Slope}$

7. $y = x + 6$ $\quad\longrightarrow m = 1 = \text{Slope}$

8. $y = -0.6x - 3.5$ $\quad\longrightarrow m = -0.6 = \text{Slope}$

Do Exercises 6–9.

To find slope from an equation, we may have to first find an equivalent form of the equation.

EXAMPLE 9 Find the slope of the line $2x + 3y = 7$.

We solve for y to get the equation in the form $y = mx + b$:

$$2x + 3y = 7$$
$$3y = -2x + 7$$
$$y = \frac{-2x + 7}{3}$$
$$y = -\frac{2}{3}x + \frac{7}{3}. \qquad \text{This is } y = mx + b.$$

The slope is $-\frac{2}{3}$.

Do Exercises 10 and 11 on the preceding page.

What about the slope of a horizontal or a vertical line?

EXAMPLE 10 Find the slope of the line $y = 5$.

We can think of $y = 5$ as $y = 0x + 5$. Then from this equation, we see that $m = 0$. Consider the points $(-3, 5)$ and $(4, 5)$, which are on the line. The change in $y = 5 - 5$, or 0. The change in $x = -3 - 4$, or -7. We have

$$m = \frac{5 - 5}{-3 - 4}$$

$$= \frac{0}{-7}$$

$$= 0.$$

Any two points on a horizontal line have the same y-coordinate. The change in y is 0. Thus the slope of a horizontal line is 0.

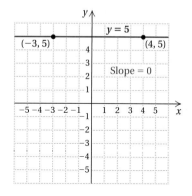

CALCULATOR CORNER

Visualizing Slope

Exercises: Graph each of the following sets of equations using the window settings $[-6, 6, -4, 4]$, Xscl = 1, Yscl = 1.

1. $y = -x$, $y = -2x$, $y = -5x$, $y = -10x$
   What do you think the graph of $y = -123x$ will look like?

2. $y = -x$, $y = -\frac{3}{4}x$, $y = -0.38x$, $y = -\frac{5}{32}x$
   What do you think the graph of $y = -0.000043x$ will look like?

EXAMPLE 11 Find the slope of the line $x = -4$.

Consider the points $(-4, 3)$ and $(-4, -2)$, which are on the line. The change in $y = 3 - (-2)$, or 5. The change in $x = -4 - (-4)$, or 0. We have

$$m = \frac{3 - (-2)}{-4 - (-4)}$$

$$= \frac{5}{0}. \qquad \text{Not defined}$$

Since division by 0 is not defined, the slope of this line is not defined. The answer in this example is "The slope of this line is not defined."

Find the slope, if it exists, of the line.

12. $x = 7$

SLOPE 0; SLOPE NOT DEFINED

The slope of a horizontal line is 0.

The slope of a vertical line is not defined.

13. $y = -5$

Do Exercises 12 and 13.

Answers on page A-15

a Find the slope, if it exists, of the line.

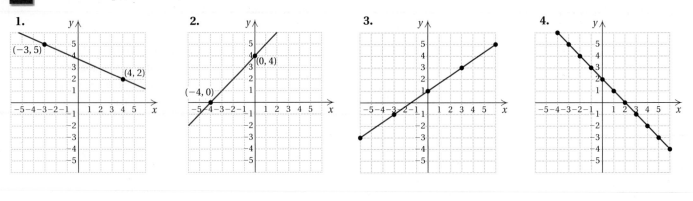

1.

2.

3.

4.

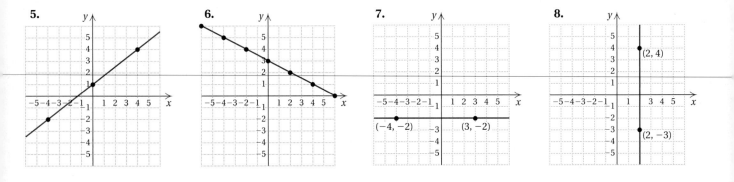

5.

6.

7.

8.

Graph the line containing the given pair of points and find the slope.

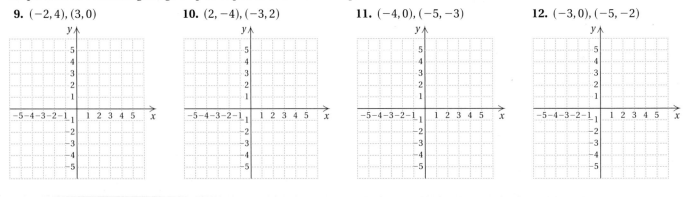

9. $(-2, 4), (3, 0)$

10. $(2, -4), (-3, 2)$

11. $(-4, 0), (-5, -3)$

12. $(-3, 0), (-5, -2)$

13. $(-4, 2), (2, -3)$

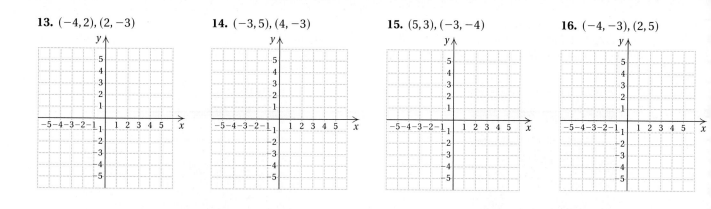

14. $(-3, 5), (4, -3)$

15. $(5, 3), (-3, -4)$

16. $(-4, -3), (2, 5)$

Find the slope, if it exists, of the line containing the given pair of points.

17. $\left(2, -\frac{1}{2}\right), \left(5, \frac{3}{2}\right)$

18. $\left(\frac{2}{3}, -1\right), \left(\frac{5}{3}, 2\right)$

19. $(4, -2), (4, 3)$

20. $(4, -3), (-2, -3)$

21. $(-11, 7), (15, -3)$

22. $(-13, 22), (8, -17)$

23. $\left(-\frac{1}{2}, \frac{3}{11}\right), \left(\frac{5}{4}, \frac{3}{11}\right)$

24. $(0.2, 4), (0.2, -0.04)$

b In Exercises 25–28, find the slope (or rate of change).

25. Find the slope (or pitch) of the roof.

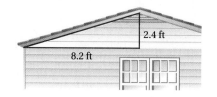

2.4 ft

8.2 ft

26. Find the slope (or grade) of the road.

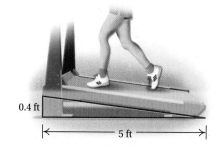

920.58 m

13,740 m

27. Find the slope of the river.

56 ft

258 ft

28. Find the slope of the treadmill.

0.4 ft

5 ft

29. *Slope of Long's Peak.* From a base elevation of 9600 ft, Long's Peak in Colorado rises to a summit elevation of 14,255 ft over a horizontal distance of 15,840 ft. Find the grade of Long's Peak.

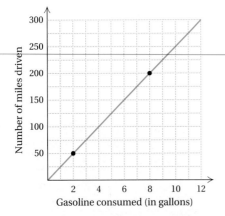

30. *Ramps for the Disabled.* In order to meet federal standards, a wheelchair ramp must not rise more than 1 ft over a horizontal distance of 12 ft. Express this slope as a grade.

In Exercises 31–34, use the graph to calculate a rate of change in which the units of the horizontal axis are used in the denominator.

31. *Gas Mileage.* The following graph shows data for a Honda Odyssey Minivan driven on interstate highways. Find the rate of change in miles per gallon, that is, the gas mileage.

Source: American Honda Motor Company, Inc.

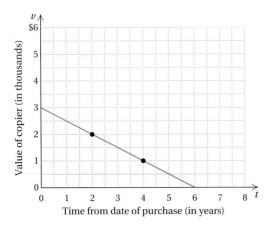

32. *Hairdresser.* Eve's Custom Cuts has a graph displaying data from a recent day of work. Find the rate of change of the number of haircuts with respect to time.

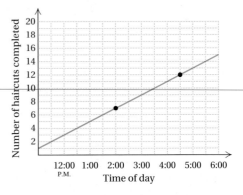

33. *Depreciation of an Office Machine.* The value of a particular color copier is represented in the following graph. Find the rate of change of the value with respect to time, in dollars per year.

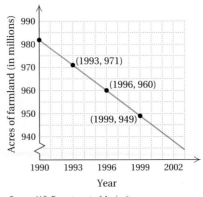

34. *Farmland.* The amount of farmland in the United States, in millions of acres, is represented in the following graph. Find the rate of change, rounded to the nearest hundred thousand, of the number of acres with respect to time, in number of acres per year.

Source: U.S. Department of Agriculture

35. *Population Growth of Alaska.* The population of Alaska is illustrated in the following graph. Find the rate of change, to the nearest hundred, of the population with respect to time, in number of people per year.

Population Growth of Alaska

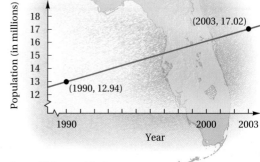

Source: U.S. Bureau of the Census

36. *Population Growth of Florida.* The population of Florida is illustrated in the following graph. Find the rate of change of the population with respect to time, in number of people per year.

Population Growth of Florida

Source: U.S. Bureau of the Census

C Find the slope, if it exists, of the line.

37. $y = -10x + 7$

38. $y = \dfrac{10}{3}x - \dfrac{5}{7}$

39. $y = 3.78x - 4$

40. $y = -\dfrac{3}{5}x + 28$

41. $3x - y = 4$

42. $-2x + y = 8$

43. $x + 5y = 10$

44. $x - 4y = 8$

45. $3x + 2y = 6$

46. $2x - 4y = 8$

47. $x = \dfrac{2}{15}$

48. $y = -\dfrac{1}{3}$

49. $y = -2.74x$

50. $y = \dfrac{219}{298}x - 6.7$

51. $9x = 3y + 5$

52. $4y = 9x - 7$

53. $5x - 4y + 12 = 0$

54. $16 + 2x - 8y = 0$

55. $y = 4$

56. $x = -3$

Assuming that the scales on each axis of each graph are the same, explain how you can estimate the slope of the line that contains segment *PQ* without knowing the coordinates of the points *P* and *Q*.

57. D_W

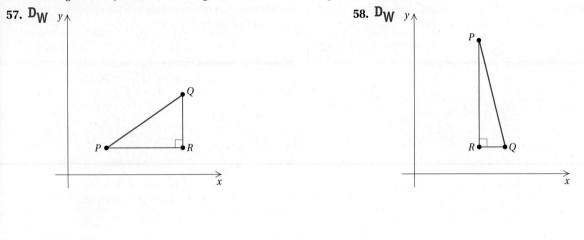

58. D_W

SKILL MAINTENANCE

Convert to fraction notation. [R.4b]

59. 16% **60.** $33\frac{1}{3}\%$ **61.** 37.5% **62.** 75%

Solve. [2.5a]

63. What is 15% of $23.80?

64. $7.29 is 15% of what number?

65. Jennifer left an $8.50 tip for a meal that cost $42.50. What percent of the cost of the meal was the tip?

66. Kristen left an 18% tip of $3.24 for a meal. What was the cost of the meal before the tip?

67. Juan left a 15% tip for a meal. The total cost of the meal, including the tip, was $51.92. What was the cost of the meal before the tip was added?

68. After a 25% reduction, a sweater is on sale for $41.25. What was the original price?

SYNTHESIS

In Exercises 69–72, find an equation for the graph shown.

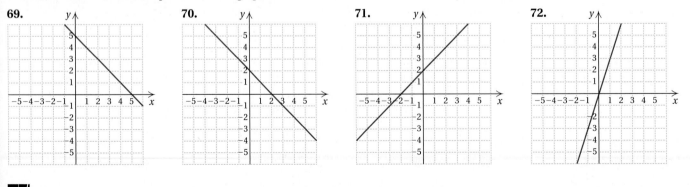

69. **70.** **71.** **72.**

Graph the equation using the standard viewing window. Then construct a table of *y*-values for *x*-values starting at $x = -10$ with $\triangle$Tbl = 0.1.

73. $y = 0.35x - 7$ **74.** $y = 5.6 - x^2$ **75.** $y = x^3 - 5$ **76.** $y = 4 + 3x - x^2$

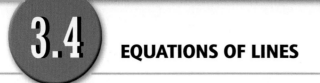

3.4 EQUATIONS OF LINES

Objectives

a Given an equation in the form $y = mx + b$, find the slope and the y-intercept; find an equation of a line when the slope and the y-intercept are given.

b Find an equation of a line when the slope and a point on the line are given.

c Find an equation of a line when two points on the line are given.

We have learned that the slope of a line and the y-intercept of the graph of the line can be read directly from the equation if it is in the form $y = mx + b$. The **slope** is m and the **y-intercept** is $(0, b)$. Here we use slope and y-intercept in order to examine linear equations in more detail.

a Finding an Equation of a Line When the Slope and the y-Intercept Are Given

We know from Sections 3.1 and 3.3 that in the equation $y = mx + b$, the slope is m and the y-intercept is $(0, b)$. Thus we call the equation $y = mx + b$ the **slope–intercept equation.**

> **THE SLOPE–INTERCEPT EQUATION:**
> $y = mx + b$
>
> The equation $y = mx + b$ is called the **slope–intercept equation.**
> The slope is m and the y-intercept is $(0, b)$.

Find the slope and the y-intercept.

1. $y = 5x$

EXAMPLE 1 Find the slope and the y-intercept of $2x - 3y = 8$.

We first solve for y:

$$2x - 3y = 8$$
$$-3y = -2x + 8 \qquad \text{Subtracting } 2x$$
$$\frac{-3y}{-3} = \frac{-2x + 8}{-3} \qquad \text{Dividing by } -3$$
$$y = \frac{-2x}{-3} + \frac{8}{-3}$$
$$y = \frac{2}{3}x - \frac{8}{3}$$

2. $y = -\dfrac{3}{2}x - 6$

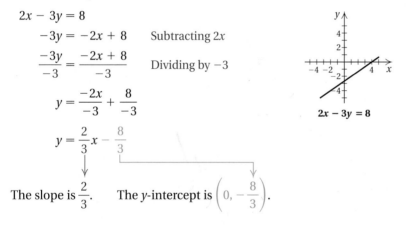

$2x - 3y = 8$

The slope is $\dfrac{2}{3}$. The y-intercept is $\left(0, -\dfrac{8}{3}\right)$.

3. $3x + 4y = 15$

Do Exercises 1–5.

4. $2y = 4x - 17$

EXAMPLE 2 A line has slope -2.4 and y-intercept $(0, 11)$. Find an equation of the line.

We use the slope–intercept equation and substitute -2.4 for m and 11 for b:

$$y = mx + b$$
$$y = -2.4x + 11. \qquad \text{Substituting}$$

5. $-7x - 5y = 22$

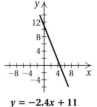

$y = -2.4x + 11$

Answers on page A-15

6. A line has slope 3.5 and y-intercept $(0, -23)$. Find an equation of the line.

EXAMPLE 3 A line has slope 0 and y-intercept $(0, -6)$. Find an equation of the line.

We use the slope–intercept equation and substitute 0 for m and -6 for b:

$$y = mx + b$$
$$y = 0x + (-6) \qquad \text{Substituting}$$
$$y = -6.$$

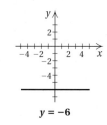

$y = -6$

EXAMPLE 4 A line has slope $-\frac{5}{3}$ and y-intercept $(0, 0)$. Find an equation of the line.

We use the slope–intercept equation and substitute $-\frac{5}{3}$ for m and 0 for b:

$$y = mx + b$$
$$y = -\tfrac{5}{3}x + 0 \qquad \text{Substituting}$$
$$y = -\tfrac{5}{3}x.$$

7. A line has slope 0 and y-intercept $(0, 13)$. Find an equation of the line.

$$y = -\frac{5}{3}x$$

Do Exercises 6–8.

b ## Finding an Equation of a Line When the Slope and a Point Are Given

Suppose we know the slope of a line and a certain point on that line. We can use the slope–intercept equation $y = mx + b$ to find an equation of the line. To write an equation in this form, we need to know the slope m and the y-intercept $(0, b)$.

8. A line has slope -7.29 and y-intercept $(0, 0)$. Find an equation of the line.

EXAMPLE 5 Find an equation of the line with slope 3 that contains the point $(4, 1)$.

We know that the slope is 3, so the equation is $y = 3x + b$. This equation is true for $(4, 1)$. Using the point $(4, 1)$, we substitute 4 for x and 1 for y in $y = 3x + b$. Then we solve for b:

$$y = 3x + b \qquad \text{Substituting 3 for } m \text{ in } y = mx + b$$
$$1 = 3(4) + b \qquad \text{Substituting 4 for } x \text{ and 1 for } y$$
$$1 = 12 + b$$
$$-11 = b. \qquad \text{Solving for } b, \text{ we find that the } y\text{-intercept is } (0, -11).$$

We use the equation $y = mx + b$ and substitute 3 for m and -11 for b:

$$y = 3x - 11.$$

Answers on page A-16

This is the equation of the line with slope 3 and y-intercept $(0, -11)$.

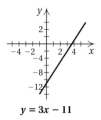

$$y = 3x - 11$$

Find an equation of the line that contains the given point and has the given slope.

9. $(4, 2)$, $m = 5$

EXAMPLE 6 Find an equation of the line with slope -5 that contains the point $(-2, 3)$.

We know that the slope is -5, so the equation is $y = -5x + b$. Using the point $(-2, 3)$, we substitute -2 for x and 3 for y in $y = -5x + b$. Then we solve for b:

10. $(-2, 1)$, $m = -3$

$y = -5x + b$	Substituting 5 for m in $y = mx + b$
$3 = -5(-2) + b$	Substituting -2 for x and 3 for y
$3 = 10 + b$	
$-7 = b.$	Solving for b

We use the equation $y = mx + b$ and substitute -5 for m and -7 for b:

$$y = -5x - 7.$$

This is the equation of the line with slope -5 and y-intercept $(0, -7)$.

11. $(3, 5)$, $m = 6$

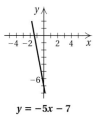

$$y = -5x - 7$$

Do Exercises 9–12.

C   Finding an Equation of a Line When Two Points Are Given

12. $(1, 4)$, $m = -\dfrac{2}{3}$

We can also use the slope–intercept equation to find an equation of a line when two points are given.

EXAMPLE 7 Find an equation of the line containing the points $(2, 3)$ and $(-6, 1)$.

First, we find the slope:

$$m = \frac{3 - 1}{2 - (-6)} = \frac{2}{8}, \text{ or } \frac{1}{4}.$$

Thus, $y = \frac{1}{4}x + b$. We then proceed as we did in Example 6, using either point to find b.

Answers on page A-16

Find an equation of the line containing the given points.

13. (2, 4) and (3, 5)

14. (−1, 2) and (−3, −2)

We choose (2, 3) and substitute 2 for x and 3 for y:

$$y = \frac{1}{4}x + b \qquad \text{Substituting } \frac{1}{4} \text{ for } m \text{ in } y = mx + b$$

$$3 = \frac{1}{4} \cdot 2 + b \qquad \text{Substituting 2 for } x \text{ and 3 for } y$$

$$3 = \frac{1}{2} + b$$

$$\frac{5}{2} = b. \qquad \text{Solving for } b$$

We use the equation $y = mx + b$ and substitute $\frac{1}{4}$ for m and $\frac{5}{2}$ for b:

$$y = \frac{1}{4}x + \frac{5}{2}.$$

This is the equation of the line with slope $\frac{1}{4}$ and y-intercept $\left(0, \frac{5}{2}\right)$.

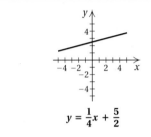

$$y = \frac{1}{4}x + \frac{5}{2}$$

Do Exercises 13 and 14.

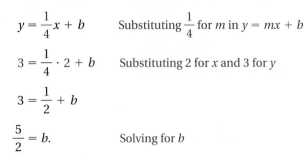

Study Tips

BETTER TEST TAKING

How often do you make the following statement after taking a test: "I was able to do the homework, but I froze during the test"? Here are two tips to help you with this difficulty. Both are intended to make test taking less stressful by getting you to practice good test-taking habits on a daily basis.

■ **Treat every homework exercise as if it were a test question.** If you had to work a problem at your job with no backup answer provided, what would you do? You would probably work it very deliberately, checking and rechecking every step. You might work it more than one time, or you might try to work it another way to check the result. Try to use this approach when doing your homework. Treat every exercise as though it were a test question with no answer at the back of the book.

■ **Be sure that you do questions without answers as part of every homework assignment whether or not the instructor has assigned them!** One reason a test may seem such a different task is that questions on a test lack answers. That is the reason for taking a test: to see if you can do the questions without assistance. As part of your test preparation, be sure you do some exercises for which you do not have the answers. Thus when you take a test, you are doing a more familiar task.

The purpose of doing your homework using these approaches is to give you more test-taking practice beforehand. Let's use a sports analogy: At a basketball game, the players take lots of practice shots before the game. They play the first half, go to the locker room, and come out for the second half. What do they do before the second half, even though they have just played 20 minutes of basketball? They shoot baskets again! We suggest the same approach here. Create more and more situations in which you practice taking test questions by treating each homework exercise like a test question and by doing exercises for which you have no answers. Good luck!

"He who does not venture has no luck."

a Find the slope and the *y*-intercept.

1. $y = -4x - 9$

2. $y = -2x + 3$

3. $y = 1.8x$

4. $y = -27.4x$

5. $-8x - 7y = 21$

6. $-2x - 8y = 16$

7. $4x = 9y + 7$

8. $5x + 4y = 12$

9. $-6x = 4y + 2$

10. $4.8x - 1.2y = 36$

11. $y = -17$

12. $y = 28$

Find an equation of the line with the given slope and *y*-intercept.

13. Slope $= -7$,
  y-intercept $= (0, -13)$

14. Slope $= 73$,
  y-intercept $= (0, 54)$

15. Slope $= 1.01$,
  y-intercept $= (0, -2.6)$

16. Slope $= -\dfrac{3}{8}$,

  y-intercept $= \left(0, \dfrac{7}{11}\right)$

b Find an equation of the line containing the given point and having the given slope.

17. $(-3, 0)$, $m = -2$

18. $(2, 5)$, $m = 5$

19. $(2, 4)$, $m = \dfrac{3}{4}$

20. $\left(\dfrac{1}{2}, 2\right), m = -1$

21. $(2, -6)$, $m = 1$

22. $(4, -2)$, $m = 6$

23. $(0, 3)$, $m = -3$

24. $(-2, -4)$, $m = 0$

c Find an equation of the line that contains the given pair of points.

25. $(12, 16)$ and $(1, 5)$

26. $(-6, 1)$ and $(2, 3)$

27. $(0, 4)$ and $(4, 2)$

28. $(0, 0)$ and $(4, 2)$

29. $(3, 2)$ and $(1, 5)$ **30.** $(-4, 1)$ and $(-1, 4)$ **31.** $(-4, 5)$ and $(-2, -3)$ **32.** $(-2, -4)$ and $(2, -1)$

33. *Aerobic Exercise.* The line graph below describes the *target heart rate T*, in beats per minute, of a person of age *a*, who is exercising. The goal is to get the number of beats per minute to this target level.

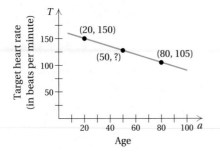

a) Find an equation of the line.
b) What is the rate of change of target heart rate with respect to time?
c) Use the equation to calculate the target heart rate of a person of age 50.

34. *Diabetes Cases.* The line graph below describes the number *N*, in millions, of persons diagnosed with diabetes in the United States in years *x* since 1992.

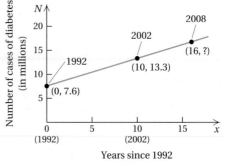

Source: U.S. National Center for Health Statistics

a) Find an equation of the line.
b) What is the rate of change of the number of cases of diabetes with respect to time?
c) Use the equation to predict the number of cases of diabetes in 2008.

35. D_W Do all graphs of linear equations have *y*-intercepts? Why or why not?

36. D_W Do all graphs of linear equations have *x*-intercepts? Why or why not?

SKILL MAINTENANCE

Solve.   [2.3b, c]

37. $3x - 4(9 - x) = 17$

38. $2(5 + 2y) + 4y = 13$

39. $40(2x - 7) = 50(4 - 6x)$

40. $\dfrac{2}{3}(x - 5) = \dfrac{3}{8}(x + 5)$

41. $3x - 9x + 21x - 15x = 6x - 12 - 24x + 18$

42. $3x - (9x + 21x) - 15x = 6x - (12 - 24x) + 18$

43. $3(x - 9x) + 21(x - 15x) = 6(x - 12) - 24(x + 18)$

44. $3x - (9x + 21x - 15x) = 6x - (12 - 24x + 18)$

SYNTHESIS

45. Find an equation of the line that contains the point $(2, -3)$ and has the same slope as the line $3x - y + 4 = 0$.

46. Find an equation of the line that has the same *y*-intercept as the line $x - 3y = 6$ and contains the point $(5, -1)$.

47. Find an equation of the line with the same slope as the line $3x - 2y = 8$ and the same *y*-intercept as the line $2y + 3x = -4$.

a   Graphs Using the Slope and the *y*-Intercept

We can graph a line if we know the coordinates of two points on that line. We can also graph a line if we know the slope and the *y*-intercept.

EXAMPLE 1   Draw a line that has slope $\frac{1}{4}$ and *y*-intercept $(0, 2)$.

We plot $(0, 2)$ and from there move *up* 1 unit (since the numerator is *positive* and corresponds to the change in *y*) and *to the right* 4 units (since the denominator is *positive* and corresponds to the change in *x*). This locates the point $(4, 3)$. We plot $(4, 3)$ and draw a line passing through $(0, 2)$ and $(4, 3)$, as shown on the right below.

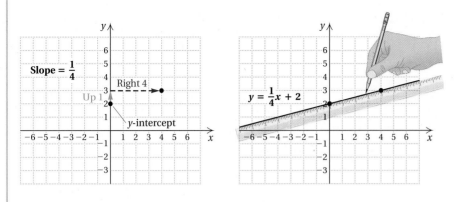

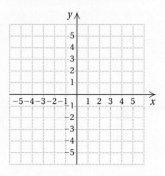

We are actually graphing the equation $y = \frac{1}{4}x + 2$.

EXAMPLE 2   Draw a line that has slope $-\frac{2}{3}$ and *y*-intercept $(0, 4)$.

We can think of $-\frac{2}{3}$ as $\frac{-2}{3}$. We plot $(0, 4)$ and from there move *down* 2 units (since the numerator is *negative*) and *to the right* 3 units (since the denominator is *positive*). We plot the point $(3, 2)$ and draw a line passing through $(0, 4)$ and $(3, 2)$.

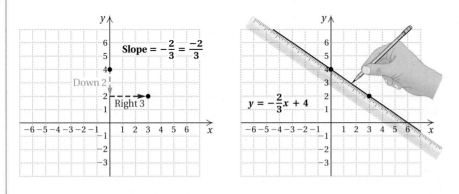

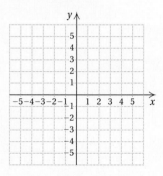

We are actually graphing the equation $y = -\frac{2}{3}x + 4$.

Do Exercises 1–3.

1. Draw a line that has slope $\frac{2}{5}$ and *y*-intercept $(0, -3)$. What equation is graphed?

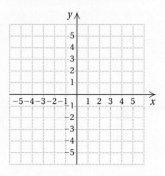

2. Draw a line that has slope $-\frac{2}{5}$ and *y*-intercept $(0, -3)$. What equation is graphed?

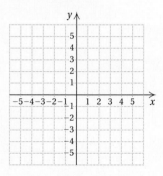

3. Draw a line that has slope 6 and *y*-intercept $(0, -3)$. Think of 6 as $\frac{6}{1}$. What equation is graphed?

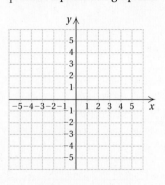

Answers on page A-16

4. Graph $y = \frac{3}{5}x - 4$ using the slope and the y-intercept.

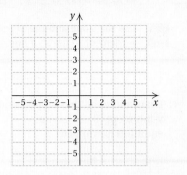

We now use our knowledge of the slope–intercept equation to graph linear equations.

EXAMPLE 3 Graph $y = \frac{3}{4}x + 5$ using the slope and the y-intercept.

From the equation $y = \frac{3}{4}x + 5$, we see that the slope of the graph is $\frac{3}{4}$ and the y-intercept is $(0, 5)$. We plot $(0, 5)$ and then consider the slope, $\frac{3}{4}$. Starting at $(0, 5)$, we plot a second point by moving *up* 3 units (since the numerator is *positive*) and *to the right* 4 units (since the denominator is *positive*). We reach a new point, $(4, 8)$.

We can also rewrite the slope as $\frac{-3}{-4}$. We again start at the y-intercept, $(0, 5)$, but move *down* 3 units (since the numerator is *negative* and corresponds to the change in y) and *to the left* 4 units (since the denominator is *negative* and corresponds to the change in x). We reach another point, $(-4, 2)$. Once two or three points have been plotted, the line representing all solutions of $y = \frac{3}{4}x + 5$ can be drawn.

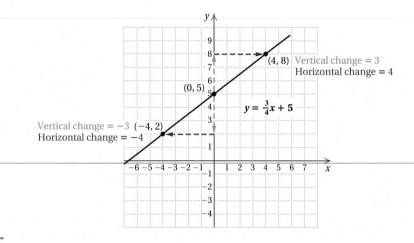

Do Exercise 4.

EXAMPLE 4 Graph $2x + 3y = 3$ using the slope and the y-intercept.

To graph $2x + 3y = 3$, we first rewrite the equation in slope–intercept form:

$$2x + 3y = 3$$
$$3y = -2x + 3 \qquad \text{Adding } -2x$$
$$\tfrac{1}{3} \cdot 3y = \tfrac{1}{3}(-2x + 3) \qquad \text{Multiplying by } \tfrac{1}{3}$$
$$y = -\tfrac{2}{3}x + 1. \qquad \text{Simplifying}$$

To graph $y = -\frac{2}{3}x + 1$, we first plot the y-intercept, $(0, 1)$. We can think of the slope as $\frac{-2}{3}$. Starting at $(0, 1)$ and using the slope, we find a second point by moving *down* 2 units (since the numerator is *negative*) and *to the right* 3 units (since the denominator is *positive*). We plot the new point, $(3, -1)$. In a similar manner, we can move from the point $(3, -1)$ to locate a third point, $(6, -3)$. The line can then be drawn.

Answer on page A-16

Since $-\frac{2}{3} = \frac{2}{-3}$, an alternative approach is to again plot $(0, 1)$, but this time move *up* 2 units (since the numerator is *positive*) and *to the left* 3 units (since the denominator is *negative*). This leads to another point on the graph, $(-3, 3)$.

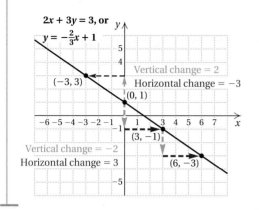

It helps to use both $\frac{2}{-3}$ and $\frac{-2}{3}$ to draw the graph.

Do Exercise 5.

5. Graph: $3x + 4y = 12$.

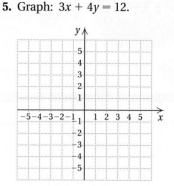

Answer on page A-16

Study Tips

TURNING NEGATIVES INTO POSITIVES

B. C. Forbes said, "History has demonstrated that notable winners usually encountered heartbreaking obstacles before they triumphed. They won because they refused to become discouraged by their defeats."

Here are some anecdotes about well-known people who turned what could have been a negative experience into a positive outcome.

- *Richard Bach* sold more than 7 million copies of his story about a "soaring" seagull, Jonathan Livingston Seagull. His work was turned down by 18 publishers before Macmillan finally published it in 1970.

- *Walt Disney* was once fired by a newspaper for what they said was his "lack of ideas." He went bankrupt several times before he built an entertainment empire that now includes Disneyland and Disney World.

- *Erik Weihenmayer*, a blind man, has climbed the tallest mountains in Africa and North and South America and recently climbed the tallest mountain in the world, Mt. Everest.

- *Hank Aaron* holds the all-time Major League home run record with a total of 755, topping the former record holder, Babe Ruth, who had 714. But Aaron also held the all-time record for many years for striking out 1383 times, also topping Babe Ruth, who struck out 1330 times!

- At the age of 15, *Michael Jordan* was cut from his school basketball team. He was told he was too small to play. Yet in 2000, he was selected by ESPN as the top athlete of the 20th century.

- *Albert Einstein* didn't speak until he was 4 years old and was not able to read until he was 7. He is now recognized as one of the greatest physicists of all time, having developed the famous theory of relativity.

In an article entitled "*Mistakes–Important Teacher*," Josh Hinds writes, "Another approach (to negative experiences) is to remind ourselves that failures are not always failures, rather they are lessons. I would challenge you to find one occurrence in your own life where you have learned from a past mistake. While it can be true that we don't gain direct rewards from them, we still gain something of great importance. Therefore we need to explore our failures and take the time to use them as our teachers …"

"Whoever makes no mistakes is doing nothing."

Dutch proverb

275

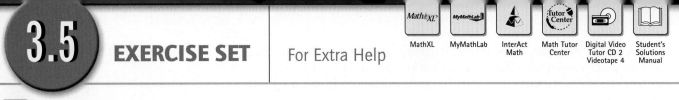

3.5 EXERCISE SET

For Extra Help

MathXL MyMathLab InterAct Math Math Tutor Center Digital Video Tutor CD 2 Videotape 4 Student's Solutions Manual

a Draw a line that has the given slope and *y*-intercept.

1. Slope $\frac{2}{5}$; *y*-intercept $(0, 1)$

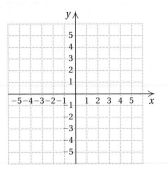

2. Slope $\frac{3}{5}$; *y*-intercept $(0, -1)$

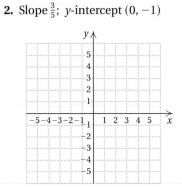

3. Slope $\frac{5}{3}$; *y*-intercept $(0, -2)$

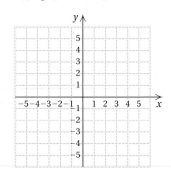

4. Slope $\frac{5}{2}$; *y*-intercept $(0, 1)$

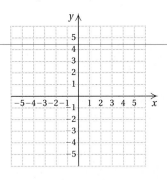

5. Slope $-\frac{3}{4}$; *y*-intercept $(0, 5)$

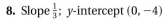

6. Slope $-\frac{4}{5}$; *y*-intercept $(0, 6)$

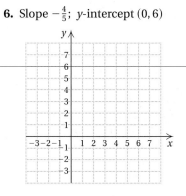

7. Slope $-\frac{1}{2}$; *y*-intercept $(0, 3)$

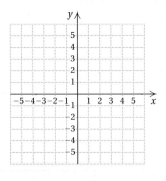

8. Slope $\frac{1}{3}$; *y*-intercept $(0, -4)$

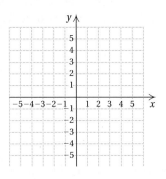

9. Slope 2; *y*-intercept $(0, -4)$

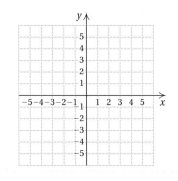

10. Slope -2; y-intercept $(0, -3)$

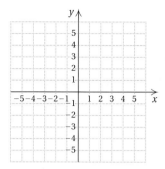

11. Slope -3; y-intercept $(0, 2)$

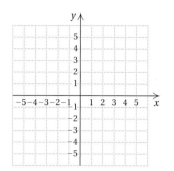

12. Slope 3; y-intercept $(0, 4)$

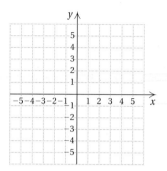

Graph using the slope and the y-intercept.

13. $y = \frac{3}{5}x + 2$

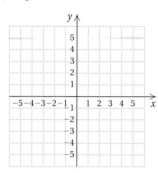

14. $y = -\frac{3}{5}x - 1$

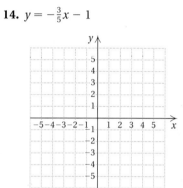

15. $y = -\frac{3}{5}x + 1$

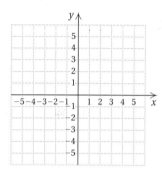

16. $y = \frac{3}{5}x - 2$

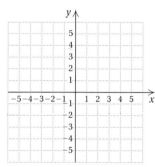

17. $y = \frac{5}{3}x + 3$

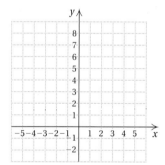

18. $y = \frac{5}{3}x - 2$

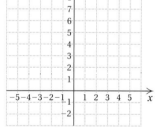

19. $y = -\frac{3}{2}x - 2$

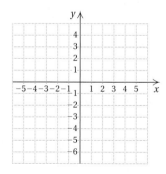

20. $y = -\frac{4}{3}x + 3$

21. $2x + y = 1$

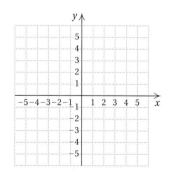

22. $3x + y = 2$

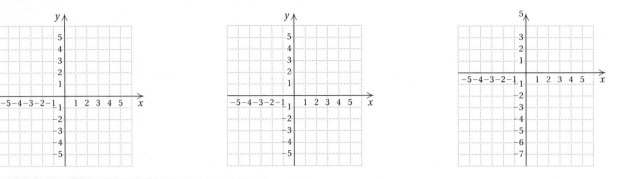

23. $3x - y = 4$

24. $2x - y = 5$

25. $2x + 3y = 9$

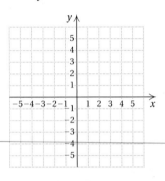

26. $4x + 5y = 15$

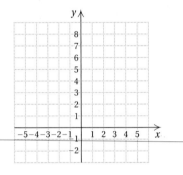

27. $x - 4y = 12$

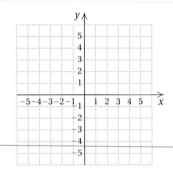

28. $x + 5y = 20$

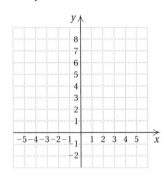

29. $x + 2y = 6$

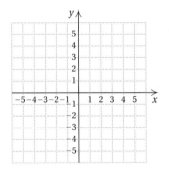

30. $x - 3y = 9$

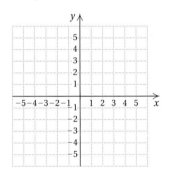

31. $\mathbf{D_W}$ Can a horizontal line be graphed using the method of Examples 3 and 4? Why or why not?

32. $\mathbf{D_W}$ Can a vertical line be graphed using the method of Examples 3 and 4? Why or why not?

Find the slope of the line containing the given pair of points.   [3.3a]

33. $(-2, -6), (8, 7)$

34. $(2, -6), (8, -7)$

35. $(4.5, -2.3), (14.5, 4.6)$

36. $(-0.8, -2.3), (-4.8, 0.1)$

37. $(-2, -6), (8, -6)$

38. $(-2, -6), (-2, 7)$

39. $(11, -1), (11, -4)$

40. $(-3, 5), (8, 5)$

41. *Kidney Transplants.*   The number of kidney transplants in the United States has increased in recent years, as shown in the following graph. Find the rate of change in the number of kidney transplants with respect to time. Find the slope of the graph.   [3.3b]

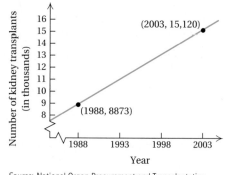

Source: National Organ Procurement and Transplantation Network

42. *Liver Transplants.*   The number of liver transplants in the United States has increased in recent years, as shown in the following graph. Find the rate of change in the number of liver transplants with respect to time. Find the slope of the graph.   [3.3b]

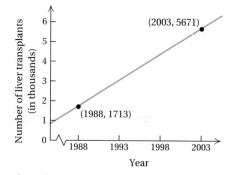

Source: National Organ Procurement and Transplantation Network

43. *Refrigerator Size.*   Kitchen designers recommend that a refrigerator be selected on the basis of the number of people in the household. For 1–2 people, a 16 ft^3 model is suggested. For each additional person, an additional 1.5 ft^3 is recommended. If x is the number of residents in excess of 2, find the slope–intercept equation for the recommended size of a refrigerator.

44. *Telephone Service.*   In a recent promotion, AT&T charged a monthly fee of $3.95 plus 7¢ for each minute of long-distance phone calls. If x is the number of minutes of long-distance calls, find the slope–intercept equation for the monthly bill.

45. Graph the line with slope 2 that passes through the point $(-3, 1)$.

Objectives

a Determine whether the graphs of two linear equations are parallel.

b Determine whether the graphs of two linear equations are perpendicular.

When we graph a pair of linear equations, there are three possibilities:

1. The graphs are the same.
2. The graphs intersect at exactly one point.
3. The graphs are parallel (they do not intersect).

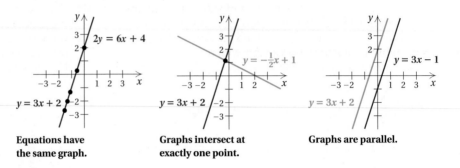

Equations have the same graph.

Graphs intersect at exactly one point.

Graphs are parallel.

a Parallel Lines

The graphs shown below are of the linear equations

$$y = 2x + 5 \quad \text{and} \quad y = 2x - 3.$$

The slope of each line is 2. The y-intercepts are $(0, 5)$ and $(0, -3)$ and are different. The lines do not intersect and are parallel.

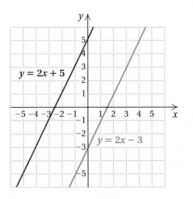

PARALLEL LINES

- Parallel nonvertical lines have the *same* slope, $m_1 = m_2$, and *different* y-intercepts, $b_1 \neq b_2$.
- Parallel horizontal lines have equations $y = p$ and $y = q$, where $p \neq q$.
- Parallel vertical lines have equations $x = p$ and $x = q$, where $p \neq q$.

By simply graphing, we may find it difficult to determine whether lines are parallel. Sometimes they may intersect only very far from the origin. We can use the preceding statements about slopes, y-intercepts, and parallel lines to determine for certain whether lines are parallel.

EXAMPLE 1 Determine whether the graphs of the lines $y = -3x + 4$ and $6x + 2y = -10$ are parallel.

The graphs of these equations are shown below, but they are not necessary in order to determine whether the lines are parallel.

We first solve each equation for y. In this case, the first equation is already solved for y.

a) $y = -3x + 4$

b) $6x + 2y = -10$

$$2y = -6x - 10$$

$$y = \frac{1}{2}(-6x - 10)$$

$$y = -3x - 5$$

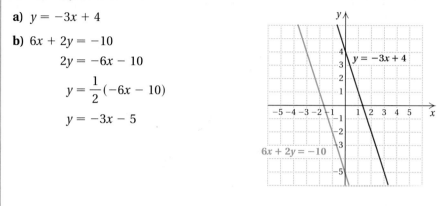

The slope of each line is -3. The y-intercepts are $(0, 4)$ and $(0, -5)$ and are different. The lines are parallel.

Do Exercises 1 and 2.

b Perpendicular Lines

Perpendicular lines in a plane are lines that intersect at a right angle. The measure of a right angle is 90°. The lines whose graphs are shown below are perpendicular. You can check this approximately by using a protractor or placing a rectangular piece of paper at the intersection.

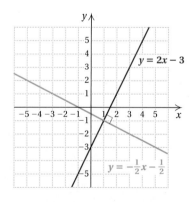

The slopes of the lines are 2 and $-\frac{1}{2}$. Note that $2\left(-\frac{1}{2}\right) = -1$. That is, the product of the slopes is -1.

PERPENDICULAR LINES

- Two nonvertical lines are perpendicular if the product of their slopes is -1, $m_1 \cdot m_2 = -1$. (If one line has slope m, the slope of the line perpendicular to it is $-1/m$.)

- If one equation in a pair of perpendicular lines is vertical, then the other is horizontal. These equations are of the form $x = a$ and $y = b$.

Determine whether the graphs of the pair of equations are parallel.

1. $y - 3x = 1,$
$-2y = 3x + 2$

2. $3x - y = -5,$
$y - 3x = -2$

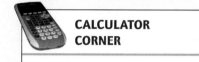

CALCULATOR CORNER

Parallel Lines Graph each pair of equations in Margin Exercises 1 and 2 in the standard viewing window, $[-10, 10, -10, 10]$. (Note that each equation must be solved for y so that it can be entered in "$y =$" form on the graphing calculator.) Determine whether the lines appear to be parallel.

Determine whether the graphs of the pair of equations are perpendicular.

3. $y = -\frac{3}{4}x + 7,$

$y = \frac{4}{3}x - 9$

4. $4x - 5y = 8,$
$6x + 9y = -12$

Answers on page A-17

EXAMPLE 2 Determine whether the graphs of the lines $3y = 9x + 3$ and $6y + 2x = 6$ are perpendicular.

The graphs are shown below, but they are not necessary in order to determine whether the lines are perpendicular.

We first solve each equation for y in order to determine the slopes:

a) $3y = 9x + 3$

$y = \frac{1}{3}(9x + 3)$

$y = 3x + 1;$

b) $6y + 2x = 6$

$6y = -2x + 6$

$y = \frac{1}{6}(-2x + 6)$

$y = -\frac{1}{3}x + 1.$

The slopes are 3 and $-\frac{1}{3}$. The product of the slopes is $3\left(-\frac{1}{3}\right) = -1$. The lines are perpendicular.

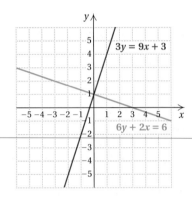

Do Exercises 3 and 4 on the preceding page.

Study Tips

SPECIAL VIDEOTAPES

In addition to the videotaped lectures for the books, there is a special VHS tape, *Math Problem Solving in the Real World*. Check with your instructor to see whether this tape is available on your campus.

There is also a special Math Study Skills for Students Video on CD that is designed to help you make better use of your math study time and improve your retention of concepts and procedures taught in classes from basic mathematics through intermediate algebra. (See the Preface for more information.)

EXERCISE SET   For Extra Help

a   Determine whether the graphs of the equations are parallel lines.

1. $x + 4 = y$,
$y - x = -3$

2. $3x - 4 = y$,
$y - 3x = 8$

3. $y + 3 = 6x$,
$-6x - y = 2$

4. $y = -4x + 2$,
$-5 = -2y + 8x$

5. $10y + 32x = 16.4$,
$y + 3.5 = 0.3125x$

6. $y = 6.4x + 8.9$,
$5y - 32x = 5$

7. $y = 2x + 7$,
$5y + 10x = 20$

8. $y + 5x = -6$,
$3y + 5x = -15$

9. $3x - y = -9$,
$2y - 6x = -2$

10. $y - 6 = -6x$,
$-2x + y = 5$

11. $x = 3$,
$x = 4$

12. $y = 1$,
$y = -2$

b   Determine whether the graphs of the equations are perpendicular lines.

13. $y = -4x + 3$,
$4y + x = -1$

14. $y = -\dfrac{2}{3}x + 4$,
$3x + 2y = 1$

15. $x + y = 6$,
$4y - 4x = 12$

16. $2x - 5y = -3$,
$5x + 2y = 6$

17. $y = -0.3125x + 11$,
$y - 3.2x = -14$

18. $y = -6.4x - 7$,
$64y - 5x = 32$

19. $y = -x + 8$,
$x - y = -1$

20. $2x + 6y = -3$,
$12y = 4x + 20$

21. $\dfrac{3}{8}x - \dfrac{y}{2} = 1$,
$\dfrac{4}{3}x - y + 1 = 0$

22. $\dfrac{1}{2}x + \dfrac{3}{4}y = 6$,
$-\dfrac{3}{2}x + y = 4$

23. $x = 0$,
$y = -2$

24. $x = -3$,
$y = 5$

a , **b**   Determine whether the graphs of the equations are parallel, perpendicular, or neither.

25. $3y + 21 = 2x$,
$3y = 2x + 24$

26. $3y + 21 = 2x$,
$2y = 16 - 3x$

27. $3y = 2x - 21$,
$2y - 16 = 3x$

28. $3y + 2x + 7 = 0$,
$3y = 2x + 24$

29. **D**w Consider two equations of the type $Ax + By = C$. Explain how you would go about showing that their graphs are perpendicular.

30. **D**w Consider two equations of the type $Ax + By = C$. Explain how you would go about showing that their graphs are parallel.

VOCABULARY REINFORCEMENT

In each of Exercises 31–38, fill in the blank with the correct term from the given list. Some of the choices may not be used.

31. Equations with the same solutions are called _____. [2.1b]

32. The _____ for equations asserts that when we subtract the same number on both sides of an equation, we get equivalent equations. [2.1b]

33. The _____ for equations asserts that when we multiply or divide by the same nonzero number on both sides of an equation, we get equivalent equations. [2.2a]

34. _____ lines are graphs of equations of the type $y = b$. [3.2b]

35. _____ lines are graphs of equations of the type $x = a$. [3.2b]

36. The _____ of a line is a number that indicates how the line slants. [3.3a]

37. The _____ of a line, if it exists, indicates where the line crosses the x-axis. [3.3a]

38. The _____ of a line, if it exists, indicates where the line crosses the y-axis. [3.2a]

vertical
horizontal
variable
addition principle
multiplication principle
coefficient
equivalent equations
slope
x-intercept
y-intercept
parallel
perpendicular

SYNTHESIS

39. Find an equation of a line that contains the point $(0, 6)$ and is parallel to $y - 3x = 4$.

40. Find an equation of the line that contains the point $(-2, 4)$ and is parallel to $y = 2x - 3$.

41. Find an equation of the line that contains the point $(0, 2)$ and is perpendicular to $3y - x = 0$.

42. Find an equation of the line that contains the point $(1, 0)$ and is perpendicular to $2x + y = -4$.

43. Find an equation of the line that has x-intercept $(-2, 0)$ and is parallel to $4x - 8y = 12$.

44. Find the value of k such that $4y = kx - 6$ and $5x + 20y = 12$ are parallel.

45. Find the value of k such that $4y = kx - 6$ and $5x + 20y = 12$ are perpendicular.

The lines in the graphs in Exercises 46 and 47 are perpendicular and the lines in the graph in Exercise 48 are parallel. Find an equation of each line.

46.
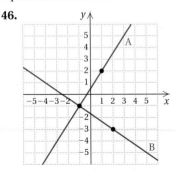

47.
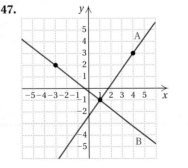

48.
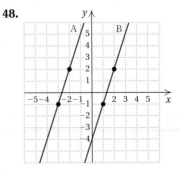

3.7 GRAPHING INEQUALITIES IN TWO VARIABLES

A graph of an inequality is a drawing that represents its solutions. An inequality in one variable can be graphed on a number line. An inequality in two variables can be graphed on a coordinate plane.

a Solutions of Inequalities in Two Variables

The solutions of inequalities in two variables are ordered pairs.

EXAMPLE 1 Determine whether $(-3, 2)$ is a solution of $5x + 4y < 13$.

We use alphabetical order to replace x with -3 and y with 2.

$$\begin{array}{c} 5x + 4y < 13 \\ \hline 5(-3) + 4 \cdot 2 \ ? \ 13 \\ -15 + 8 \ | \\ -7 \ | \quad \text{TRUE} \end{array}$$

Since $-7 < 13$ is true, $(-3, 2)$ is a solution.

EXAMPLE 2 Determine whether $(6, 8)$ is a solution of $5x + 4y < 13$.

We use alphabetical order to replace x with 6 and y with 8.

$$\begin{array}{c} 5x + 4y < 13 \\ \hline 5(6) + 4(8) \ ? \ 13 \\ 30 + 32 \ | \\ 62 \ | \quad \text{FALSE} \end{array}$$

Since $62 < 13$ is false, $(6, 8)$ is not a solution.

Do Exercises 1 and 2.

b Graphing Inequalities in Two Variables

EXAMPLE 3 Graph: $y > x$.

We first graph the line $y = x$. Every solution of $y = x$ is an ordered pair like $(3, 3)$. The first and second coordinates are the same. We draw the line $y = x$ dashed because its points (as shown on the left below) are *not* solutions of $y > x$.

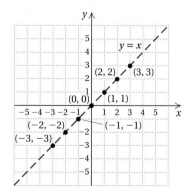 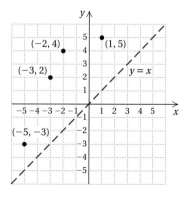

Objectives

a Determine whether an ordered pair of numbers is a solution of an inequality in two variables.

b Graph linear inequalities.

1. Determine whether $(4, 3)$ is a solution of $3x - 2y < 1$.

2. Determine whether $(2, -5)$ is a solution of $4x + 7y \geq 12$.

Answers on page A-17

3. Graph: $y < x$.

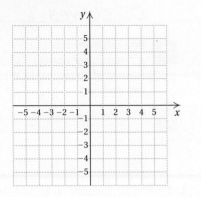

Now look at the graph on the right on the preceding page. Several ordered pairs are plotted in the half-plane above the line $y = x$. Each is a solution of $y > x$.

We can check a pair such as $(-2, 4)$ as follows:

$$\frac{y > x}{4\ ?\ -2}\ \text{TRUE}$$

It turns out that any point on the same side of $y = x$ as $(-2, 4)$ is also a solution. *If we know that one point in a half-plane is a solution, then all points in that half-plane are solutions.* We could have chosen other points to check. The graph of $y > x$ is shown below. (Solutions are indicated by color shading throughout.) We shade the half-plane above $y = x$.

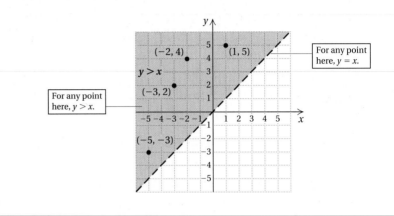

Do Exercise 3.

A **linear inequality** is one that we can get from a linear equation by changing the equals symbol to an inequality symbol. Every linear equation has a graph that is a straight line. The graph of a linear inequality is a half-plane, sometimes including the line along the edge.

> **To graph an inequality in two variables:**
>
> 1. Replace the inequality symbol with an equals sign and graph this related linear equation.
> 2. If the inequality symbol is $<$ or $>$, draw the line dashed. If the inequality symbol is $\leq$ or $\geq$, draw the line solid.
> 3. The graph consists of a half-plane, either above or below or left or right of the line, and, if the line is solid, the line as well. To determine which half-plane to shade, choose a point *not on the line* as a test point. Substitute to find whether that point is a solution of the *inequality*. If it is, shade the half-plane containing that point. If it is not, shade the half-plane on the opposite side of the line.

Answer on page A-17

EXAMPLE 4 Graph: $5x - 2y < 10$.

1. We first graph the line $5x - 2y = 10$. The intercepts are $(0, -5)$ and $(2, 0)$. This line forms the boundary of the solutions of the inequality.

2. Since the inequality contains the $<$ symbol, points on the line are not solutions of the inequality, so we draw a dashed line.

3. To determine which half-plane to shade, we consider a test point *not* on the line. We try $(3, -2)$ and substitute:

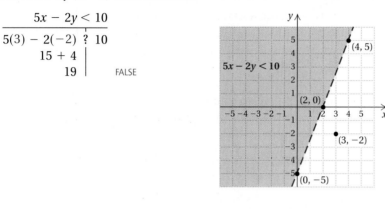

$$\frac{5x - 2y < 10}{\begin{array}{c|c} 5(3) - 2(-2) \ ? \ 10 \\ 15 + 4 \\ 19 \end{array}} \quad \text{FALSE}$$

Since this inequality is false, the point $(3, -2)$ is *not* a solution; no point in the half-plane containing $(3, -2)$ is a solution. Thus the points in the opposite half-plane are solutions. The graph is shown above.

Do Exercise 4.

EXAMPLE 5 Graph: $2x + 3y \le 6$.

1. First, we graph the line $2x + 3y = 6$. The intercepts are $(0, 2)$ and $(3, 0)$.

2. Since the inequality contains the $\le$ symbol, we draw the line solid to indicate that any pair on the line is a solution.

3. Next, we choose a test point that does not belong to the line. We substitute to determine whether this point is a solution. The origin $(0, 0)$ is generally an easy one to use:

$$\frac{2x + 3y \le 6}{\begin{array}{c|c} 2 \cdot 0 + 3 \cdot 0 \ ? \ 6 \\ 0 \end{array}} \quad \text{TRUE}$$

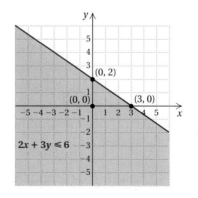

We see that $(0, 0)$ is a solution, so we shade the lower half-plane. Had the substitution given us a false inequality, we would have shaded the other half-plane.

Do Exercises 5 and 6.

4. Graph: $2x + 4y < 8$.

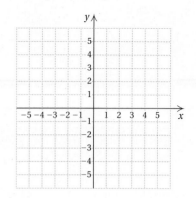

Graph.

5. $3x - 5y < 15$

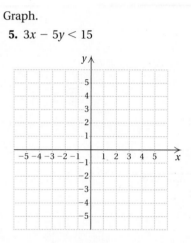

6. $2x + 3y \ge 12$

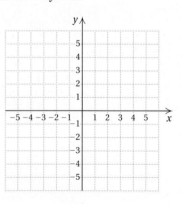

Answers on page A-17

Graph.

7. $x > -3$

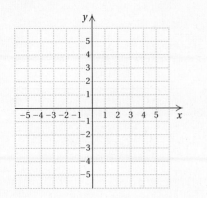

8. $y \leq 4$

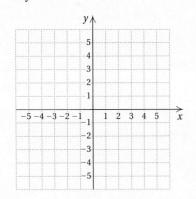

EXAMPLE 6 Graph $x < 3$ on a plane.

There is no y-term in this inequality, but we can rewrite this inequality as $x + 0y < 3$. We use the same technique that we have used with the other examples.

1. We graph the related equation $x = 3$ on the plane.

2. Since the inequality symbol is $<$, we use a dashed line.

3. The graph is a half-plane either to the left or to the right of the line $x = 3$. To determine which, we consider a test point, $(-4, 5)$:

$$\frac{x + 0y < 3}{-4 + 0(5) \ ? \ 3}$$
$$-4 \ \mid \quad \text{TRUE}$$

We see that $(-4, 5)$ is a solution, so all the pairs in the half-plane containing $(-4, 5)$ are solutions. We shade that half-plane.

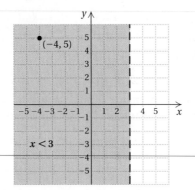

We see from the graph that the solutions of $x < 3$ are all those ordered pairs whose first coordinates are less than 3.

If we graph the inequality in Example 6 on a line rather than on a plane, its graph is as follows:

EXAMPLE 7 Graph: $y \geq -4$.

1. We first graph $y = -4$.

2. We use a solid line to indicate that all points on the line are solutions.

3. We then use $(2, 3)$ as a test point and substitute:

$$\frac{0x + y \geq -4}{0(2) + 3 \ ? \ -4}$$
$$3 \ | \qquad \text{TRUE}$$

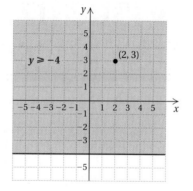

Since $(2, 3)$ is a solution, all points in the half-plane containing $(2, 3)$ are solutions. Note that this half-plane consists of all ordered pairs whose second coordinate is greater than or equal to -4.

Do Exercises 7 and 8 on the preceding page.

CALCULATOR CORNER

Graphs of Inequalities   We can graph inequalities on a graphing calculator, shading the region of the solution set. To graph the inequality in Example 5,

$$2x + 3y \leq 6,$$

we first graph the line $2x + 3y = 6$. Solving for y, we get $y = \dfrac{6 - 2x}{3}$, or $y = -\dfrac{2}{3}x + 2$. We enter this equation on the equation-editor screen.

After determining algebraically that the solution set consists of all points below the line, we use the graphing calculator's "shade below" graph style to shade this region. On the equation-editor screen, we position the cursor over the graphstyle icon to the left of the equation and press **ENTER** repeatedly until the "shade below" icon appears. Then we press **GRAPH** to display the graph of the inequality.

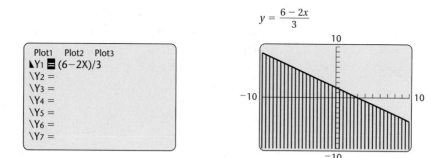

$$y = \frac{6 - 2x}{3}$$

Note that we cannot graph an inequality like the one in Example 6, $x < 3$, on a graphing calculator because the related equation has no y-term and thus cannot be entered in "$y =$" form.

Exercises:

1. Use a graphing calculator to graph the inequalities in Margin Exercises 6 and 8.

2. Use a graphing calculator to graph the inequality in Example 7.

Visualizing for Success

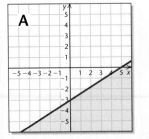

A

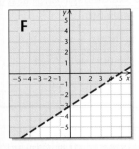

F

Match the equation or inequality with its graph.

1. $3x - 5y \leq 15$

2. $3x + 5y = 15$

3. $3x + 5y \leq 15$

4. $3x - 5y \geq 15$

5. $3x - 5y = 15$

6. $3x - 5y < 15$

7. $3x + 5y \geq 15$

8. $3x + 5y > 15$

9. $3x - 5y > 15$

10. $3x + 5y < 15$

Answers on page A-17

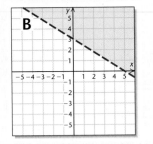

B

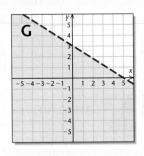

G

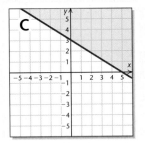

C

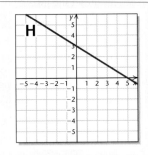

H

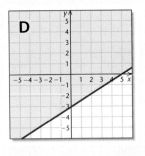

D

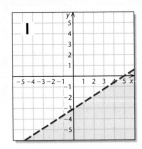

I

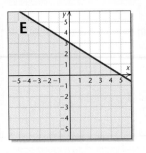

E

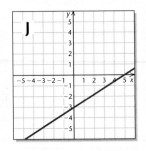

J

EXERCISE SET

For Extra Help

a

1. Determine whether $(-3, -5)$ is a solution of
$$-x - 3y < 18.$$

2. Determine whether $(2, -3)$ is a solution of
$$5x - 4y \geq 1.$$

3. Determine whether $\left(\frac{1}{2}, -\frac{1}{4}\right)$ is a solution of
$$7y - 9x \leq -3.$$

4. Determine whether $(-8, 5)$ is a solution of
$$x + 0 \cdot y > 4.$$

b   Graph on a plane.

5. $x > 2y$

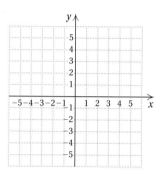

6. $x > 3y$

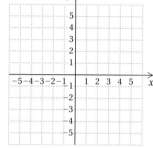

7. $y \leq x - 3$

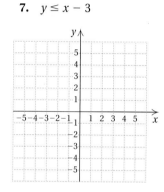

8. $y \leq x - 5$

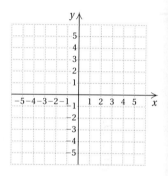

9. $y < x + 1$

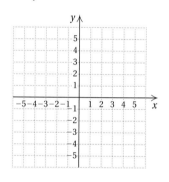

10. $y < x + 4$

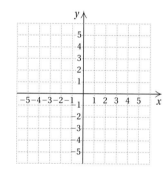

11. $y \geq x - 2$

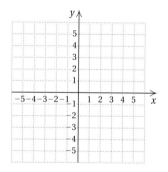

12. $y \geq x - 1$

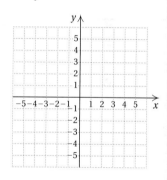

13. $y \leq 2x - 1$

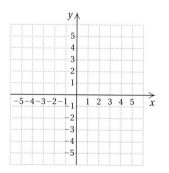

14. $y \leq 3x + 2$

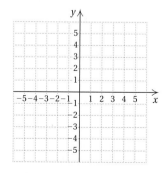

15. $x + y \leq 3$

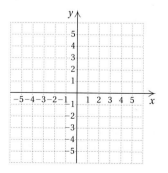

16. $x + y \leq 4$

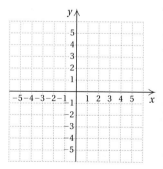

In which quadrant is the point located? [3.1a]

7. $(3, -8)$ **8.** $(-20, -14)$ **9.** $(4.9, 1.3)$

Determine whether the ordered pair is a solution of
$2y - x = 10$. [3.1c]

10. $(2, -6)$ **11.** $(0, 5)$

12. Show that the ordered pairs $(0, -3)$ and $(2, 1)$ are
solutions of the equation $2x - y = 3$. Then use the
graph of the two points to determine another solution.
Answers may vary. [3.1c]

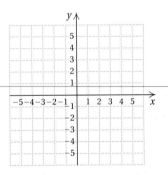

Graph the equation, identifying the y-intercept. [3.1d]

13. $y = 2x - 5$

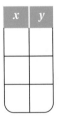

14. $y = -\dfrac{3}{4}x$

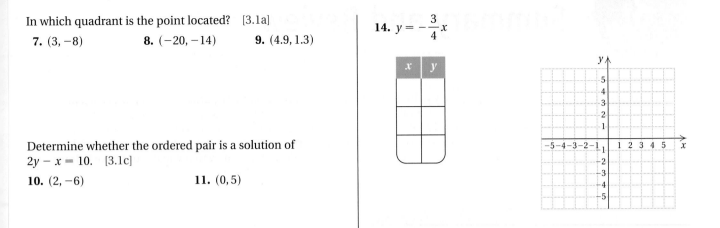

15. $y = -x + 4$

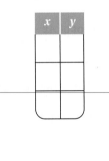
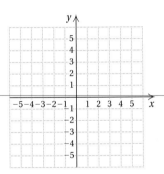

16. $y = 3 - 4x$

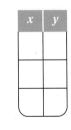
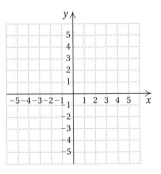

Graph the equation. [3.2b]

17. $y = 3$

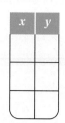

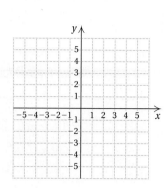

18. $5x - 4 = 0$

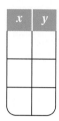

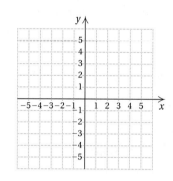

Find the intercepts of the equation. Then graph the equation. [3.2a]

19. $x - 2y = 6$

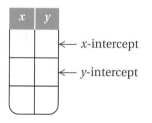
← x-intercept
← y-intercept

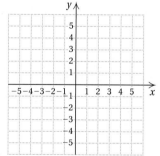

20. $5x - 2y = 10$

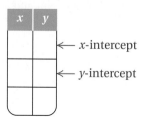
← x-intercept
← y-intercept

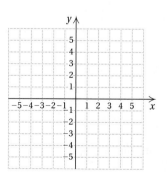

Solve. [3.1e]

21. *Kitchen Design.* Kitchen designers recommend that a refrigerator be selected on the basis of the number of people *n* in the household. The appropriate size *S*, in cubic feet, is given by

$$S = \frac{3}{2}n + 13.$$

a) Determine the recommended size of a refrigerator if the number of people is 1, 2, 5, and 10.

b) Graph the equation and use the graph to estimate the recommended size of a refrigerator for 3 people sharing an apartment.

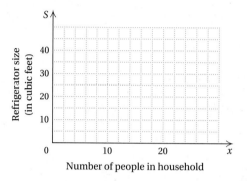

c) A refrigerator is 22 ft³. For how many residents is it the recommended size?

22. *Snow Removal.* By 3:00 P.M., Erin had plowed 7 driveways and by 5:30 P.M. she had completed 13.

a) Find Erin's plowing rate in number of driveways per hour. [3.3b]

b) Find Erin's plowing rate in minutes per driveway. [3.3b]

23. *Manicures.* The following graph shows data from a recent day's work at the O'Hara School of Cosmetology. What is the rate of change, in number of manicures per hour? [3.3b]

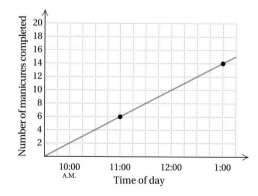

Find the slope.   [3.3a]

24.

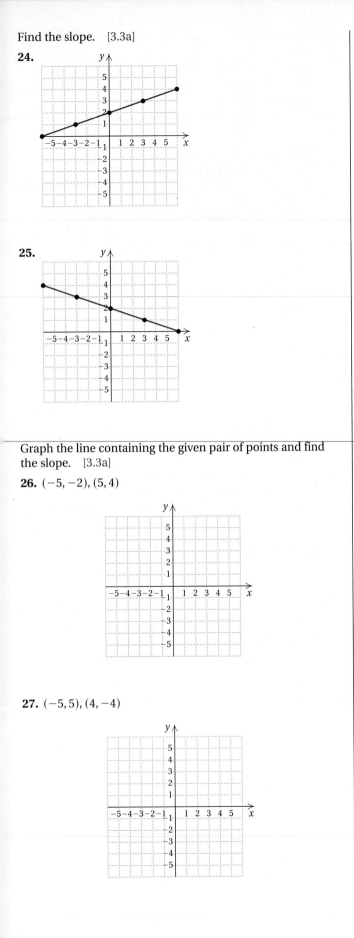

25.

Graph the line containing the given pair of points and find the slope.   [3.3a]

26. $(-5, -2), (5, 4)$

27. $(-5, 5), (4, -4)$

28. *Road Grade.*   At one point, Beartooth Highway in Yellowstone National Park rises 315 ft over a horizontal distance of 4500 ft. Find the slope, or grade, of the road. [3.3b]

Find the slope, if it exists.   [3.3c]

29. $y = -\dfrac{5}{8}x - 3$

30. $2x - 4y = 8$

31. $x = -2$

32. $y = 9$

Find the slope and the *y*-intercept.   [3.4a]

33. $y = -9x + 46$

34. $x + y = 9$

35. $3x - 5y = 4$

Find an equation of the line with the given slope and *y*-intercept.   [3.4a]

36. Slope $= -2.8$; *y*-intercept: $(0, 19)$

37. Slope $= \frac{5}{8}$; *y*-intercept: $\left(0, -\frac{7}{8}\right)$

Find an equation of the line containing the given point and with the given slope.   [3.4b]

38. $(1, 2), \; m = 3$

39. $(-2, -5), \; m = \frac{2}{3}$

40. $(0, -4), \; m = -2$

Find an equation of the line containing the given pair of points. [3.4c]

41. $(5, 7)$ and $(-1, 1)$

42. $(2, 0)$ and $(-4, -3)$

Solve. [3.4c]

43. *Women in the Labor Force.* The line graph below illustrates the percent of the female population age 16 and older in the work force for years since 1950.

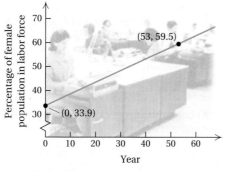

Source: U.S. Department of Labor

a) Find an equation of the line.
b) What is the rate of change in the percent of female workers in the labor force with respect to time?
c) Use the equation to find the percent of female workers in the labor force in 2005.

44. Draw a line that has slope -1 and y-intercept $(0, 4)$. [3.5a]

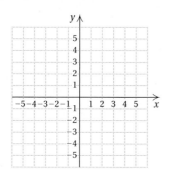

45. Draw a line that has slope $\frac{5}{3}$ and y-intercept $(0, -3)$. [3.5a]

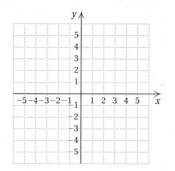

46. Graph $y = -\frac{3}{5}x + 2$ using the slope and the y-intercept. [3.5a]

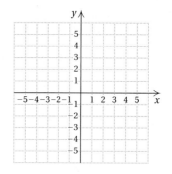

47. Graph $2y - 3x = 6$ using the slope and the y-intercept. [3.5a]

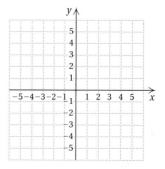

Determine whether the graphs of the equations are parallel, perpendicular, or neither. [3.6a, b]

48. $4x + y = 6$,
$4x + y = 8$

49. $2x + y = 10$,
$y = \frac{1}{2}x - 4$

50. $x + 4y = 8$,
$x = -4y - 10$

51. $3x - y = 6$,
$3x + y = 8$

Determine whether the given point is a solution of the inequality $x - 2y > 1$. [3.7a]

52. $(0, 0)$

53. $(1, 3)$

54. $(4, -1)$

Graph on a plane. [3.7b]

55. $x < y$

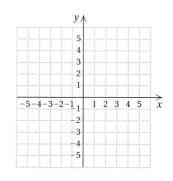

56. $x + 2y \geq 4$

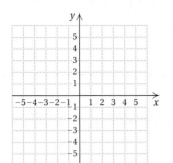

57. $x > -2$

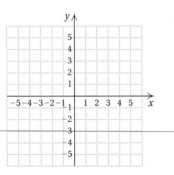

58. $\mathbf{D_W}$ Explain why the first coordinate of the y-intercept is always 0.   [3.1d]

59. $\mathbf{D_W}$ Graph $x < 1$ on both a number line and a plane, and explain the difference between the graphs.   [3.7b]

60. $\mathbf{D_W}$ Describe how you would graph $y = 0.37x + 2458$ using the slope and the y-intercept. You need not actually draw the graph.   [3.5a]

SYNTHESIS

61. Find the value of m in $y = mx + 3$ such that $(-2, 5)$ is on the graph.   [3.2a]

62. Find the area and the perimeter of a rectangle for which $(-2, 2)$, $(7, 2)$, and $(7, -3)$ are three of the vertices.   [3.1a]

63. *Mountaineering.*   As part of an ill-fated expedition to climb Mount Everest in 1996, author Jon Krakauer departed "The Balcony," elevation 27,600 ft, at 7:00 A.M. and reached the summit, elevation 29,028 ft, at 1:25 P.M. [3.3c]

Source: Jon Krakauer, *Into Thin Air*. New York: Villard, 1998.

a) Find Krakauer's rate of ascent in feet per minute.
b) Find Krakauer's rate of ascent in minutes per foot.

64. In chess, the knight can move to any of the eight squares shown by a, b, c, d, e, f, g, and h below. If lines are drawn from the beginning to the end of the move, what slopes are possible for these lines?   [3.3a]

In which quadrant is the point located?

1. $\left(-\frac{1}{2}, 7\right)$

2. $(-5, -6)$

Find the coordinates of the point.

3. A

4. B

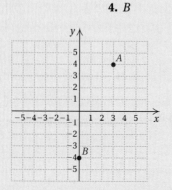

5. Show that the ordered pairs $(-4, -3)$ and $(-1, 3)$ are solutions of the equation $y - 2x = 5$. Then use the graph of the straight line containing the two points to determine another solution. Answers may vary.

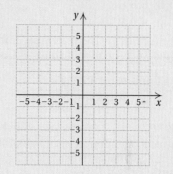

Graph the equation. Identify the *y*-intercept.

6. $y = 2x - 1$

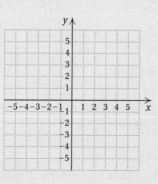

7. $y = -\frac{3}{2}x$

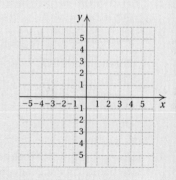

Graph the equation.

8. $2x + 8 = 0$

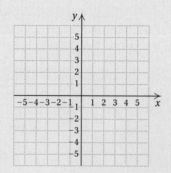

9. $y = 5$

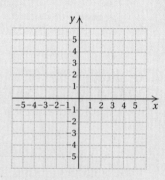

Find the intercepts of the equation. Then graph the equation.

10. $2x - 4y = -8$

x	y
		←x-intercept
		←y-intercept

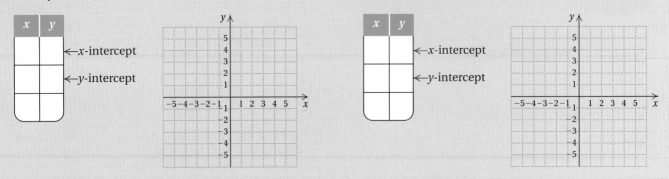

11. $2x - y = 3$

x	y
		←x-intercept
		←y-intercept

12. *Private-College Costs.*   The yearly cost T, in thousands of dollars, of tuition and required fees at a private college (includes two- and four-year schools and does not include room and board) can be approximated by

$$T = \frac{3}{5}n + 5,$$

where n is the number of years since 1985. That is, $n = 0$ corresponds to 1985, $n = 5$ corresponds to 1990, and so on.

Source: *Statistical Abstract of the United States,* 2003

a) Find the cost of tuition in 1985, 1996, 2000, and 2004.

b) Graph the equation and then use the graph to estimate the cost of tuition in 2005.

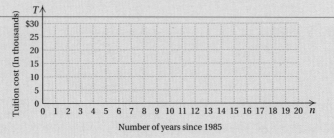

c) Predict the year in which the cost of tuition will be $23,000.

13. *Elevators.*   At 2:38, Serge entered an elevator on the 34th floor of the Regency Hotel. At 2:40, he stepped off at the 5th floor.

a) Find the elevator's average rate of travel in number of floors per minute.

b) Find the elevator's average rate of travel in seconds per floor.

14. *Train Travel.*   The following graph shows data concerning a recent train ride from Denver to Kansas City. At what rate did the train travel?

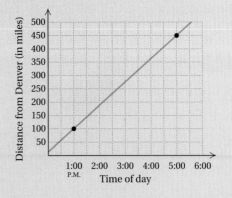

15. Find the slope.

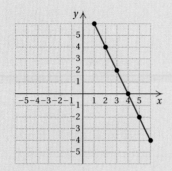

16. Graph the line containing $(-3, 1)$ and $(5, 4)$ and find the slope.

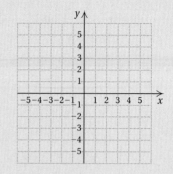

17. *Navigation.*   Capital Rapids drops 54 ft vertically over a horizontal distance of 1080 ft. What is the slope of the rapids?

18. Find the slope, if it exists.

a) $2x - 5y = 10$

b) $x = -2$

19. Draw a graph of the line with slope $-\frac{3}{2}$ and y-intercept $(0, 1)$.

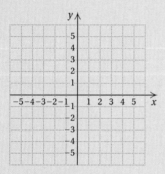

20. Graph $y = 2x - 3$ using the slope and the y-intercept.

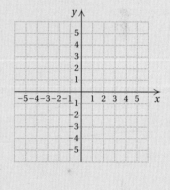

Find the slope and the y-intercept.

21. $y = 2x - \frac{1}{4}$

22. $-4x + 3y = -6$

Find an equation of the line with the given slope and y-intercept.

23. Slope $= 1.8$; y-intercept: $(0, -7)$

24. Slope $= -\frac{3}{8}$; y-intercept: $\left(0, -\frac{1}{8}\right)$

Find an equation of the line containing the given point and with the given slope.

25. $(3, 5)$, $m = 1$

26. $(-2, 0)$, $m = -3$

Find an equation of the line containing the given pair of points.

27. $(1, 1)$ and $(2, -2)$

28. $(4, -1)$ and $(-4, -3)$

29. *Lung Transplants.* The number of lung transplants in the United States has increased in recent years. The line graph at right describes the increase in the number of lung transplants for years since 1988.

a) Find an equation of the line.

b) What is the rate of change in the number of lung transplants with respect to time?

c) Use the equation to determine the number of lung transplants in 2005.

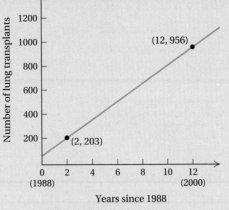

Number of lung transplants

(12, 956)

(2, 203)

0 2 4 6 8 10 12
(1988)   (2000)

Years since 1988

Source: National Organ Procurement and Transplantation Network

---

Determine whether the graphs of the equations are parallel, perpendicular, or neither.

30. $2x + y = 8$,
$2x + y = 4$

31. $2x + 5y = 2$,
$y = 2x + 4$

32. $x + 2y = 8$,
$-2x + y = 8$

Determine whether the given point is a solution of the inequality $3y - 2x < -2$.

33. $(0, 0)$

34. $(-4, -10)$

Graph on a plane.

35. $y > x - 1$

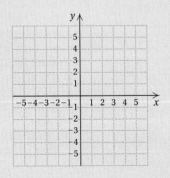

36. $2x - y \leq 4$

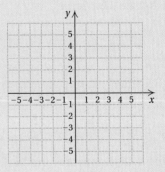

SYNTHESIS

37. A diagonal of a square connects the points $(-3, -1)$ and $(2, 4)$. Find the area and the perimeter of the square.

38. Find the value of k such that $3x + 7y = 14$ and $ky - 7x = -3$ are perpendicular.

CHAPTER 3: Graphs of Linear Equations

Systems of Equations

Real-World Application

At a local "paint swap," Kari found large supplies of Skylite Pink (12.5% red pigment) and MacIntosh Red (20% red pigment). How many gallons of each color should Kari pick up in order to mix a gallon of Summer Rose (17% red pigment)?

This problem appears as Exercise 6 in Section 7.4.

SYSTEMS OF EQUATIONS IN TWO VARIABLES

Objectives

a Determine whether an ordered pair is a solution of a system of equations.

b Solve systems of two linear equations in two variables by graphing.

a Systems of Equations and Solutions

Many problems can be solved more easily by translating to two equations in two variables. The following is such a **system of equations:**

$$x + y = 8,$$
$$2x - y = 1.$$

> **SOLUTION OF A SYSTEM OF EQUATIONS**
>
> A **solution** of a system of two equations is an ordered pair that makes both equations true.

Look at the graphs shown below. Recall that a graph of an equation is a drawing that represents its solution set. Each point on the graph corresponds to a solution of that equation. Which points (ordered pairs) are solutions of *both* equations?

The graph shows that there is only one. It is the point P where the graphs cross. This point looks as if its coordinates are $(3, 5)$. We check to see if $(3, 5)$ is a solution of *both* equations, substituting 3 for x and 5 for y.

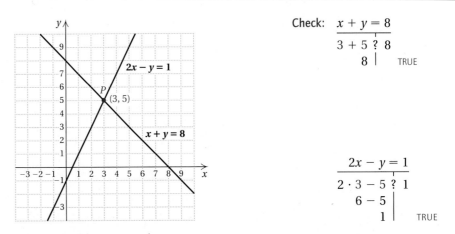

Check: $\quad x + y = 8$
$$\overline{3 + 5\ ?\ 8}$$
$$8\ \Big|\quad \text{TRUE}$$

$$2x - y = 1$$
$$\overline{2 \cdot 3 - 5\ ?\ 1}$$
$$6 - 5\ \Big|$$
$$1\ \Big|\quad \text{TRUE}$$

There is just one solution of the system of equations. It is $(3, 5)$. In other words, $x = 3$ and $y = 5$.

EXAMPLE 1 Determine whether $(1, 2)$ is a solution of the system

$$y = x + 1,$$
$$2x + y = 4.$$

We check by substituting alphabetically 1 for x and 2 for y.

Check: $\quad y = x + 1$
$$\overline{2\ ?\ 1 + 1}$$
$$\Big|\ 2 \qquad \text{TRUE}$$

$$2x + y = 4$$
$$\overline{2 \cdot 1 + 2\ ?\ 4}$$
$$2 + 2\ \Big|$$
$$4\ \Big|\quad \text{TRUE}$$

This checks, so $(1, 2)$ is a solution of the system.

EXAMPLE 2 Determine whether $(-3, 2)$ is a solution of the system

$$p + q = -1,$$
$$q + 3p = 4.$$

We check by substituting alphabetically -3 for p and 2 for q.

Check:
$$\begin{array}{c|c} p + q = -1 & q + 3p = 4 \\ \hline -3 + 2 \,?\, -1 & 2 + 3(-3) \,?\, 4 \\ -1 \mid \quad \text{TRUE} & 2 - 9 \mid \\ & -7 \mid \quad \text{FALSE} \end{array}$$

The point $(-3, 2)$ is not a solution of $q + 3p = 4$. Thus it is not a solution of the system.

Example 2 illustrates that an ordered pair may be a solution of one equation while *not* a solution of *both* equations. If that is the case, it is *not* a solution of the system.

Do Exercises 1 and 2.

b Graphing Systems of Equations

Recall that the **graph** of an equation is a drawing that represents its solution set. If the graph of an equation is a line, then every point on the line corresponds to an ordered pair that is a solution of the equation. If we graph a **system** of two linear equations, we graph both equations and find the coordinates of the points of intersection, if any exist.

EXAMPLE 3 Solve this system of equations by graphing:

$$x + y = 6,$$
$$x = y + 2.$$

We graph the equations using any of the methods studied in Chapter 3. Point P with coordinates $(4, 2)$ looks as if it is the solution.

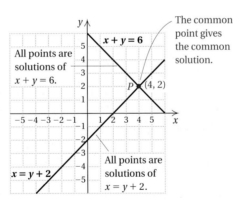

We check the pair as follows.

Check:
$$\begin{array}{c|c} x + y = 6 & x = y + 2 \\ \hline 4 + 2 \,?\, 6 & 4 \,?\, 2 + 2 \\ 6 \mid \quad \text{TRUE} & \mid 4 \quad \text{TRUE} \end{array}$$

The solution is $(4, 2)$.

Do Exercise 3.

Determine whether the given ordered pair is a solution of the system of equations.

1. $(2, -3)$; $x = 2y + 8,$
$\qquad\qquad\quad\; 2x + y = 1$

Check:

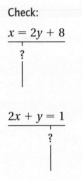

2. $(20, 40)$; $a = \dfrac{1}{2}b,$
$\qquad\qquad\quad b - a = 60$

Check:

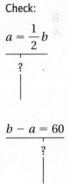

3. Solve this system by graphing:

$$2x + y = 1,$$
$$x = 2y + 8.$$

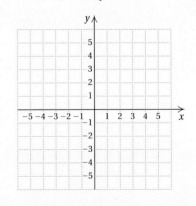

Answers on page A-35

4. Solve this system by graphing:

$$x = -4,$$
$$y = 3.$$

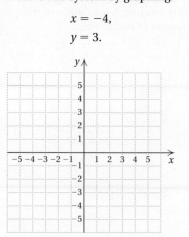

5. Solve this system by graphing:

$$y + 4 = x,$$
$$x - y = -2.$$

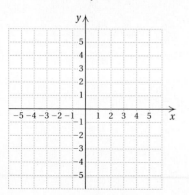

6. Solve this system by graphing:

$$2x + y = 4,$$
$$-6x - 3y = -12.$$

Answers on page A-35

EXAMPLE 4 Solve this system of equations by graphing:

$$x = 2,$$
$$y = -3.$$

The graph of $x = 2$ is a vertical line, and the graph of $y = -3$ is a horizontal line. They intersect at the point $(2, -3)$. The solution is $(2, -3)$.

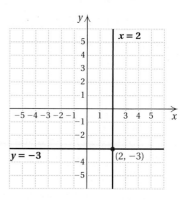

Do Exercise 4.

Sometimes the equations in a system have graphs that are parallel lines.

EXAMPLE 5 Solve this system of equations by graphing:

$$y = 3x + 4,$$
$$y = 3x - 3.$$

We graph the equations, again using any of the methods studied in Chapter 3. The lines have the same slope, 3, and different y-intercepts, $(0, 4)$ and $(0, -3)$, so they are parallel.

There is no point at which the lines cross, so the system has no solution. The solution set is the empty set, denoted $\varnothing$, or $\{\ \}$.

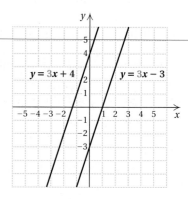

Do Exercise 5.

Sometimes the equations in a system have the same graph.

EXAMPLE 6 Solve this system of equations by graphing:

$$2x + 3y = 6,$$
$$-8x - 12y = -24.$$

We graph the equations and see that the graphs are the same. Thus any solution of one of the equations is a solution of the other. Each equation has an infinite number of solutions, some of which are indicated on the graph.

On the following page, we check one such solution, $(0, 2)$: the y-intercept of each equation.

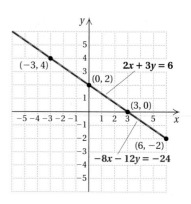

Check:

$$\begin{array}{c|c} 2x + 3y = 6 \\ \hline 2(0) + 3(2) \ ? \ 6 \\ 0 + 6 \ \Big| \\ 6 \ \Big| \quad \text{TRUE} \end{array} \qquad \begin{array}{c|c} -8x - 12y = -24 \\ \hline -8(0) - 12(2) \ ? \ -24 \\ 0 - 24 \ \Big| \\ -24 \ \Big| \quad \text{TRUE} \end{array}$$

We leave it to the student to check that $(-3, 4)$ is also a solution of the system. If $(0, 2)$ and $(-3, 4)$ are solutions, then all points on the line containing them are solutions. The system has an infinite number of solutions.

Do Exercise 6 on the preceding page.

When we graph a system of two equations in two variables, we obtain one of the following three results.

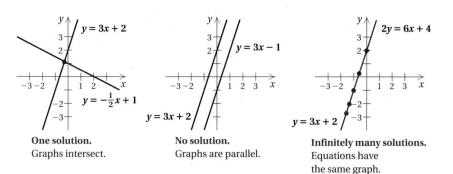

One solution.
Graphs intersect.

No solution.
Graphs are parallel.

Infinitely many solutions.
Equations have
the same graph.

AG ALGEBRAIC–GRAPHICAL CONNECTION

To bring together the concepts of Chapters 1–7, let's take an algebraic–graphical look at equation solving. Such interpretation is useful when using a graphing calculator.

Consider the equation $6 - x = x - 2$. Let's solve it algebraically as we did in Chapter 2:

$$\begin{aligned} 6 - x &= x - 2 \\ 6 &= 2x - 2 \qquad \text{Adding } x \\ 8 &= 2x \qquad \text{Adding 2} \\ 4 &= x. \qquad \text{Dividing by 2} \end{aligned}$$

Can we also solve the equation graphically? We can, as we see in the following two methods.

METHOD 1 Solve $6 - x = x - 2$ graphically.

We let $y = 6 - x$ and $y = x - 2$. Graphing the system of equations gives us the graph at right. The point of intersection is $(4, 2)$. Note that the x-coordinate of the intersection is 4. This value for x is also the *solution* of the equation $6 - x = x - 2$.

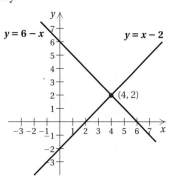

Do Exercise 7.

---

7. a) Solve $2x - 1 = 8 - x$ algebraically.

b) Solve $2x - 1 = 8 - x$ graphically using method 1.

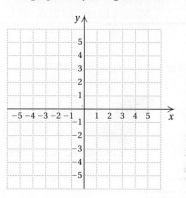

c) Compare your answers to parts (a) and (b).

Answers on page A-35

8. a) Solve $2x - 1 = 8 - x$ graphically using method 2.

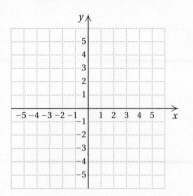

b) Compare your answers to Margin Exercises 7(a), 7(b), and 8(a).

Answers on page A-35

METHOD 2 Solve $6 - x = x - 2$ graphically.

Adding x and -6 on both sides, we obtain the form $0 = 2x - 8$. In this case, we let $y = 0$ and $y = 2x - 8$. Since $y = 0$ is the x-axis, we need graph only $y = 2x - 8$ and see where it crosses the x-axis. Note that the x-intercept of $y = 2x - 8$ is $(4, 0)$. The x-coordinate of this ordered pair is also the *solution* of the equation $6 - x = x - 2$.

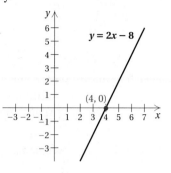

Do Exercise 8.

Let's compare the two methods. Using method 1, we graph two equations. The solution of the original equation is the x-coordinate of the point of intersection. Using method 2, we find that the solution of the original equation is the x-coordinate of the x-intercept of the graph.

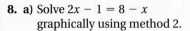

CALCULATOR CORNER

Solving Systems of Equations We can solve a system of two equations in two variables on a graphing calculator. Consider the system of equations in Example 3,

$$x + y = 6,$$
$$x = y + 2.$$

First, we solve the equations for y, obtaining $y = -x + 6$ and $y = x - 2$. Then we enter $y_1 = -x + 6$ and $y_2 = x - 2$ on the equation-editor screen and graph the equations. We can use the standard viewing window, $[-10, 10, -10, 10]$.

We will use the **INTERSECT** feature to find the coordinates of the point of intersection of the lines. To access this feature, we press **2ND** **CALC** **5**. (CALC is the second operation associated with the **TRACE** key.) The query "First curve?" appears on the graph screen. The blinking cursor is positioned on the graph of y_1. We press **ENTER** to indicate that this is the first curve involved in the intersection. Next, the query "Second curve?" appears and the blinking cursor is positioned on the graph of y_2. We press **ENTER** to indicate that this is the second curve. Now the query "Guess?" appears, so we use the ▷ and ◁ keys to move the cursor close to the point of intersection and press **ENTER**. The coordinates of the point of intersection of the graphs, $x = 4$, $y = 2$, appear at the bottom of the screen. Thus the solution of the system of equations is $(4, 2)$.

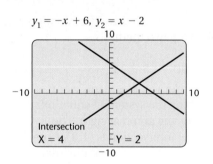

Exercises: Use a graphing calculator to solve the system of equations.

1. $x + y = 2,$
   $y = x + 4$

2. $y = x + 5,$
   $2x + y = 5$

3. $x - y = 5,$
   $y = 2x - 7$

4. $x + 3y = -1,$
   $x - y = -5$

5. $3x + 5y = 19,$
   $4x = 10 + y$

6. $3x = y + 6,$
   $1 = 2x + y$

a Determine whether the given ordered pair is a solution of the system of equations. Use alphabetical order of the variables.

1. $(1, 5);$ $5x - 2y = -5,$
           $3x - 7y = -32$

2. $(3, 2);$ $2x + 3y = 12,$
           $x - 4y = -5$

3. $(4, 2);$ $3b - 2a = -2,$
           $b + 2a = 8$

4. $(6, -6);$ $t + 2s = 6,$
             $t - s = -12$

5. $(15, 20);$ $3x - 2y = 5,$
             $6x - 5y = -10$

6. $(-1, -5);$ $4r + s = -9,$
              $3r = 2 + s$

7. $(-1, 1);$ $x = -1,$
           $x - y = -2$

8. $(-3, 4);$ $2x = -y - 2,$
           $y = -4$

9. $(18, 3);$ $y = \dfrac{1}{6}x,$
           $2x - y = 33$

10. $(-3, 1);$ $y = -\dfrac{1}{3}x,$
            $3y = -5x - 12$

b Solve the system of equations by graphing.

11. $x - y = 2,$
     $x + y = 6$

12. $x + y = 3,$
     $x - y = 1$

13. $8x - y = 29,$
     $2x + y = 11$

14. $4x - y = 10,$
     $3x + 5y = 19$

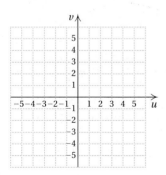 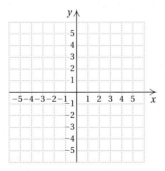 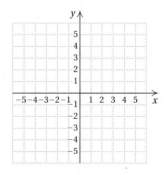 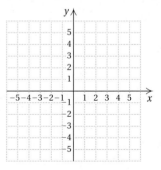

15. $u = v,$
     $4u = 2v - 6$

16. $x = 3y,$
     $3y - 6 = 2x$

17. $x = -y,$
     $x + y = 4$

18. $-3x = 5 - y,$
     $2y = 6x + 10$

19. $a = \dfrac{1}{2}b + 1,$

$a - 2b = -2$

20. $x = \dfrac{1}{3}y + 2,$

$-2x - y = 1$

21. $y - 2x = 0,$

$y = 6x - 2$

22. $y = 3x,$

$y = -3x + 2$

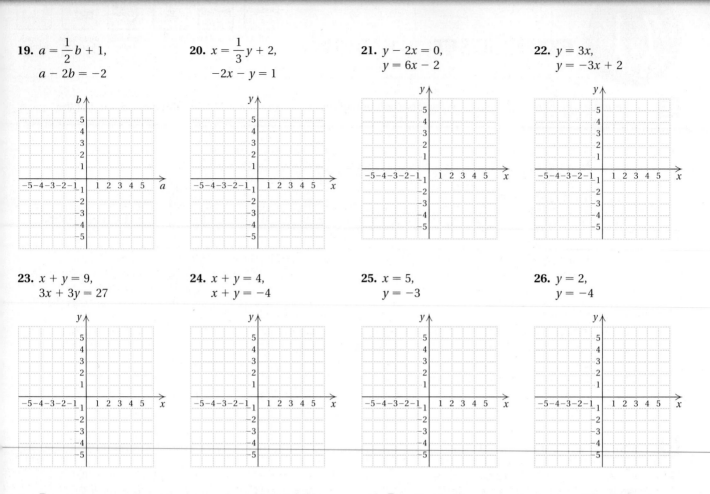

23. $x + y = 9,$

$3x + 3y = 27$

24. $x + y = 4,$

$x + y = -4$

25. $x = 5,$

$y = -3$

26. $y = 2,$

$y = -4$

27. **D$_W$** Suppose you have shown that the solution of the equation $3x - 1 = 9 - 2x$ is 2. How can this result be used to determine where the graphs of $y = 3x - 1$ and $y = 9 - 2x$ intersect?

28. **D$_W$** Graph this system of equations. What happens when you try to determine a solution from the graph?

$x - 2y = 6,$

$3x + 2y = 4$

Simplify.

29. $\dfrac{1}{x} - \dfrac{1}{x^2} + \dfrac{1}{x + 1}$ [6.5b]

30. $\dfrac{3 - x}{x - 2} - \dfrac{x - 7}{2 - x}$ [6.5a]

31. $\dfrac{x + 2}{x - 4} - \dfrac{x + 1}{x + 4}$ [6.5a]

32. $\dfrac{2x^2 - x - 15}{x^2 - 9}$ [6.1c]

Classify the polynomial as a monomial, a binomial, a trinomial, or none of these.   [4.3i]

33. $5x^2 - 3x + 7$

34. $4x^3 - 2x^2$

35. $1.8x^5$

36. $x^3 + 2x^2 - 3x + 1$

SYNTHESIS

37. The solution of the following system is $(2, -3)$. Find A and B.

$Ax - 3y = 13,$

$x - By = 8$

38. Find an equation to go with $5x + 2y = 11$ such that the solution of the system is $(3, -2)$. Answers may vary.

39. Find a system of equations with $(6, -2)$ as a solution. Answers may vary.

40.–47. Use the TABLE feature on a graphing calculator to check your answers to Exercises 11–18.

566

7.2 THE SUBSTITUTION METHOD

Objectives

a Solve a system of two equations in two variables by the substitution method when one of the equations has a variable alone on one side.

b Solve a system of two equations in two variables by the substitution method when neither equation has a variable alone on one side.

c Solve applied problems by translating to a system of two equations and then solving using the substitution method.

Consider the following system of equations:

$$3x + 7y = 5,$$
$$6x - 7y = 1.$$

Suppose we try to solve this system graphically. We obtain the graph shown at right.

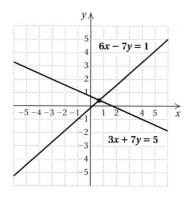

What is the solution? It is rather difficult to tell exactly. It would appear that the coordinates of the point are not integers. It turns out that the solution is $\left(\frac{2}{3}, \frac{3}{7}\right)$. We need techniques involving algebra to determine the solution exactly. Graphing helps us picture the solution of a system of equations, but solving by graphing, though practical in many applications, is not always fast or accurate in cases where solutions are not integers. We now learn other methods using algebra. Because they use algebra, they are called **algebraic.**

a Solving by the Substitution Method

One nongraphical method for solving systems is known as the **substitution method.** In Example 1, we use the substitution method to solve a system we graphed in Example 3 of Section 7.1.

EXAMPLE 1 Solve the system

$$x + y = 6, \quad \textbf{(1)}$$
$$x = y + 2. \quad \textbf{(2)}$$

Equation (2) says that x and $y + 2$ name the same thing. Thus in equation (1), we can substitute $y + 2$ for x:

$$x + y = 6 \qquad \text{Equation (1)}$$
$$(y + 2) + y = 6. \qquad \text{Substituting } y + 2 \text{ for } x$$

This last equation has only one variable. We solve it:

$$y + 2 + y = 6 \qquad \text{Removing parentheses}$$
$$2y + 2 = 6 \qquad \text{Collecting like terms}$$
$$2y + 2 - 2 = 6 - 2 \qquad \text{Subtracting 2 on both sides}$$
$$2y = 4 \qquad \text{Simplifying}$$
$$\frac{2y}{2} = \frac{4}{2} \qquad \text{Dividing by 2}$$
$$y = 2. \qquad \text{Simplifying}$$

We have found the y-value of the solution. To find the x-value, we return to the original pair of equations. Substituting into either equation will give us the x-value.

Study Tips

BEGINNING TO STUDY FOR THE FINAL EXAM (PART 1)

It is never too soon to begin to study for the final examination. Take a few minutes each week to review the highlighted information, such as formulas, properties, and procedures. Make special use of the Summary and Reviews, Chapter Tests, and Cumulative Reviews, as well as the supplements such as the Work It Out! Chapter Test Video on CD, the Interact Math Tutorial Web site, and MathXL. The Cumulative Review/Final Examination for Chapters 1–9 is a sample final exam.

"Practice does not make perfect; practice makes permanent."

Dr. Richard Chase, former president, Wheaton College

1. Solve by the substitution method. Do not graph.

$$x + y = 5,$$
$$x = y + 1$$

We choose equation (2) because it has x alone on one side:

$$x = y + 2 \qquad \text{Equation (2)}$$
$$ = 2 + 2 \qquad \text{Substituting 2 for } y$$
$$ = 4.$$

The ordered pair $(4, 2)$ may be a solution. Note that we are using alphabetical order in listing the coordinates in an ordered pair. That is, since x precedes y, we list 4 before 2 in the pair $(4, 2)$.

We check as follows.

Check:
$$\frac{x + y = 6}{4 + 2 \ ? \ 6}$$
$$ 6 \ | \qquad \text{TRUE}$$

$$\frac{x = y + 2}{4 \ ? \ 2 + 2}$$
$$ | \ 4 \qquad \text{TRUE}$$

Since $(4, 2)$ checks, we have the solution. We could also express the answer as $x = 4$, $y = 2$.

Note in Example 1 that substituting 2 for y in equation (1) will also give us the x-value of the solution:

$$x + y = 6$$
$$x + 2 = 6$$
$$x = 4.$$

Do Exercise 1.

---

2. Solve by the substitution method:

$$a - b = 4,$$
$$b = 2 - a.$$

EXAMPLE 2 Solve the system

$$t = 1 - 3s, \qquad \textbf{(1)}$$
$$s - t = 11. \qquad \textbf{(2)}$$

We substitute $1 - 3s$ for t in equation (2):

$$s - t = 11 \qquad \text{Equation (2)}$$
$$s - (1 - 3s) = 11. \qquad \text{Substituting } 1 - 3s \text{ for } t$$

| Remember to use parentheses when you substitute. |

Now we solve for s:

$$s - 1 + 3s = 11 \qquad \text{Removing parentheses}$$
$$4s - 1 = 11 \qquad \text{Collecting like terms}$$
$$4s = 12 \qquad \text{Adding 1}$$
$$s = 3. \qquad \text{Dividing by 4}$$

Next, we substitute 3 for s in equation (1) of the original system:

$$t = 1 - 3s \qquad \text{Equation (1)}$$
$$ = 1 - 3 \cdot 3 \qquad \text{Substituting 3 for } s$$
$$ = -8.$$

The pair $(3, -8)$ checks and is the solution. Remember: We list the answer in alphabetical order, (s, t). That is, since s comes before t in the alphabet, 3 is listed first and -8 second.

Do Exercise 2.

b Solving for the Variable First

Sometimes neither equation of a pair has a variable alone on one side. Then we solve one equation for one of the variables and proceed as before, substituting into the *other* equation. If possible, we solve in either equation for a variable that has a coefficient of 1.

EXAMPLE 3 Solve the system

$$x - 2y = 6, \quad \textbf{(1)}$$
$$3x + 2y = 4. \quad \textbf{(2)}$$

We solve one equation for one variable. Since the coefficient of x is 1 in equation (1), it is easier to solve that equation for x:

$$x - 2y = 6 \qquad \text{Equation (1)}$$
$$x = 6 + 2y. \qquad \text{Adding } 2y \qquad \textbf{(3)}$$

We substitute $6 + 2y$ for x in equation (2) of the original pair and solve for y:

$$3x + 2y = 4 \qquad\qquad \text{Equation (2)}$$
$$3(6 + 2y) + 2y = 4 \qquad \text{Substituting } 6 + 2y \text{ for } x$$
$$18 + 6y + 2y = 4 \qquad \text{Removing parentheses}$$
$$18 + 8y = 4 \qquad \text{Collecting like terms}$$
$$8y = -14 \qquad \text{Subtracting 18}$$
$$y = \frac{-14}{8}, \text{ or } -\frac{7}{4}. \qquad \text{Dividing by 8}$$

To find x, we go back to either of the original equations (1) or (2) or to equation (3), which we solved for x. It is generally easier to use an equation like equation (3) where we have solved for a specific variable. We substitute $-\frac{7}{4}$ for y in equation (3) and compute x:

$$x = 6 + 2y \qquad \text{Equation (3)}$$
$$= 6 + 2\left(-\frac{7}{4}\right) \qquad \text{Substituting } -\frac{7}{4} \text{ for } y$$
$$= 6 - \frac{7}{2} = \frac{5}{2}.$$

We check the ordered pair $\left(\frac{5}{2}, -\frac{7}{4}\right)$.

Check:

$$\begin{array}{c|c}
x - 2y = 6 \\
\hline
\frac{5}{2} - 2\left(-\frac{7}{4}\right) \,?\, 6 \\
\frac{5}{2} + \frac{7}{2} \\
\frac{12}{2} \\
6 \quad\quad \text{TRUE}
\end{array}
\qquad
\begin{array}{c|c}
3x + 2y = 4 \\
\hline
3 \cdot \frac{5}{2} + 2\left(-\frac{7}{4}\right) \,?\, 4 \\
\frac{15}{2} - \frac{7}{2} \\
\frac{8}{2} \\
4 \quad\quad \text{TRUE}
\end{array}$$

Since $\left(\frac{5}{2}, -\frac{7}{4}\right)$ checks, it is the solution. This solution would have been difficult to find graphically because it involves fractions.

Do Exercise 3.

c Solving Applied Problems

Now let's solve an applied problem using systems of equations and the substitution method.

---

3. Solve:

$$x - 2y = 8,$$
$$2x + y = 8.$$

> **Caution!**
>
> A solution of a system of equations in two variables is an ordered *pair* of numbers. Once you have solved for one variable, don't forget the other. A common mistake is to solve for only one variable.

Answer on page A-35

4. Community Garden. A rectangular community garden is to be enclosed with 92 m of fencing. In order to allow for compost storage, the garden must be 4 m longer than it is wide. Determine the dimensions of the garden.

EXAMPLE 4 *Standard Billboard.* A standard rectangular highway billboard has a perimeter of 124 ft. The length is 34 ft more than the width. Find the length and the width.

Source: Eller Sign Company

1. **Familiarize.** We make a drawing and label it. We let l = the length and w = the width.

$l = 34 + w$

w

2. **Translate.** The perimeter of the rectangle is given by the formula $2l + 2w$. We translate each statement, as follows.

$\underbrace{\text{The perimeter}}$ $\underbrace{\text{is}}$ $\underbrace{\text{124 ft.}}$
$\quad\quad 2l + 2w \quad\quad = \quad\quad 124$

$\underbrace{\text{The length}}$ $\underbrace{\text{is}}$ $\underbrace{\text{34 ft longer than the width.}}$
$\quad\quad l \quad\quad = \quad\quad\quad 34 + w$

We now have a system of equations:

$$2l + 2w = 124, \quad\quad \textbf{(1)}$$
$$l = 34 + w. \quad\quad\quad \textbf{(2)}$$

3. **Solve.** We solve the system. To begin, we substitute $34 + w$ for l in the first equation and solve:

$2(34 + w) + 2w = 124$ Substituting $34 + w$ for l in equation (1)
$2 \cdot 34 + 2 \cdot w + 2w = 124$ Removing parentheses
$4w + 68 = 124$ Collecting like terms
$4w = 56$ Subtracting 68
$w = 14.$ Dividing by 4

We go back to one of the original equations and substitute 14 for w:

$l = 34 + w = 34 + 14 = 48.$ Substituting in equation (2)

4. **Check.** If the length is 48 ft and the width is 14 ft, then the length is 34 ft more than the width ($48 - 14 = 34$), and the perimeter is $2(48 \text{ ft}) + 2(14 \text{ ft})$, or 124 ft. Thus these dimensions check.

5. **State.** The width is 14 ft and the length is 48 ft.

The problem in Example 4 illustrates that many problems that can be solved by translating to *one* equation in *one* variable may actually be easier to solve by translating to *two* equations in *two* variables.

Answer on page A-35

Do Exercise 4.

7.2

EXERCISE SET | For Extra Help

MathXL | MyMathLab | InterAct Math | Math Tutor Center | Digital Video Tutor CD 4 Videotape 8 | Student's Solutions Manual

a Solve using the substitution method.

1. $x + y = 10,$
$y = x + 8$

2. $x + y = 4,$
$y = 2x + 1$

3. $y = x - 6,$
$x + y = -2$

4. $y = x + 1,$
$2x + y = 4$

5. $y = 2x - 5,$
$3y - x = 5$

6. $y = 2x + 1,$
$x + y = -2$

7. $x = -2y,$
$x + 4y = 2$

8. $r = -3s,$
$r + 4s = 10$

b Solve using the substitution method. First, solve one equation for one variable.

9. $x - y = 6,$
$x + y = -2$

10. $s + t = -4,$
$s - t = 2$

11. $y - 2x = -6,$
$2y - x = 5$

12. $x - y = 5,$
$x + 2y = 7$

13. $2x + 3y = -2,$
$2x - y = 9$

14. $x + 2y = 10,$
$3x + 4y = 8$

15. $x - y = -3,$
$2x + 3y = -6$

16. $3b + 2a = 2,$
$-2b + a = 8$

17. $r - 2s = 0,$
$4r - 3s = 15$

18. $y - 2x = 0,$
$3x + 7y = 17$

c Solve.

19. *Perimeter of NBA Court.* The perimeter of an NBA-sized basketball court is 288 ft. The length is 44 ft longer than the width. Find the dimensions of the court.

Source: National Basketball Association

20. *Perimeter of High School Court.* The perimeter of a standard high school basketball court is 268 ft. The length is 34 ft longer than the width. Find the dimensions of the court.

Source: Indiana High School Athletic Association

21. *Two-by-Four.* The perimeter of a cross section of a "two-by-four" piece of lumber is 10 in. The length is 2 in. more than the width. Find the actual dimensions of a cross section of a two-by-four.

22. *Rose Garden.* The perimeter of a rectangular rose garden is 400 m. The length is 3 m more than twice the width. Find the length and the width.

23. *Dimensions of Wyoming.* The state of Wyoming is a rectangle with a perimeter of 1280 mi. The width is 90 mi less than the length. Find the length and the width.

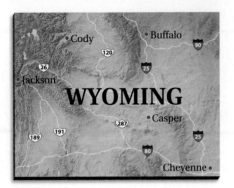

24. *Dimensions of Colorado.* The state of Colorado is roughly in the shape of a rectangle whose perimeter is 1300 mi. The width is 110 mi less than the length. Find the length and the width.

25. *Racquetball.* A regulation racquetball court should have a perimeter of 120 ft, with a length that is twice the width. Find the length and the width of a court.

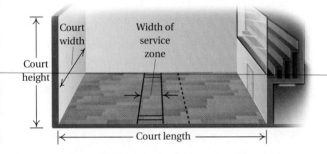

26. *Racquetball.* The height of the front wall of a standard racquetball court is four times the width of the service zone (see the figure). Together, these measurements total 25 ft. Find the height and the width.

27. *Lacrosse.* The perimeter of a lacrosse field is 340 yd. The length is 10 yd less than twice the width. Find the length and the width.

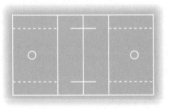

28. *Soccer.* The perimeter of a soccer field is 280 yd. The width is 5 more than half the length. Find the length and the width.

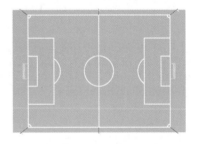

29. The sum of two numbers is 37. One number is 5 more than the other. Find the numbers.

30. The sum of two numbers is 26. One number is 12 more than the other. Find the numbers.

31. Find two numbers whose sum is 52 and whose difference is 28.

32. Find two numbers whose sum is 63 and whose difference is 5.

33. The difference between two numbers is 12. Two times the larger is five times the smaller. What are the numbers?

34. The difference between two numbers is 18. Twice the smaller number plus three times the larger is 74. What are the numbers?

35. D_W Janine can tell by inspection that the system
$$x = 2y - 1,$$
$$x = 2y + 3$$
has no solution. How can she tell?

36. D_W Joel solves every system of two equations (in x and y) by first solving for y in the first equation and then substituting into the second equation. Is he using the best approach? Why or why not?

SKILL MAINTENANCE

Graph.   [3.2a, b]

37. $2x - 3y = 6$

38. $2x + 3y = 6$

39. $y = 2x - 5$

40. $y = 4$

Factor completely.   [5.6a]

41. $6x^2 - 13x + 6$

42. $4p^2 - p - 3$

43. $4x^2 + 3x + 2$

44. $9a^2 - 25$

Simplify.   [4.1d, e, f]

45. $\dfrac{x^{-2}}{x^{-5}}$

46. $x^2 \cdot x^5$

47. $x^{-2} \cdot x^{-5}$

48. $\dfrac{a^2 b^{-3}}{a^5 b^{-6}}$

SYNTHESIS

Solve using a graphing calculator and its CALC-INTERSECT feature. Then solve algebraically and decide which method you prefer to use.

49. $x - y = 5,$
$x + 2y = 7$

50. $y - 2x = -6,$
$2y - x = 5$

51. $y - 2.35x = -5.97,$
$2.14y - x = 4.88$

52. $y = 1.2x - 32.7,$
$y = -0.7x + 46.15$

53. *Softball.*   The perimeter of a softball diamond is two-thirds of the perimeter of a baseball diamond. Together, the two perimeters measure 200 yd. Find the distance between the bases in each sport.

54. Write a system of two linear equations that can be solved more quickly—but still precisely—by a graphing calculator than by substitution. Time yourself using both methods to solve the system.

573

Objectives

a Solve a system of two equations in two variables using the elimination method when no multiplication is necessary.

b Solve a system of two equations in two variables using the elimination method when multiplication is necessary.

7.3 THE ELIMINATION METHOD

a Solving by the Elimination Method

The **elimination method** for solving systems of equations makes use of the *addition principle*. Some systems are much easier to solve using this method. For example, to solve the system

$$2x + 3y = 13, \quad \textbf{(1)}$$
$$4x - 3y = 17 \quad \textbf{(2)}$$

by substitution, we would need to first solve for a variable in one of the equations. Were we to solve equation (1) for y, we would find (after several steps) that $y = \frac{13}{3} - \frac{2}{3}x$. We could then use the expression $\frac{13}{3} - \frac{2}{3}x$ in equation (2) as a replacement for y:

$$4x - 3\left(\frac{13}{3} - \frac{2}{3}x\right) = 17.$$

As you can see, although substitution could be used to solve this system, doing so is not easy. Fortunately, another method, elimination, can be used to solve systems and, on problems like this, is simpler to use.

EXAMPLE 1 Solve the system

$$2x + 3y = 13, \quad \textbf{(1)}$$
$$4x - 3y = 17. \quad \textbf{(2)}$$

The key to the advantage of the elimination method for solving this system involves the $3y$ in one equation and the $-3y$ in the other. The terms are opposites. If we add the terms on the sides of the equations, the y-terms will add to 0, and in effect, the variable y will be eliminated.

We will use the addition principle for equations. According to equation (2), $4x - 3y$ and 17 are the same number. Thus we can use a vertical form and add $4x - 3y$ to the left side of equation (1) and 17 to the right side—in effect, adding the same number on both sides of equation (1):

$$
\begin{array}{ll}
2x + 3y = 13 & \textbf{(1)} \\
\underline{4x - 3y = 17} & \textbf{(2)} \\
6x + 0y = 30, \text{ or} & \text{Adding} \\
6x \quad\ \ = 30.
\end{array}
$$

We have "eliminated" one variable. This is why we call this the **elimination method.** We now have an equation with just one variable that can be solved for x:

$$6x = 30$$
$$x = 5.$$

Next, we substitute 5 for x in either of the original equations:

$$
\begin{array}{ll}
2x + 3y = 13 & \text{Equation (1)} \\
2(5) + 3y = 13 & \text{Substituting 5 for } x \\
10 + 3y = 13 & \\
3y = 3 & \\
y = 1. & \text{Solving for } y
\end{array}
$$

We check the ordered pair $(5, 1)$.

Check:

$$2x + 3y = 13$$
$$\overline{2(5) + 3(1) \;?\; 13}$$
$$10 + 3 \;\big|$$
$$13 \;\big| \quad \text{TRUE}$$

$$4x - 3y = 17$$
$$\overline{4(5) - 3(1) \;?\; 17}$$
$$20 - 3 \;\big|$$
$$17 \;\big| \quad \text{TRUE}$$

Since $(5, 1)$ checks, it is the solution. We can see the solution in the graph shown below.

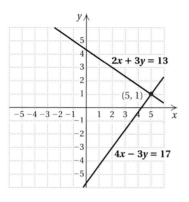

Do Exercises 1 and 2.

b   Using the Multiplication Principle First

The elimination method allows us to eliminate a variable. We may need to multiply by certain numbers first, however, so that terms become opposites.

EXAMPLE 2   Solve the system

$$2x + 3y = 8, \quad \textbf{(1)}$$
$$x + 3y = 7. \quad \textbf{(2)}$$

If we add, we will not eliminate a variable. However, if the $3y$ were $-3y$ in one equation, we could eliminate y. Thus we multiply by -1 on both sides of equation (2) and then add, using a vertical form:

$$2x + 3y = 8 \qquad \text{Equation (1)}$$
$$\underline{-x - 3y = -7} \qquad \text{Multiplying equation (2) by } -1$$
$$x = 1. \qquad \text{Adding}$$

Next, we substitute 1 for x in one of the original equations:

$$x + 3y = 7 \qquad \text{Equation (2)}$$
$$1 + 3y = 7 \qquad \text{Substituting 1 for } x$$
$$3y = 6$$
$$y = 2. \qquad \text{Solving for } y$$

Solve using the elimination method.

1. $x + y = 5,$
    $2x - y = 4$

2. $-2x + y = -4,$
    $2x - 5y = 12$

Answers on page A-35

3. Solve. Multiply one equation by -1 first.

$$5x + 3y = 17,$$
$$5x - 2y = -3$$

We check the ordered pair $(1, 2)$.

Check:

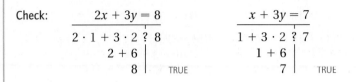

$$
\begin{array}{c|c}
2x + 3y = 8 & x + 3y = 7 \\
\hline
2 \cdot 1 + 3 \cdot 2 \ ? \ 8 & 1 + 3 \cdot 2 \ ? \ 7 \\
2 + 6 & 1 + 6 \\
8 \ \text{TRUE} & 7 \ \text{TRUE}
\end{array}
$$

Since $(1, 2)$ checks, it is the solution.

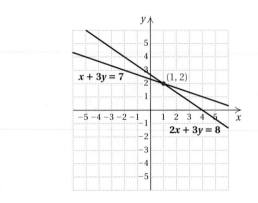

Do Exercises 3 and 4.

In Example 2, we used the multiplication principle, multiplying by -1. However, we often need to multiply by something other than -1.

4. Solve the system

$$3x - 2y = -30,$$
$$5x - 2y = -46.$$

EXAMPLE 3 Solve the system

$$3x + 6y = -6, \qquad \textbf{(1)}$$
$$5x - 2y = 14. \qquad \textbf{(2)}$$

Looking at the terms with variables, we see that if $-2y$ were $-6y$, we would have terms that are opposites. We can achieve this by multiplying by 3 on both sides of equation (2). Then we add and solve for x:

$$
\begin{array}{ll}
3x + 6y = -6 & \text{Equation (1)} \\
\underline{15x - 6y = 42} & \text{Multiplying by 3 on both sides of equation (2)} \\
18x = 36 & \text{Adding} \\
x - 2. & \text{Solving for } x
\end{array}
$$

Next, we substitute 2 for x in either of the original equations. We choose the first:

$$
\begin{array}{ll}
3x + 6y = -6 & \text{Equation (1)} \\
3 \cdot 2 + 6y = -6 & \text{Substituting 2 for } x \\
6 + 6y = -6 & \\
6y = -12 & \\
y = -2. & \text{Solving for } y
\end{array}
$$

We check the ordered pair $(2, -2)$.

Check:

$$
\begin{array}{c|c}
3x + 6y = -6 & 5x - 2y = 14 \\
\hline
3 \cdot 2 + 6 \cdot (-2) \ ? \ -6 & 5 \cdot 2 - 2 \cdot (-2) \ ? \ 14 \\
6 + (-12) & 10 - (-4) \\
-6 \ \text{TRUE} & 14 \ \text{TRUE}
\end{array}
$$

Answers on page A-35

Since $(2, -2)$ checks, it is the solution.

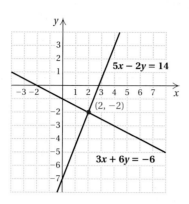

Do Exercises 5 and 6.

Solve the system.

5. $4a + 7b = 11,$
$2a + 3b = 5$

6. $3x - 8y = 2,$
$5x + 2y = -12$

Part of the strategy in using the elimination method is making a decision about which variable to eliminate. So long as the algebra has been carried out correctly, the solution can be found by eliminating *either* variable. We multiply so that terms involving the variable to be eliminated are opposites. It is helpful to first get each equation in a form equivalent to $Ax + By = C$.

EXAMPLE 4 Solve the system

$$3y + 1 + 2x = 0, \qquad \textbf{(1)}$$
$$5x = 7 - 4y. \qquad \textbf{(2)}$$

We first rewrite each equation in a form equivalent to $Ax + By = C$:

$2x + 3y = -1,$ **(1)**   Subtracting 1 on both sides and rearranging terms

$5x + 4y = 7.$ **(2)**   Adding $4y$ on both sides

We decide to eliminate the x-term. We do this by multiplying by 5 on both sides of equation (1) and by -2 on both sides of equation (2). Then we add and solve for y:

$$
\begin{array}{ll}
10x + 15y = -5 & \text{Multiplying by 5 on both sides of equation (1)} \\
\underline{-10x - 8y = -14} & \text{Multiplying by } -2 \text{ on both sides of equation (2)} \\
 7y = -19 & \text{Adding} \\
 y = \dfrac{-19}{7}, \text{ or } -\dfrac{19}{7}. & \text{Solving for } y
\end{array}
$$

Next, we substitute $-\frac{19}{7}$ for y in one of the original equations:

$$
\begin{array}{ll}
2x + 3y = -1 & \text{Equation (1)} \\
2x + 3\left(-\frac{19}{7}\right) = -1 & \text{Substituting } -\frac{19}{7} \text{ for } y \\
2x - \frac{57}{7} = -1 & \\
2x = -1 + \frac{57}{7} & \\
2x = -\frac{7}{7} + \frac{57}{7} & \\
2x = \frac{50}{7} & \\
\frac{1}{2} \cdot 2x = \frac{1}{2} \cdot \frac{50}{7} & \text{Multiplying by } \frac{1}{2} \text{ on both sides of the equation} \\
x = \frac{50}{14} & \\
x = \frac{25}{7}. & \text{Simplifying}
\end{array}
$$

CALCULATOR CORNER

Solving Systems of Equations   Use the INTERSECT feature to solve the systems of equations in Margin Exercises 1–6. (See the Calculator Corner on p. 564 for the procedure.)

Answers on page A-35

Caution!

Solving a *system* of equations in two variables requires finding an ordered *pair* of numbers. Once you have solved for one variable, don't forget the other, and remember to list the ordered-pair solution using alphabetical order.

7. Solve the system

$$3x = 5 + 2y,$$
$$2x + 3y - 1 = 0.$$

We check the ordered pair $\left(\frac{25}{7}, -\frac{19}{7}\right)$.

Check:

$$\frac{3y + 1 + 2x = 0}{3\left(-\frac{19}{7}\right) + 1 + 2\left(\frac{25}{7}\right) \; ? \; 0}$$
$$-\frac{57}{7} + \frac{7}{7} + \frac{50}{7} \;\Big|$$
$$0 \;\Big| \quad \text{TRUE}$$

$$\frac{5x = 7 - 4y}{5\left(\frac{25}{7}\right) \; ? \; 7 - 4\left(-\frac{19}{7}\right)}$$
$$\frac{125}{7} \;\Big|\; \frac{49}{7} + \frac{76}{7}$$
$$\Big|\; \frac{125}{7}$$
$$\quad\quad\quad \text{TRUE}$$

The solution is $\left(\frac{25}{7}, -\frac{19}{7}\right)$.

Do Exercise 7.

Let's consider a system with no solution and see what happens when we apply the elimination method.

EXAMPLE 5 Solve the system

$$y - 3x = 2, \quad \textbf{(1)}$$
$$y - 3x = 1. \quad \textbf{(2)}$$

We multiply by -1 on both sides of equation (2) and then add:

$$
\begin{array}{ll}
y - 3x = 2 & \text{Equation (1)} \\
\underline{-y + 3x = -1} & \text{Multiplying by } -1 \text{ on both sides of equation (2)} \\
0 = 1. & \text{Adding}
\end{array}
$$

We obtain a false equation, $0 = 1$, so there is *no solution*. (See Section 2.3c.)
The slope–intercept forms of these equations are

$$y = 3x + 2,$$
$$y = 3x + 1.$$

The slopes, 3, are the same and the y-intercepts, $(0, 2)$ and $(0, 1)$, are different. Thus the lines are parallel. They do not intersect.

8. Solve the system

$$2x + y = 15,$$
$$4x + 2y = 23.$$

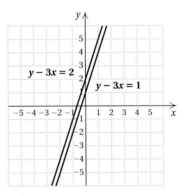

Do Exercise 8.

Answers on page A-35

Sometimes there is an infinite number of solutions. Let's look at a system that we graphed in Example 6 of Section 7.1.

EXAMPLE 6 Solve the system

$$2x + 3y = 6, \qquad \textbf{(1)}$$
$$-8x - 12y = -24. \qquad \textbf{(2)}$$

We multiply by 4 on both sides of equation (1) and then add the two equations:

$$\begin{array}{ll} 8x + 12y = 24 & \text{Multiplying by 4 on both sides of equation (1)} \\ \underline{-8x - 12y = -24} & \\ 0 = 0. & \text{Adding} \end{array}$$

We have eliminated both variables, and what remains, $0 = 0$, is an equation easily seen to be true. If this happens when we use the elimination method, we have an infinite number of solutions. (See Section 2.3c.)

Do Exercise 9.

When decimals or fractions appear, we first multiply to clear them. Then we proceed as before.

EXAMPLE 7 Solve the system

$$\frac{1}{3}x + \frac{1}{2}y = -\frac{1}{6}, \qquad \textbf{(1)}$$
$$\frac{1}{2}x + \frac{2}{5}y = \frac{7}{10}. \qquad \textbf{(2)}$$

The number 6 is a multiple of all the denominators of equation (1). The number 10 is a multiple of all the denominators of equation (2). We multiply by 6 on both sides of equation (1) and by 10 on both sides of equation (2):

$$6\left(\frac{1}{3}x + \frac{1}{2}y\right) = 6\left(-\frac{1}{6}\right) \qquad\qquad 10\left(\frac{1}{2}x + \frac{2}{5}y\right) = 10\left(\frac{7}{10}\right)$$

$$6 \cdot \frac{1}{3}x + 6 \cdot \frac{1}{2}y = -1 \qquad\qquad 10 \cdot \frac{1}{2}x + 10 \cdot \frac{2}{5}y = 7$$

$$2x + 3y = -1; \qquad\qquad 5x + 4y = 7.$$

The resulting system is

$$2x + 3y = -1,$$
$$5x + 4y = 7.$$

As we saw in Example 4, the solution of this system is $\left(\frac{25}{7}, -\frac{19}{7}\right)$.

Do Exercises 10 and 11 on the following page.

9. Solve the system

$$5x - 2y = 3,$$
$$-15x + 6y = -9.$$

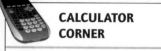

Answer on page A-35

Solve the system.

10. $\frac{1}{2}x + \frac{3}{10}y = \frac{1}{5}$,

$\frac{3}{5}x + \quad y = -\frac{2}{5}$

11. $3.3x + 6.6y = -6.6$,

$0.1x - 0.04y = 0.28$

Answers on page A-35

The following is a summary that compares the graphical, substitution, and elimination methods for solving systems of equations.

METHOD	STRENGTHS	WEAKNESSES
Graphical	Can "see" solution.	Inexact when solution involves numbers that are not integers or are very large and off the graph.
Substitution	Works well when solutions are not integers. Easy to use when a variable is alone on one side.	Introduces extensive computations with fractions for more complicated systems where coefficients are not 1 or −1. Cannot "see" solution.
Elimination	Works well when solutions are not integers, when coefficients are not 1 or −1, and when coefficients involve decimals or fractions.	Cannot "see" solution.

Study Tips

THE 20 BEST JOBS

Although this does not qualify as a Study Tip, you can use the information to motivate your study of mathematics. The book Best Jobs for the 21st Century, *3rd ed., developed by Michael Farr with database work by Laurence Shatkin, Ph.D., ranks 500 jobs on the basis of overall scores for pay, growth rate through 2010, and number of annual openings. Note that the use of mathematics is significant in most of the 20 top jobs.*

JOB	ANNUAL EARNINGS	GROWTH RATE THROUGH 2010	ANNUAL OPENINGS
1. Computer software engineers, applications	$70,210	100.0%	28,000
2. Computer systems analysts	61,990	59.7	34,000
3. Computer and information systems managers	82,480	47.9	28,000
4. Teachers, postsecondary	52,115	23.5	184,000
5. Management analysts	57,970	28.9	50,000
6. Registered nurses	46,670	25.6	140,000
7. Computer software engineers, systems software	73,280	89.7	23,000
8. Medical and health services managers	59,220	32.3	27,000
9. Sales agents, financial services	59,690	22.3	55,000
10. Sales agents, securities and commodities	59,690	22.3	55,000
11. Securities, commodities, and financial services sales agents	59,690	22.3	55,000
12. Computer support specialists	38,560	97.0	40,000
13. Sales managers	71,620	32.8	21,000
14. Computer security specialists	53,770	81.9	18,000
15. Network and computer systems administrators	53,770	81.9	18,000
16. Financial managers	70,210	18.5	53,000
17. Financial managers, branch or department	70,210	18.5	53,000
18. Treasurers, comptrollers, and chief financial officers	70,210	18.5	53,000
19. Accountants	45,380	18.5	100,000
20. Accountants and auditors	45,380	18.5	100,000

Source: Based on "The 20 Best Jobs," from *Best Jobs for the 21st Century*, 3rd ed. Indianapolis: Jist Works, 2004, p. 16.

a   Solve using the elimination method.

1. $x - y = 7,$
$x + y = 5$

2. $x + y = 11,$
$x - y = 7$

3. $x + y = 8,$
$-x + 2y = 7$

4. $x + y = 6,$
$-x + 3y = -2$

5. $5x - y = 5,$
$3x + y = 11$

6. $2x - y = 8,$
$3x + y = 12$

7. $4a + 3b = 7,$
$-4a + b = 5$

8. $7c + 5d = 18,$
$c - 5d = -2$

9. $8x - 5y = -9,$
$3x + 5y = -2$

10. $3a - 3b = -15,$
$-3a - 3b = -3$

11. $4x - 5y = 7,$
$-4x + 5y = 7$

12. $2x + 3y = 4,$
$-2x - 3y = -4$

b   Solve using the multiplication principle first. Then add.

13. $x + y = -7,$
$3x + y = -9$

14. $-x - y = 8,$
$2x - y = -1$

15. $3x - y = 8,$
$x + 2y = 5$

16. $x + 3y = 19,$
$x - y = -1$

17. $x - y = 5,$
$4x - 5y = 17$

18. $x + y = 4,$
$5x - 3y = 12$

19. $2w - 3z = -1,$
$3w + 4z = 24$

20. $7p + 5q = 2,$
$8p - 9q = 17$

21. $2a + 3b = -1,$
$\quad 3a + 5b = -2$

22. $3x - 4y = 16,$
$\quad 5x + 6y = 14$

23. $x = 3y,$
$\quad 5x + 14 = y$

24. $5a = 2b,$
$\quad 2a + 11 = 3b$

25. $2x + 5y = 16,$
$\quad 3x - 2y = 5$

26. $3p - 2q = 8,$
$\quad 5p + 3q = 7$

27. $p = 32 + q,$
$\quad 3p = 8q + 6$

28. $3x = 8y + 11,$
$\quad x + 6y - 8 = 0$

29. $3x - 2y = 10,$
$\quad -6x + 4y = -20$

30. $2x + y = 13,$
$\quad 4x + 2y = 23$

31. $0.06x + 0.05y = 0.07,$
$\quad 0.4x - 0.3y = 1.1$

32. $1.8x - 2y = 0.9,$
$\quad 0.04x + 0.18y = 0.15$

33. $\dfrac{1}{3}x + \dfrac{3}{2}y = \dfrac{5}{4},$
$\quad \dfrac{3}{4}x - \dfrac{5}{6}y = \dfrac{3}{8}$

34. $x - \dfrac{3}{2}y = 13,$
$\quad \dfrac{3}{2}x - y = 17$

35. $-4.5x + 7.5y = 6,$
$\quad -x + 1.5y = 5$

36. $0.75x + 0.6y = -0.3,$
$\quad 3.9x + 5.2y = 96.2$

37. **D$_W$** The following lists the steps a student uses to solve a system of equations, but an error has been made. Find and describe the error and correct the answer.

$$\begin{array}{rl} 3x - y = & 4 \\ 2x + y = & 16 \\ \hline 5x \quad\;\; = & 20 \\ x = & 4 \end{array}$$

$$3x - y = 4$$
$$3(4) - y = 4$$
$$y = 4 - 12$$
$$y = -8$$

The solution is $(4, -8)$.

38. **D$_W$** Explain how the addition and multiplication principles are used in this section. Then count the number of times that these principles are used in Example 4.

✍ VOCABULARY REINFORCEMENT

In each of Exercises 39–46, fill in the blank with the correct term from the given list. Some of the choices may not be used.

39. Parallel lines have the same _____ and different _____.   [3.6a]

40. Two nonvertical lines are _____ if the product of their slopes is -1.   [3.6b]

41. A(n) _____ of a system of two equations is an ordered pair that makes both equations true.   [7.1a]

42. If a situation gives rise to an equation $y = kx$, where k is a positive constant, we say that we have _____ variation.   [6.9a]

43. The graph of $y = b$ is a(n) _____ line.   [3.2b]

44. If a situation gives rise to an equation $y = k/x$, where k is a positive constant, we say that we have _____ variation.   [6.9c]

45. The equation $y = mx + b$ is called the _____ equation.   [3.4a]

46. The _____ of an equation is a drawing that represents its solution set.   [3.1c]

horizontal

vertical

nonvertical

direct

inverse

parallel

perpendicular

x-intercepts

y-intercepts

solution

slope

slope–intercept

graph

SYNTHESIS

47.–56. 📊 Use the TABLE feature to check the possible solutions to Exercises 1–10.

57.–66. 📊 Use a graphing calculator and the CALC-INTERSECT feature to solve the systems in Exercises 21–30.

Solve using the substitution method, the elimination method, or the graphing method.

67. $3(x - y) = 9,$
$\quad x + y = 7$

68. $2(x - y) = 3 + x,$
$\quad x = 3y + 4$

69. $2(5a - 5b) = 10,$
$\quad -5(6a + 2b) = 10$

70. $\dfrac{x}{3} + \dfrac{y}{2} = 1\dfrac{1}{3},$
$\quad x + 0.05y = 4$

71. $y = -\dfrac{2}{7}x + 3,$
$\quad y = \dfrac{4}{5}x + 3$

72. $y = \dfrac{2}{5}x - 7,$
$\quad y = \dfrac{2}{5}x + 4$

Solve for x and y.

73. $y = ax + b,$
$\quad y = x + c$

74. $ax + by + c = 0,$
$\quad ax + cy + b = 0$

Objective

a Solve applied problems by translating to a system of two equations in two variables.

a We now use systems of equations to solve applied problems that involve two equations in two variables.

EXAMPLE 1 *Pizza and Soda Prices.* A campus vendor charges $3.50 for one slice of pizza and one medium soda and $9.15 for three slices of pizza and two medium sodas. Determine the price of one medium soda and the price of one slice of pizza.

1. **Familiarize.** We let p = the price of one slice of pizza and s = the price of one medium soda.

2. **Translate.** The price of one slice of pizza and one medium soda is $3.50. This gives us one equation:

   $$p + s = 3.50.$$

   The price of three slices of pizza and two medium sodas is $9.15. This gives us another equation:

   $$3p + 2s = 9.15.$$

3. **Solve.** We solve the system of equations

   $$p + s = 3.50, \quad \textbf{(1)}$$
   $$3p + 2s = 9.15. \quad \textbf{(2)}$$

   Which method should we use? As we discussed in Section 7.3, any method can be used. Each has its advantages and disadvantages. We decide to proceed with the elimination method, because we see that if we multiply each side of equation (1) by -2 and add, the s-terms can be eliminated. (We could also multiply equation (1) by -3 and eliminate p.)

   $$
   \begin{array}{ll}
   -2p - 2s = -7.00 & \text{Multiplying equation (1) by } -2 \\
   \underline{3p + 2s = 9.15} & \text{Equation (2)} \\
   p = 2.15. & \text{Adding}
   \end{array}
   $$

   Next, we substitute 2.15 for p in equation (1) and solve for s:

   $$p + s = 3.50$$
   $$2.15 + s = 3.50$$
   $$s = 1.35.$$

4. **Check.** The sum of the prices for one slice of pizza and one medium soda is

   $$\$2.15 + \$1.35, \quad \text{or} \quad \$3.50.$$

   Three times the price of one slice of pizza plus twice the price of a medium soda is

   $$3(\$2.15) + 2(\$1.35), \quad \text{or} \quad \$9.15.$$

   The prices check.

5. **State.** The price of one slice of pizza is $2.15, and the price of one medium soda is $1.35.

1. **Chicken and Hamburger Prices.** Fast Rick's Burger restaurant decides to include chicken on its menu. It offers a special two-and-one promotion. The price of one hamburger and two pieces of chicken is $5.39, and the price of two hamburgers and one piece of chicken is $5.68. Find the price of one hamburger and the price of one piece of chicken.

Answer on page A-36

Do Exercise 1.

EXAMPLE 2 *IMAX Movie Prices.* There were 322 people at a recent showing of the IMAX 3D movie *Nascar 3D: The IMAX Experience.* Admission was $8.75 each for adults and $6.00 each for children, and receipts totaled $2531.50. How many adults and how many children attended?

1. **Familiarize.** There are many ways in which to familiarize ourselves with a problem situation. This time, let's make a guess and do some calculations. The total number of people at the movie was 322, so we choose numbers that total 322. Let's try

   242 adults and

   80 children.

   How much money was taken in? The problem says that adults paid $8.75 each, so the total amount of money collected from the adults was

   242($8.75), or $2117.50.

   Children paid $6.00 each, so the total amount of money collected from the children was

   80($6.00), or $480.

   This makes the total receipts $2117.50 + $480, or $2597.50.

   Our guess is not the answer to the problem because the total taken in, according to the problem, was $2531.50. If we were to continue guessing, we would need to add more children and fewer adults, since our first guess gave us an amount of total receipts that was higher than $2351.50. The steps we have used to see if our guesses are correct help us to understand the actual steps involved in solving the problem.

   Let's list the information in a table. That usually helps in the familiarization process. We let a = the number of adults and c = the number of children.

	ADULTS	CHILDREN	TOTAL
Admission	$8.75	$6.00	
Number Attending	a	c	322
Money Taken In	8.75a	6.00c	$2531.50

$\longrightarrow a + c = 322$

$\longrightarrow \begin{array}{c} 8.75a + 6.00c \\ = 2531.50 \end{array}$

2. **Translate.** The total number of people attending was 322, so

   $a + c = 322.$

   The amount taken in from the adults was 8.75a, and the amount taken in from the children was 6.00c. These amounts are in dollars. The total was $2531.50, so we have

   $8.75a + 6.00c = 2531.50.$

   We can multiply by 100 on both sides to clear decimals. Thus we have a translation to a system of equations:

   $$a + c = 322, \qquad \textbf{(1)}$$
   $$875a + 600c = 253{,}150. \qquad \textbf{(2)} \qquad \text{Multiplying by 100}$$

2. Game Admissions. There were 166 paid admissions to a game. The price was $3.10 each for adults and $1.75 each for children. The amount taken in was $459.25. How many adults and how many children attended?

Complete the following table to aid with the familiarization.

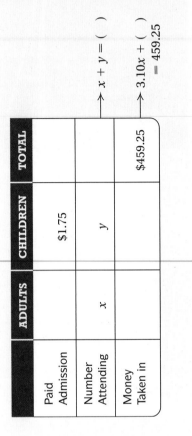

	ADULTS	CHILDREN	TOTAL
Paid Admission		$1.75	
Number Attending	x	y	
Money Taken in			$459.25

$x + y = (\ \ \ )$

$3.10x + (\ \ \ ) = 459.25$

Answer on page A-36

3. Solve. We solve the system. We use the elimination method since the equations are both in the form $Ax + By = C$. (A case can certainly be made for using the substitution method since we can solve for one of the variables quite easily in the first equation. Very often a decision is just a matter of choice.) We multiply by -600 on both sides of equation (1) and then add and solve for a:

$$-600a - 600c = -193,200 \qquad \text{Multiplying by } -600$$
$$\underline{875a + 600c = 253,150}$$
$$275a = 59,950 \qquad \text{Adding}$$
$$a = \frac{59,950}{275} \qquad \text{Dividing by } 275$$
$$a = 218.$$

Next, we go back to equation (1), substituting 218 for a, and solve for c:

$$a + c = 322$$
$$218 + c = 322$$
$$c = 104.$$

4. Check. The check is left to the student. It is similar to what we did in the *Familiarize* step.

5. State. Attending the showing were 218 adults and 104 children.

Do Exercise 2.

EXAMPLE 3 *Mixture of Solutions.* A chemist has one solution that is 80% acid (that is, 8 parts are acid and 2 parts are water) and another solution that is 30% acid. What is needed is 200 L of a solution that is 62% acid. The chemist will prepare it by mixing the two solutions. How much of each should be used?

1. Familiarize. We can make a drawing of the situation. The chemist uses x liters of the first solution and y liters of the second solution. We can also arrange the information in a table.

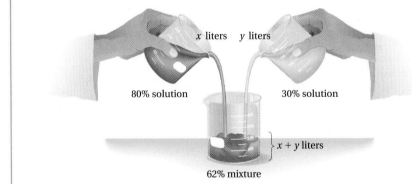

x liters y liters

80% solution   30% solution

$x + y$ liters

62% mixture

	FIRST SOLUTION	SECOND SOLUTION	MIXTURE	
Amount of Solution	x	y	200 L	$\rightarrow x + y = 200$
Percent of Acid	80%	30%	62%	
Amount of Acid In Solution	80%x	30%y	62% × 200, or 124 L	$\rightarrow$ 80%x + 30%y = 124

2. **Translate.** The chemist uses x liters of the first solution and y liters of the second. Since the total is to be 200 L, we have

Total amount of solution: $\quad x + y = 200.$

The amount of acid in the new mixture is to be 62% of 200 L, or 124 L. The amounts of acid from the two solutions are 80%x and 30%y. Thus,

Total amount of acid: $\quad 80\%x + 30\%y = 124$

or $\qquad\qquad\qquad\qquad 0.8x + 0.3y = 124.$

We clear decimals by multiplying by 10 on both sides:

$$10(0.8x + 0.3y) = 10 \cdot 124$$
$$8x + 3y = 1240.$$

Thus we have a translation to a system of equations:

$$x + y = 200, \qquad \textbf{(1)}$$
$$8x + 3y = 1240. \qquad \textbf{(2)}$$

3. **Solve.** We solve the system. We use the elimination method, again because equations are in the form $Ax + By = C$ and a multiplication in one equation will allow us to eliminate a variable, but substitution would also work. We multiply by -3 on both sides of equation (1) and then add and solve for x:

$$\begin{array}{rl} -3x - 3y = -600 & \text{Multiplying by } -3 \\ \underline{8x + 3y = 1240} & \\ 5x = 640 & \text{Adding} \\ x = \dfrac{640}{5} & \text{Dividing by 5} \\ x = 128. & \end{array}$$

Next, we go back to equation (1) and substitute 128 for x:

$$x + y = 200$$
$$128 + y = 200$$
$$y = 72.$$

The solution is $x = 128$ and $y = 72$.

4. **Check.** The sum of 128 and 72 is 200. Also, 80% of 128 is 102.4 and 30% of 72 is 21.6. These add up to 124.

5. **State.** The chemist should use 128 L of the 80%-acid solution and 72 L of the 30%-acid solution.

Do Exercise 3.

EXAMPLE 4 *Candy Mixtures.* A bulk wholesaler wishes to mix some candy worth 45 cents per pound and some worth 80 cents per pound to make 350 lb of a mixture worth 65 cents per pound. How much of each type of candy should be used?

1. **Familiarize.** Arranging the information in a table will help. We let $x =$ the amount of 45-cents candy and $y =$ the amount of 80-cents candy.

3. **Mixture of Solutions.** One solution is 50% alcohol and a second is 70% alcohol. How much of each should be mixed in order to make 30 L of a solution that is 55% alcohol?

Complete the following table to aid in the familiarization.

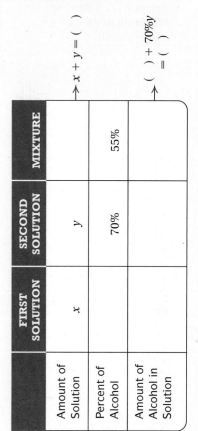

Answer on page A-36

4. Mixture of Grass Seeds.

Grass seed A is worth $1.40 per pound and seed B is worth $1.75 per pound. How much of each should be mixed in order to make 50 lb of a mixture worth $1.54 per pound?

Complete the following table to aid in the familiarization.

	SEED A	SEED B	MIXTURE
Cost of Seed	$1.40		$1.54
Amount (in pounds)	x	y	
Mixture		$1.75y$	

$$x + y = (\quad)$$
$$1.40x + 1.75y = (\quad)$$

	INEXPENSIVE CANDY	EXPENSIVE CANDY	MIXTURE	
Cost of Candy	45 cents	80 cents	65 cents	
Amount (in pounds)	x	y	350	$\longrightarrow x + y = 350$
Total Cost	$45x$	$80y$	65 cents $\cdot$ (350), or 22,750 cents	$\longrightarrow 45x + 80y = 22{,}750$

Note the similarity of this problem to Example 2. Here we consider types of candy instead of groups of people.

2. **Translate.** We translate as follows. From the second row of the table, we find that

Total amount of candy: $x + y = 350$.

Our second equation will come from the costs. The value of the inexpensive candy, in cents, is $45x$ (x pounds at 45 cents per pound). The value of the expensive candy is $80y$, and the value of the mixture is 65×350, or 22,750 cents. Thus we have

Total cost of mixture: $45x + 80y = 22{,}750$.

Remember the problem-solving tip about dimension symbols. In this last equation, all expressions are given in cents. We could have expressed them all in dollars, but we do not want some in cents and some in dollars. Thus we have a translation to a system of equations:

$$x + \quad y = 350, \qquad \textbf{(1)}$$
$$45x + 80y = 22{,}750. \qquad \textbf{(2)}$$

3. **Solve.** We solve the system using the elimination method again. We multiply by -45 on both sides of equation (1) and then add and solve for y:

$$
\begin{array}{ll}
-45x - 45y = -15{,}750 & \text{Multiplying by } -45 \\
\underline{45x + 80y = 22{,}750} & \\
35y = 7{,}000 & \text{Adding} \\
y = \dfrac{7{,}000}{35} & \\
y = 200. &
\end{array}
$$

Next, we go back to equation (1), substituting 200 for y, and solve for x:

$$x + y = 350$$
$$x + 200 = 350$$
$$x = 150.$$

4. **Check.** We consider $x = 150$ lb and $y = 200$ lb. The sum is 350 lb. The value of the candy is $45(150) + 80(200)$, or 22,750 cents and each pound of the mixture is worth $22{,}750 \div 350$, or 65 cents. These values check.

5. **State.** The grocer should mix 150 lb of the 45-cents candy with 200 lb of the 80-cents candy.

Answer on page A-36

Do Exercise 4.

EXAMPLE 5 *Coin Value.* A student assistant at the university copy center has some nickels and dimes to use for change when students make copies. The value of the coins is $7.40. There are 26 more dimes than nickels. How many of each kind of coin are there?

5. Coin Value. On a table are 20 coins, quarters and dimes. Their value is $3.05. How many of each kind of coin are there?

1. **Familiarize.** We let d = the number of dimes and n = the number of nickels.

2. **Translate.** We have one equation at once:

   $d = n + 26.$

   The value of the nickels, in cents, is $5n$, since each coin is worth 5 cents. The value of the dimes, in cents, is $10d$, since each coin is worth 10 cents. The total value is given as $7.40. Since we have the values of the nickels and dimes *in cents*, we must use cents for the total value. This is 740. This gives us another equation:

   $10d + 5n = 740.$

   We now have a system of equations:

   $d = n + 26,$ **(1)**
   $10d + 5n = 740.$ **(2)**

3. **Solve.** Since we have d alone on one side of one equation, we use the substitution method. We substitute $n + 26$ for d in equation (2):

$10d + 5n = 740$	Equation (2)
$10(n + 26) + 5n = 740$	Substituting $n + 26$ for d
$10n + 260 + 5n = 740$	Removing parentheses
$15n + 260 = 740$	Collecting like terms
$15n = 480$	Subtracting 260
$n = \dfrac{480}{15}$, or 32.	Dividing by 15

   Next, we substitute 32 for n in either of the original equations to find d. We use equation (1):

   $d = n + 26 = 32 + 26 = 58.$

4. **Check.** We have 58 dimes and 32 nickels. There are 26 more dimes than nickels. The value of the coins is 58($0.10) + 32($0.05), which is $7.40. This checks.

5. **State.** The student assistant has 58 dimes and 32 nickels.

Answer on page A-36

589

Do Exercise 5 on the preceding page.

Look back over Examples 2–5. The problems are quite similar in their structure. Compare them and try to see the similarities. The problems in Examples 2–5 are often called *mixture problems*. These problems provide a pattern, or model, for many related problems.

PROBLEM-SOLVING TIP

When solving problems, see if they are patterned or modeled after other problems that you have studied.

Study Tips

TROUBLE SPOTS

By now you have probably encountered certain topics that gave you more difficulty than others. It is important to know that this happens to every person who studies mathematics. Unfortunately, frustration is often part of the learning process and it is important not to give up when difficulty arises.

One source of frustration for many students is not being able to set aside sufficient time for studying. Family commitments, work schedules, and extracurricular activities are just a few of the time demands that many students face. Couple these demands with a math lesson that seems to require a greater than usual amount of study time, and it is no wonder that many students often feel frustrated. Below are some study tips that might be useful if and when troubles arise.

- **Realize that everyone—even your instructor—has been stumped at times when studying math.** You are not the first person, nor will you be the last, to encounter a "roadblock."

- **Whether working alone or with a classmate, try to allow enough study time so that you won't need to constantly glance at a clock.** Difficult material is best mastered when your mind is completely focused on the subject matter. Thus, if you are tired, it is usually best to study early the next morning or to take a ten-minute "power-nap" in order to make the most productive use of your time. Consider redoing the weekly planner on the Student Organizer in the Preface. You may need to adjust your schedule frequently. PLAN FOR SUCCESS with extra study time!

- **Talk about your trouble spot with a classmate.** It is possible that she or he is also having difficulty with the same material. If that is the case, perhaps the majority of your class is confused and your instructor's coverage of the topic is not yet finished. If your classmate *does* understand the topic that is troubling you, patiently allow him or her to explain it to you. By verbalizing the math in question, your classmate may help clarify the material for both of you. Perhaps you will be able to return the favor for your classmate when he or she is struggling with a topic that you understand.

- **Try to study in a "controlled" environment.** What we mean by this is that you can often put yourself in a setting that will enable you to maximize your powers of concentration. For example, some students may succeed in studying at home or in a dorm room, but for many these settings are filled with distractions. Consider a trip to a library, classroom building, or perhaps the attic or basement if such a setting is more conducive to studying. If you plan on working with a classmate, try to find a location in which conversation will not be bothersome to others.

- **When working on difficult material, it is often helpful to first "back up" and review the most recent material that did make sense.** This can build your confidence and create a momentum that can often carry you through the roadblock. Sometimes a small piece of information that appeared in a previous section is all that is needed for your problem spot to disappear. When the difficult material is finally mastered, try to make use of what is fresh in your mind by taking a "sneak preview" of what your next topic for study will be.

a Solve.

1. *Basketball Scoring.* In a recent game of the 2004–2005 basketball season, the San Antonio Spurs scored 85 of their points on a combination of 39 two- and three-point baskets. How many of each type of shot were made?

Source: National Basketball Association

2. *Basketball Scoring.* Shaquille O'Neill of the Miami Heat once scored 36 points on 22 shots in an NBA game, shooting only two-pointers and foul shots (one point). How many of each type of shot did he make?

Source: National Basketball Association

3. *Film Processing.* Cord Camera charges $9.00 for processing a 24-exposure roll of film and $12.60 for processing a 36-exposure roll of film. After Jack's field trip to observe a variety of architectural styles, he took 17 rolls of film to Cord Camera and paid $171 for processing. How many rolls of each type were processed?

Source: Cord Camera

4. *Paid Admissions.* Following the baseball season, the players on a junior college team decided to go to a major-league baseball game. Ticket prices for the game are shown in the table below. They bought 29 tickets of two types, Upper Box and Lower Reserved. The cost of all the tickets was $318. How many of each kind of ticket did they buy?

TICKET INFORMATION	
Lower Box	$18.50
Upper Box	$12.00
Lower Reserved	$ 9.50
Upper Reserved	$ 8.00
General Admission	$ 6.50

5. *Grain Mixtures for Horses.* Brianna is a barn manager at a horse stable. She needs to calculate the correct mix of grain and hay to feed her horse. On the basis of her horse's age, weight, and workload, she determines that he needs to eat 15 lb of feed per day, with an average protein content of 8%. Hay contains 6% protein, whereas grain has a 12% protein content. How many pounds of hay and grain should she feed her horse each day?

Source: *Michael Plumb's Horse Journal*, February 1996, pp. 26–29

6. *Paint Mixtures.* At a local "paint swap," Kari found large supplies of Skylite Pink (12.5% red pigment) and MacIntosh Red (20% red pigment). How many gallons of each color should Kari pick up in order to mix a gallon of Summer Rose (17% red pigment)?

7. *Investments.* Cassandra has a number of $50 and $100 savings bonds to use for part of her college expenses. The total value of the bonds is $1250. There are 7 more $50 bonds than $100 bonds. How many of each type of bond does she have?

8. *Food Prices.* Mr. Chooeydough's Pizza Parlor charges $3.70 for a slice of pizza and a soda and $9.65 for three slices of pizza and two sodas. Determine the cost of one soda and the cost of one slice of pizza.

9. *Ticket Sales.* There were 203 tickets sold for a volleyball game. For activity-card holders, the price was $2.25 each, and for non-cardholders, the price was $3 each. The total amount of money collected was $513. How many of each type of ticket were sold?

10. *Paid Admissions.* There were 429 people at a play. Admission was $8 each for adults and $4.50 each for children. The total receipts were $2641. How many adults and how many children attended?

11. *The Butterfly Exhibit.* On one day during a weekend, 1630 people visited The Butterfly Exhibit at White River Gardens in Indianapolis, Indiana. Admission was $7 each for adults and $6 each for children. The receipts totaled $11,080. How many adults and how many children visited that day?

12. *Zoo Admissions.* During the summer months, the Bronx Zoo charges $12 each for adults and $9 each for children and seniors. One July day, a total of $9780 was collected from 960 admissions. How many adult admissions were there?

Source: Bronx Zoo

13. *Mixture of Solutions.* Solution A is 50% acid and solution B is 80% acid. How many liters of each should be used in order to make 100 L of a solution that is 68% acid? Complete the following table to aid in the familiarization.

14. *Mixture of Solutions.* Solution A is 30% alcohol and solution B is 75% alcohol. How much of each should be used in order to make 100 L of a solution that is 50% alcohol?

	SOLUTION A	SOLUTION B	MIXTURE
Amount of Solution	x	y	L
Percent of Acid	50%		68%
Amount of Acid in Solution		80%y	68% × 100 or L

$\rightarrow x + y = (\quad)$

$\rightarrow 50\%x + (\quad) = (\quad)$

15. *Coin Value.* A parking meter contains dimes and quarters worth $15.25. There are 103 coins in all. How many of each type of coin are there?

16. *Coin Value.* A vending machine contains nickels and dimes worth $14.50. There are 95 more nickels than dimes. How many of each type of coin are there?

17. *Coffee Blends.* Cafebucks coffee shop mixes Brazilian coffee worth $19 per pound with Turkish coffee worth $22 per pound. The mixture is to sell for $20 per pound. How much of each type of coffee should be used in order to make a 300-lb mixture? Complete the following table to aid in the familiarization.

	BRAZILIAN COFFEE	TURKISH COFFEE	MIXTURE	
Cost of Coffee	$19		$20	
Amount (in pounds)	x	y	300	$\rightarrow x + y = (\ \ )$
Mixture		$22y$	20(300), or $6000	$\rightarrow 19x + (\ \ )$ $= 6000$

18. *Coffee Blends.* The Java Joint wishes to mix organic Kenyan coffee beans that sell for $7.25 per pound with organic Venezuelan beans that sell for $8.50 per pound in order to form a 50-lb batch of Morning Blend that sells for $8.00 per pound. How many pounds of each type of bean should be used to make the blend?

19. *Horticulture.* A solution containing 28% fungicide is to be mixed with a solution containing 40% fungicide to make 300 L of a solution containing 36% fungicide. How much of each solution should be used?

20. *Production.* Clear Shine window cleaner is 12% alcohol and Sunstream window cleaner is 30% alcohol. How much of each should be used to make 90 oz of a cleaner that is 20% alcohol?

21. *Printing.* A printer knows that a page of print contains 830 words if large type is used and 1050 words if small type is used. A document containing 11,720 words fills exactly 12 pages. How many pages are in the large type? in the small type?

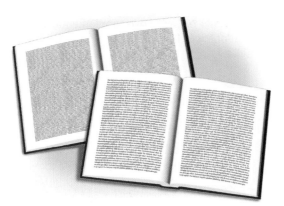

22. *Paint Mixture.* A merchant has two kinds of paint. If 9 gal of the inexpensive paint is mixed with 7 gal of the expensive paint, the mixture will be worth $19.70 per gallon. If 3 gal of the inexpensive paint is mixed with 5 gal of the expensive paint, the mixture will be worth $19.825 per gallon. What is the price per gallon of each type of paint?

23. *Mixed Nuts.* A customer has asked a caterer to provide 60 lb of nuts, 60% of which are to be cashews. The caterer has available mixtures of 70% cashews and 45% cashews. How many pounds of each mixture should be used?

24. *Mixture of Grass Seeds.* Grass seed A is worth $2.50 per pound and seed B is worth $1.75 per pound. How much of each would you use in order to make 75 lb of a mixture worth $2.14 per pound?

25. *Test Scores.* You are taking a test in which items of type A are worth 10 points and items of type B are worth 15 points. It takes 3 min to complete each item of type A and 6 min to complete each item of type B. The total time allowed is 60 min and you do exactly 16 questions. How many questions of each type did you complete? Assuming that all your answers were correct, what was your score?

26. *Gold Alloys.* A goldsmith has two alloys that are different purities of gold. The first is three-fourths pure gold and the second is five-twelfths pure gold. How many ounces of each should be melted and mixed in order to obtain a 6-oz mixture that is two-thirds pure gold?

27. *Ages.* The Kuyatts' house is twice as old as the Marconis' house. Eight years ago, the Kuyatts' house was three times as old as the Marconis' house. How old is each house?

28. *Ages.* David is twice as old as his daughter. In 4 yr, David's age will be three times what his daughter's age was 6 yr ago. How old are they now?

29. *Ages.* Randy is four times as old as Mandy. In 12 yr, Mandy's age will be half of Randy's. How old are they now?

30. *Ages.* Jennifer is twice as old as Ramon. The sum of their ages 7 yr ago was 13. How old are they now?

31. *Supplementary Angles.* **Supplementary angles** are angles whose sum is 180°. Two supplementary angles are such that one is 30° more than two times the other. Find the angles.

Supplementary angles
$x + y = 180°$

32. *Supplementary Angles.* Two supplementary angles are such that one is 8° less than three times the other. Find the angles.

33. *Complementary Angles.* **Complementary angles** are angles whose sum is 90°. Two complementary angles are such that their difference is 34°. Find the angles.

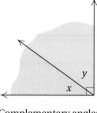

Complementary angles
$x + y = 90°$

34. *Complementary Angles.* Two angles are complementary. One angle is 42° more than one-half the other. Find the angles.

35. *Octane Ratings.* In most areas of the United States, gas stations offer three grades of gasoline, indicated by octane ratings on the pumps, such as 87, 89, and 93. When a tanker delivers gas, it brings only two grades of gasoline, the highest and the lowest, filling two large underground tanks. If you purchase the middle grade, the pump's computer mixes the other two grades appropriately. How much 87-octane gas and 93-octane gas should be blended in order to make 18 gal of 89-octane gas?

Source: Exxon

36. *Octane Ratings.* Referring to Exercise 35, suppose the pump grades offered are 85, 87, and 91. How much 85-octane gas and 91-octane gas should be blended in order to make 12 gal of 87-octane gas?

Source: Exxon

37. *Cough Syrup.* Dr. Zeke's cough syrup is 2% alcohol. Vitabrite cough syrup is 5% alcohol. How much of each type should be used in order to prepare an 80-oz batch of cough syrup that is 3% alcohol?

38. *Suntan Lotion.* Lisa has a tube of Kinney's suntan lotion that is rated 15 spf and a second tube of Coppertone that is 30 spf. How many fluid ounces of each type of lotion should be mixed in order to create 50 fluid ounces of sunblock that is rated 20 spf?

39. **D**_W Look over Example 4 of this section. What new equation-solving skills have we developed in this chapter that enable us to solve this problem? How do these equations differ from others in the preceding parts of this book?

40. **D**_W Look over Example 4 of this section. What equation-solving skills learned elsewhere in this book are most important in solving systems of equations?

Factor.   [5.6a]

41. $25x^2 - 81$

42. $36 - a^2$

43. $4x^2 + 100$

44. $4x^2 - 100$

Find the intercepts. Then graph the equation.   [3.2a]

45. $y = -2x - 3$

46. $y = -0.1x + 0.4$

47. $5x - 2y = -10$

48. $2.5x + 4y = 10$

Simplify.   [6.1c]

49. $\dfrac{x^2 - 5x + 6}{x^2 - 4}$

50. $\dfrac{x^2 - 25}{x^2 - 10x + 25}$

Subtract.   [6.5a]

51. $\dfrac{x - 2}{x + 3} - \dfrac{2x - 5}{x - 4}$

52. $\dfrac{x + 7}{x^2 - 1} - \dfrac{3}{x + 1}$

53. *Milk Mixture.*   A farmer has 100 L of milk that is 4.6% butterfat. How much skim milk (no butterfat) should be mixed with it in order to make milk that is 3.2% butterfat?

54. One year, Shannon made $288 from two investments: $1100 was invested at one yearly rate and $1800 at a rate that was 1.5% higher. Find the two rates of interest.

55. *Automobile Maintenance.*   An automobile radiator contains 16 L of antifreeze and water. This mixture is 30% antifreeze. How much of this mixture should be drained and replaced with pure antifreeze so that the mixture will be 50% antifreeze?

56. *Employer Payroll.*   An employer has a daily payroll of $1225 when employing some workers at $80 per day and others at $85 per day. When the number of $80 workers is increased by 50% and the number of $85 workers is decreased by $\frac{1}{5}$, the new daily payroll is $1540. How many were originally employed at each rate?

57. A two-digit number is six times the sum of its digits. The tens digit is 1 more than the units digit. Find the number.

7.5 APPLICATIONS WITH MOTION

Objective

a Solve motion problems using the formula $d = rt$.

a We first studied problems involving motion in Chapter 6. Here we extend our problem-solving skills by solving certain motion problems whose solutions can be found using systems of equations. Recall the motion formula.

THE MOTION FORMULA

Distance = Rate (or speed) · Time

$$d = rt$$

We have five steps for problem solving. The tips in the margin at right are also helpful when solving motion problems.

As we saw in Chapter 6, there are motion problems that can be solved with just one equation. Let's start with another such problem.

EXAMPLE 1 *Car Travel.* Two cars leave Ashland at the same time traveling in opposite directions. One travels at 60 mph and the other at 30 mph. In how many hours will they be 150 mi apart?

1. Familiarize. We first make a drawing.

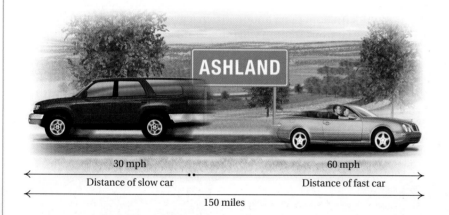

	30 mph			60 mph	
	Distance of slow car			Distance of fast car	

150 miles

From the wording of the problem and the drawing, we see that the distances may *not* be the same. But the times that the cars travel are the same, so we can use just t for time. We can organize the information in a chart.

$$d = r \cdot t$$

	DISTANCE	SPEED	TIME
Fast Car	Distance of fast car	60	t
Slow Car	Distance of slow car	30	t
Total	150		

TIPS FOR SOLVING MOTION PROBLEMS

1. Draw a diagram using an arrow or arrows to represent distance and the direction of each object in motion.
2. Organize the information in a chart.
3. Look for as many things as you can that are the same so that you can write equations.

597

1. Car Travel. Two cars leave town at the same time traveling in opposite directions. One travels at 48 mph and the other at 60 mph. How far apart will they be 3 hr later? (*Hint*: The times are the same. Be *sure* to make a drawing.)

2. Translate. From the drawing, we see that

(Distance of fast car) + (Distance of slow car) = 150.

Then using $d = rt$ in each row of the table, we get

$$60t + 30t = 150.$$

3. Solve. We solve the equation:

$$60t + 30t = 150$$
$$90t = 150 \qquad \text{Collecting like terms}$$
$$t = \frac{150}{90}, \text{ or } \frac{5}{3}, \text{ or } 1\frac{2}{3} \text{ hr.} \qquad \text{Dividing by 90}$$

4. Check. When $t = \frac{5}{3}$ hr,

$$(\text{Distance of fast car}) + (\text{Distance of slow car}) = 60\left(\frac{5}{3}\right) + 30\left(\frac{5}{3}\right)$$
$$= 100 + 50, \text{ or } 150 \text{ mi.}$$

Thus the time of $\frac{5}{3}$ hr, or $1\frac{2}{3}$ hr, checks.

5. State. In $1\frac{2}{3}$ hr, the cars will be 150 mi apart.

Do Exercises 1 and 2.

Now let's solve some motion problems using systems of equations.

EXAMPLE 2 *Train Travel.* A train leaves Stanton traveling east at 35 miles per hour (mph). An hour later, another train leaves Stanton on a parallel track at 40 mph. How far from Stanton will the second (or faster) train catch up with the first (or slower) train?

1. Familiarize. We first make a drawing.

2. Car Travel. Two cars leave town at the same time traveling in the same direction. One travels at 35 mph and the other at 40 mph. In how many hours will they be 15 mi apart? (*Hint*: The times are the same. Be *sure* to make a drawing.)

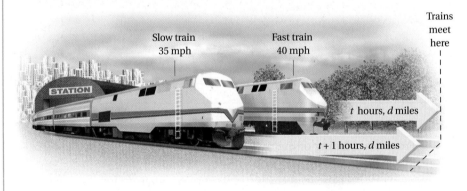

From the drawing, we see that the distances are the same. Let's call the distance d. We don't know the times. We let $t =$ the time for the faster train. Then the time for the slower train $= t + 1$, since it left 1 hr earlier. We can organize the information in a chart.

	DISTANCE	SPEED	TIME	
Slow Train	d	35	$t + 1$	→ $d = 35(t + 1)$
Fast Train	d	40	t	→ $d = 40t$

$$d \quad = \quad r \quad \cdot \quad t$$

2. **Translate.** In motion problems, we look for quantities that are the same so that we can write equations. From each row of the chart, we get an equation, $d = rt$. Thus we have two equations:

$$d = 35(t + 1), \qquad \textbf{(1)}$$
$$d = 40t. \qquad \textbf{(2)}$$

3. **Solve.** Since we have a variable alone on one side, we solve the system using the substitution method:

$35(t + 1) = 40t$	Using the substitution method (substituting $35(t + 1)$ for d in equation 2)
$35t + 35 = 40t$	Removing parentheses
$35 = 5t$	Subtracting $35t$
$\dfrac{35}{5} = t$	Dividing by 5
$7 = t.$	

The problem asks us to find how far from Stanton the fast train catches up with the other. Thus we need to find d. We can do this by substituting 7 for t in the equation $d = 40t$:

$$d = 40(7)$$
$$= 280.$$

4. **Check.** If the time is 7 hr, then the distance that the slow train travels is $35(7 + 1)$, or 280 mi. The fast train travels $40(7)$, or 280 mi. Since the distances are the same, we know how far from Stanton the trains will be when the fast train catches up with the other.

5. **State.** The fast train will catch up with the slow train 280 mi from Stanton.

Do Exercise 3.

EXAMPLE 3 *Boat Travel.* A motorboat took 3 hr to make a downstream trip with a 6-km/h current. The return trip against the same current took 5 hr. Find the speed of the boat in still water.

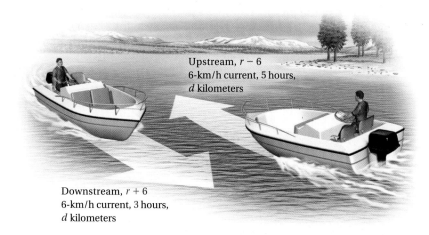

Upstream, $r - 6$
6-km/h current, 5 hours,
d kilometers

Downstream, $r + 6$
6-km/h current, 3 hours,
d kilometers

1. **Familiarize.** We first make a drawing. From the drawing, we see that the distances are the same. Let's call the distance d. We let $r =$ the speed of the boat in still water. Then, when the boat is traveling downstream, its speed is $r + 6$ (the current helps the boat along). When it is traveling upstream, its speed is $r - 6$ (the current holds the boat back).

3. **Car Travel.** A car leaves Spokane traveling north at 56 km/h. Another car leaves Spokane 1 hr later traveling north at 84 km/h. How far from Spokane will the second car catch up with the first? (*Hint*: The cars travel the same distance.)

Answer on page A-36

4. Air Travel. An airplane flew for 5 hr with a 25-km/h tail wind. The return flight against the same wind took 6 hr. Find the speed of the airplane in still air. (*Hint:* The distance is the same both ways. The speeds are $r + 25$ and $r - 25$, where r is the speed in still air.)

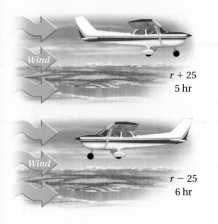

We can organize the information in a chart. In this case, the distances are the same, so we use the formula $d = rt$.

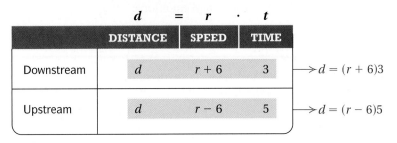

	DISTANCE	SPEED	TIME	
Downstream	d	$r + 6$	3	$\rightarrow d = (r + 6)3$
Upstream	d	$r - 6$	5	$\rightarrow d = (r - 6)5$

2. **Translate.** From each row of the chart, we get an equation, $d = rt$:

$$d = (r + 6)3, \quad \textbf{(1)}$$
$$d = (r - 6)5. \quad \textbf{(2)}$$

3. **Solve.** Since there is a variable alone on one side of an equation, we solve the system using substitution:

$(r + 6)3 = (r - 6)5$	Substituting $(r + 6)3$ for d in equation (2)
$3r + 18 = 5r - 30$	Removing parentheses
$-2r + 18 = -30$	Subtracting $5r$
$-2r = -48$	Subtracting 18
$r = \dfrac{-48}{-2}$, or 24.	Dividing by -2

4. **Check.** When $r = 24$, $r + 6 = 30$, and $30 \cdot 3 = 90$, the distance downstream. When $r = 24$, $r - 6 = 18$, and $18 \cdot 5 = 90$, the distance upstream. In both cases, we get the same distance.

5. **State.** The speed in still water is 24 km/h.

**MORE TIPS FOR SOLVING
MOTION PROBLEMS**

1. Translating to a system of equations eases the solution of many motion problems.
2. At the end of the problem, always ask yourself, "Have I found what the problem asked for?" You might have solved for a certain variable but still not have answered the question of the original problem. For instance, in Example 2 we solve for t but the question of the original problem asks for d. Thus we need to continue the *Solve* step.

Do Exercise 4.

Answer on page A-36

Translating for Success

1. *Car Travel.* Two cars leave town at the same time traveling in different directions. One travels 50 mph and the other travels 55 mph. In how many hours will they be 50 mi apart?

2. *Mixture of Solutions* Solution A is 20% alcohol and solution B is 60% alcohol. How much of each should be used in order to make 10 L of a solution that is 50% alcohol?

3. *Triangle Dimensions.* The height of a triangle is 3 cm less than the base. The area is 27 cm². Find the height and the base.

4. *Fish Population.* To determine the number of fish in a lake, a conservationist catches 85 fish, tags them, and throws them back into the lake. Later, 60 fish are caught, 25 of which are tagged. How many fish are in the lake?

5. *Supplementary Angles.* Two angles are supplementary. One angle measures 36° more than three times the measure of the other. Find the measure of each angle.

The goal of these matching questions is to practice step (2), *Translate*, of the five-step problem-solving process. Translate each word problem to an equation or a system of equations and select a correct translation from A–O.

A. $20\%x + 60\%y = 50\% \cdot 10,$
$x + y = 10$

B. $18 + 0.35x = 100$

C. $55x + 50x = 50$

D. $x + (3x + 36) + (x + 7) = 90$

E. $\dfrac{85}{x} = \dfrac{25}{60}$

F. $\dfrac{1}{15} + \dfrac{1}{9} = \dfrac{1}{x}$

G. $\dfrac{1}{2}x(x - 3) = 27$

H. $x^2 + (x + 4)^2 = 8^2$

I. $8^2 + x^2 = (x + 4)^2$

J. $x + (3x + 36) = 180$

K. $20x + 60y = 5,$
$x + y = 10$

L. $x + (3x + 36) + (x - 7) = 180$

M. $18 + 35x = 100$

N. $\dfrac{x}{85} = \dfrac{25}{60}$

O. $x + (3x + 36) = 90$

Answers on page A-36

---

6. *Triangle Dimensions.* The length of one leg of a right triangle is 8 m. The length of the hypotenuse is 4 m longer than the length of the other leg. Find the lengths of the hypotenuse and the other leg.

7. *Costs of Promotional Buttons.* The vice-president of a fraternity has $100 to spend on promotional buttons for pledge week. There is a setup fee of $18 and a cost of 35¢ per button. How many buttons can he purchase?

8. *Triangle Measures.* The second angle of a triangle measures 36° more than three times the measure of the first. The measure of the third angle is 7° less than the first. Find the measure of each angle of the triangle.

9. *Complementary Angles.* Two angles are complementary. One angle measures 36° more than three times the measure of the other. Find the measure of each angle.

10. *Work Time.* It takes Maggie 15 hr to put a roof on a house. It takes Claire 9 hr to put a roof on the same type of house. How long would it take to complete the house if they worked together?

a   Solve. In Exercises 1–6, complete the table to aid the translation.

1. *Car Travel.* Two cars leave town at the same time going in the same direction. One travels at 30 mph and the other travels at 46 mph. In how many hours will they be 72 mi apart?

$$d = r \cdot t$$

	DISTANCE	SPEED	TIME
Slow Car	Distance of slow car		t
Fast Car	Distance of fast car	46	

2. *Car and Truck Travel.* A truck and a car leave a service station at the same time and travel in the same direction. The truck travels at 55 mph and the car at 40 mph. They can maintain CB radio contact within a range of 10 mi. When will they lose contact?

$$d = r \cdot t$$

	DISTANCE	SPEED	TIME
Truck	Distance of truck	55	
Car	Distance of car		t

3. *Train Travel.* A train leaves a station and travels east at 72 mph. Three hours later, a second train leaves on a parallel track and travels east at 120 mph. When will it overtake the first train?

$$d = r \cdot t$$

	DISTANCE	SPEED	TIME
Slow Train	d		$t + 3$
Fast Train	d	120	

→ $d = 72(\quad)$

→ $d = (\quad)t$

4. *Airplane Travel.* A private airplane leaves an airport and flies due south at 192 mph. Two hours later, a jet leaves the same airport and flies due south at 960 mph. When will the jet overtake the plane?

$$d = r \cdot t$$

	DISTANCE	SPEED	TIME
Private Plane	d	192	
Jet	d		t

→ $d = 192(\quad)$

→ $d = (\quad)(t)$

5. *Canoeing.* A canoeist paddled for 4 hr with a 6-km/h current to reach a campsite. The return trip against the same current took 10 hr. Find the speed of the canoe in still water.

$$d = r \cdot t$$

	DISTANCE	SPEED	TIME
Down- stream	d	$r + 6$	
Upstream	d		10

→ $d = (\quad)4$

→ $= (r - 6)10$

6. *Airplane Travel.* An airplane flew for 4 hr with a 20-km/h tail wind. The return flight against the same wind took 5 hr. Find the speed of the plane in still air.

$$d = r \cdot t$$

	DISTANCE	SPEED	TIME
With Wind	d		4
Against Wind	d	$r - 20$	

→ $d = (\quad)4$

→ $d = (\quad)5$

7. *Train Travel.* It takes a passenger train 2 hr less time than it takes a freight train to make the trip from Central City to Clear Creek. The passenger train averages 96 km/h, while the freight train averages 64 km/h. How far is it from Central City to Clear Creek?

8. *Airplane Travel.* It takes a small jet 4 hr less time than it takes a propeller-driven plane to travel from Glen Rock to Oakville. The jet averages 637 km/h, while the propeller plane averages 273 km/h. How far is it from Glen Rock to Oakville?

9. *Motorboat Travel.* On a weekend outing, Antoine rents a motorboat for 8 hr to travel down the river and back. The rental operator tells him to go for 3 hr downstream, leaving him 5 hr to return upstream.

    a) If the river current flows at a speed of 6 mph, how fast must Antoine travel in order to return in 8 hr?

    b) How far downstream did Antoine travel before he turned back?

10. *Airplane Travel.* For spring break some students flew to Cancun. From Mexico City, the airplane took 2 hr to fly 600 mi against a head wind. The return trip with the wind took $1\frac{2}{3}$ hr. Find the speed of the plane in still air.

11. *Running.* A toddler takes off running down the sidewalk at 230 ft/min. One minute later, a worried mother runs after the child at 660 ft/min. When will the mother overtake the toddler?

12. *Airplane Travel.* Two airplanes start at the same time and fly toward each other from points 1000 km apart at rates of 420 km/h and 330 km/h. When will they meet?

13. *Motorcycle Travel.* A motorcycle breaks down and the rider must walk the rest of the way to work. The motorcycle was being driven at 45 mph, and the rider walks at a speed of 6 mph. The distance from home to work is 25 mi, and the total time for the trip was 2 hr. How far did the motorcycle go before it broke down?

14. *Walking and Jogging.* A student walks and jogs to college each day. She averages 5 km/h walking and 9 km/h jogging. The distance from home to college is 8 km, and she makes the trip in 1 hr. How far does the student jog?

15. **Dw** Discuss the advantages of using a table to organize information when solving a motion problem.

16. **Dw** From the formula $d = rt$, derive two other formulas, one for r and one for t. Discuss the kinds of problems for which each formula might be useful.

SKILL MAINTENANCE

Simplify.   [6.1c]

17. $\dfrac{8x^2}{24x}$

18. $\dfrac{5x^8y^4}{10x^3y}$

19. $\dfrac{5a + 15}{10}$

20. $\dfrac{12x - 24}{48}$

21. $\dfrac{2x^2 - 50}{x^2 - 25}$

22. $\dfrac{x^2 - 1}{x^4 - 1}$

23. $\dfrac{x^2 - 3x - 10}{x^2 - 2x - 15}$

24. $\dfrac{6x^2 + 15x - 36}{2x^2 - 5x + 3}$

25. $\dfrac{(x^2 + 6x + 9)(x - 2)}{(x^2 - 4)(x + 3)}$

26. $\dfrac{x^2 + 25}{x^2 - 25}$

27. $\dfrac{6x^2 + 18x + 12}{6x^2 - 6}$

28. $\dfrac{x^3 + 3x^2 + 2x + 6}{2x^3 + 6x^2 + x + 3}$

SYNTHESIS

29. *Lindbergh's Flight.* Charles Lindbergh flew the Spirit of St. Louis in 1927 from New York to Paris at an average speed of 107.4 mph. Eleven years later, Howard Hughes flew the same route, averaged 217.1 mph, and took 16 hr and 57 min less time. Find the length of their route.

30. *Car Travel.* A car travels from one town to another at a speed of 32 mph. If it had gone 4 mph faster, it could have made the trip in $\frac{1}{2}$ hr less time. How far apart are the towns?

31. *River Cruising.* An afternoon sightseeing cruise up river and back down river is scheduled to last 1 hr. The speed of the current is 4 mph, and the speed of the riverboat in still water is 12 mph. How far upstream should the pilot travel before turning around?

7 Summary and Review

The review that follows is meant to prepare you for a chapter exam. It consists of three parts. The first part, Concept Reinforcement, is designed to increase understanding of the concepts through true/false exercises. The second part is a list of important properties and formulas. The third part is the Review Exercises. These provide practice exercises for the exam, together with references to section objectives so you can go back and review. Before beginning, stop and look back over the skills you have obtained. What skills in mathematics do you have now that you did not have before studying this chapter?

CONCEPT REINFORCEMENT

Determine whether the statement is true or false. Answers are given at the back of the book.

_____ **1.** Every system of two equations has one and only one ordered pair as a solution.

_____ **2.** The system of equations $y = \dfrac{a}{c}x + b$ and $y = \dfrac{a}{c}x - b$, $b \neq 0$, has no solution.

_____ **3.** The solution of the system of equations $x = a$ and $y = b$ is (a, b).

_____ **4.** The solution of the system of equations $y = \dfrac{a}{c}x + b$ and $y = -\dfrac{c}{a}x + b$ is $(b, 0)$.

_____ **5.** A solution of a system of two equations is an ordered pair that makes at least one equation true.

IMPORTANT PROPERTIES AND FORMULAS

Motion Formula: $d = rt$

Review Exercises

Determine whether the given ordered pair is a solution of the system of equations. [7.1a]

1. $(6, -1)$; $x - y = 3$,
$\quad\quad\quad\quad 2x + 5y = 6$

2. $(2, -3)$; $2x + y = 1$,
$\quad\quad\quad\quad\; x - y = 5$

3. $(-2, 1)$; $x + 3y = 1$,
$\quad\quad\quad\quad\; 2x - y = -5$

4. $(-4, -1)$; $x - y = 3$,
$\quad\quad\quad\quad\quad x + y = -5$

Solve the system by graphing. [7.1b]

5. $x + y = 4$,
$\quad\; x - y = 8$

6. $x + 3y = 12$,
$\quad\; 2x - 4y = 4$

7. $y = 5 - x$,
$\quad\; 3x - 4y = -20$

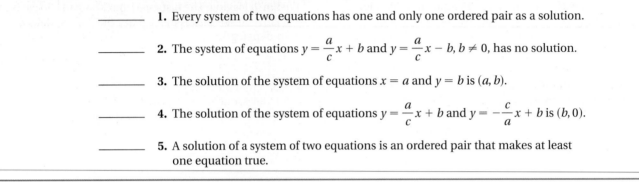

8. $3x - 2y = -4,$
$2y - 3x = -2$

Solve the system using the substitution method. [7.2a]

9. $y = 5 - x,$
$3x - 4y = -20$

10. $x + y = 6,$
$y = 3 - 2x$

11. $x - y = 4,$
$y = 2 - x$

12. $s + t - 5,$
$s = 13 - 3t$

Solve the system using the substitution method. [7.2b]

13. $x + 2y = 6,$
$2x + 3y = 8$

14. $3x + y = 1,$
$x - 2y = 5$

Solve the system using the elimination method. [7.3a]

15. $x + y = 4,$
$2x - y = 5$

16. $x + 2y = 9,$
$3x - 2y = -5$

17. $x - y = 8,$
$2x + y = 7$

Solve the system using the elimination method. [7.3b]

18. $2x + 3y = 8,$
$5x + 2y = -2$

19. $5x - 2y = 2,$
$3x - 7y = 36$

20. $-x - y = -5,$
$2x - y = 4$

21. $6x + 2y = 4,$
$10x + 7y = -8$

22. $-6x - 2y = 5,$
$12x + 4y = -10$

23. $\frac{2}{3}x + y = -\frac{5}{3},$
$x - \frac{1}{3}y = -\frac{13}{3}$

Solve. [7.2c], [7.4a]

24. *Rectangle Dimensions.* The perimeter of a rectangle is 96 cm. The length is 27 cm more than the width. Find the length and the width.

25. *Paid Admissions.* There were 508 people at a rock concert. Orchestra seats cost $25 each and balcony seats cost $18 each. The total receipts were $11,223. Find the number of orchestra seats and the number of balcony seats sold for the concert.

26. *Window Cleaner.* Clear Shine window cleaner is 30% alcohol, whereas Sunstream window cleaner is 60% alcohol. How much of each is needed to make 80 L of a cleaner that is 45% alcohol?

27. *Weights of Elephants.* A zoo has both an Asian and an African elephant. The African elephant weighs 2400 kg more than the Asian elephant. Together, they weigh 12,000 kg. How much does each elephant weigh?

Asian elephant   African elephant

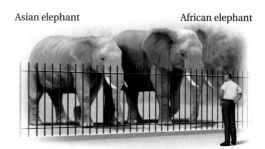

28. *Mixed Nuts.* Sandy's Catering needs to provide 13 lb of mixed nuts for a wedding reception. The wedding couple has allocated $71 for nuts. Peanuts cost $4.50 per pound and fancy nuts cost $7.00 per pound. How many pounds of each type should be mixed?

29. *Phone Rates.* Recently, AT&T offered an unlimited long-distance calling plan to anyone in the United States, 24 hours a day, 7 days a week, for $29.95 a month. Another plan charges 7¢ a minute all day every day, but costs an additional $3.95 per month. For what number of minutes will the two plans cost the same?

30. *Octane Ratings.* The octane rating of a gasoline is a measure of the amount of isooctane in the gas. How much 87-octane gas and 95-octane gas should be blended in order to end up with a 10-gal batch of 93-octane gas?

Source: Champlain Electric and Petroleum Equipment

31. *Age.* Jeff is three times as old as his son. In 13 yr, Jeff will be twice as old as his son. How old is each now?

32. *Complementary Angles.* Two angles are complementary. Their difference is 26°. Find the measure of each angle.

33. *Supplementary Angles.* Two angles are supplementary. Their difference is 26°. Find the measure of each angle.

Solve. [7.5a]

34. *Air Travel.* An airplane flew for 4 hr with a 15-km/h tail wind. The return flight against the wind took 5 hr. Find the speed of the airplane in still air.

d	$=$	r	$\cdot$	t
	DISTANCE	SPEED	TIME
Going			
Returning			

35. *Car Travel.* One car leaves Phoenix, Arizona, on Interstate highway I-10 traveling at a speed of 55 mph. Two hours later, another car leaves Phoenix on the same highway, but travels at a speed limit of 75 mph. How far from Phoenix will the second car catch up to the other?

d	$=$	r	$\cdot$	t
	DISTANCE	SPEED	TIME
Slow Car			
Fast Car			

36. $\mathbf{D_W}$ Janine can tell by inspection that the system
$$y = 2x - 1,$$
$$y = 2x + 3$$
has no solution. How did she determine this? [7.1b]

37. $\mathbf{D_W}$ Which of the five problem-solving steps have you found the most challenging? Why? [7.4a], [7.5b]

38. *Value of a Horse.* Stephanie agreed to work as a stablehand for 1 yr. At the end of that time, she was to receive $2400 and one horse. After 7 months, she quit the job, but still received the horse and $1000. What was the value of the horse? [7.4a]

39. The solution of the following system is $(6, 2)$. Find C and D. [7.1a]
$$2x - Dy = 6,$$
$$Cx + 4y = 14$$

40. Solve: [7.2a]
$$3(x - y) = 4 + x,$$
$$x = 5y + 2.$$

Each of the following shows the graph of a system of equations. Find the equations. [3.4c], [7.1b]

41. **42.**

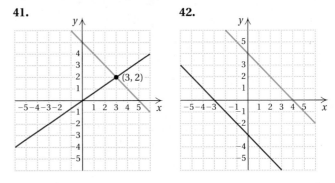

43. *Ancient Chinese Math Problem.* Several ancient Chinese books included problems that can be solved by translating to systems of equations. *Arithmetical Rules in Nine Sections* is a book of 246 problems compiled by a Chinese mathematician, Chang Tsang, who died in 152 B.C. One of the problems is: Suppose there are a number of rabbits and pheasants confined in a cage. In all, there are 35 heads and 94 feet. How many rabbits and how many pheasants are there? Solve the problem. [7.4a]

1. Determine whether the given ordered pair is a solution of the system of equations.

$$(-2, -1); \quad x = 4 + 2y,$$
$$2y - 3x = 4$$

2. Solve this system by graphing. Show your work.

$$x - y = 3,$$
$$x - 2y = 4.$$

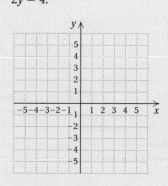

Solve the system using the substitution method.

3. $y = 6 - x,$
   $2x - 3y = 22$

4. $x + 2y = 5,$
   $x + y = 2$

5. $y = 5x - 2,$
   $y - 2 = 5x$

Solve the system using the elimination method.

6. $x - y = 6,$
   $3x + y = -2$

7. $\frac{1}{2}x - \frac{1}{3}y = 8,$
   $\frac{2}{3}x + \frac{1}{2}y = 5$

8. $-4x - 9y = 4,$
   $6x + 3y = 1$

9. $2x + 3y = 13,$
   $3x - 5y = 10$

Solve.

10. *Rectangle Dimensions.* The perimeter of a rectangular field is 8266 yd. The length is 84 yd more than the width. Find the length and the width.

11. *Mixture of Solutions.* Solution A is 25% acid, and solution B is 40% acid. How much of each is needed to make 60 L of a solution that is 30% acid?

12. *Motorboat Travel.* A motorboat traveled for 2 hr with an 8-km/h current. The return trip against the same current took 3 hr. Find the speed of the motorboat in still water.

13. *Carnival Prices.* A carnival comes to town and makes an income of $4275 one day. Twice as much was made on concessions as on the rides. How much did the concessions bring in? How much did the rides bring in?

14. *Farm Acreage.* The Rolling Velvet Horse Farm allots 650 acres to plant hay and oats. The owners know that their needs are best met if they plant 180 acres more of hay than of oats. How many acres of each should they plant?

15. *Supplementary Angles.* Two angles are supplementary. One angle measures 45° more than twice the measure of the other. Find the measure of each angle.

16. *Octane Ratings.* The octane rating of a gasoline is a measure of the amount of isooctane in the gas. How much 87-octane gas and 93-octane gas should be blended in order to end up with 12 gal of 91-octane gas?

Source: Champlain Electric and Petroleum Equipment

17. *Phone Rates.* Recently, SBC offered a domestic calling plan for $2.95 per month plus 10¢ per minute. Another plan charges $1.95 per month plus 15¢ per minute. For what number of minutes will the two plans cost the same?

18. *Ski Trip.* A group of students drive both a car and an SUV on a ski trip. The car left first and traveled at 55 mph. The SUV left 2 hr later and traveled at 65 mph. How long will it take the SUV to catch up to the car?

SYNTHESIS

19. Find the numbers C and D such that $(-2, 3)$ is a solution of the system

$$Cx - 4y = 7,$$
$$3x + Dy = 8.$$

20. *Ticket Line.* You are in line at a ticket window. There are two more people ahead of you than there are behind you. In the entire line, there are three times as many people as there are behind you. How many are ahead of you in line?

Each of the following shows the graph of a system of equations. Find the equations.

21.

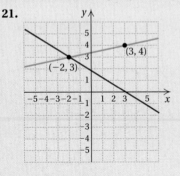

22.

(3, −2)

Appendixes

A FACTORING SUMS OR DIFFERENCES OF CUBES

B FINDING EQUATIONS OF LINES: POINT–SLOPE EQUATION

C HIGHER ROOTS

D SETS

E MEAN, MEDIAN, AND MODE

Objective

a Factor sums and differences of two cubes.

N	N^3
0.2	0.008
0.1	0.001
0	0
1	1
2	8
3	27
4	64
5	125
6	216
7	343
8	512
9	729
10	1000

Factor.

1. $x^3 - 27$

2. $64 - y^3$

Factor.

3. $y^3 + 8$

4. $125 + t^3$

Answers on page A-46

A FACTORING SUMS OR DIFFERENCES OF CUBES

a Factoring Sums or Differences of Cubes

We can factor the sum or the difference of two expressions that are cubes. Consider the following products:

$$(A + B)(A^2 - AB + B^2) = A(A^2 - AB + B^2) + B(A^2 - AB + B^2)$$
$$= A^3 - A^2B + AB^2 + A^2B - AB^2 + B^3$$
$$= A^3 + B^3$$

and

$$(A - B)(A^2 + AB + B^2) = A(A^2 + AB + B^2) - B(A^2 + AB + B^2)$$
$$= A^3 + A^2B + AB^2 - A^2B - AB^2 - B^3$$
$$= A^3 - B^3.$$

The above equations (reversed) show how we can factor a sum or a difference of two cubes.

> **FACTORING SUMS OR DIFFERENCES OF CUBES**
>
> $A^3 + B^3 = (A + B)(A^2 - AB + B^2),$
> $A^3 - B^3 = (A - B)(A^2 + AB + B^2)$

Note that what we are considering here is a sum or a difference of cubes. We are not cubing a binomial. For example, $(A + B)^3$ is *not* the same as $A^3 + B^3$. The table of cubes in the margin is helpful.

EXAMPLE 1 Factor: $x^3 - 8$.

We have

$$x^3 - 8 = x^3 - 2^3 = (x - 2)(x^2 + x \cdot 2 + 2^2).$$
$$A^3 - B^3 = (A - B)(A^2 + A \ B + B^2)$$

This tells us that $x^3 - 8 = (x - 2)(x^2 + 2x + 4)$. Note that we cannot factor $x^2 + 2x + 4$. (It is not a trinomial square nor can it be factored by trial and error or the *ac*-method.) The check is left to the student.

Do Exercises 1 and 2.

EXAMPLE 2 Factor: $x^3 + 125$.

We have

$$x^3 + 125 = x^3 + 5^3 = (x + 5)(x^2 - x \cdot 5 + 5^2).$$
$$A^3 + B^3 = (A + B)(A^2 - A \ B + B^2)$$

Thus, $x^3 + 125 = (x + 5)(x^2 - 5x + 25)$. The check is left to the student.

Do Exercises 3 and 4.

EXAMPLE 3 Factor: $x^3 - 27t^3$.

We have

$$x^3 - 27t^3 = x^3 - (3t)^3 = (x - 3t)(x^2 + x \cdot 3t + (3t)^2)$$
$$A^3 - B^3 = (A - B)(A^2 + A \quad B + B^2)$$
$$= (x - 3t)(x^2 + 3xt + 9t^2)$$

Do Exercises 5 and 6.

EXAMPLE 4 Factor: $128y^7 - 250x^6y$.

We first look for a common factor:

$$128y^7 - 250x^6y = 2y(64y^6 - 125x^6) = 2y[(4y^2)^3 - (5x^2)^3]$$
$$= 2y(4y^2 - 5x^2)(16y^4 + 20x^2y^2 + 25x^4).$$

EXAMPLE 5 Factor: $a^6 - b^6$.

We can express this polynomial as a difference of squares:

$$(a^3)^2 - (b^3)^2.$$

We factor as follows:

$$a^6 - b^6 = (a^3 + b^3)(a^3 - b^3).$$

One factor is a sum of two cubes, and the other factor is a difference of two cubes. We factor them:

$$(a + b)(a^2 - ab + b^2)(a - b)(a^2 + ab + b^2).$$

We have now factored completely.

In Example 5, had we thought of factoring first as a difference of two cubes, we would have had

$$(a^2)^3 - (b^2)^3 = (a^2 - b^2)(a^4 + a^2b^2 + b^4)$$
$$= (a + b)(a - b)(a^4 + a^2b^2 + b^4).$$

In this case, we might have missed some factors; $a^4 + a^2b^2 + b^4$ can be factored as $(a^2 - ab + b^2)(a^2 + ab + b^2)$, but we probably would not have known to do such factoring.

EXAMPLE 6 Factor: $64a^6 - 729b^6$.

$$64a^6 - 729b^6 = (8a^3 - 27b^3)(8a^3 + 27b^3) \qquad \text{Factoring a difference of squares}$$

$$= [(2a)^3 - (3b)^3][(2a)^3 + (3b)^3].$$

Each factor is a sum or a difference of cubes. We factor each:

$$= (2a - 3b)(4a^2 + 6ab + 9b^2)(2a + 3b)(4a^2 - 6ab + 9b^2)$$

Sum of cubes:	$A^3 + B^3 = (A + B)(A^2 - AB + B^2)$;
Difference of cubes:	$A^3 - B^3 = (A - B)(A^2 + AB + B^2)$;
Difference of squares:	$A^2 - B^2 = (A + B)(A - B)$;
Sum of squares:	$A^2 + B^2$ cannot be factored using real numbers if the largest common factor has been removed.

Do Exercises 7–10.

Factor.

5. $27x^3 - y^3$

6. $8y^3 + z^3$

Factor.

7. $m^6 - n^6$

8. $16x^7y + 54xy^7$

9. $729x^6 - 64y^6$

10. $x^3 - 0.027$

Answers on page A-46

a Factor.

1. $z^3 + 27$

2. $a^3 + 8$

3. $x^3 - 1$

4. $c^3 - 64$

5. $y^3 + 125$

6. $x^3 + 1$

7. $8a^3 + 1$

8. $27x^3 + 1$

9. $y^3 - 8$

10. $p^3 - 27$

11. $8 - 27b^3$

12. $64 - 125x^3$

13. $64y^3 + 1$

14. $125x^3 + 1$

15. $8x^3 + 27$

16. $27y^3 + 64$

17. $a^3 - b^3$

18. $x^3 - y^3$

19. $a^3 + \dfrac{1}{8}$

20. $b^3 + \dfrac{1}{27}$

21. $2y^3 - 128$

22. $3z^3 - 3$

23. $24a^3 + 3$

24. $54x^3 + 2$

25. $rs^3 + 64r$

26. $ab^3 + 125a$

27. $5x^3 - 40z^3$

APPENDIX A: Factoring Sums or
Differences of Cubes

28. $2y^3 - 54z^3$

29. $x^3 + 0.001$

30. $y^3 + 0.125$

31. $64x^6 - 8t^6$

32. $125c^6 - 8d^6$

33. $2y^4 - 128y$

34. $3z^5 - 3z^2$

35. $z^6 - 1$

36. $t^6 + 1$

37. $t^6 + 64y^6$

38. $p^6 - q^6$

SYNTHESIS

Consider these polynomials:

$(a + b)^3$; $a^3 + b^3$; $(a + b)(a^2 - ab + b^2)$;
$(a + b)(a^2 + ab + b^2)$; $(a + b)(a + b)(a + b)$.

39. Evaluate each polynomial when $a = -2$ and $b = 3$.

40. Evaluate each polynomial when $a = 4$ and $b = -1$.

Factor. Assume that variables in exponents represent natural numbers.

41. $x^{6a} + y^{3b}$

42. $a^3x^3 - b^3y^3$

43. $3x^{3a} + 24y^{3b}$

44. $\frac{8}{27}x^3 + \frac{1}{64}y^3$

45. $\frac{1}{24}x^3y^3 + \frac{1}{3}z^3$

46. $7x^3 - \frac{7}{8}$

47. $(x + y)^3 - x^3$

48. $(1 - x)^3 + (x - 1)^6$

49. $(a + 2)^3 - (a - 2)^3$

50. $y^4 - 8y^3 - y + 8$

FINDING EQUATIONS OF LINES: POINT-SLOPE EQUATION

Objectives

a Find an equation of a line when the slope and a point are given.

b Find an equation of a line when two points are given.

In Section 3.4, we found equations of lines using the slope–intercept equation, $y = mx + b$. Here we introduce another form, the *point–slope equation,* and find equations of lines using both forms.

 Finding an Equation of a Line When the Slope and a Point Are Given

Suppose we know the slope of a line and the coordinates of one point on the line. We can use the slope–intercept equation to find an equation of the line. Or, we can use what is called a **point–slope equation.** We first develop a formula for such a line.

Suppose that a line of slope m passes through the point (x_1, y_1). For any other point (x, y) to lie on this line, we must have

$$\frac{y - y_1}{x - x_1} = m.$$

It is tempting to use this last equation as an equation of the line of slope m that passes through (x_1, y_1). The only problem with this form is that when x and y are replaced with x_1 and y_1, we have $\frac{0}{0} = m$, a false equation. To avoid this difficulty, we multiply by $x - x_1$ on both sides and simplify:

$$(x - x_1)\frac{y - y_1}{x - x_1} = m(x - x_1) \qquad \text{Multiplying by } x - x_1 \text{ on both sides}$$

$$y - y_1 = m(x - x_1). \qquad \text{Removing a factor of 1: } \frac{x - x_1}{x - x_1} = 1$$

This is the *point–slope* form of a linear equation.

POINT–SLOPE EQUATION

The **point–slope equation** of a line with slope m, passing through (x_1, y_1), is

$$y - y_1 = m(x - x_1).$$

If we know the slope of a line and a certain point on the line, we can find an equation of the line using either the point–slope equation,

$$y - y_1 = m(x - x_1),$$

or the slope–intercept equation,

$$y = mx + b.$$

EXAMPLE 1 Find an equation of the line with slope -2 and containing the point $(-1, 3)$.

Using the Point–Slope Equation: We consider $(-1, 3)$ to be (x_1, y_1) and -2 to be the slope m, and substitute:

$$y - y_1 = m(x - x_1)$$
$$y - 3 = -2[x - (-1)] \qquad \text{Substituting}$$
$$y - 3 = -2(x + 1)$$
$$y - 3 = -2x - 2$$
$$y = -2x - 2 + 3$$
$$y = -2x + 1.$$

Using the Slope–Intercept Equation: The point $(-1, 3)$ is on the line, so it is a solution. Thus we can substitute -1 for x and 3 for y in $y = mx + b$. We also substitute -2 for m, the slope. Then we solve for b:

$$y = mx + b$$
$$3 = -2 \cdot (-1) + b \qquad \text{Substituting}$$
$$3 = 2 + b$$
$$1 = b. \qquad \text{Solving for } b$$

We then use the equation $y = mx + b$ and substitute -2 for m and 1 for b:

$$y = -2x + 1.$$

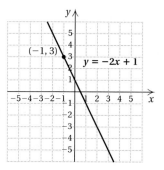

Do Exercises 1–4.

Find an equation of the line with the given slope and containing the given point.

1. $m = -3$, $(-5, 4)$

2. $m = 5$, $(-2, 1)$

3. $m = 6$, $(3, -5)$

4. $m = -\dfrac{2}{3}$, $(1, 2)$

Answers on page A-46

5. Find an equation of the line containing the points $(3, -5)$ and $(-1, 4)$.

b Finding an Equation of a Line When Two Points Are Given

We can also use the point–slope equation or the slope–intercept equation to find an equation of a line when two points are given.

EXAMPLE 2   Find an equation of the line containing the points $(3, 4)$ and $(-5, 2)$.

First, we find the slope:

$$m = \frac{4 - 2}{3 - (-5)} = \frac{2}{8}, \text{ or } \frac{1}{4}.$$

Now we have the slope and two points. We then proceed as we did in Example 1, using either point, and either the point–slope equation or the slope–intercept equation.

Using the Point–Slope Equation: We choose $(3, 4)$ and substitute 3 for x_1, 4 for y_1, and $\frac{1}{4}$ for m:

$$y - y_1 = m(x - x_1)$$
$$y - 4 = \tfrac{1}{4}(x - 3) \qquad \text{Substituting}$$
$$y - 4 = \tfrac{1}{4}x - \tfrac{3}{4}$$
$$y = \tfrac{1}{4}x - \tfrac{3}{4} + 4$$
$$y = \tfrac{1}{4}x - \tfrac{3}{4} + \tfrac{16}{4}$$
$$y = \tfrac{1}{4}x + \tfrac{13}{4}.$$

6. Find an equation of the line containing the points $(-3, 11)$ and $(-4, 20)$.

Using the Slope–Intercept Equation: We choose $(3, 4)$ and substitute 3 for x, 4 for y, and $\frac{1}{4}$ for m and solve for b:

$$y = mx + b$$
$$4 = \tfrac{1}{4} \cdot 3 + b \qquad \text{Substituting}$$
$$4 = \tfrac{3}{4} + b$$
$$4 - \tfrac{3}{4} = b$$
$$\tfrac{16}{4} - \tfrac{3}{4} = b$$
$$\tfrac{13}{4} = b. \qquad \text{Solving for } b$$

Finally, we use the equation $y = mx + b$ and substitute $\frac{1}{4}$ for m and $\frac{13}{4}$ for b:

$$y = \tfrac{1}{4}x + \tfrac{13}{4}.$$

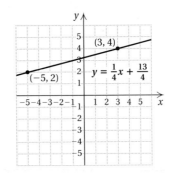

Do Exercises 5 and 6.

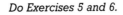

Answers on page A-46

EXERCISE SET

a   Find an equation of the line having the given slope and containing the given point.

1. $m = 4$, $(5,2)$ **2.** $m = 5$, $(4,3)$ **3.** $m = -2$, $(2,8)$ **4.** $m = -3$, $(9,6)$

5. $m = 3$, $(-2,-2)$ **6.** $m = 1$, $(-1,-7)$ **7.** $m = -3$, $(-2,0)$ **8.** $m = -2$, $(8,0)$

9. $m = 0$, $(0,4)$ **10.** $m = 0$, $(0,-7)$ **11.** $m = -\frac{4}{5}$, $(2,3)$ **12.** $m = \frac{2}{3}$, $(1,-2)$

b   Find an equation of the line containing the given pair of points.

13. $(2,5)$ and $(4,7)$ **14.** $(1,4)$ and $(5,6)$ **15.** $(-1,-1)$ and $(9,9)$ **16.** $(-3,-3)$ and $(2,2)$

17. $(0,-5)$ and $(3,0)$ **18.** $(-4,0)$ and $(0,7)$ **19.** $(-4,-7)$ and $(-2,-1)$ **20.** $(-2,-3)$ and $(-4,-6)$

21. $(0,0)$ and $(-4,7)$ **22.** $(0,0)$ and $(6,1)$ **23.** $\left(\frac{2}{3},\frac{3}{2}\right)$ and $\left(-3,\frac{5}{6}\right)$ **24.** $\left(\frac{1}{4},-\frac{1}{2}\right)$ and $\left(\frac{3}{4},6\right)$

SYNTHESIS

25. Find an equation of the line that has the same y-intercept as the line $2x - y = -3$ and contains the point $(-1,-2)$.

26. Find an equation of the line with the same slope as the line $\frac{1}{2}x - \frac{1}{3}y = 10$ and the same y-intercept as the line $\frac{1}{4}x + 3y = -2$.

Objectives

a Find higher roots of real numbers.

b Simplify radical expressions using the product and quotient rules.

C **HIGHER ROOTS**

In this appendix, we study *higher* roots, such as cube roots, or fourth roots.

a Higher Roots

Recall that c is a square root of a if $c^2 = a$. A similar definition can be made for *cube roots*.

CUBE ROOT

The number c is the **cube root** of a if $c^3 = a$.

---

1. Find $\sqrt[3]{27}$.

Every real number has exactly *one* real-number cube root. The symbolism $\sqrt[3]{a}$ is used to represent the cube root of a. In the radical $\sqrt[3]{a}$, the number 3 is called the **index** and a is called the **radicand**.

2. Find $\sqrt[3]{-8}$.

EXAMPLE 1 Find $\sqrt[3]{8}$.

The cube root of 8 is the number whose cube is 8. Since $2^3 = 2 \cdot 2 \cdot 2 = 8$, the cube root of 8 is 2, so $\sqrt[3]{8} = 2$.

3. Find $\sqrt[3]{216}$.

EXAMPLE 2 Find $\sqrt[3]{-125}$.

The cube root of -125 is the number whose cube is -125. Since $(-5)^3 = (-5)(-5)(-5) = -125$, the cube root of -125 is -5, so $\sqrt[3]{-125} = -5$.

Find the root, if it exists, of each of the following.

4. $\sqrt[5]{1}$

Do Exercises 1–3.

5. $\sqrt[5]{-1}$

Positive real numbers always have *two* nth roots (one positive and one negative) when n is even, but we refer to the *positive nth root* of a positive number a as the *nth root* and denote it $\sqrt[n]{a}$. For example, although both -3 and 3 are fourth roots of 81, since $(-3)^4 = 81$ and $3^4 = 81$, 3 is considered to be *the* fourth root of 81. In symbols, $\sqrt[4]{81} = 3$.

6. $\sqrt[4]{-81}$

---

nTH ROOT

The number c is the **nth root** of a if $c^n = a$.

If n is odd, then there is exactly one real-number nth root of a and $\sqrt[n]{a}$ represents that root.

7. $\sqrt[4]{81}$

If n is even and a is positive, then $\sqrt[n]{a}$ represents the nonnegative nth root.

Even roots of negative numbers are not real numbers.

---

8. $\sqrt[3]{-216}$

EXAMPLES Find the root of each of the following.

9. $-\sqrt[3]{216}$

3. $\sqrt[4]{16} = 2$ Since $2^4 = 2 \cdot 2 \cdot 2 \cdot 2 = 16$

4. $\sqrt[4]{-16}$ is not a real number, because it is an even root of a negative number.

Answers on page A-46

5. $\sqrt[5]{32} = 2$ Since $2^5 = 2 \cdot 2 \cdot 2 \cdot 2 \cdot 2 = 32$

6. $\sqrt[5]{-32} = -2$ Since $(-2)^5 = (-2)(-2)(-2)(-2)(-2) = -32$

7. $-\sqrt[3]{64} = -\left(\sqrt[3]{64}\right)$ This is the opposite of $\sqrt[3]{64}$.
$\qquad\quad = -4$ Since $4^3 = 4 \cdot 4 \cdot 4 = 64$

Do Exercises 4–9 on the preceding page.

Some roots occur so frequently that you may want to memorize them.

SQUARE ROOTS		CUBE ROOTS	FOURTH ROOTS	FIFTH ROOTS
$\sqrt{1} = 1$	$\sqrt{4} = 2$	$\sqrt[3]{1} = 1$	$\sqrt[4]{1} = 1$	$\sqrt[5]{1} = 1$
$\sqrt{9} = 3$	$\sqrt{16} = 4$	$\sqrt[3]{8} = 2$	$\sqrt[4]{16} = 2$	$\sqrt[5]{32} = 2$
$\sqrt{25} = 5$	$\sqrt{36} = 6$	$\sqrt[3]{27} = 3$	$\sqrt[4]{81} = 3$	$\sqrt[5]{243} = 3$
$\sqrt{49} = 7$	$\sqrt{64} = 8$	$\sqrt[3]{64} = 4$	$\sqrt[4]{256} = 4$	
$\sqrt{81} = 9$	$\sqrt{100} = 10$	$\sqrt[3]{125} = 5$	$\sqrt[4]{625} = 5$	
$\sqrt{121} = 11$	$\sqrt{144} = 12$	$\sqrt[3]{216} = 6$		

b   Products and Quotients Involving Higher Roots

The rules for working with products and quotients of square roots can be extended to products and quotients of *n*th roots.

> **THE PRODUCT AND QUOTIENT RULES FOR RADICALS**
>
> For any nonnegative real numbers A and B and any index n, $n \geq 2$,
>
> $$\sqrt[n]{AB} = \sqrt[n]{A} \cdot \sqrt[n]{B} \quad \text{and} \quad \sqrt[n]{\frac{A}{B}} = \frac{\sqrt[n]{A}}{\sqrt[n]{B}}.$$

  EXAMPLES   Simplify.

8. $\sqrt[3]{40} = \sqrt[3]{8 \cdot 5}$ Factoring the radicand. 8 is a perfect cube.
$\qquad\quad = \sqrt[3]{8} \cdot \sqrt[3]{5}$ Using the product rule
$\qquad\quad = 2\sqrt[3]{5}$

9. $\sqrt[3]{\dfrac{125}{27}} = \dfrac{\sqrt[3]{125}}{\sqrt[3]{27}}$ Using the quotient rule

$\qquad\quad = \dfrac{5}{3}$ Simplifying. 125 and 27 are perfect cubes.

10. $\sqrt[4]{1250} = \sqrt[4]{2 \cdot 625}$ Factoring the radicand. 625 is a perfect fourth power.

$\qquad\quad = \sqrt[4]{2 \cdot 5 \cdot 5 \cdot 5 \cdot 5}$

$\qquad\quad = 5\sqrt[4]{2}$ Simplifying

11. $\sqrt[5]{\dfrac{2}{243}} = \dfrac{\sqrt[5]{2}}{\sqrt[5]{243}}$ Using the quotient rule

$\qquad\quad = \dfrac{\sqrt[5]{2}}{3}$ Simplifying. 243 is a perfect fifth power.

Do Exercises 10–13.

Simplify.
10. $\sqrt[3]{24}$

11. $\sqrt[4]{\dfrac{81}{256}}$

12. $\sqrt[5]{96}$

13. $\sqrt[3]{\dfrac{4}{125}}$

Answers on page A-46

EXERCISE SET

Simplify. If an expression does not represent a real number, state this.

1. $\sqrt[3]{125}$

2. $\sqrt[3]{-27}$

3. $\sqrt[3]{-1000}$

4. $\sqrt[3]{8}$

5. $\sqrt[4]{1}$

6. $-\sqrt[5]{32}$

7. $\sqrt[4]{-256}$

8. $\sqrt[6]{-1}$

9. $-\sqrt[3]{-216}$

10. $\sqrt[3]{-125}$

11. $\sqrt[4]{256}$

12. $-\sqrt[3]{-8}$

13. $\sqrt[4]{10,000}$

14. $\sqrt[3]{-64}$

15. $-\sqrt[4]{81}$

16. $-\sqrt[3]{1}$

17. $-\sqrt[4]{-16}$

18. $\sqrt[6]{64}$

19. $-\sqrt[3]{125}$

20. $\sqrt[3]{1000}$

21. $\sqrt[5]{t^5}$

22. $\sqrt[7]{y^7}$

23. $-\sqrt[3]{x^3}$

24. $-\sqrt[9]{a^9}$

25. $\sqrt[3]{64}$

26. $-\sqrt[3]{216}$

27. $\sqrt[3]{-343}$

28. $\sqrt[5]{-243}$

29. $\sqrt[5]{-3125}$

30. $\sqrt[4]{625}$

31. $\sqrt[6]{1,000,000}$

32. $\sqrt[5]{243}$

33. $-\sqrt[5]{-100,000}$

34. $-\sqrt[4]{-10,000}$

35. $-\sqrt[3]{343}$

36. $\sqrt[3]{512}$

37. $\sqrt[8]{-1}$

38. $\sqrt[6]{-64}$

39. $\sqrt[5]{3125}$

40. $\sqrt[4]{-625}$

41. $\sqrt[3]{54}$

42. $\sqrt[5]{64}$

43. $\sqrt[4]{324}$

44. $\sqrt[3]{81}$

45. $\sqrt[3]{\dfrac{27}{64}}$

46. $\sqrt[3]{\dfrac{125}{64}}$

47. $\sqrt[4]{512}$

48. $\sqrt[3]{375}$

49. $\sqrt[5]{128}$

50. $\sqrt[4]{112}$

51. $\sqrt[4]{\dfrac{256}{625}}$

52. $\sqrt[5]{\dfrac{243}{32}}$

53. $\sqrt[3]{\dfrac{17}{8}}$

54. $\sqrt[5]{\dfrac{11}{32}}$

55. $\sqrt[3]{250}$

56. $\sqrt[5]{160}$

57. $\sqrt[5]{486}$

58. $\sqrt[3]{128}$

59. $\sqrt[4]{\dfrac{13}{81}}$

60. $\sqrt[3]{\dfrac{10}{27}}$

61. $\sqrt[4]{\dfrac{7}{16}}$

62. $\sqrt[4]{\dfrac{27}{256}}$

63. $\sqrt[4]{\dfrac{16}{625}}$

64. $\sqrt[3]{\dfrac{216}{27}}$

Simplify. If an expression does not represent a real number, state this.

65. $\sqrt[3]{\sqrt{64}}$

66. $\sqrt{\sqrt[3]{-64}}$

67. $\sqrt[3]{\sqrt[3]{1{,}000{,}000{,}000}}$

68. $\sqrt{-\sqrt[3]{-1}}$

Objectives

a Name sets using the roster method.

b Classify statements regarding set membership and subsets as true or false.

c Find the intersection and the union of sets.

Name the set using the roster method.

1. The set of whole numbers 0 through 7

2. {*x* | the square of *x* is 25}

Determine whether each of the following is true or false.

3. 8 ∈ {*x* | *x* is an even whole number}

4. 2 ∈ {*x* | *x* is a prime number}

Answers on page A-46

D SETS

a Naming Sets

To name the set of whole numbers less than 6, we can use the **roster method,** as follows: {0, 1, 2, 3, 4, 5}.

The set of real numbers *x* such that *x* is less than 6 cannot be named by listing all its members because there are infinitely many. We name such a set using **set-builder notation,** as follows: {*x* | *x* < 6}. This is read "The set of all *x* such that *x* is less than 6." See Section 2.7 for more on this notation.

Do Exercises 1 and 2.

b Set Membership and Subsets

The symbol ∈ means **is a member of** or **belongs to,** or **is an element of.** Thus, *x* ∈ *A* means *x* is a member of *A* or *x* belongs to *A* or *x* is an element of *A*.

EXAMPLE 1 Classify each of the following as true or false.

a) 1 ∈ {1, 2, 3}

b) 1 ∈ {2, 3}

c) 4 ∈ {*x* | *x* is an even whole number}

d) 5 ∈ {*x* | *x* is an even whole number}

a) Since 1 *is* listed as a member of the set, 1 ∈ {1, 2, 3} is true.

b) Since 1 *is not* a member of {2, 3}, the statement 1 ∈ {2, 3} is false.

c) Since 4 *is* an even whole number, 4 ∈ {*x* | *x* is an even whole number} is a true statement.

d) Since 5 *is not* even, 5 ∈ {*x* | *x* is an even whole number} is false.

Set membership can be illustrated with a diagram, as shown here.

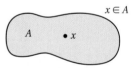

Do Exercises 3 and 4.

If every element of *A* is an element of *B*, then *A* is a **subset** of *B*. This is denoted *A* ⊆ *B*. The set of whole numbers is a subset of the set of integers. The set of rational numbers is a subset of the set of real numbers.

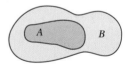

EXAMPLE 2 Classify each of the following as true or false.

a) {1, 2} ⊆ {1, 2, 3, 4}   **b)** {p, q, r, w} ⊆ {a, p, r, z}

c) {*x* | *x* < 6} ⊆ {*x* | *x* ≤ 11}

a) Since every element of {1, 2} is in the set {1, 2, 3, 4}, the statement {1, 2} ⊆ {1, 2, 3, 4} is true.

b) Since $q \in \{p, q, r, w\}$, but $q \notin \{a, p, r, z\}$, the statement $\{p, q, r, w\} \subseteq \{a, p, r, z\}$ is false.

c) Since every number that is less than 6 is also less than 11, the statement $\{x \mid x < 6\} \subseteq \{x \mid x \leq 11\}$ is true.

Do Exercises 5–7.

Intersections and Unions

The **intersection** of sets A and B, denoted $A \cap B$, is the set of members that are common to both sets.

EXAMPLE 3 Find the intersection.

a) $\{0, 1, 3, 5, 25\} \cap \{2, 3, 4, 5, 6, 7, 9\}$ **b)** $\{a, p, q, w\} \cap \{p, q, t\}$

a) $\{0, 1, 3, 5, 25\} \cap \{2, 3, 4, 5, 6, 7, 9\} = \{3, 5\}$

b) $\{a, p, q, w\} \cap \{p, q, t\} = \{p, q\}$

Set intersection can be illustrated with a diagram, as shown here.

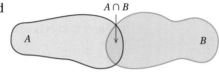

The set without members is known as the **empty set,** and is often named $\varnothing$, and sometimes $\{\ \}$. Each of the following is a description of the empty set:

$\{2, 3\} \cap \{5, 6, 7\};$

$\{x \mid x \text{ is an even natural number}\} \cap \{x \mid x \text{ is an odd natural number}\}.$

Do Exercises 8–10.

Two sets A and B can be combined to form a set that contains the members of A as well as those of B. The new set is called the **union** of A and B, denoted $A \cup B$.

EXAMPLE 4 Find the union.

a) $\{0, 5, 7, 13, 27\} \cup \{0, 2, 3, 4, 5\}$ **b)** $\{a, c, e, g\} \cup \{b, d, f\}$

a) $\{0, 5, 7, 13, 27\} \cup \{0, 2, 3, 4, 5\} = \{0, 2, 3, 4, 5, 7, 13, 27\}$

       Note that the 0 and the 5 are *not* listed twice in the solution.

b) $\{a, c, e, g\} \cup \{b, d, f\} = \{a, b, c, d, e, f, g\}$

Set union can be illustrated with a diagram, as shown here.

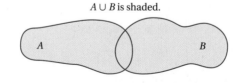

The solution set of the equation $(x - 3)(x + 2) = 0$ is $\{3, -2\}$. This set is the union of the solution sets of $x - 3 = 0$ and $x + 2 = 0$, which are $\{3\}$ and $\{-2\}$.

Do Exercises 11–13.

Determine whether each of the following is true or false.

5. $\{-2, -3, 4\} \subseteq$
$\{-5, -4, -2, 7, -3, 5, 4\}$

6. $\{a, e, i, o, u\} \subseteq$
The set of all consonants

7. $\{x \mid x \leq -8\} \subseteq \{x \mid x \leq -7\}$

Find the intersection.
8. $\{-2, -3, 4, -4, 8\} \cap$
$\{-5, -4, -2, 7, -3, 5, 4\}$

9. $\{a, e, i, o, u\} \cap \{m, a, r, v, i, n\}$

10. $\{a, e, i, o, u\} \cap$
The set of all consonants

Find the union.
11. $\{-2, -3, 4, -4, 8\} \cup$
$\{-5, -4, -2, 7, -3, 5, 4\}$

12. $\{a, e, i, o, u\} \cup \{m, a, r, v, i, n\}$

13. $\{a, e, i, o, u\} \cup$
The set of all consonants

Answers on page A-46

a   Name the set using the roster method.

1. The set of whole numbers 3 through 8

2. The set of whole numbers 101 through 107

3. The set of odd numbers between 40 and 50

4. The set of multiples of 5 between 11 and 39

5. $\{x \mid$ the square of x is $9\}$

6. $\{x \mid x$ is the cube of $0.2\}$

b   Classify the statement as true or false.

7. $2 \in \{x \mid x$ is an odd number$\}$

8. $7 \in \{x \mid x$ is an odd number$\}$

9. Jeff Gordon $\in$ The set of all NASCAR drivers

10. Apple $\in$ The set of all fruit

11. $-3 \in \{-4, -3, 0, 1\}$

12. $0 \in \{-4, -3, 0, 1\}$

13. $\frac{2}{3} \in \{x \mid x$ is a rational number$\}$

14. Heads $\in$ The set of outcomes of flipping a penny

15. $\{4, 5, 8,\} \subseteq \{1, 3, 4, 5, 6, 7, 8, 9\}$

16. The set of vowels $\subseteq$ The set of consonants

17. $\{-1, -2, -3, -4, -5\} \subseteq \{-1, 2, 3, 4, 5\}$

18. The set of integers $\subseteq$ The set of rational numbers

c   Find the intersection.

19. $\{a, b, c, d, e\} \cap \{c, d, e, f, g\}$

20. $\{a, e, i, o, u\} \cap \{q, u, i, c, k\}$

21. $\{1, 2, 5, 10\} \cap \{0, 1, 7, 10\}$

APPENDIX D: Sets

22. $\{0, 1, 7, 10\} \cap \{0, 1, 2, 5\}$ **23.** $\{1, 2, 5, 10\} \cap \{3, 4, 7, 8\}$ **24.** $\{a, e, i, o, u\} \cap \{m, n, f, g, h\}$

Find the union.

25. $\{a, e, i, o, u\} \cup \{q, u, i, c, k\}$

26. $\{a, b, c, d, e\} \cup \{c, d, e, f, g\}$

27. $\{0, 1, 7, 10\} \cup \{0, 1, 2, 5\}$

28. $\{1, 2, 5, 10\} \cup \{0, 1, 7, 10\}$

29. $\{a, e, i, o, u\} \cup \{m, n, f, g, h\}$

30. $\{1, 2, 5, 10\} \cup \{a, b\}$

| SYNTHESIS |

31. Find the union of the set of integers and the set of whole numbers.

32. Find the intersection of the set of odd integers and the set of even integers.

33. Find the union of the set of rational numbers and the set of irrational numbers.

34. Find the intersection of the set of even integers and the set of positive rational numbers.

35. Find the intersection of the set of rational numbers and the set of irrational numbers.

36. Find the union of the set of negative integers, the set of positive integers, and the set containing 0.

37. For a set A, find each of the following.
     a) $A \cup \varnothing$ **b)** $A \cup A$
     c) $A \cap A$ **d)** $A \cap \varnothing$

38. A set is *closed* under an operation if, when the operation is performed on its members, the result is in the set. For example, the set of real numbers is closed under the operation of addition since the sum of any two real numbers is a real number.
     a) Is the set of even numbers closed under addition?
     b) Is the set of odd numbers closed under addition?
     c) Is the set $\{0, 1\}$ closed under addition?
     d) Is the set $\{0, 1\}$ closed under multiplication?
     e) Is the set of real numbers closed under multiplication?
     f) Is the set of integers closed under division?

39. Experiment with sets of various types and determine whether the following distributive law for sets is true:
$$A \cap (B \cup C) = (A \cap B) \cup (A \cap C).$$

Objective

a Find the mean (average), the median, and the mode of a set of data and solve related applied problems.

MEAN, MEDIAN, AND MODE

a Mean, Median, and Mode

One way to analyze data is to look for a single representative number, called a **center point** or **measure of central tendency.** Those most often used are the **mean** (or **average**), the **median,** and the **mode.**

MEAN

Let's first consider the *mean*, or *average*.

> **MEAN, OR AVERAGE**
>
> The **mean,** or **average,** of a set of numbers is the sum of the numbers divided by the number of addends.

EXAMPLE 1 Consider the following data on total net revenue, in billions of dollars, for Starbucks Corporation for the years 2000–2004:

$2.2, $2.6, $3.3, $4.1, $5.3

What is the mean of the numbers?

Source: Starbucks Corporation

First we add the numbers:

$$2.2 + 2.6 + 3.3 + 4.1 + 5.3 = 17.5.$$

Then we divide by the number of addends, 5:

$$\frac{(2.2 + 2.6 + 3.3 + 4.1 + 5.3)}{5} = \frac{17.5}{5} = 3.5.$$

The mean, or average, revenue of Starbucks for those five years is $3.5 billion.

Note that $3.5 + 3.5 + 3.5 + 3.5 + 3.5 = 17.5$. If we use this center point, 3.5, repeatedly as the addend, we get the same sum that we do when adding the individual data numbers.

Do Exercises 1–3.

Find the mean. Round to the nearest tenth.

1. 28, 103, 39

2. 85, 46, 105.7, 22.1

3. A student scored the following on five tests:

   78, 95, 84, 100, 82.

   What was the average score?

Answers on page A-47

MEDIAN

The *median* is useful when we wish to de-emphasize extreme values. For example, suppose five workers in a technology company manufactured the following number of computers during one day's work:

Sarah:	88	Jen:	94
Matt:	92	Mark:	91
Pat:	66		

Let's first list the values in order from smallest to largest:

66 88 91 92 94.
           ↑
     Middle number

The middle number—in this case, 91—is the **median.**

MEDIAN

Once a set of data has been arranged from smallest to largest, the **median** of the set of data is the middle number if there is an odd number of data numbers. If there is an even number of data numbers, then there are two middle numbers and the median is the *average* of the two middle numbers.

EXAMPLE 2 What is the median of the following set of yearly salaries?

$76,000, $58,000, $87,000, $32,500, $64,800, $62,500

We first rearrange the numbers in order from smallest to largest.

$32,500, $58,000, $62,500, $64,800, $76,000, $87,000

↑
Median

There is an even number of numbers. We look for the middle two, which are $62,500 and $64,800. In this case, the median is the average of $62,500 and $64,800:

$$\frac{\$62,500 + \$64,800}{2} = \$63,650.$$

Do Exercises 4–6.

MODE

The last center point we consider is called the *mode*. A number that occurs most often in a set of data can be considered a representative number or center point.

MODE

The **mode** of a set of data is the number or numbers that occur most often. If each number occurs the same number of times, there is *no* mode.

EXAMPLE 3 Find the mode of the following data:

23, 24, 27, 18, 19, 27

The number that occurs most often is 27. Thus the mode is 27.

EXAMPLE 4 Find the mode of the following data:

83, 84, 84, 84, 85, 86, 87, 87, 87, 88, 89, 90.

There are two numbers that occur most often, 84 and 87. Thus the modes are 84 and 87.

EXAMPLE 5 Find the mode of the following data:

115, 117, 211, 213, 219.

Each number occurs the same number of times. The set of data has *no* mode.

Do Exercises 7–10.

Find the median.
4. 17, 13, 18, 14, 19

5. 17, 18, 16, 19, 13, 14

6. 122, 102, 103, 91, 83, 81, 78, 119, 88

Find any modes that exist.
7. 33, 55, 55, 88, 55

8. 90, 54, 88, 87, 87, 54

9. 23.7, 27.5, 54.9, 17.2, 20.1

10. In conducting laboratory tests, Carole discovers bacteria in different lab dishes grew to the following areas, in square millimeters:

25, 19, 29, 24, 28.
a) What is the mean?

b) What is the median?

c) What is the mode?

Answers on page A-47

EXERCISE SET

E

a For each set of numbers, find the mean (average), the median, and any modes that exist.

1. 17, 19, 29, 18, 14, 29

2. 72, 83, 85, 88, 92

3. 5, 37, 20, 20, 35, 5, 25

4. 13, 32, 25, 27, 13

5. 4.3, 7.4, 1.2, 5.7, 7.4

6. 13.4, 13.4, 12.6, 42.9

7. 234, 228, 234, 229, 234, 278

8. $29.95, $28.79, $30.95, $29.95

9. *Atlantic Storms and Hurricanes.* The following bar graph shows the number of Atlantic storms or hurricanes that formed in various months from 1980 to 2000. What is the average number for the 9 months given? the median? the mode?

10. *Cheddar Cheese Prices.* The following prices per pound of sharp cheddar cheese were found at five supermarkets:

$5.99, $6.79, $5.99, $6.99, $6.79.

What was the average price per pound? the median price? the mode?

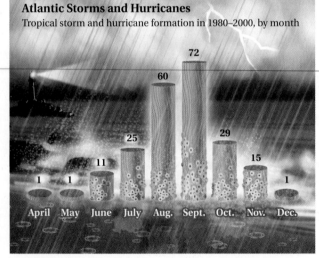

Atlantic Storms and Hurricanes
Tropical storm and hurricane formation in 1980–2000, by month

Source: Colorado State University

11. *Coffee Consumption.* The following lists the annual coffee consumption, in cups per person, for various countries. Find the mean, the median, and the mode.

Germany	1113
United States	610
Switzerland	1215
France	798
Italy	750

Source: Beverage Marketing Corporation

12. *NBA Tall Men.* The following is a list of the heights, in inches, of the tallest men in the NBA in a recent year. Find the mean, the median, and the mode.

Shaquille O'Neal	85
Gheorghe Muresan	91
Shawn Bradley	90
Priest Lauderdale	88
Rik Smits	88
David Robinson	85
Arvydas Sabonis	87

Source: National Basketball Association

13. *Salmon Prices.* The following prices per pound of Atlantic salmon were found at five fish markets:

$6.99, $8.49, $8.99, $6.99, $9.49.

What was the average price per pound? the median price? the mode?

14. *PBA Scores.* Chris Barnes rolled scores of 224, 224, 254, and 187 in a recent tournament of the Professional Bowlers Association. What was his average? his median? his mode?

Source: Professional Bowlers Association

SYNTHESIS

Grade Point Average. The tables in Exercises 15 and 16 show the grades of a student for one semester. In each case, find the grade point average. Assume that the grade point values are 4.0 for an A, 3.0 for a B, and so on. Round to the nearest tenth.

15.

GRADE	NUMBER OF CREDIT HOURS IN COURSE
B	4
A	5
D	3
C	4

16.

GRADE	NUMBER OF CREDIT HOURS IN COURSE
A	5
C	4
F	3
B	5

17. *Hank Aaron.* Hank Aaron averaged $34\frac{7}{22}$ home runs per year over a 22-yr career. After 21 yr, Aaron had averaged $35\frac{10}{21}$ home runs per year. How many home runs did Aaron hit in his final year?

18. The ordered set of data 18, 21, 24, a, 36, 37, b has a median of 30 and an average of 32. Find a and b.

19. *Length of Pregnancy.* Marta was pregnant 270 days, 259 days, and 272 days for her first three pregnancies. In order for Marta's average length of pregnancy to equal the worldwide average of 266 days, how long must her fourth pregnancy last?

Source: David Crystal (ed.), *The Cambridge Factfinder.* Cambridge CB2 1RP: Cambridge University Press, 1993, p. 84.

20. *Male Height.* Jason's brothers are 174 cm, 180 cm, 179 cm, and 172 cm tall. The average male is 176.5 cm tall. How tall is Jason if he and his brothers have an average height of 176.5 cm?

Answers

CHAPTER R

Margin Exercises, Section R.1, pp. 2–5

1. 1, 3, 9 **2.** 1, 2, 4, 8, 16 **3.** 1, 2, 3, 4, 6, 8, 12, 24
4. 1, 2, 3, 4, 5, 6, 9, 10, 12, 15, 18, 20, 30, 36, 45, 60, 90, 180
5. 13 **6.** $2 \cdot 2 \cdot 2 \cdot 2 \cdot 3$ **7.** $2 \cdot 5 \cdot 5$ **8.** $2 \cdot 5 \cdot 7 \cdot 11$
9. 15, 30, 45, 60, ... **10.** 45, 90, 135, 180, ... **11.** 40
12. 54 **13.** 360 **14.** 18 **15.** 24 **16.** 36 **17.** 210

Exercise Set R.1, p. 6

1. 1, 2, 4, 5, 10, 20 **3.** 1, 2, 3, 4, 6, 8, 9, 12, 18, 24, 36, 72
5. $3 \cdot 5$ **7.** $2 \cdot 11$ **9.** $3 \cdot 3$ **11.** $7 \cdot 7$ **13.** $2 \cdot 3 \cdot 3$
15. $2 \cdot 2 \cdot 2 \cdot 5$ **17.** $2 \cdot 3 \cdot 3 \cdot 5$ **19.** $2 \cdot 3 \cdot 5 \cdot 7$
21. $7 \cdot 13$ **23.** $7 \cdot 17$ **25.** $2 \cdot 2; 5; 20$
27. $2 \cdot 2 \cdot 2 \cdot 3; 2 \cdot 2 \cdot 3 \cdot 3; 72$ **29.** $3; 3 \cdot 5; 15$
31. $2 \cdot 3 \cdot 5; 2 \cdot 2 \cdot 2 \cdot 5; 120$ **33.** 13; 23; 299
35. $2 \cdot 3 \cdot 3; 2 \cdot 3 \cdot 5; 90$ **37.** $2 \cdot 3 \cdot 5; 2 \cdot 2 \cdot 3 \cdot 3; 180$
39. $2 \cdot 2 \cdot 2 \cdot 3; 2 \cdot 3 \cdot 5; 120$ **41.** 17; 29; 493
43. $2 \cdot 2 \cdot 3; 2 \cdot 2 \cdot 7; 84$ **45.** 2; 3; 5; 30
47. $2 \cdot 2 \cdot 2 \cdot 3; 2 \cdot 2 \cdot 3 \cdot 3; 2 \cdot 2 \cdot 3; 72$
49. $5; 2 \cdot 2 \cdot 3; 3 \cdot 5; 60$ **51.** $2 \cdot 3; 2 \cdot 2 \cdot 3; 2 \cdot 3 \cdot 3; 36$
53. Every 60 yr **55.** Every 420 yr **57.** 30 strands
59. **(a)** No; not a multiple of 8; **(b)** No; it is a multiple of
both 8 and 12, but it is not the least common multiple;
(c) no; not a multiple of 8 or 12; **(d)** yes; it is a multiple of
both 8 and 12 and is the smallest such multiple.
61. 70,200

Margin Exercises, Section R.2, pp. 9–15

1. $\frac{8}{12}$ **2.** $\frac{21}{28}$ **3.** $\frac{14}{16}, \frac{21}{24}, \frac{28}{32}$; answers may vary **4.** $\frac{2}{5}$
5. $\frac{19}{9}$ **6.** $\frac{8}{3}$ **7.** $\frac{1}{2}$ **8.** 4 **9.** $\frac{5}{2}$ **10.** $\frac{35}{16}$ **11.** $\frac{7}{5}$
12. 2 **13.** $\frac{23}{15}$ **14.** $\frac{43}{60}$ **15.** $\frac{19}{40}$ **16.** $\frac{7}{36}$ **17.** $\frac{11}{4}$
18. $\frac{7}{15}$ **19.** $\frac{1}{5}$ **20.** 3 **21.** $\frac{21}{20}$ **22.** $\frac{8}{21}$ **23.** $\frac{5}{6}$
24. $\frac{8}{15}$ **25.** $\frac{1}{64}$ **26.** 81

Calculator Corner, p. 16

1. $\frac{7}{12}$ **2.** $\frac{41}{24}$ **3.** $\frac{11}{10}$ **4.** $\frac{153}{112}$ **5.** $\frac{35}{16}$ **6.** $\frac{4}{3}$ **7.** $\frac{3}{10}$
8. $\frac{35}{12}$

Exercise Set R.2, p. 17

1. $\frac{9}{12}$ **3.** $\frac{60}{100}$ **5.** $\frac{104}{160}$ **7.** $\frac{21}{24}$ **9.** $\frac{20}{16}$ **11.** $\frac{391}{437}$
13. $\frac{2}{3}$ **15.** 4 **17.** $\frac{1}{7}$ **19.** 8 **21.** $\frac{1}{4}$ **23.** 5
25. $\frac{17}{21}$ **27.** $\frac{13}{7}$ **29.** $\frac{4}{3}$ **31.** $\frac{1}{12}$ **33.** $\frac{45}{16}$ **35.** $\frac{2}{3}$
37. $\frac{7}{6}$ **39.** $\frac{5}{6}$ **41.** $\frac{13}{20}$ **43.** $\frac{1}{2}$ **45.** $\frac{13}{24}$ **47.** $\frac{31}{60}$
49. $\frac{35}{18}$ **51.** $\frac{10}{3}$ **53.** $\frac{1}{2}$ **55.** $\frac{5}{36}$ **57.** 500 **59.** $\frac{3}{40}$
61. $\mathbf{D_W}$ **63.** $2 \cdot 2 \cdot 7$ **64.** $2 \cdot 2 \cdot 2 \cdot 7$
65. $2 \cdot 2 \cdot 2 \cdot 5 \cdot 5 \cdot 5$ **66.** $2 \cdot 2 \cdot 2 \cdot 2 \cdot 2 \cdot 2 \cdot 3$
67. $3 \cdot 23 \cdot 29$ **68.** 126 **69.** 48 **70.** 392 **71.** 192
72. 150 **73.** $\frac{3}{4}$ **75.** 4 **77.** 1

Margin Exercises, Section R.3, pp. 19–24

1. $\frac{568}{1000}$ **2.** $\frac{23}{10}$ **3.** $\frac{8904}{100}$ **4.** 4.131 **5.** 0.4131
6. 5.73 **7.** 284.455 **8.** 268.63 **9.** 27.676
10. 64.683 **11.** 99.59 **12.** 239.883 **13.** 5.868
14. 0.5868 **15.** 51.53808 **16.** 48.9 **17.** 15.82
18. 1.28 **19.** 17.95 **20.** 856 **21.** 0.85 **22.** 0.625
23. $0.\overline{6}$ **24.** $7.\overline{63}$ **25.** 2.8 **26.** 13.9 **27.** 7.0
28. 7.83 **29.** 34.68 **30.** 0.03 **31.** 0.943 **32.** 8.004
33. 43.112 **34.** 37.401 **35.** 7459.355 **36.** 7459.35
37. 7459.4 **38.** 7459 **39.** 7460

Calculator Corner, p. 23

1. 40.42 **2.** 2.6 **3.** 3.33 **4.** 0.69324 **5.** 7.5
6. 2.38

Exercise Set R.3, p. 25

1. $\dfrac{53}{10}$ **3.** $\dfrac{67}{100}$ **5.** $\dfrac{20,007}{10,000}$ **7.** $\dfrac{78,898}{10}$ **9.** 0.1

11. 0.0001   **13.** 9.999   **15.** 0.4578   **17.** 444.94
19. 390.617   **21.** 155.724   **23.** 63.79   **25.** 32.234
27. 26.835   **29.** 47.91   **31.** 1.9193   **33.** 13.212
35. 0.7998   **37.** 179.5   **39.** 1.40756   **41.** 3.60558
43. 2.3   **45.** 5.2   **47.** 0.023   **49.** 18.75   **51.** 660
53. 0.68   **55.** 0.34375   **57.** $1.\overline{18}$ **59.** $0.\overline{5}$ **61.** $2.\overline{1}$
63. 745.07; 745.1; 745; 750; 700   **65.** 6780.51; 6780.5; 6781;
6780; 6800   **67.** $17.99; $18   **69.** $346.08; $346
71. $17   **73.** $190   **75.** 12.3457; 12.346; 12.35; 12.3; 12

77. 0.5897; 0.590; 0.59; 0.6; 1   **79.** $\mathbf{D_W}$ **81.** $\dfrac{33}{32}$ **82.** $\dfrac{1}{48}$

83. $\dfrac{55}{64}$ **84.** $\dfrac{5}{4}$ **85.** $\dfrac{139}{210}$ **86.** $\dfrac{449}{336}$ **87.** $\dfrac{1023}{1000}$

88. $\dfrac{259}{210}$, or $\dfrac{37}{30}$ **89.** $2 \cdot 2 \cdot 2 \cdot 2 \cdot 13$
90. $2 \cdot 2 \cdot 2 \cdot 2 \cdot 2 \cdot 2 \cdot 2$ **91.** $2 \cdot 5 \cdot 5 \cdot 5 \cdot 5$
92. $2 \cdot 2 \cdot 2 \cdot 2 \cdot 2 \cdot 2 \cdot 2 \cdot 2 \cdot 2 \cdot 5$

Margin Exercises, Section R.4, pp. 27–29

1. 0.125   **2.** 1   **3.** 0.6667   **4.** $\dfrac{90}{100}$ **5.** $\dfrac{53}{100}$ **6.** $\dfrac{459}{1000}$

7. $\dfrac{23}{10,000}$ **8.** 51%   **9.** 677%   **10.** 99.44%

11. $33.\overline{3}\%$, or $33\dfrac{1}{3}\%$ **12.** 25%   **13.** 87.5%

Exercise Set R.4, p. 30

1. 0.21   **3.** 0.0345   **5.** 0.63   **7.** 0.941   **9.** 0.01

11. 0.0061   **13.** 2.4   **15.** 0.0325   **17.** $\dfrac{2}{100}$ **19.** $\dfrac{109}{1000}$

21. $\dfrac{77}{100}$ **23.** $\dfrac{60}{100}$ **25.** $\dfrac{289}{1000}$ **27.** $\dfrac{110}{100}$ **29.** $\dfrac{42}{100,000}$

31. $\dfrac{250}{100}$ **33.** $\dfrac{347}{10,000}$ **35.** 73%   **37.** 41%   **39.** 100%

41. 99.6%   **43.** 0.47%   **45.** 7.2%   **47.** 920%

49. 0.68%   **51.** $16.\overline{6}\%$, or $16\dfrac{2}{3}\%$ **53.** 65%   **55.** 29%

57. 80%   **59.** 60%   **61.** $66.\overline{6}\%$, or $66\dfrac{2}{3}\%$ **63.** 175%

65. 75%   **67.** 0.1186%   **69.** 0.49; $\dfrac{49}{100}$ **71.** $\dfrac{29}{100}$; 29%

73. 0.3; 30%   **75.** 0.36; $\dfrac{36}{100}$, or $\dfrac{9}{25}$ **77.** $\mathbf{D_W}$ **79.** 2.25

80. 1.375   **81.** $1.41\overline{6}$ **82.** $0.\overline{8}$ **83.** $0.\overline{90}$ **84.** $1.\overline{54}$
85. 164.90974   **86.** 56.43   **87.** 896.559   **88.** 722.579
89. 32%   **91.** 70%   **93.** 2700%   **95.** 345%   **97.** 2.5%

Margin Exercises, Section R.5, pp. 33–36

1. 4^3 **2.** 6^5 **3.** $(1.08)^2$ **4.** 10,000   **5.** 512   **6.** 1.331
7. 5   **8.** 14   **9.** 13   **10.** 1000   **11.** 250   **12.** 178

13. 2   **14.** 125   **15.** 48   **16.** $\dfrac{11}{2}$

Calculator Corner, p. 34

1. 1024   **2.** 40,353,607   **3.** 361   **4.** 32.695524

5. 10.4976   **6.** 12,812.904   **7.** $\dfrac{243}{1024}$ **8.** $\dfrac{64}{729}$

Calculator Corner, p. 36

1. 38   **2.** 81   **3.** 72   **4.** 5932   **5.** 25.011   **6.** 743.027
7. 450   **8.** 14,321,949.1   **9.** 4   **10.** 2   **11.** 783
12. 228,112.96   **13.** 40; the calculator adds 39 to $141 \div 47$
to get 42 and then subtracts 2 to get 40.

Exercise Set R.5, p. 37

1. 5^4 **3.** 10^3 **5.** 10^6 **7.** 49   **9.** 59,049   **11.** 100

13. 1   **15.** 5.29   **17.** 0.008   **19.** 416.16   **21.** $\dfrac{9}{64}$

23. 125   **25.** 1061.208   **27.** 25   **29.** 114   **31.** 33
33. 5   **35.** 12   **37.** 324   **39.** 100   **41.** 1000   **43.** 22
45. 1   **47.** 4   **49.** 102   **51.** 96   **53.** 24   **55.** 90

57. 8   **59.** 1   **61.** 50,000   **63.** 5   **65.** 27   **67.** $\dfrac{22}{45}$

69. $\dfrac{19}{66}$ **71.** 9   **73.** $\mathbf{D_W}$ **75.** 31.25%   **76.** $183.\overline{3}\%$, or

$183\dfrac{1}{3}\%$ **77.** $\dfrac{3}{667}$ **78.** $\dfrac{401}{728}$ **79.** $2 \cdot 2 \cdot 2 \cdot 2 \cdot 3$

80. 168   **81.** 10^2 **83.** 5^6 **85.** $3 = \dfrac{5+5}{5} + \dfrac{5}{5}$;

$4 = \dfrac{5+5+5+5}{5}$; $5 = \dfrac{5(5+5)}{5} - 5$; $6 = \dfrac{5}{5} + \dfrac{5 \cdot 5}{5}$;

$7 = \dfrac{5}{5} + \dfrac{5}{5} + 5$; $8 = 5 + \dfrac{5+5+5}{5}$; $9 = \dfrac{5 \cdot 5 - 5}{5} + 5$;

$10 = \dfrac{5 \cdot 5 + 5 \cdot 5}{5}$

Margin Exercises, Section R.6, pp. 39–45

1. 26 cm   **2.** 46 in.   **3.** 12 cm   **4.** 17.5 yd   **5.** 40 km
6. 21 yd   **7.** 8 cm^2 **8.** 56 km^2 **9.** 16.96 yd^2

10. 118.81 m^2 **11.** $\dfrac{25}{64}$ yd^2 **12.** 43.8 cm^2

13. 12.375 km^2 **14.** 96 m^2 **15.** 18.7 cm^2 **16.** 9 in.

17. 7 ft   **18.** 62.8 mi   **19.** 88 m   **20.** $78\dfrac{4}{7}$ km^2

21. 339.62 cm^2 **22.** 128 ft^3

Calculator Corner, p. 44

1. Varies by calculator; 3.141592654 gives 9 decimal places.
2. 1417.98926 in.; 160,005.9081 in^2 **3.** 1705.539236 in^2
4. 125,663.7061 ft^2

Exercise Set R.6, p. 46

1. 17 mm   **3.** 15.25 in.   **5.** 30 ft   **7.** 79.14 cm

9. $81\dfrac{1}{2}$ ft   **11.** 182 mm   **13.** (a) 228 ft; (b) $1046.52

15. 15 km²   **17.** 1.4 in²   **19.** $\frac{4}{9}$ yd²   **21.** 8100 ft²

23. 50 ft²   **25.** 169.883 cm²   **27.** $\frac{5}{9}$ in²   **29.** $495\frac{1}{16}$ ft²

31. 3237.61 km²   **33.** $\frac{9}{64}$ yd²   **35.** 630.36 m²

37. 32 cm²   **39.** $63\frac{3}{4}$ in²   **41.** 8.05 cm²   **43.** 7 mi²

45. 14 cm; 44 cm; 154 cm²   **47.** $1\frac{1}{2}$ in.; $4\frac{5}{7}$ in.; $1\frac{43}{56}$ in²

49. 16 ft; 100.48 ft; 803.84 ft²   **51.** 0.7 cm; 4.396 cm; 1.5386 cm²   **53.** 154 ft²   **55.** 768 cm³   **57.** 45 in³

59. 75 m³   **61.** 357.5 yd³   **63.** 2772 in³   **65.** $\mathbf{D_W}$

67. 87.5%   **68.** $66.\overline{6}\%$, or $66\frac{2}{3}\%$ **69.** 37.5%

70. $33.\overline{3}\%$, or $33\frac{1}{3}\%$ **71.** $\frac{163}{360}$ **72.** $\frac{163}{108}$ **73.** $\frac{41}{108}$

74. $\frac{127}{360}$ **75.** 803.84 in³   **77.** 353.25 cm³

Concept Reinforcement, p. 51

1. True   **2.** False   **3.** False   **4.** True   **5.** True

Summary and Review: Chapter R, p. 51

1. $2 \cdot 2 \cdot 23$ **2.** $2 \cdot 2 \cdot 2 \cdot 5 \cdot 5 \cdot 7$ **3.** 416   **4.** 90
5. $\frac{12}{30}$ **6.** $\frac{96}{184}$ **7.** $\frac{40}{64}$ **8.** $\frac{91}{84}$ **9.** $\frac{5}{12}$ **10.** $\frac{51}{91}$
11. $\frac{31}{36}$ **12.** $\frac{1}{4}$ **13.** $\frac{3}{5}$ **14.** $\frac{72}{25}$ **15.** $\frac{205}{144}$ **16.** $\frac{139}{72}$
17. $\frac{101}{54}$ **18.** $\frac{109}{84}$ **19.** $\frac{13}{72}$ **20.** $\frac{29}{144}$ **21.** $\frac{1}{12}$ **22.** $\frac{23}{90}$
23. $\frac{1797}{100}$ **24.** 0.2337   **25.** 2442.905   **26.** 86.0298
27. 9.342   **28.** 133.264   **29.** 430.8   **30.** 110.483
31. 55.6   **32.** 0.45   **33.** $1.58\overline{3}$ **34.** 34.1   **35.** 0.155
36. 12.7%   **37.** $\frac{311}{10,000}$ **38.** 0.1141%   **39.** 62.5%
40. 116%   **41.** 6^3 **42.** 1.1236   **43.** 119   **44.** 4
45. 29   **46.** 1   **47.** 7   **48.** 64   **49.** $\frac{103}{17}$ **50.** 23 m
51. 4.4 m   **52.** 228 ft; 2808 ft²   **53.** 36 ft; 81 ft²
54. 17.6 cm; 12.6 cm²   **55.** 60 cm²   **56.** 22.5 m²
57. 27.5 cm²   **58.** 126 in²   **59.** 840 ft²   **60.** 8 m
61. $\frac{14}{11}$ in.   **62.** 14 ft   **63.** 20 cm   **64.** 50.24 m
65. 8 in.   **66.** 200.96 m²   **67.** $5\frac{1}{11}$ in²   **68.** 93.6 m³
69. 193.2 cm³   **70.** $\mathbf{D_W}$ See the formulas for area listed at the beginning of the Summary and Review for Chapter R.
71. $\mathbf{D_W}$ All represent the same number. When expressed in simplified fraction notation, the numerator is 11 and the denominator is 16.   **72.** 139.36 ft²   **73.** 60.75 yd²
74. 100.48 in²   **75.** 157 m²   **76.** 20.5632 cm²
77. 0.077104 m²

Test: Chapter R, p. 55

1. [R.1a] $2 \cdot 2 \cdot 3 \cdot 5 \cdot 5$ **2.** [R.1b] 120   **3.** [R.2a] $\frac{21}{49}$
4. [R.2a] $\frac{33}{48}$ **5.** [R.2b] $\frac{2}{3}$ **6.** [R.2b] $\frac{37}{61}$ **7.** [R.2c] $\frac{5}{36}$
8. [R.2c] $\frac{11}{40}$ **9.** [R.2c] $\frac{67}{36}$ **10.** [R.2c] $\frac{5}{36}$
11. [R.3a] $\frac{678}{100}$ **12.** [R.3a] 1.895   **13.** [R.3b] 99.0187
14. [R.3b] 1796.58   **15.** [R.3b] 435.072   **16.** [R.3b] 1.6
17. [R.3b] $2.\overline{09}$ **18.** [R.3c] 234.7   **19.** [R.3c] 234.728
20. [R.4a] 0.007   **21.** [R.4b] $\frac{91}{100}$ **22.** [R.4d] 44%
23. [R.5b] 625   **24.** [R.5b] 1.44   **25.** [R.5c] 242
26. [R.5c] 20,000   **27.** [R.4d] 0.1014%   **28.** [R.4a] 0.0214
29. [R.6a, b] 32.82 cm; 65.894 cm²
30. [R.6a, b] 100 m; 625 m²   **31.** [R.6b] 25 cm²
32. [R.6b] 12 m²   **33.** [R.6d] 84 cm³   **34.** [R.6c] $\frac{1}{4}$ in.;
$\frac{11}{14}$ in.; $\frac{11}{224}$ in²   **35.** [R.6c] 9 cm; 56.52 cm; 254.34 cm²
36. [R.6b, c] 26.28 ft²

CHAPTER 1

Margin Exercises, Section 1.1, pp. 58–62

1. $14{,}410 + x = 15{,}300$; 890 ft   **2.** 64   **3.** 28   **4.** 60
5. 192 ft²   **6.** 25   **7.** 16   **8.** 12 hr   **9.** $x - 8$
10. $y + 8$, or $8 + y$ **11.** $m - 4$ **12.** $\frac{1}{2}p$
13. $6 + 8x$, or $8x + 6$ **14.** $a - b$
15. $59\%x$, or $0.59x$ **16.** $xy - 200$ **17.** $p + q$

Calculator Corner, p. 60

1. 56   **2.** 11.9   **3.** 1.8   **4.** 34,427.16   **5.** 20.1
6. 29.9

Exercise Set 1.1, p. 63

1. 32 min; 69 min; 81 min   **3.** 1935 m²   **5.** 260 mi
7. 24 ft²   **9.** 56   **11.** 8   **13.** 1   **15.** 6   **17.** 2
19. $b + 7$, or $7 + b$ **21.** $c - 12$ **23.** $q + 4$, or $4 + q$
25. $a + b$, or $b + a$ **27.** $x \div y$, or $\frac{x}{y}$, or x/y, or $x \cdot \frac{1}{y}$
29. $x + w$, or $w + x$ **31.** $n - m$ **33.** $x + y$, or $y + x$
35. $2z$ **37.** $3m$ **39.** $4a + 6$, or $6 + 4a$ **41.** $xy - 8$
43. $2t - 5$ **45.** $3n + 11$, or $11 + 3n$
47. $4x + 3y$, or $3y + 4x$
49. $89\%s$, or $0.89s$, where s is the salary   **51.** $s + 0.05s$
53. $65t$ miles   **55.** $\$50 - x$ **57.** $\mathbf{D_W}$ **59.** $2 \cdot 3 \cdot 3 \cdot 3$
60. $2 \cdot 2 \cdot 2 \cdot 2 \cdot 2$ **61.** $2 \cdot 2 \cdot 3 \cdot 3 \cdot 3$
62. $2 \cdot 2 \cdot 2 \cdot 2 \cdot 2 \cdot 3$ **63.** $3 \cdot 11 \cdot 31$ **64.** 18
65. 96   **66.** 60   **67.** 96   **68.** 396   **69.** $\frac{1}{4}$ **71.** 0

Margin Exercises, Section 1.2, pp. 68–74

1. 8; −5 **2.** 125; −50 **3.** −3 **4.** −10; 156
5. −120; 50; −80 **6.**

$$-\frac{7}{2}$$
number line from −6 to 6 with point at −7/2

7.
number line from −6 to 6 with point at −1.4

8.
$$\frac{11}{4}$$
number line from −6 to 6 with point at 11/4

9. −0.375

10. $-0.5\overline{4}$ **11.** $1.\overline{3}$ **12.** < **13.** < **14.** > **15.** >
16. > **17.** < **18.** < **19.** > **20.** 7 > −5
21. 4 < x **22.** False **23.** True **24.** True **25.** 8
26. 9 **27.** $\frac{2}{3}$ **28.** 5.6

Calculator Corner, p. 69

1. −0.75 **2.** −0.45 **3.** −0.125 **4.** −1.8 **5.** −0.675
6. −0.6875 **7.** −3.5 **8.** −0.76

Calculator Corner, p. 70

1. 8.717797887 **2.** 17.80449381 **3.** 67.08203932
4. 35.4807407 **5.** 3.141592654 **6.** 91.10618695
7. 530.9291585 **8.** 138.8663978

Calculator Corner, p. 73

1. 5 **2.** 17 **3.** 0 **4.** 6.48 **5.** 12.7 **6.** 0.9
7. $\frac{5}{7}$ **8.** $\frac{4}{3}$

Exercise Set 1.2, p. 75

1. −34,000,000 **3.** 24; −2 **5.** 950,000,000; −460
7. Alley Cats: −34; Strikers: 34
9.
$$\frac{10}{3}$$
number line from −6 to 6 with point at 10/3

11.
$$-5.2$$
number line from −6 to 6 with point at −5.2

13.
$$-4\frac{2}{5}$$
number line from −6 to 6 with point at −4 2/5

15. −0.875

17. $0.8\overline{3}$ **19.** $-1.1\overline{6}$ **21.** $0.\overline{6}$ **23.** 0.1 **25.** −0.5
27. 0.16 **29.** > **31.** < **33.** < **35.** < **37.** >
39. < **41.** > **43.** < **45.** < **47.** > **49.** <
51. < **53.** True **55.** False **57.** x < −6
59. y ≥ −10 **61.** 3 **63.** 10 **65.** 0 **67.** 30.4
69. $\frac{2}{3}$ **71.** 0 **73.** $3\frac{5}{8}$ **75.** **D**W **77.** 0.63
78. 0.238 **79.** 1.1 **80.** 0.2276 **81.** 52% **82.** 125%
83. $83.\overline{3}\%$, or $83\frac{1}{3}\%$ **84.** 59.375%, or $59\frac{3}{8}\%$

85. $-\frac{5}{6}, -\frac{3}{4}, -\frac{2}{3}, \frac{1}{6}, \frac{3}{8}, \frac{1}{2}$
87. −8.76, −5.16, −4.24, −2.13, 1.85, 5.23
89. $\frac{1}{9}$ **91.** $5\frac{5}{9}$, or $\frac{50}{9}$

Margin Exercises, Section 1.3, pp. 78–82

1. −3 **2.** −3 **3.** −5 **4.** 4 **5.** 0 **6.** −2 **7.** −11
8. −12 **9.** 2 **10.** −4 **11.** −2 **12.** 0 **13.** −22
14. 3 **15.** 0.53 **16.** 2.3 **17.** −7.7 **18.** −6.2
19. $-\frac{2}{9}$ **20.** $-\frac{19}{20}$ **21.** −58 **22.** −56 **23.** −14
24. −12 **25.** 4 **26.** −8.7 **27.** 7.74 **28.** $\frac{8}{9}$ **29.** 0
30. −12 **31.** −14; 14 **32.** −1; 1 **33.** 19; −19
34. 1.6; −1.6 **35.** $-\frac{2}{3}; \frac{2}{3}$ **36.** $\frac{9}{8}; -\frac{9}{8}$ **37.** 4
38. 13.4 **39.** 0 **40.** $-\frac{1}{4}$ **41.** −2 students

Exercise Set 1.3, p. 83

1. −7 **3.** −6 **5.** 0 **7.** −8 **9.** −7 **11.** −27
13. 0 **15.** −42 **17.** 0 **19.** 0 **21.** 3 **23.** −9
25. 7 **27.** 0 **29.** 35 **31.** −3.8 **33.** −8.1
35. $-\frac{1}{5}$ **37.** $-\frac{7}{9}$ **39.** $-\frac{3}{8}$ **41.** $-\frac{19}{24}$ **43.** $\frac{1}{24}$
45. $\frac{8}{15}$ **47.** $\frac{16}{45}$ **49.** 37 **51.** 50 **53.** −1409
55. −24 **57.** 26.9 **59.** −8 **61.** $\frac{13}{8}$ **63.** −43
65. $\frac{4}{3}$ **67.** 24 **69.** $\frac{3}{8}$ **71.** 13,796 ft **73.** −3°F
75. −$20,300 **77.** He owes $85. **79.** **D**W **81.** 0.713
82. 0.92875 **83.** 12.5% **84.** 40.625% **85.** $\frac{8}{5}$
86. $\frac{1}{4}$ **87.** All positive **89.** (b)

Margin Exercises, Section 1.4, pp. 86–88

1. −10 **2.** 3 **3.** −5 **4.** −1 **5.** 2 **6.** −4 **7.** −2
8. −11 **9.** 4 **10.** −2 **11.** −6 **12.** −16 **13.** 7.1
14. 3 **15.** 0 **16.** $\frac{3}{2}$ **17.** −8 **18.** 7 **19.** −3
20. −23.3 **21.** 0 **22.** −9 **23.** $-\frac{6}{5}$ **24.** 12.7
25. 214°F higher

Exercise Set 1.4, p. 89

1. −7 **3.** −6 **5.** 0 **7.** −4 **9.** −7 **11.** −6
13. 0 **15.** 14 **17.** 11 **19.** −14 **21.** 5 **23.** −1

25. 18 **27.** −3 **29.** −21 **31.** 5 **33.** −8 **35.** 12 **37.** −23 **39.** −68 **41.** −73 **43.** 116 **45.** 0 **47.** −1 **49.** $\frac{1}{12}$ **51.** $-\frac{17}{12}$ **53.** $\frac{1}{8}$ **55.** 19.9 **57.** −8.6 **59.** −0.01 **61.** −193 **63.** 500 **65.** −2.8 **67.** −3.53 **69.** $-\frac{1}{2}$ **71.** $\frac{6}{7}$ **73.** $-\frac{41}{30}$ **75.** $-\frac{2}{15}$ **77.** $-\frac{1}{48}$ **79.** $-\frac{43}{60}$ **81.** 37 **83.** −62 **85.** −139 **87.** 6 **89.** 108.5 **91.** $\frac{1}{4}$ **93.** 2319 m **95.** $347.94 **97.** (a) 77; (b) −41 **99.** 381 ft **101.** $\mathbf{D_W}$ **103.** 100.5 **104.** 226 **105.** 13 **106.** 50 **107.** $\frac{11}{12}$ **108.** $\frac{41}{64}$ **109.** False; $3 − 0 \neq 0 − 3$ **111.** True **113.** True

Margin Exercises, Section 1.5, pp. 93–96

1. 20; 10; 0; −10; −20; −30 **2.** −18 **3.** −100 **4.** −80 **5.** $-\frac{5}{9}$ **6.** −30.033 **7.** $-\frac{7}{10}$ **8.** −10; 0; 10; 20; 30 **9.** 27 **10.** 32 **11.** 35 **12.** $\frac{20}{63}$ **13.** $\frac{2}{3}$ **14.** 13.455 **15.** −30 **16.** 30 **17.** 0 **18.** $-\frac{8}{3}$ **19.** 0 **20.** 0 **21.** −30 **22.** −30.75 **23.** $-\frac{5}{3}$ **24.** 120 **25.** −120 **26.** 6 **27.** 4; −4 **28.** 9; −9 **29.** 48; 48 **30.** 55°C

Exercise Set 1.5, p. 97

1. −8 **3.** −48 **5.** −24 **7.** −72 **9.** 16 **11.** 42 **13.** −120 **15.** −238 **17.** 1200 **19.** 98 **21.** −72 **23.** −12.4 **25.** 30 **27.** 21.7 **29.** $-\frac{2}{5}$ **31.** $\frac{1}{12}$ **33.** −17.01 **35.** $-\frac{5}{12}$ **37.** 420 **39.** $\frac{2}{7}$ **41.** −60 **43.** 150 **45.** $-\frac{2}{45}$ **47.** 1911 **49.** 50.4 **51.** $\frac{10}{189}$ **53.** −960 **55.** 17.64 **57.** $-\frac{5}{784}$ **59.** 0 **61.** −720 **63.** −30,240 **65.** 1 **67.** 16, −16; 16, −16 **69.** 441; −147 **71.** 20; 20 **73.** −2; 2 **75.** −20 lb **77.** −54°C **79.** $12.71 **81.** −32 m **83.** $\mathbf{D_W}$ **85.** 180 **86.** $2 \cdot 2 \cdot 2 \cdot 2 \cdot 2 \cdot 2 \cdot 2 \cdot 2 \cdot 2 \cdot 3 \cdot 3$ **87.** $\frac{2}{3}$ **88.** $\frac{8}{9}$ **89.** $\frac{6}{11}$ **90.** $\frac{41}{265}$ **91.** $\frac{11}{32}$ **92.** $\frac{37}{67}$ **93.** $\frac{1}{24}$ **94.** 6 **95.** (a)

97.

Margin Exercises, Section 1.6, pp. 100–105

1. −2 **2.** 5 **3.** −3 **4.** 8 **5.** −6 **6.** $-\frac{30}{7}$ **7.** Not defined **8.** 0 **9.** $\frac{3}{2}$ **10.** $-\frac{4}{5}$ **11.** $-\frac{1}{3}$ **12.** −5 **13.** $\frac{1}{1.6}$ **14.** $\frac{2}{3}$

15.

NUMBER	OPPOSITE	RECIPROCAL
$\frac{2}{3}$	$-\frac{2}{3}$	$\frac{3}{2}$
$-\frac{5}{4}$	$\frac{5}{4}$	$-\frac{4}{5}$
0	0	Not defined
1	−1	1
−8	8	$-\frac{1}{8}$
−4.5	4.5	$-\frac{1}{4.5}$

16. $\frac{4}{7} \cdot \left(-\frac{5}{3}\right)$ **17.** $5 \cdot \left(-\frac{1}{8}\right)$ **18.** $(a − b) \cdot \left(\frac{1}{7}\right)$ **19.** $-23 \cdot a$ **20.** $-5 \cdot \left(\frac{1}{7}\right)$ **21.** $-\frac{20}{21}$ **22.** $-\frac{12}{5}$ **23.** $\frac{16}{7}$ **24.** −7 **25.** $\frac{5}{-6}, -\frac{5}{6}$ **26.** $\frac{-8}{7}, \frac{8}{-7}$ **27.** $\frac{-10}{3}, -\frac{10}{3}$ **28.** −3.4°F per minute

Calculator Corner, p. 105

1. −4 **2.** −0.3 **3.** −12 **4.** −9.5 **5.** −12 **6.** 2.7 **7.** −2 **8.** −5.7 **9.** −32 **10.** −1.8 **11.** 35 **12.** 14.44 **13.** −2 **14.** −0.8 **15.** 1.4 **16.** 4

Exercise Set 1.6, p. 106

1. −8 **3.** −14 **5.** −3 **7.** 3 **9.** −8 **11.** 2 **13.** −12 **15.** −8 **17.** Not defined **19.** 0 **21.** $\frac{7}{15}$ **23.** $-\frac{13}{47}$ **25.** $\frac{1}{13}$ **27.** $\frac{1}{4.3}$ **29.** −7.1 **31.** $\frac{q}{p}$ **33.** $4y$ **35.** $\frac{3b}{2a}$ **37.** $4 \cdot \left(\frac{1}{17}\right)$ **39.** $8 \cdot \left(-\frac{1}{13}\right)$ **41.** $13.9 \cdot \left(-\frac{1}{1.5}\right)$ **43.** $x \cdot y$ **45.** $(3x + 4)\left(\frac{1}{5}\right)$

47. $(5a - b)\left(\dfrac{1}{5a + b}\right)$ **49.** $-\dfrac{9}{8}$ **51.** $\dfrac{5}{3}$ **53.** $\dfrac{9}{14}$

55. $\dfrac{9}{64}$ **57.** -2 **59.** $\dfrac{11}{13}$ **61.** -16.2 **63.** Not defined

65. 44.3% **67.** -5.1% **69.** $\mathbf{D_W}$ **71.** 33 **72.** 129

73. 1 **74.** 1296 **75.** $\dfrac{22}{39}$ **76.** 0.477 **77.** 87.5%

78. $\dfrac{2}{3}$ **79.** $\dfrac{9}{8}$ **80.** $\dfrac{128}{625}$ **81.** $\dfrac{1}{-10.5}$; -10.5, the
reciprocal of the reciprocal is the original number
83. Negative **85.** Positive **87.** Negative

Margin Exercises, Section 1.7, pp. 109–117

1.

Value	$x + x$	$2x$
$x = 3$	6	6
$x = -6$	-12	-12
$x = 4.8$	9.6	9.6

2.

Value	$x + 3x$	$5x$
$x = 2$	8	10
$x = -6$	-24	-30
$x = 4.8$	19.2	24

3. $\dfrac{6}{8}$ **4.** $\dfrac{3t}{4t}$ **5.** $\dfrac{3}{4}$ **6.** $-\dfrac{4}{3}$ **7.** $\dfrac{x}{8}$ **8.** $\dfrac{3}{4q}$ **9.** 1; 1

10. $-10; -10$ **11.** $9 + x$ **12.** qp
13. $t + xy$, or $yx + t$, or $t + yx$ **14.** 19; 19 **15.** 150; 150
16. $(r + s) + 7$ **17.** $(9a)b$
18. $(4t)u$, $(tu)4$, $t(4u)$; answers may vary
19. $(2 + r) + s$, $(r + s) + 2$, $s + (r + 2)$; answers may vary
20. (a) 63; **(b)** 63 **21. (a)** 80; **(b)** 80 **22. (a)** 28; **(b)** 28
23. (a) 8; **(b)** 8 **24. (a)** -4; **(b)** -4 **25. (a)** -25; **(b)** -25
26. $5x, -8y, 3$ **27.** $-4y, -2x, 3z$ **28.** $3x - 15$
29. $5x + 5$ **30.** $\dfrac{3}{5}p + \dfrac{3}{5}q - \dfrac{3}{5}t$ **31.** $-2x + 6$
32. $5x - 10y + 20z$ **33.** $-5x + 10y - 20z$
34. Associative law of multiplication
35. Identity property of 1
36. Commutative law of addition
37. Distributive law of multiplication over addition
38. Identity property of 0
39. Commutative law of multiplication
40. Associative law of addition
41. $6(x - 2)$ **42.** $3(x - 2y + 3)$ **43.** $b(x + y - z)$
44. $2(8a - 18b + 21)$ **45.** $\dfrac{1}{8}(3x - 5y + 7)$
46. $-4(3x - 8y + 4z)$ **47.** $3x$ **48.** $6x$ **49.** $-8x$
50. $0.59x$ **51.** $3x + 3y$ **52.** $-4x - 5y - 7$
53. $-\dfrac{2}{3} + \dfrac{1}{10}x + \dfrac{7}{9}y$

Exercise Set 1.7, p. 118

1. $\dfrac{3y}{5y}$ **3.** $\dfrac{10x}{15x}$ **5.** $\dfrac{2x}{x^2}$ **7.** $-\dfrac{3}{2}$ **9.** $-\dfrac{7}{6}$ **11.** $\dfrac{4s}{3}$
13. $8 + y$ **15.** nm **17.** $xy + 9$, or $9 + yx$
19. $c + ab$, or $ba + c$ **21.** $(a + b) + 2$ **23.** $8(xy)$
25. $a + (b + 3)$ **27.** $(3a)b$
29. $2 + (b + a), (2 + a) + b, (b + 2) + a$;
answers may vary **31.** $(5 + w) + v; (v + 5) + w$;
$(w + v) + 5$; answers may vary
33. $(3x)y, y(x \cdot 3), 3(yx)$; answers may vary
35. $a(7b), b(7a), (7b)a$; answers may vary **37.** $2b + 10$
39. $7 + 7t$ **41.** $30x + 12$ **43.** $7x + 28 + 42y$
45. $7x - 21$ **47.** $-3x + 21$ **49.** $\dfrac{2}{3}b - 4$
51. $7.3x - 14.6$ **53.** $-\dfrac{3}{5}x + \dfrac{3}{5}y - 6$
55. $45x + 54y - 72$ **57.** $-4x + 12y + 8z$
59. $-3.72x + 9.92y - 3.41$ **61.** $4x, 3z$ **63.** $7x, 8y, -9z$
65. $2(x + 2)$ **67.** $5(6 + y)$ **69.** $7(2x + 3y)$
71. $5(x + 2 + 3y)$ **73.** $8(x - 3)$
75. $4(-y + 8)$, or $-4(y - 8)$ **77.** $2(4x + 5y - 11)$
79. $a(x - 1)$ **81.** $a(x - y - z)$
83. $6(-3x + 2y + 1)$, or $-6(3x - 2y - 1)$
85. $\dfrac{1}{3}(2x - 5y + 1)$ **87.** $19a$ **89.** $9a$ **91.** $8x + 9z$
93. $7x + 15y^2$ **95.** $-19a + 88$ **97.** $4t + 6y - 4$
99. b **101.** $\dfrac{13}{4}y$ **103.** $8x$ **105.** $5n$ **107.** $-16y$
109. $17a - 12b - 1$ **111.** $4x + 2y$ **113.** $7x + y$
115. $0.8x + 0.5y$ **117.** $\dfrac{35}{6}a + \dfrac{3}{2}b - 42$ **119.** $\mathbf{D_W}$
121. 144 **122.** 72 **123.** 144 **124.** 60 **125.** 32
126. 72 **127.** 90 **128.** 108 **129.** $\dfrac{89}{48}$ **130.** $\dfrac{5}{24}$
131. $-\dfrac{5}{24}$ **132.** 30% **133.** Not equivalent;
$3 \cdot 2 + 5 \neq 3 \cdot 5 + 2$ **135.** Equivalent; commutative law
of addition **137.** $q(1 + r + rs + rst)$

Margin Exercises, Section 1.8, pp. 122–127

1. $-x - 2$ **2.** $-5x - 2y - 8$ **3.** $-6 + t$ **4.** $-x + y$
5. $4a - 3t + 10$ **6.** $-18 + m + 2n - 4z$ **7.** $2x - 9$
8. $3y + 2$ **9.** $2x - 7$ **10.** $3y + 3$ **11.** $-2a + 8b - 3c$
12. $-9x - 8y$ **13.** $-16a + 18$ **14.** $-26a + 41b - 48c$
15. $3x - 7$ **16.** $-18.6x - 19y$ **17.** 2 **18.** 18 **19.** 6
20. 17 **21.** $5x - y - 8$ **22.** -1237 **23.** 8 **24.** 4
25. 317 **26.** -12

Calculator Corner, p. 126

1. -11 **2.** 9 **3.** 114 **4.** 117,649 **5.** $-1{,}419{,}857$
6. $-1{,}124{,}864$ **7.** $-117{,}649$ **8.** $-1{,}419{,}857$
9. $-1{,}124{,}864$ **10.** -4 **11.** -2 **12.** 787

Exercise Set 1.8, p. 128

1. $-2x - 7$ **3.** $-8 + x$ **5.** $-4a + 3b - 7c$
7. $-6x + 8y - 5$ **9.** $-3x + 5y + 6$ **11.** $8x + 6y + 43$
13. $5x - 3$ **15.** $-3a + 9$ **17.** $5x - 6$ **19.** $-19x + 2y$
21. $9y - 25z$ **23.** $-7x + 10y$ **25.** $37a - 23b + 35c$
27. 7   **29.** -40 **31.** 19   **33.** $12x + 30$ **35.** $3x + 30$
37. $9x - 18$ **39.** $-4x - 64$ **41.** -7 **43.** -7
45. -16 **47.** -334 **49.** 14   **51.** 1880   **53.** 12
55. 8   **57.** -86 **59.** 37   **61.** -1 **63.** -10
65. -67 **67.** -7988 **69.** -3000 **71.** 60   **73.** 1
75. 10   **77.** $-\dfrac{13}{45}$ **79.** $-\dfrac{23}{18}$ **81.** -122 **83.** $\mathbf{D_W}$
85. Integers   **86.** Additive inverses
87. Commutative law   **88.** Identity property of 1
89. Associative law   **90.** Associative law
91. Multiplicative inverses   **92.** Identity property of 0
93. $6y - (-2x + 3a - c)$ **95.** $6m - (-3n + 5m - 4b)$
97. $-2x - f$ **99.** (a) 52; 52; 28.130169; (b) -24; -24;
-108.307025 **101.** -6

Concept Reinforcement, p. 132

1. True   **2.** True   **3.** False   **4.** True   **5.** False
6. True   **7.** False

Summary and Review: Chapter 1, p. 132

1. 4   **2.** $19\% x$, or $0.19x$ **3.** $-45, 72$ **4.** 38
5.
6.
7. $<$ **8.** $>$
9. $>$ **10.** $<$ **11.** -3.8 **12.** $\dfrac{3}{4}$ **13.** $\dfrac{8}{3}$ **14.** $-\dfrac{1}{7}$
15. 34   **16.** 5   **17.** -3 **18.** -4 **19.** -5 **20.** 1
21. $-\dfrac{7}{5}$ **22.** -7.9 **23.** 54   **24.** -9.18 **25.** $-\dfrac{2}{7}$
26. -210 **27.** -7 **28.** -3 **29.** $\dfrac{3}{4}$ **30.** 40.4
31. -2 **32.** 2   **33.** -9 **34.** 8-yd gain   **35.** $-\$130$
36. $\$4.64$ **37.** $\$18.95$ **38.** $15x - 35$ **39.** $-8x + 10$
40. $4x + 15$ **41.** $-24 + 48x$ **42.** $2(x - 7)$
43. $6(-x + 1)$, or $-6(x - 1)$ **44.** $5(x + 2)$
45. $3(-x + 4y - 4)$, or $-3(x - 4y + 4)$ **46.** $7a - 3b$
47. $-2x + 5y$ **48.** $5x - y$ **49.** $-a + 8b$ **50.** $-3a + 9$
51. $-2b + 21$ **52.** 6   **53.** $12y - 34$ **54.** $5x + 24$
55. $-15x + 25$ **56.** True   **57.** False   **58.** $x > -3$
59. $\mathbf{D_W}$ If the sum of two numbers is 0, they are
opposites, or additive inverses of each other. For every
real number a, the opposite of a can be named $-a$, and
$a + (-a) = (-a) + a = 0$.   **60.** $\mathbf{D_W}$ No; $|0| = 0$, and 0
is not positive.   **61.** $-\dfrac{5}{8}$ **62.** -2.1 **63.** 1000
64. $4a + 2b$

Test: Chapter 1, p. 135

1. [1.1a] 6   **2.** [1.1b] $x - 9$ **3.** [1.1a] 240 ft^2
4. [1.2d] $<$ **5.** [1.2d] $>$ **6.** [1.2d] $>$ **7.** [1.2d] $<$
8. [1.2e] 7   **9.** [1.2e] $\dfrac{9}{4}$ **10.** [1.2e] 2.7   **11.** [1.3b] $-\dfrac{2}{3}$
12. [1.3b] 1.4   **13.** [1.3b] 8   **14.** [1.6b] $-\dfrac{1}{2}$
15. [1.6b] $\dfrac{7}{4}$ **16.** [1.4a] 7.8   **17.** [1.3a] -8
18. [1.3a] $\dfrac{7}{40}$ **19.** [1.4a] 10   **20.** [1.4a] -2.5
21. [1.4a] $\dfrac{7}{8}$ **22.** [1.5a] -48 **23.** [1.5a] $\dfrac{3}{16}$
24. [1.6a] -9 **25.** [1.6c] $\dfrac{3}{4}$ **26.** [1.6c] -9.728
27. [1.8d] -173 **28.** [1.8d] -5 **29.** [1.4b] 14°F
30. [1.3c], [1.4b] Up 15 points   **31.** [1.5b] 16,080
32. [1.6d] $\dfrac{33}{35}$°C per minute   **33.** [1.7c] $18 - 3x$
34. [1.7c] $-5y + 5$ **35.** [1.7d] $2(6 - 11x)$
36. [1.7d] $7(x + 3 + 2y)$ **37.** [1.4a] 12
38. [1.8b] $2x + 7$ **39.** [1.8b] $9a - 12b - 7$
40. [1.8c] $68y - 8$ **41.** [1.8d] -4 **42.** [1.8d] 448
43. [1.2d] $-2 \geq x$ **44.** [1.2e], [1.8d] 15
45. [1.8c] $4a$ **46.** [R.6a], [1.7e] $4x + 4y$

CHAPTER 2

Margin Exercises, Section 2.1, pp. 138–141

1. False   **2.** True   **3.** Neither   **4.** Yes   **5.** No
6. No   **7.** Yes   **8.** 9   **9.** -13 **10.** 22   **11.** 13.2
12. -6.5 **13.** -2 **14.** $\dfrac{31}{8}$

Exercise Set 2.1, p. 142

1. Yes   **3.** No   **5.** No   **7.** Yes   **9.** No   **11.** No
13. 4   **15.** -20 **17.** -14 **19.** -18 **21.** 15
23. -14 **25.** 2   **27.** 20   **29.** -6 **31.** $6\frac{1}{2}$ **33.** 19.9
35. $\frac{7}{3}$ **37.** $-\frac{7}{4}$ **39.** $\frac{41}{24}$ **41.** $-\frac{1}{20}$ **43.** 5.1   **45.** 12.4
47. -5 **49.** $1\frac{5}{6}$ **51.** $-\frac{10}{21}$ **53.** $\mathbf{D_W}$ **55.** -11 **56.** 5
57. $-\frac{5}{12}$ **58.** $\frac{1}{3}$ **59.** $-\frac{3}{2}$ **60.** -5.2 **61.** $-\frac{1}{24}$
62. 172.72   **63.** $\$83 - x$ **64.** $65t$ miles   **65.** 342.246
67. $-\frac{26}{15}$ **69.** -10 **71.** All real numbers   **73.** $-\frac{5}{17}$
75. $13, -13$

Margin Exercises, Section 2.2, pp. 144–147

1. 15   **2.** $-\frac{7}{4}$ **3.** -18 **4.** 10   **5.** 10   **6.** $-\frac{4}{5}$
7. 7800   **8.** -3 **9.** 28

Exercise Set 2.2, p. 148

1. 6   **3.** 9   **5.** 12   **7.** -40 **9.** 1   **11.** -7 **13.** -6
15. 6   **17.** -63 **19.** 36   **21.** -21 **23.** $-\frac{3}{5}$ **25.** $-\frac{3}{2}$

27. $\frac{9}{2}$ **29.** 7 **31.** -7 **33.** 8 **35.** 15.9 **37.** -50
39. -14 **41.** D_W **43.** $7x$ **44.** $-x + 5$ **45.** $8x + 11$
46. $-32y$ **47.** $x - 4$ **48.** $-5x - 23$ **49.** $-10y - 42$
50. $-22a + 4$ **51.** $8r$ miles **52.** $\frac{1}{2}b \cdot 10 \text{ m}^2$, or $5b \text{ m}^2$
53. -8655 **55.** No solution **57.** No solution
59. $\frac{b}{3a}$ **61.** $\frac{4b}{a}$

Margin Exercises, Section 2.3, pp. 150–156

1. 5 **2.** 4 **3.** 4 **4.** 39 **5.** $-\frac{3}{2}$ **6.** -4.3 **7.** -3
8. 800 **9.** 1 **10.** 2 **11.** 2 **12.** $\frac{17}{2}$ **13.** $\frac{8}{3}$
14. $-\frac{43}{10}$, or -4.3 **15.** 2 **16.** 3 **17.** -2 **18.** $-\frac{1}{2}$
19. Yes **20.** Yes **21.** Yes **22.** Yes **23.** No
24. No **25.** No **26.** No **27.** All real numbers
28. No solution

Calculator Corner, p. 157

1. Left to the student **2.** Left to the student

Exercise Set 2.3, p. 158

1. 5 **3.** 8 **5.** 10 **7.** 14 **9.** -8 **11.** -8 **13.** -7
15. $\frac{2}{3}$ **17.** 6 **19.** 4 **21.** 6 **23.** -3 **25.** 1
27. 6 **29.** -20 **31.** 7 **33.** 2 **35.** 5 **37.** 2
39. 10 **41.** 4 **43.** 0 **45.** -1 **47.** $-\frac{4}{3}$ **49.** $\frac{2}{5}$
51. -2 **53.** -4 **55.** $\frac{4}{5}$ **57.** $-\frac{28}{27}$ **59.** 6 **61.** 2
63. No solution **65.** All real numbers **67.** 6 **69.** 8
71. 1 **73.** All real numbers **75.** No solution
77. 17 **79.** $-\frac{5}{3}$ **81.** -3 **83.** 2 **85.** $\frac{4}{7}$
87. No solution **89.** All real numbers **91.** $-\frac{51}{31}$
93. D_W **95.** -6.5 **96.** -75.14 **97.** $7(x - 3 - 2y)$
98. $8(y - 11x + 1)$ **99.** -160 **100.** $-17x + 18$
101. $91x - 242$ **102.** 0.25 **103.** $-\frac{5}{32}$ **105.** $\frac{52}{45}$

Margin Exercises, Section 2.4, pp. 162–165

1. 2.8 mi **2.** 280,865 socks **3.** 341 mi **4.** $q = 3B$
5. $r = \frac{d}{t}$ **6.** $I = \frac{E}{R}$ **7.** $x = y - 5$ **8.** $x = y + 7$
9. $x = y + b$ **10.** $y = \frac{5x}{9}$, or $\frac{5}{9}x$ **11.** $p = \frac{bq}{a}$
12. $x = \frac{y - b}{m}$ **13.** $Q = \frac{a + p}{t}$ **14.** $D = \frac{C}{\pi}$
15. $c = 4A - a - b - d$

Exercise Set 2.4, p. 166

1. (a) 57,000 Btu's; (b) $a = \dfrac{B}{30}$ **3.** (a) $1\frac{3}{5}$ mi; (b) $t = 5M$
5. (a) 1423 students; (b) $n = 15f$
7. 10.5 calories per ounce **9.** 42 games **11.** $x = \dfrac{y}{5}$
13. $c = \dfrac{a}{b}$ **15.** $x = y - 13$ **17.** $x = y - b$

19. $x = 5 - y$ **21.** $x = a - y$ **23.** $y = \dfrac{5x}{8}$, or $\dfrac{5}{8}x$
25. $x = \dfrac{By}{A}$ **27.** $t = \dfrac{W - b}{m}$ **29.** $x = \dfrac{y - c}{b}$
31. $b = 3A - a - c$ **33.** $t = \dfrac{A - b}{a}$ **35.** $h = \dfrac{A}{b}$
37. $w = \dfrac{P - 2l}{2}$, or $\dfrac{1}{2}P - l$ **39.** $a = 2A - b$
41. $a = \dfrac{F}{m}$ **43.** $c^2 = \dfrac{E}{m}$ **45.** $x = \dfrac{c - By}{A}$ **47.** $t = \dfrac{3k}{v}$
49. D_W **51.** 0.92 **52.** -90 **53.** -9.325 **54.** 44
55. -13.2 **56.** $-21a + 12b$ **57.** 0.031 **58.** 0.671
59. $\frac{1}{6}$ **60.** $-\frac{3}{2}$
61. (a) 1901 calories;

(b) $a = \dfrac{917 + 6w + 6h - K}{6}$;

$h = \dfrac{K - 917 - 6w + 6a}{6}$;

$w = \dfrac{K - 917 - 6h + 6a}{6}$

63. $b = \dfrac{Ha - 2}{H}$, or $a - \dfrac{2}{H}$; $a = \dfrac{2 + Hb}{H}$, or $\dfrac{2}{H} + b$
65. A quadruples. **67.** A increases by $2h$ units.

Margin Exercises, Section 2.5, pp. 170–173

1. $13\% \cdot 80 = a$ **2.** $a = 60\% \cdot 70$ **3.** $43 = 20\% \cdot b$
4. $110\% \cdot b = 30$ **5.** $16 = n \cdot 80$ **6.** $n \cdot 94 = 10.5$
7. 1.92 **8.** 115 **9.** 36% **10.** 111,416 mi^2
11. About 1.2 million **12.** About 58%

Exercise Set 2.5, p. 174

1. 20% **3.** 150 **5.** 546 **7.** 24% **9.** 2.5 **11.** 5%
13. 25% **15.** 84 **17.** 24% **19.** 16% **21.** $46\frac{2}{3}$
23. 0.8 **25.** 5 **27.** 40 **29.** $198 **31.** $1584
33. $528 **35.** Japan: 44.3%; Germany: 24.9%
37. About 603 at-bats **39.** $195 **41.** (a) 16%; (b) $29
43. (a) $3.75; (b) $28.75 **45.** (a) $28.80; (b) $33.12
47. 200 women **49.** About 31.5 lb **51.** $655; 196%
53. $2190; $1455 **55.** $3935; 261% **57.** D_W
59. 181.52 **60.** 0.4538 **61.** 12.0879 **62.** 844.1407
63. $a + c$ **64.** $7x - 9y$ **65.** -3.9 **66.** $-6\frac{1}{8}$
67. Division; subtraction **68.** Exponential; division;
subtraction **69.** 6 ft 7 in.

Margin Exercises, Section 2.6, pp. 179–188

1. $62\frac{2}{3}$ mi **2.** Jenny: 8 in.; Emma: 4 in.; Sarah: 6 in.
3. 313 and 314 **4.** 60,417 copies
5. Length: 84 ft; width: 50 ft **6.** First: 30°; second: 90°;
third: 60° **7.** Second: 80; third: 89 **8.** $8400 **9.** $658

Translating for Success, p. 189

1. B **2.** H **3.** G **4.** N **5.** J **6.** C **7.** L **8.** E
9. F **10.** D

Exercise Set 2.6, p. 190

1. 180 in.; 60 in.　**3.** $4.29　**5.** $6.3 billion　**7.** $699\frac{1}{3}$ mi
9. 1204 and 1205　**11.** 41, 42, 43　**13.** 61, 63, 65
15. Length: 48 ft; width: 14 ft　**17.** $75　**19.** $85
21. 11 visits　**23.** 28°, 84°, 68°　**25.** 33°, 38°, 109°
27. $350　**29.** $852.94　**31.** 12 mi　**33.** $36
35. $25 and $50　**37.** D_W　**39.** $-\frac{47}{40}$　**40.** $-\frac{17}{40}$
41. $-\frac{3}{10}$　**42.** $-\frac{32}{15}$　**43.** -10　**44.** 1.6　**45.** 409.6
46. -9.6　**47.** -41.6　**48.** 0.1　**49.** 120 apples
51. About 0.65 in.　**53.** $9.17, not $9.10

Margin Exercises, Section 2.7, pp. 195–202

1. (a) No; (b) no; (c) no; (d) yes; (e) no; (f) no
2. (a) Yes; (b) yes; (c) yes; (d) no; (e) yes; (f) yes
3. $x \le 4$
4. $x > -2$
5. $-2 < x \le 4$
6. $\{x \mid x > 2\}$;
7. $\{x \mid x \le 3\}$;
8. $\{x \mid x < -3\}$;
9. $\{x \mid x \ge \frac{2}{15}\}$　**10.** $\{y \mid y \le -3\}$
11. $\{x \mid x < 8\}$;
12. $\{y \mid y \ge 32\}$;
13. $\{x \mid x \ge -6\}$　**14.** $\{y \mid y < -\frac{13}{5}\}$
15. $\{x \mid x > -\frac{1}{4}\}$　**16.** $\{y \mid y \ge \frac{19}{9}\}$　**17.** $\{y \mid y \ge \frac{19}{9}\}$
18. $\{x \mid x \ge -2\}$　**19.** $\{x \mid x \ge -4\}$　**20.** $\{x \mid x > \frac{8}{3}\}$

Exercise Set 2.7, p. 203

1. (a) Yes; (b) yes; (c) no; (d) yes; (e) yes
3. (a) No; (b) no; (c) no; (d) yes; (e) no
5. $x > 4$
7. $t < -3$
9. $m \ge -1$
11. $-3 < x \le 4$
13. $0 < x < 3$
15. $\{x \mid x > -5\}$;
17. $\{x \mid x \le -18\}$;
19. $\{y \mid y > -5\}$
21. $\{x \mid x > 2\}$　**23.** $\{x \mid x \le -3\}$　**25.** $\{x \mid x < 4\}$
27. $\{t \mid t > 14\}$　**29.** $\{y \mid y \le \frac{1}{4}\}$　**31.** $\{x \mid x > \frac{7}{12}\}$
33. $\{x \mid x < 7\}$;
35. $\{x \mid x < 3\}$;
37. $\{y \mid y \ge -\frac{2}{5}\}$　**39.** $\{x \mid x \ge -6\}$　**41.** $\{y \mid y \le 4\}$
43. $\{x \mid x > \frac{17}{3}\}$　**45.** $\{y \mid y < -\frac{1}{14}\}$　**47.** $\{x \mid x \le \frac{3}{10}\}$
49. $\{x \mid x < 8\}$　**51.** $\{x \mid x \le 6\}$　**53.** $\{x \mid x < -3\}$
55. $\{x \mid x > -3\}$　**57.** $\{x \mid x \le 7\}$　**59.** $\{x \mid x > -10\}$

---

61. $\{y \mid y < 2\}$　**63.** $\{y \mid y \ge 3\}$　**65.** $\{y \mid y > -2\}$
67. $\{x \mid x > -4\}$　**69.** $\{x \mid x \le 9\}$　**71.** $\{y \mid y \le -3\}$
73. $\{y \mid y < 6\}$　**75.** $\{m \mid m \ge 6\}$　**77.** $\{t \mid t < -\frac{5}{3}\}$
79. $\{r \mid r > -3\}$　**81.** $\{x \mid x \ge -\frac{57}{34}\}$　**83.** $\{x \mid x > -2\}$
85. D_W　**87.** -74　**88.** 4.8　**89.** $-\frac{5}{8}$　**90.** -1.11
91. -38　**92.** $-\frac{7}{8}$　**93.** -9.4　**94.** 1.11　**95.** 140
96. 41　**97.** $-2x - 23$　**98.** $37x - 1$　**99.** (a) Yes;
(b) yes; (c) no; (d) no; (e) no; (f) yes; (g) yes
101. No solution

Margin Exercises, Section 2.8, pp. 207–209

1. $m \ge 92$　**2.** $c \ge 4000$　**3.** $p \le 21{,}900$
4. $45 < t < 55$　**5.** $d > 15$　**6.** $w < 110$　**7.** $n > -2$
8. $c \le 12{,}500$　**9.** $d \le 11.4\%$　**10.** $s \ge 23$
11. $\frac{9}{5}C + 32 < 88; \{C \mid C < 31\frac{1}{9}°\}$
12. $\dfrac{91 + 86 + 89 + s}{4} \ge 90; \{s \mid s \ge 94\}$

Exercise Set 2.8, p. 210

1. $n \ge 7$　**3.** $w > 2$ kg　**5.** 90 mph $< s <$ 110 mph
7. $a \le 1{,}200{,}000$　**9.** $c \ge \$1.50$　**11.** $x > 8$　**13.** $y \le -4$
15. $n \ge 1300$　**17.** $A \le 500$ L　**19.** $3x + 2 < 13$
21. $\{x \mid x \ge 84\}$　**23.** $\{C \mid C < 1063°\}$　**25.** $\{Y \mid Y \ge 1935\}$
27. $\{L \mid L \ge 5$ in.$\}$　**29.** 15 or fewer copies　**31.** 5 min or
more　**33.** 2 courses　**35.** 4 servings or more
37. Lengths greater than or equal to 92 ft; lengths less than
or equal to 92 ft　**39.** Lengths less than 21.5 cm
41. The blue-book value is greater than or equal to $10,625.
43. It has at least 16 g of fat.　**45.** Dates at least 6 weeks
after July 1　**47.** Heights greater than or equal to 4 ft
49. 21 calls or more　**51.** D_W　**53.** Even　**54.** Odd
55. Additive　**56.** Multiplicative　**57.** Equivalent
58. Addition principle　**59.** Multiplication principle;
is reversed　**60.** Solution
61. Temperatures between $-15°$C and $-9\frac{4}{9}°$C
63. They contain at least 7.5 g of fat per serving.

Concept Reinforcement, p. 215

1. True　**2.** True　**3.** True　**4.** False　**5.** True
6. False

Summary and Review: Chapter 2, p. 215

1. -22　**2.** 1　**3.** 25　**4.** 9.99　**5.** $\frac{1}{4}$　**6.** 7　**7.** -192
8. $-\frac{7}{3}$　**9.** $-\frac{15}{64}$　**10.** -8　**11.** 4　**12.** -5　**13.** $-\frac{1}{3}$
14. 3　**15.** 4　**16.** 16　**17.** All real numbers　**18.** 6
19. -3　**20.** 28　**21.** 4　**22.** No solution　**23.** Yes
24. No　**25.** Yes　**26.** $\{y \mid y \ge -\frac{1}{2}\}$　**27.** $\{x \mid x \ge 7\}$
28. $\{y \mid y > 2\}$　**29.** $\{y \mid y \le -4\}$　**30.** $\{x \mid x < -11\}$
31. $\{y \mid y > -7\}$　**32.** $\{x \mid x > -\frac{9}{11}\}$　**33.** $\{x \mid x \ge -\frac{1}{12}\}$
34. $x < 3$
35. $-2 < x \le 5$

36.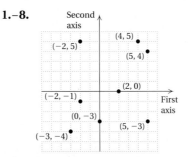

37. $d = \dfrac{C}{\pi}$ **38.** $B = \dfrac{3V}{h}$

39. $a = 2A - b$ **40.** $x = \dfrac{y - b}{m}$ **41.** Length: 365 mi;
width: 275 mi   **42.** 345, 346   **43.** $2117
44. 27 appliances   **45.** $35°, 85°, 60°$ **46.** 15
47. 18.75%   **48.** 600   **49.** About 26%   **50.** $220
51. $53,400   **52.** $138.95   **53.** 86   **54.** $\{w \mid w > 17 \text{ cm}\}$
55. **D$_W$** The end result is the same either way. If s is the original salary, the new salary after a 5% raise followed by an 8% raise is $1.08(1.05s)$. If the raises occur the other way around, the new salary is $1.05(1.08s)$. By the commutative and associative laws of multiplication, we see that these are equal. However, it would be better to receive the 8% raise first, because this increase yields a higher salary initially than a 5% raise.   **56.** **D$_W$** The inequalities are equivalent by the multiplication principle for inequalities. If we multiply both sides of one inequality by -1, the other inequality results.   **57.** $23, -23$ **58.** $20, -20$
59. $a = \dfrac{y - 3}{2 - b}$

Test: Chapter 2, p. 218

1. [2.1b] 8   **2.** [2.1b] 26   **3.** [2.2a] -6 **4.** [2.2a] 49
5. [2.3b] -12 **6.** [2.3a] 2   **7.** [2.3a] -8 **8.** [2.1b] $-\frac{7}{20}$
9. [2.3c] 7   **10.** [2.3c] $\frac{5}{3}$ **11.** [2.3b] $\frac{5}{2}$
12. [2.3c] No solution   **13.** [2.3c] All real numbers
14. [2.7c] $\{x \mid x \le -4\}$ **15.** [2.7c] $\{x \mid x > -13\}$
16. [2.7d] $\{x \mid x \le 5\}$ **17.** [2.7d] $\{y \mid y \le -13\}$
18. [2.7d] $\{y \mid y \ge 8\}$ **19.** [2.7d] $\left\{x \mid x \le -\frac{1}{20}\right\}$
20. [2.7e] $\{x \mid x < -6\}$ **21.** [2.7e] $\{x \mid x \le -1\}$
22. [2.7b]   **23.** [2.7b, e]

24. [2.7b]   **25.** [2.5a] 18

26. [2.5a] 16.5%   **27.** [2.5a] 40,000
28. [2.5a] About 53.4%   **29.** [2.6a] Width: 7 cm; length: 11 cm   **30.** [2.5a] About $240.7 billion
31. [2.6a] 2509, 2510, 2511   **32.** [2.6a] $880
33. [2.6a] 3 m, 5 m   **34.** [2.8b] $\{l \mid l \ge 174 \text{ yd}\}$
35. [2.8b] $\{b \mid b \le \$105\}$ **36.** [2.8a] $\{c \mid c \le 143{,}750\}$
37. [2.4b] $r = \dfrac{A}{2\pi h}$ **38.** [2.4b] $x = \dfrac{y - b}{8}$
39. [2.4b] $d = \dfrac{1 - ca}{-c}$, or $\dfrac{ca - 1}{c}$
40. [1.2e], [2.3a] $15, -15$ **41.** [2.6a] 60 tickets

Cumulative Review: Chapters 1–2, p. 220

1. [1.1a] $\frac{3}{2}$ **2.** [1.1a] $\frac{15}{4}$ **3.** [1.1a] 0   **4.** [1.1b] $2w - 4$
5. [1.2d] $>$ **6.** [1.2d] $>$ **7.** [1.2d] $<$
8. [1.3b], [1.6b] $-\frac{2}{5}, \frac{5}{2}$ **9.** [1.2e] 3   **10.** [1.2e] $\frac{3}{4}$
11. [1.2e] 0   **12.** [1.3a] -4.4

13. [1.4a] $-\frac{5}{2}$ **14.** [1.5a] $\frac{5}{6}$ **15.** [1.5a] -105
16. [1.6a] -9 **17.** [1.6c] -3 **18.** [1.6c] $\frac{32}{125}$
19. [1.7c] $15x + 25y + 10z$ **20.** [1.7c] $-12x - 8$
21. [1.7c] $-12y + 24x$ **22.** [1.7d] $2(32 + 9x + 12y)$
23. [1.7d] $8(2y - 7)$ **24.** [1.7d] $5(a - 3b + 5)$
25. [1.7e] $15b + 22y$ **26.** [1.7e] $4 + 9y + 6z$
27. [1.7e] $1 - 3a - 9d$ **28.** [1.7e] $-2.6x - 5.2y$
29. [1.8b] $3x - 1$ **30.** [1.8b] $-2x - y$
31. [1.8b] $-7x + 6$ **32.** [1.8b] $8x$ **33.** [1.8c] $5x - 13$
34. [2.1b] 4.5   **35.** [2.2a] $\frac{4}{25}$ **36.** [2.1b] 10.9
37. [2.1b] $3\frac{5}{6}$ **38.** [2.2a] -48 **39.** [2.2a] 12
40. [2.2a] -6.2 **41.** [2.3a] -3 **42.** [2.3b] $-\frac{12}{5}$
43. [2.3b] 8   **44.** [2.3c] 7   **45.** [2.3b] $-\frac{4}{5}$
46. [2.3b] $-\frac{10}{3}$ **47.** [2.3c] All real numbers
48. [2.3c] No solution   **49.** [2.3c] All real numbers
50. [2.7c] $\{x \mid x < 2\}$ **51.** [2.7e] $\{y \mid y \ge 4\}$
52. [2.7e] $\{y \mid y < -3\}$ **53.** [2.4b] $m = 65 - H$
54. [2.4b] $P = \dfrac{I}{rt}$ **55.** [2.5a] 25.2   **56.** [2.5a] 45%
57. [2.5a] $363.56   **58.** [2.5a] 174.6 million
59. [2.8b] $\{s \mid s \ge 84\}$ **60.** [2.6a] $45   **61.** [2.6a] $1050
62. [2.6a] 50 m, 53 m, 40 m   **63.** [2.8b] $\left\{d \mid d \le 128\frac{1}{3} \text{ mi}\right\}$
64. [2.6a] $24.60   **65.** [1.8d] (c)   **66.** [1.8c] (d)
67. [2.4b] (b)   **68.** [2.5a] $45,200   **69.** [2.5a] 30%
70. [1.2e], [2.3a] $4, -4$ **71.** [2.3b] 3
72. [2.4b] $Q = \dfrac{2 - pm}{p}$

CHAPTER 3

Margin Exercises, Section 3.1, pp. 224–234

1.–8.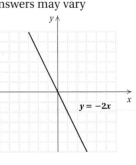

9. Both are negative numbers.   **10.** First, positive; second, negative   **11.** I   **12.** III   **13.** IV   **14.** II
15. On an axis   **16.** $A: (-5, 1)$; $B: (-3, 2)$; $C: (0, 4)$; $D: (3, 3)$; $E: (1, 0)$; $F: (0, -3)$; $G: (-5, -4)$ **17.** No
18. Yes   **19.** $(-2, -3), (1, 3)$; answers may vary
20.

x	y	(x, y)
-3	6	$(-3, 6)$
-1	2	$(-1, 2)$
0	0	$(0, 0)$
1	-2	$(1, -2)$
3	-6	$(3, -6)$

21.

x	y	(x, y)
4	2	(4, 2)
2	1	(2, 1)
0	0	(0, 0)
−2	−1	(−2, −1)
−4	−2	(−4, −2)
−1	−$\frac{1}{2}$	(−1, −$\frac{1}{2}$)

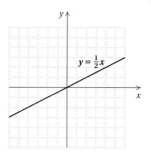

22.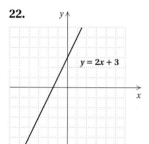

23.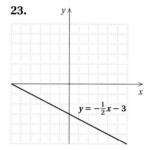

24.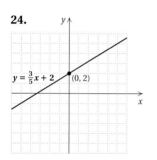

25.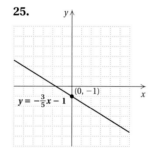

26.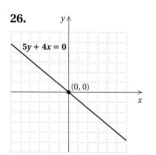

27.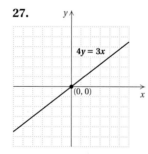

28.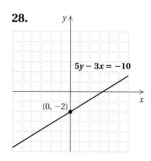

29.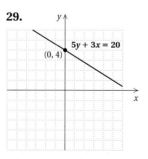

30. **(a)** $2720; $2040; $680; $0;
(b) about $1700;
(c) about 2.8 yr

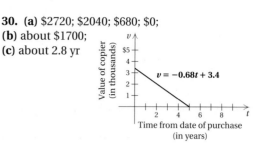

Value of copier (in thousands) — $v = -0.68t + 3.4$

Time from date of purchase (in years)

Calculator Corner, p. 230

1. Left to the student

Calculator Corner, p. 235

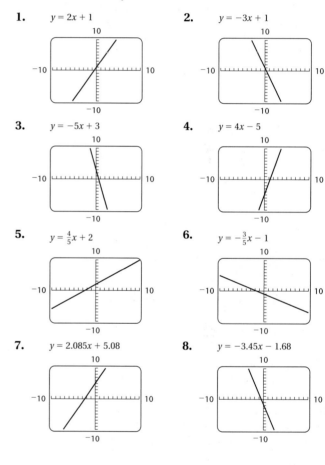

1. $y = 2x + 1$

2. $y = -3x + 1$

3. $y = -5x + 3$

4. $y = 4x - 5$

5. $y = \frac{4}{5}x + 2$

6. $y = -\frac{3}{5}x - 1$

7. $y = 2.085x + 5.08$

8. $y = -3.45x - 1.68$

Exercise Set 3.1, p. 236

1.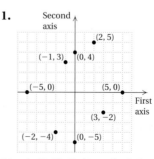

3. II **5.** IV **7.** III
9. On an axis **11.** II
13. IV **15.** II
17. I, IV **19.** I, III

21. A: (3, 3); B: (0, −4); C: (−5, 0); D: (−1, −1); E: (2, 0)

23. No   **25.** No   **27.** Yes

29.
$$y = x - 5$$
$$\frac{}{-1 \; ? \; 4 - 5}$$
$$\quad | \; -1 \qquad \text{TRUE}$$

$$y = x - 5$$
$$\frac{}{-4 \; ? \; 1 - 5}$$
$$\quad | \; -4 \qquad \text{TRUE}$$

31.
$$y = \tfrac{1}{2}x + 3$$
$$\frac{}{5 \; ? \; \tfrac{1}{2} \cdot 4 + 3}$$
$$\quad | \; 2 + 3$$
$$\quad | \; 5 \qquad \text{TRUE}$$

$$y = \tfrac{1}{2}x + 3$$
$$\frac{}{2 \; ? \; \tfrac{1}{2}(-2) + 3}$$
$$\quad | \; -1 + 3$$
$$\quad | \; 2 \qquad \text{TRUE}$$

33.
$$4x - 2y = 10$$
$$\frac{}{4 \cdot 0 - 2(-5) \; ? \; 10}$$
$$\quad 0 + 10 \; |$$
$$\quad\quad 10 \; | \qquad \text{TRUE}$$

$$4x - 2y = 10$$
$$\frac{}{4 \cdot 4 - 2 \cdot 3 \; ? \; 10}$$
$$\quad 16 - 6 \; |$$
$$\quad\quad 10 \; | \qquad \text{TRUE}$$

35.

x	y
-2	-1
-1	0
0	1
1	2
2	3
3	4

37.

x	y
-2	-2
-1	-1
0	0
1	1
2	2
3	3

39.

x	y
-2	-1
0	0
4	2

41.

43.

45.

47.

49.

51.

53.

55.

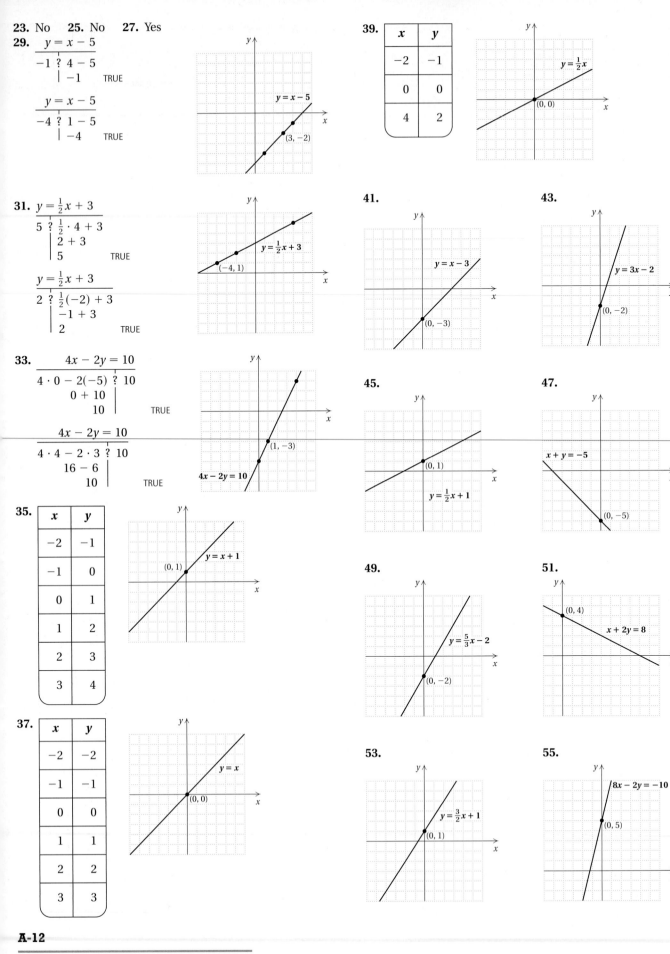

57.

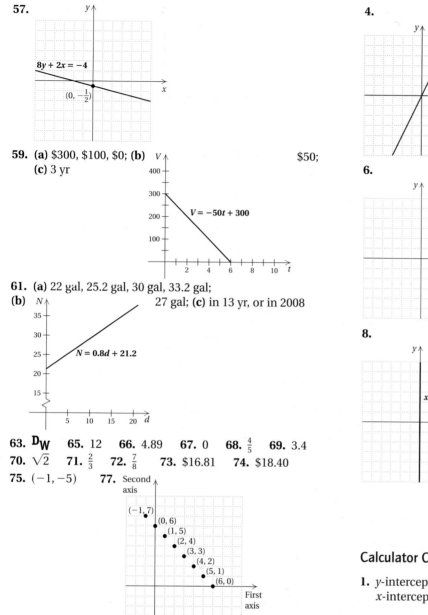

$8y + 2x = -4$

$(0, -\frac{1}{2})$

59. (a) \$300, \$100, \$0; **(b)** \$50; **(c)** 3 yr

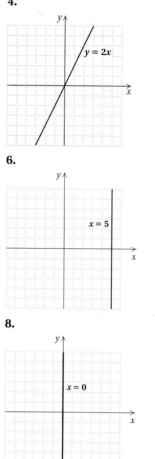

$V = -50t + 300$

61. (a) 22 gal, 25.2 gal, 30 gal, 33.2 gal;
(b) 27 gal; **(c)** in 13 yr, or in 2008

$N = 0.8d + 21.2$

63. D_W **65.** 12   **66.** 4.89   **67.** 0   **68.** $\frac{4}{5}$ **69.** 3.4
70. $\sqrt{2}$ **71.** $\frac{2}{3}$ **72.** $\frac{7}{8}$ **73.** \$16.81   **74.** \$18.40
75. $(-1, -5)$ **77.**

Second axis

$(-1, 7)$
$(0, 6)$
$(1, 5)$
$(2, 4)$
$(3, 3)$
$(4, 2)$
$(5, 1)$
$(6, 0)$

First axis

79. 26 linear units   **81.** A: $(10, 18)$; B: $(8, 15)$; C: $(3, 13)$;
D: $(8, 11)$; E: $(3, 8)$; F: $(8, 5)$; G: $(12, 5)$; H: $(17, 8)$; I: $(12, 11)$;
J: $(17, 13)$; K: $(12, 15)$
83. The figure is translated 3 units down.

Margin Exercises, Section 3.2, pp. 243–247

1. (a) $(0, 3)$; **(b)** $(4, 0)$
2.

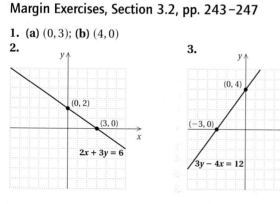

$(0, 2)$
$(3, 0)$
$2x + 3y = 6$

3.

$(0, 4)$
$(-3, 0)$
$3y - 4x = 12$

4.

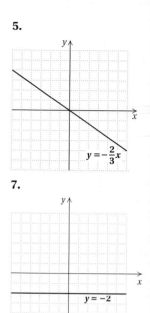

$y = 2x$

5.

$y = -\frac{2}{3}x$

6.

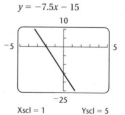

$x = 5$

7.

$y = -2$

8.

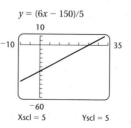

$x = 0$

9.

$x = -3$

Calculator Corner, p. 245

1. y-intercept: $(0, -15)$;
x-intercept: $(-2, 0)$;

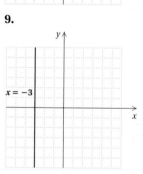

$y = -7.5x - 15$

Xscl = 1   Yscl = 5

2. y-intercept: $(0, 43)$;
x-intercept: $(-20, 0)$;

$y = 2.15x + 43$

Xscl = 5   Yscl = 5

3. y-intercept: $(0, -30)$;
x-intercept: $(25, 0)$;

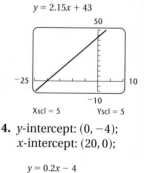

$y = (6x - 150)/5$

Xscl = 5   Yscl = 5

4. y-intercept: $(0, -4)$;
x-intercept: $(20, 0)$;

$y = 0.2x - 4$

Xscl = 5   Yscl = 1

5. y-intercept: $(0, -15)$;
x-intercept: $(10, 0)$;

$y = 1.5x - 15$

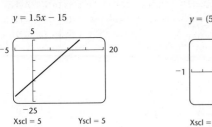

Xscl = 5   Yscl = 5

6. y-intercept: $\left(0, -\frac{1}{2}\right)$;
x-intercept: $\left(\frac{2}{5}, 0\right)$;

$y = (5x - 2)/4$

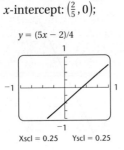

Xscl = 0.25   Yscl = 0.25

Visualizing for Success, p. 248

1. E   **2.** C   **3.** G   **4.** A   **5.** I   **6.** D   **7.** F   **8.** J
9. B   **10.** H

Exercise Set 3.2, p. 249

1. (a) $(0, 5)$; **(b)** $(2, 0)$ **3. (a)** $(0, -4)$; **(b)** $(3, 0)$
5. (a) $(0, 3)$; **(b)** $(5, 0)$ **7. (a)** $(0, -14)$; **(b)** $(4, 0)$
9. (a) $\left(0, \frac{10}{3}\right)$; **(b)** $\left(-\frac{5}{2}, 0\right)$ **11. (a)** $\left(0, -\frac{1}{3}\right)$; **(b)** $\left(\frac{1}{2}, 0\right)$
13.   **15.**

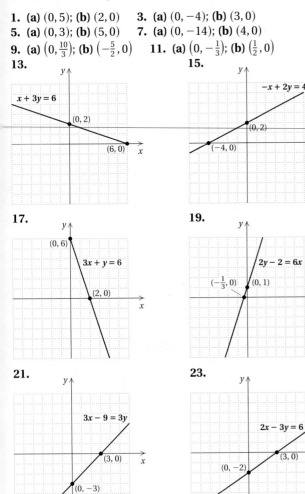

17.   **19.**

21.   **23.**

25.

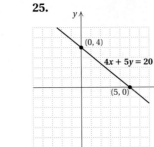

27.

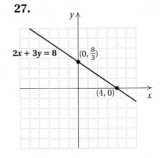

29.

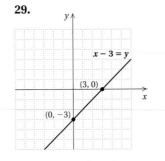

31.

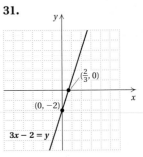

33.

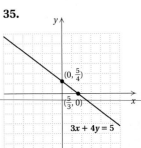

35.

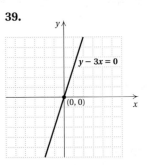

37.

39.

41.

43.

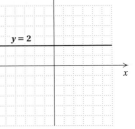

45.

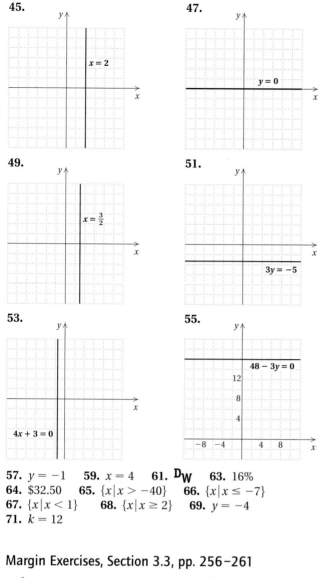

x = 2

47.

y = 0

49.

x = 3/2

51.

3*y* = −5

53.

4*x* + 3 = 0

55.

48 − 3*y* = 0

12

8

4

−8 −4   4   8   *x*

57. $y = -1$ **59.** $x = 4$ **61.** $\mathbf{D}_{\mathbf{W}}$ **63.** 16%
64. \$32.50   **65.** $\{x \mid x > -40\}$ **66.** $\{x \mid x \le -7\}$
67. $\{x \mid x < 1\}$ **68.** $\{x \mid x \ge 2\}$ **69.** $y = -4$
71. $k = 12$

Margin Exercises, Section 3.3, pp. 256–261

1. $\frac{2}{5}$ **2.** $-\frac{5}{3}$

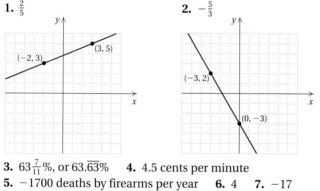

(−2, 3)   (3, 5)

(−3, 2)   (0, −3)

3. $63\frac{7}{11}\%$, or $63.\overline{63}\%$ **4.** 4.5 cents per minute
5. −1700 deaths by firearms per year   **6.** 4   **7.** −17
8. −1   **9.** $\frac{2}{3}$ **10.** −1   **11.** $\frac{5}{4}$ **12.** Not defined   **13.** 0

Calculator Corner, p. 260

1. This line will pass through the origin and slant up from left to right. This line will be steeper than $y = 10x$.
2. This line will pass through the origin and slant up from left to right. This line will be less steep than $y = \frac{5}{32}x$.

Calculator Corner, p. 261

1. This line will pass through the origin and slant down from left to right. This line will be steeper than $y = -10x$.
2. This line will pass through the origin and slant down from left to right. This line will be less steep than $y = -\frac{5}{32}x$.

Exercise Set 3.3, p. 262

1. $-\frac{3}{7}$ **3.** $\frac{2}{3}$ **5.** $\frac{3}{4}$ **7.** 0
9. $-\frac{4}{5}$;   **11.** 3;

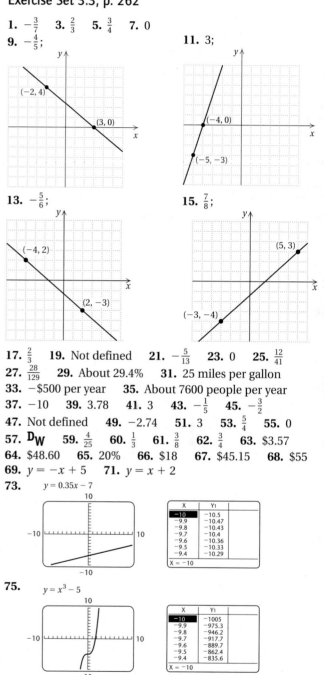

(−2, 4)   (3, 0)

(−4, 0)   (−5, −3)

13. $-\frac{5}{6}$;   **15.** $\frac{7}{8}$;

(−4, 2)   (2, −3)

(5, 3)   (−3, −4)

17. $\frac{2}{3}$ **19.** Not defined   **21.** $-\frac{5}{13}$ **23.** 0   **25.** $\frac{12}{41}$
27. $\frac{28}{129}$ **29.** About 29.4%   **31.** 25 miles per gallon
33. −\$500 per year   **35.** About 7600 people per year
37. −10   **39.** 3.78   **41.** 3   **43.** $-\frac{1}{5}$ **45.** $-\frac{3}{2}$
47. Not defined   **49.** −2.74   **51.** 3   **53.** $\frac{5}{4}$ **55.** 0
57. $\mathbf{D}_{\mathbf{W}}$ **59.** $\frac{4}{25}$ **60.** $\frac{1}{3}$ **61.** $\frac{3}{8}$ **62.** $\frac{3}{4}$ **63.** \$3.57
64. \$48.60   **65.** 20%   **66.** \$18   **67.** \$45.15   **68.** \$55
69. $y = -x + 5$ **71.** $y = x + 2$
73. $y = 0.35x - 7$

X	Y₁
−10	−10.5
−9.9	−10.47
−9.8	−10.43
−9.7	−10.4
−9.6	−10.36
−9.5	−10.33
−9.4	−10.29

X = −10

75. $y = x^3 - 5$

X	Y₁
−10	−1005
−9.9	−975.3
−9.8	−946.2
−9.7	−917.7
−9.6	−889.7
−9.5	−862.4
−9.4	−835.6

X = −10

Margin Exercises, Section 3.4, pp. 267–270

1. Slope: 5; *y*-intercept: (0, 0)
2. Slope: $-\frac{3}{2}$; *y*-intercept: (0, −6)
3. Slope: $-\frac{3}{4}$; *y*-intercept: $\left(0, \frac{15}{4}\right)$

4. Slope: 2; y-intercept: $\left(0, -\frac{17}{2}\right)$
5. Slope: $-\frac{7}{5}$; y-intercept: $\left(0, -\frac{22}{5}\right)$
6. $y = 3.5x - 23$ **7.** $y = 13$ **8.** $y = -7.29x$
9. $y = 5x - 18$ **10.** $y = -3x - 5$ **11.** $y = 6x - 13$
12. $y = -\frac{2}{3}x + \frac{14}{3}$ **13.** $y = x + 2$ **14.** $y = 2x + 4$

Exercise Set 3.4, p. 271

1. Slope: -4; y-intercept: $(0, -9)$
3. Slope: 1.8; y-intercept: $(0, 0)$
5. Slope: $-\frac{8}{7}$; y-intercept: $(0, -3)$
7. Slope: $\frac{4}{9}$; y-intercept: $\left(0, -\frac{7}{9}\right)$
9. Slope: $-\frac{3}{2}$; y-intercept: $\left(0, -\frac{1}{2}\right)$
11. Slope: 0; y-intercept: $(0, -17)$ **13.** $y = -7x - 13$
15. $y = 1.01x - 2.6$ **17.** $y = -2x - 6$
19. $y = \frac{3}{4}x + \frac{5}{2}$ **21.** $y = x - 8$ **23.** $y = -3x + 3$
25. $y = x + 4$ **27.** $y = -\frac{1}{2}x + 4$ **29.** $y = -\frac{3}{2}x + \frac{13}{2}$
31. $y = -4x - 11$ **33. (a)** $T = -0.75a + 165$;
(b) -0.75 beat per minute per year; **(c)** 127.5 beats per
minute   **35.** **D$_W$**   **37.** $\frac{53}{7}$ **38.** $\frac{3}{8}$ **39.** $\frac{24}{19}$
40. $\frac{125}{7}$ **41.** $\frac{1}{3}$ **42.** $-\frac{1}{12}$ **43.** $\frac{42}{25}$ **44.** $\frac{5}{7}$
45. $y = 3x - 9$ **47.** $y = \frac{3}{2}x - 2$

Margin Exercises, Section 3.5, pp. 273–275

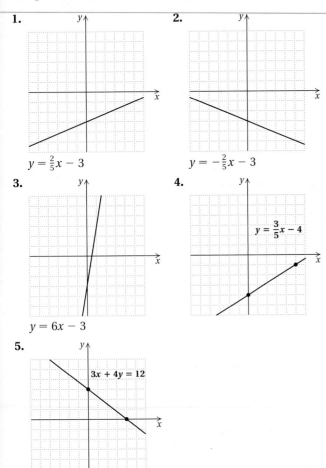

1. $y = \frac{2}{5}x - 3$

2. $y = -\frac{2}{5}x - 3$

3. $y = 6x - 3$

4. $y = \frac{3}{5}x - 4$

5. $3x + 4y = 12$

Exercise Set 3.5, p. 276

1.

3.

5.

7.

9.

11.

13. $y = \frac{3}{5}x + 2$

15. $y = -\frac{3}{5}x + 1$

17. $y = \frac{5}{3}x + 3$

19. $y = -\frac{3}{2}x - 2$

21.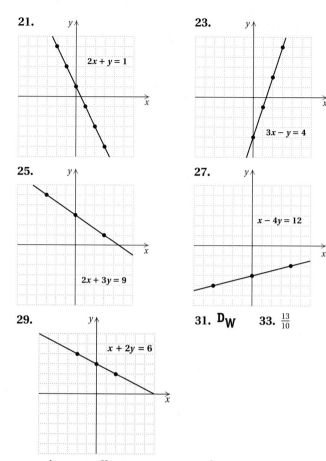

23.

25.

27.

29.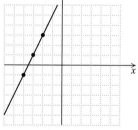

31. $\mathbf{D_W}$ **33.** $\frac{13}{10}$

34. $-\frac{1}{6}$ **35.** $\frac{69}{100}$, or 0.69   **36.** $-\frac{3}{5}$, or -0.6 **37.** 0
38. Not defined   **39.** Not defined   **40.** 0
41. Increase of about 416 kidney transplants per year; 416
42. Increase of about 264 liver transplants per year; 264
43. $y = 1.5x + 16$ **45.**

38. y-intercept   **39.** $y = 3x + 6$
41. $y = -3x + 2$ **43.** $y = \frac{1}{2}x + 1$ **45.** 16
47. $A: y = \frac{4}{3}x - \frac{7}{3}$; $B: y = -\frac{3}{4}x - \frac{1}{4}$

Margin Exercises, Section 3.7, pp. 285–288

1. No   **2.** No   **3.**

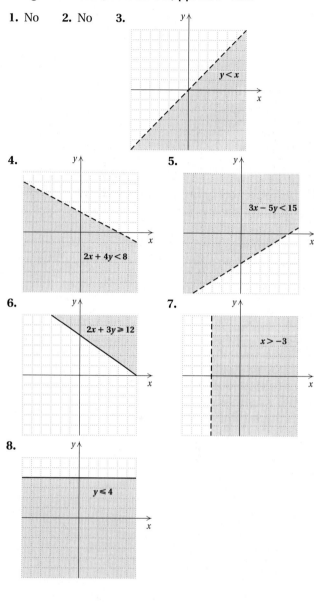

4.   **5.**

6.   **7.**

8.

Margin Exercises, Section 3.6, p. 281

1. No   **2.** Yes   **3.** Yes   **4.** No

Exercise Set 3.6, p. 283

1. Yes   **3.** No   **5.** No   **7.** No   **9.** Yes   **11.** Yes
13. No   **15.** Yes   **17.** Yes   **19.** Yes   **21.** No
23. Yes   **25.** Parallel   **27.** Neither   **29.** $\mathbf{D_W}$
31. Equivalent equations   **32.** Addition principle
33. Multiplication principle   **34.** Horizontal
35. Vertical   **36.** Slope   **37.** x-intercept

Calculator Corner, p. 289

1. Left to the student   **2.** Left to the student

Visualizing for Success, p. 290

1. D   **2.** H   **3.** E   **4.** A   **5.** J   **6.** F   **7.** C   **8.** B
9. I   **10.** G

Exercise Set 3.7, p. 291

1. No **3.** Yes **5.**

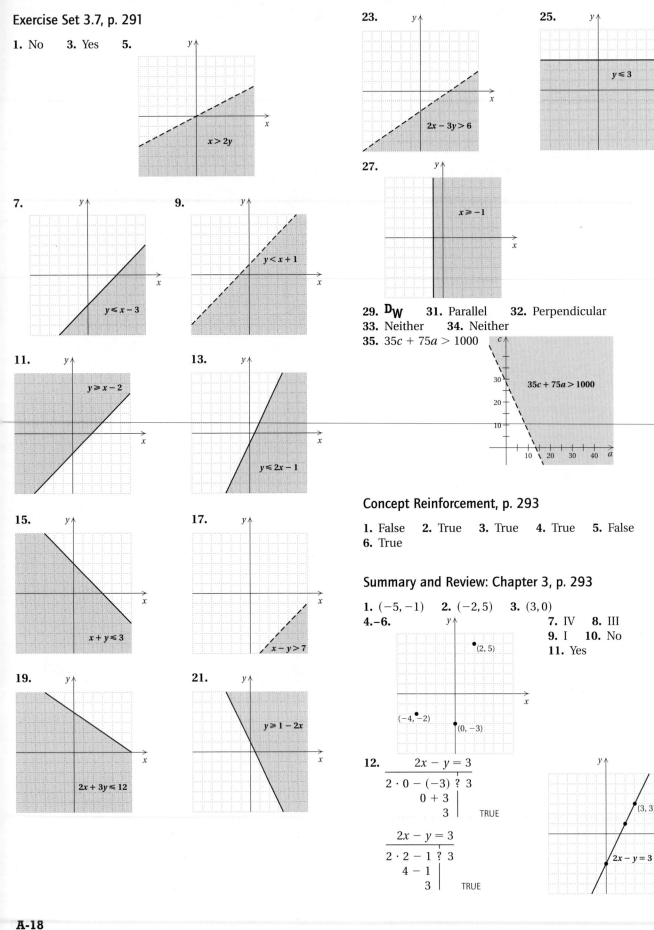

7.

9.

11.

13.

15.

17.

19.

21.

23.

25.

27.

29. D_W **31.** Parallel **32.** Perpendicular
33. Neither **34.** Neither
35. $35c + 75a > 1000$

Concept Reinforcement, p. 293

1. False **2.** True **3.** True **4.** True **5.** False
6. True

Summary and Review: Chapter 3, p. 293

1. $(-5, -1)$ **2.** $(-2, 5)$ **3.** $(3, 0)$
4.–6. **7.** IV **8.** III
9. I **10.** No
11. Yes

12.

$$
\begin{array}{c}
2x - y = 3 \\
\hline
2 \cdot 0 - (-3) \;?\; 3 \\
0 + 3 \\
3 \quad\quad \text{TRUE}
\end{array}
$$

$$
\begin{array}{c}
2x - y = 3 \\
\hline
2 \cdot 2 - 1 \;?\; 3 \\
4 - 1 \\
3 \quad\quad \text{TRUE}
\end{array}
$$

13.

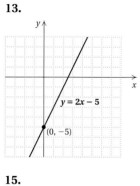

14.

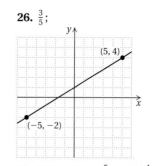

26. $\frac{3}{5}$;

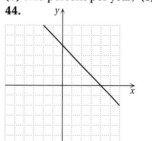

27. -1;

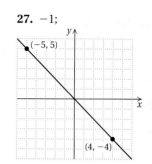

28. 7%   **29.** $-\frac{5}{8}$ **30.** $\frac{1}{2}$ **31.** Not defined   **32.** 0
33. Slope: -9; y-intercept: $(0, 46)$ **34.** Slope: -1;
y-intercept: $(0, 9)$ **35.** Slope: $\frac{3}{5}$; y-intercept: $\left(0, -\frac{4}{5}\right)$
36. $y = -2.8x + 19$ **37.** $y = \frac{5}{8}x - \frac{7}{8}$ **38.** $y = 3x - 1$
39. $y = \frac{2}{3}x - \frac{11}{3}$ **40.** $y = -2x - 4$ **41.** $y = x + 2$
42. $y = \frac{1}{2}x - 1$ **43.** **(a)** $y = 0.48x + 33.9$;
(b) 0.48 percent per year; **(c)** 60.3%

15.

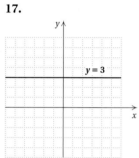

16.

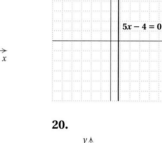

44.

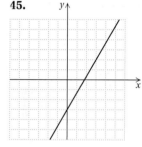

45.

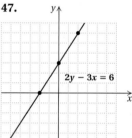

17.

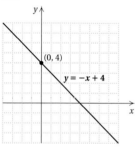

18.

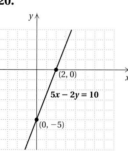

46.

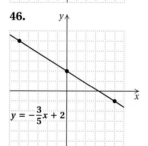

47.

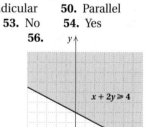

48. Parallel   **49.** Perpendicular   **50.** Parallel
51. Neither   **52.** No   **53.** No   **54.** Yes

55.

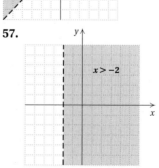

56.

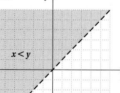

19.

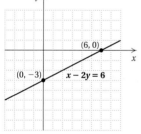

20.

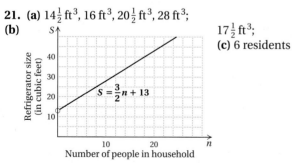

57.

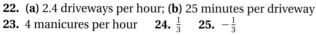

21. **(a)** $14\frac{1}{2}$ ft^3, 16 ft^3, $20\frac{1}{2}$ ft^3, 28 ft^3;
(b)

$17\frac{1}{2}$ ft^3;
(c) 6 residents

22. **(a)** 2.4 driveways per hour; **(b)** 25 minutes per driveway
23. 4 manicures per hour   **24.** $\frac{1}{3}$ **25.** $-\frac{1}{3}$

58. **Dᴡ** The *y*-intercept is the point at which the graph crosses the *y*-axis. Since a point on the *y*-axis is neither left nor right of the origin, the first or *x*-coordinate of the point is 0.

59. **Dᴡ**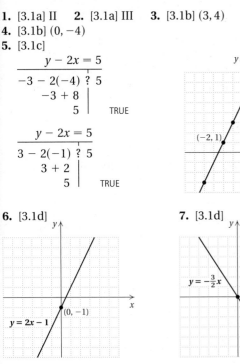
The graph of $x < 1$ on a number line consists of the points in the set $\{x \mid x < 1\}$. The graph of $x < 1$ on a plane consists of the points, or ordered pairs, in the set $\{(x, y) \mid x + 0 \cdot y < 1\}$. This is the set of ordered pairs with first coordinate less than 1.

60. **Dᴡ** First plot the *y*-intercept, (0, 2458). Then, thinking of the slope as $\frac{37}{100}$, plot a second point on the line by moving up 37 units and to the right 100 units from the *y*-intercept. Next, thinking of the slope as $\frac{-37}{-100}$, start at the *y*-intercept and plot a third point by moving down 37 units and to the left 100 units. Finally, draw a line through the three points.

61. $m = -1$ **62.** 45 square units; 28 linear units

63. **(a)** 3.709 feet per minute; **(b)** about 0.2696 minute per foot   **64.** $-\frac{1}{2}, \frac{1}{2}, -2, 2$

Test: Chapter 3, p. 299

1. [3.1a] II   **2.** [3.1a] III   **3.** [3.1b] (3, 4)

4. [3.1b] (0, −4)

5. [3.1c]

$$y - 2x = 5$$

$$\overline{-3 - 2(-4) \overset{?}{\vert} 5}$$
$$-3 + 8$$
$$5 \qquad \text{TRUE}$$

$$y - 2x = 5$$
$$\overline{3 - 2(-1) \overset{?}{\vert} 5}$$
$$3 + 2$$
$$5 \qquad \text{TRUE}$$

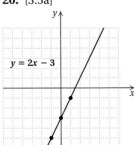

6. [3.1d]

7. [3.1d]

8. [3.2b]

9. [3.2b]

10. [3.2a]

11. [3.2a]

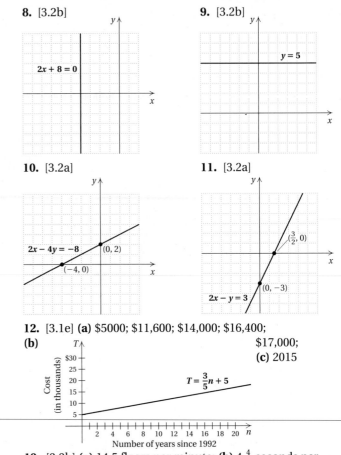

12. [3.1e] **(a)** $5000; $11,600; $14,000; $16,400; $17,000; **(c)** 2015

(b)

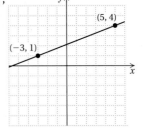

13. [3.3b] **(a)** 14.5 floors per minute; **(b)** $4\frac{4}{29}$ seconds per floor   **14.** [3.3b] 87.5 miles per hour   **15.** [3.3a] −2

16. [3.3a] $\frac{3}{8}$;

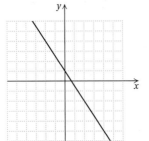

17. [3.3b] $-\frac{1}{20}$ **18.** [3.3c] **(a)** $\frac{2}{5}$; **(b)** not defined

19. [3.5a]

20. [3.5a]

21. [3.4a] Slope: 2; y-intercept: $\left(0, -\frac{1}{4}\right)$
22. [3.4a] Slope: $\frac{4}{3}$; y-intercept: $(0, -2)$
23. [3.4a] $y = 1.8x - 7$ **24.** [3.4a] $y = -\frac{3}{8}x - \frac{1}{8}$
25. [3.4b] $y = x + 2$ **26.** [3.4b] $y = -3x - 6$
27. [3.4c] $y = -3x + 4$ **28.** [3.4c] $y = \frac{1}{4}x - 2$
29. [3.4c] **(a)** $y = 75.3x + 52.4$; **(b)** about 75 lung transplants per year; **(c)** about 1333 lung transplants
30. [3.6a, b] Parallel **31.** [3.6a, b] Neither
32. [3.6a, b] Perpendicular **33.** [3.7a] No
34. [3.7a] Yes **35.** [3.7b]

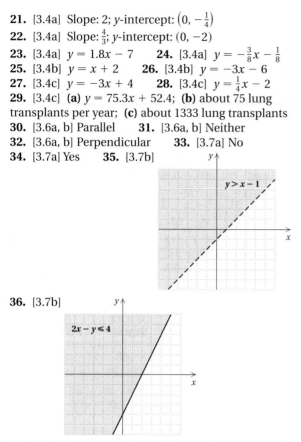

36. [3.7b]

37. [3.1a] 25 square units; 20 linear units **38.** [3.6b] 3

CHAPTER 4

Margin Exercises, Section 4.1, pp. 304–309

1. $5 \cdot 5 \cdot 5 \cdot 5$ **2.** $x \cdot x \cdot x \cdot x \cdot x$ **3.** $3t \cdot 3t$ **4.** $3 \cdot t \cdot t$
5. $(-x) \cdot (-x) \cdot (-x) \cdot (-x)$ **6.** $-1 \cdot y \cdot y \cdot y$ **7.** 6
8. 1 **9.** 8.4 **10.** 1 **11.** -1.4 **12.** 0 **13.** 125
14. 160 **15.** 3215.36 cm² **16.** 119 **17.** 3; -3
18. **(a)** 144; **(b)** 36; **(c)** no **19.** 3^{10} **20.** x^{10} **21.** p^{24}
22. x^5 **23.** $a^9 b^8$ **24.** 4^3 **25.** y^4 **26.** p^9 **27.** $a^4 b^2$
28. $\frac{1}{4^3} = \frac{1}{64}$ **29.** $\frac{1}{5^2} = \frac{1}{25}$ **30.** $\frac{1}{2^4} = \frac{1}{16}$
31. $\frac{1}{(-2)^3} = -\frac{1}{8}$ **32.** $\frac{4}{p^3}$ **33.** x^2 **34.** 5^2 **35.** $\frac{1}{x^7}$
36. $\frac{1}{7^5}$ **37.** b **38.** t^6

Exercise Set 4.1, p. 310

1. $3 \cdot 3 \cdot 3 \cdot 3$ **3.** $(-1.1)(-1.1)(-1.1)(-1.1)(-1.1)$
5. $\left(\frac{2}{3}\right)\left(\frac{2}{3}\right)\left(\frac{2}{3}\right)\left(\frac{2}{3}\right)$ **7.** $(7p)(7p)$ **9.** $8 \cdot k \cdot k \cdot k$
11. $-6 \cdot y \cdot y \cdot y \cdot y$ **13.** 1 **15.** b **17.** 1
19. -7.03 **21.** 1 **23.** ab **25.** a **27.** 27 **29.** 19
31. -81 **33.** 256 **35.** 93 **37.** 136 **39.** 10; 4

41. 3629.84 ft² **43.** $\frac{1}{3^2} = \frac{1}{9}$ **45.** $\frac{1}{10^3} = \frac{1}{1000}$
47. $\frac{1}{7^3} = \frac{1}{343}$ **49.** $\frac{1}{a^3}$ **51.** $8^2 = 64$ **53.** y^4 **55.** z^n
57. 4^{-3} **59.** x^{-3} **61.** a^{-5} **63.** 2^7 **65.** 8^{14} **67.** x^7
69. 9^{38} **71.** $(3y)^{12}$ **73.** $(7y)^{17}$ **75.** 3^3 **77.** $\frac{1}{x}$
79. x^{17} **81.** $\frac{1}{x^{13}}$ **83.** $\frac{1}{a^{10}}$ **85.** 1 **87.** 7^3 **89.** 8^6
91. y^4 **93.** $\frac{1}{16^6}$ **95.** $\frac{1}{m^6}$ **97.** $\frac{1}{(8x)^4}$ **99.** 1 **101.** x^2
103. x^9 **105.** $\frac{1}{z^4}$ **107.** x^3 **109.** 1
111. $5^2 = 25$; $5^{-2} = \frac{1}{25}$; $\left(\frac{1}{5}\right)^2 = \frac{1}{25}$; $\left(\frac{1}{5}\right)^{-2} = 25$; $-5^2 = -25$; $(-5)^2 = 25$; $-\left(\frac{1}{5}\right)^2 = -\frac{1}{25}$; $\left(-\frac{1}{5}\right)^{-2} = 25$ **113.** $\mathbf{D_W}$
115. 8 in., 4 in. **116.** 228, 229 **117.** 25,543.75 ft²
118. 51°, 27°, 102° **119.** $\frac{23}{14}$ **120.** $\frac{11}{10}$
121. $4(x - 3 + 6y)$ **122.** $2(128 - a - 2b)$ **123.** No
125. No **127.** y^{5x} **129.** a^{4t} **131.** 1 **133.** >
135. < **137.** $-\frac{1}{10,000}$

Margin Exercises, Section 4.2, pp. 314–321

1. 3^{20} **2.** $\frac{1}{x^{12}}$ **3.** y^{15} **4.** $\frac{1}{x^{32}}$ **5.** $\frac{16x^{20}}{y^{12}}$ **6.** $\frac{25x^{10}}{y^{12}z^6}$
7. x^{74} **8.** $\frac{27z^{24}}{y^6 x^{15}}$ **9.** $-\frac{1}{y^{24}}$ **10.** $-\frac{1}{8x^{12}}$ **11.** $-\frac{y^{15}}{27x^6}$
12. $\frac{x^{12}}{25}$ **13.** $\frac{8t^{15}}{w^{12}}$ **14.** $\frac{9}{x^8}$ **15.** 5.17×10^{-4}
16. 5.23×10^8 **17.** 689,300,000,000 **18.** 0.0000567
19. 5.6×10^{-15} **20.** 7.462×10^{-13} **21.** 2.0×10^3
22. 5.5×10^2 **23.** 1.884672×10^{11} L
24. The mass of Saturn is 9.5×10 times the mass of Earth.

Calculator Corner, p. 319

1. 1.3545×10^{-4} **2.** 9.044×10^5 **3.** 3.2×10^5
4. 3.6×10^{12} **5.** 3×10^{-6} **6.** 4×10^5 **7.** 8×10^{-26}
8. 3×10^{13}

Exercise Set 4.2, p. 322

1. 2^6 **3.** $\frac{1}{5^6}$ **5.** x^{12} **7.** $\frac{1}{a^{18}}$ **9.** t^{18} **11.** $\frac{1}{t^{12}}$
13. x^8 **15.** $a^3 b^3$ **17.** $\frac{1}{a^3 b^3}$ **19.** $\frac{1}{m^3 n^6}$ **21.** $16x^6$
23. $\frac{9}{x^8}$ **25.** $\frac{1}{x^{12} y^{15}}$ **27.** $x^{24} y^8$ **29.** $\frac{a^{10}}{b^{35}}$ **31.** $\frac{25t^6}{r^8}$
33. $\frac{b^{21}}{a^{15} c^6}$ **35.** $\frac{9x^6}{y^{16} z^6}$ **37.** $\frac{16x^6}{y^4}$ **39.** $a^{12} b^8$ **41.** $\frac{y^6}{4}$
43. $\frac{a^8}{b^{12}}$ **45.** $\frac{8}{y^6}$ **47.** $49x^6$ **49.** $\frac{x^6 y^3}{z^3}$ **51.** $\frac{c^2 d^6}{a^4 b^2}$
53. 2.8×10^{10} **55.** 9.07×10^{17} **57.** 3.04×10^{-6}
59. 1.8×10^{-8} **61.** 10^{11} **63.** 2.96×10^8 **65.** 10^{-7}
67. 87,400,000 **69.** 0.00000005704 **71.** 10,000,000
73. 0.00001 **75.** 6×10^9 **77.** 3.38×10^4

Exercise Set 4.6, p. 363

1. $x^3 + x^2 + 3x + 3$ **3.** $x^4 + x^3 + 2x + 2$
5. $y^2 - y - 6$ **7.** $9x^2 + 12x + 4$ **9.** $5x^2 + 4x - 12$
11. $9t^2 - 1$ **13.** $4x^2 - 6x + 2$ **15.** $p^2 - \frac{1}{16}$
17. $x^2 - 0.01$ **19.** $2x^3 + 2x^2 + 6x + 6$
21. $-2x^2 - 11x + 6$ **23.** $a^2 + 14a + 49$
25. $1 - x - 6x^2$ **27.** $\frac{9}{64}y^2 - \frac{5}{8}y + \frac{25}{36}$
29. $x^5 + 3x^3 - x^2 - 3$ **31.** $3x^6 - 2x^4 - 6x^2 + 4$
33. $13.16x^2 + 18.99x - 13.95$ **35.** $6x^7 + 18x^5 + 4x^2 + 12$
37. $8x^6 + 65x^3 + 8$ **39.** $4x^3 - 12x^2 + 3x - 9$
41. $4y^6 + 4y^5 + y^4 + y^3$ **43.** $x^2 - 16$ **45.** $4x^2 - 1$
47. $25m^2 - 4$ **49.** $4x^4 - 9$ **51.** $9x^8 - 16$
53. $x^{12} - x^4$ **55.** $x^8 - 9x^2$ **57.** $x^{24} - 9$
59. $4y^{16} - 9$ **61.** $\frac{25}{64}x^2 - 18.49$ **63.** $x^2 + 4x + 4$
65. $9x^4 + 6x^2 + 1$ **67.** $a^2 - a + \frac{1}{4}$ **69.** $9 + 6x + x^2$
71. $x^4 + 2x^2 + 1$ **73.** $4 - 12x^4 + 9x^8$
75. $25 + 60t^2 + 36t^4$ **77.** $x^2 - \frac{5}{4}x + \frac{25}{64}$
79. $9 - 12x^3 + 4x^6$ **81.** $4x^3 + 24x^2 - 12x$
83. $4x^4 - 2x^2 + \frac{1}{4}$ **85.** $9p^2 - 1$ **87.** $15t^5 - 3t^4 + 3t^3$
89. $36x^8 + 48x^4 + 16$ **91.** $12x^3 + 8x^2 + 15x + 10$
93. $64 - 96x^4 + 36x^8$ **95.** $t^3 - 1$ **97.** $25; 49$
99. $56; 16$ **101.** $a^2 + 2a + 1$ **103.** $t^2 + 10t + 24$
105. D_W **107.** Lamps: 500 watts; air conditioner: 2000 watts; television: 50 watts   **108.** $\frac{28}{27}$ **109.** $-\frac{41}{7}$
110. $\frac{27}{4}$ **111.** $y = \dfrac{3x - 12}{2}$, or $y = \dfrac{3}{2}x - 6$
112. $a = \dfrac{5d + 4}{3}$, or $a = \dfrac{5}{3}d + \dfrac{4}{3}$
113. $30x^3 + 35x^2 - 15x$ **115.** $a^4 - 50a^2 + 625$
117. $81t^{16} - 72t^8 + 16$ **119.** -7 **121.** First row: 90, $-432, -63$; second row: 7, $-18, -36, -14, 12, -6, -21, -11$; third row: 9, $-2, -2, 10, -8, -8, -8, -10, 21$; fourth row: $-19, -6$ **123.** Yes   **125.** No

Margin Exercises, Section 4.7, pp. 367–370

1. -7940 **2.** -176 **3.** 1889 calories   **4.** $-3, 3, -2, 1, 2$
5. $3, 7, 1, 1, 0; 7$ **6.** $2x^2y + 3xy$ **7.** $5pq - 8$
8. $-4x^3 + 2x^2 - 4y + 2$ **9.** $14x^3y + 7x^2y - 3xy - 2y$
10. $-5p^2q^4 + 2p^2q^2 + 3p^2q + 6pq^2 + 3q + 5$
11. $-8s^4t + 6s^3t^2 + 2s^2t^3 - s^2t^2$
12. $-9p^4q + 9p^3q^2 - 4p^2q^3 - 9q^4 + 5$
13. $x^5y^5 + 2x^4y^2 + 3x^3y^3 + 6x^2$
14. $p^5q - 4p^3q^3 + 3pq^3 + 6q^4$
15. $3x^3y + 6x^2y^3 + 2x^3 + 4x^2y^2$
16. $2x^2 - 11xy + 15y^2$ **17.** $16x^2 + 40xy + 25y^2$
18. $9x^4 - 12x^3y^2 + 4x^2y^4$ **19.** $4x^2y^4 - 9x^2$
20. $16y^2 - 9x^2y^4$ **21.** $9y^2 + 24y + 16 - 9x^2$
22. $4a^2 - 25b^2 - 10bc - c^2$

Exercise Set 4.7, p. 371

1. -1 **3.** -15 **5.** 240   **7.** -145 **9.** 3.715 liters
11. 92.4 m   **13.** 44.46 in^2 **15.** 63.78125 in^2
17. Coefficients: $1, -2, 3, -5$; degrees: 4, 2, 2, 0; 4
19. Coefficients: $17, -3, -7$; degrees: 5, 5, 0; 5
21. $-a - 2b$ **23.** $3x^2y - 2xy^2 + x^2$ **25.** $20au + 10av$
27. $8u^2v - 5uv^2$ **29.** $x^2 - 4xy + 3y^2$ **31.** $3r + 7$

33. $-b^2a^3 - 3b^3a^2 + 5ba + 3$ **35.** $ab^2 - a^2b$
37. $2ab - 2$ **39.** $-2a + 10b - 5c + 8d$
41. $6z^2 + 7zu - 3u^2$ **43.** $a^4b^2 - 7a^2b + 10$
45. $a^6 - b^2c^2$ **47.** $y^6x + y^4x + y^4 + 2y^2 + 1$
49. $12x^2y^2 + 2xy - 2$ **51.** $12 - c^2d^2 - c^4d^4$
53. $m^3 + m^2n - mn^2 - n^3$
55. $x^9y^9 - x^6y^6 + x^5y^5 - x^2y^2$ **57.** $x^2 + 2xh + h^2$
59. $r^6t^4 - 8r^3t^2 + 16$ **61.** $p^8 + 2m^2n^2p^4 + m^4n^4$
63. $4a^6 - 2a^3b^3 + \frac{1}{4}b^6$ **65.** $3a^3 - 12a^2b + 12ab^2$
67. $4a^2 - b^2$ **69.** $c^4 - d^2$ **71.** $a^2b^2 - c^2d^4$
73. $x^2 + 2xy + y^2 - 9$ **75.** $x^2 - y^2 - 2yz - z^2$
77. $a^2 - b^2 - 2bc - c^2$
79. $3x^4 - 7x^2y + 3x^2 - 20y^2 + 22y - 6$ **81.** D_W
83. IV   **84.** III   **85.** I   **86.** II
87.   **88.**

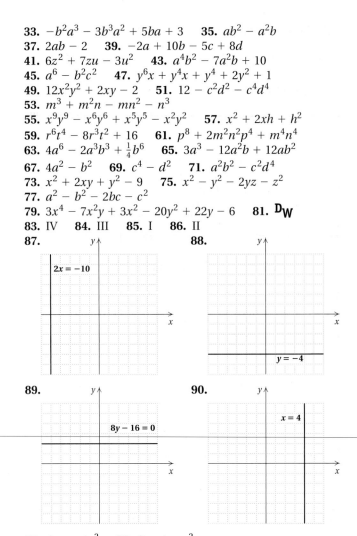

89.   **90.**

91. $4xy - 4y^2$ **93.** $2xy + \pi x^2$
95. $2\pi nh + 2\pi mh + 2\pi n^2 - 2\pi m^2$ **97.** 16 gal
99. \$15,638.03

Margin Exercises, Section 4.8, pp. 376–379

1. $4x^2$ **2.** $-7x^{11}$ **3.** $-28p^3q$ **4.** $\frac{1}{4}x^4$ **5.** $7x^4 + 8x^2$
6. $x^2 + 3x + 2$ **7.** $2x^2 + x - \frac{2}{3}$ **8.** $4x^2 - \frac{3}{2}x + \frac{1}{2}$
9. $2x^2y^4 - 3xy^2 + 5y$ **10.** $x - 2$ **11.** $x + 4$
12. $x + 4$, R -2, or $x + 4 + \dfrac{-2}{x + 3}$ **13.** $x^2 + x + 1$
14. $2x^3 - x^2 + 3x - 1$ with R $= 11$; or
$$2x^3 - x^2 + 3x - 1 + \frac{11}{4x + 2}$$

Exercise Set 4.8, p. 380

1. $3x^4$ **3.** $5x$ **5.** $18x^3$ **7.** $4a^3b$
9. $3x^4 - \frac{1}{2}x^3 + \frac{1}{8}x^2 - 2$ **11.** $1 - 2u - u^4$
13. $5t^2 + 8t - 2$ **15.** $-4x^4 + 4x^2 + 1$
17. $6x^2 - 10x + \frac{3}{2}$ **19.** $9x^2 - \frac{5}{2}x + 1$
21. $6x^2 + 13x + 4$ **23.** $3rs + r - 2s$ **25.** $x + 2$
27. $x - 5 + \dfrac{-50}{x - 5}$ **29.** $x - 2 + \dfrac{-2}{x + 6}$ **31.** $x - 3$
33. $x^4 - x^3 + x^2 - x + 1$ **35.** $2x^2 - 7x + 4$

37. $x^3 - 6$ **39.** $3x^2 + x + 2 + \dfrac{10}{5x+1}$ **41.** $t^2 + 1$
43. **D$_W$**   **45.** Product   **46.** Monomial
47. Multiplication; equivalent   **48.** $x = a$
49. Trinomial   **50.** Quotient   **51.** Absolute value
52. Slope   **53.** $x^2 + 5$ **55.** $a + 3 + \dfrac{5}{5a^2 - 7a - 2}$
57. $2x^2 + x - 3$ **59.** $a^5 + a^4b + a^3b^2 + a^2b^3 + ab^4 + b^5$
61. -5 **63.** 1

Concept Reinforcement, p. 383

1. False   **2.** True   **3.** False   **4.** True   **5.** False
6. True

Summary and Review: Chapter 4, p. 383

1. $\dfrac{1}{7^2}$ **2.** y^{11} **3.** $(3x)^{14}$ **4.** t^8 **5.** 4^3 **6.** $\dfrac{1}{a^3}$ **7.** 1

8. $9t^8$ **9.** $36x^8$ **10.** $\dfrac{y^3}{8x^3}$ **11.** t^{-5} **12.** $\dfrac{1}{y^4}$

13. 3.28×10^{-5} **14.** 8,300,000   **15.** 2.09×10^4
16. 5.12×10^{-5} **17.** 4.4676×10^9 gal   **18.** 10
19. $-4y^5, 7y^2, -3y, -2$ **20.** x^2, x^0 **21.** 3, 2, 1, 0; 3
22. Binomial   **23.** None of these   **24.** Monomial
25. $-2x^2 - 3x + 2$ **26.** $10x^4 - 7x^2 - x - \frac{1}{2}$
27. $x^5 - 2x^4 + 6x^3 + 3x^2 - 9$
28. $-2x^5 - 6x^4 - 2x^3 - 2x^2 + 2$ **29.** $2x^2 - 4x$
30. $x^5 - 3x^3 - x^2 + 8$ **31.** Perimeter: $4w + 6$; area:
$w^2 + 3w$ **32.** $(t+3)(t+4)$, $t^2 + 7t + 12$
33. $x^2 + \frac{7}{6}x + \frac{1}{3}$ **34.** $49x^2 + 14x + 1$
35. $12x^3 - 23x^2 + 13x - 2$ **36.** $9x^4 - 16$
37. $15x^7 - 40x^6 + 50x^5 + 10x^4$ **38.** $x^2 - 3x - 28$
39. $9y^4 - 12y^3 + 4y^2$ **40.** $2t^4 - 11t^2 - 21$ **41.** 49
42. Coefficients: 1, -7, 9, -8; degrees: 6, 2, 2, 0; 6
43. $-y + 9w - 5$
44. $m^6 - 2m^2n + 2m^2n^2 + 8n^2m - 6m^3$
45. $-9xy - 2y^2$ **46.** $11x^3y^2 - 8x^2y - 6x^2 - 6x + 6$
47. $p^3 - q^3$ **48.** $9a^8 - 2a^4b^3 + \frac{1}{9}b^6$ **49.** $5x^2 - \frac{1}{2}x + 3$
50. $3x^2 - 7x + 4 + \dfrac{1}{2x+3}$ **51.** 0, 3.75, -3.75, 0
52. **D$_W$** 578.6×10^{-7} is not in scientific notation because 578.6 is larger than 10.   **53.** **D$_W$** A monomial is an expression of the type ax^n, where n is a whole number and a is a real number. A binomial is a sum of two monomials and has two terms. A trinomial is a sum of three monomials and has three terms. A general polynomial is a monomial or a sum of monomials and has one or more terms.
54. $\frac{1}{2}x^2 - \frac{1}{2}y^2$ **55.** $400 - 4a^2$ **56.** $-28x^8$ **57.** $\frac{94}{13}$
58. $x^4 + x^3 + x^2 + x + 1$ **59.** 16 ft by 8 ft

Test: Chapter 4, p. 386

1. [4.1d, f] $\dfrac{1}{6^5}$ **2.** [4.1d] x^9 **3.** [4.1d] $(4a)^{11}$

4. [4.1e] 3^3 **5.** [4.1e, f] $\dfrac{1}{x^5}$ **6.** [4.1b, e] 1   **7.** [4.2a] x^6

8. [4.2a, b] $-27y^6$ **9.** [4.2a, b] $16a^{12}b^4$ **10.** [4.2b] $\dfrac{a^3b^3}{c^3}$
11. [4.1d], [4.2a, b] $-216x^{21}$ **12.** [4.1d], [4.2a, b] $-24x^{21}$
13. [4.1d], [4.2a, b] $162x^{10}$ **14.** [4.1d], [4.2a, b] $324x^{10}$
15. [4.1f] $\dfrac{1}{5^3}$ **16.** [4.1f] y^{-8} **17.** [4.2c] 3.9×10^9
18. [4.2c] 0.00000005   **19.** [4.2d] 1.75×10^{17}
20. [4.2d] 1.296×10^{22} **21.** [4.2e] 1.5×10^4 files
22. [4.3a] -43 **23.** [4.3d] $\frac{1}{3}, -1, 7$ **24.** [4.3g] 3, 0, 1, 6; 6
25. [4.3i] Binomial   **26.** [4.3e] $5a^2 - 6$
27. [4.3e] $\frac{7}{4}y^2 - 4y$ **28.** [4.3f] $x^5 + 2x^3 + 4x^2 - 8x + 3$
29. [4.4a] $4x^5 + x^4 + 2x^3 - 8x^2 + 2x - 7$
30. [4.4a] $5x^4 + 5x^2 + x + 5$
31. [4.4c] $-4x^4 + x^3 - 8x - 3$
32. [4.4c] $-x^5 + 0.7x^3 - 0.8x^2 - 21$
33. [4.5b] $-12x^4 + 9x^3 + 15x^2$ **34.** [4.6c] $x^2 - \frac{2}{3}x + \frac{1}{9}$
35. [4.6b] $9x^2 - 100$ **36.** [4.6a] $3b^2 - 4b - 15$
37. [4.6a] $x^{14} - 4x^8 + 4x^6 - 16$
38. [4.6a] $48 + 34y + 5y^2$ **39.** [4.5d] $6x^3 - 7x^2 - 11x - 3$
40. [4.6c] $25t^2 + 20t + 4$
41. [4.7c] $-5x^3y - y^3 + xy^3 - x^2y^2 + 19$
42. [4.7e] $8a^2b^2 + 6ab - 4b^3 + 6ab^2 + ab^3$
43. [4.7f] $9x^{10} - 16y^{10}$ **44.** [4.8a] $4x^2 + 3x - 5$
45. [4.8b] $2x^2 - 4x - 2 + \dfrac{17}{3x+2}$
46. [4.3a] 3, 1.5, -3.5, -5, -5.25 **47.** [4.4d] $28a + 90$
48. [4.4d] $(t+2)(t+2)$, $t^2 + 4t + 4$
49. [4.5b], [4.6a] $V = l^3 - 3l^2 + 2l$ **50.** [2.3b], [4.6b, c] $-\frac{61}{12}$

Cumulative Review: Chapters 1–4, p. 388

1. [4.3a] 66.6 ft, 86.6 ft, 66.6 ft, 41.6 ft   **2.** [1.1a] $\frac{5}{2}$
3. [4.3a] -4 **4.** [4.7a] -14 **5.** [1.2e] 4   **6.** [1.6b] $\frac{1}{5}$
7. [1.3a] $-\frac{11}{60}$ **8.** [1.4a] 4.2   **9.** [1.5a] 7.28
10. [1.6c] $-\frac{5}{12}$ **11.** [4.2d] 2.2×10^{22} **12.** [4.2d] 4×10^{-5}
13. [1.7a] -3 **14.** [1.8b] $-2y - 7$ **15.** [1.8c] $5x + 11$
16. [1.8d] -2 **17.** [4.4a] $2x^5 - 2x^4 + 3x^3 + 2$
18. [4.7d] $3x^2 + xy - 2y^2$ **19.** [4.4c] $x^3 + 5x^2 - x - 7$
20. [4.4c] $-\frac{1}{3}x^2 - \frac{3}{4}x$ **21.** [1.7c] $12x - 15y + 21$
22. [4.5a] $6x^8$ **23.** [4.5b] $2x^5 - 4x^4 + 8x^3 - 10x^2$
24. [4.5d] $3y^4 + 5y^3 - 10y - 12$
25. [4.7f] $2p^4 + 3p^3q + 2p^2q^2 - 2p^4q - p^3q^2 - p^2q^3 + pq^3$
26. [4.6a] $6x^2 + 13x + 6$ **27.** [4.6c] $9x^4 + 6x^2 + 1$
28. [4.6b] $t^2 - \frac{1}{4}$ **29.** [4.6b] $4y^4 - 25$
30. [4.6a] $4x^6 + 6x^4 - 6x^2 - 9$ **31.** [4.6c] $t^2 - 4t^3 + 4t^4$
32. [4.7f] $15p^2 - pq - 2q^2$ **33.** [4.8a] $6x^2 + 2x - 3$
34. [4.8b] $3x^2 - 2x - 7$ **35.** [2.1b] -1.2 **36.** [2.2a] -21
37. [2.3a] 9   **38.** [2.2a] $-\frac{20}{3}$ **39.** [2.3b] 2   **40.** [2.1b] $\frac{13}{8}$
41. [2.3c] $-\frac{17}{21}$ **42.** [2.3b] -17 **43.** [2.3b] 2
44. [2.7e] $\{x \,|\, x < 16\}$ **45.** [2.7e] $\left\{x \,|\, x \leq -\frac{11}{8}\right\}$
46. [2.4b] $x = \dfrac{A - P}{Q}$ **47.** [4.4d] $(\pi r^2 - 18)$ ft^2
48. [2.6a] 18 and 19   **49.** [2.6a] 20 ft, 24 ft   **50.** [2.6a] 10°
51. [2.5a] \$3.50   **52.** [4.2e] 6.2245×10^9 gal
53. [4.1d, f] y^4 **54.** [4.1e, f] $\dfrac{1}{x}$ **55.** [4.2a, b] $-\dfrac{27x^9}{y^6}$
56. [4.1d, e, f] x^3 **57.** [4.3d] $\frac{2}{3}, 4, -6$ **58.** [4.3g] 4, 2, 1, 0; 4
59. [4.3i] Binomial   **60.** [4.3i] Trinomial

61. [3.3a]

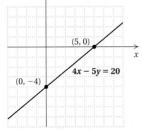

62. [3.4c] $y = \frac{1}{3}x + \frac{17}{3}$

63. [4.4d] $(x + 4)(x + 4)$, $x^2 + 8x + 16$

64. [4.1a, f] $3^2 = 9$, $3^{-2} = \frac{1}{9}$, $\left(\frac{1}{3}\right)^2 = \frac{1}{9}$, $\left(\frac{1}{3}\right)^{-2} = 9$, $-3^2 = -9$,

$(-3)^2 = 9$, $\left(-\frac{1}{3}\right)^2 = \frac{1}{9}$, $\left(-\frac{1}{3}\right)^{-2} = 9$ **65.** [3.6a, b] Neither

66. [3.6a, b] Parallel   **67.** [3.6a, b] Perpendicular

68. [4.4d] $(4x - 4)$ in^2

69. [4.1d], [4.2a, b], [4.4a] $12x^5 - 15x^4 - 27x^3 + 4x^2$

70. [4.4a], [4.6c] $5x^2 - 2x + 10$

71. [4.4a], [4.8b] $4x^2 - 2x + 7$ **72.** [2.3b], [4.6a, c] $\frac{11}{7}$

73. [2.3b], [4.8b] 1   **74.** [1.2e], [2.3a] $-5, 5$

75. [2.3b], [4.6a], [4.8b] All real numbers except 5

76. [4.5c, d] $V = (x^3 + 6x^2 + 12x + 8)$ cm^3

63. **64.** **65.** **66.**

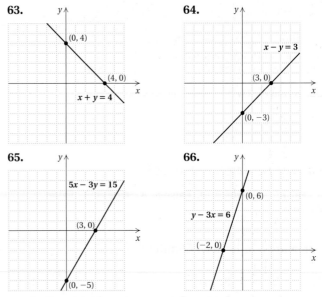

67. $(2x^3 + 3)(2x^2 + 3)$ **69.** $(x^7 + 1)(x^5 + 1)$

71. Not factorable by grouping

CHAPTER 5

Margin Exercises, Section 5.1, pp. 393–398

1. 20   **2.** 7   **3.** 72   **4.** 1   **5.** $4x^2$ **6.** y^2 **7.** $4mn^2$

8. $7x^3$ **9.** (a) $3x + 6$; (b) $3(x + 2)$

10. (a) $2x^3 + 10x^2 + 8x$; (b) $2x(x^2 + 5x + 4)$

11. $x(x + 3)$ **12.** $y^2(3y^4 - 5y + 2)$

13. $3x^2y(3x^2y - 5x + 1)$ **14.** $\frac{1}{4}(3t^3 + 5t^2 + 7t + 1)$

15. $7x^3(5x^4 - 7x^3 + 2x^2 - 9)$ **16.** $28(3x^2 - 2x + 1)$

17. $(x^2 + 3)(x + 7)$ **18.** $(x^2 + 2)(a + b)$

19. $(x^2 + 3)(x + 7)$ **20.** $(2t^2 + 3)(4t + 1)$

21. $(3m^3 + 2)(m^2 - 5)$ **22.** $(3x^2 - 1)(x - 2)$

23. $(2x^2 - 3)(2x - 3)$ **24.** Not factorable using factoring by grouping

Exercise Set 5.1, p. 399

1. x **3.** x^2 **5.** 2   **7.** $17xy$ **9.** x **11.** x^2y^2

13. $x(x - 6)$ **15.** $2x(x + 3)$ **17.** $x^2(x + 6)$

19. $8x^2(x^2 - 3)$ **21.** $2(x^2 + x - 4)$

23. $17xy(x^4y^2 + 2x^2y + 3)$ **25.** $x^2(6x^2 - 10x + 3)$

27. $x^2y^2(x^3y^3 + x^2y + xy - 1)$

29. $2x^3(x^4 - x^3 - 32x^2 + 2)$

31. $0.8x(2x^3 - 3x^2 + 4x + 8)$

33. $\frac{1}{3}x^3(5x^3 + 4x^2 + x + 1)$ **35.** $(x^2 + 2)(x + 3)$

37. $(5a^3 - 1)(2a - 7)$ **39.** $(x^2 + 2)(x + 3)$

41. $(2x^2 + 1)(x + 3)$ **43.** $(4x^2 + 3)(2x - 3)$

45. $(4p^2 + 1)(3p - 4)$ **47.** $(5x^2 - 1)(x - 1)$

49. $(x^2 - 3)(x + 8)$ **51.** $(2x^2 - 9)(x - 4)$ **53.** $\mathbf{D_W}$

55. $\{x | x > -24\}$ **56.** $\{x | x \le \frac{14}{5}\}$ **57.** 27

58. $p = 2A - q$ **59.** $y^2 + 12y + 35$ **60.** $y^2 + 14y + 49$

61. $y^2 - 49$ **62.** $y^2 - 14y + 49$

Margin Exercises, Section 5.2, pp. 401–406

1. (a) $-13, 8, -8, 7, -7$; (b) 13, 8, 7; both 7 and 12 are positive; (c) $(x + 3)(x + 4)$ **2.** $(x + 9)(x + 4)$

3. The coefficient of the middle term, -8, is negative.

4. $(x - 5)(x - 3)$ **5.** $(t - 5)(t - 4)$ **6.** (a) 23, 10, 5, 2; the positive factor has the larger absolute value; (b) -23, $-10, -5, -2$; the negative factor has the larger absolute value; (c) $(x + 3)(x - 8)$ **7.** (a) $-23, -10, -5, -2$; the negative factor has the larger absolute value; (b) 23, 10, 5, 2; the positive factor has the larger absolute value;

(c) $(x - 2)(x + 12)$ **8.** $(a - 2)(a + 12)$

9. $(t + 2)(t - 12)$ **10.** $(y - 6)(y + 2)$

11. $(t^2 + 7)(t^2 - 2)$ **12.** Prime   **13.** $x(x + 6)(x - 2)$

14. $p(p - q - 3q^2)$ **15.** $3x(x + 4)^2$

16. $-1(x + 2)(x - 7)$, or $(-x - 2)(x - 7)$, or $(x + 2)(-x + 7)$ **17.** $-1(x + 3)(x - 6)$, or $(-x - 3)(x - 6)$, or $(x + 3)(-x + 6)$

Exercise Set 5.2, p. 407

1.

PAIRS OF FACTORS	SUMS OF FACTORS
1, 15	16
$-1, -15$	-16
3, 5	8
$-3, -5$	-8

$(x + 3)(x + 5)$

3.

PAIRS OF FACTORS	SUMS OF FACTORS
1, 12	13
−1, −12	−13
2, 6	8
−2, −6	−8
3, 4	7
−3, −4	−7

$(x + 3)(x + 4)$

5.

PAIRS OF FACTORS	SUMS OF FACTORS
1, 9	10
−1, −9	−10
3, 3	6
−3, −3	−6

$(x - 3)^2$

7.

PAIRS OF FACTORS	SUMS OF FACTORS
−1, 14	13
1, −14	−13
−2, 7	5
2, −7	−5

$(x + 2)(x - 7)$

9.

PAIRS OF FACTORS	SUMS OF FACTORS
1, 4	5
−1, −4	−5
2, 2	4
−2, −2	−4

$(b + 1)(b + 4)$

11.

PAIRS OF FACTORS	SUMS OF FACTORS
$\frac{1}{3}, \frac{1}{3}$	$\frac{2}{3}$
$-\frac{1}{3}, -\frac{1}{3}$	$-\frac{2}{3}$
$1, \frac{1}{9}$	$\frac{10}{9}$
$-1, -\frac{1}{9}$	$-\frac{10}{9}$

$\left(x + \frac{1}{3}\right)^2$

13. $(d - 2)(d - 5)$ **15.** $(y - 1)(y - 10)$ **17.** Prime
19. $(x - 9)(x + 2)$ **21.** $x(x - 8)(x + 2)$
23. $y(y - 9)(y + 5)$ **25.** $(x - 11)(x + 9)$
27. $(c^2 + 8)(c^2 - 7)$ **29.** $(a^2 + 7)(a^2 - 5)$
31. $(x - 6)(x + 7)$ **33.** Prime **35.** $(x + 10)^2$
37. $-1(x - 10)(x + 3)$, or $(-x + 10)(x + 3)$, or
$(x - 10)(-x - 3)$ **39.** $-1(a - 2)(a + 12)$, or
$(-a + 2)(a + 12)$, or $(a - 2)(-a - 12)$
41. $x^2(x - 25)(x + 4)$ **43.** $(x - 24)(x + 3)$
45. $(x - 9)(x - 16)$ **47.** $(a + 12)(a - 11)$

49. $(x - 15)(x - 8)$ **51.** $-1(x + 12)(x - 9)$, or
$(-x - 12)(x - 9)$, or $(x + 12)(-x + 9)$
53. $(y - 0.4)(y + 0.2)$ **55.** $(p + 5q)(p - 2q)$
57. $-1(t + 14)(t - 6)$, or $(-t - 14)(t - 6)$, or
$(t + 14)(-t + 6)$ **59.** $(m + 4n)(m + n)$
61. $(s + 3t)(s - 5t)$ **63.** $6a^8(a + 2)(a - 7)$ **65.** **D**_W
67. **D**_W **69.** $16x^3 - 48x^2 + 8x$ **70.** $28w^2 - 53w - 66$
71. $49w^2 + 84w + 36$ **72.** $16w^2 - 88w + 121$
73. $16w^2 - 121$ **74.** $y^3 - 3y^2 + 5y$
75. $6x^2 + 11xy - 35y^2$ **76.** $27x^{12}$ **77.** $\frac{8}{3}$ **78.** $-\frac{7}{2}$
79. 29,555 **80.** 100°, 25°, 55° **81.** 15, −15, 27, −27, 51,
−51 **83.** $\left(x + \frac{1}{4}\right)\left(x - \frac{3}{4}\right)$ **85.** $(x + 5)\left(x - \frac{5}{7}\right)$
87. $(b^n + 5)(b^n + 2)$ **89.** $2x^2(4 - \pi)$

Margin Exercises, Section 5.3, pp. 412–415

1. $(2x + 5)(x - 3)$ **2.** $(4x + 1)(3x - 5)$
3. $(3x - 4)(x - 5)$ **4.** $2(5x - 4)(2x - 3)$
5. $(2x + 1)(3x + 2)$ **6.** $-1(2x - 1)(3x + 2)$, or
$(2x - 1)(-3x - 2)$, or $(-2x + 1)(3x + 2)$
7. $-2(3x - 4)(x + 1)$, or $2(-3x + 4)(x + 1)$, or
$2(3x - 4)(-x - 1)$ **8.** $(2a - b)(3a - b)$
9. $3(2x + 3y)(x + y)$

Calculator Corner, p. 416

1. Correct **2.** Correct **3.** Not correct **4.** Not correct
5. Not correct **6.** Correct **7.** Not correct **8.** Correct

Exercise Set 5.3, p. 417

1. $(2x + 1)(x - 4)$ **3.** $(5x + 9)(x - 2)$
5. $(3x + 1)(2x + 7)$ **7.** $(3x + 1)(x + 1)$
9. $(2x - 3)(2x + 5)$ **11.** $(2x + 1)(x - 1)$
13. $(3x - 2)(3x + 8)$ **15.** $(3x + 1)(x - 2)$
17. $(3x + 4)(4x + 5)$ **19.** $(7x - 1)(2x + 3)$
21. $(3x + 2)(3x + 4)$ **23.** $(3x - 7)^2$
25. $(24x - 1)(x + 2)$ **27.** $(5x - 11)(7x + 4)$
29. $-2(x - 5)(x + 2)$, or $2(-x + 5)(x + 2)$, or
$2(x - 5)(-x - 2)$ **31.** $4(3x - 2)(x + 3)$
33. $6(5x - 9)(x + 1)$ **35.** $2(3y + 5)(y - 1)$
37. $(3x - 1)(x - 1)$ **39.** $4(3x + 2)(x - 3)$
41. $(2x + 1)(x - 1)$ **43.** $(3x + 2)(3x - 8)$
45. $5(3x + 1)(x - 2)$ **47.** $p(3p + 4)(4p + 5)$
49. $-1(3x + 2)(3x - 8)$, or $(-3x - 2)(3x - 8)$, or
$(3x + 2)(-3x + 8)$ **51.** $-1(5x - 3)(3x - 2)$, or
$(-5x + 3)(3x - 2)$, or $(5x - 3)(-3x + 2)$
53. $x^2(7x - 1)(2x + 3)$ **55.** $3x(8x - 1)(7x - 1)$
57. $(5x^2 - 3)(3x^2 - 2)$ **59.** $(5t + 8)^2$
61. $2x(3x + 5)(x - 1)$ **63.** Prime **65.** Prime
67. $(4m + 5n)(3m - 4n)$ **69.** $(2a + 3b)(3a - 5b)$
71. $(3a + 2b)(3a + 4b)$ **73.** $(5p + 2q)(7p + 4q)$
75. $6(3x - 4y)(x + y)$ **77.** **D**_W **79.** $q = \dfrac{A + 7}{p}$
80. $x = \dfrac{y - b}{m}$ **81.** $y = \dfrac{6 - 3x}{2}$ **82.** $q = p + r - 2$
83. $\{x \mid x > 4\}$ **84.** $\left\{x \mid x \leq \frac{8}{11}\right\}$

85.

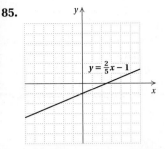

The graph shows the line $y = \frac{2}{5}x - 1$.

86. y^8　**87.** y-intercept: $(0, -4)$; x-intercept: $(16, 0)$
88. y-intercept: $(0, 4)$; x-intercept: $(16, 0)$
89. y-intercept: $(0, -5)$; x-intercept: $(6.5, 0)$
90. y-intercept: $\left(0, \frac{2}{3}\right)$; x-intercept: $\left(\frac{5}{8}, 0\right)$
91. y-intercept: $(0, 4)$; x-intercept: $\left(\frac{4}{5}, 0\right)$
92. y-intercept: $(0, -5)$; x-intercept: $\left(\frac{5}{2}, 0\right)$
93. $(2x^n + 1)(10x^n + 3)$　**95.** $(x^{3a} - 1)(3x^{3a} + 1)$
97.–105. Left to the student

Margin Exercises, Section 5.4, p. 421

1. $(2x + 1)(3x + 2)$　**2.** $(4x + 1)(3x - 5)$
3. $3(2x + 3)(x + 1)$　**4.** $2(5x - 4)(2x - 3)$

Exercise Set 5.4, p. 422

1. $(x + 7)(x + 2)$　**3.** $(x - 1)(x - 4)$
5. $(2x + 3)(3x + 2)$　**7.** $(x - 4)(3x - 4)$
9. $(5x + 3)(7x - 8)$　**11.** $(2x - 3)(2x + 3)$
13. $(2x^2 + 5)(x^2 + 3)$　**15.** $(2x - 1)(x + 4)$
17. $(3x + 5)(x - 3)$　**19.** $(2x + 7)(3x + 1)$
21. $(3x - 1)(x - 1)$　**23.** $(2x + 3)(2x - 5)$
25. $(2x - 1)(x + 1)$　**27.** $(3x + 2)(3x - 8)$
29. $(3x - 1)(x + 2)$　**31.** $(3x - 4)(4x - 5)$
33. $(7x + 1)(2x - 3)$　**35.** $(3x + 2)(3x + 4)$
37. $(3x - 7)^2$　**39.** $(24x + 1)(x - 2)$
41. $-1(3a - 1)(3a + 5)$, or $(-3a + 1)(3a + 5)$, or $(3a - 1)(-3a - 5)$　**43.** $-2(x - 5)(x + 2)$, or $2(-x + 5)(x + 2)$, or $2(x - 5)(-x - 2)$
45. $4(3x - 2)(x + 3)$　**47.** $6(5x - 9)(x + 1)$
49. $2(3y + 5)(y - 1)$　**51.** $(3x - 1)(x - 1)$
53. $4(3x + 2)(x - 3)$　**55.** $(2x + 1)(x - 1)$
57. $(3x - 2)(3x + 8)$　**59.** $5(3x + 1)(x - 2)$
61. $p(3p + 4)(4p + 5)$　**63.** $-1(5x - 4)(x + 1)$, or $(-5x + 4)(x + 1)$, or $(5x - 4)(-x - 1)$
65. $-3(2t - 1)(t - 5)$, or $3(-2t + 1)(t - 5)$, or $3(2t - 1)(-t + 5)$　**67.** $x^2(7x - 1)(2x + 3)$
69. $3x(8x - 1)(7x - 1)$　**71.** $(5x^2 - 3)(3x^2 - 2)$
73. $(5t + 8)^2$　**75.** $2x(3x + 5)(x - 1)$　**77.** Prime
79. Prime　**81.** $(4m + 5n)(3m - 4n)$
83. $(2a + 3b)(3a - 5b)$　**85.** $(3a - 2b)(3a - 4b)$
87. $(5p + 2q)(7p + 4q)$　**89.** $6(3x - 4y)(x + y)$
91. $-6x(x - 5)(x + 2)$, or $6x(-x + 5)(x + 2)$, or $6x(x - 5)(-x - 2)$　**93.** $x^3(5x - 11)(7x + 4)$　**95.** $\mathbf{D_W}$
97. $\{x \mid x < -100\}$　**98.** $\{x \mid x \geq 217\}$　**99.** $\{x \mid x \leq 8\}$
100. $\{x \mid x < 2\}$　**101.** $\left\{x \mid x \geq \frac{20}{3}\right\}$　**102.** $\{x \mid x > 17\}$
103. $\left\{x \mid x > \frac{26}{7}\right\}$　**104.** $\left\{x \mid x \geq \frac{77}{17}\right\}$
105. About 6369 km, or 3949 mi　**106.** $40°$
107. $(3x^5 - 2)^2$　**109.** $(4x^5 + 1)^2$
111.–119. Left to the student

Margin Exercises, Section 5.5, pp. 427–431

1. Yes　**2.** No　**3.** No　**4.** Yes　**5.** No　**6.** Yes
7. No　**8.** Yes　**9.** $(x + 1)^2$　**10.** $(x - 1)^2$
11. $(t + 2)^2$　**12.** $(5x - 7)^2$　**13.** $(7 - 4y)^2$
14. $3(4m + 5)^2$　**15.** $(p^2 + 9)^2$　**16.** $z^3(2z - 5)^2$
17. $(3a + 5b)^2$　**18.** Yes　**19.** No　**20.** No　**21.** No
22. Yes　**23.** Yes　**24.** Yes　**25.** $(x + 3)(x - 3)$
26. $4(t + 4)(t - 4)$　**27.** $(a + 5b)(a - 5b)$
28. $x^4(8 + 5x)(8 - 5x)$　**29.** $5(1 + 2t^3)(1 - 2t^3)$
30. $(9x^2 + 1)(3x + 1)(3x - 1)$
31. $\left(4 + \frac{1}{9}y^4\right)\left(2 - \frac{1}{3}y^2\right)\left(2 + \frac{1}{3}y^2\right)$
32. $(7p^2 + 5q^3)(7p^2 - 5q^3)$

Exercise Set 5.5, p. 432

1. Yes　**3.** No　**5.** No　**7.** No　**9.** $(x - 7)^2$
11. $(x + 8)^2$　**13.** $(x - 1)^2$　**15.** $(x + 2)^2$　**17.** $(q^2 - 3)^2$
19. $(4y + 7)^2$　**21.** $2(x - 1)^2$　**23.** $x(x - 9)^2$
25. $3(2q - 3)^2$　**27.** $(7 - 3x)^2$　**29.** $5(y^2 + 1)^2$
31. $(1 + 2x^2)^2$　**33.** $(2p + 3q)^2$　**35.** $(a - 3b)^2$
37. $(9a - b)^2$　**39.** $4(3a + 4b)^2$　**41.** Yes　**43.** No
45. No　**47.** Yes　**49.** $(y + 2)(y - 2)$
51. $(p + 3)(p - 3)$　**53.** $(t + 7)(t - 7)$
55. $(a + b)(a - b)$　**57.** $(5t + m)(5t - m)$
59. $(10 + k)(10 - k)$　**61.** $(4a + 3)(4a - 3)$
63. $(2x + 5y)(2x - 5y)$　**65.** $2(2x + 7)(2x - 7)$
67. $x(6 + 7x)(6 - 7x)$　**69.** $\left(\frac{1}{4} + 7x^4\right)\left(\frac{1}{4} - 7x^4\right)$
71. $(0.3y + 0.02)(0.3y - 0.02)$　**73.** $(7a^2 + 9)(7a^2 - 9)$
75. $(a^2 + 4)(a + 2)(a - 2)$　**77.** $5(x^2 + 9)(x + 3)(x - 3)$
79. $(1 + y^4)(1 + y^2)(1 + y)(1 - y)$
81. $(x^6 + 4)(x^3 + 2)(x^3 - 2)$　**83.** $\left(y + \frac{1}{4}\right)\left(y - \frac{1}{4}\right)$
85. $\left(5 + \frac{1}{7}x\right)\left(5 - \frac{1}{7}x\right)$　**87.** $(4m^2 + t^2)(2m + t)(2m - t)$
89. $\mathbf{D_W}$　**91.** -11　**92.** 400　**93.** $-\frac{5}{6}$　**94.** -0.9
95. 2　**96.** -160　**97.** $x^2 - 4xy + 4y^2$　**98.** $\frac{1}{2}\pi x^2 + 2xy$
99. y^{12}　**100.** $25a^4b^6$　**101.**

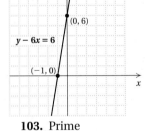

The graph shows the line $y - 6x = 6$ passing through $(0, 6)$ and $(-1, 0)$.

102.

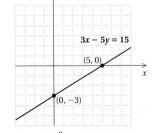

The graph shows the line $3x - 5y = 15$ passing through $(5, 0)$ and $(0, -3)$.

103. Prime
105. $(x + 11)^2$　**107.** $2x(3x + 1)^2$
109. $(x^4 + 2^4)(x^2 + 2^2)(x + 2)(x - 2)$
111. $3x^3(x + 2)(x - 2)$　**113.** $2x\left(3x + \frac{2}{5}\right)\left(3x - \frac{2}{5}\right)$
115. $p(0.7 + p)(0.7 - p)$　**117.** $(0.8x + 1.1)(0.8x - 1.1)$

119. $x(x + 6)$ **121.** $\left(x + \dfrac{1}{x}\right)\left(x - \dfrac{1}{x}\right)$
123. $(9 + b^{2k})(3 - b^k)(3 + b^k)$ **125.** $(3b^n + 2)^2$
127. $(y + 4)^2$ **129.** 9   **131.** Not correct
133. Not correct

Margin Exercises, Section 5.6, pp. 437–439

1. $3(m^2 + 1)(m + 1)(m - 1)$ **2.** $(x^3 + 4)^2$
3. $2x^2(x + 1)(x + 3)$ **4.** $(3x^2 - 2)(x + 4)$
5. $8x(x - 5)(x + 5)$ **6.** $5(3x^2 - 2y)(x^2 + y)$
7. $2p^4q^2(5p^2 + 2pq + q^2)$ **8.** $(a - b)(2x + 5 + y^2)$
9. $(a + b)(x^2 + y)$ **10.** $(x^2 + y^2)^2$ **11.** $(xy + 1)(xy + 4)$
12. $(p^2 + 9q^2)(p + 3q)(p - 3q)$

Exercise Set 5.6, p. 440

1. $3(x + 8)(x - 8)$ **3.** $(a - 5)^2$ **5.** $(2x - 3)(x - 4)$
7. $x(x + 12)^2$ **9.** $(x + 2)(x - 2)(x + 3)$
11. $3(4x + 1)(4x - 1)$ **13.** $3x(3x - 5)(x + 3)$
15. Prime   **17.** $x(x - 3)(x^2 + 7)$ **19.** $x^3(x - 7)^2$
21. $-2(x - 2)(x + 5)$, or $2(-x + 2)(x + 5)$, or
$2(x - 2)(-x - 5)$ **23.** Prime
25. $4(x^2 + 4)(x + 2)(x - 2)$
27. $(1 + y^4)(1 + y^2)(1 + y)(1 - y)$ **29.** $x^3(x - 3)(x - 1)$
31. $\dfrac{1}{9}\left(\dfrac{1}{3}x^3 - 4\right)^2$ **33.** $m(x^2 + y^2)$ **35.** $9xy(xy - 4)$
37. $2\pi r(h + r)$ **39.** $(a + b)(2x + 1)$
41. $(x + 1)(x - 1 - y)$ **43.** $(n + p)(n + 2)$
45. $(3q + p)(2q - 1)$ **47.** $(2b - a)^2$, or $(a - 2b)^2$
49. $(4x + 3y)^2$ **51.** $(7m^2 - 8n)^2$ **53.** $(y^2 + 5z^2)^2$
55. $\left(\dfrac{1}{2}a + \dfrac{1}{3}b\right)^2$ **57.** $(a + b)(a - 2b)$
59. $(m + 20n)(m - 18n)$ **61.** $(mn - 8)(mn + 4)$
63. $r^3(rs - 2)(rs - 8)$ **65.** $a^3(a - b)(a + 5b)$
67. $\left(a + \dfrac{1}{5}b\right)\left(a - \dfrac{1}{5}b\right)$ **69.** $(x + y)(x - y)$
71. $(4 + p^2q^2)(2 + pq)(2 - pq)$
73. $(1 + 4x^6y^6)(1 + 2x^3y^3)(1 - 2x^3y^3)$
75. $(q + 1)(q - 1)(q + 8)$ **77.** $(7x + 8y)^2$ **79.** $\mathbf{D_W}$
81. $y = -3x - 12$ **82.** $y = 8x - 4$ **83.** $y = -\dfrac{2}{3}x + \dfrac{7}{3}$
84. $y = -0.28x - 1.16$ **85.** $-\dfrac{14}{11}$ **86.** $25x^2 - 10xt + t^2$
87. $X = \dfrac{A + 7}{a + b}$ **88.** $\{x \mid x < 32\}$ **89.** $(a + 1)^2(a - 1)^2$
91. $(3.5x - 1)^2$ **93.** $(5x + 4)(x + 1.8)$
95. $(y + 3)(y - 3)(y - 2)$ **97.** $(a^2 + 1)(a + 4)$
99. $(x + 2)(x - 2)(x - 1)$ **101.** $(y - 1)^3$
103. $(y + 4 + x)^2$

Margin Exercises, Section 5.7, pp. 445–448

1. $3, -4$ **2.** $7, 3$ **3.** $-\dfrac{1}{4}, \dfrac{2}{3}$ **4.** $0, \dfrac{17}{3}$ **5.** $-2, 3$
6. $-4, 7$ **7.** 3   **8.** $0, 4$ **9.** $-\dfrac{4}{3}, \dfrac{4}{3}$ **10.** $3, \dfrac{7}{2}$ **11.** $-5, 2$
12. $-3, 3$ **13.** $(-5, 0), (1, 0)$ **14.** $0, 3$

Calculator Corner, p. 449

1. Left to the student

Exercise Set 5.7, p. 450

1. $-4, -9$ **3.** $-3, 8$ **5.** $-12, 11$ **7.** $0, -3$ **9.** $0, -18$
11. $-\dfrac{5}{2}, -4$ **13.** $-\dfrac{1}{5}, 3$ **15.** $4, \dfrac{1}{4}$ **17.** $0, \dfrac{2}{3}$ **19.** $-\dfrac{1}{10}, \dfrac{1}{27}$
21. $\dfrac{1}{3}, -20$ **23.** $0, \dfrac{2}{3}, \dfrac{1}{2}$ **25.** $-5, -1$ **27.** $-9, 2$
29. $3, 5$ **31.** $0, 8$ **33.** $0, -18$ **35.** $-4, 4$ **37.** $-\dfrac{2}{3}, \dfrac{2}{3}$
39. -3 **41.** 4   **43.** $0, \dfrac{6}{5}$ **45.** $-1, \dfrac{5}{3}$ **47.** $-\dfrac{1}{4}, \dfrac{2}{3}$
49. $-1, \dfrac{2}{3}$ **51.** $-\dfrac{7}{10}, \dfrac{7}{10}$ **53.** $-2, 9$ **55.** $\dfrac{4}{5}, \dfrac{3}{2}$
57. $(-4, 0), (1, 0)$ **59.** $\left(-\dfrac{5}{2}, 0\right), (2, 0)$ **61.** $(-3, 0), (5, 0)$
63. $-1, 4$ **65.** $-1, 3$ **67.** $\mathbf{D_W}$ **69.** $(a + b)^2$
70. $a^2 + b^2$ **71.** -16
72. -4.5 **73.** $-\dfrac{10}{3}$ **74.** $\dfrac{3}{10}$
75. $-5, 4$ **77.** $-3, 9$ **79.** $-\dfrac{1}{8}, \dfrac{1}{8}$ **81.** $-4, 4$
83. Answers may vary. **(a)** $x^2 - x - 12 = 0$;
(b) $x^2 + 7x + 12 = 0$; **(c)** $4x^2 - 4x + 1 = 0$;
(d) $x^2 - 25 = 0$; **(e)** $40x^3 - 14x^2 + x = 0$ **85.** $2.33, 6.77$
87. $0, 2.74$

Margin Exercises, Section 5.8, pp. 453–458

1. Length: 24 in.; width: 12 in.   **2.** Height: 25 ft; width: 10 ft
3. (a) 342 games; **(b)** 9 teams   **4.** 22 and 23   **5.** 24 ft
6. 3 m, 4 m

Translating for Success, p. 459

1. O   **2.** M   **3.** K   **4.** I   **5.** G   **6.** E   **7.** C   **8.** A
9. H   **10.** B

Exercise Set 5.8, p. 460

1. Length: 6 cm; width: 4 cm   **3.** Length: 12 ft; width: 2 ft
5. Height: 4 cm; base: 14 cm   **7.** Base: 8 m; height: 16 m
9. 182 games   **11.** 12 teams   **13.** 4950 handshakes
15. 25 people   **17.** 20 people   **19.** 14 and 15
21. 12 and 14; -12 and -14 **23.** 15 and 17; -15 and -17
25. Hypotenuse: 17 ft; leg: 15 ft   **27.** 32 ft   **29.** 9 ft
31. Dining room: 12 ft by 12 ft; kitchen: 12 ft by 10 ft
33. 4 sec   **35.** 5 and 7   **37.** $\mathbf{D_W}$ **39.** Factor
40. Factor   **41.** Product   **42.** Common factor
43. Trinomial   **44.** Quotient rule   **45.** y-intercept
46. Slope   **47.** 35 ft   **49.** 5 ft   **51.** 30 cm by 15 cm
53. 7 ft

Concept Reinforcement, p. 466

1. True   **2.** False   **3.** True   **4.** False   **5.** True

Summary and Review: Chapter 5, p. 466

1. $5y^2$ **2.** $12x$ **3.** $5(1 + 2x^3)(1 - 2x^3)$ **4.** $x(x - 3)$
5. $(3x + 2)(3x - 2)$ **6.** $(x + 6)(x - 2)$ **7.** $(x + 7)^2$
8. $3x(2x^2 + 4x + 1)$ **9.** $(x^2 + 3)(x + 1)$
10. $(3x - 1)(2x - 1)$ **11.** $(x^2 + 9)(x + 3)(x - 3)$
12. $3x(3x - 5)(x + 3)$ **13.** $2(x + 5)(x - 5)$

14. $(x^3 - 2)(x + 4)$ **15.** $(4x^2 + 1)(2x + 1)(2x - 1)$
16. $4x^4(2x^2 - 8x + 1)$ **17.** $3(2x + 5)^2$ **18.** Prime
19. $x(x - 6)(x + 5)$ **20.** $(2x + 5)(2x - 5)$
21. $(3x - 5)^2$ **22.** $2(3x + 4)(x - 6)$ **23.** $(x - 3)^2$
24. $(2x + 1)(x - 4)$ **25.** $2(3x - 1)^2$
26. $3(x + 3)(x - 3)$ **27.** $(x - 5)(x - 3)$ **28.** $(5x - 2)^2$
29. $(7b^5 - 2a^4)^2$ **30.** $(xy + 4)(xy - 3)$ **31.** $3(2a + 7b)^2$
32. $(m + t)(m + 5)$ **33.** $32(x^2 - 2y^2z^2)(x^2 + 2y^2z^2)$
34. $1, -3$ **35.** $-7, 5$ **36.** $-4, 3$ **37.** $\frac{2}{3}, 1$ **38.** $-4, \frac{3}{2}$
39. $-2, 8$ **40.** Height: 6 cm; base: 5 cm   **41.** -18 and
-16; 16 and 18   **42.** -19 and -17; 17 and 19   **43.** 3 ft
44. 6 km   **45.** $(-5, 0), (-4, 0)$ **46.** $\left(-\frac{3}{2}, 0\right), (5, 0)$
47. $\mathbf{D_W}$ Answers may vary. The area of a rectangle is 90 m². The length is 1 m greater than the width. Find the length and the width.   **48.** $\mathbf{D_W}$ Because Sheri did not first factor out the largest common factor, 4, her factorization will not be "complete" until she removes a common factor of 2 from each binomial.   **49.** 2.5 cm   **50.** 0, 2   **51.** Length: 12; width: 6   **52.** No solution   **53.** $2, -3, \frac{5}{2}$ **54.** $-2, \frac{5}{4}, 3$
55. $(\pi - 2)x^2$

Test: Chapter 5, p. 469

1. [5.1a] $4x^3$ **2.** [5.2a] $(x - 5)(x - 2)$ **3.** [5.5b] $(x - 5)^2$
4. [5.1b] $2y^2(2y^2 - 4y + 3)$ **5.** [5.1c] $(x^2 + 2)(x + 1)$
6. [5.1b] $x(x - 5)$ **7.** [5.2a] $x(x + 3)(x - 1)$
8. [5.3a], [5.4a] $2(5x - 6)(x + 4)$
9. [5.5d] $(2x + 3)(2x - 3)$ **10.** [5.2a] $(x - 4)(x + 3)$
11. [5.3a], [5.4a] $3m(2m + 1)(m + 1)$
12. [5.5d] $3(w + 5)(w - 5)$ **13.** [5.5b] $5(3x + 2)^2$
14. [5.5d] $3(x^2 + 4)(x + 2)(x - 2)$ **15.** [5.5b] $(7x - 6)^2$
16. [5.3a], [5.4a] $(5x - 1)(x - 5)$
17. [5.1c] $(x^3 - 3)(x + 2)$
18. [5.5d] $5(4 + x^2)(2 + x)(2 - x)$
19. [5.3a], [5.4a] $(2x + 3)(2x - 5)$
20. [5.3a], [5.4a] $3t(2t + 5)(t - 1)$
21. [5.2a] $3(m + 2n)(m - 5n)$ **22.** [5.7b] $-4, 5$
23. [5.7b] $-5, \frac{3}{2}$ **24.** [5.7b] $-4, 7$ **25.** [5.8a] Length: 8 m; width: 6 m   **26.** [5.8a] Height: 4 cm; base: 14 cm
27. [5.8a] 5 ft   **28.** [5.7b] $(-5, 0), (7, 0)$
29. [5.7b] $\left(\frac{2}{3}, 0\right), (1, 0)$ **30.** [5.8a] Length: 15; width: 3
31. [5.2a] $(a - 4)(a + 8)$ **32.** [5.7b] $-\frac{8}{3}, 0, \frac{2}{5}$
33. [4.6b], [5.5d] (d)

CHAPTER 6

Margin Exercises, Section 6.1, pp. 472–477

1. 3   **2.** $-8, 3$ **3.** None   **4.** $\dfrac{(2x + 1)x}{(3x - 2)x}$
5. $\dfrac{(x + 1)(x + 2)}{(x - 2)(x + 2)}$ **6.** $\dfrac{(x - 8)(-1)}{(x - y)(-1)}$ **7.** 5   **8.** $\dfrac{x}{4}$
9. $\dfrac{2x + 1}{3x + 2}$ **10.** $\dfrac{x + 1}{2x + 1}$ **11.** $x + 2$ **12.** $\dfrac{y + 2}{4}$
13. -1 **14.** -1 **15.** -1 **16.** $\dfrac{a - 2}{a - 3}$ **17.** $\dfrac{x - 5}{2}$

Calculator Corner, p. 478

1. Correct   **2.** Correct   **3.** Not correct   **4.** Not correct
5. Not correct   **6.** Not correct   **7.** Correct   **8.** Correct

Exercise Set 6.1, p. 479

1. 0   **3.** 8   **5.** $-\dfrac{5}{2}$ **7.** $-4, 7$ **9.** $-5, 5$ **11.** None
13. $\dfrac{(4x)(3x^2)}{(4x)(5y)}$ **15.** $\dfrac{2x(x - 1)}{2x(x + 4)}$ **17.** $\dfrac{-1(3 - x)}{-1(4 - x)}$
19. $\dfrac{(y + 6)(y - 7)}{(y + 6)(y + 2)}$ **21.** $\dfrac{x^2}{4}$ **23.** $\dfrac{8p^2q}{3}$ **25.** $\dfrac{x - 3}{x}$
27. $\dfrac{m + 1}{2m + 3}$ **29.** $\dfrac{a - 3}{a + 2}$ **31.** $\dfrac{a - 3}{a - 4}$ **33.** $\dfrac{x + 5}{x - 5}$
35. $a + 1$ **37.** $\dfrac{x^2 + 1}{x + 1}$ **39.** $\dfrac{3}{2}$ **41.** $\dfrac{6}{t - 3}$
43. $\dfrac{t + 2}{2(t - 4)}$ **45.** $\dfrac{t - 2}{t + 2}$ **47.** -1 **49.** -1 **51.** -6
53. $-x - 1$ **55.** $\dfrac{56x}{3}$ **57.** $\dfrac{2}{dc^2}$ **59.** $\dfrac{x + 2}{x - 2}$
61. $\dfrac{(a + 3)(a - 3)}{a(a + 4)}$ **63.** $\dfrac{2a}{a - 2}$ **65.** $\dfrac{(t + 2)(t - 2)}{(t + 1)(t - 1)}$
67. $\dfrac{x + 4}{x + 2}$ **69.** $\dfrac{5(a + 6)}{a - 1}$ **71.** $\mathbf{D_W}$ **73.** 18 and 20;
-18 and -20 **74.** 3.125 L   **75.** $(x - 8)(x + 7)$
76. $(a - 8)^2$ **77.** $x^3(x - 7)(x + 5)$
78. $(2y^2 + 1)(y - 5)$ **79.** $(2 + t)(2 - t)(4 + t^2)$
80. $10(x + 7)(x + 1)$ **81.** $(x - 7)(x - 2)$ **82.** Prime
83. $(4x - 5y)^2$ **84.** $(a - 7b)(a - 2b)$ **85.** $x + 2y$
87. $\dfrac{(t - 9)^2(t - 1)}{(t^2 + 9)(t + 1)}$ **89.** $\dfrac{x - y}{x - 5y}$
91. $\dfrac{5(2x + 5) - 25}{10} = \dfrac{10x + 25 - 25}{10}$
$$= \dfrac{10x}{10}$$
$$= x$$
You get the same number you selected. To do a number trick, ask someone to select a number and then perform these operations. The person will probably be surprised that the result is the original number.

Margin Exercises, Section 6.2, pp. 483–485

1. $\dfrac{2}{7}$ **2.** $\dfrac{2x^3 - 1}{x^2 + 5}$ **3.** $\dfrac{1}{x - 5}$ **4.** $x^2 - 3$ **5.** $\dfrac{6}{7}$
6. $\dfrac{5}{8}$ **7.** $\dfrac{(x - 3)(x - 2)}{(x + 5)(x + 5)}$ **8.** $\dfrac{3a^2}{a - 5}$ **9.** $\dfrac{x - 3}{x + 2}$
10. $\dfrac{(x - 3)(x - 2)}{x + 2}$ **11.** $\dfrac{y + 1}{y - 1}$

Exercise Set 6.2, p. 486

1. $\dfrac{x}{4}$ **3.** $\dfrac{1}{x^2 - y^2}$ **5.** $a + b$ **7.** $\dfrac{x^2 - 4x + 7}{x^2 + 2x - 5}$ **9.** $\dfrac{3}{10}$
11. $\dfrac{1}{4}$ **13.** $\dfrac{b}{a}$ **15.** $\dfrac{(a + 2)(a + 3)}{(a - 3)(a - 1)}$ **17.** $\dfrac{(x - 1)^2}{x}$

19. $\dfrac{1}{2}$ **21.** $\dfrac{15}{8}$ **23.** $\dfrac{15}{4}$ **25.** $\dfrac{a-5}{3(a-1)}$ **27.** $\dfrac{(x+2)^2}{x}$

29. $\dfrac{3}{2}$ **31.** $\dfrac{c+1}{c-1}$ **33.** $\dfrac{y-3}{2y-1}$ **35.** $\dfrac{x+1}{x-1}$ **37.** $\mathbf{D_W}$

39. $\{x \mid x \geq 77\}$ **40.** Height: 7 in.; base: 10 in.

41. $8x^3 - 11x^2 - 3x + 12$ **42.** $-2p^2 + 4pq - 4q^2$

43. $\dfrac{4y^8}{x^6}$ **44.** $\dfrac{125x^{18}}{y^{12}}$ **45.** $\dfrac{4x^6}{y^{10}}$ **46.** $\dfrac{1}{a^{15}b^{20}}$ **47.** $-\dfrac{1}{b^2}$

49. $\dfrac{a+1}{5ab^2(a^2+4)}$

Margin Exercises, Section 6.3, pp. 488–489

1. 144 **2.** 12 **3.** 10 **4.** 120 **5.** $\frac{35}{144}$ **6.** $\frac{1}{4}$ **7.** $\frac{11}{10}$
8. $\frac{9}{40}$ **9.** $60x^3y^2$ **10.** $(y+1)^2(y+4)$
11. $7(t^2+16)(t-2)$ **12.** $3x(x+1)^2(x-1)$

Exercise Set 6.3, p. 490

1. 108 **3.** 72 **5.** 126 **7.** 360 **9.** 500 **11.** $\frac{65}{72}$
13. $\frac{29}{120}$ **15.** $\frac{23}{180}$ **17.** $12x^3$ **19.** $18x^2y^2$
21. $6(y-3)$ **23.** $t(t+2)(t-2)$
25. $(x+2)(x-2)(x+3)$ **27.** $t(t+2)^2(t-4)$
29. $(a+1)(a-1)^2$ **31.** $(m-3)(m-2)^2$
33. $(2+3x)(2-3x)$ **35.** $10v(v+4)(v+3)$
37. $18x^3(x-2)^2(x+1)$ **39.** $6x^3(x+2)^2(x-2)$
41. $\mathbf{D_W}$ **43.** $(x-3)^2$ **44.** $2x(3x+2)$
45. $(x+3)(x-3)$ **46.** $(x+7)(x-3)$ **47.** $(x+3)^2$
48. $(x-7)(x+3)$ **49.** $120x^4; 8x^3; 960x^7$
50. $48x^6; 16x^5; 768x^{11}$ **51.** $20x^2; 10x; 200x^3$
52. $48ab^3; 4ab; 192a^2b^4$ **53.** $120x^3; 2x^2; 240x^5$
54. $a^{15}; a^5; a^{20}$ **55.** 24 min

Margin Exercises, Section 6.4, pp. 492–495

1. $\dfrac{7}{9}$ **2.** $\dfrac{3+x}{x-2}$ **3.** $\dfrac{6x+4}{x-1}$ **4.** $\dfrac{10x^2+9x}{48}$ **5.** $\dfrac{9x+10}{48x^2}$

6. $\dfrac{4x^2-x+3}{x(x-1)(x+1)^2}$ **7.** $\dfrac{2x^2+16x+5}{(x+3)(x+8)}$

8. $\dfrac{8x+88}{(x+16)(x+1)(x+8)}$ **9.** $\dfrac{x-5}{4}$ **10.** $\dfrac{x-1}{x-3}$

11. $\dfrac{-2x-11}{3(x+4)(x-4)}$

Exercise Set 6.4, p. 496

1. 1 **3.** $\dfrac{6}{3+x}$ **5.** $\dfrac{2x+3}{x-5}$ **7.** $\dfrac{2x+5}{x^2}$ **9.** $\dfrac{41}{24r}$

11. $\dfrac{4x+6y}{x^2y^2}$ **13.** $\dfrac{4+3t}{18t^3}$ **15.** $\dfrac{x^2+4xy+y^2}{x^2y^2}$

17. $\dfrac{6x}{(x-2)(x+2)}$ **19.** $\dfrac{11x+2}{3x(x+1)}$ **21.** $\dfrac{x^2+6x}{(x+4)(x-4)}$

23. $\dfrac{6}{z+4}$ **25.** $\dfrac{3x-1}{(x-1)^2}$ **27.** $\dfrac{11a}{10(a-2)}$

29. $\dfrac{2x^2+8x+16}{x(x+4)}$ **31.** $\dfrac{7a+6}{(a-2)(a+1)(a+3)}$

33. $\dfrac{2x^2-4x+34}{(x-5)(x+3)}$ **35.** $\dfrac{3a+2}{(a+1)(a-1)}$ **37.** $\dfrac{1}{4}$

39. $-\dfrac{1}{t}$ **41.** $\dfrac{-x+7}{x-6}$ **43.** $y+3$ **45.** $\dfrac{2b-14}{b^2-16}$

47. $a+b$ **49.** $\dfrac{5x+2}{x-5}$ **51.** -1 **53.** $\dfrac{-x^2+9x-14}{(x-3)(x+3)}$

55. $\dfrac{2x+6y}{(x+y)(x-y)}$ **57.** $\dfrac{a^2+7a+1}{(a+5)(a-5)}$

59. $\dfrac{5t-12}{(t+3)(t-3)(t-2)}$ **61.** $\mathbf{D_W}$ **63.** x^2-1

64. $13y^3 - 14y^2 + 12y - 73$ **65.** $\dfrac{1}{8x^{12}y^9}$ **66.** $\dfrac{x^6}{25y^2}$

67. $\dfrac{1}{x^{12}y^{21}}$ **68.** $\dfrac{25}{x^4y^6}$ **69.**

$y = \frac{1}{2}x - 5$

70.

$2y + x + 10 = 0$

71.

$y = 3$

72.

$x = -5$

73. -8 **74.** $\dfrac{5}{6}$

75. 3, 5 **76.** $-2, 9$

77. Perimeter: $\dfrac{16y+28}{15}$;

area: $\dfrac{y^2+2y-8}{15}$

79. $\dfrac{(z+6)(2z-3)}{(z+2)(z-2)}$

81. $\dfrac{11z^4 - 22z^2 + 6}{(z^2+2)(z^2-2)(2z^2-3)}$

83.–85. Left to the student

Margin Exercises, Section 6.5, pp. 500–503

1. $\dfrac{4}{11}$ **2.** $\dfrac{5}{y}$ **3.** $\dfrac{x^2+2x+1}{2x+1}$ **4.** $\dfrac{-x-7}{15x}$

5. $\dfrac{x^2-48}{(x+7)(x+8)(x+6)}$ **6.** $\dfrac{3x-1}{3}$ **7.** $\dfrac{4x-3}{x-2}$

8. $\dfrac{-8y-28}{(y+4)(y-4)}$ **9.** $\dfrac{x-13}{(x+3)(x-3)}$ **10.** $\dfrac{6x^2-2x-2}{3x(x+1)}$

Exercise Set 6.5, p. 504

1. $\dfrac{4}{x}$ **3.** 1 **5.** $\dfrac{1}{x-1}$ **7.** $\dfrac{-a-4}{10}$ **9.** $\dfrac{7z-12}{12z}$

11. $\dfrac{4x^2 - 13xt + 9t^2}{3x^2t^2}$ **13.** $\dfrac{2x-40}{(x+5)(x-5)}$ **15.** $\dfrac{3-5t}{2t(t-1)}$

17. $\dfrac{2s - st - s^2}{(t+s)(t-s)}$ **19.** $\dfrac{y-19}{4y}$ **21.** $\dfrac{-2a^2}{(x+a)(x-a)}$

23. $\dfrac{8}{3}$ **25.** $\dfrac{13}{a}$ **27.** $\dfrac{8}{y-1}$ **29.** $\dfrac{x-2}{x-7}$ **31.** $\dfrac{4}{a^2-25}$

33. $\dfrac{2x-4}{x-9}$ **35.** $\dfrac{9x+12}{(x+3)(x-3)}$ **37.** $\dfrac{1}{2}$

39. $\dfrac{x-3}{(x+3)(x+1)}$ **41.** $\dfrac{18x+5}{x-1}$ **43.** 0 **45.** $\dfrac{-9}{2x-3}$

47. $\dfrac{20}{2y-1}$ **49.** $\dfrac{2a-3}{2-a}$ **51.** $\dfrac{z-3}{2z-1}$ **53.** $\dfrac{2}{x+y}$

55. D_W **57.** x^5 **58.** $30x^{12}$ **59.** $\dfrac{b^{20}}{a^8}$ **60.** $18x^3$

61. $\dfrac{6}{x^3}$ **62.** $\dfrac{10}{x^3}$ **63.** $x^2 - 9x + 18$ **64.** $(4-\pi)r^2$

65. $\dfrac{30}{(x-3)(x+4)}$ **67.** $\dfrac{x^2 + xy - x^3 + x^2y - xy^2 + y^3}{(x^2 + y^2)(x+y)^2(x-y)}$

69. Missing side: $\dfrac{-2a-15}{a-6}$; area: $\dfrac{-2a^3 - 15a^2 + 12a + 90}{2(a-6)^2}$

71.–73. Left to the student

Margin Exercises, Section 6.6, pp. 508–511

1. $\dfrac{33}{2}$ **2.** $\dfrac{3}{2}$ **3.** 3 **4.** $-\dfrac{1}{8}$ **5.** 1 **6.** 2 **7.** 4

Calculator Corner, p. 512

1.–12. Left to the student

Study Tip, p. 513

1. Rational expression   **2.** Solutions   **3.** Rational expression   **4.** Rational expression   **5.** Rational expression   **6.** Solutions   **7.** Rational expression   **8.** Solutions   **9.** Solutions   **10.** Solutions   **11.** Rational expression   **12.** Solutions   **13.** Rational expression

Exercise Set 6.6, p. 514

1. $\dfrac{6}{5}$ **3.** $\dfrac{40}{29}$ **5.** $\dfrac{47}{2}$ **7.** -6 **9.** $\dfrac{24}{7}$ **11.** $-4, -1$

13. $-4, 4$ **15.** 3 **17.** $\dfrac{14}{3}$ **19.** 5 **21.** 5 **23.** $\dfrac{5}{2}$

25. -2 **27.** $-\dfrac{13}{2}$ **29.** $\dfrac{17}{2}$ **31.** No solution   **33.** -5

35. $\dfrac{5}{3}$ **37.** $\dfrac{1}{2}$ **39.** No solution   **41.** No solution

43. 4 **45.** No solution   **47.** $-2, 2$ **49.** 7

51. D_W **53.** Quotient   **54.** Product   **55.** Reciprocals

56. Factoring   **57.** Greatest   **58.** Not   **59.** Subtract

60. Additive inverses   **61.** $-\dfrac{1}{6}$ **63.** Left to the student

Margin Exercises, Section 6.7, pp. 520–525

1. $3\frac{3}{7}$ hr   **2.** Greg: 40 mph; Nancy: 60 mph   **3.** 58 km/L
4. 0.28   **5.** 124 km/h   **6.** 2.4 fish/yd^2 **7.** About
34.6 gal   **8.** 90 whales   **9.** Yes; approximately 224 walks
10. 24.75 ft   **11.** About 34.9 ft

Translating for Success, p. 526

1. K   **2.** E   **3.** C   **4.** N   **5.** D   **6.** O   **7.** F   **8.** H
9. B   **10.** A

Exercise Set 6.7, p. 527

1. $2\frac{2}{9}$ hr   **3.** $25\frac{5}{7}$ min   **5.** $3\frac{15}{16}$ hr   **7.** $22\frac{2}{9}$ min
9. $3\frac{3}{4}$ min   **11.** Sarah: 30 km/h; Rick: 70 km/h
13. Passenger: 80 mph; freight: 66 mph   **15.** 20 mph
17. Hank: 14 km/h; Kelly: 19 km/h   **19.** Ralph: 5 km/h;
Bonnie: 8 km/h   **21.** 3 hr   **23.** $\frac{5}{9}$ divorce/marriage
25. 2.3 km/h   **27.** 66 g   **29.** 1.92 g   **31.** 1.75 lb
33. $1\frac{11}{39}$ kg   **35.** (a) 0.332; (b) 243 hits; (c) 232 hits
37. 22 in.; 55.8 cm   **39.** $7\frac{1}{4}$; 57.9 cm   **41.** $7\frac{1}{2}$; $23\frac{3}{5}$ in.
43. 287 trout   **45.** 200 duds   **47.** (a) 4.8 tons; (b) 48 lb
49. $\frac{21}{2}$ **51.** $\frac{8}{3}$ **53.** $\frac{35}{3}$ **55.** 15 ft   **57.** D_W

59. x^{11} **60.** x **61.** $\dfrac{1}{x^{11}}$ **62.** $\dfrac{1}{x}$

63.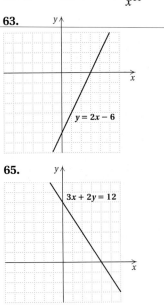

64.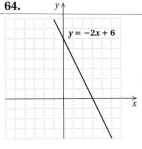

65.

66.

67.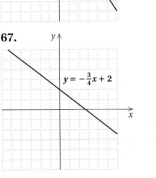

68.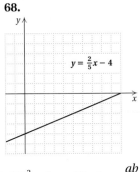

69. Ann: 6 hr; Betty: 12 hr   **71.** $27\frac{3}{11}$ min   **73.** $t = \dfrac{ab}{b+a}$

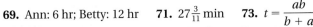

Margin Exercises, Section 6.8, pp. 535–537

1. $\dfrac{136}{5}$ **2.** $\dfrac{7x^2}{3(2-x^2)}$ **3.** $\dfrac{x}{x-1}$ **4.** $\dfrac{136}{5}$ **5.** $\dfrac{7x^2}{3(2-x^2)}$

6. $\dfrac{x}{x-1}$

Exercise Set 6.8, p. 538

1. $\dfrac{25}{4}$ **3.** $\dfrac{1}{3}$ **5.** -6 **7.** $\dfrac{1+3x}{1-5x}$ **9.** $\dfrac{2x+1}{x}$ **11.** 8

13. $x-8$ **15.** $\dfrac{y}{y-1}$ **17.** $-\dfrac{1}{a}$ **19.** $\dfrac{ab}{b-a}$

21. $\dfrac{p^2+q^2}{q+p}$ **23.** $\dfrac{2a^2+4a}{5-3a^2}$ **25.** $\dfrac{60-15a^3}{126a^2+28a^3}$

27. $\dfrac{ac}{bd}$ **29.** 1 **31.** $\dfrac{4x+1}{5x+3}$ **33.** $\mathbf{D_W}$

35. $4x^4+3x^3+2x-7$ **36.** 0 **37.** $(p-5)^2$
38. $(p+5)^2$ **39.** $50(p^2-2)$ **40.** $5(p+2)(p-10)$
41. 14 yd **42.** 12 ft, 5 ft **43.** $\dfrac{(x-1)(3x-2)}{5x-3}$

45. $\dfrac{5x+3}{3x+2}$

Margin Exercises, Section 6.9, pp. 541–545

1. $y=7x;\ 287$ **2.** $y=\frac{5}{8}x;\ \frac{25}{2}$ **3. (a)** $C=\frac{7}{360}n;$
(b) \$0.4667; \$0.0194 **4. (a)** $V=0.88E;$ **(b)** 174.24 lb
5. $y=\dfrac{63}{x};\ 3.15$ **6.** $y=\dfrac{900}{x};\ 562.5$ **7.** 8 hr
8. (a) $t=\dfrac{300}{r};$ **(b)** 7.5 hr

Exercise Set 6.9, p. 546

1. $y=4x;\ 80$ **3.** $y=\frac{8}{5}x;\ 32$ **5.** $y=3.6x;\ 72$
7. $y=\frac{25}{3}x;\ \frac{500}{3}$ **9. (a)** $P=5.6H;$ **(b)** \$196
11. (a) $C=11.25S;$ **(b)** \$101.25 **13. (a)** $M=\frac{1}{6}E;$
(b) $18.\overline{3}$ lb; **(c)** 30 lb **15. (a)** $N=80{,}000S;$
(b) 16,000,000 instructions/sec **17.** $93\frac{1}{3}$ servings
19. $y=\dfrac{75}{x};\ \frac{15}{2}$, or 7.5 **21.** $y=\dfrac{80}{x};\ 8$ **23.** $y=\dfrac{1}{x};\ \frac{1}{10}$
25. $y=\dfrac{2100}{x};\ 210$ **27.** $y=\dfrac{0.06}{x};\ 0.006$
29. (a) Direct; **(b)** $69\frac{3}{8}$ players **31. (a)** Inverse; **(b)** $4\frac{1}{2}$ hr
33. (a) $N=\dfrac{280}{P};$ **(b)** 10 gal **35. (a)** $I=\dfrac{1920}{R};$
(b) 32 amperes **37. (a)** $m=\dfrac{40}{n};$ **(b)** 10 questions
39. 8.25 ft **41.** $\mathbf{D_W}$ **43.** $\mathbf{D_W}$ **45.** $\frac{8}{5}$ **46.** 11
47. 9, 16 **48.** $-12,-9$ **49.** $\frac{2}{5},\frac{4}{7}$ **50.** $-\frac{1}{7},\frac{3}{2}$
51. $\frac{1}{3}$ **52.** $\frac{47}{20}$ **53.** -1 **54.** 49
55. The y-values become larger. **57.** $P^2=kt$
59. $P=kV^3$

Concept Reinforcement, p. 551

1. False **2.** True **3.** True **4.** True **5.** False

Summary and Review: Chapter 6, p. 551

1. 0 **2.** 6 **3.** $-6,6$ **4.** $-6,5$ **5.** -2 **6.** None
7. $\dfrac{x-2}{x+1}$ **8.** $\dfrac{7x+3}{x-3}$ **9.** $\dfrac{y-5}{y+5}$ **10.** $\dfrac{a-6}{5}$
11. $\dfrac{6}{2t-1}$ **12.** $-20t$ **13.** $\dfrac{2x^2-2x}{x+1}$ **14.** $30x^2y^2$
15. $4(a-2)$ **16.** $(y-2)(y+2)(y+1)$ **17.** $\dfrac{-3x+18}{x+7}$
18. -1 **19.** $\dfrac{2a}{a-1}$ **20.** $d+c$ **21.** $\dfrac{4}{x-4}$ **22.** $\dfrac{x+5}{2x}$
23. $\dfrac{2x+3}{x-2}$ **24.** $\dfrac{-x^2+x+26}{(x-5)(x+5)(x+1)}$ **25.** $\dfrac{2(x-2)}{x+2}$
26. $\dfrac{z}{1-z}$ **27.** c d **20.** 0 **29.** $-5,3$ **30.** $5\frac{1}{7}$ lu
31. 240 km/h, 280 km/h **32.** 95 mph, 175 mph
33. 160 defective calculators **34. (a)** $\frac{12}{13}$ c; **(b)** $4\frac{1}{5}$ c; **(c)** $9\frac{1}{3}$ c
35. 10,000 blue whales **36.** 6 **37.** $y=3x;\ 60$
38. $y=\frac{1}{2}x;\ 10$ **39.** $y=\frac{4}{5}x;\ 16$ **40.** $y=\dfrac{30}{x};\ 6$
41. $y=\dfrac{1}{x};\ \frac{1}{5}$ **42.** $y=\dfrac{0.65}{x};\ 0.13$ **43.** \$288.75 **44.** 1 hr
45. $\mathbf{D_W}$ $\dfrac{5x+6}{(x+2)(x-2)}$; used to find an equivalent
expression for each rational expression with the LCM as the
least common denominator **46.** $\mathbf{D_W}$ $\dfrac{3x+10}{(x-2)(x+2)}$;
used to find an equivalent expression for each rational
expression with the LCM as the least common denominator
47. $\mathbf{D_W}$ 4; used to clear fractions **48.** $\mathbf{D_W}$ $\dfrac{4(x-2)}{x(x+4)}$;
method 1: used to multiply by 1 using LCM/LCM; method 2:
LCM of the denominators in the numerator used to subtract
in the numerator and LCM of the denominators in the
denominator used to add in the denominator
49. $\dfrac{5(a+3)^2}{a}$ **50.** $\dfrac{10a}{(a-b)(b-c)}$
51. They are equivalent proportions.

Test: Chapter 6, p. 554

1. [6.1a] 0 **2.** [6.1a] -8 **3.** [6.1a] $-7,7$ **4.** [6.1a] 1, 2
5. [6.1a] 1 **6.** [6.1a] None **7.** [6.1c] $\dfrac{3x+7}{x+3}$
8. [6.1d] $\dfrac{a+5}{2}$ **9.** [6.2b] $\dfrac{(5x+1)(x+1)}{3x(x+2)}$
10. [6.3c] $(y-3)(y+3)(y+7)$ **11.** [6.4a] $\dfrac{23-3x}{x^3}$
12. [6.5a] $\dfrac{8-2t}{t^2+1}$ **13.** [6.4a] $\dfrac{-3}{x-3}$ **14.** [6.5a] $\dfrac{2x-5}{x-3}$
15. [6.4a] $\dfrac{8t-3}{t(t-1)}$ **16.** [6.5a] $\dfrac{-x^2-7x-15}{(x+4)(x-4)(x+1)}$

17. [6.5b] $\dfrac{x^2 + 2x - 7}{(x - 1)^2(x + 1)}$ **18.** [6.8a] $\dfrac{3y + 1}{y}$

19. [6.6a] 12   **20.** [6.6a] $-3, 5$ **21.** [6.9a] $y = 2x$; 50

22. [6.9a] $y = 0.5x$; 12.5   **23.** [6.9c] $y = \dfrac{18}{x}; \frac{9}{50}$

24. [6.9c] $y = \dfrac{22}{x}; \frac{11}{50}$ **25.** [6.9b] 240 km

26. [6.9d] $1\frac{1}{5}$ hr   **27.** [6.7b] 16 defective spark plugs
28. [6.7b] 50 zebras   **29.** [6.7a] 12 min
30. [6.7a] Craig: 65 km/h; Marilyn: 45 km/h   **31.** [6.7b] 15
32. [6.7a] Rema: 4 hr; Reggie: 10 hr   **33.** [6.8a] $\dfrac{3a + 2}{2a + 1}$

Cumulative Review: Chapters 1–6, p. 556

1. [1.2e] 3.5   **2.** [4.3d] 1, -2, 1, -1
3. [4.3g] 3, 2, 1, 0; 3   **4.** [4.3i] None of these
5. [2.5a] \$16.74   **6.** [6.7b] 27 lb   **7.** [6.7a] 30 min
8. [6.9b] **(a)** Let M = muscle weight, in pounds, and B = body weight, in pounds; $M = 0.4B$; **(b)** 76.8 lb
9. [2.5a] \$2500   **10.** [6.7a] 35 mph, 25 mph
11. [5.8a] 14 ft   **12.** [2.6a] 34 and 35
13. [4.3e] $2x^3 - 3x^2 - 2$ **14.** [1.8c] $\frac{3}{8}x + 1$
15. [4.1e], [4.2a, b] $\dfrac{9}{4x^8}$ **16.** [6.8a] $\dfrac{8x - 12}{17x}$
17. [4.7e] $-2xy^2 - 4x^2y^2 + xy^3$
18. [4.4a] $2x^5 + 6x^4 + 2x^3 - 10x^2 + 3x - 9$
19. [6.1d] $\dfrac{2}{3(y + 2)}$ **20.** [6.2b] 2   **21.** [6.4a] $x + 4$
22. [6.5a] $\dfrac{2x - 6}{(x + 2)(x - 2)}$ **23.** [4.6a] $a^2 - 9$
24. [4.6c] $36x^2 - 60x + 25$ **25.** [4.6b] $4x^6 - 1$
26. [5.3a], [5.4a] $(9a - 2)(a + 6)$ **27.** [5.5b] $(3x - 5y)^2$
28. [5.5d] $(7x - 1)(7x + 1)$ **29.** [2.3c] 3
30. [5.7b] $-4, \frac{1}{2}$ **31.** [5.7b] $-5, 4$
32. [2.7e] $\{x | x \geq -26\}$ **33.** [5.7a] 0, 4
34. [5.7b] 0, 10   **35.** [5.7b] $-20, 20$
36. [2.4b] $a = \dfrac{t}{x + y}$ **37.** [6.6a] 2
38. [6.6a] No solution
39. [3.1d]

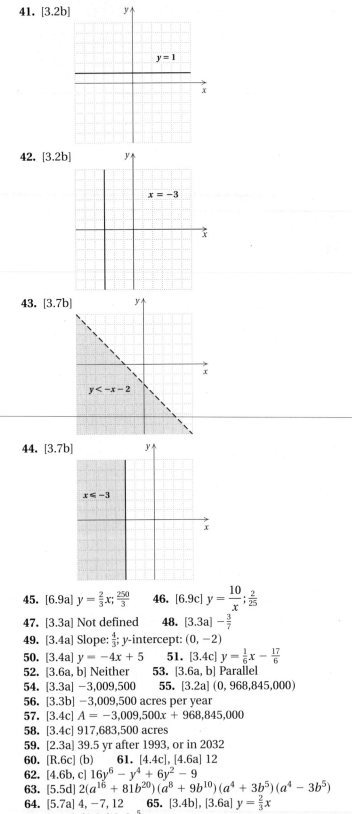

40. [3.2a]

41. [3.2b]

42. [3.2b]

43. [3.7b]

44. [3.7b]

45. [6.9a] $y = \frac{2}{3}x; \frac{250}{3}$ **46.** [6.9c] $y = \dfrac{10}{x}; \frac{2}{25}$
47. [3.3a] Not defined   **48.** [3.3a] $-\frac{3}{7}$
49. [3.4a] Slope: $\frac{4}{3}$; y-intercept: $(0, -2)$
50. [3.4a] $y = -4x + 5$ **51.** [3.4c] $y = \frac{1}{6}x - \frac{17}{6}$
52. [3.6a, b] Neither   **53.** [3.6a, b] Parallel
54. [3.3a] $-3,009,500$ **55.** [3.2a] $(0, 968,845,000)$
56. [3.3b] $-3,009,500$ acres per year
57. [3.4c] $A = -3,009,500x + 968,845,000$
58. [3.4c] 917,683,500 acres
59. [2.3a] 39.5 yr after 1993, or in 2032
60. [R.6c] (b)   **61.** [4.4c], [4.6a] 12
62. [4.6b, c] $16y^6 - y^4 + 6y^2 - 9$
63. [5.5d] $2(a^{16} + 81b^{20})(a^8 + 9b^{10})(a^4 + 3b^5)(a^4 - 3b^5)$
64. [5.7a] 4, -7, 12   **65.** [3.4b], [3.6a] $y = \frac{2}{3}x$
66. [6.1a], [6.8a] 0, 3, $\frac{5}{2}$

CHAPTER 7

Margin Exercises, Section 7.1, p. 561–564

1. Yes **2.** No **3.** $(2, -3)$ **4.** $(-4, 3)$ **5.** No solution
6. Infinite number of solutions **7. (a)** 3; **(b)** 3; **(c)** same
8. (a) 3; **(b)** same

Calculator Corner, p. 564

1. $(-1, 3)$ **2.** $(0, 5)$ **3.** $(2, -3)$ **4.** $(-4, 1)$ **5.** $(3, 2)$
6. $\left(\frac{7}{5}, -\frac{9}{5}\right)$

Exercise Set 7.1, p. 565

1. Yes **3.** No **5.** Yes **7.** Yes **9.** Yes **11.** $(4, 2)$
13. $(4, 3)$ **15.** $(-3, -3)$ **17.** No solution **19.** $(2, 2)$
21. $\left(\frac{1}{2}, 1\right)$ **23.** Infinite number of solutions
25. $(5, -3)$ **27.** $\mathbf{D_W}$ **29.** $\dfrac{2x^2 - 1}{x^2(x + 1)}$ **30.** $\dfrac{-4}{x - 2}$
31. $\dfrac{9x + 12}{(x - 4)(x + 4)}$ **32.** $\dfrac{2x + 5}{x + 3}$ **33.** Trinomial
34. Binomial **35.** Monomial **36.** None of these
37. $A = 2, B = 2$ **39.** $x + 2y = 2, x - y = 8$
41.–47. Left to the student

Margin Exercises, Section 7.2, pp. 568–570

1. $(3, 2)$ **2.** $(3, -1)$ **3.** $\left(\frac{24}{5}, -\frac{8}{5}\right)$
4. Length: 25 m; width: 21 m

Exercise Set 7.2, p. 571

1. $(1, 9)$ **3.** $(2, -4)$ **5.** $(4, 3)$ **7.** $(-2, 1)$ **9.** $(2, -4)$
11. $\left(\frac{17}{3}, \frac{16}{3}\right)$ **13.** $\left(\frac{25}{8}, -\frac{11}{4}\right)$ **15.** $(-3, 0)$ **17.** $(6, 3)$
19. Length: 94 ft; width: 50 ft
21. Length: $3\frac{1}{2}$ in.; width: $1\frac{1}{2}$ in.
23. Length: 365 mi; width: 275 mi
25. Length: 40 ft; width: 20 ft
27. Length: 110 yd; width: 60 yd **29.** 16 and 21
31. 12 and 40 **33.** 20 and 8 **35.** $\mathbf{D_W}$
37.

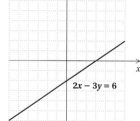
$2x - 3y = 6$

38.

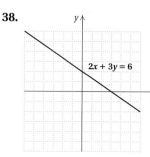
$2x + 3y = 6$

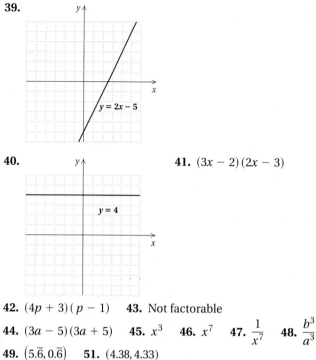

39.
$y = 2x - 5$

40.
$y = 4$

41. $(3x - 2)(2x - 3)$

42. $(4p + 3)(p - 1)$ **43.** Not factorable
44. $(3a - 5)(3a + 5)$ **45.** x^3 **46.** x^7 **47.** $\dfrac{1}{x^7}$ **48.** $\dfrac{b^3}{a^3}$
49. $(5.\overline{6}, 0.\overline{6})$ **51.** $(4.38, 4.33)$
53. Baseball: 30 yd; softball: 20 yd

Margin Exercises, Section 7.3, pp. 575–580

1. $(3, 2)$ **2.** $(1, -2)$ **3.** $(1, 4)$ **4.** $(-8, 3)$ **5.** $(1, 1)$
6. $(-2, -1)$ **7.** $\left(\frac{17}{13}, -\frac{7}{13}\right)$ **8.** No solution
9. Infinite number of solutions **10.** $(1, -1)$
11. $(2, -2)$

Calculator Corner, p. 579

1. We get equations of two lines with the same slope but
different y-intercepts. This indicates that the lines are
parallel, so the system of equations has no solution.
2. We get equivalent equations. This indicates that the lines
are the same, so the system of equations has an infinite
number of solutions.

Exercise Set 7.3, p. 581

1. $(6, -1)$ **3.** $(3, 5)$ **5.** $(2, 5)$ **7.** $\left(-\frac{1}{2}, 3\right)$
9. $\left(-1, \frac{1}{5}\right)$ **11.** No solution **13.** $(-1, -6)$ **15.** $(3, 1)$
17. $(8, 3)$ **19.** $(4, 3)$ **21.** $(1, -1)$ **23.** $(-3, -1)$
25. $(3, 2)$ **27.** $(50, 18)$ **29.** Infinite number of solutions
31. $(2, -1)$ **33.** $\left(\frac{231}{202}, \frac{117}{202}\right)$ **35.** $(-38, -22)$ **37.** $\mathbf{D_W}$
39. Slope; y-intercepts **40.** Perpendicular **41.** Solution
42. Direct **43.** Horizontal **44.** Inverse
45. Slope–intercept **46.** Graph
47.–65. Left to the student **67.** $(5, 2)$ **69.** $(0, -1)$
71. $(0, 3)$ **73.** $x = \dfrac{c - b}{a - 1}, y = \dfrac{ac - b}{a - 1}$

Margin Exercises, Section 7.4, pp. 584–589

1. Hamburger: $1.99; chicken: $1.70   **2.** Adults: 125; children: 41   **3.** 50% alcohol: 22.5 L; 70% alcohol: 7.5 L
4. Seed A: 30 lb; seed B: 20 lb   **5.** Quarters: 7; dimes: 13

Exercise Set 7.4, p. 591

1. Two-pointers: 32; three-pointers: 7
3. 24-exposure: 12; 36-exposure: 5   **5.** Hay: 10 lb; grain: 5 lb   **7.** $50 bonds: 13; $100 bonds: 6
9. Cardholders: 128; non-cardholders: 75
11. Adults: 1300; children: 330
13. Solution A: 40 L; solution B: 60 L   **15.** Dimes: 70; quarters: 33   **17.** Brazilian: 200 lb; Turkish: 100 lb
19. 28% fungicide: 100 L; 40% fungicide: 200 L
21. Large type: 4 pages; small type: 8 pages
23. 70% cashews: 36 lb; 45% cashews: 24 lb
25. Type A: 12; type B: 4; 180   **27.** Kuyatts': 32 yr; Marconis': 16 yr   **29.** Randy: 24; Mandy: 6   **31.** 50°, 130°
33. 28°, 62°   **35.** 87-octane: 12 gal; 93-octane: 6 gal
37. Dr. Zeke's $53\frac{1}{3}$ oz; Vitabrite: $26\frac{2}{3}$ oz   **39.** $\mathbf{D_W}$
41. $(5x + 9)(5x - 9)$ **42.** $(6 + a)(6 - a)$
43. $4(x^2 + 25)$ **44.** $4(x + 5)(x - 5)$

45.

$y = -2x - 3$; points $(-\frac{3}{2}, 0)$, $(0, -3)$

46.

$y = -0.1x + 0.4$; points $(0, 0.4)$, $(4, 0)$

47.

$5x - 2y = -10$; points $(0, 5)$, $(-2, 0)$

48.

$2.5x + 4y = 10$; points $(0, 2.5)$, $(4, 0)$

49. $\dfrac{x - 3}{x + 2}$ **50.** $\dfrac{x + 5}{x - 5}$ **51.** $\dfrac{-x^2 - 7x + 23}{(x + 3)(x - 4)}$
52. $\dfrac{-2x + 10}{(x + 1)(x - 1)}$ **53.** 43.75 L   **55.** $4\frac{4}{7}$ L   **57.** 54

Margin Exercises, Section 7.5, pp. 598–600

1. 324 mi   **2.** 3 hr   **3.** 168 km   **4.** 275 km/h

Translating for Success, p. 601

1. C   **2.** A   **3.** G   **4.** E   **5.** J   **6.** I   **7.** B   **8.** L
9. O   **10.** F

Exercise Set 7.5, p. 602

1.

SPEED	TIME
30	t
46	t

4.5 hr

3.

SPEED	TIME	
72	$t + 3$	$\rightarrow d = 72(t + 3)$
120	t	$\rightarrow d = 120t$

$4\frac{1}{2}$ hr

5.

SPEED	TIME	
$r + 6$	4	$\rightarrow d = (r + 6)4$
$r - 6$	10	$\rightarrow d = (r - 6)10$

14 km/h

7. 384 km   **9. (a)** 24 mph; **(b)** 90 mi
11. $1\frac{23}{43}$ min after the toddler starts running, or $\frac{23}{43}$ min after the mother starts running   **13.** 15 mi   **15.** $\mathbf{D_W}$
17. $\dfrac{x}{3}$ **18.** $\dfrac{x^5 y^3}{2}$ **19.** $\dfrac{a + 3}{2}$ **20.** $\dfrac{x - 2}{4}$ **21.** 2
22. $\dfrac{1}{x^2 + 1}$ **23.** $\dfrac{x + 2}{x + 3}$ **24.** $\dfrac{3(x + 4)}{x - 1}$ **25.** $\dfrac{x + 3}{x + 2}$
26. $\dfrac{x^2 + 25}{x^2 - 25}$ **27.** $\dfrac{x + 2}{x - 1}$ **28.** $\dfrac{x^2 + 2}{2x^2 + 1}$
29. Approximately 3603 mi   **31.** $5\frac{1}{3}$ mi

Concept Reinforcement, p. 604

1. False   **2.** True   **3.** True   **4.** False   **5.** False

Summary and Review: Chapter 7, p. 604

1. No   **2.** Yes   **3.** Yes   **4.** No   **5.** $(6, -2)$ **6.** $(6, 2)$
7. $(0, 5)$ **8.** No solution   **9.** $(0, 5)$ **10.** $(-3, 9)$
11. $(3, -1)$ **12.** $(1, 4)$ **13.** $(-2, 4)$ **14.** $(1, -2)$
15. $(3, 1)$ **16.** $(1, 4)$ **17.** $(5, -3)$ **18.** $(-2, 4)$
19. $(-2, -6)$ **20.** $(3, 2)$ **21.** $(2, -4)$
22. Infinite number of solutions   **23.** $(-4, 1)$
24. Length: 37.5 cm; width: 10.5 cm
25. Orchestra: 297; balcony: 211   **26.** 40 L of each
27. Asian: 4800 kg; African: 7200 kg
28. Peanuts: 8 lb; fancy nuts: 5 lb   **29.** About 371 min
30. 87-octane: 2.5 gal; 95-octane: 7.5 gal   **31.** Jeff: 39; his son: 13   **32.** 32°, 58°   **33.** 77°, 103°   **34.** 135 km/h
35. 412.5 mi   **36.** $\mathbf{D_W}$ The equations have the same slope but different y-intercepts, so they represent parallel lines. Thus the system of equations has no solution.

37. **D_W** Translating. It is difficult to define the variables and write equations that represent the mathematical relationships in the exercises. Answers may vary.
38. $960   **39.** $C = 1, D = 3$ **40.** $(2, 0)$
41. $y = -x + 5, y = \frac{2}{3}x$ **42.** $x + y = 4, x + y = -3$
43. Rabbits: 12; pheasants: 23

Test: Chapter 7, p. 607

1. [7.1a] No
2. [7.1b]

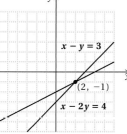

3. [7.2a] $(8, -2)$ **4.** [7.2b] $(-1, 3)$ **5.** [7.2a] No solution
6. [7.3a] $(1, -5)$ **7.** [7.3b] $(12, -6)$ **8.** [7.3b] $\left(\frac{1}{2}, -\frac{2}{3}\right)$
9. [7.3b] $(5, 1)$ **10.** [7.2c] Length: 2108.5 yd;
width: 2024.5 yd   **11.** [7.4a] Solution A: 40 L;
solution B: 20 L   **12.** [7.5a] 40 km/h
13. [7.2c] Concessions: $2850; rides: $1425
14. [7.2c] Hay: 415 acres; oats: 235 acres
15. [7.2c] 45°, 135°   **16.** [7.4a] 87-octane: 4 gal;
93-octane: 8 gal   **17.** [7.4a] 20 min
18. [7.5a] 11 hr   **19.** [7.1a] $C = -\frac{19}{2}; D = \frac{14}{3}$ **20.** [7.4a] 5
21. [3.4c], [7.1b] $y = \frac{1}{5}x + \frac{17}{5}, y = -\frac{3}{5}x + \frac{9}{5}$
22. [3.4c], [7.1b] $x = 3, y = -2$

CHAPTER 8

Margin Exercises, Section 8.1, pp. 610–614

1. $6, -6$ **2.** $8, -8$ **3.** $11, -11$ **4.** $12, -12$ **5.** 4
6. 7   **7.** 10   **8.** 21   **9.** -7 **10.** -13 **11.** 3.873
12. 5.477   **13.** 31.305   **14.** -25.842 **15.** 0.816
16. -1.732 **17.** **(a)** About 28.3 mph; **(b)** about 49.6 mph
18. 227   **19.** $45 + x$ **20.** $\frac{x}{x + 2}$ **21.** $x^2 + 4$ **22.** Yes
23. No   **24.** No   **25.** Yes   **26.** 13   **27.** $|7w|$ **28.** $|xy|$
29. $|xy|$ **30.** $|x - 11|$ **31.** $|x + 4|$ **32.** xy **33.** xy
34. $x - 11$ **35.** $x + 4$ **36.** $5y$ **37.** $\frac{1}{2}t$

Calculator Corner, p. 611

1. 6.557   **2.** 10.050   **3.** 102.308   **4.** 0.632
5. -96.985 **6.** -0.804

Exercise Set 8.1, p. 615

1. $2, -2$ **3.** $3, -3$ **5.** $10, -10$ **7.** $13, -13$
9. $16, -16$ **11.** 2   **13.** -3 **15.** -6 **17.** -15
19. 19   **21.** 2.236   **23.** 20.785   **25.** -18.647
27. 2.779   **29.** -120 **31.** **(a)** 13 spaces; **(b)** 24 spaces
33. 0.833 sec   **35.** 0.911 sec   **37.** 200   **39.** $a - 4$

41. $t^2 + 1$ **43.** $\frac{3}{x + 2}$ **45.** No   **47.** Yes   **49.** No
51. c **53.** $3x$ **55.** $8p$ **57.** ab **59.** $34d$ **61.** $x + 3$
63. $a - 5$ **65.** $2a - 5$ **67.** **D_W**   **69.** 61°, 119°
70. 38°, 52°   **71.** $10,660   **72.** $\frac{1}{x + 3}$ **73.** 1
74. $\frac{(x + 2)(x - 2)}{(x + 1)(x - 1)}$ **75.** 1.7, 2.2, 2.6   **77.** $16, -16$
79. $7, -7$

Margin Exercises, Section 8.2, pp. 618–621

1. **(a)** 20; **(b)** 20   **2.** $\sqrt{33}$ **3.** 5   **4.** $\sqrt{\frac{30}{77}}$
5. $\sqrt{x^2 + x}$ **6.** $\sqrt{x^2 - 4}$ **7.** $4\sqrt{2}$ **8.** $2\sqrt{23}$
9. $8\sqrt{2t}$ **10.** $11\sqrt{3q}$ **11.** $3x\sqrt{7}$ **12.** $x + 7$ **13.** $9m$
14. $\sqrt{3}(x - 10)$ **15.** t^2 **16.** t^{10} **17.** h^{23} **18.** $x^3\sqrt{x}$
19. $2x^5\sqrt{6x}$ **20.** $3\sqrt{2}$ **21.** 10   **22.** $4x^3y^2$
23. $5xy^2\sqrt{2xy}$ **24.** $14q^7r^4\sqrt{3q}$

Calculator Corner, p. 621

1. False   **2.** False   **3.** False   **4.** True

Exercise Set 8.2, p. 622

1. $2\sqrt{3}$ **3.** $5\sqrt{3}$ **5.** $2\sqrt{5}$ **7.** $10\sqrt{6}$ **9.** $9\sqrt{6}$
11. $3\sqrt{x}$ **13.** $4\sqrt{3x}$ **15.** $4\sqrt{a}$ **17.** $8y$ **19.** $x\sqrt{13}$
21. $2t\sqrt{2}$ **23.** $6\sqrt{5}$ **25.** $12\sqrt{2y}$ **27.** $2x\sqrt{7}$
29. $x - 3$ **31.** $\sqrt{2}(2x + 1)$ **33.** $\sqrt{y}(6 + y)$ **35.** t^3
37. x^6 **39.** $x^2\sqrt{x}$ **41.** $t^9\sqrt{t}$ **43.** $(y - 2)^4$
45. $2(x + 5)^5$ **47.** $6m\sqrt{m}$ **49.** $2a^2\sqrt{2a}$
51. $2p^8\sqrt{26p}$ **53.** $8x^3y\sqrt{7y}$ **55.** $3\sqrt{6}$ **57.** $3\sqrt{10}$
59. $6\sqrt{7x}$ **61.** $6\sqrt{xy}$ **63.** 13   **65.** $5b\sqrt{3}$ **67.** $2t$
69. $a\sqrt{bc}$ **71.** $2xy\sqrt{2xy}$ **73.** 18   **75.** $\sqrt{10x - 5}$
77. $x + 2$ **79.** $6xy^3\sqrt{3xy}$ **81.** $10x^2y^3\sqrt{5xy}$
83. $33p^4q^2\sqrt{2pq}$ **85.** $16a^3b^3c^5\sqrt{3abc}$ **87.** **D_W**
89. $(-2, 4)$ **90.** $\left(\frac{1}{8}, \frac{9}{8}\right)$ **91.** $(2, 1)$ **92.** $(10, 3)$
93. 360 ft²   **94.** Adults: 350; children: 61   **95.** 80 L of
30%; 120 L of 50%   **96.** 10 mph   **97.** $\sqrt{5}\sqrt{x - 1}$
99. $\sqrt{x + 6}\sqrt{x - 6}$ **101.** $x\sqrt{x - 2}$ **103.** 0.5
105. $4y\sqrt{3}$ **107.** $18(x + 1)\sqrt{y(x + 1)}$ **109.** $2x^3\sqrt{5x}$

Margin Exercises, Section 8.3, pp. 626–629

1. 4   **2.** 5   **3.** $x\sqrt{6x}$ **4.** $\frac{4}{3}$ **5.** $\frac{1}{5}$ **6.** $\frac{6}{x}$ **7.** $\frac{3}{4}$
8. $\frac{15}{16}$ **9.** $\frac{7}{y^5}$ **10.** **(a)** $\frac{\sqrt{15}}{5}$; **(b)** $\frac{\sqrt{15}}{5}$ **11.** $\frac{\sqrt{10}}{4}$
12. $\frac{10\sqrt{3}}{3}$ **13.** $\frac{\sqrt{21}}{7}$ **14.** $\frac{\sqrt{5r}}{r}$ **15.** $\frac{8y\sqrt{7}}{7}$

Exercise Set 8.3, p. 630

1. 3   **3.** 6   **5.** $\sqrt{5}$ **7.** $\frac{1}{5}$ **9.** $\frac{2}{5}$ **11.** 2   **13.** $3y$
15. $\frac{4}{7}$ **17.** $\frac{1}{6}$ **19.** $-\frac{4}{9}$ **21.** $\frac{8}{17}$ **23.** $\frac{13}{14}$ **25.** $\frac{5}{x}$
27. $\frac{3a}{25}$ **29.** $\frac{5}{y^5}$ **31.** $\frac{x^9}{7}$ **33.** $\frac{\sqrt{10}}{5}$ **35.** $\frac{\sqrt{14}}{4}$

37. $\dfrac{\sqrt{3}}{6}$ **39.** $\dfrac{\sqrt{10}}{6}$ **41.** $\dfrac{3\sqrt{5}}{5}$ **43.** $\dfrac{2\sqrt{6}}{3}$ **45.** $\dfrac{\sqrt{3x}}{x}$

47. $\dfrac{\sqrt{xy}}{y}$ **49.** $\dfrac{x\sqrt{5}}{10}$ **51.** $\dfrac{\sqrt{14}}{2}$ **53.** $\dfrac{3\sqrt{2}}{4}$ **55.** $\dfrac{\sqrt{6}}{2}$

57. $\sqrt{2}$ **59.** $\dfrac{\sqrt{55}}{11}$ **61.** $\dfrac{\sqrt{21}}{6}$ **63.** $\dfrac{\sqrt{6}}{2}$ **65.** 5

67. $\dfrac{\sqrt{3x}}{x}$ **69.** $\dfrac{4y\sqrt{5}}{5}$ **71.** $\dfrac{a\sqrt{2a}}{4}$ **73.** $\dfrac{\sqrt{42x}}{3x}$

75. $\dfrac{3\sqrt{6}}{8c}$ **77.** $\dfrac{y\sqrt{xy}}{x}$ **79.** $\dfrac{3n\sqrt{10}}{8}$ **81.** $\mathbf{D_W}$

83. $(4, 2)$ **84.** $(10, 30)$ **85.** No solution
86. Infinite number of solutions **87.** $\left(-\frac{5}{2}, -\frac{9}{2}\right)$

88. $\left(\frac{26}{23}, \frac{44}{23}\right)$ **89.** $\dfrac{(x+7)^2}{x-7}$ **90.** $\dfrac{(x-2)(x-5)}{(x-3)(x-4)}$

91. $\dfrac{a-5}{2}$ **92.** $\dfrac{x-3}{x-2}$ **93.** $9x^2 - 49$ **94.** $16a^2 - 25b^2$

95. $21x - 9y$ **96.** $14a - 6b$ **97.** 1.57 sec; 3.14 sec;
8.88 sec; 11.10 sec **99.** 1 sec

101. $\dfrac{\sqrt{5}}{40}$ **103.** $\dfrac{\sqrt{5x}}{5x^2}$ **105.** $\dfrac{\sqrt{3ab}}{b}$ **107.** $\dfrac{3\sqrt{10}}{100}$

109. $\dfrac{y-x}{xy}$

Margin Exercises, Section 8.4, pp. 634–637

1. $12\sqrt{2}$ **2.** $5\sqrt{5}$ **3.** $-12\sqrt{10}$ **4.** $5\sqrt{6}$ **5.** $\sqrt{x+1}$

6. $\frac{3}{2}\sqrt{2}$ **7.** $\dfrac{8\sqrt{15}}{15}$ **8.** $\sqrt{15} + \sqrt{6}$

9. $4 + 3\sqrt{5} - 4\sqrt{2} - 3\sqrt{10}$ **10.** $2 - a$
11. $25 + 10\sqrt{x} + x$ **12.** 2 **13.** $7 - \sqrt{5}$

14. $\sqrt{5} + \sqrt{2}$ **15.** $1 + \sqrt{x}$ **16.** $\dfrac{21 - 3\sqrt{5}}{44}$

17. $-6 - \sqrt{35}$ **18.** $\dfrac{7 + 7\sqrt{x}}{1 - x}$

Exercise Set 8.4, p. 638

1. $16\sqrt{3}$ **3.** $4\sqrt{5}$ **5.** $13\sqrt{x}$ **7.** $-9\sqrt{d}$ **9.** $25\sqrt{2}$
11. $\sqrt{3}$ **13.** $\sqrt{5}$ **15.** $13\sqrt{2}$ **17.** $3\sqrt{3}$ **19.** $2\sqrt{2}$
21. 0 **23.** $(2 + 9x)\sqrt{x}$ **25.** $(3 - 2x)\sqrt{3}$
27. $3\sqrt{2x + 2}$ **29.** $(x + 3)\sqrt{x^3 - 1}$

31. $(4a^2 + a^2b - 5b)\sqrt{b}$ **33.** $\dfrac{2\sqrt{3}}{3}$ **35.** $\dfrac{13\sqrt{2}}{2}$

37. $\dfrac{\sqrt{6}}{6}$ **39.** $\sqrt{15} - \sqrt{3}$ **41.** $10 + 5\sqrt{3} - 2\sqrt{7} - \sqrt{21}$

43. $9 - 4\sqrt{5}$ **45.** -62 **47.** 1 **49.** $13 + \sqrt{5}$
51. $x - 2\sqrt{xy} + y$ **53.** $-\sqrt{3} - \sqrt{5}$ **55.** $5 - 2\sqrt{6}$

57. $\dfrac{4\sqrt{10} - 4}{9}$ **59.** $5 - 2\sqrt{7}$ **61.** $\dfrac{12 - 3\sqrt{x}}{16 - x}$

63. $\dfrac{24 + 3\sqrt{x} + 8\sqrt{2} + \sqrt{2x}}{64 - x}$ **65.** $\mathbf{D_W}$ **67.** $\frac{5}{11}$

68. $-\frac{38}{13}$ **69.** $-1, 6$ **70.** 2, 5 **71.** $\dfrac{x^6}{3}$ **72.** $\dfrac{x-3}{4(x+3)}$

73. Jolly Juice: 1.6 L; Real Squeeze: 6.4 L **74.** $\frac{1}{3}$ hr
75. $-9, -2, -5, -17, -0.678375$ **77.** Not equivalent
79. Not correct **81.** $11\sqrt{3} - 10\sqrt{2}$

83. True; $\left(3\sqrt{x+2}\right)^2 = \left(3\sqrt{x+2}\right)\left(3\sqrt{x+2}\right) =$
$(3 \cdot 3)\left(\sqrt{x+2} \cdot \sqrt{x+2}\right) = 9(x+2)$

Margin Exercises, Section 8.5, pp. 642–646

1. $\frac{64}{3}$ **2.** 2 **3.** $\frac{3}{8}$ **4.** 4 **5.** 1 **6.** 4 **7.** About
276 mi **8.** About 9 mi **9.** About 52 ft

Calculator Corner, p. 645

1. Left to the student **2.** Left to the student

Exercise Set 8.5, p. 647

1. 36 **3.** 18.49 **5.** 165 **7.** $\frac{621}{2}$ **9.** 5 **11.** 3
13. $\frac{17}{4}$ **15.** No solution **17.** No solution **19.** 9
21. 12 **23.** 1, 5 **25.** 3 **27.** 5 **29.** No solution
31. $-\frac{10}{3}$ **33.** 3 **35.** No solution **37.** 9 **39.** 1
41. 8 **43.** 256 **45.** About 232 mi **47.** 16,200 ft
49. 211.25 ft; 281.25 ft **51.** $\mathbf{D_W}$ **53.** Slope; y-intercepts
54. Square root **55.** Principal square root
56. Positive; direct **57.** Quotient **58.** Positive; inverse
59. Quotient **60.** Product **61.** $-2, 2$ **63.** $-\frac{57}{16}$
65. 13 **67.** Left to the student **69.** Left to the student

Margin Exercises, Section 8.6, pp. 652–653

1. $\sqrt{65} \approx 8.062$ **2.** $\sqrt{75} \approx 8.660$ **3.** $\sqrt{10} \approx 3.162$
4. $\sqrt{175} \approx 13.229$ **5.** $\sqrt{325}$ ft ≈ 18.028 ft

Translating for Success, p. 654

1. J **2.** K **3.** N **4.** H **5.** G **6.** E **7.** O **8.** D
9. B **10.** C

Exercise Set 8.6, p. 655

1. 17 **3.** $\sqrt{32} \approx 5.657$ **5.** 12 **7.** 4 **9.** 26 **11.** 12
13. 2 **15.** $\sqrt{2} \approx 1.414$ **17.** 5 **19.** 3
21. $\sqrt{211,200,000}$ ft $\approx 14,533$ ft **23.** 240 ft
25. $\sqrt{18}$ cm ≈ 4.243 cm **27.** $\sqrt{208}$ ft ≈ 14.422 ft
29. $\mathbf{D_W}$ **31.** $\left(-\frac{3}{2}, -\frac{1}{16}\right)$ **32.** $\left(\frac{8}{5}, 9\right)$ **33.** $\left(-\frac{9}{19}, \frac{91}{38}\right)$
34. $(-10, 1)$ **35.** $-\frac{1}{3}$ **36.** $\frac{5}{8}$ **37.** $12 - 2\sqrt{6} \approx 7.101$

Concept Reinforcement, p. 657

1. True **2.** True **3.** True **4.** False **5.** False
6. False **7.** True **8.** True

Summary and Review: Chapter 8, p. 657

1. $8, -8$ **2.** $20, -20$ **3.** 6 **4.** -13 **5.** 1.732
6. 9.950 **7.** -17.892 **8.** 0.742 **9.** -2.055
10. 394.648 **11.** $x^2 + 4$ **12.** $5ab^3$ **13.** No **14.** Yes
15. No **16.** No **17.** No **18.** No **19.** m
20. $x - 4$ **21.** $\sqrt{21}$ **22.** $\sqrt{x^2 - 9}$ **23.** $-4\sqrt{3}$
24. $4t\sqrt{2}$ **25.** $\sqrt{t-7}\sqrt{t+7}$ **26.** $x + 8$ **27.** x^4

28. $m^7\sqrt{m}$ **29.** $2\sqrt{15}$ **30.** $2x\sqrt{10}$ **31.** $5xy\sqrt{2}$

32. $10a^2b\sqrt{ab}$ **33.** $\frac{5}{8}$ **34.** $\frac{2}{3}$ **35.** $\frac{7}{t}$ **36.** $\frac{\sqrt{2}}{2}$

37. $\frac{\sqrt{2}}{4}$ **38.** $\frac{\sqrt{5y}}{y}$ **39.** $\frac{2\sqrt{3}}{3}$ **40.** $\frac{\sqrt{15}}{5}$ **41.** $\frac{x\sqrt{30}}{6}$

42. $8 - 4\sqrt{3}$ **43.** $13\sqrt{5}$ **44.** $\sqrt{5}$ **45.** $\frac{\sqrt{2}}{2}$

46. $7 + 4\sqrt{3}$ **47.** 1 **48.** 52 **49.** No solution
50. $0, 3$ **51.** 9 **52.** 20 **53.** $\sqrt{3} \approx 1.732$
54. $\sqrt{2{,}600{,}000{,}000}$ ft $\approx 50{,}990$ ft **55.** 9 ft
56. (a) About 63 mph; **(b)** 405 ft
57. $\mathbf{D_W}$ It is incorrect to take the square roots of the terms in the numerator individually—that is, $\sqrt{a + b}$ and $\sqrt{a} + \sqrt{b}$ are not equivalent. The following is correct:
$$\sqrt{\frac{9 + 100}{25}} = \frac{\sqrt{9 + 100}}{\sqrt{25}} = \frac{\sqrt{109}}{5}.$$
58. $\mathbf{D_W}$ **(a)** $\sqrt{5x^2} = \sqrt{5}\sqrt{x^2} = \sqrt{5} \cdot |x| = |x|\sqrt{5}$. The given statement is correct.
(b) Let $b = 3$. Then $\sqrt{b^2 - 4} = \sqrt{3^2 - 4} = \sqrt{9 - 4} = \sqrt{5}$, but $b - 2 = 3 - 2 = 1$. The given statement is false.
(c) Let $x = 3$. Then $\sqrt{x^2 + 16} = \sqrt{3^2 + 16} = \sqrt{9 + 16} = \sqrt{25} = 5$, but $x + 4 = 3 + 4 = 7$. The given statement is false.
59. $\sqrt{1525}$ mi ≈ 39.051 mi **60.** 2 **61.** $b = \pm\sqrt{A^2 - a^2}$
62. 6

Test: Chapter 8, p. 660

1. [8.1a] $9, -9$ **2.** [8.1a] 8 **3.** [8.1a] -5 **4.** [8.1b] 10.770 **5.** [8.1b] -9.349 **6.** [8.1b] 4.127 **7.** [8.1d] $4 - y^3$ **8.** [8.1e] Yes **9.** [8.1e] No **10.** [8.1f] a
11. [8.1f] $6y$ **12.** [8.2c] $\sqrt{30}$ **13.** [8.2c] $\sqrt{x^2 - 64}$
14. [8.2a] $3\sqrt{3}$ **15.** [8.2a] $5\sqrt{x - 1}$ **16.** [8.2b] $t^2\sqrt{t}$
17. [8.2c] $5\sqrt{2}$ **18.** [8.2c] $3ab^2\sqrt{2}$ **19.** [8.3b] $\frac{3}{2}$
20. [8.3b] $\frac{12}{a}$ **21.** [8.3c] $\frac{\sqrt{10}}{5}$ **22.** [8.3c] $\frac{\sqrt{2xy}}{y}$
23. [8.3a, c] $\frac{3\sqrt{6}}{8}$ **24.** [8.3a] $\frac{\sqrt{7}}{4y}$ **25.** [8.4a] $-6\sqrt{2}$
26. [8.4a] $\frac{6\sqrt{5}}{5}$ **27.** [8.4b] $21 - 8\sqrt{5}$ **28.** [8.4b] 11
29. [8.4c] $\frac{40 + 10\sqrt{5}}{11}$ **30.** [8.6a] $\sqrt{80} \approx 8.944$
31. [8.5a] 48 **32.** [8.5a] $-2, 2$ **33.** [8.5b] -3
34. [8.5c] **(a)** About 237 mi; **(b)** 34,060.5 ft
35. [8.6b] $\sqrt{15{,}700}$ yd ≈ 125.300 yd **36.** [8.1a] $\sqrt{5}$
37. [8.2b] y^{8n}

Cumulative Review: Chapters 1–8, p. 662

1. [4.3a] -15 **2.** [4.3e] $-4x^3 - \frac{1}{7}x^2 - 2$ **3.** [6.1a] $-\frac{1}{2}$
4. [8.1e] No **5.** [8.4b] 1 **6.** [8.1a] -14 **7.** [8.2c] 15
8. [8.4b] $3 - 2\sqrt{2}$ **9.** [8.3a, c] $\frac{9\sqrt{10}}{25}$ **10.** [8.4a] $12\sqrt{5}$
11. [4.7f] $9x^8 - 4y^{10}$ **12.** [4.6c] $x^4 + 8x^2 + 16$
13. [4.6a] $8x^2 - \frac{1}{8}$ **14.** [6.5a] $\frac{4x + 2}{2x - 1}$
15. [4.4a, c] $-3x^3 + 8x^2 - 5x$ **16.** [6.1d] $\frac{2(x - 5)}{3(x - 1)}$

17. [6.2b] $\frac{(x + 1)(x - 3)}{2(x + 3)}$ **18.** [4.8b] $3x^2 + 4x + 9 + \frac{13}{x - 2}$
19. [8.2a] $\sqrt{2}(x - 1)$ **20.** [4.1d, f] $\frac{1}{x^{12}}$ **21.** [8.3b] $\frac{5}{x^4}$
22. [6.8a] $2(x - 1)$ **23.** [5.5d] $3(1 + 2x^4)(1 - 2x^4)$
24. [5.1b] $4t(3 - t - 12t^3)$ **25.** [5.3a], [5.4a] $2(3x - 2)(x - 4)$ **26.** [5.6a] $(2x + 1)(2x - 1)(x + 1)$
27. [5.5b] $(4x^2 - 7)^2$ **28.** [5.2a] $(x + 15)(x - 12)$
29. [5.7b] $-17, 0$ **30.** [2.7e] $\{x \mid x > -6\}$ **31.** [6.6a] $-\frac{12}{5}$
32. [5.7b] $-5, 6$ **33.** [2.7e] $\{x \mid x \le -\frac{9}{2}\}$ **34.** [5.7b] $-9, 9$
35. [8.5a] 41 **36.** [8.5b] 9 **37.** [2.3b] $\frac{2}{5}$ **38.** [6.8a] $\frac{1}{3}$
39. [7.2a] $(4, 1)$ **40.** [7.3a] $(3, -8)$ **41.** [2.4b] $p = \frac{4A}{r + q}$
42. [3.7b]

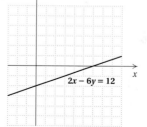

43. [3.2b]

$x = 5$

44. [3.2a]

$2x - 6y = 12$

45. [3.4c] $y = \frac{11}{4}x - \frac{19}{4}$ **46.** [3.4a] Slope: $\frac{5}{3}$; y-intercept: $(0, -3)$ **47.** [4.3a] $-2; 1; -2; -5; -2$ **48.** [6.7b] About 72 home runs **49.** [6.9d] 0.4 ft **50.** [7.4a] Hamburger: $2.95; milkshake: $2.50 **51.** [8.6b] $\sqrt{48}$ m ≈ 6.9 m
52. [2.6a] $38°, 76°, 66°$ **53.** [6.7b] 20 defective resistors
54. [5.8a] Length: 15 m; width: 12 m **55.** [7.4a] Dimes: 65; quarters: 50 **56.** [2.5a] $2600 **57.** [6.7a] 60 mph
58. [8.3c] (a) **59.** [6.6a] (b) **60.** [6.8a] (a)
61. [4.7f] (e) **62.** [1.2d, e] $<$ **63.** [1.2d, e] $>$
64. [7.4a] 300 L **65.** [7.3b], [8.5a] $(9, 4)$ **66.** [8.6b] Yes
67. [8.6a] $\frac{\sqrt{3}}{2} \approx 0.866$

CHAPTER 9

Margin Exercises, Section 9.1, pp. 666–672

1. **(a)** y-intercept: $(0, -3)$; x-intercept: $\left(-\frac{9}{2}, 0\right)$;

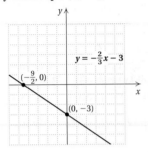

(b) $-\frac{9}{2}$; **(c)** $-\frac{9}{2}$; first coordinate; $\left(-\frac{9}{2}, 0\right)$
2. **(a)** $-1, 3$; **(b)** $-1, 3$; first coordinates, $(-1, 0)$, $(3, 0)$
3. $6x^2 + 7x - 3 = 0$; $a = 6$, $b = 7$, $c = -3$
4. $y^2 - 8y = 0$; $a = 1$, $b = -8$, $c = 0$
5. $x^2 + 9x - 3 = 0$; $a = 1$, $b = 9$, $c = -3$
6. $4x^2 + x + 4 = 0$; $a = 4$, $b = 1$, $c = 4$
7. $5x^2 - 21 = 0$; $a = 5$, $b = 0$, $c = -21$ **8.** $0, -4$
9. $0, \frac{3}{5}$ **10.** $-2, \frac{3}{4}$ **11.** $1, 4$ **12.** $5, 13$
13. **(a)**

14 diagonals;

(b) 14 diagonals; **(c)** 11 sides

Calculator Corner, p. 672

1. $0.6, 1$ **2.** $-1.5, 5$ **3.** $3, 8$ **4.** $2, 4$

Exercise Set 9.1, p. 673

1. $x^2 - 3x + 2 = 0$; $a = 1$, $b = -3$, $c = 2$
3. $7x^2 - 4x + 3 = 0$; $a = 7$, $b = -4$, $c = 3$
5. $2x^2 - 3x + 5 = 0$; $a = 2$, $b = -3$, $c = 5$
7. $0, -5$ **9.** $0, -2$ **11.** $0, \frac{2}{5}$ **13.** $0, -1$
15. $0, 3$ **17.** $0, \frac{1}{5}$ **19.** $0, \frac{3}{14}$ **21.** $0, \frac{81}{2}$ **23.** $-12, 4$
25. $-5, -1$ **27.** $-9, 2$ **29.** $3, 5$ **31.** -5 **33.** 4
35. $-\frac{2}{3}, \frac{1}{2}$ **37.** $-\frac{2}{3}, 4$ **39.** $-1, \frac{5}{3}$ **41.** $-5, -1$
43. $-2, 7$ **45.** $-5, 4$ **47.** 4 **49.** $-2, 1$
51. $-\frac{2}{5}, 10$ **53.** $-4, 6$ **55.** 1 **57.** $2, 5$
59. No solution   **61.** $-\frac{5}{2}, 1$ **63.** 35 diagonals
65. 7 sides   **67.** $\mathbf{D_W}$ **69.** 8 **70.** -13 **71.** $2\sqrt{2}$
72. $2\sqrt{3}$ **73.** $2\sqrt{5}$ **74.** $2\sqrt{22}$ **75.** $9\sqrt{5}$
76. $2\sqrt{255}$ **77.** 2.646 **78.** 4.796 **79.** 1.528
80. 22.908 **81.** $-\frac{1}{3}, 1$ **83.** $0, \dfrac{\sqrt{5}}{5}$ **85.** $-1.7, 4$
87. $-1.7, 3$ **89.** $-2, 3$ **91.** 4

Margin Exercises, Section 9.2, pp. 675–680

1. $\sqrt{10}, -\sqrt{10}$ **2.** 0 **3.** $\dfrac{\sqrt{6}}{2}, -\dfrac{\sqrt{6}}{2}$ **4.** $7, -1$
5. $-4 \pm \sqrt{11}$ **6.** $-5, 11$ **7.** $1 \pm \sqrt{5}$ **8.** $2, 4$
9. $-10, 2$ **10.** $6 \pm \sqrt{13}$ **11.** $-2, 5$ **12.** $\dfrac{-3 \pm \sqrt{33}}{4}$
13. About 7.5 sec

Exercise Set 9.2, p. 681

1. $11, -11$ **3.** $\sqrt{7}, -\sqrt{7}$ **5.** $\dfrac{\sqrt{15}}{5}, -\dfrac{\sqrt{15}}{5}$ **7.** $\frac{5}{2}, -\frac{5}{2}$
9. $\dfrac{7\sqrt{3}}{3}, -\dfrac{7\sqrt{3}}{3}$ **11.** $\sqrt{3}, -\sqrt{3}$ **13.** $\frac{8}{7}, -\frac{8}{7}$
15. $-7, 1$ **17.** $-3 \pm \sqrt{21}$ **19.** $-13 \pm 2\sqrt{2}$
21. $7 \pm 2\sqrt{3}$ **23.** $-9 \pm \sqrt{34}$ **25.** $\dfrac{-3 \pm \sqrt{14}}{2}$
27. $-5, 11$ **29.** $-15, 1$ **31.** $-2, 8$ **33.** $-21, -1$
35. $1 \pm \sqrt{6}$ **37.** $11 \pm \sqrt{19}$ **39.** $-5 \pm \sqrt{29}$
41. $\dfrac{7 \pm \sqrt{57}}{2}$ **43.** $-7, 4$ **45.** $\dfrac{-3 \pm \sqrt{17}}{4}$
47. $\dfrac{-3 \pm \sqrt{145}}{4}$ **49.** $\dfrac{-2 \pm \sqrt{7}}{3}$ **51.** $-\frac{1}{2}, 5$
53. $-\frac{5}{2}, \frac{2}{3}$ **55.** About 9.6 sec   **57.** About 4.4 sec
59. $\mathbf{D_W}$ **61.** Product   **62.** Quadratic; equivalent
63. Principal square root   **64.** Square root
65. Quotient   **66.** Product   **67.** Quotient
68. Power; multiply   **69.** $-12, 12$ **71.** $-16\sqrt{2}, 16\sqrt{2}$
73. $-2\sqrt{c}, 2\sqrt{c}$ **75.** $49.896, -49.896$ **77.** $-9, 9$

Margin Exercises, Section 9.3, pp. 685–688

1. $-4, \frac{1}{2}$ **2.** $-2, 5$ **3.** $-2 \pm \sqrt{11}$
4. No real-number solutions   **5.** $\dfrac{4 \pm \sqrt{31}}{5}$
6. $-0.3, 1.9$

Calculator Corner, p. 687

1. The equations $x^2 + x = -1$ and $x^2 + x + 1 = 0$ are equivalent. The graph of $y = x^2 + x + 1$ has no x-intercepts, so the equation $x^2 + x = -1$ has no real-number solutions.
2. Yes   **3.** No

Calculator Corner, p. 688

1. $-1.3, 5.3$ **2.** $-5.3, 1.3$ **3.** $-0.3, 1.9$

Exercise Set 9.3, p. 689

1. $-3, 7$ **3.** 3 **5.** $-\frac{4}{3}, 2$ **7.** $-\frac{5}{2}, \frac{3}{2}$ **9.** $-3, 3$
11. $1 \pm \sqrt{3}$ **13.** $5 \pm \sqrt{3}$ **15.** $-2 \pm \sqrt{7}$
17. $\dfrac{-4 \pm \sqrt{10}}{3}$ **19.** $\dfrac{5 \pm \sqrt{33}}{4}$ **21.** $\dfrac{1 \pm \sqrt{3}}{2}$
23. No real-number solutions   **25.** $\dfrac{5 \pm \sqrt{73}}{6}$

27. $\dfrac{3 \pm \sqrt{29}}{2}$　**29.** $-\sqrt{5}, \sqrt{5}$　**31.** $-2 \pm \sqrt{3}$

33. $\dfrac{5 \pm \sqrt{37}}{2}$　**35.** $-1.3, 5.3$　**37.** $-0.2, 6.2$

39. $-1.2, 0.2$　**41.** $0.3, 2.4$　**43.** $\mathbf{D_W}$　**45.** $3\sqrt{10}$
46. $\sqrt{6}$　**47.** $2\sqrt{2}$　**48.** $(9x-2)\sqrt{x}$　**49.** $4\sqrt{5}$

50. $3x^2\sqrt{3x}$　**51.** $30x^5\sqrt{10}$　**52.** $\dfrac{\sqrt{21}}{3}$　**53.** $y = \dfrac{141}{x}$

54. $3\frac{1}{3}$ hr　**55.** $0, 2$　**57.** $\dfrac{3 \pm \sqrt{5}}{2}$　**59.** $\dfrac{-7 \pm \sqrt{61}}{2}$

61. $\dfrac{-2 \pm \sqrt{10}}{2}$　**63.–69.** Left to the student

Margin Exercises, Section 9.4, pp. 691–693

1. (a) $I = \dfrac{9R}{E}$;　**(b)** $R = \dfrac{EI}{9}$　**2.** $x = \dfrac{y-5}{a-b}$　**3.** $f = \dfrac{pq}{q+p}$

4. $L = \dfrac{r^2}{20}$　**5.** $L = \dfrac{T^2 g}{4\pi^2}$　**6.** $m = \dfrac{E}{c^2}$　**7.** $r = \sqrt{\dfrac{A}{\pi}}$

8. $n = \dfrac{1 + \sqrt{1 + 4N}}{2}$

Exercise Set 9.4, p. 694

1. $I = \dfrac{VQ}{q}$　**3.** $m = \dfrac{Sd^2}{kM}$　**5.** $d^2 = \dfrac{kmM}{S}$

7. $W = \sqrt{\dfrac{10t}{T}}$　**9.** $t = \dfrac{A}{a+b}$　**11.** $x = \dfrac{y-c}{a+b}$

13. $a = \dfrac{bt}{b-t}$　**15.** $p = \dfrac{qf}{q-f}$　**17.** $b = \dfrac{2A}{h}$

19. $h = \dfrac{S - 2\pi r^2}{2\pi r}$, or $h = \dfrac{S}{2\pi r} - r$　**21.** $R = \dfrac{r_1 r_2}{r_2 + r_1}$

23. $Q = \dfrac{P^2}{289}$　**25.** $E = \dfrac{mv^2}{2g}$　**27.** $r = \dfrac{1}{2}\sqrt{\dfrac{S}{\pi}}$

29. $A = \dfrac{-m + \sqrt{m^2 + 4kP}}{2k}$　**31.** $a = \sqrt{c^2 - b^2}$

33. $t = \dfrac{\sqrt{s}}{4}$　**35.** $r = \dfrac{-\pi h + \sqrt{\pi^2 h^2 + \pi A}}{\pi}$

37. $v = 20\sqrt{\dfrac{F}{A}}$　**39.** $a = \sqrt{c^2 - b^2}$　**41.** $a = \dfrac{2h\sqrt{3}}{3}$

43. $T = \dfrac{2 + \sqrt{4 - a(m-n)}}{a}$　**45.** $T = \dfrac{v^2 \pi m}{8k}$

47. $x = \dfrac{d\sqrt{3}}{3}$　**49.** $n = \dfrac{1 + \sqrt{1 + 8N}}{2}$　**51.** $b = \dfrac{a}{3S - 1}$

53. $B = \dfrac{A}{QA + 1}$　**55.** $n = \dfrac{S + 360}{180}$, or $n = \dfrac{S}{180} + 2$

57. $t = \dfrac{A - P}{Pr}$　**59.** $D = \dfrac{BC}{A}$　**61.** $a = \dfrac{-b}{C - K}$, or

$a = \dfrac{b}{K - C}$　**63.** $\mathbf{D_W}$　**65.** $\sqrt{65} \approx 8.062$

66. $\sqrt{75} \approx 8.660$　**67.** $\sqrt{41} \approx 6.403$　**68.** $\sqrt{44} \approx 6.633$
69. $\sqrt{1084} \approx 32.924$　**70.** $\sqrt{5} \approx 2.236$
71. $\sqrt{424}$ ft ≈ 20.591 ft　**72.** $\sqrt{12{,}500}$ yd ≈ 111.803 yd
73. $3x\sqrt{2}$　**74.** $8x^2\sqrt{3x}$　**75.** $3t$　**76.** $x^3\sqrt{x}$

77. (a) $r = \dfrac{C}{2\pi}$;　**(b)** $A = \dfrac{C^2}{4\pi}$　**79.** $\dfrac{1}{3a}, 1$

Margin Exercises, Section 9.5, pp. 697–699

1. Length: 14.8 yd; width: 4.6 yd　**2.** 3.8 yd, 5.8 yd
3. 3 km/h

Translating for Success, p. 700

1. M　**2.** G　**3.** F　**4.** L　**5.** D　**6.** N　**7.** J
8. E　**9.** B　**10.** C

Exercise Set 9.5, p. 701

1. Width: about 61 in.; height: about 34 in.
3. Length: 10 ft; width: 7 ft　**5.** 16 in.; 24 in.
7. Length: 20 cm; width: 16 cm
9. 4.6 m; 6.6 m　**11.** Length: 5.6 in.; width: 3.6 in.
13. Length: 6.4 cm; width: 3.2 cm　**15.** 3 cm
17. 7 km/h　**19.** 0 km/h (no wind) or 40 km/h
21. 0 km/h (stream is still) or 4 km/h　**23.** 8 mph
25. 1 km/h　**27.** $\mathbf{D_W}$　**29.** $8\sqrt{2}$　**30.** $12\sqrt{10}$

31. $(2x - 7)\sqrt{x}$　**32.** $-\sqrt{6}$　**33.** $\dfrac{3\sqrt{2}}{2}$　**34.** $\dfrac{2\sqrt{3}}{3}$

35. $5\sqrt{6} - 4\sqrt{3}$　**36.** $(9x + 2)\sqrt{x}$
37. $12\sqrt{2}$ in. ≈ 16.97 in.; two 12-in. pizzas

Margin Exercises, Section 9.6, pp. 707–708

1. $(0, -3)$

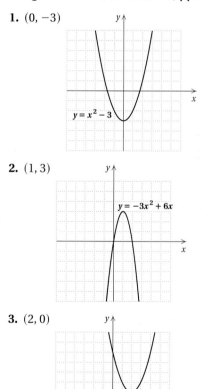

2. $(1, 3)$

3. $(2, 0)$　　**4.** $\left(-\sqrt{3}, 0\right); \left(\sqrt{3}, 0\right)$

5. $(-4, 0); (-2, 0)$ **6.** $\left(\dfrac{-2 - \sqrt{6}}{2}, 0\right); \left(\dfrac{-2 + \sqrt{6}}{2}, 0\right)$

7. None

Visualizing for Success, p. 709

1. J   **2.** F   **3.** H   **4.** G   **5.** B   **6.** E   **7.** D
8. I   **9.** C   **10.** A

Calculator Corner, p. 706

Left to the student

Calculator Corner, p. 708

Left to the student

Exercise Set 9.6, p. 710

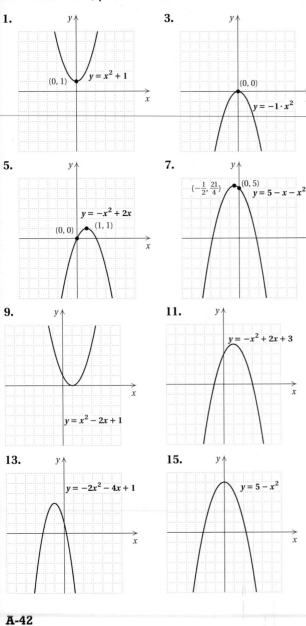

1. $y = x^2 + 1$, $(0, 1)$

3. $y = -1 \cdot x^2$, $(0, 0)$

5. $y = -x^2 + 2x$, $(0, 0)$, $(1, 1)$

7. $y = 5 - x - x^2$, $\left(-\dfrac{1}{2}, \dfrac{21}{4}\right)$, $(0, 5)$

9. $y = x^2 - 2x + 1$

11. $y = -x^2 + 2x + 3$

13. $y = -2x^2 - 4x + 1$

15. $y = 5 - x^2$

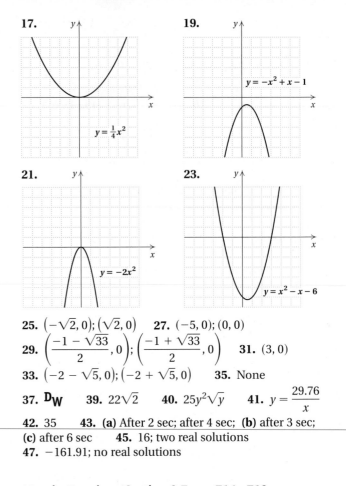

17. $y = \tfrac{1}{4}x^2$

19. $y = -x^2 + x - 1$

21. $y = -2x^2$

23. $y = x^2 - x - 6$

25. $(-\sqrt{2}, 0); (\sqrt{2}, 0)$ **27.** $(-5, 0); (0, 0)$

29. $\left(\dfrac{-1 - \sqrt{33}}{2}, 0\right); \left(\dfrac{-1 + \sqrt{33}}{2}, 0\right)$ **31.** $(3, 0)$

33. $(-2 - \sqrt{5}, 0); (-2 + \sqrt{5}, 0)$ **35.** None

37. $\mathbf{D_W}$ **39.** $22\sqrt{2}$ **40.** $25y^2\sqrt{y}$ **41.** $y = \dfrac{29.76}{x}$

42. 35   **43. (a)** After 2 sec; after 4 sec; **(b)** after 3 sec;
(c) after 6 sec   **45.** 16; two real solutions
47. -161.91; no real solutions

Margin Exercises, Section 9.7, pp. 714–719

1. Yes   **2.** No   **3.** Yes   **4.** No   **5.** Yes   **6.** Yes
7. (a) -33; **(b)** -3; **(c)** 2; **(d)** 97; **(e)** -9
8. (a) 21; **(b)** 9; **(c)** 14; **(d)** 69
9.

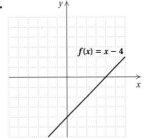

$f(x) = x - 4$

10.

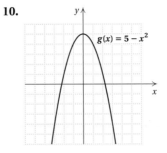

$g(x) = 5 - x^2$

11.

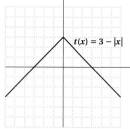

12. Yes   **13.** No

14. No   **15.** Yes   **16.** About $43 million
17. About $6 million

Calculator Corner, p. 716

1. -12.8 **2.** -9.2 **3.** -2 **4.** 20

Exercise Set 9.7, p. 720

1. Yes   **3.** Yes   **5.** No   **7.** Yes   **9.** Yes   **11.** Yes
13. A relation but not a function   **15.** (a) 9; (b) 12;
(c) 2; (d) 5; (e) 7.4; (f) $5\frac{2}{3}$ **17.** (a) -21; (b) 15;
(c) 42; (d) 0; (e) 2; (f) -162.6 **19.** (a) 7; (b) -17;
(c) 24.1; (d) 4; (e) -26; (f) 6   **21.** (a) 0; (b) 5; (c) 2;
(d) 170; (e) 65; (f) 230   **23.** (a) 1; (b) 3; (c) 3; (d) 4;
(e) 11; (f) 23   **25.** (a) 0; (b) -1; (c) 8; (d) 1000;
(e) -125; (f) -1000 **27.** (a) 159.48 cm; (b) 153.98 cm
29. $1\frac{20}{33}$ atm; $1\frac{10}{11}$ atm; $4\frac{1}{33}$ atm   **31.** 1.792 cm; 2.8 cm; 11.2 cm
33.

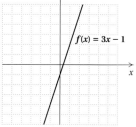

35.

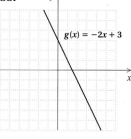

37.

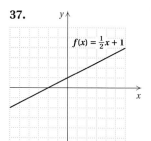

39.

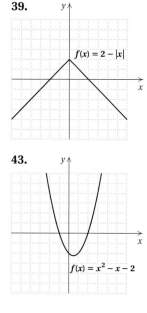

41.

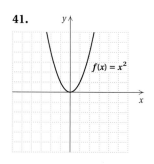

43.

45. Yes   **47.** Yes   **49.** No   **51.** No   **53.** About 75
per 10,000 men   **55.** $\mathbf{D_W}$ **57.** No   **58.** Yes
59. No solution   **60.** Infinite number of solutions
61.

63.

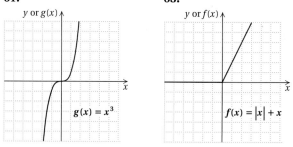

Concept Reinforcement, p. 724

1. True   **2.** False   **3.** True   **4.** True   **5.** True
6. False

Summary and Review: Chapter 9, p. 724

1. $-\sqrt{3}, \sqrt{3}$ **2.** $-2\sqrt{2}, 2\sqrt{2}$ **3.** $\frac{3}{5}, 1$ **4.** $-2, \frac{1}{3}$
5. $-8 \pm \sqrt{13}$ **6.** 0   **7.** $0, \frac{7}{5}$ **8.** $1 \pm \sqrt{11}$
9. $\frac{1 \pm \sqrt{10}}{3}$ **10.** $-3 \pm 3\sqrt{2}$ **11.** $\frac{2 \pm \sqrt{3}}{2}$
12. $\frac{3 \pm \sqrt{33}}{2}$ **13.** No real-number solutions
14. $0, \frac{4}{3}$ **15.** $-5, 3$ **16.** 1   **17.** $\frac{5 \pm \sqrt{17}}{2}$
18. $-1, \frac{5}{3}$ **19.** 0.4, 4.6   **20.** $-1.9, -0.1$
21. $T = L(4V^2 - 1)$ **22.**

23.

24. $\left(-\sqrt{2}, 0\right); \left(\sqrt{2}, 0\right)$

25. $\left(2 - \sqrt{6}, 0\right); \left(2 + \sqrt{6}, 0\right)$ **26.** 4.7 cm, 1.7 cm
27. 15 ft   **28.** About 6.3 sec   **29.** $-1, -7, 2$
30. 0, 0, 19   **31.** 2700 calories

A-43

32.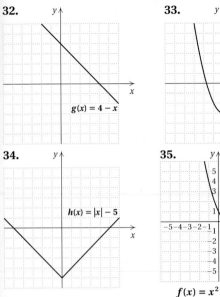
$g(x) = 4 - x$

33.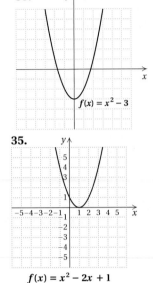
$f(x) = x^2 - 3$

34.
$h(x) = |x| - 5$

35.
5
4
3
1
−5−4−3−2−1   1 2 3 4 5 x
−1
−2
−3
−4
−5
$f(x) = x^2 - 2x + 1$

36. No   **37.** Yes

38. **D**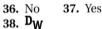

Equation	Form	Example
Linear	Reducible to $x = a$	$3x - 5 = 8$
Quadratic	$ax^2 + bx + c = 0$	$2x^2 - 3x + 1 = 0$
Rational	Contains one or more rational expressions	$\dfrac{x}{3} + \dfrac{4}{x-1} = 1$
Radical	Contains one or more radical expressions	$\sqrt{3x - 1} = x - 7$
Systems of equations	$Ax + By = C,$ $Dx + Ey = F$	$4x - 5y = 3,$ $3x + 2y = 1$

39. **D_W** **(a)** The third line should be $x = 0$ or $x + 20 = 0$; the solution 0 is lost in the given procedure. Also, the last line should be $x = -20$. **(b)** The addition principle should be used at the outset to get 0 on one side of the equation. Since this was not done in the given procedure, the principle of zero products was not applied correctly.
40. 31 and 32; −32 and −31   **41.** $5\sqrt{\pi}$ in., or about 8.9 in.
42. 25   **43.** −4, −2   **44.** −5, −1   **45.** −6, 0
46. −3

Test: Chapter 9, p. 727

1. [9.2a] $-\sqrt{5}, \sqrt{5}$ **2.** [9.1b] $-\frac{8}{7}, 0$
3. [9.1c] −8, 6   **4.** [9.1c] $-\frac{1}{3}, 2$ **5.** [9.2b] $8 \pm \sqrt{13}$
6. [9.3a] $\dfrac{1 \pm \sqrt{13}}{2}$ **7.** [9.3a] $\dfrac{3 \pm \sqrt{37}}{2}$
8. [9.3a] $-2 \pm \sqrt{14}$ **9.** [9.3a] $\dfrac{7 \pm \sqrt{37}}{6}$
10. [9.1c] −1, 2   **11.** [9.1c] −4, 2
12. [9.2c] $2 \pm \sqrt{14}$ **13.** [9.3b] −1.7, 5.7
14. [9.4a] $n = \dfrac{-b + \sqrt{b^2 + 4ad}}{2a}$

15. [9.6b] $\left(\dfrac{1 - \sqrt{21}}{2}, 0\right), \left(\dfrac{1 + \sqrt{21}}{2}, 0\right)$

16. [9.6a]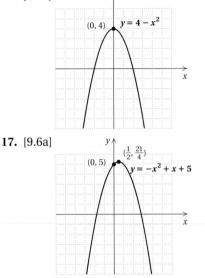
$(0, 4)$ $y = 4 - x^2$

17. [9.6a]
$\left(\frac{1}{2}, \frac{21}{4}\right)$
$(0, 5)$ $y = -x^2 + x + 5$

18. [9.7b] 1; $1\frac{1}{2}$; 2   **19.** [9.7b] 1; 3; −3
20. [9.5a] Length: 6.5 m; width: 2.5 m
21. [9.5a] 24 km/h   **22.** [9.7e] 25.98 min
23. [9.7c]
$h(x) = x - 4$

24. [9.7c]
$g(x) = x^2 - 4$
25. [9.7d] Yes

26. [9.7d] No   **27.** [9.5a] $5 + 5\sqrt{2}$
28. [7.2b], [9.3a] $1 \pm \sqrt{5}$

Cumulative Review/Final Examination:
Chapters 1–9, p. 729

1. [4.1a] $x \cdot x \cdot x$ **2.** [4.1c] 54   **3.** [1.2c] $-0.\overline{27}$
4. [6.3a] 240   **5.** [1.2e] 7   **6.** [1.3a] 9   **7.** [1.4a] 15
8. [1.6c] $-\frac{3}{20}$ **9.** [1.8d] 4   **10.** [1.8b] $-2m - 4$
11. [2.2a] −8   **12.** [2.3b] −12   **13.** [2.3c] 7
14. [5.7b] 3, 5   **15.** [7.2a] (1, 2)   **16.** [7.3a] (12, 5)
17. [7.3b] (6, 7)   **18.** [5.7b] −2, 3
19. [9.3a] $\dfrac{-3 \pm \sqrt{29}}{2}$ **20.** [8.5a] 2
21. [2.7e] $\{x \,|\, x \geq -1\}$ **22.** [2.3b] 8   **23.** [2.3b] −3

24. [2.7d] $\{x \mid x < -8\}$ **25.** [2.7e] $\{y \mid y \le \frac{35}{22}\}$

26. [9.2a] $-\sqrt{10}, \sqrt{10}$ **27.** [9.2b] $3 \pm \sqrt{6}$

28. [6.6a] $\frac{2}{9}$ **29.** [6.6a] -5

30. [6.6a], [9.1b] No solution **31.** [8.5a] 12

32. [2.4b] $b = \dfrac{At}{4}$ **33.** [9.4a] $m = \dfrac{tn}{t + n}$

34. [9.4a] $A = \pi r^2$ **35.** [9.4a] $x = \dfrac{b + \sqrt{b^2 + 4ay}}{2a}$

36. [4.1d, f] $\dfrac{1}{x^4}$ **37.** [4.1e, f] y^7 **38.** [4.2a, b] $4y^{12}$

39. [4.3f] $10x^3 + 3x - 3$ **40.** [4.4a] $7x^3 - 2x^2 + 4x - 17$

41. [4.4c] $8x^2 - 4x - 6$ **42.** [4.5b] $-8y^4 + 6y^3 - 2y^2$

43. [4.5d] $6t^3 - 17t^2 + 16t - 6$ **44.** [4.6b] $t^2 - \frac{1}{16}$

45. [4.6c] $9m^2 - 12m + 4$

46. [4.7e] $15x^2y^3 + x^2y^2 + 5xy^2 + 7$

47. [4.7f] $x^4 - 0.04y^2$ **48.** [4.7f] $9p^2 + 24pq^2 + 16q^4$

49. [6.1d] $\dfrac{2}{x + 3}$ **50.** [6.2b] $\dfrac{3a(a - 1)}{2(a + 1)}$

51. [6.4a] $\dfrac{27x - 4}{5x(3x - 1)}$ **52.** [6.5a] $\dfrac{-x^2 + x + 2}{(x + 4)(x - 4)(x - 5)}$

53. [5.1b] $4x(2x - 1)$ **54.** [5.5d] $(5x - 2)(5x + 2)$

55. [5.3a], [5.4a] $(3y + 2)(2y - 3)$ **56.** [5.5b] $(m - 4)^2$

57. [5.1c] $(x^2 - 5)(x - 8)$

58. [5.6a] $3(a^2 + 6)(a + 2)(a - 2)$

59. [5.5d] $(4x^2 + 1)(2x + 1)(2x - 1)$

60. [5.5d] $(7ab + 2)(7ab - 2)$ **61.** [5.5b] $(3x + 5y)^2$

62. [5.1c] $(2a + d)(c - 3b)$

63. [5.3a], [5.4a] $(5x - 2y)(3x + 4y)$

64. [6.8a] $-\frac{42}{5}$ **65.** [8.1a] 7 **66.** [8.1a] -25

67. [8.1f] $8x$ **68.** [8.2c] $\sqrt{a^2 - b^2}$

69. [8.2c] $8a^2b\sqrt{3ab}$ **70.** [8.2a] $5\sqrt{6}$

71. [8.2b] $9xy\sqrt{3x}$ **72.** [8.3b] $\frac{10}{9}$ **73.** [8.3b] $\dfrac{8}{x}$

74. [8.4a] $12\sqrt{3}$ **75.** [8.3a, c] $\dfrac{2\sqrt{10}}{5}$ **76.** [8.6a] 40

77. [3.1d]

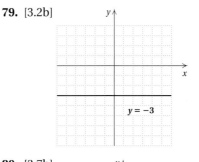

78. [3.2a]

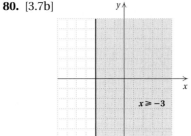

79. [3.2b]

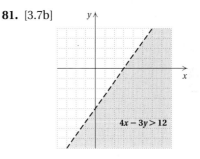

80. [3.7b]

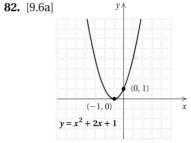

81. [3.7b]

82. [9.6a]

83. [9.2c] $\dfrac{2 \pm \sqrt{6}}{3}$

84. [9.3b] $-0.2, 1.2$ **85.** [2.5a] 25% **86.** [2.5a] 60

87. [6.7a] $4\frac{4}{9}$ hr **88.** [9.5a] Length: 12 ft; width: 8 ft

89. [9.5a] 2 km/h **90.** [5.8a] 12 m

91. [9.5a] 5 and 7; -7 and -5

92. [7.4a] 40 L of A; 20 L of B **93.** [9.2d] About 7.8 sec

94. [6.9b] $451.20; the variation constant is the amount earned per hour **95.** [2.6a] 6090 cars

96. [7.4a] $3.30 per pound: 14 lb; $2.40 per pound: 28 lb

97. [7.5a] 140 mph **98.** [9.6b] $-3, 2$

99. [9.6b] $\left(-2 - \sqrt{3}, 0\right), \left(-2 + \sqrt{3}, 0\right)$

100. [3.4a] Slope: 2; y-intercept: $(0, -8)$

101. [3.6a, b] Neither **102.** [3.3a] 15

103. [6.9a] $y = 10x$; 640 **104.** [6.9c] $y = \dfrac{1000}{x}$; 8

105. [9.7d] Yes **106.** [9.7d] No

107. [9.7c]

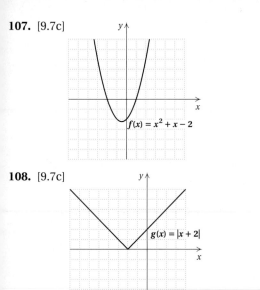

$f(x) = x^2 + x - 2$

108. [9.7c]

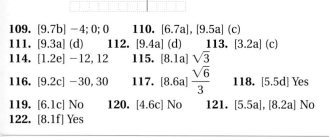

$g(x) = |x + 2|$

109. [9.7b] $-4; 0; 0$ **110.** [6.7a], [9.5a] (c)
111. [9.3a] (d)   **112.** [9.4a] (d)   **113.** [3.2a] (c)
114. [1.2e] $-12, 12$ **115.** [8.1a] $\sqrt{3}$

116. [9.2c] $-30, 30$ **117.** [8.6a] $\dfrac{\sqrt{6}}{3}$ **118.** [5.5d] Yes

119. [6.1c] No   **120.** [4.6c] No   **121.** [5.5a], [8.2a] No
122. [8.1f] Yes

APPENDIXES

Margin Exercises, Appendix A, pp. 736–737

1. $(x - 3)(x^2 + 3x + 9)$ **2.** $(4 - y)(16 + 4y + y^2)$
3. $(y + 2)(y^2 - 2y + 4)$ **4.** $(5 + t)(25 - 5t + t^2)$
5. $(3x - y)(9x^2 + 3xy + y^2)$ **6.** $(2y + z)(4y^2 - 2yz + z^2)$
7. $(m + n)(m^2 - mn + n^2)(m - n)(m^2 + mn + n^2)$
8. $2xy(2x^2 + 3y^2)(4x^4 - 6x^2y^2 + 9y^4)$
9. $(3x + 2y)(9x^2 - 6xy + 4y^2)(3x - 2y)(9x^2 + 6xy + 4y^2)$
10. $(x - 0.3)(x^2 + 0.3x + 0.09)$

Exercise Set A, p. 738

1. $(z + 3)(z^2 - 3z + 9)$ **3.** $(x - 1)(x^2 + x + 1)$
5. $(y + 5)(y^2 - 5y + 25)$ **7.** $(2a + 1)(4a^2 - 2a + 1)$
9. $(y - 2)(y^2 + 2y + 4)$ **11.** $(2 - 3b)(4 + 6b + 9b^2)$
13. $(4y + 1)(16y^2 - 4y + 1)$ **15.** $(2x + 3)(4x^2 - 6x + 9)$
17. $(a - b)(a^2 + ab + b^2)$ **19.** $\left(a + \frac{1}{2}\right)\left(a^2 - \frac{1}{2}a + \frac{1}{4}\right)$
21. $2(y - 4)(y^2 + 4y + 16)$
23. $3(2a + 1)(4a^2 - 2a + 1)$
25. $r(s + 4)(s^2 - 4s + 16)$
27. $5(x - 2z)(x^2 + 2xz + 4z^2)$
29. $(x + 0.1)(x^2 - 0.1x + 0.01)$
31. $8(2x^2 - t^2)(4x^4 + 2x^2t^2 + t^4)$
33. $2y(y - 4)(y^2 + 4y + 16)$
35. $(z - 1)(z^2 + z + 1)(z + 1)(z^2 - z + 1)$
37. $(t^2 + 4y^2)(t^4 - 4t^2y^2 + 16y^4)$ **39.** $1; 19; 19; 7; 1$
41. $(x^{2a} + y^b)(x^{4a} - x^{2a}y^b + y^{2b})$

43. $3(x^a + 2y^b)(x^{2a} - 2x^ay^b + 4y^{2b})$
45. $\frac{1}{3}\left(\frac{1}{2}xy + z\right)\left(\frac{1}{4}x^2y^2 - \frac{1}{2}xyz + z^2\right)$
47. $y(3x^2 + 3xy + y^2)$ **49.** $4(3a^2 + 4)$

Margin Exercises, Appendix B, pp. 741–742

1. $y = -3x - 11$ **2.** $y = 5x + 11$ **3.** $y = 6x - 23$
4. $y = -\frac{2}{3}x + \frac{8}{3}$ **5.** $y = -\frac{9}{4}x + \frac{7}{4}$ **6.** $y = -9x - 16$

Exercise Set B, p. 743

1. $y = 4x - 18$ **3.** $y = -2x + 12$ **5.** $y = 3x + 4$
7. $y = -3x - 6$ **9.** $y = 4$ **11.** $y = -\frac{4}{5}x + \frac{23}{5}$
13. $y = x + 3$ **15.** $y = x$ **17.** $y = \frac{5}{3}x - 5$
19. $y = 3x + 5$ **21.** $y = -\frac{7}{4}x$ **23.** $y = \frac{2}{11}x + \frac{91}{66}$
25. $y = 5x + 3$

Margin Exercises, Appendix C, pp. 744–745

1. 3   **2.** -2 **3.** 6   **4.** 1   **5.** -1 **6.** Not a real
number   **7.** 3   **8.** -6 **9.** -6 **10.** $2\sqrt[3]{3}$ **11.** $\frac{3}{4}$
12. $2\sqrt[5]{3}$ **13.** $\dfrac{\sqrt[3]{4}}{5}$

Exercise Set C, p. 746

1. 5   **3.** -10 **5.** 1   **7.** Not a real number   **9.** 6
11. 4   **13.** 10   **15.** -3 **17.** Not a real number
19. -5 **21.** t **23.** $-x$ **25.** 4   **27.** -7 **29.** -5
31. 10   **33.** 10   **35.** -7 **37.** Not a real number
39. 5   **41.** $3\sqrt[3]{2}$ **43.** $3\sqrt[4]{4}$ **45.** $\frac{3}{4}$ **47.** $4\sqrt[4]{2}$
49. $2\sqrt[5]{4}$ **51.** $\frac{4}{5}$ **53.** $\dfrac{\sqrt[3]{17}}{2}$ **55.** $5\sqrt[3]{2}$ **57.** $3\sqrt[5]{2}$
59. $\dfrac{\sqrt[4]{13}}{3}$ **61.** $\dfrac{\sqrt[4]{7}}{2}$ **63.** $\frac{2}{5}$ **65.** 2   **67.** 10

Margin Exercises, Appendix D, pp. 748–749

1. $\{0, 1, 2, 3, 4, 5, 6, 7\}$ **2.** $\{-5, 5\}$ **3.** True   **4.** True
5. True   **6.** False   **7.** True   **8.** $\{-2, -3, 4, -4\}$
9. $\{a, i\}$ **10.** $\{\ \}$, or $\varnothing$ **11.** $\{-2, -3, 4, -4, 8, -5, 7, 5\}$
12. $\{a, e, i, o, u, m, r, v, n\}$
13. $\{a, b, c, d, e, f, g, h, i, j, k, l, m, n, o, p, q, r, s, t, u, v, w, x, y, z\}$

Exercise Set D, p. 750

1. $\{3, 4, 5, 6, 7, 8\}$ **3.** $\{41, 43, 45, 47, 49\}$ **5.** $\{-3, 3\}$
7. False   **9.** True   **11.** True   **13.** True   **15.** True
17. False   **19.** $\{c, d, e\}$ **21.** $\{1, 10\}$ **23.** $\{\ \}$, or $\varnothing$
25. $\{a, e, i, o, u, q, c, k\}$ **27.** $\{0, 1, 7, 10, 2, 5\}$
29. $\{a, e, i, o, u, m, n, f, g, h\}$ **31.** $\{x \mid x \text{ is an integer}\}$
33. $\{x \mid x \text{ is a real number}\}$ **35.** $\{\ \}$, or $\varnothing$ **37.** (a) A;
(b) A; (c) A; (d) $\{\ \}$, or $\varnothing$ **39.** True

Margin Exercises, Appendix E, pp. 752–753

1. 56.7   **2.** 64.7   **3.** 87.8   **4.** 17   **5.** 16.5   **6.** 91
7. 55   **8.** 54, 87   **9.** No mode exists.   **10.** (a) 25 mm^2;
(b) 25 mm^2; (c) No mode exists.

Exercise Set E, p. 754

1. Mean: 21; median: 18.5; mode: 29   **3.** Mean: 21;
median: 20; modes: 5, 20   **5.** Mean: 5.2; median: 5.7;
mode: 7.4   **7.** Mean: 239.5; median: 234; mode: 234
9. Mean: 23.$\overline{8}$; median: 15; mode: 1   **11.** Mean: 897.2;
median: 798; no mode exists   **13.** Mean: $8.19;
median: $8.49; mode: $6.99   **15.** 2.7   **17.** 10 home runs
19. 263 days

Photo Credits

Glossary

A

Abscissa   The first coordinate in an ordered pair of numbers

Absolute value   The distance that a number is from 0 on the number line

ac-method   A method for factoring trinomials of the type $ax^2 + bx + c, a \neq 1$, involving the product, ac, of the leading coefficient a and the last term c

Additive identity   The number 0

Additive inverse   A number's opposite; two numbers are additive inverses of each other if their sum is 0

Algebraic expression   An expression consisting of variables, constants, numerals, and operation signs

Area   The number of square units that fill a plane region

Arithmetic numbers   The whole numbers and the positive fractions

Ascending order   When a polynomial is written with the terms arranged according to degree from least to greatest, it is said to be in ascending order.

Associative law of addition   The statement that when three numbers are added, regrouping the addends gives the same sum

Associative law of multiplication   The statement that when three numbers are multiplied, regrouping the factors gives the same product

Average   A center point of a set of numbers found by adding the numbers and dividing by the number of items of data; also called the *arithmetic mean* or *mean*

Axes   Two perpendicular number lines used to identify points in a plane

B

Bar graph   A graphic display of data using bars proportional in length to the numbers represented

Base   In exponential notation, the number being raised to a power

Binomial   A polynomial composed of two terms

C

Circumference   The distance around a circle

Coefficient   The numerical multiplier of a variable

Commutative law of addition   The statement that when two numbers are added, changing the order in which the numbers are added does not affect the sum

Commutative law of multiplication   The statement that when two numbers are multiplied, changing the order in which the numbers are multiplied does not affect the product

Completing the square   Adding a particular constant to an expression so that the resulting sum is a perfect square

Complex fraction expression   A rational expression that has one or more rational expressions within its numerator and/or denominator

Complex rational expression   A rational expression that has one or more rational expressions within its numerator and/or denominator

Complex-number system   A number system that contains the real-number system and is designed so that negative numbers have square roots

Composite number   A natural number, other than 1, that is not prime

Conjugates   Pairs of radical terms, like $\sqrt{a} + \sqrt{b}$ and $\sqrt{a} - \sqrt{b}$ or $c + \sqrt{d}$ and $c - \sqrt{d}$, for which the product does not have a radical term

Consecutive even integers   Even integers that are two units apart

Consecutive integers   Integers that are one unit apart

Consecutive odd integers   Odd integers that are two units apart

Constant   A known number

Constant of proportionality   The constant in an equation of direct or inverse variation

Coordinates   The numbers in an ordered pair

Cube root   The number c is called a cube root of a if $c^3 = a.$

D

Degree of a polynomial   The degree of the term of highest degree in a polynomial

Degree of a term   The sum of the exponents of the variables

Denominator   The number below the fraction bar in a fraction

Descending order When a polynomial is written with the terms arranged according to degree from greatest to least, it is said to be in descending order.

Diameter A segment that passes through the center of a circle and has its endpoints on the circle

Difference of cubes Any expression that can be written in the form $a^3 - b^3$

Difference of squares Any expression that can be written in the form $a^2 - b^2$

Direct variation A situation that translates to an equation of the form $y = kx$, with k a positive constant

Discriminant The radicand, $b^2 - 4ac$, from the quadratic formula

Distributive law of multiplication over addition The statement that multiplying a factor by the sum of two numbers gives the same result as multiplying the factor by each of the two numbers and then adding

Distributive law of multiplication over subtraction The statement that multiplying a factor by the difference of two numbers gives the same result as multiplying the factor by each of the two numbers and then subtracting

Domain The set of all first coordinates of the ordered pairs in a function

E

Elimination method An algebraic method that uses the addition principle to solve a system of equations

Empty set The set without members

Equation A number sentence that says that the expressions on either side of the equals sign, $=$, represent the same number

Equation of direct variation An equation, described by $y = kx$ with k a positive constant, used to represent direct variation

Equation of inverse variation An equation, described by $y = k/x$ with k a positive constant, used to represent inverse variation

Equivalent equations Equations with the same solution set

Equivalent expressions Expressions that have the same value for all allowable replacements

Equivalent inequalities Inequalities that have the same solution set

Evaluate To substitute a value for each occurrence of a variable in an expression

Exponent In expressions of the form a^n, the number n is an exponent. For n a natural number, a^n represents n factors of a.

Exponential notation A representation of a number using a base raised to a power

F

Factor *Verb*: To write an equivalent expression that is a product. *Noun*: A multiplier

Factorization of a polynomial An expression that names the polynomial as a product

FOIL To multiply two binomials by multiplying the First terms, the Outside terms, the Inside terms, and then the Last terms

Formula An equation that uses numbers or letters to represent a relationship between two or more quantities

Fraction equation An equation containing one or more rational expressions; also called a *rational equation*

Fraction expression A quotient, or ratio, of polynomials; also called a *rational expression*

Fraction notation A number written using a numerator and a denominator

Function A correspondence that assigns to each member of a set called the domain exactly one member of a set called the range

G

Grade The measure of a road's steepness

Graph A picture or diagram of the data in a table; a line, curve, or collection of points that represents all the solutions of an equation

Greatest common factor (GCF) The common factor of a polynomial with the largest possible coefficient and the largest possible exponent(s)

H

Hypotenuse In a right triangle, the side opposite the right angle

I

Identity Property of 1 The statement that the product of a number and 1 is always the original number

Identity Property of 0 The statement that the sum of a number and 0 is always the original number

Index In the radical $\sqrt[n]{a}$, the number n is called the index.

Inequality A mathematical sentence using $<$, $>$, $\leq$, $\geq$, or $\neq$

Input A member of the domain of a function

Integers The whole numbers and their opposites

Intercept The point at which a graph intersects the x- or y-axis

Intersection of two sets The set of all elements that are common to both sets

Inverse variation A situation that translates to an equation of the form $y = k/x$, with k a positive constant

Irrational number A real number that cannot be named as a ratio of two integers

L

Leading coefficient The coefficient of the term of highest degree in a polynomial

Leading term The term of highest degree in a polynomial

Least common denominator (LCD) The least common multiple of the denominators

Legs In a right triangle, the two sides that form the right angle

Like terms Terms that have exactly the same variable factors

Line of symmetry A line that can be drawn through a graph such that the part of the graph on one side of the line is an exact reflection of the part on the opposite side

Linear equation Any equation that can be written in the form $y = mx + b$ or $Ax + By = C$, where x and y are variables

Linear function A function that can be described by an equation of the form $y = mx + b$, where x and y are variables

Linear inequality An inequality whose related equation is a linear equation

M

Mean A center point of a set of numbers found by adding the numbers and dividing by the number of items of data; also called the *arithmetic mean* or *average*

Median In a set of data listed in order from smallest to largest, the middle number if there is an odd number of data items, or the average of the two middle numbers if there is an even number of data items

Mode The number or numbers that occur most often in a set of data

Monomial A constant, a variable, or a product of a constant and one or more variables

Motion problem A problem that deals with distance, speed, and time

Multiple of a number A product of the number and some natural number

Multiplication property of 0 The statement that the product of 0 and any real number is 0

Multiplicative identity The number 1

Multiplicative inverses Reciprocals; two numbers whose product is 1

N

Natural numbers The counting numbers: 1, 2, 3, 4, 5, ...

Numerator The number above the fraction bar in a fraction

O

Opposite The opposite, or additive inverse, of a number a is written $-a$. Opposites are the same distance from 0 on the number line but on different sides of 0.

Opposite of a polynomial To find the opposite of a polynomial, replace each term with its opposite— that is, change the sign of every term.

Ordered pair A pair of numbers of the form (h, k) for which the order in which the numbers are listed is important

Ordinate The second coordinate in an ordered pair of numbers

Origin The point on a graph where the two axes intersect

Output A member of the range of a function

P

Parabola A graph of a quadratic equation

Parallel lines Lines in the same plane that never intersect; two lines are parallel if they have the same slope.

Parallelogram A four-sided polygon with two pairs of parallel sides

Percent notation A representation of a number as parts per 100

Perfect square A rational number p for which there exists a number a for which $a^2 = p$

Perfect-square trinomial A trinomial that is the square of a binomial

Perimeter The sum of the lengths of the sides of a polygon

Perpendicular lines Lines that form a right angle

Pi (π) The number that results when the circumference of a circle is divided by its diameter; $\pi \approx 3.14$, or 22/7

Polygon A closed geometric figure with three or more sides

Polynomial A monomial or sum of monomials

Polynomial equation An equation in which two polynomials are set equal to each other

Prime factorization A factorization of a composite number as a product of prime numbers

Prime number A natural number that has exactly two different factors: itself and 1

Prime polynomial A polynomial that cannot be factored using only integer coefficients

Principal square root The nonnegative square root of a number

Principle of zero products The statement that an equation $ab = 0$ is true if and only if $a = 0$ is true or $b = 0$ is true, or both are true

Proportion An equation stating that two ratios are equal

Proportional numbers Two pairs of numbers having the same ratio

Pythagorean theorem In any right triangle, if a and b are the lengths of the legs and c is the length of the hypotenuse, then $a^2 + b^2 = c^2$.

Q

Quadrants The four regions into which the axes divide a plane

Quadratic equation An equation of the form $ax^2 + bx + c = 0$, where $a \neq 0$

Quadratic formula The solutions of $ax^2 + bx + c = 0$, $a \neq 0$, are given by the equation $x = \dfrac{-b \pm \sqrt{b^2 - 4ac}}{2a}$.

Quadratic function A second-degree polynomial function in one variable

R

Radical equation An equation in which a variable appears in a radicand

Radical expression An algebraic expression in which a radical symbol appears

Radical symbol The symbol $\sqrt{}$

Radicand The expression under the radical symbol

Radius A segment with one endpoint on the center of a circle and the other endpoint on the circle

Range The set of all second coordinates of the ordered pairs in a function

Ratio   The quotient of two quantities

Rational equation   An equation containing one or more rational expressions

Rational expression   A quotient of two polynomials

Rational number   A number that can be written in the form a/b, where a and b are integers and $b \neq 0$

Rationalizing the denominator   A procedure for finding an equivalent expression without a radical in the denominator

Real numbers   All rational and irrational numbers

Reciprocal   A multiplicative inverse; two numbers are reciprocals if their product is 1.

Rectangle   A four-sided polygon with four right angles

Relation   A correspondence between a first set, the domain, and a second set, the range, such that each member of the domain corresponds to at least one member of the range

Repeating decimal   A decimal in which a number pattern repeats indefinitely

Right triangle   A triangle that includes a right angle

Rise   The change in the second coordinate between two points on a line

Roster notation   A way of naming sets by listing all the elements in the set

Rounding   Approximating the value of a number; used when estimating

Run   The change in the first coordinate between two points on a line

S

Scientific notation   A representation of a number of the form $M \times 10^n$, where n is an integer, $1 \leq M < 10$, and M is expressed in decimal notation

Set   A collection of objects

Set-builder notation   The naming of a set by describing basic characteristics of the elements in the set

Similar triangles   Triangles in which corresponding sides are proportional

Simplify   To rewrite an expression in an equivalent, abbreviated, form

Slope   The ratio of the rise to the run for any two points on a line

Slope–intercept equation   An equation of the form $y = mx + b$, where x and y are variables

Solution   A replacement or substitution that makes an equation or inequality true

Solution set   The set of all solutions of an equation, an inequality, or a system of equations or inequalities

Solve   To find all solutions of an equation, an inequality, or a system of equations or inequalities; to find the solution(s) of a problem

Square   A four-sided polygon with four right angles and all sides of equal length

Square of a number   A number multiplied by itself

Square root   The number c is a square root of a if $c^2 = a$.

Substitute   To replace a variable with a number

Substitution method   An algebraic method for solving systems of equations

Sum of cubes   An expression that can be written in the form $a^3 + b^3$

Sum of squares   An expression that can be written in the form $a^2 + b^2$

System of equations   A set of two or more equations that are to be solved simultaneously

T

Term   A number, a variable, or a product or a quotient of numbers and/or variables

Terminating decimal   A decimal that can be written using a finite number of decimal places

Trinomial   A polynomial that is composed of three terms

Trinomial square   The square of a binomial expressed as three terms

U

Union of sets A and B   The set of all elements belonging to either A or B

V

Value   The numerical result after a number has been substituted into an expression

Variable   A letter that represents an unknown number

Variable expression   An expression containing a variable

Variation constant   The constant in an equation of direct or inverse variation

Vertex   The point at which the graph of a quadratic equation crosses its axis of symmetry

Vertical-line test   The statement that a graph represents a function if it is impossible to draw a vertical line that intersects the graph more than once

W

Whole numbers   The natural numbers and 0: 0, 1, 2, 3, ...

X

x-intercept   The point at which a graph crosses the x-axis

Y

y-intercept   The point at which a graph crosses the y-axis

Index

and multiplying by -1, 122
  of an opposite, 81
  of a polynomial, 342
  in subtraction, 87, 342
  of a sum, 122
Opposites
  in rational expressions, 476
  sum of, 82
Order
  ascending, 333
  descending, 332
  on number line, 71, 72
  of operations, 34, 36, 125, 126
Ordered pairs, 224, 560
Ordinate, 224
Origin, 224
Output, 715

P

Pairs, ordered, 224, 560
Parabolas, 705
Parallel lines, 280, 293
Parallelogram, area of, 41, 51
Parentheses
  in equations, 154
  within parentheses, 124
  removing, 123
Parking-lot arrival spaces, 615
Pendulum, period of, 633
Percent, applications of, 170
Percent notation, 27, 51
  converting to/from decimal
    notation, 27, 28
  converting to/from fraction
    notation, 28, 29
Perfect-square radicand, 613
Perfect-square trinomial, 426, 427,
  466
Perimeter. *See also Index of*
  Applications.
  of a polygon, 39
  of a rectangle, 39, 51
  of a square, 40, 51
Period of a pendulum, 633
Perpendicular lines, 281, 293
Pi (π), 43, 70
Place-value chart, 19
Plotting points, 224
Point–slope equation, 740
Points, coordinates of, 224
Polygon
  number of diagonals, 670
  perimeter, 39
Polynomial equation, 328
Polynomials, 327
  addition of, 341, 369
  additive inverse of, 342
  in ascending order, 333
  binomials, 334

coefficients in, 331
  collecting like terms (or combining
    similar terms), 332
  degree of, 333, 368
  in descending order, 332
  division of, 376–379
  evaluating, 327, 330, 367
  factoring, *see* Factoring,
    polynomials
  and geometry, 343
  like terms in, 331
  missing terms in, 334
  monomials, 327, 334
  multiplication of, 349–352,
    356–361, 370, 383
  opposite of, 342
  perfect-square trinomial, 426
  prime, 405
  quadratic, 705
  in several variables, 367
  subtraction of, 342, 369
  terms of, 330, 368
  trinomial squares, 426
  trinomials, 334
  value of, 327
Positive integers, 67
Positive square root, 610
Power, 33. *See also* Exponents, raising
  to a power.
Power rule, 314, 321
Powers, square roots of, 620
Prime factorization, 3
  and LCM, 4
Prime number, 2, 3
Prime polynomial, 405
Principal square root, 610
Principle of square roots, 675, 724
Principle of squaring, 642, 657
Principle of zero products, 445, 466
Problem solving, five-step process,
  178. *See also Index of*
  Applications.
Procedure for solving equations, 155
Product, raising to a power, 315, 321
Product rule
  for exponential notation, 306, 309,
    321
  for radicals, 618, 657, 745
Products. *See also* Multiplication;
  Multiplying.
  of radical expressions, 618, 635, 745
  raising to a power, 315, 321
  of sums and differences, 357, 383
  of two binomials, 350, 356–359,
    383
Projectile height, 712
Properties of reciprocals, 102
Property of -1, 122
Proportion, 522
Proportional, 522

Proportionality, constant of, 540, 543
Pythagoras, 651
Pythagorean equation, 651, 657
Pythagorean theorem, 457, 466, 657

Q

Quadrants, 225
Quadratic equation, 444, 667
  approximating solutions, 687, 688
  discriminant, 708, 724
  graphs of, 705
  solving, 685
    by completing the square,
      677–679
    by factoring, 446, 668, 669
    on a graphing calculator, 449, 672
    using the principle of square
      roots, 675
    using the quadratic formula, 684
  standard form, 667, 724
  x-intercepts, 708
Quadratic formula, 684, 724
Quadratic function, 714
Quadratic polynomial, 705
Quotient
  of integers, 100
  of polynomials, 376–379
  raising to a power, 316, 321
  involving square roots, 626, 657
Quotient rule
  for exponential notation, 307, 309,
    321
  for radicals, 626, 657, 745

R

Radical equations, 642
Radical expressions, 612. *See also*
  Square roots.
  adding, 634
  conjugates, 636
  dividing, 626, 657, 745
  in equations, 642
  factoring, 618
  index, 744
  meaningful, 612
  multiplying, 618, 635, 745
  perfect-square radicands, 613
  product rule, 618, 657
  quotient rule, 626, 657
  involving quotients, 626, 657, 745
  radicand, 612
  rationalizing denominators, 627,
    636
  simplifying, 618
  subtracting, 634
Radical symbol, 610
Radicals, like, 634

Radicand, 612, 744
  negative, 612
  perfect square, 613
Radius, 43, 51
Raising a power to a power, 314, 321
Raising a product to a power, 315, 321
Raising a quotient to a power, 316, 321
Range, 713, 714
Rate, 522
  of change, 258. *See also* Slope.
Ratio, 522. *See also* Proportion.
Rational equations, 508
Rational expressions, 472. *See also*
        Fraction expressions; Rational
        numbers.
  addition, 492–495
  complex, 534
  division, 483
  multiplying, 473, 477
  reciprocals, 483
  simplifying, 474
  subtraction, 500–503
  undefined, 472
Rational numbers, 68. *See also*
        Fraction expressions; Rational
        expressions.
  decimal notation, 69, 70, 71
  nonnegative, 8
Rationalizing denominators, 627, 636
Real numbers, 71
  addition, 78, 79, 105
  division, 100–105
  multiplication, 93–96, 105
  order, 71
  subsets of, 66, 71
  subtraction, 86, 87, 105
Real-number system, 71. *See also* Real
        numbers.
Reciprocals, 14, 101
  and division, 15, 103, 483
  properties, 102
  of rational expressions, 483
  sign of, 102
Rectangle, 39
  area, 40, 51
  golden, 704
  perimeter, 39, 51
Rectangular solid, volume, 45, 51
Related equation, 286
Relation, 714
Remainder, 378, 379
Removing a factor of one, 9, 110, 474
Removing parentheses, 123
Repeating decimal notation, 23, 70
Reversing equations, 146
Right circular cylinder, surface area,
        372
Right triangle, 456, 651
Rise, 255

Roots
  cube, 744
  even, 744
  higher, 744
  *n*th, 744
  odd, 744
  of products, 745
  of quotients, 745
  square, *see* Radical expressions;
        Square roots
Roster notation, 66, 748
Rounding, 24
Run, 255

S

Scientific notation, 316, 317, 321,
        383
  on a calculator, 319
  converting from/to decimal
        notation, 317, 318
  dividing using, 319
  multiplying using, 318, 319
Second coordinate, 224
Set, 66, 748
  closed under an operation, 751
  element of, 748
  empty, 562, 749
  intersection, 749
  membership, 748
  notation, 66, 98
  roster notation, 66, 748
  set-builder notation, 198, 748
  solution, 195
  subset, 66, 748
  union, 749
Set-builder notation, 198, 748
Several variables, polynomial in, 367
Sighting to the horizon, 646
Sign changes in fraction notation, 104
Sign of a reciprocal, 102
Signs of numbers, 82
Similar triangles, 524, 525
Simplest fraction notation, 9
Simplifying
  checking, 478
  complex rational (or fraction)
        expressions, 534–537
  fraction expressions, 9, 474
  fraction notation, 9
  radical expressions, 618
  rational expressions, 474
  removing parentheses, 123
Skidding car, speed, 611
Slant, *see* Slope
Slope, 255, 293
  applications, 257–259
  from equations, 260
  of horizontal line, 261
  of parallel lines, 280, 293

  of perpendicular lines, 281, 293
  as rate of change, 258
  slope–intercept equation, 267, 293
  of vertical line, 261
Slope–intercept equation, 267, 293
Solution set, 195
Solutions
  of equations, 138, 226, 230
  of inequalities, 195, 285
  of systems of equations, 560
Solve, in problem-solving process, 178
Solving equations, 155. *See also*
        Solving formulas.
  using the addition principle, 139,
        215
  clearing decimals, 152, 154
  clearing fractions, 152, 153
  collecting like terms, 151
  containing parentheses, 154
  by factoring, 446, 668, 669
  fraction, 508
  on a graphing calculator, 449, 645,
        672
  using the multiplication principle,
        144, 215
  with parentheses, 154
  using the principle of zero
        products, 446, 668
  procedure, 155
  quadratic, 685
    by completing the square,
        677–679
    by factoring, 446, 668
    on a graphing calculator, 449, 672
    using the principle of square
        roots, 675
    using the quadratic formula, 684
    with radicals, 642–645
  rational, 508
  systems of
    by elimination method, 574
    by graphing, 561, 564
    by substitution method, 567
Solving formulas, 163–165, 691
Solving inequalities, 195
  using the addition principle, 197,
        215
  using the multiplication principle,
        199, 215
  solution set, 195
Special products of polynomials
  squaring binomials, 358, 359, 383
  sum and difference of two
        expressions, 357, 383
  two binomials (FOIL), 356, 383
Speed, 522
  of a skidding car, 611
Square, 40
  area, 41, 51
  perimeter, 40, 51